BENSENVILLE COMMUNITY PUBLIC LIBRARY

3 1457 00516 8635

W9-AUI-307

KILROY ~~WAS~~ IS HERE™

Bensenville Community Public Library
200 S. Church Road
Bensenville, IL 60106

Created by

Joe Pruett

pg 6   "REFLECTIONS," epilogue
"Tiananmen Square"
originally presented in Negative Burn #1
art by Guy Burwell and Tim Bradstreet

"Safe Haven"
originally presented in Negative Burn #6
art by Ken Meyer Jr.

pg 19   "REFLECTIONS," chapter one
originally presented in Kilroy Is Here #1
art by Ken Meyer Jr.

pg 43   "REFLECTIONS," chapter two
originally presented in Kilroy Is Here #2
art by Ken Meyer Jr. and Craig Gilmore

pg 64   "REFLECTIONS," chapter three
originally presented in Kilroy Is Here #3
art by Ken Meyer Jr.

pg 85   "REFLECTIONS," chapter four
originally presented in Kilroy Is Here #4
art by Mike Perkins

pg 106   "REFLECTIONS," chapter five
originally presented in Kilroy Is Here #5
art by Ken Meyer Jr.

pg 127   "PRIDE, PREJUDICE AND PERSECUTION," chapter one
originally presented in Kilroy Is Here #6
art by Mike Perkins

pg 148   "PRIDE, PREJUDICE AND PERSECUTION," chapter two
originally presented in Kilroy Is Here #7
art by Mike Perkins

pg 170   "PRIDE, PREJUDICE AND PERSECUTION," chapter three
originally presented in Kilroy Is Here #8
art by Mike Perkins

pg 195   "STALKED"
originally presented in Kilroy Is Here #9
art by Michael Avon Oeming. Ande Parks, and Bruce McCorkindale

pg 216   "TO LIVE AND DIE IN MOGADISHU"
originally presented in Kilroy Is Here #10
art by Phil Hester and Andrew Walls, with Fredd Gorham

pg 237   "REVELATIONS"
originally presented in Kilroy: Revelations #1
art by Guy Burwell and Ray Snyder

All stories written by
Joe Pruett

art by D. Alexander Gregory and Andrew Robinson

cover art by Brian Bolland
cover colors by Len O'Grady

inside front cover art by Dan Brereton
insdie back cover by Paul Grist

pg 259   "SYMPATHY FOR THE DEVIL"
originally presented in Kilroy Is Here #0
art by Ken Meyer Jr.

pg 275   "LIVING IN HELL"
originally presented in St. Germaine #6 and #7
art by Ed Herrera and Mike Perkins

pg 293   SHORT STORIES

pg 294 "KILROY IS HERE"
originally presented in Calibrations #1
art by Bil Ruth

pg 302 "SEASONS GREETINGS"
originally presented in Negative Burn #18
art by Andrew Robinson

pg 305 "ROSEWOOD"
originally presented in Negative Burn #4
art by Guy Burwell

pg 312 "THE ACCUSED"
originally presented in High Caliber
art by Phil Hester and Jim Woodyard

pg 318 "HENRY"
originally presented in Negative Burn #13
art by Marc Erickson

pg 326 "IN REMEMBRANCE"
originally presented in Negative Burn #24
art by Kevin Landwehr

pg 331 "CAT LIVES"
originally presented in Negative Burn #50
art by Jon Haward

pg 338 "THE DEATH OF BILLY THE KID"
originally presented in Negative Burn #47
art by Guy Burwell

pg 346 "CHRISTMAS FOR CHARLIE"
originally presented in A Caliber Christmas
art by Michael Gaydos

pg 353 PIN UP AND COVERS GALLERY
*art by Brian Bolland, Joe Quesada, Don Kramer, Phil Hester, Matthew Smith,
D. Alexander Gregory and Andrew Robinson*

art by D. Alexander Gregory and Andrew Robinson

Bensenville Community Public Library
200 S. Church Road
Bensenville, IL 60106

back cover art by Andrew Robinson

DESPERADO

www.desperadopublishing.com

Joe Pruett
Publisher

April Doster
Creative Director

Gary Reed
Business Development

Brett Smith
Controller

Ian Feller
Media Liaison
www.813sands.com

Tim Hegarty
Foreign Sales
www.InternationalEnterprise.org

Shinn Uehara
Production & Design

Joe Karg
Production Assistant

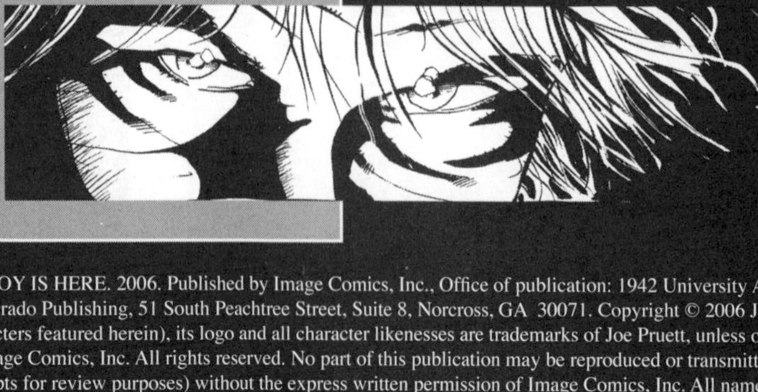

www.imagecomics.com

Erik Larsen
Publisher

Todd McFarlane
President

Marc Silvestri
CEO

Jim Valentino
Vice-President

Eric Stephenson
Executive Director

Jim Demonakos
PR & Marketing Coordinator

Mia MacHatton
Accounts Manager

Laurenn McCubbin
Art Director

Allen Hui
Production Artist

Joe Keatinge
Traffic Manager

Jonathan Chan
Production Assistant

Drew Gill
Production Assistant

Traci Hui
Administrative Assistant

KILROY IS HERE. 2006. Published by Image Comics, Inc., Office of publication: 1942 University Avenue, Suite 305, Berkeley, California 94704 and Desperado Publishing, 51 South Peachtree Street, Suite 8, Norcross, GA 30071. Copyright © 2006 Joe Pruett. KILROY™ (including all prominent characters featured herein), its logo and all character likenesses are trademarks of Joe Pruett, unless otherwise noted. Image Comics® is a trademark of Image Comics, Inc. All rights reserved. No part of this publication may be reproduced or transmitted, in any form or by any means (except for short excerpts for review purposes) without the express written permission of Image Comics, Inc. All names, characters, events and locales in this publication are entirely fictional. Any resemblance to actual persons (living or dead), events or places, without satiric intent, is coincidental. PRINTED IN CANADA.

KILROY WAS IS HERE™

Created by

Joe Pruett

"Reflections"
Epilogue

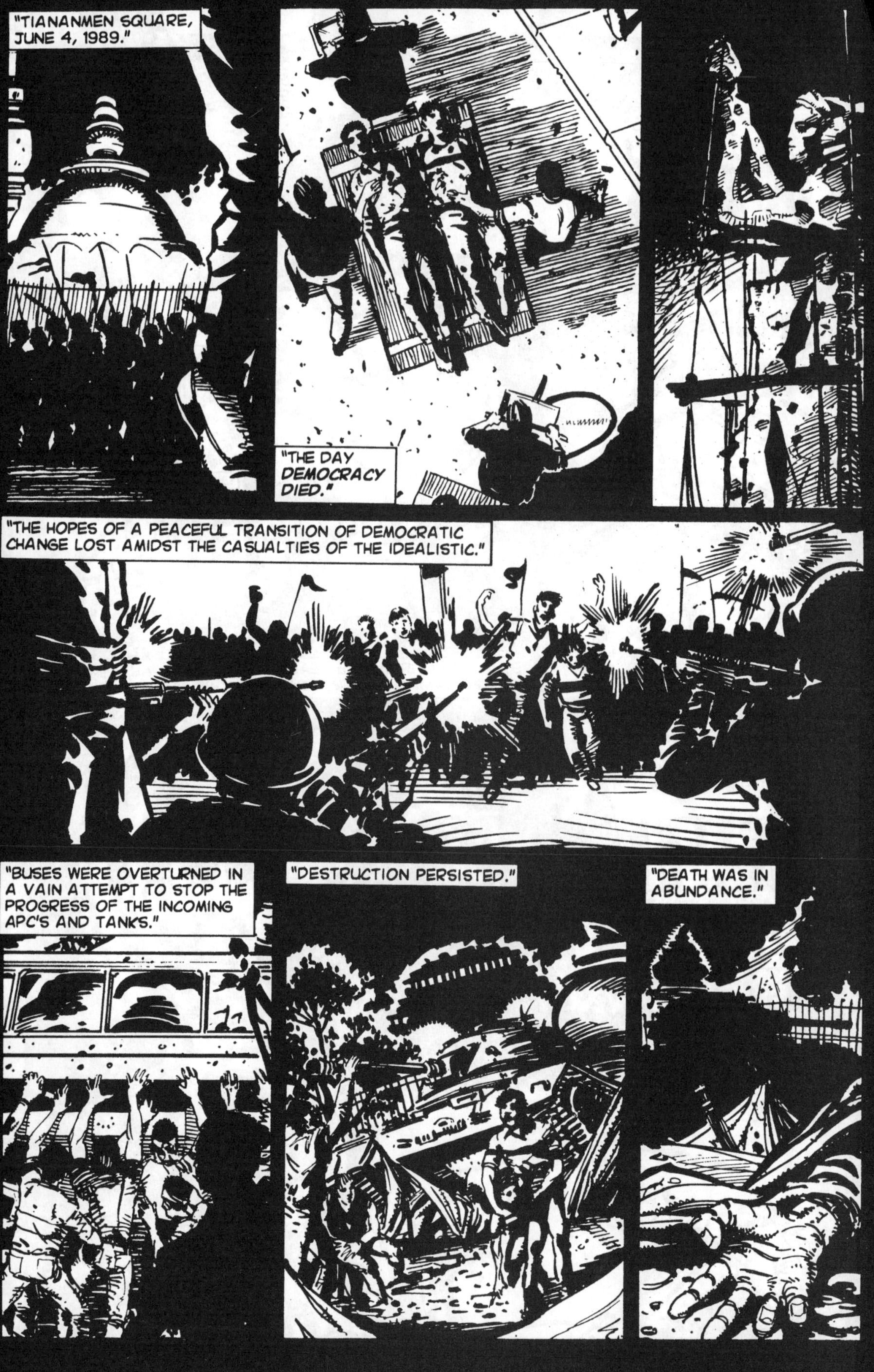
"TIANANMEN SQUARE, JUNE 4, 1989."
"THE DAY DEMOCRACY DIED."
"THE HOPES OF A PEACEFUL TRANSITION OF DEMOCRATIC CHANGE LOST AMIDST THE CASUALTIES OF THE IDEALISTIC."
"BUSES WERE OVERTURNED IN A VAIN ATTEMPT TO STOP THE PROGRESS OF THE INCOMING APC'S AND TANKS."
"DESTRUCTION PERSISTED."
"DEATH WAS IN ABUNDANCE."

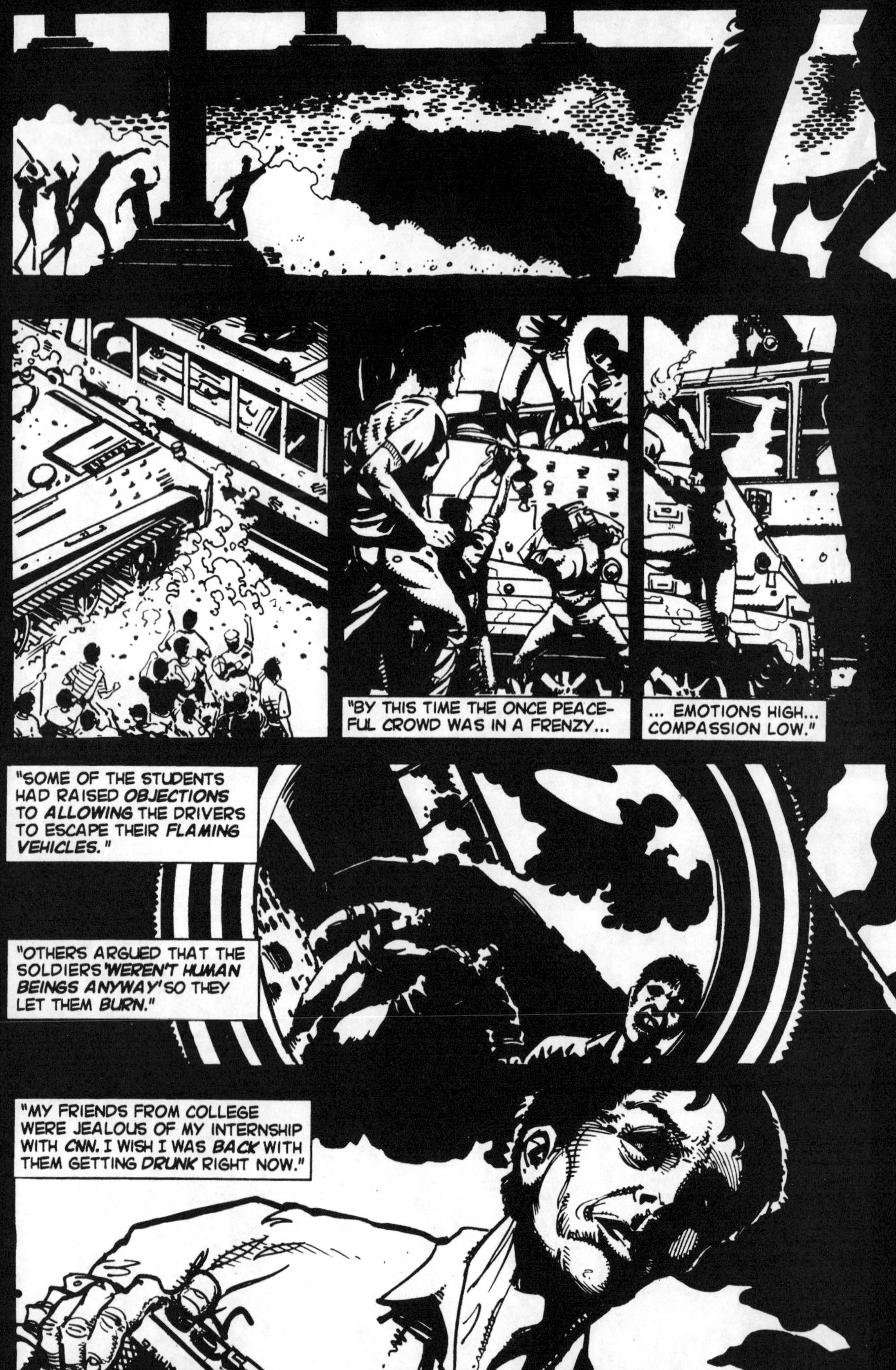
"BY THIS TIME THE ONCE PEACE-FUL CROWD WAS IN A FRENZY...
... EMOTIONS HIGH... COMPASSION LOW."
"SOME OF THE STUDENTS HAD RAISED *OBJECTIONS* TO *ALLOWING* THE DRIVERS TO ESCAPE THEIR *FLAMING VEHICLES.*"
"OTHERS ARGUED THAT THE SOLDIERS *'WEREN'T HUMAN BEINGS ANYWAY'* SO THEY LET THEM *BURN.*"
"MY FRIENDS FROM COLLEGE WERE JEALOUS OF MY INTERNSHIP WITH *CNN.* I WISH I WAS *BACK* WITH THEM GETTING *DRUNK* RIGHT NOW."

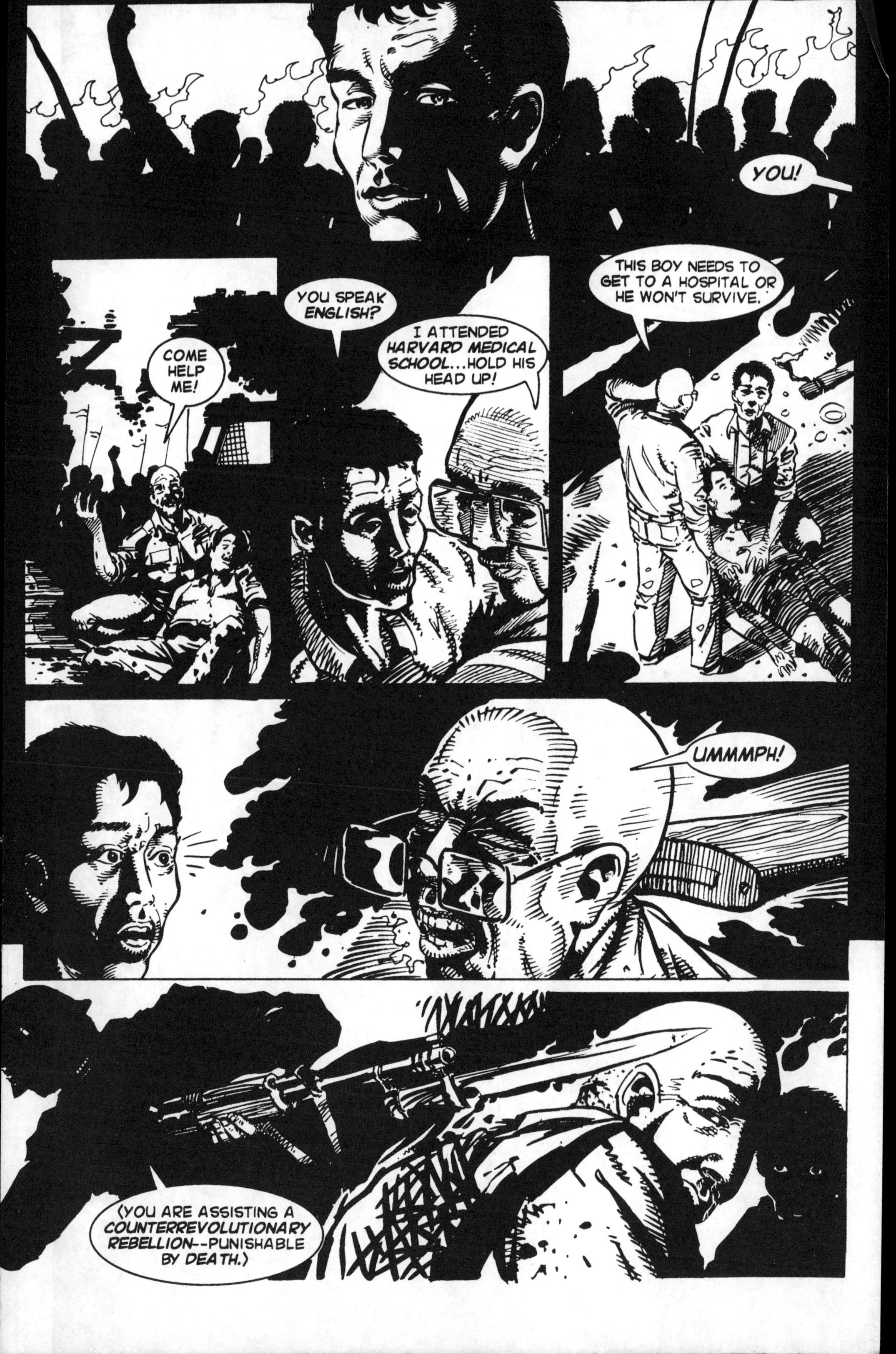
YOU!
COME HELP ME!
YOU SPEAK ENGLISH?
I ATTENDED HARVARD MEDICAL SCHOOL...HOLD HIS HEAD UP!
THIS BOY NEEDS TO GET TO A HOSPITAL OR HE WON'T SURVIVE.
UMMMPH!
(YOU ARE ASSISTING A COUNTERREVOLUTIONARY REBELLION--PUNISHABLE BY DEATH.)

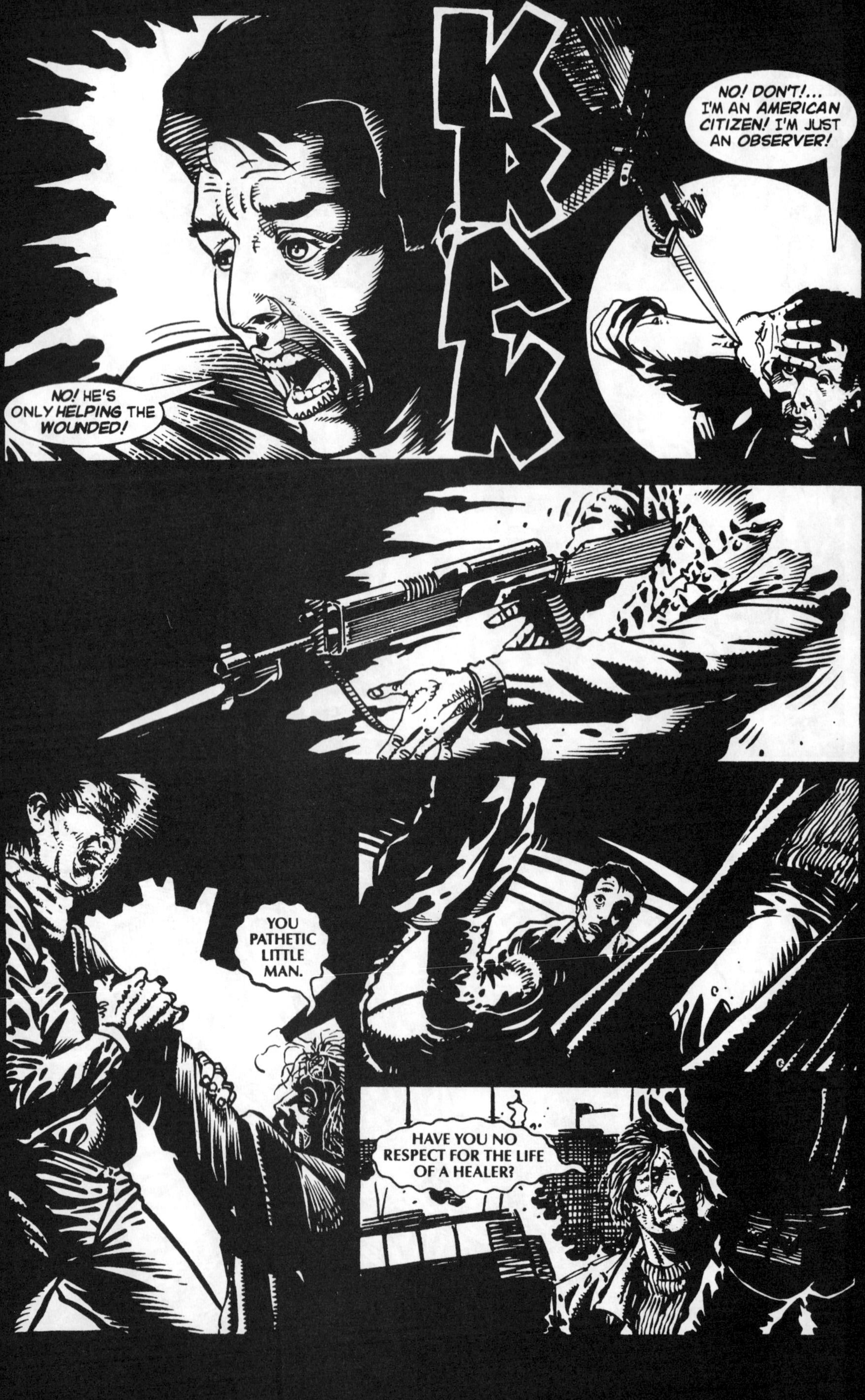
KRAK
NO! DON'T!... I'M AN AMERICAN CITIZEN! I'M JUST AN OBSERVER!
NO! HE'S ONLY HELPING THE WOUNDED!
YOU PATHETIC LITTLE MAN.
HAVE YOU NO RESPECT FOR THE LIFE OF A HEALER?

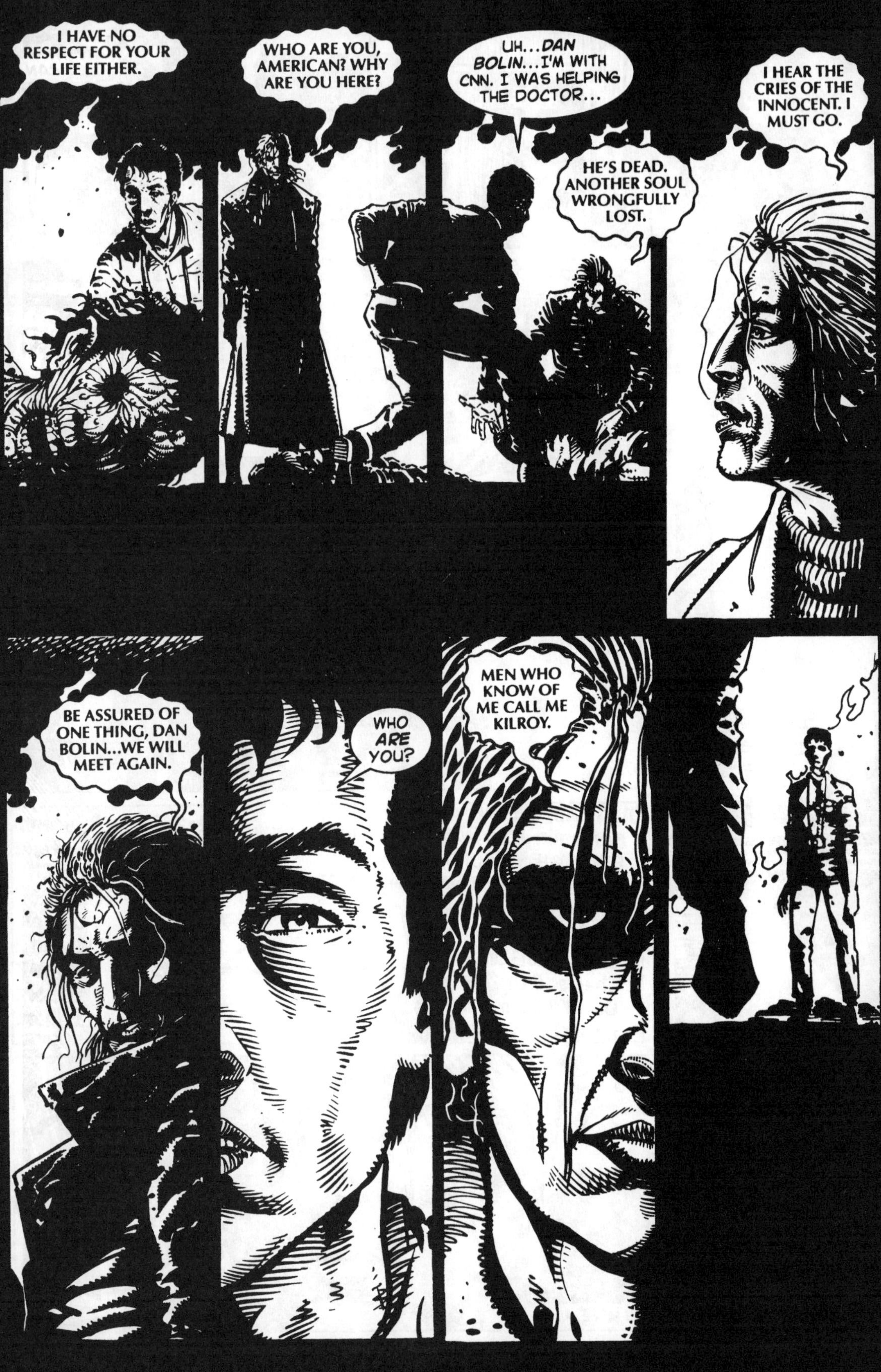
I HAVE NO RESPECT FOR YOUR LIFE EITHER.
WHO ARE YOU, AMERICAN? WHY ARE YOU HERE?
UH...DAN BOLIN...I'M WITH CNN. I WAS HELPING THE DOCTOR...
HE'S DEAD. ANOTHER SOUL WRONGFULLY LOST.
I HEAR THE CRIES OF THE INNOCENT. I MUST GO.
BE ASSURED OF ONE THING, DAN BOLIN...WE WILL MEET AGAIN.
WHO ARE YOU?
MEN WHO KNOW OF ME CALL ME KILROY.

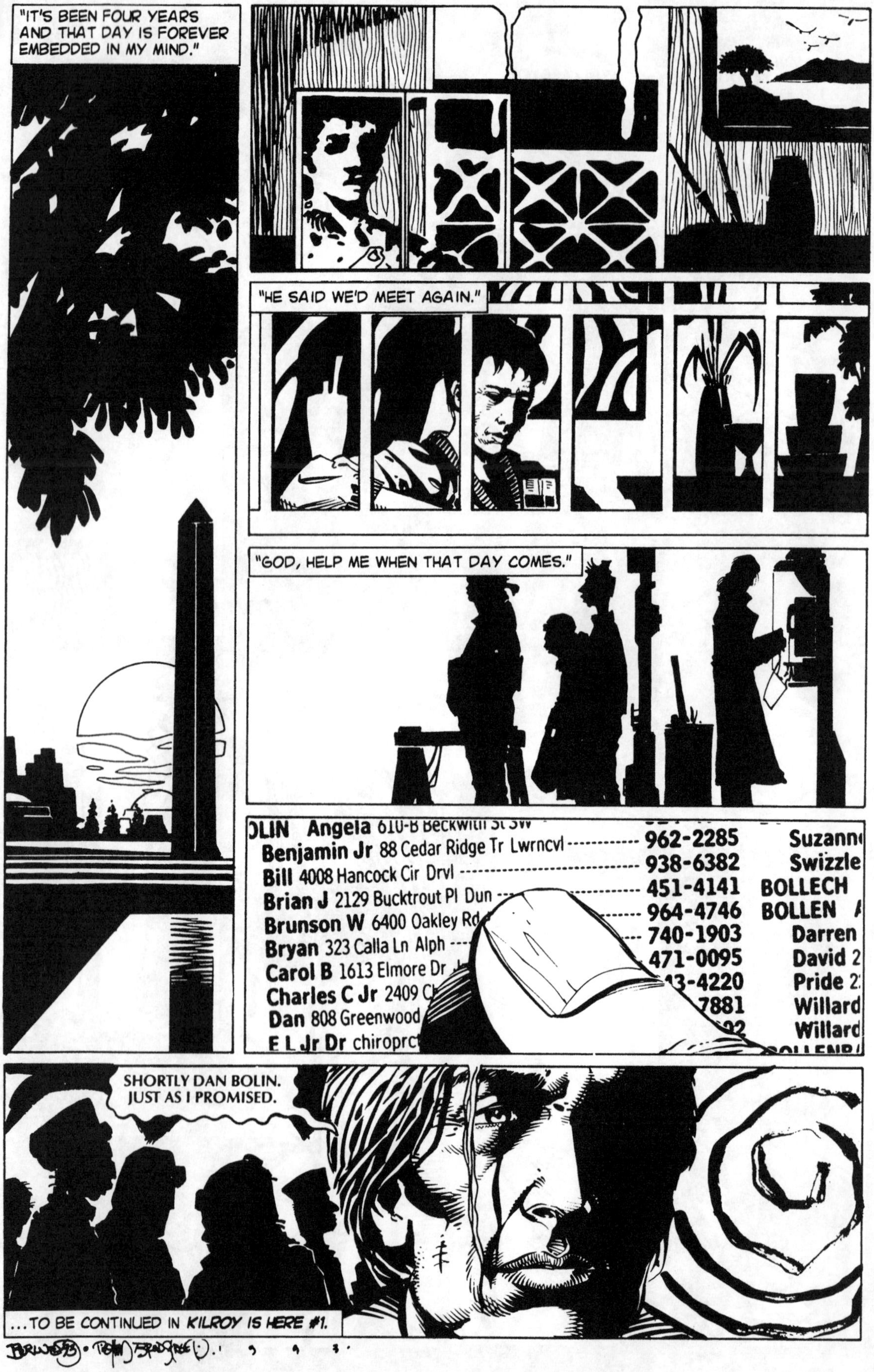

"IT'S BEEN FOUR YEARS AND THAT DAY IS FOREVER EMBEDDED IN MY MIND."
"HE SAID WE'D MEET AGAIN."
"GOD, HELP ME WHEN THAT DAY COMES."
OLIN Angela
Benjamin Jr 88 Cedar Ridge Tr Lwrncvl 962-2285 Suzann
Bill 4008 Hancock Cir Drvl 938-6382 Swizzle
Brian J 2129 Bucktrout Pl Dun 451-4141 BOLLECH
Brunson W 6400 Oakley Rd 964-4746 BOLLEN
Bryan 323 Calla Ln Alph 740-1903 Darren
Carol B 1613 Elmore Dr 471-0095 David
Charles C Jr 2409 -4220 Pride
Dan 808 Greenwood 7881 Willard
Willard
SHORTLY DAN BOLIN. JUST AS I PROMISED.
...TO BE CONTINUED IN KILROY IS HERE #1.

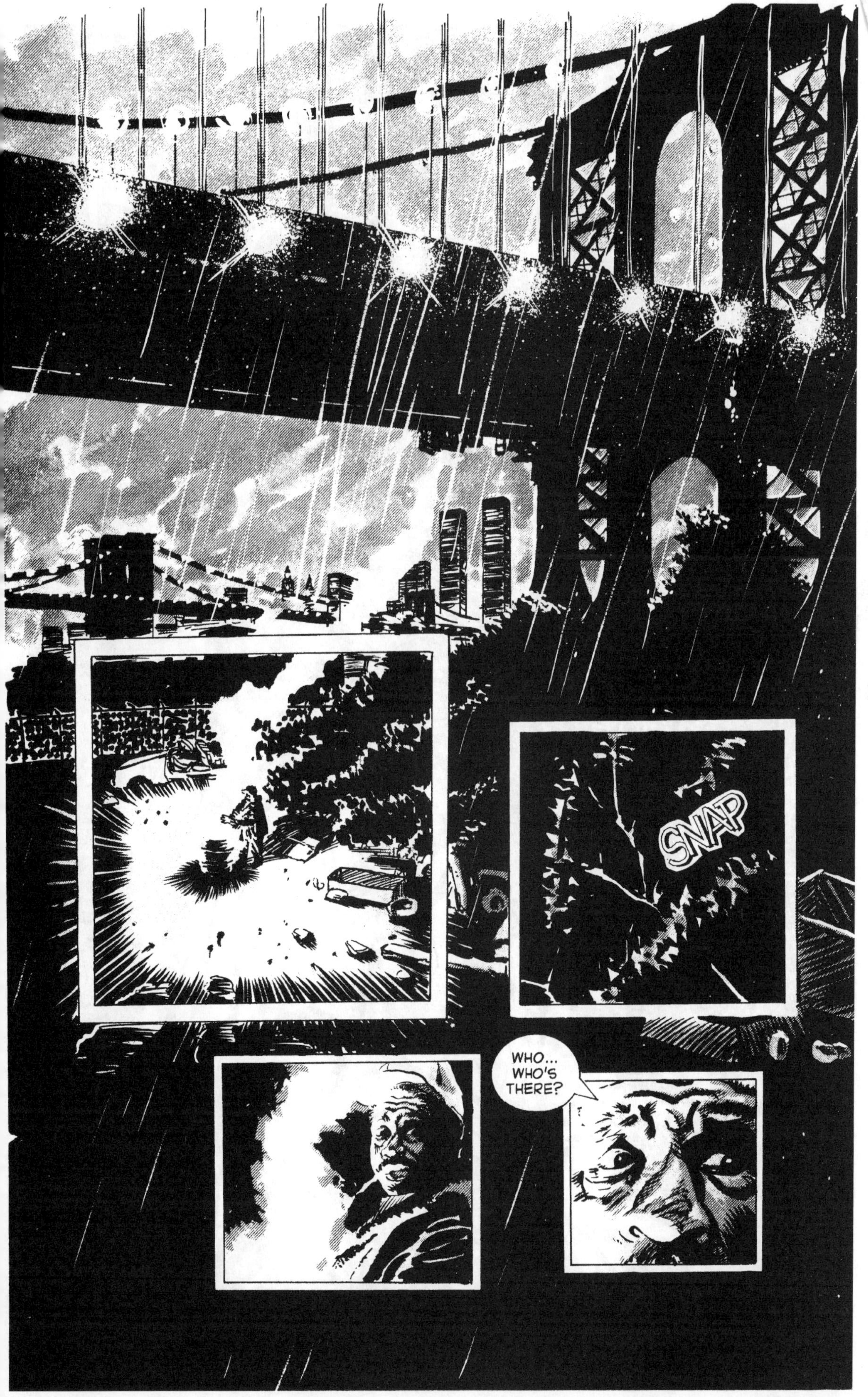
SNAP
WHO... WHO'S THERE?

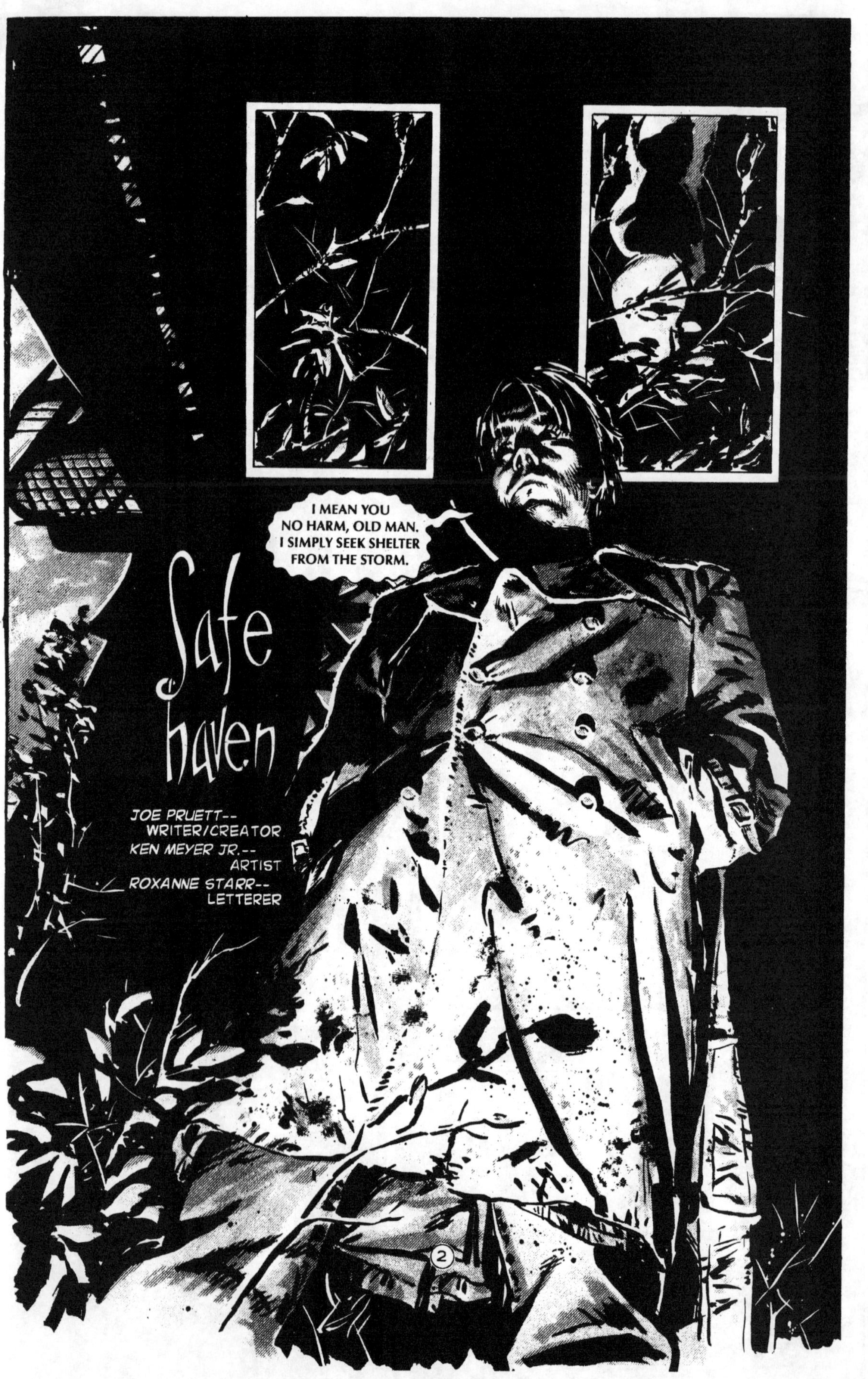
I MEAN YOU NO HARM, OLD MAN. I SIMPLY SEEK SHELTER FROM THE STORM.
Safe haven
JOE PRUETT-- WRITER/CREATOR
KEN MEYER JR.-- ARTIST
ROXANNE STARR-- LETTERER
2

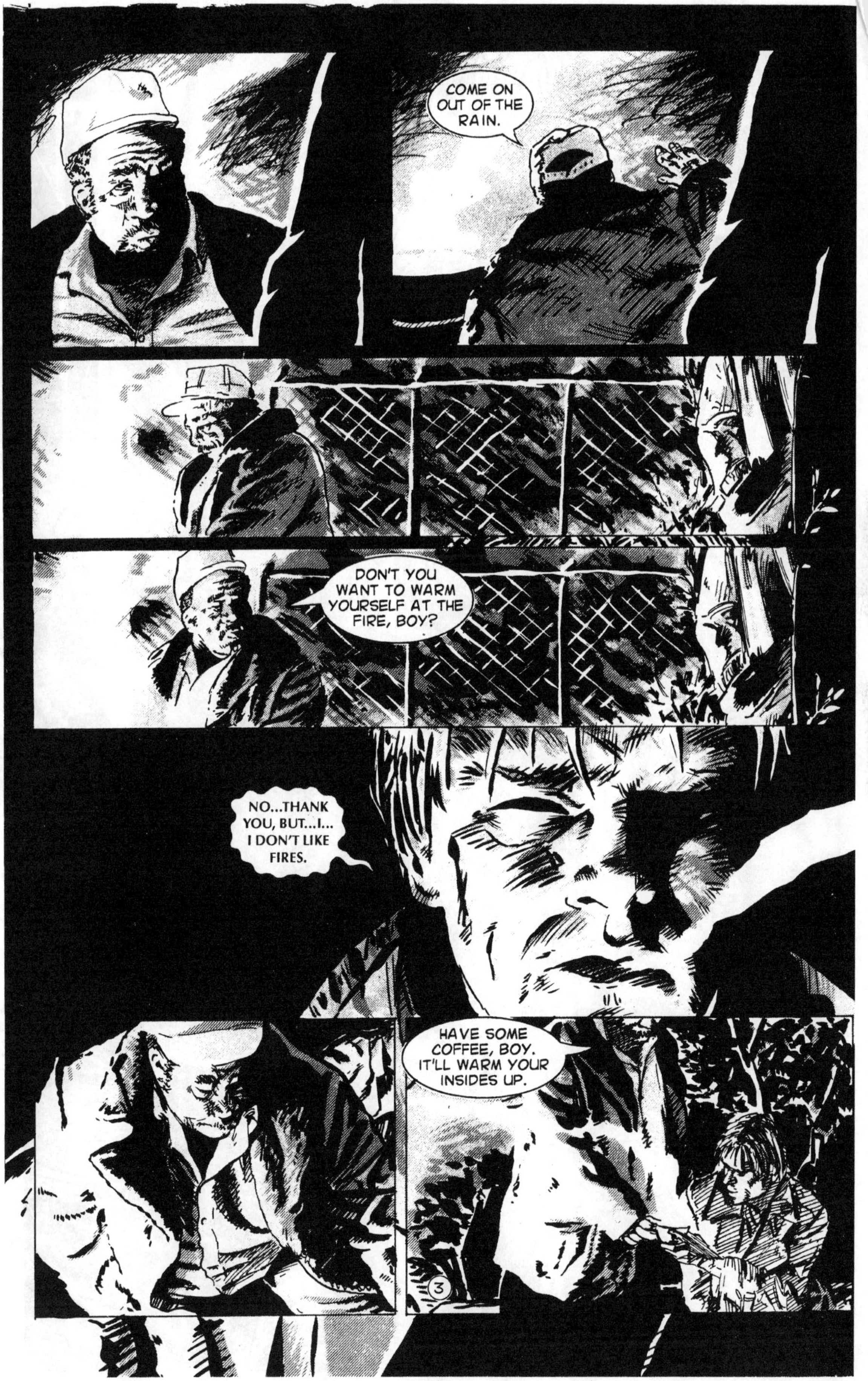
COME ON OUT OF THE RAIN.
DON'T YOU WANT TO WARM YOURSELF AT THE FIRE, BOY?
NO...THANK YOU, BUT...I... I DON'T LIKE FIRES.
HAVE SOME COFFEE, BOY. IT'LL WARM YOUR INSIDES UP.
3

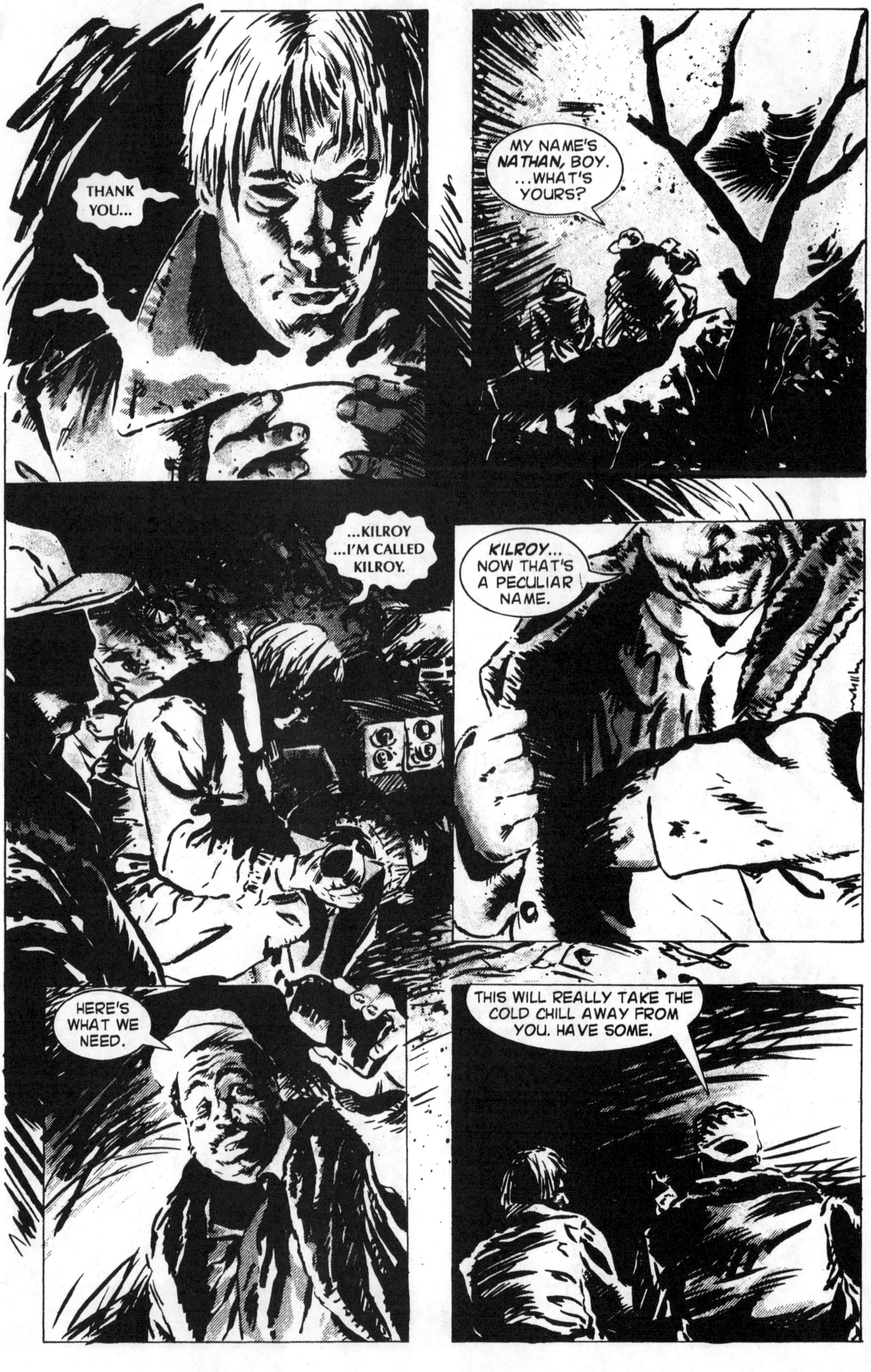
THANK YOU...
MY NAME'S NATHAN, BOY. ...WHAT'S YOURS?
...KILROY ...I'M CALLED KILROY.
KILROY... NOW THAT'S A PECULIAR NAME.
HERE'S WHAT WE NEED.
THIS WILL REALLY TAKE THE COLD CHILL AWAY FROM YOU. HAVE SOME.

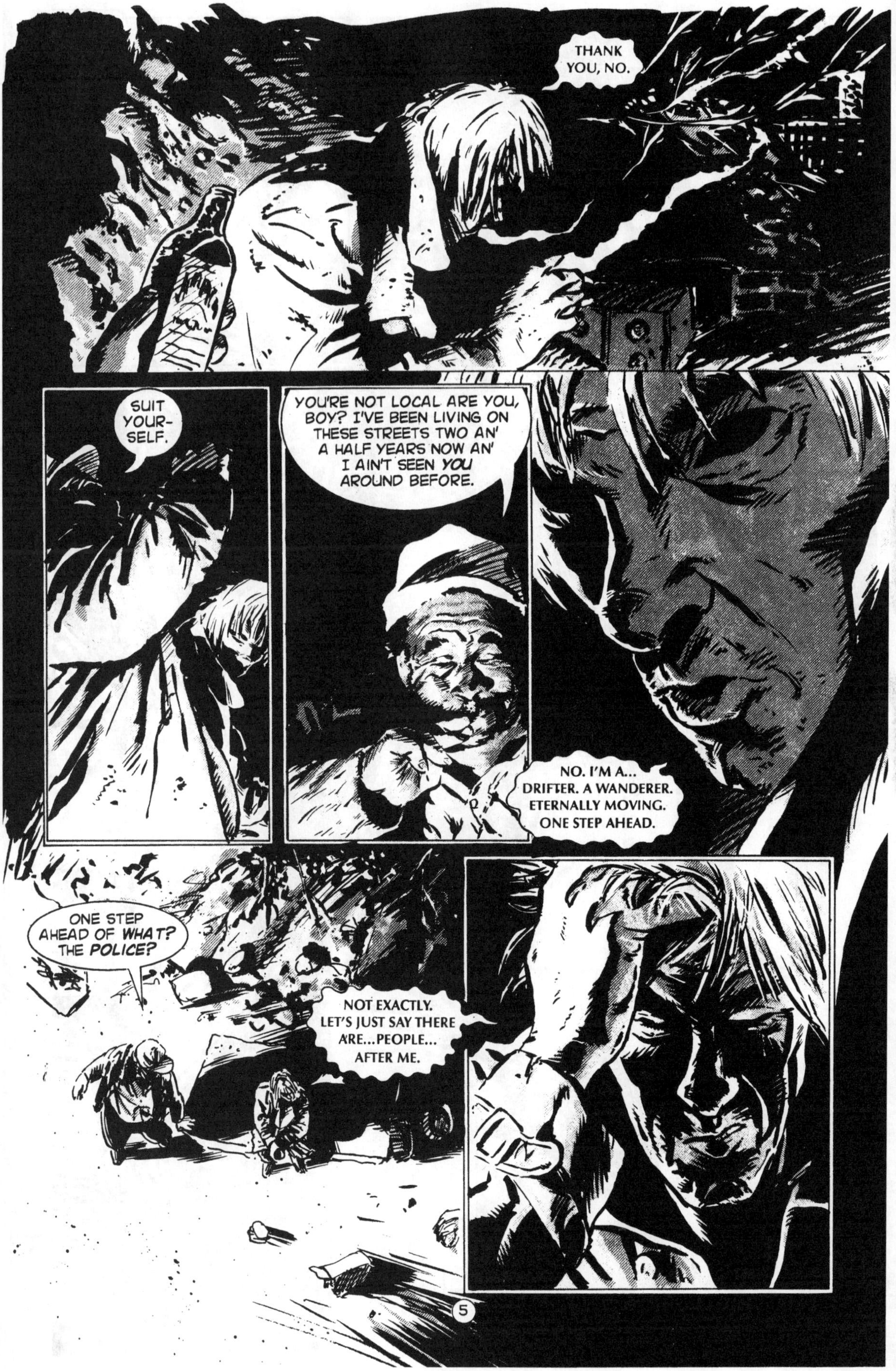
THANK YOU, NO.
SUIT YOUR-SELF.
YOU'RE NOT LOCAL ARE YOU, BOY? I'VE BEEN LIVING ON THESE STREETS TWO AN' A HALF YEARS NOW AN' I AIN'T SEEN *YOU* AROUND BEFORE.
NO. I'M A... DRIFTER. A WANDERER. ETERNALLY MOVING. ONE STEP AHEAD.
ONE STEP AHEAD OF *WHAT*? THE *POLICE*?
NOT EXACTLY. LET'S JUST SAY THERE ARE...PEOPLE... AFTER ME.

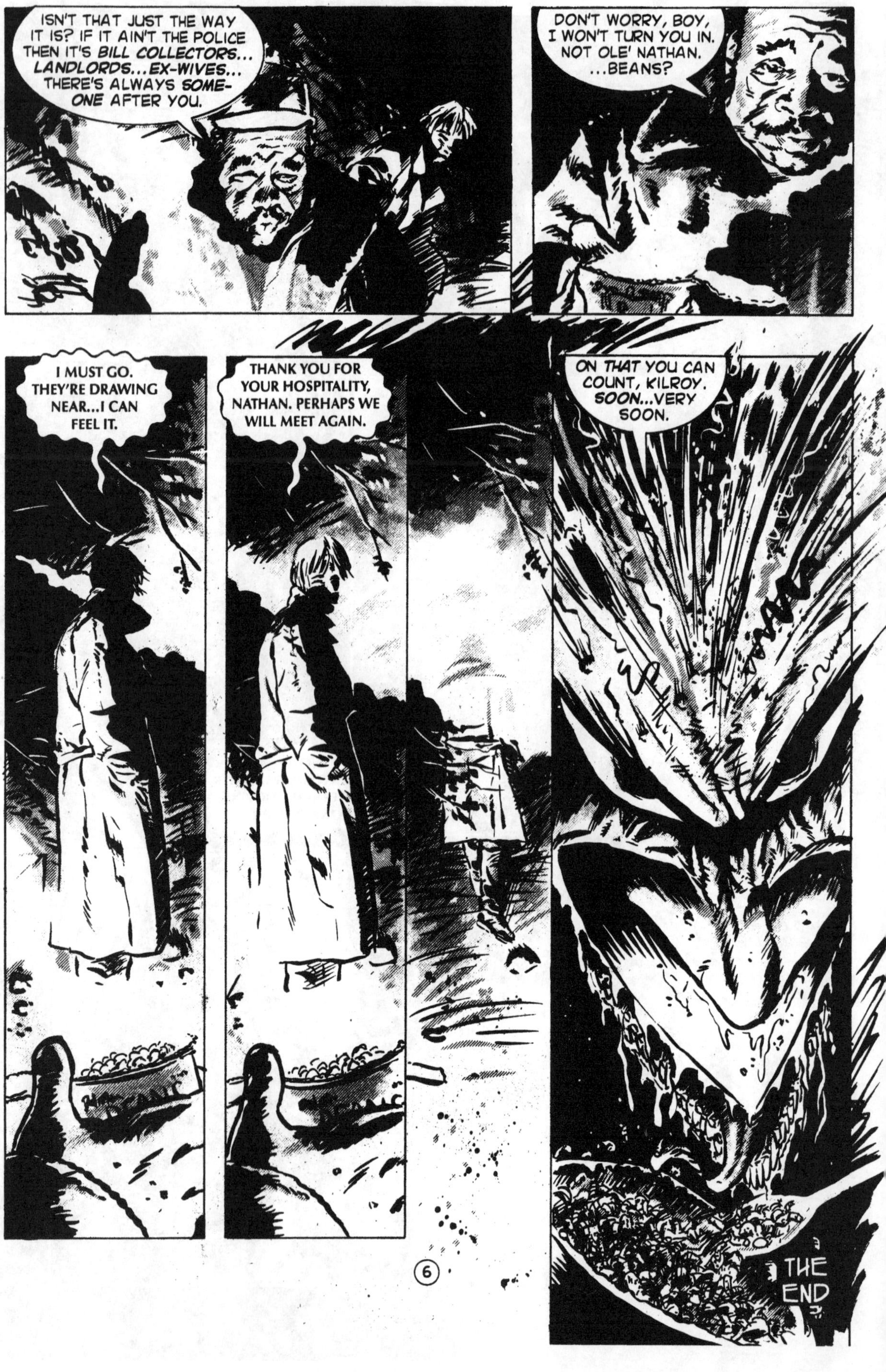
ISN'T THAT JUST THE WAY IT IS? IF IT AIN'T THE POLICE THEN IT'S BILL COLLECTORS... LANDLORDS... EX-WIVES... THERE'S ALWAYS SOME-ONE AFTER YOU.
DON'T WORRY, BOY, I WON'T TURN YOU IN. NOT OLE' NATHAN. ...BEANS?
I MUST GO. THEY'RE DRAWING NEAR...I CAN FEEL IT.
THANK YOU FOR YOUR HOSPITALITY, NATHAN. PERHAPS WE WILL MEET AGAIN.
ON THAT YOU CAN COUNT, KILROY. SOON...VERY SOON.
THE END

"Reflections"
Chapter One

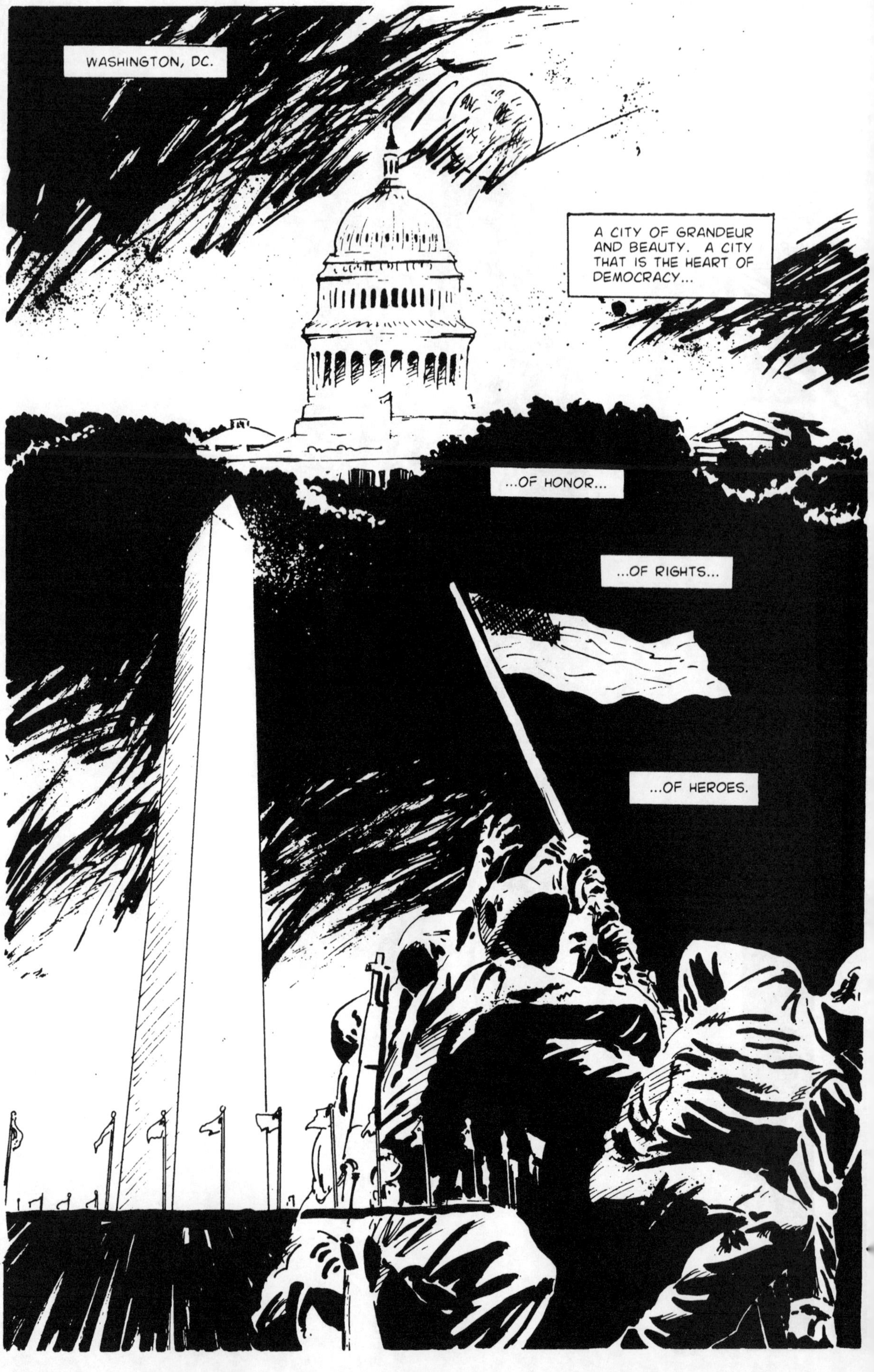
WASHINGTON, DC.
A CITY OF GRANDEUR AND BEAUTY. A CITY THAT IS THE HEART OF DEMOCRACY...
...OF HONOR...
...OF RIGHTS...
...OF HEROES.

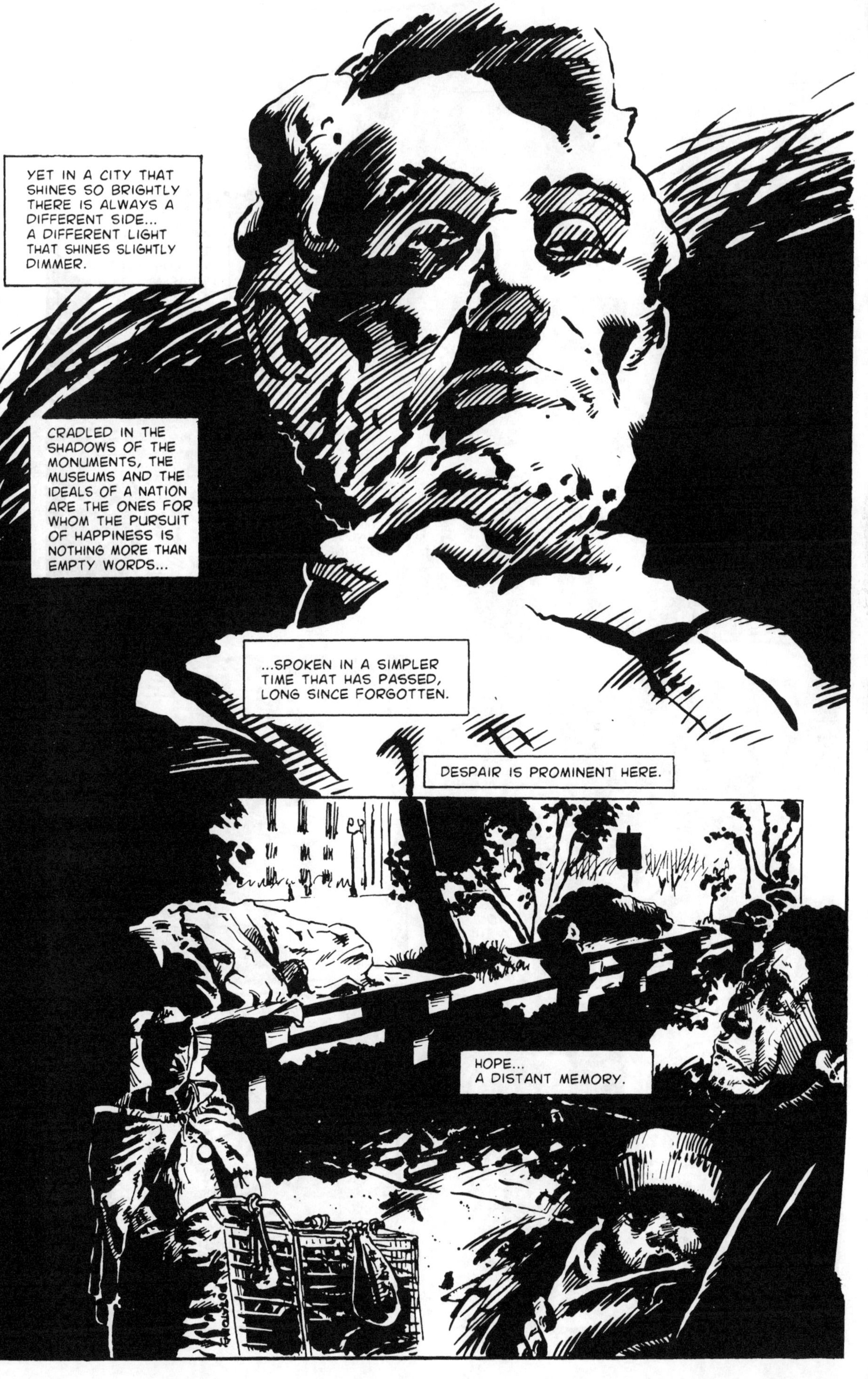
YET IN A CITY THAT SHINES SO BRIGHTLY THERE IS ALWAYS A DIFFERENT SIDE... A DIFFERENT LIGHT THAT SHINES SLIGHTLY DIMMER.
CRADLED IN THE SHADOWS OF THE MONUMENTS, THE MUSEUMS AND THE IDEALS OF A NATION ARE THE ONES FOR WHOM THE PURSUIT OF HAPPINESS IS NOTHING MORE THAN EMPTY WORDS...
...SPOKEN IN A SIMPLER TIME THAT HAS PASSED, LONG SINCE FORGOTTEN.
DESPAIR IS PROMINENT HERE.
HOPE... A DISTANT MEMORY.

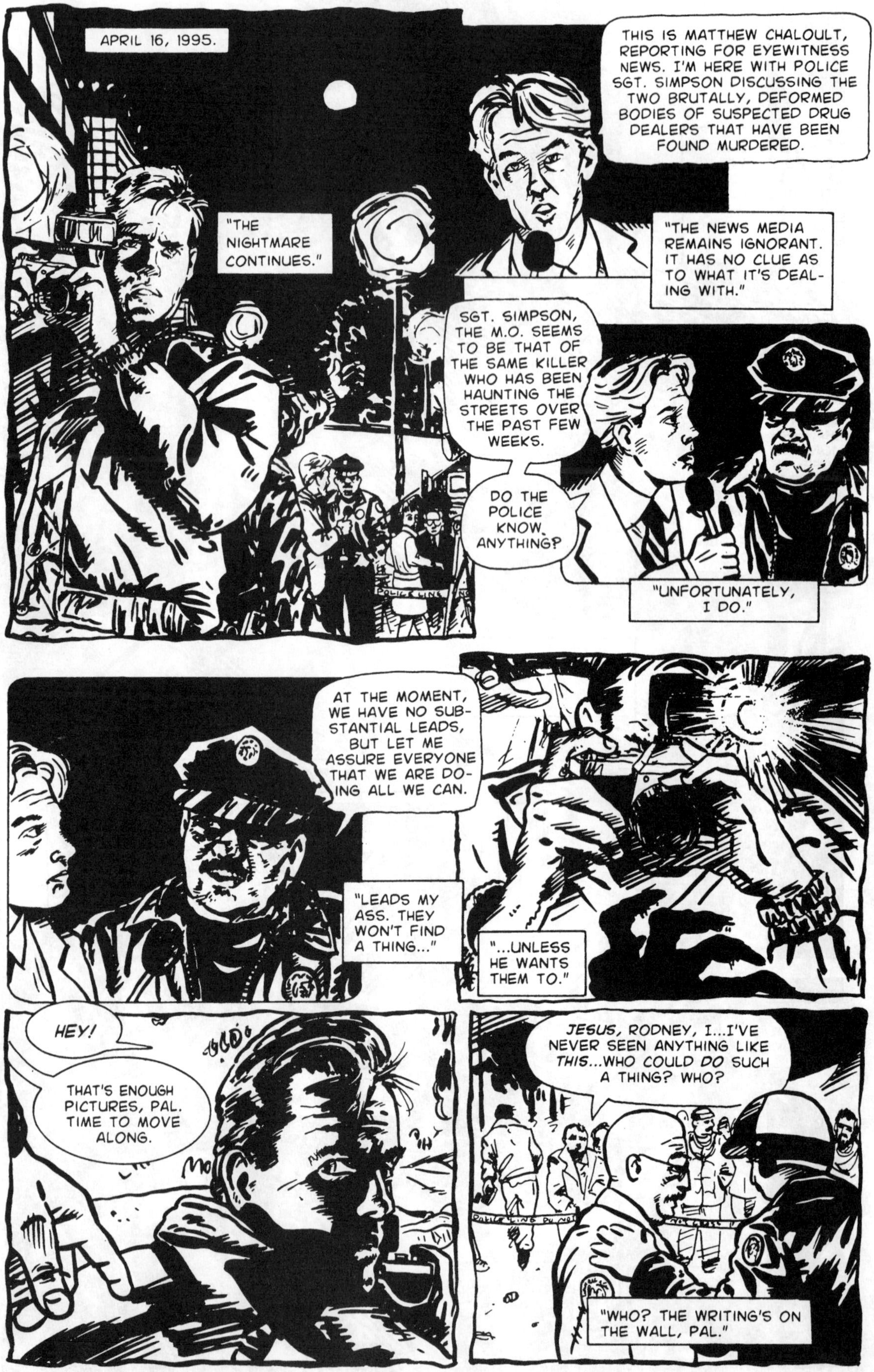
APRIL 16, 1995.
THIS IS MATTHEW CHALOULT, REPORTING FOR EYEWITNESS NEWS. I'M HERE WITH POLICE SGT. SIMPSON DISCUSSING THE TWO BRUTALLY, DEFORMED BODIES OF SUSPECTED DRUG DEALERS THAT HAVE BEEN FOUND MURDERED.
"THE NIGHTMARE CONTINUES."
"THE NEWS MEDIA REMAINS IGNORANT. IT HAS NO CLUE AS TO WHAT IT'S DEALING WITH."
SGT. SIMPSON, THE M.O. SEEMS TO BE THAT OF THE SAME KILLER WHO HAS BEEN HAUNTING THE STREETS OVER THE PAST FEW WEEKS.
DO THE POLICE KNOW ANYTHING?
"UNFORTUNATELY, I DO."
AT THE MOMENT, WE HAVE NO SUBSTANTIAL LEADS, BUT LET ME ASSURE EVERYONE THAT WE ARE DOING ALL WE CAN.
"LEADS MY ASS. THEY WON'T FIND A THING..."
"...UNLESS HE WANTS THEM TO."
HEY!
THAT'S ENOUGH PICTURES, PAL. TIME TO MOVE ALONG.
JESUS, RODNEY, I...I'VE NEVER SEEN ANYTHING LIKE THIS...WHO COULD DO SUCH A THING? WHO?
"WHO? THE WRITING'S ON THE WALL, PAL."

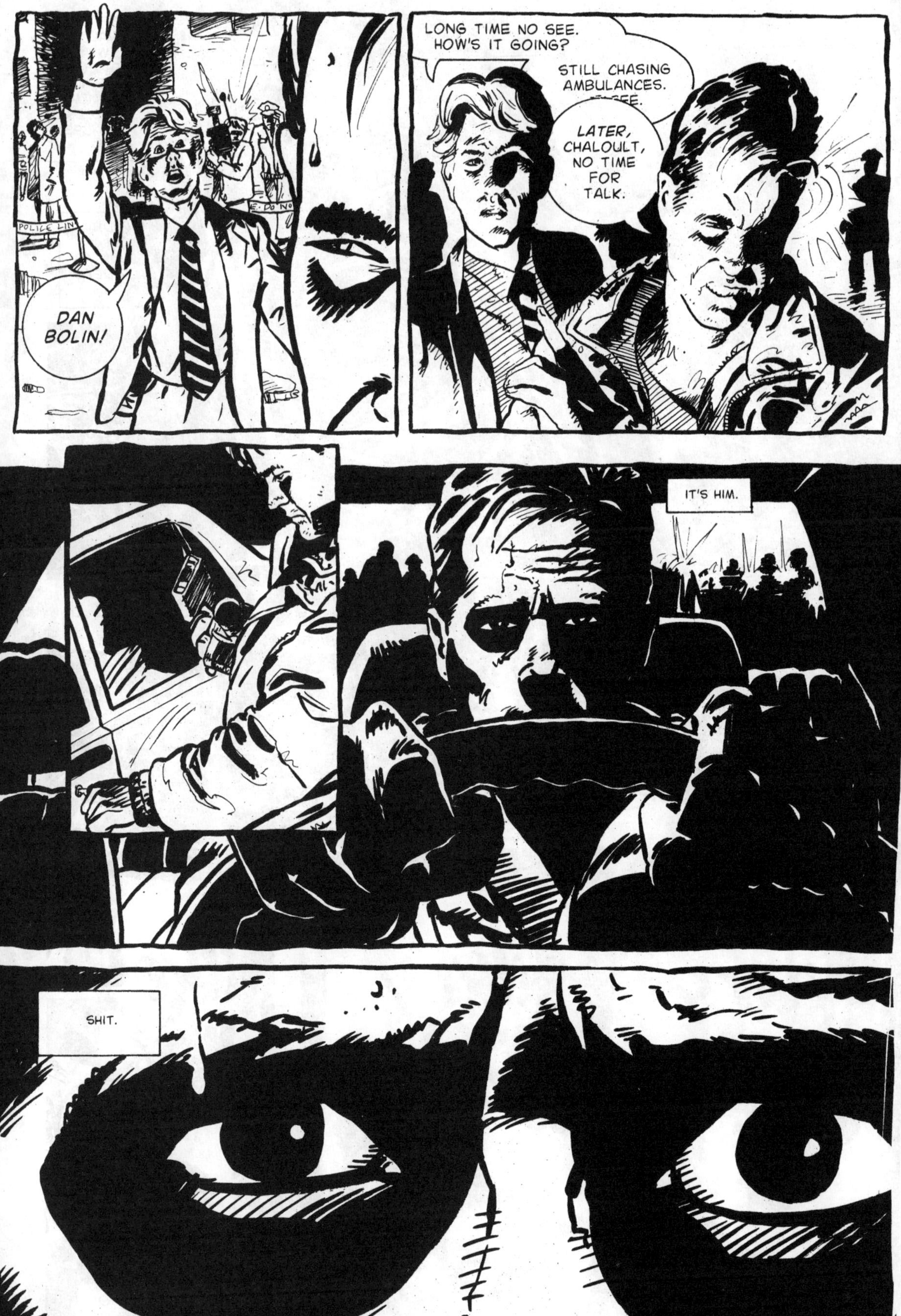
DAN BOLIN!
LONG TIME NO SEE. HOW'S IT GOING?
STILL CHASING AMBULANCES.
LATER, CHALOULT, NO TIME FOR TALK.
IT'S HIM.
SHIT.

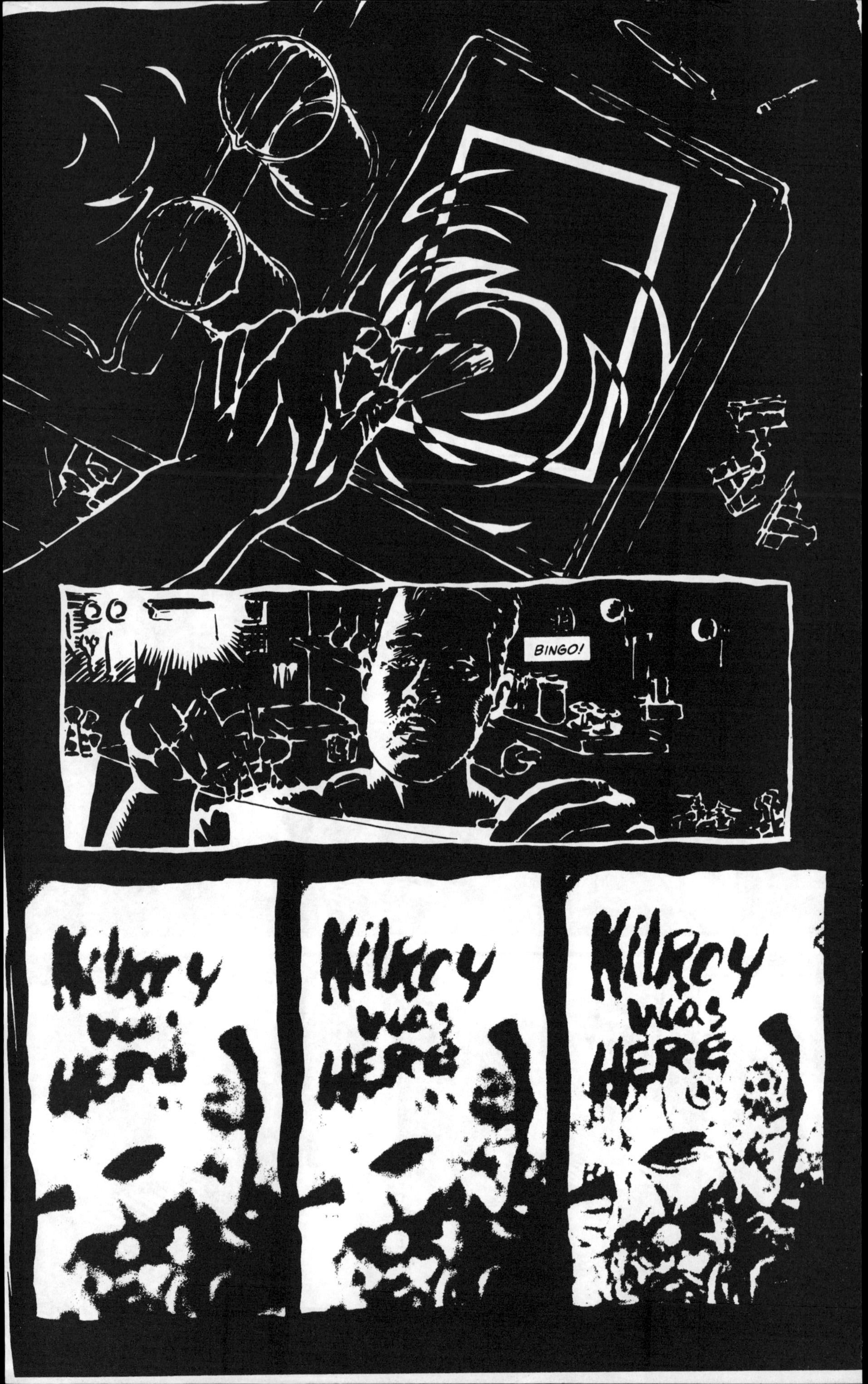
BINGO!
KILROY WAS HERE
KILROY WAS HERE
KILROY WAS HERE

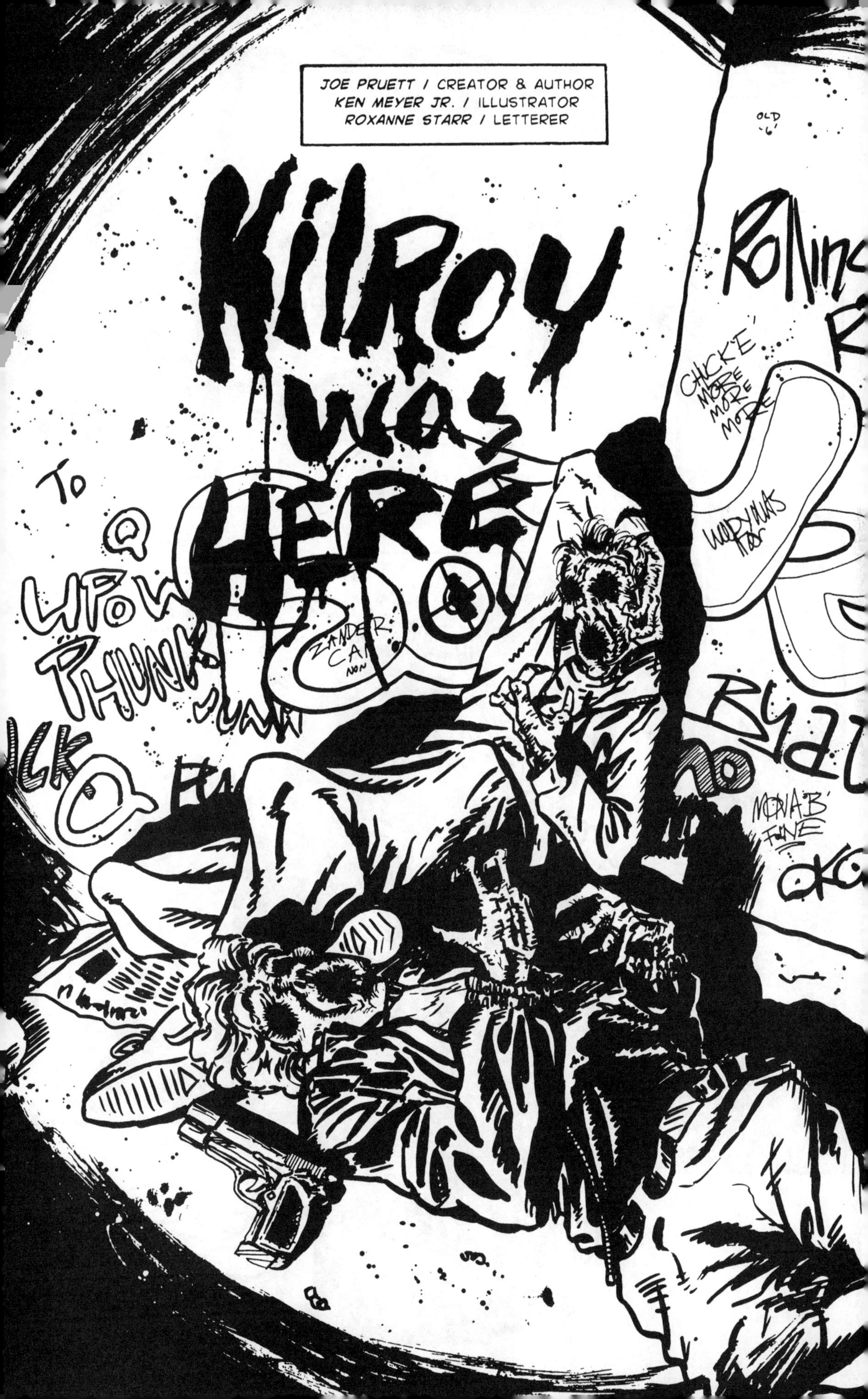
JOE PRUETT / CREATOR & AUTHOR
KEN MEYER JR. / ILLUSTRATOR
ROXANNE STARR / LETTERER
KILROY WAS HERE

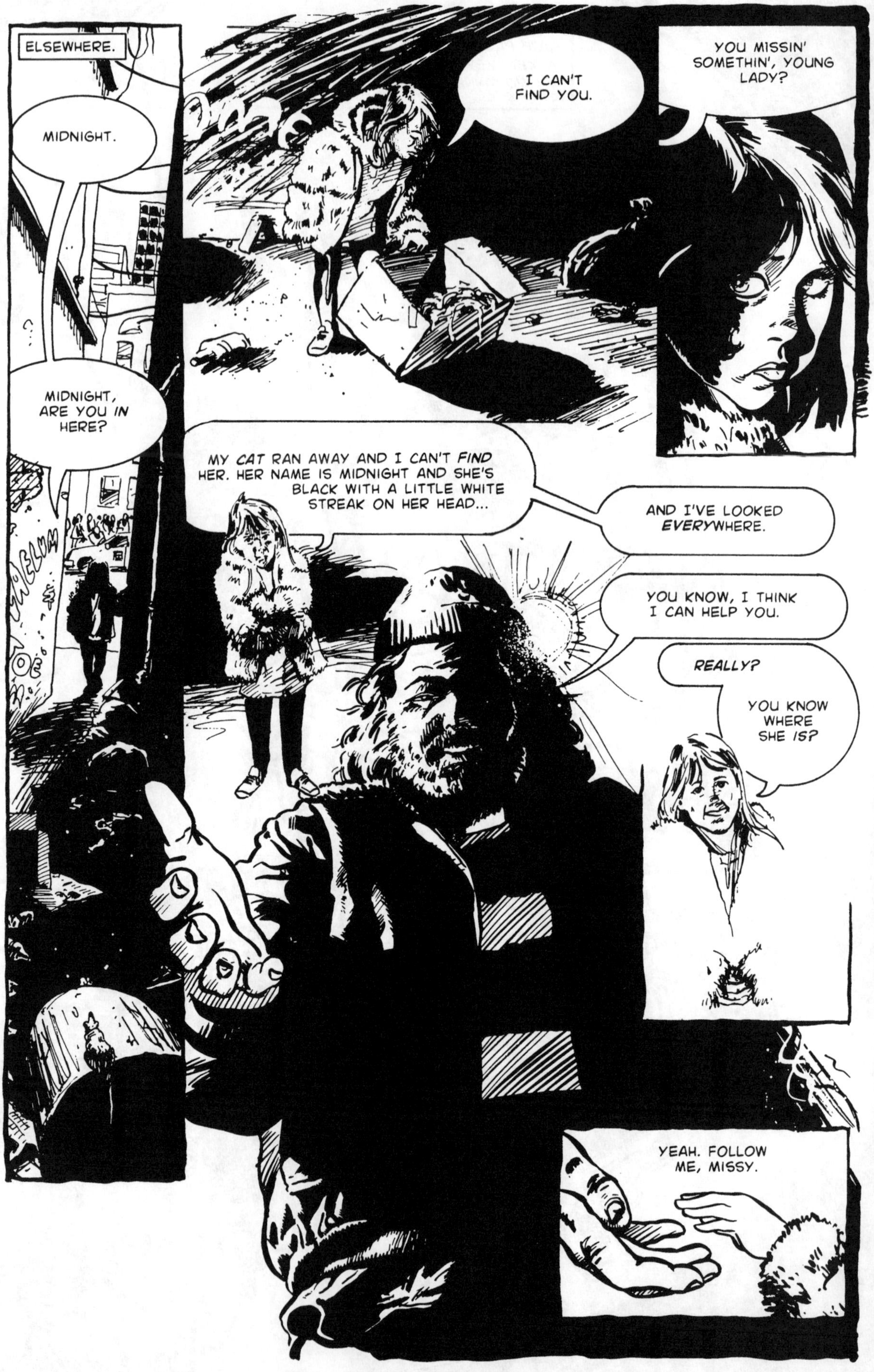

ELSEWHERE.
MIDNIGHT.
MIDNIGHT, ARE YOU IN HERE?
I CAN'T FIND YOU.
YOU MISSIN' SOMETHIN', YOUNG LADY?
MY CAT RAN AWAY AND I CAN'T FIND HER. HER NAME IS MIDNIGHT AND SHE'S BLACK WITH A LITTLE WHITE STREAK ON HER HEAD...
AND I'VE LOOKED EVERYWHERE.
YOU KNOW, I THINK I CAN HELP YOU.
REALLY?
YOU KNOW WHERE SHE IS?
YEAH. FOLLOW ME, MISSY.

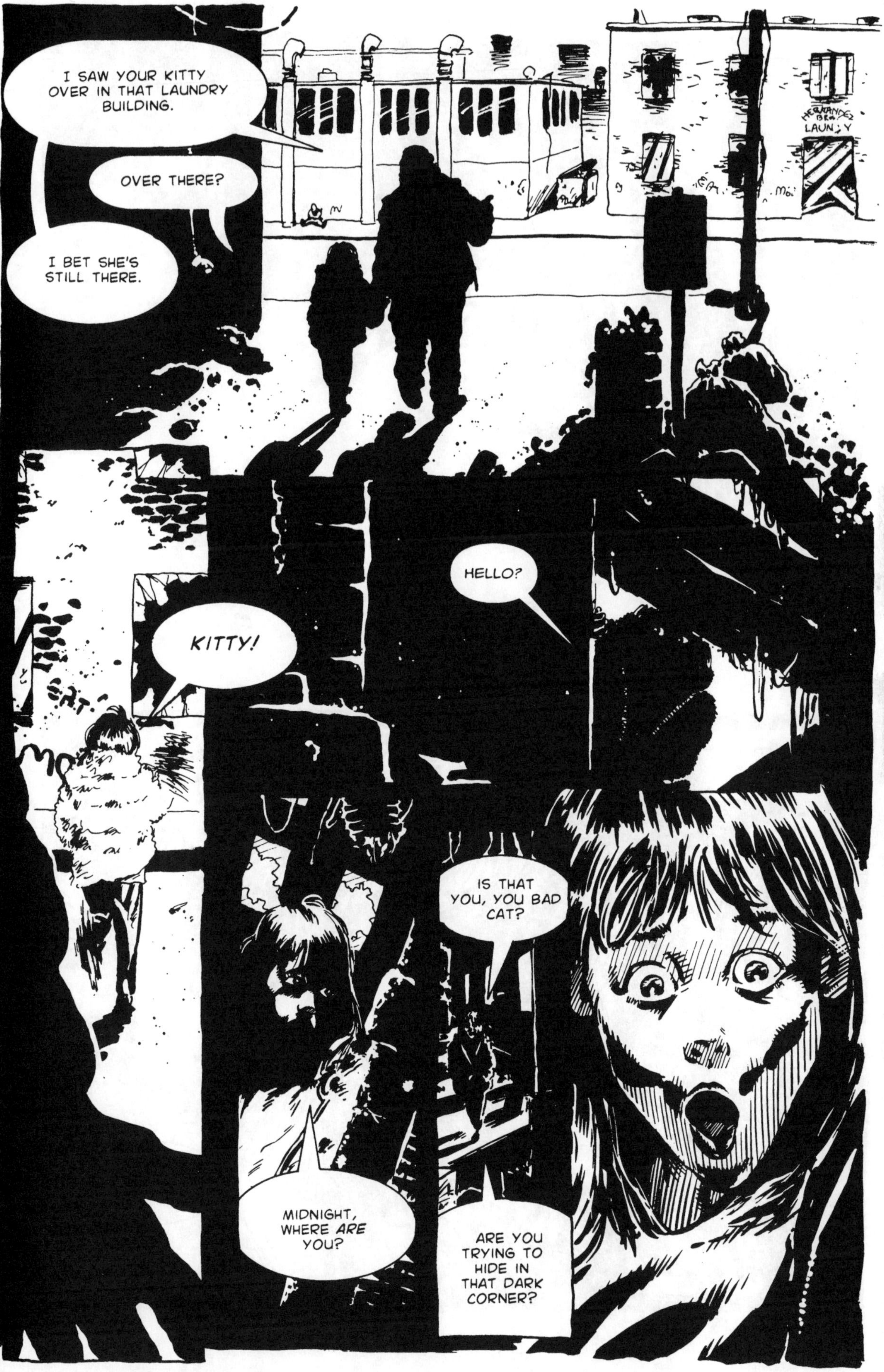
I SAW YOUR KITTY OVER IN THAT LAUNDRY BUILDING.
OVER THERE?
I BET SHE'S STILL THERE.
HERNANDEZ BROS LAUN Y
KITTY!
HELLO?
MIDNIGHT, WHERE *ARE* YOU?
IS THAT YOU, YOU BAD CAT?
ARE YOU TRYING TO HIDE IN THAT DARK CORNER?

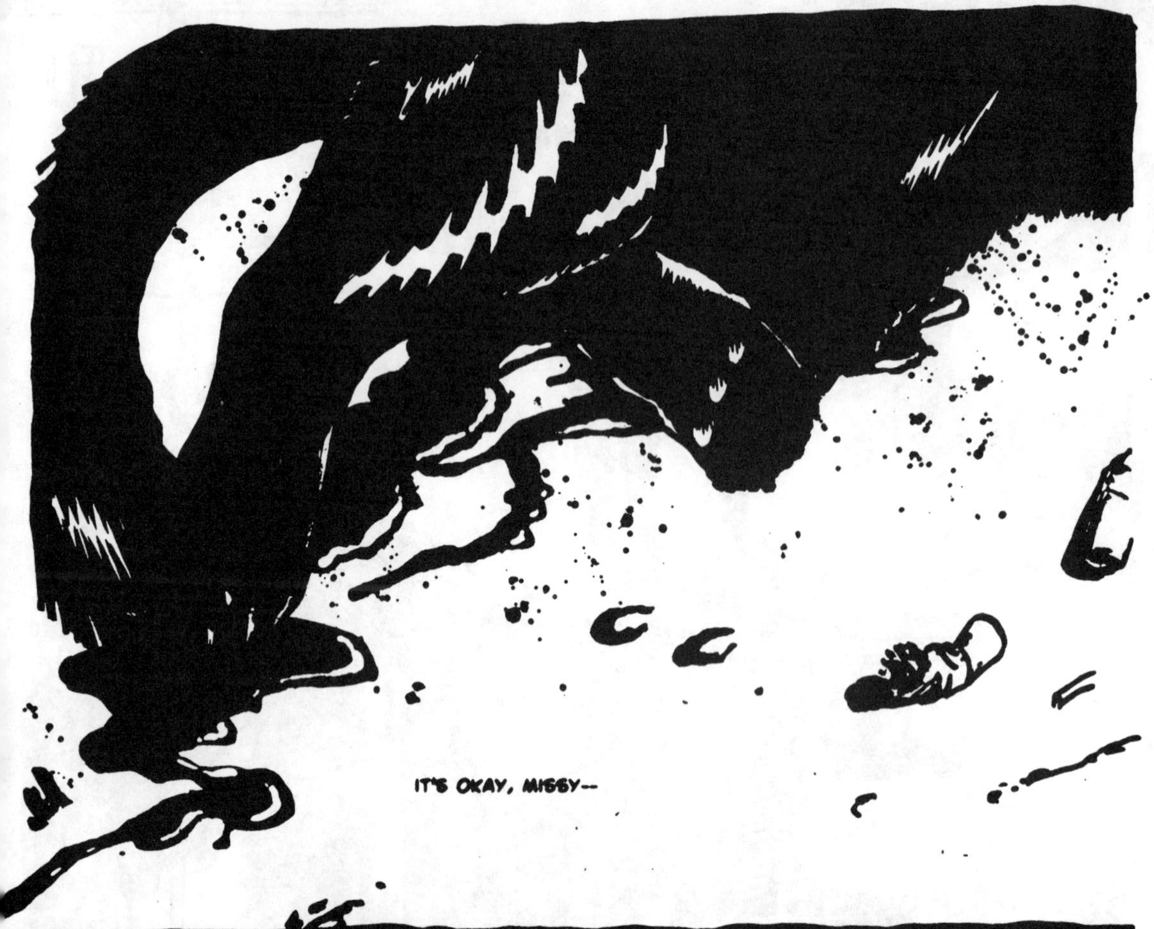
IT'S OKAY, MISSY--

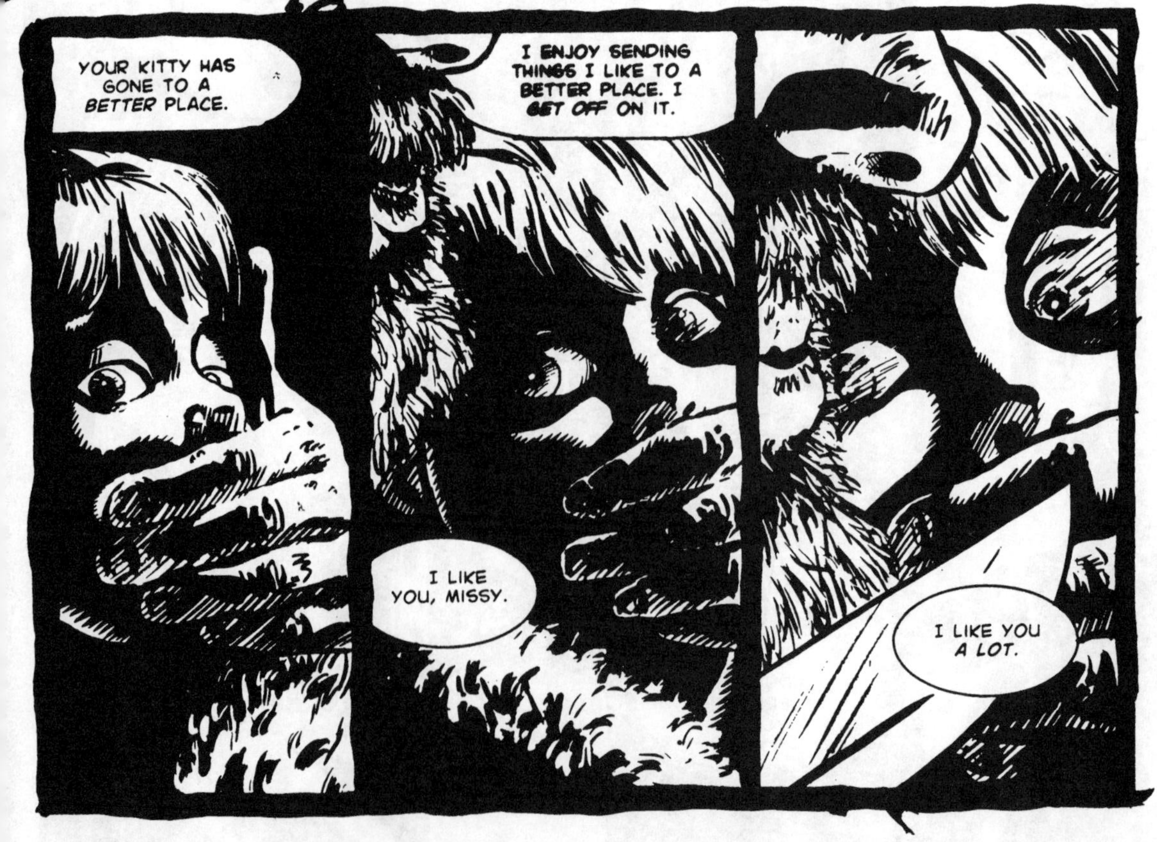
YOUR KITTY HAS GONE TO A BETTER PLACE.
I ENJOY SENDING THINGS I LIKE TO A BETTER PLACE. I GET OFF ON IT.
I LIKE YOU, MISSY.
I LIKE YOU A LOT.

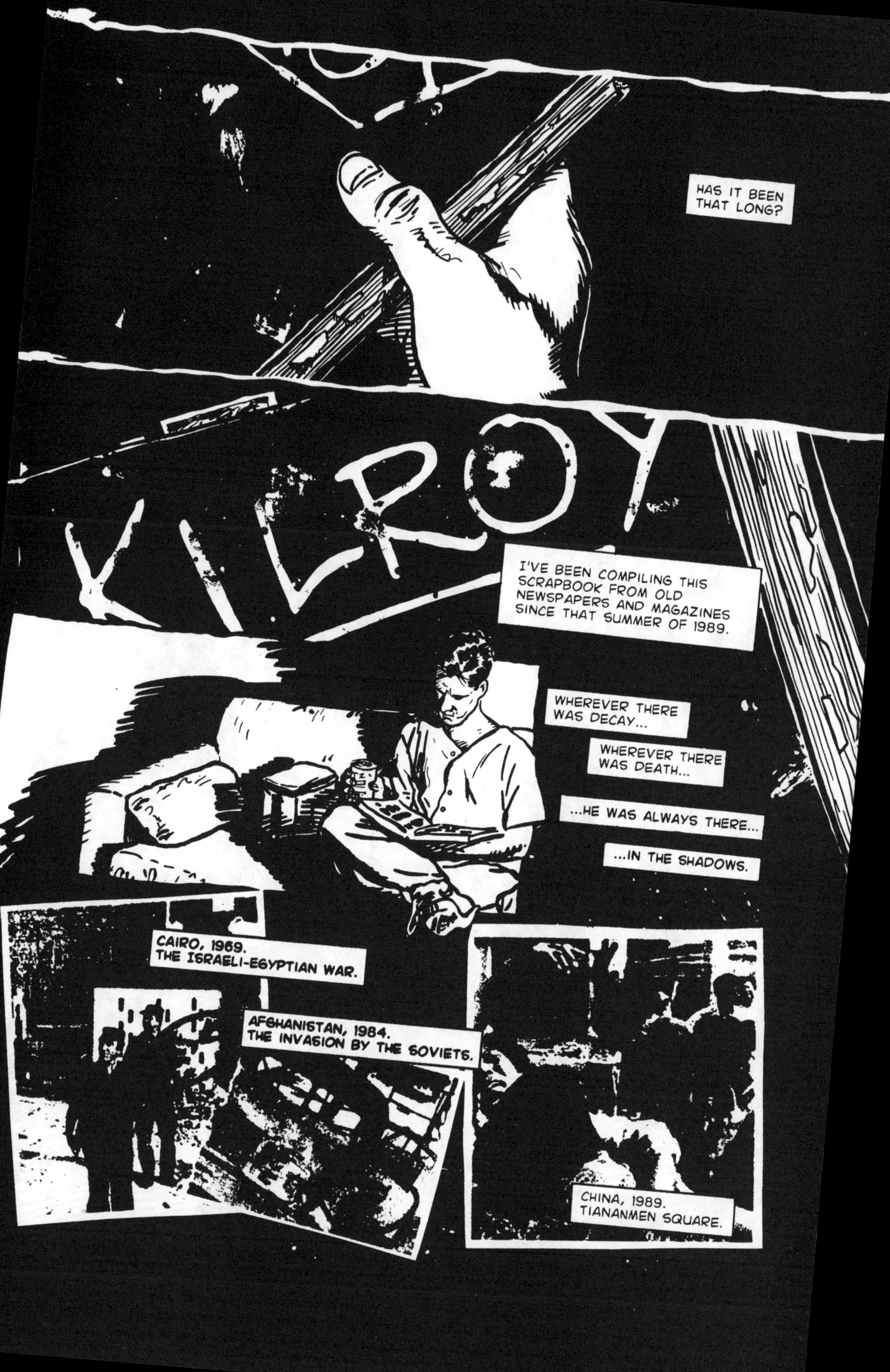
HAS IT BEEN THAT LONG?
KILROY
I'VE BEEN COMPILING THIS SCRAPBOOK FROM OLD NEWSPAPERS AND MAGAZINES SINCE THAT SUMMER OF 1989.
WHEREVER THERE WAS DECAY...
WHEREVER THERE WAS DEATH...
...HE WAS ALWAYS THERE...
...IN THE SHADOWS.
CAIRO, 1969.
THE ISRAELI-EGYPTIAN WAR.
AFGHANISTAN, 1984.
THE INVASION BY THE SOVIETS.
CHINA, 1989.
TIANANMEN SQUARE.

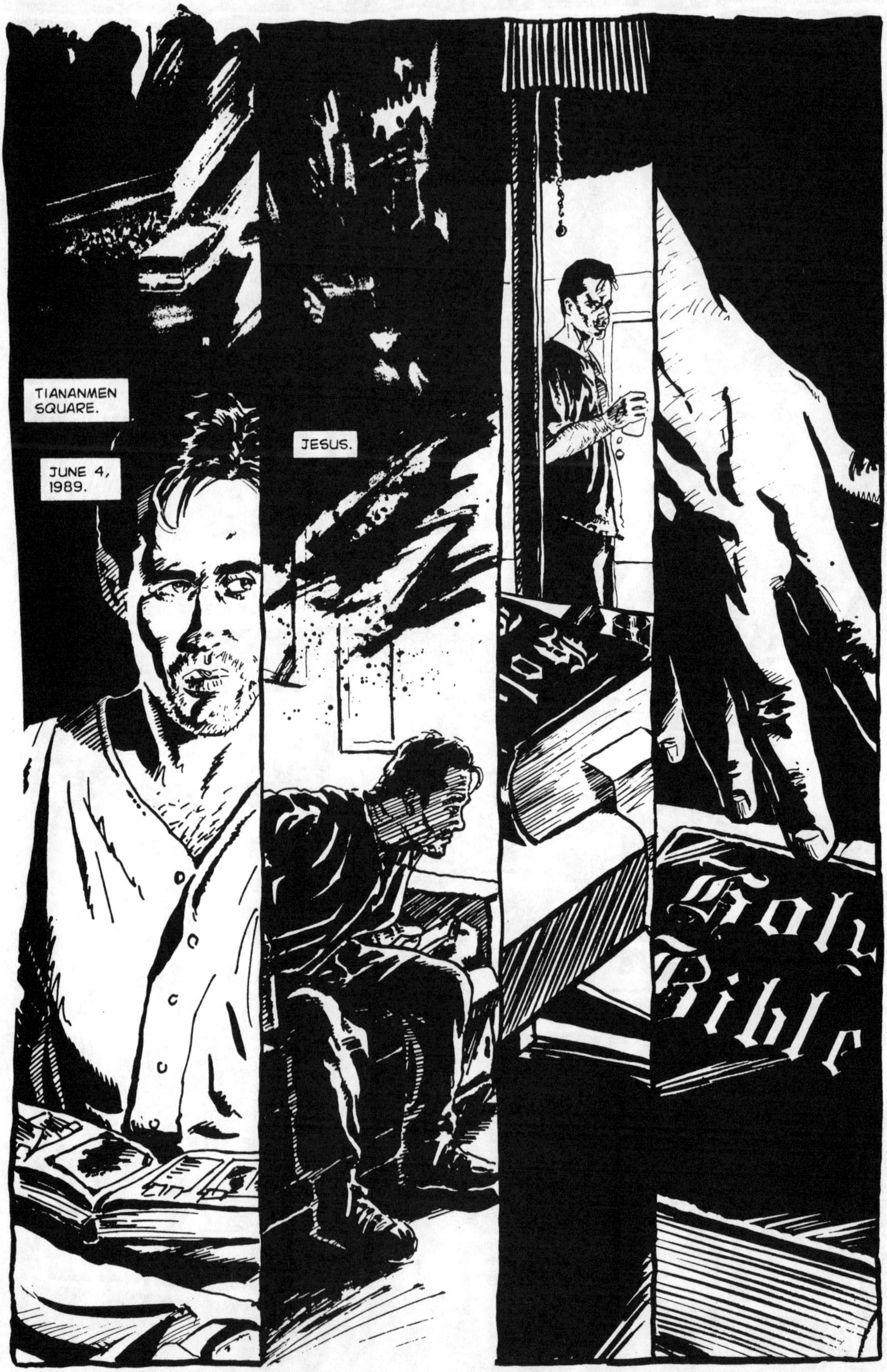
TIANANMEN SQUARE.
JUNE 4, 1989.
JESUS.
Holy Bible

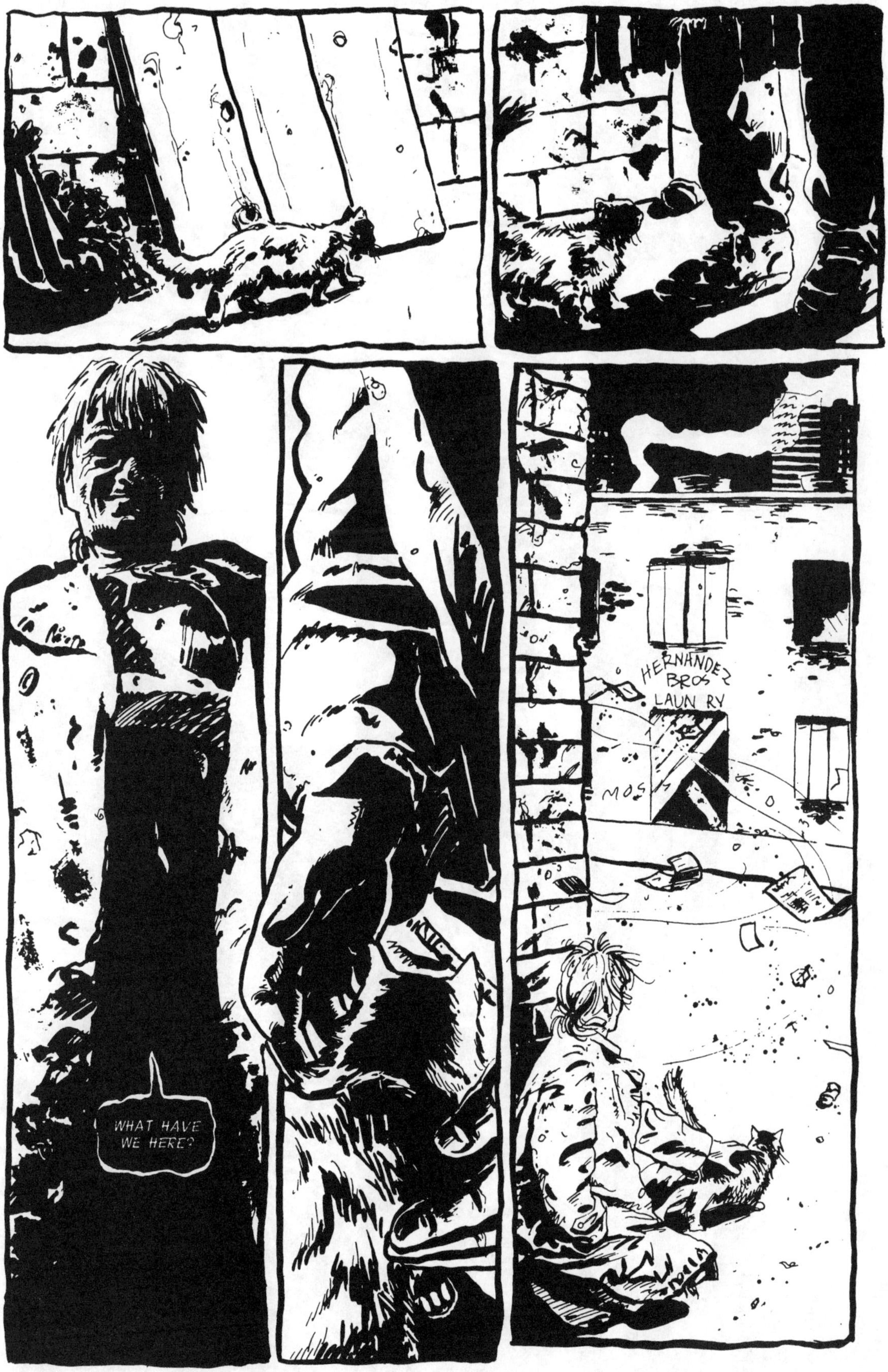
WHAT HAVE WE HERE?
HERNANDEZ BROS LAUN RY
MOS

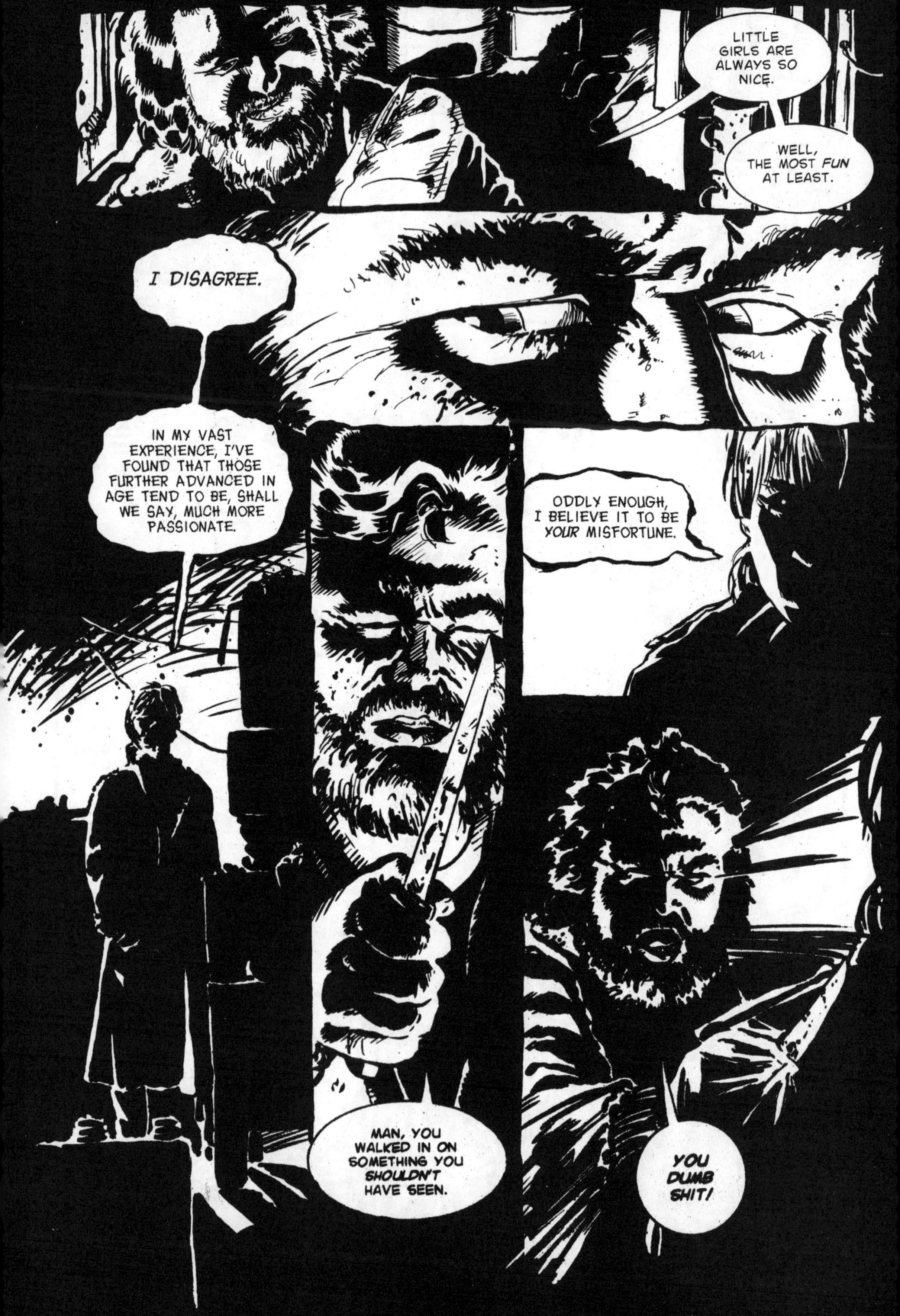
LITTLE GIRLS ARE ALWAYS SO NICE.
WELL, THE MOST *FUN* AT LEAST.
I DISAGREE.
IN MY VAST EXPERIENCE, I'VE FOUND THAT THOSE FURTHER ADVANCED IN AGE TEND TO BE, SHALL WE SAY, MUCH MORE PASSIONATE.
ODDLY ENOUGH, I BELIEVE IT TO BE *YOUR* MISFORTUNE.
MAN, YOU WALKED IN ON SOMETHING YOU *SHOULDN'T* HAVE SEEN.
YOU DUMB SHIT!

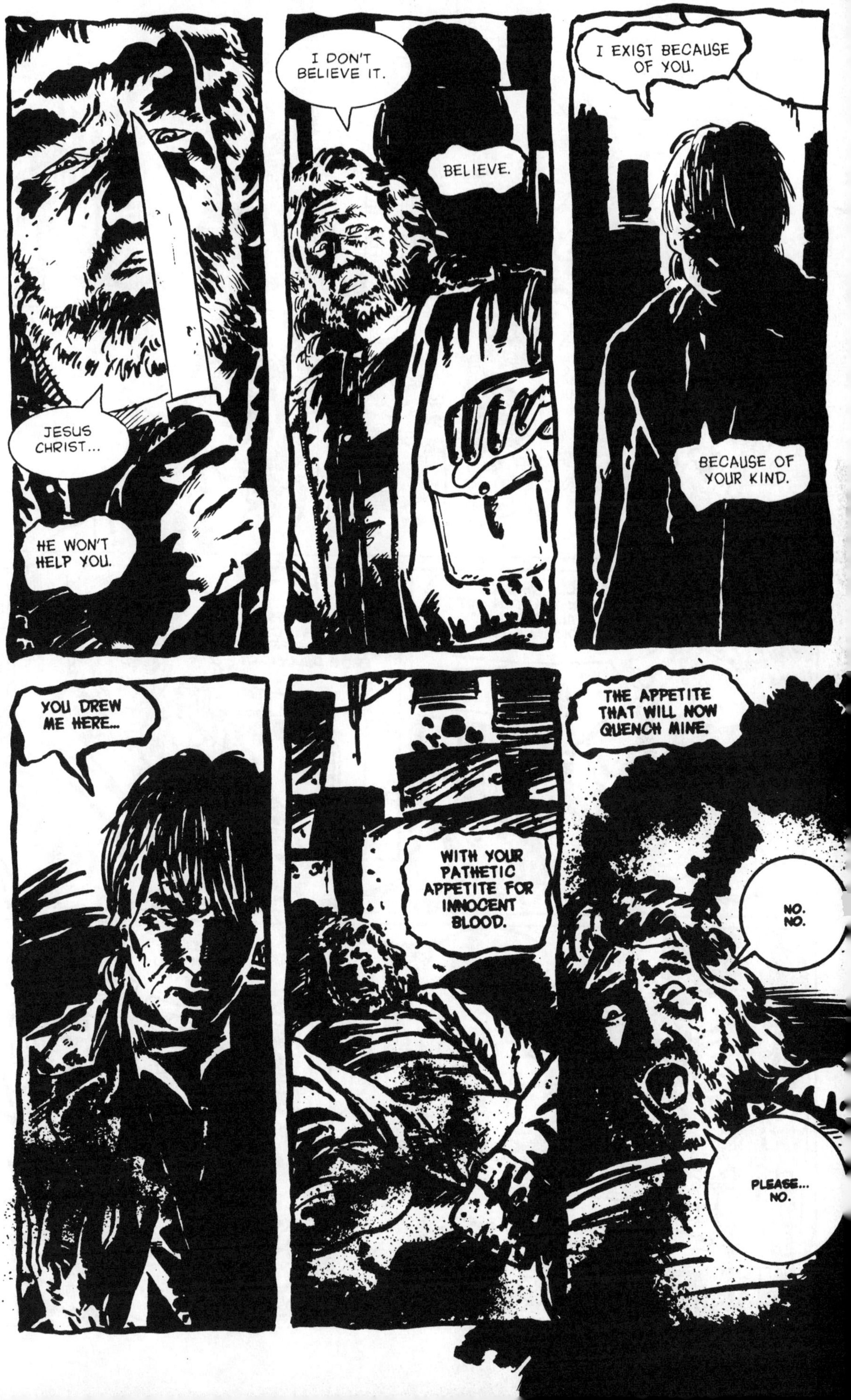
JESUS CHRIST...
HE WON'T HELP YOU.
I DON'T BELIEVE IT.
BELIEVE.
I EXIST BECAUSE OF YOU.
BECAUSE OF YOUR KIND.
YOU DREW ME HERE...
WITH YOUR PATHETIC APPETITE FOR INNOCENT BLOOD.
THE APPETITE THAT WILL NOW QUENCH MINE.
NO. NO.
PLEASE... NO.

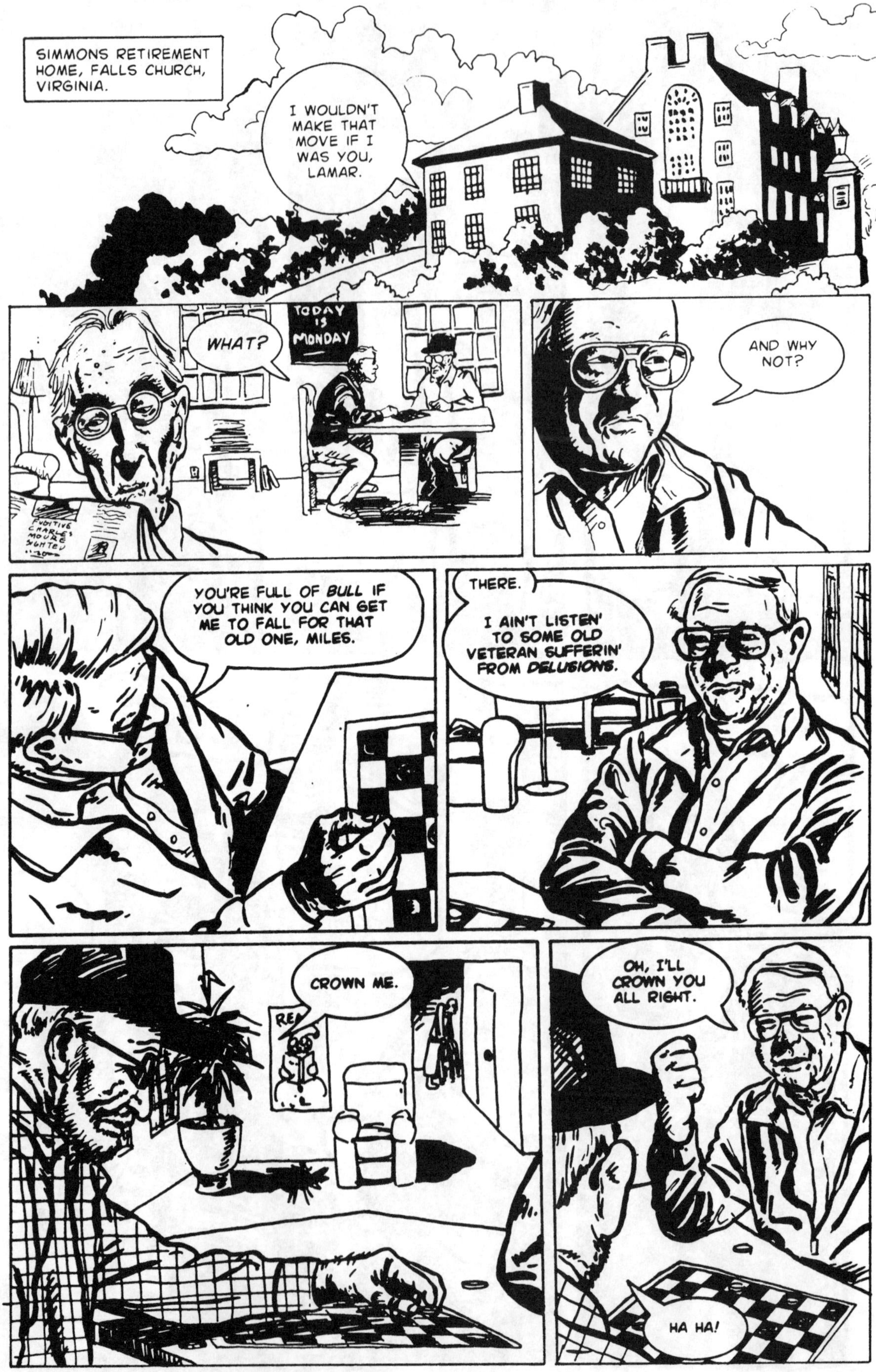
SIMMONS RETIREMENT HOME, FALLS CHURCH, VIRGINIA.
I WOULDN'T MAKE THAT MOVE IF I WAS YOU, LAMAR.
TODAY IS MONDAY
WHAT?
AND WHY NOT?
YOU'RE FULL OF BULL IF YOU THINK YOU CAN GET ME TO FALL FOR THAT OLD ONE, MILES.
THERE.
I AIN'T LISTEN' TO SOME OLD VETERAN SUFFERIN' FROM DELUSIONS.
CROWN ME.
OH, I'LL CROWN YOU ALL RIGHT.
HA HA!

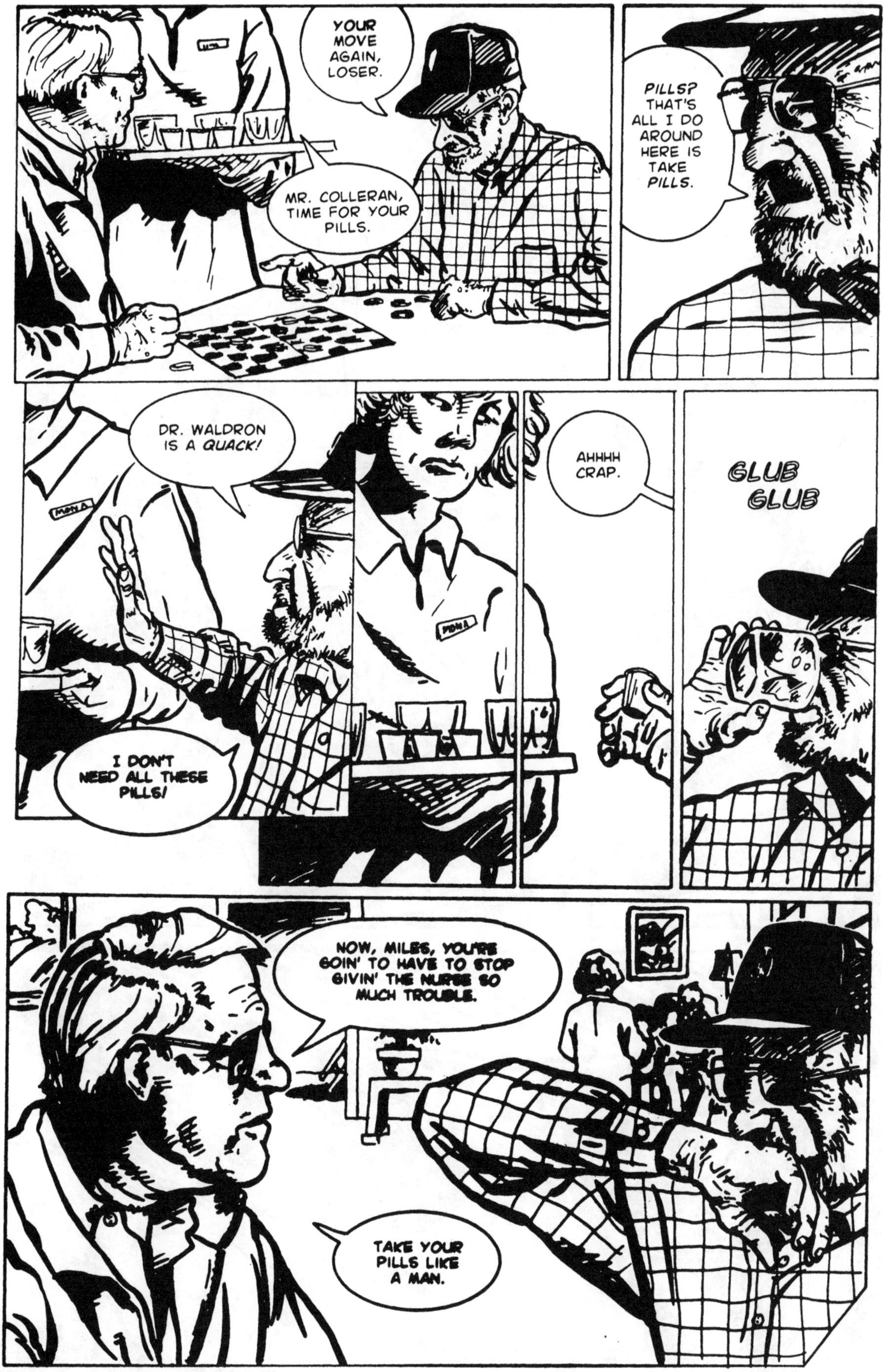
YOUR MOVE AGAIN, LOSER.
MR. COLLERAN, TIME FOR YOUR PILLS.
PILLS? THAT'S ALL I DO AROUND HERE IS TAKE PILLS.
DR. WALDRON IS A QUACK!
I DON'T NEED ALL THESE PILLS!
AHHHH CRAP.
GLUB GLUB
NOW, MILES, YOU'RE GOIN' TO HAVE TO STOP GIVIN' THE NURSE SO MUCH TROUBLE.
TAKE YOUR PILLS LIKE A MAN.

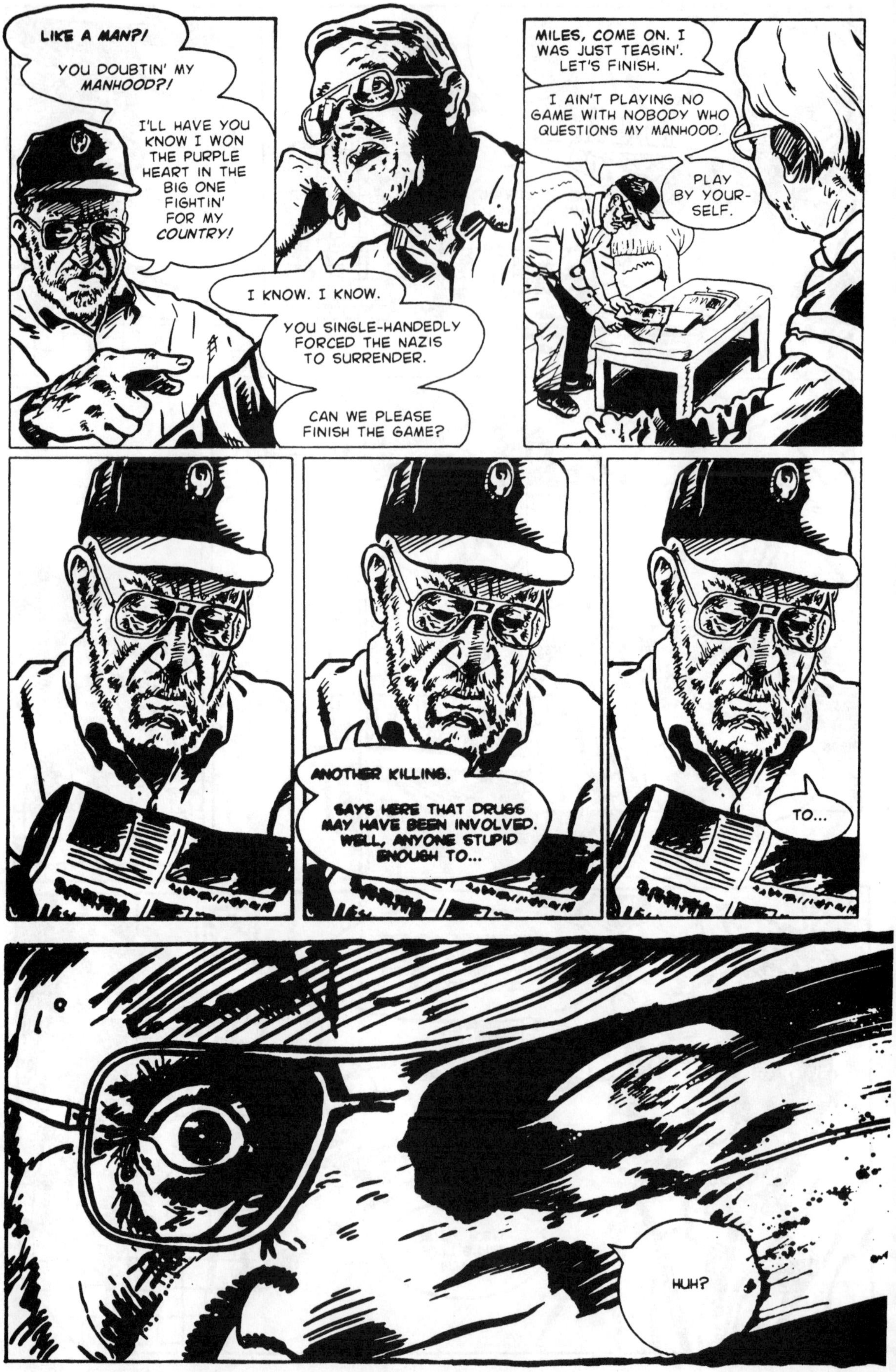
LIKE A MAN?!
YOU DOUBTIN' MY MANHOOD?!
I'LL HAVE YOU KNOW I WON THE PURPLE HEART IN THE BIG ONE FIGHTIN' FOR MY COUNTRY!
I KNOW. I KNOW.
YOU SINGLE-HANDEDLY FORCED THE NAZIS TO SURRENDER.
CAN WE PLEASE FINISH THE GAME?
MILES, COME ON. I WAS JUST TEASIN'. LET'S FINISH.
I AIN'T PLAYING NO GAME WITH NOBODY WHO QUESTIONS MY MANHOOD.
PLAY BY YOURSELF.
ANOTHER KILLING.
SAYS HERE THAT DRUGS MAY HAVE BEEN INVOLVED. WELL, ANYONE STUPID ENOUGH TO...
TO...
HUH?

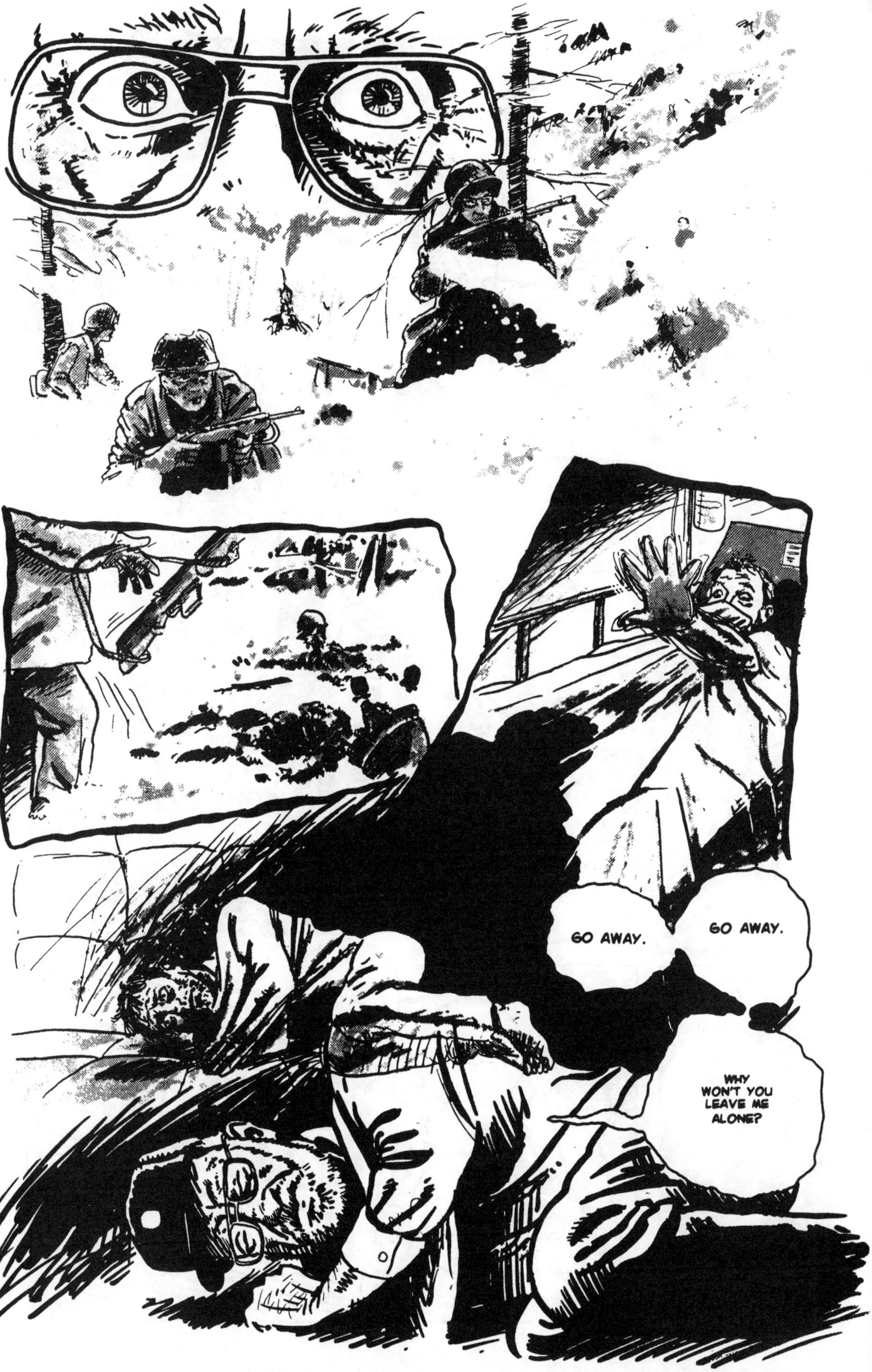
GO AWAY.
GO AWAY.
WHY WON'T YOU LEAVE ME ALONE?

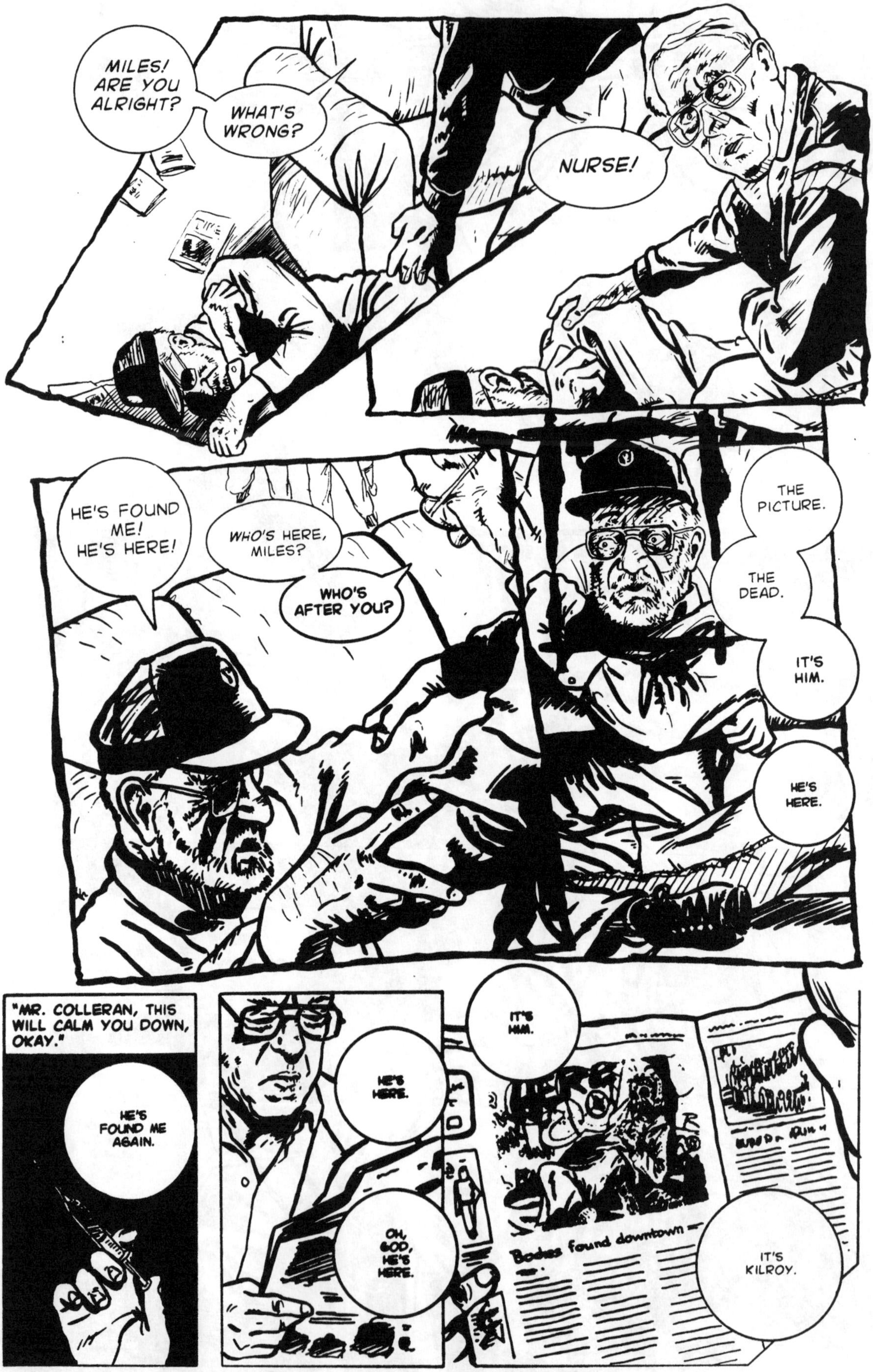
MILES! ARE YOU ALRIGHT?
WHAT'S WRONG?
NURSE!
HE'S FOUND ME! HE'S HERE!
WHO'S HERE, MILES?
WHO'S AFTER YOU?
THE PICTURE.
THE DEAD.
IT'S HIM.
HE'S HERE.
"MR. COLLERAN, THIS WILL CALM YOU DOWN, OKAY."
HE'S FOUND ME AGAIN.
IT'S HIM.
HE'S HERE.
OH, GOD, HE'S HERE.
Bodies found downtown
IT'S KILROY.

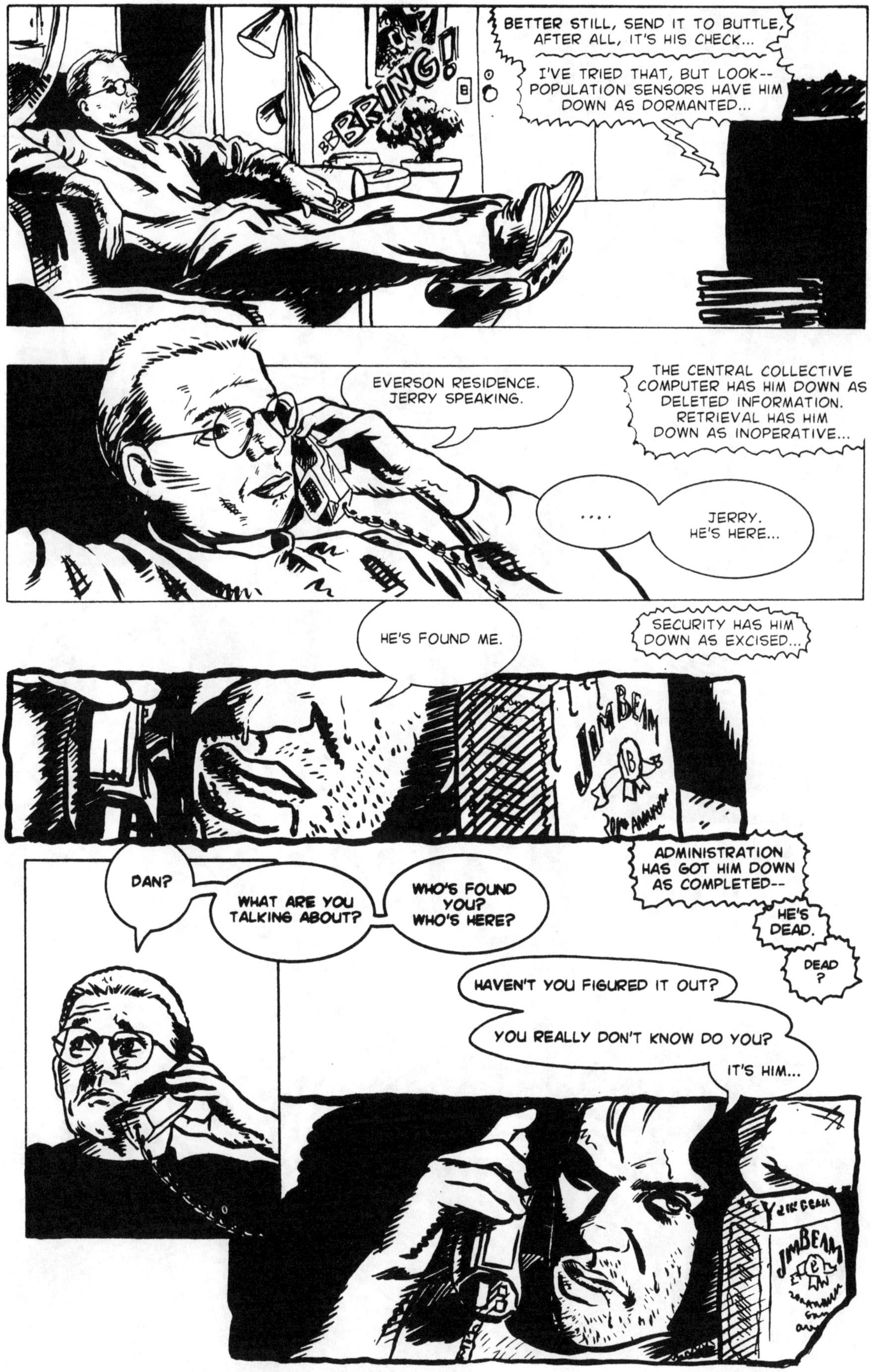
BBBRING!
BETTER STILL, SEND IT TO BUTTLE, AFTER ALL, IT'S HIS CHECK...
I'VE TRIED THAT, BUT LOOK-- POPULATION SENSORS HAVE HIM DOWN AS DORMANTED...
EVERSON RESIDENCE. JERRY SPEAKING.
THE CENTRAL COLLECTIVE COMPUTER HAS HIM DOWN AS DELETED INFORMATION. RETRIEVAL HAS HIM DOWN AS INOPERATIVE...
....
JERRY. HE'S HERE...
HE'S FOUND ME.
SECURITY HAS HIM DOWN AS EXCISED...
JIM BEAM
ADMINISTRATION HAS GOT HIM DOWN AS COMPLETED--
DAN?
WHAT ARE YOU TALKING ABOUT?
WHO'S FOUND YOU? WHO'S HERE?
HE'S DEAD.
DEAD?
HAVEN'T YOU FIGURED IT OUT?
YOU REALLY DON'T KNOW DO YOU?
IT'S HIM...
JIM BEAM

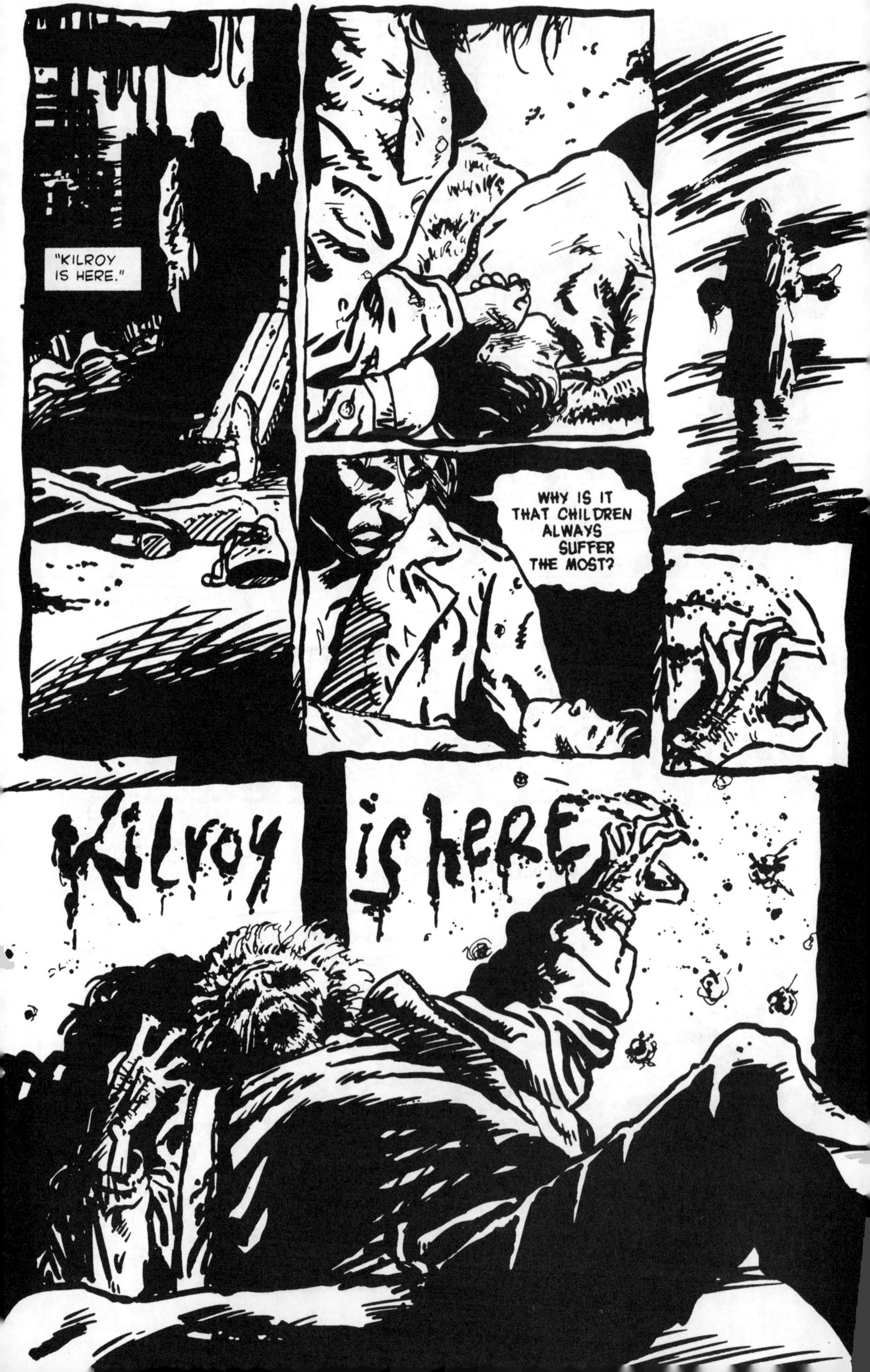
"KILROY IS HERE."
WHY IS IT THAT CHILDREN ALWAYS SUFFER THE MOST?
Kilroy is here

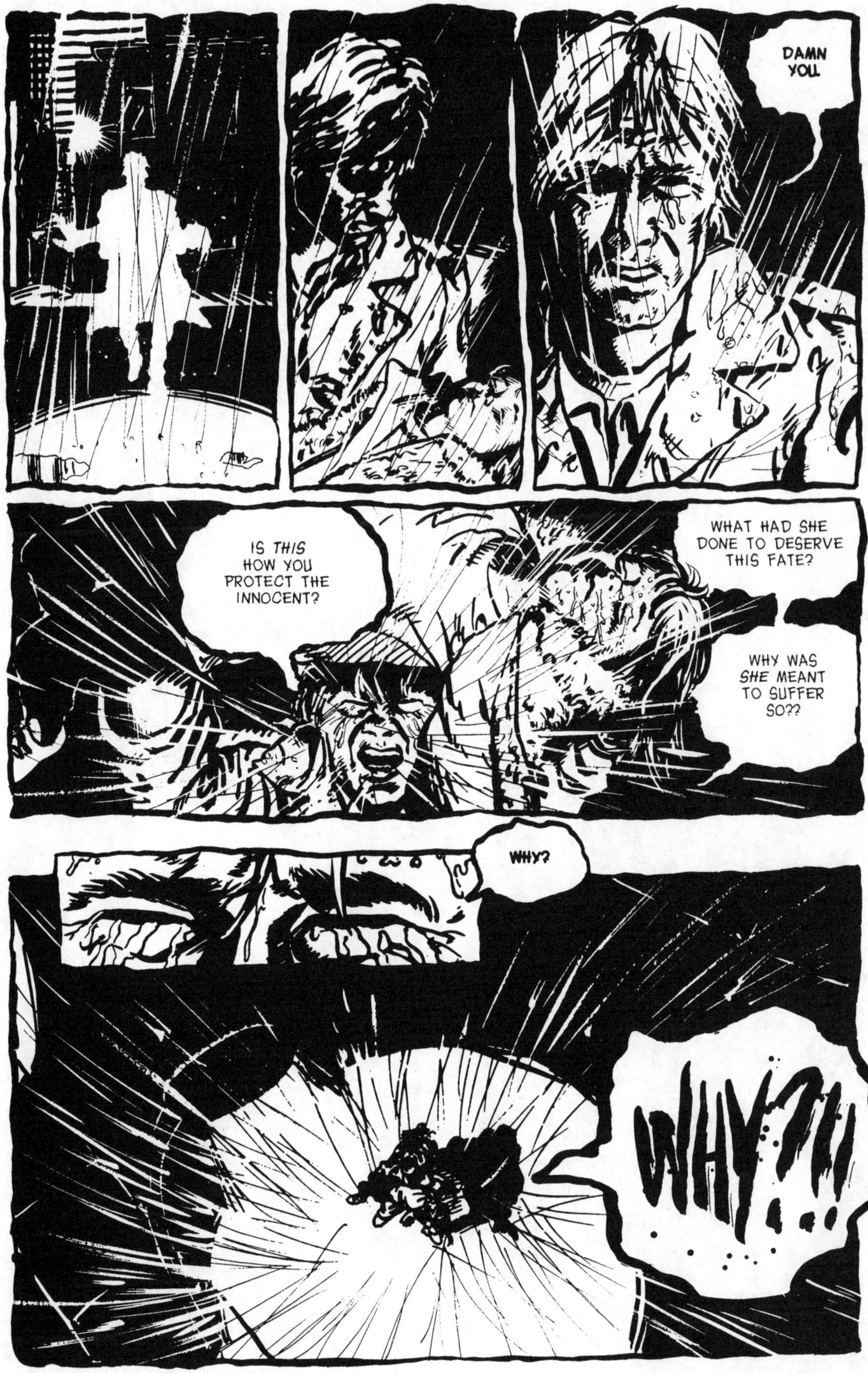
DAMN YOU
IS THIS HOW YOU PROTECT THE INNOCENT?
WHAT HAD SHE DONE TO DESERVE THIS FATE?
WHY WAS SHE MEANT TO SUFFER SO??
WHY?
WHY?!!

WHY?
TO BE CONTINUED...

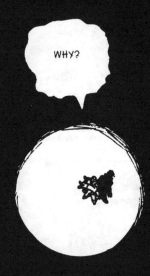

"Reflections"
Chapter Two

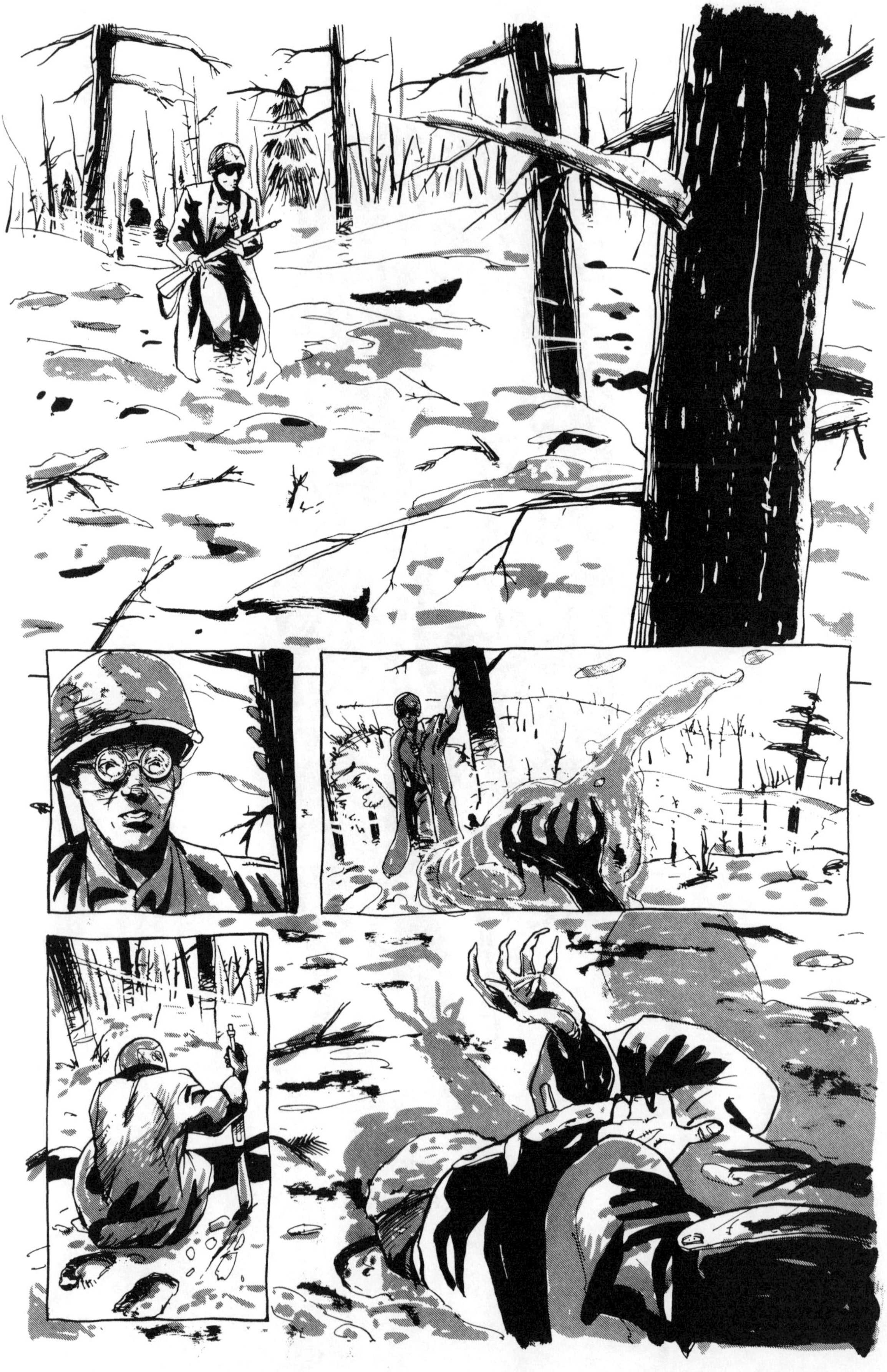

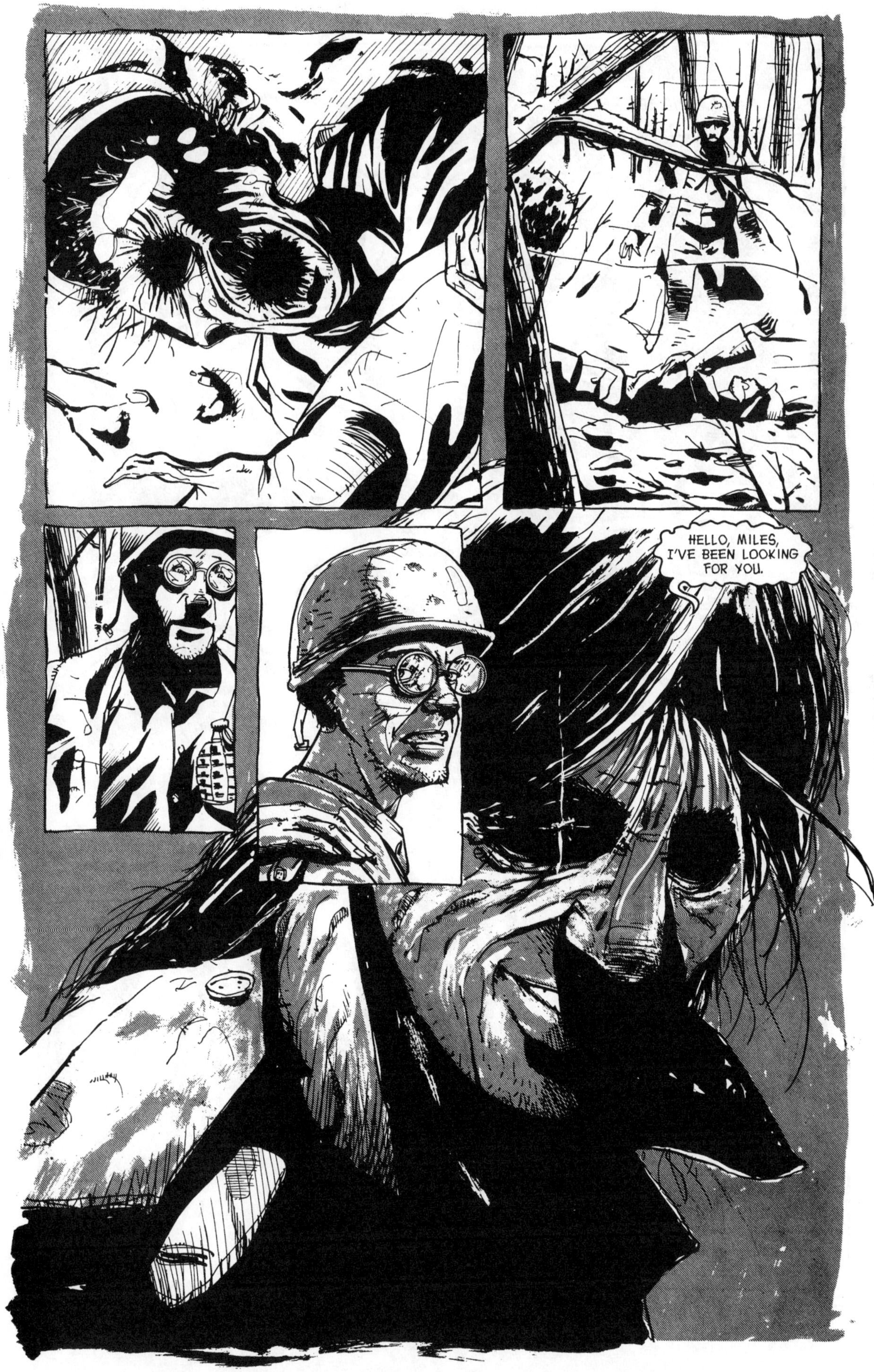
HELLO, MILES, I'VE BEEN LOOKING FOR YOU.

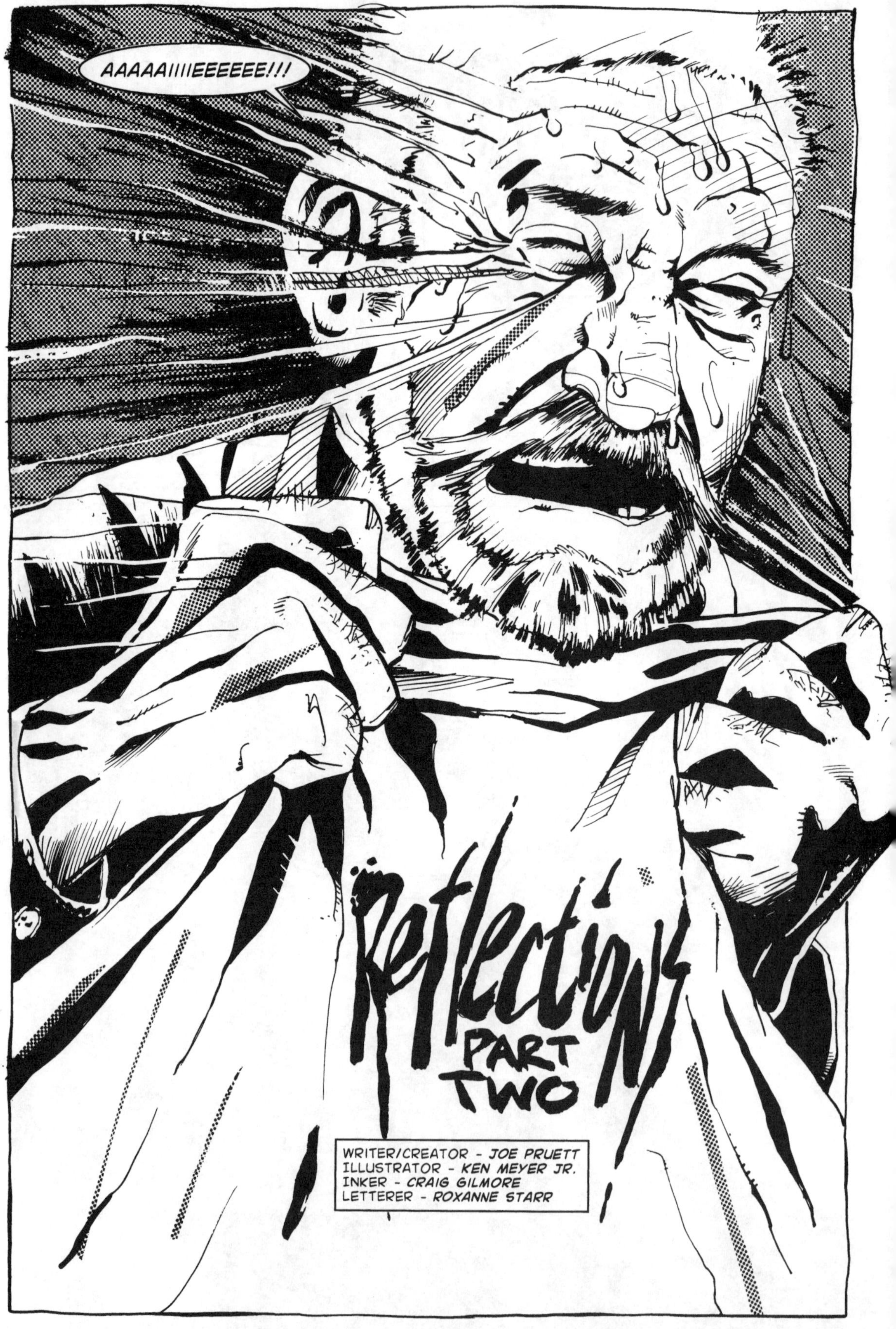
AAAAAIIIIEEEEEE!!!
Reflections
PART TWO
WRITER/CREATOR - JOE PRUETT
ILLUSTRATOR - KEN MEYER JR.
INKER - CRAIG GILMORE
LETTERER - ROXANNE STARR

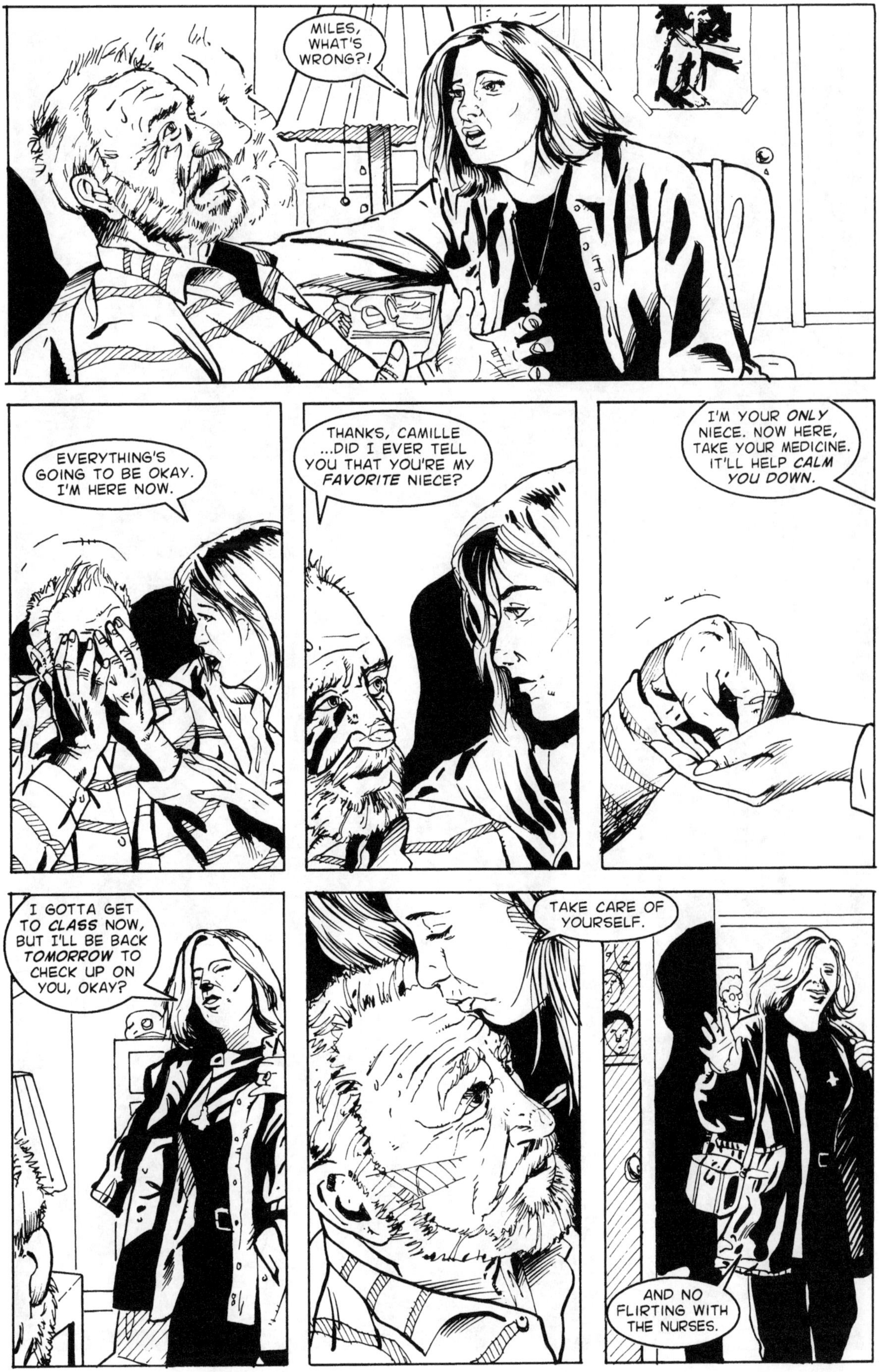
MILES, WHAT'S WRONG?!
EVERYTHING'S GOING TO BE OKAY. I'M HERE NOW.
THANKS, CAMILLE ...DID I EVER TELL YOU THAT YOU'RE MY *FAVORITE* NIECE?
I'M YOUR *ONLY* NIECE. NOW HERE, TAKE YOUR MEDICINE. IT'LL HELP *CALM YOU DOWN.*
I GOTTA GET TO *CLASS* NOW, BUT I'LL BE BACK *TOMORROW* TO CHECK UP ON YOU, OKAY?
TAKE CARE OF YOURSELF.
AND NO FLIRTING WITH THE NURSES.

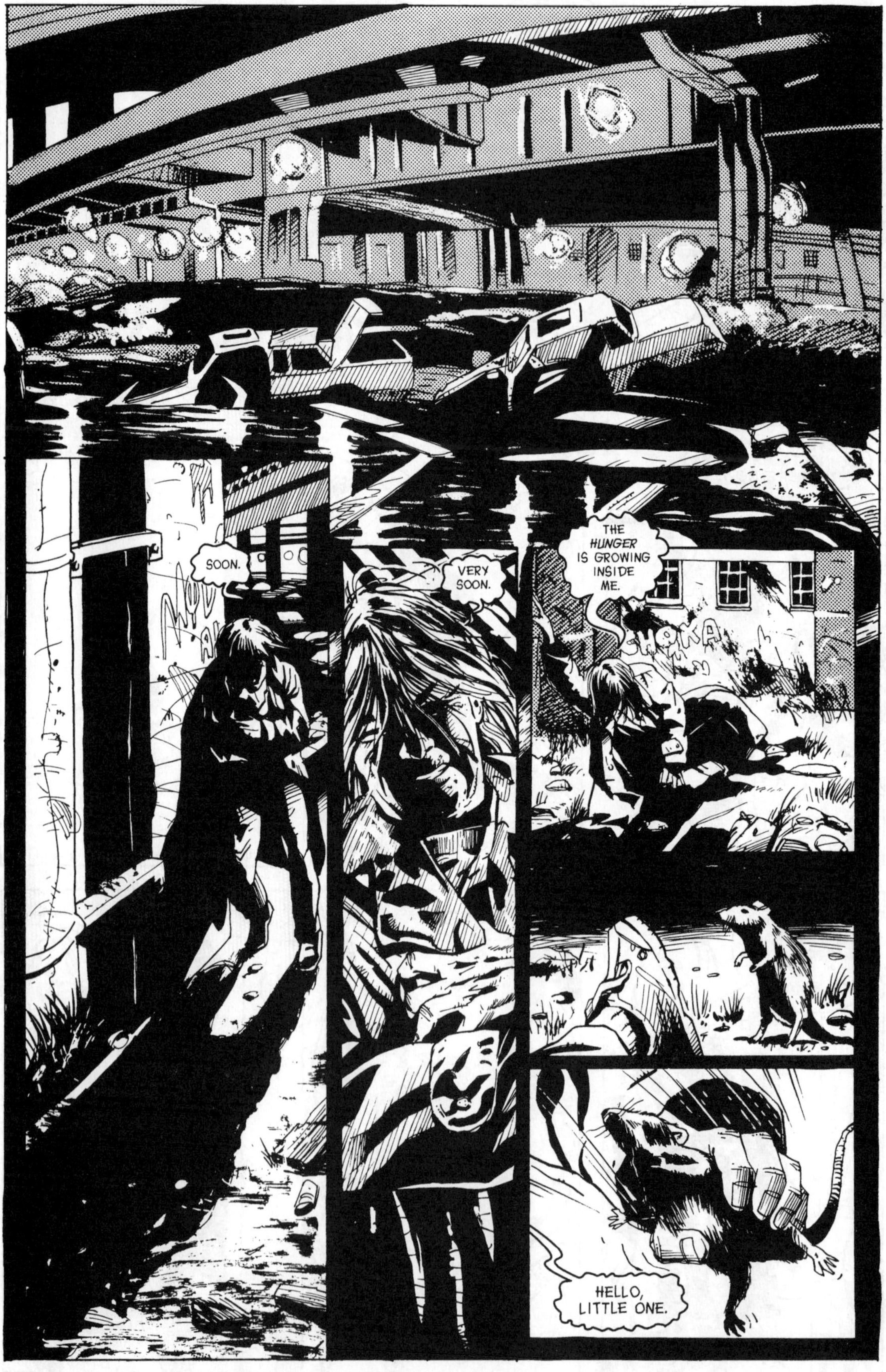
SOON.
VERY SOON.
THE HUNGER IS GROWING INSIDE ME.
HELLO, LITTLE ONE.

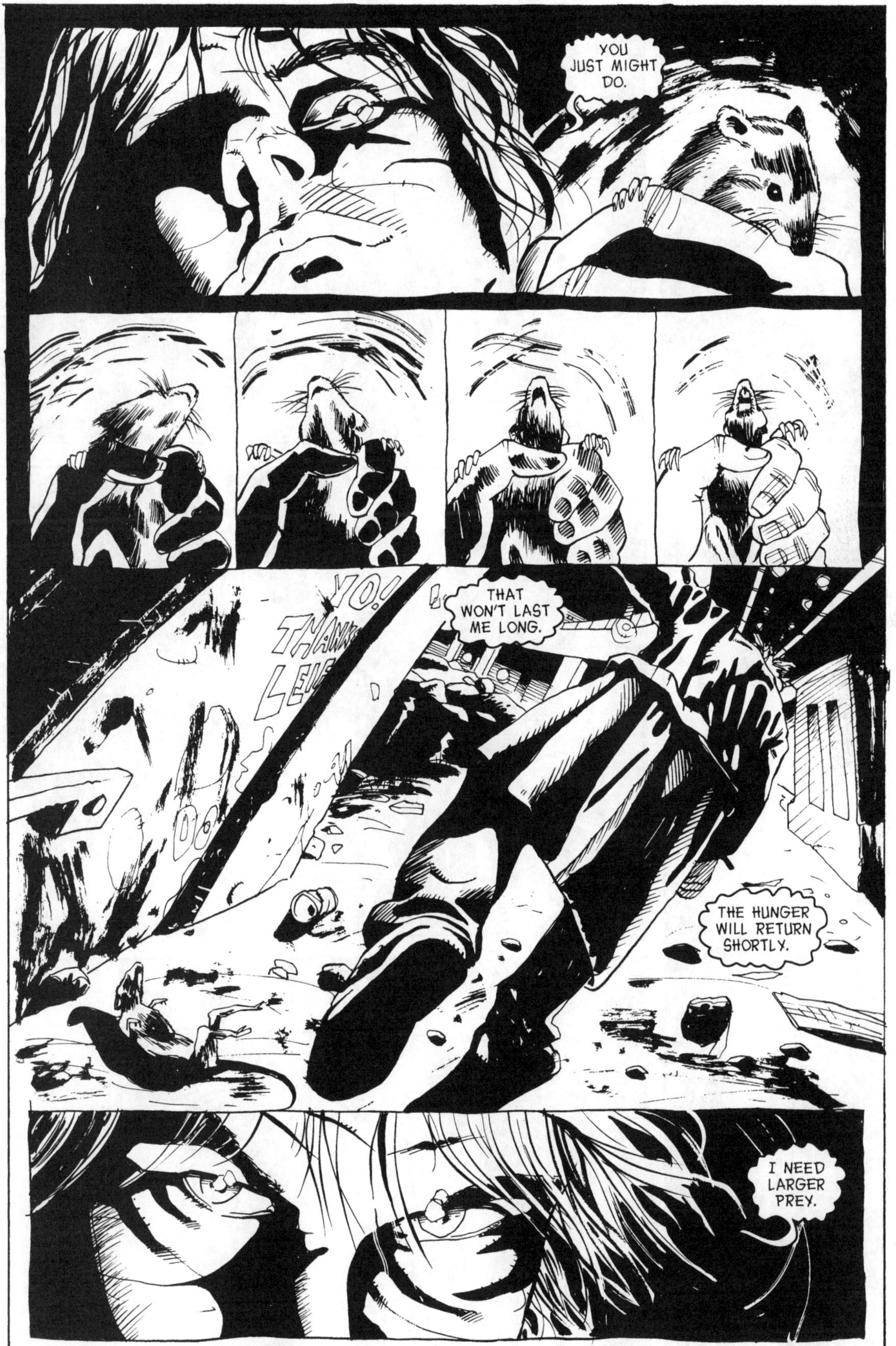
YOU JUST MIGHT DO.
YO!
THAT WON'T LAST ME LONG.
THE HUNGER WILL RETURN SHORTLY.
I NEED LARGER PREY.

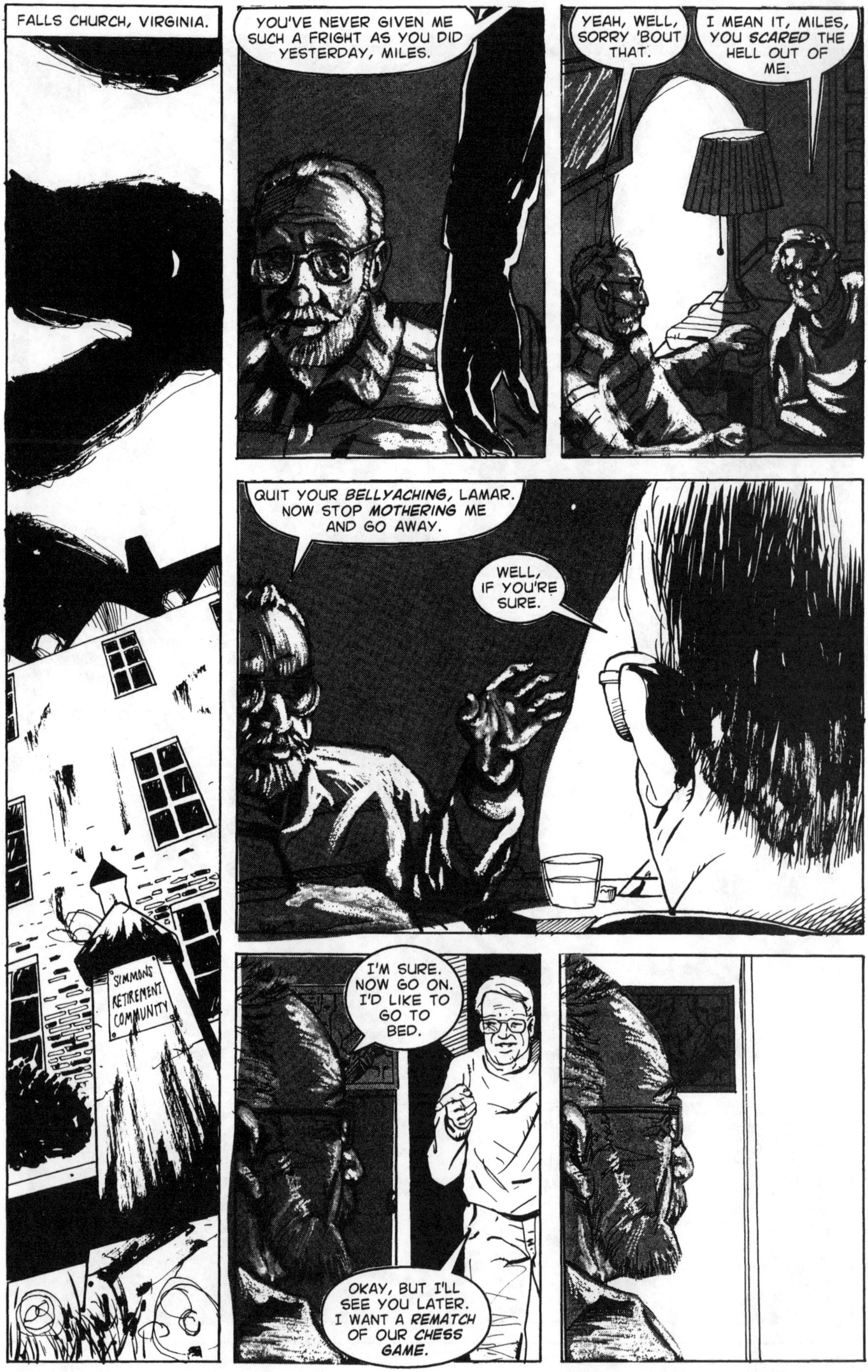
FALLS CHURCH, VIRGINIA.
YOU'VE NEVER GIVEN ME SUCH A FRIGHT AS YOU DID YESTERDAY, MILES.
YEAH, WELL, SORRY 'BOUT THAT.
I MEAN IT, MILES, YOU SCARED THE HELL OUT OF ME.
QUIT YOUR BELLYACHING, LAMAR. NOW STOP MOTHERING ME AND GO AWAY.
WELL, IF YOU'RE SURE.
SIMMONS RETIREMENT COMMUNITY
I'M SURE. NOW GO ON. I'D LIKE TO GO TO BED.
OKAY, BUT I'LL SEE YOU LATER. I WANT A REMATCH OF OUR CHESS GAME.

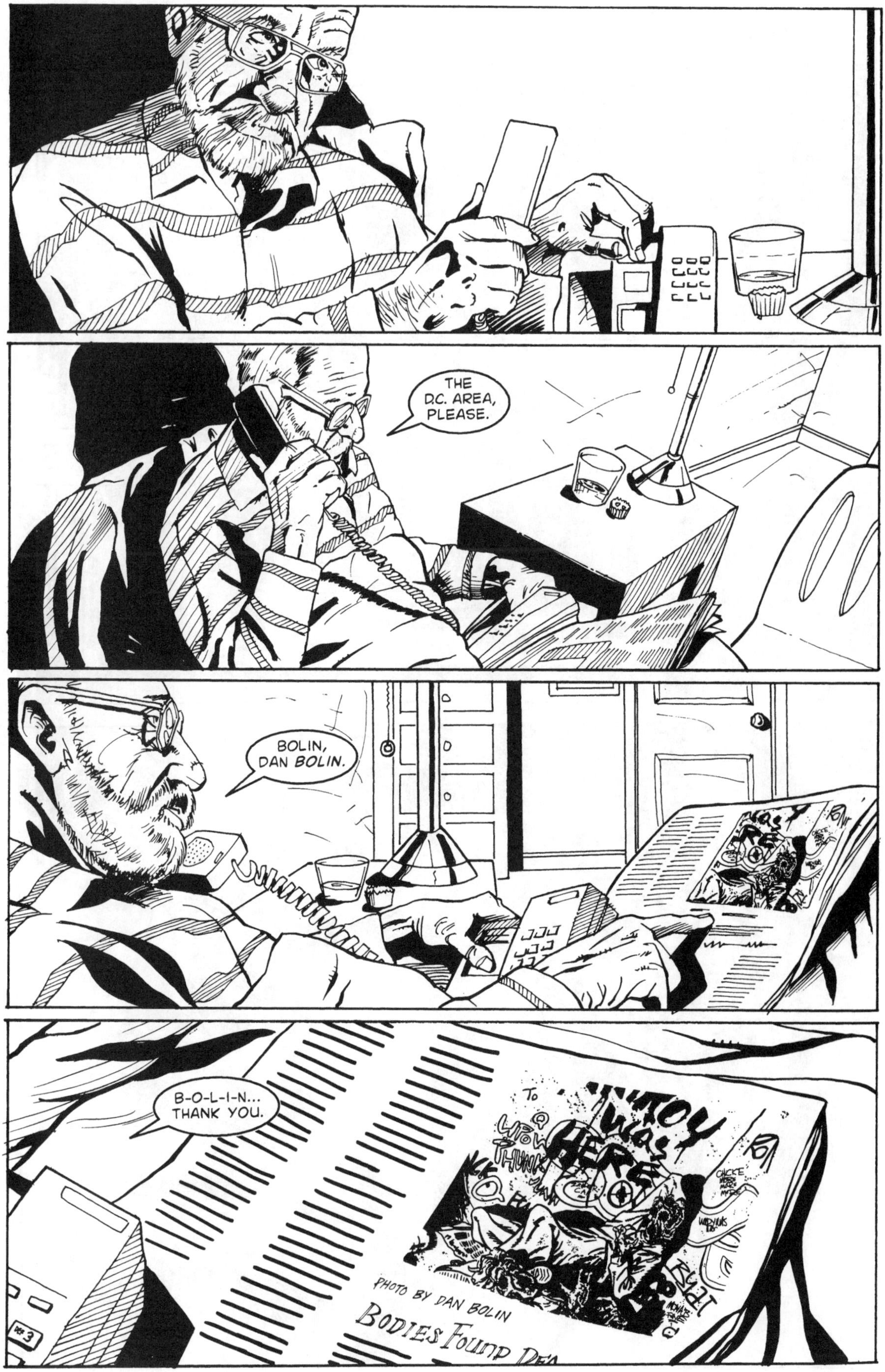

THE D.C. AREA, PLEASE.
BOLIN, DAN BOLIN.
B-O-L-I-N... THANK YOU.
PHOTO BY DAN BOLIN
BODIES FOUND

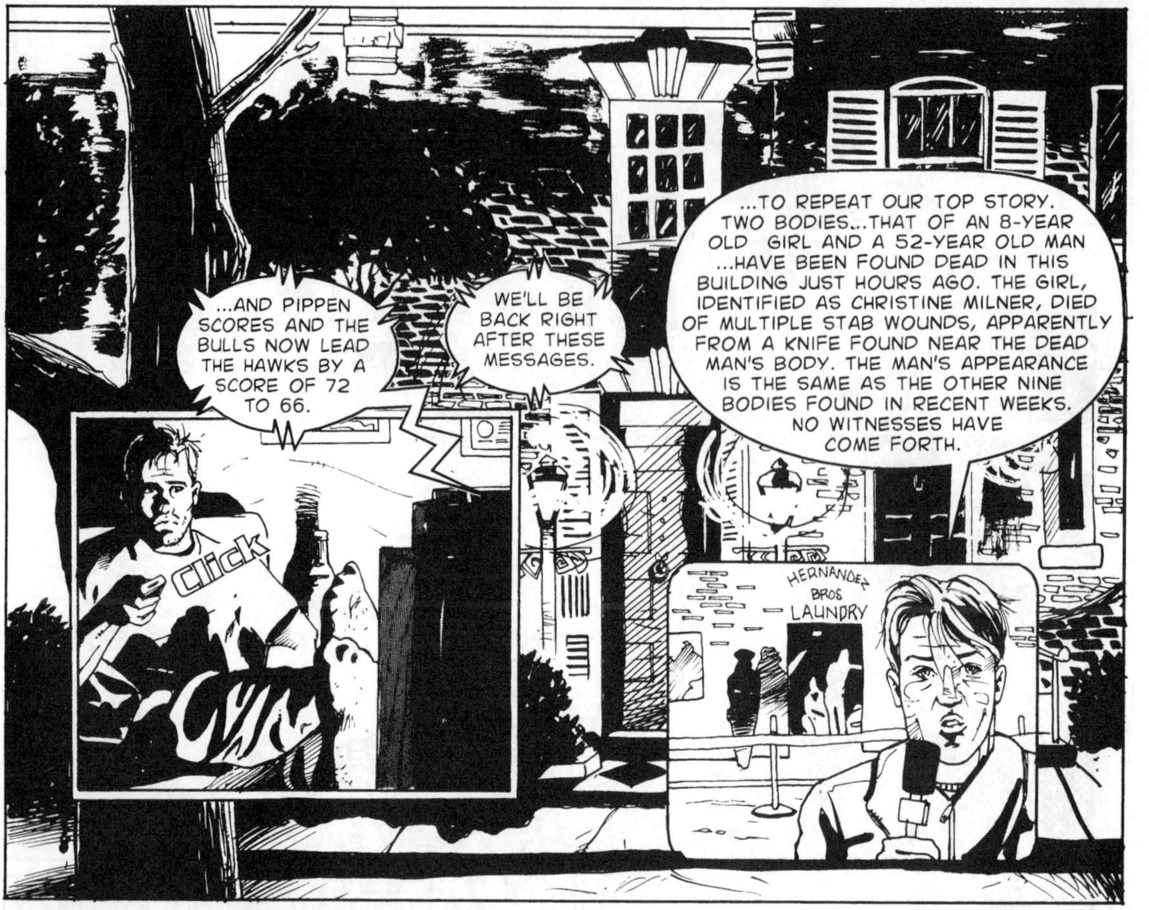
...AND PIPPEN SCORES AND THE BULLS NOW LEAD THE HAWKS BY A SCORE OF 72 TO 66.
WE'LL BE BACK RIGHT AFTER THESE MESSAGES.
...TO REPEAT OUR TOP STORY. TWO BODIES...THAT OF AN 8-YEAR OLD GIRL AND A 52-YEAR OLD MAN ...HAVE BEEN FOUND DEAD IN THIS BUILDING JUST HOURS AGO. THE GIRL, IDENTIFIED AS CHRISTINE MILNER, DIED OF MULTIPLE STAB WOUNDS, APPARENTLY FROM A KNIFE FOUND NEAR THE DEAD MAN'S BODY. THE MAN'S APPEARANCE IS THE SAME AS THE OTHER NINE BODIES FOUND IN RECENT WEEKS. NO WITNESSES HAVE COME FORTH.
CLICK
HERNANDEZ BROS LAUNDRY

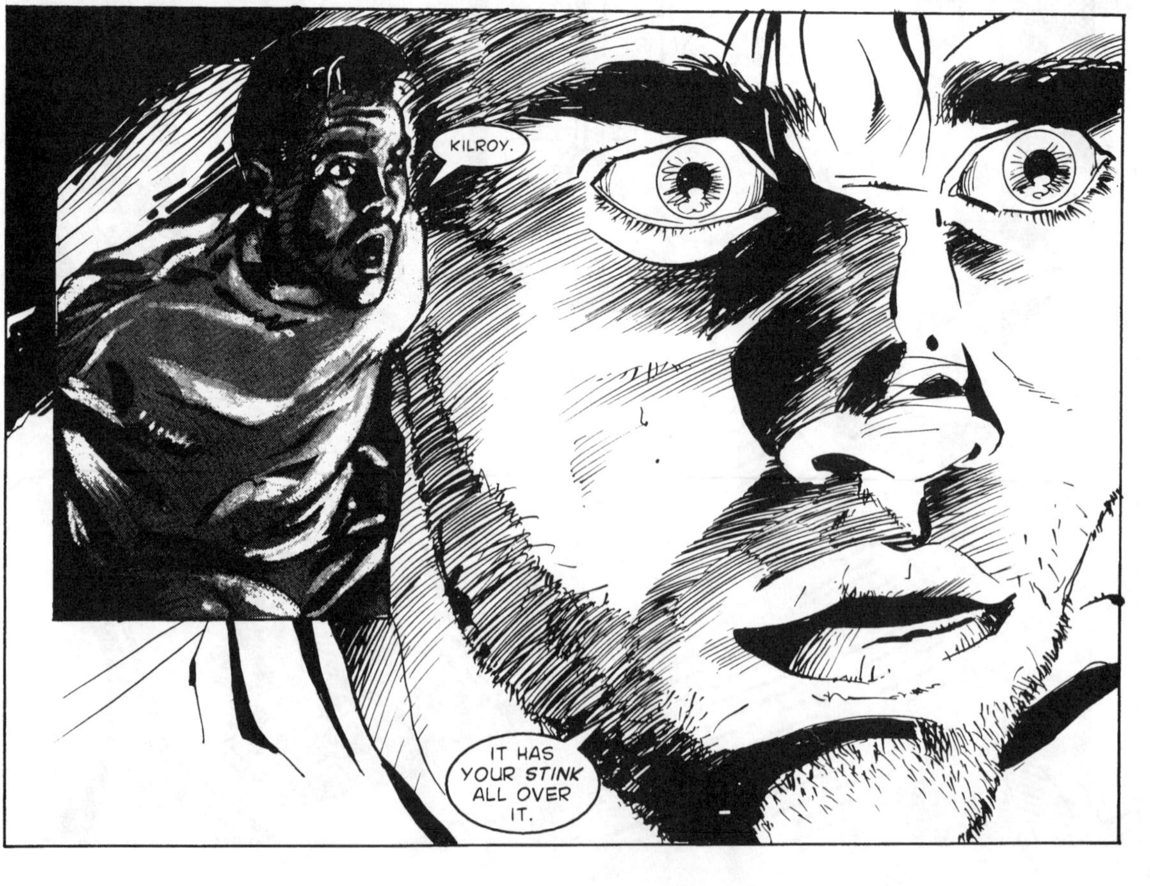
KILROY.
IT HAS YOUR *STINK* ALL OVER IT.

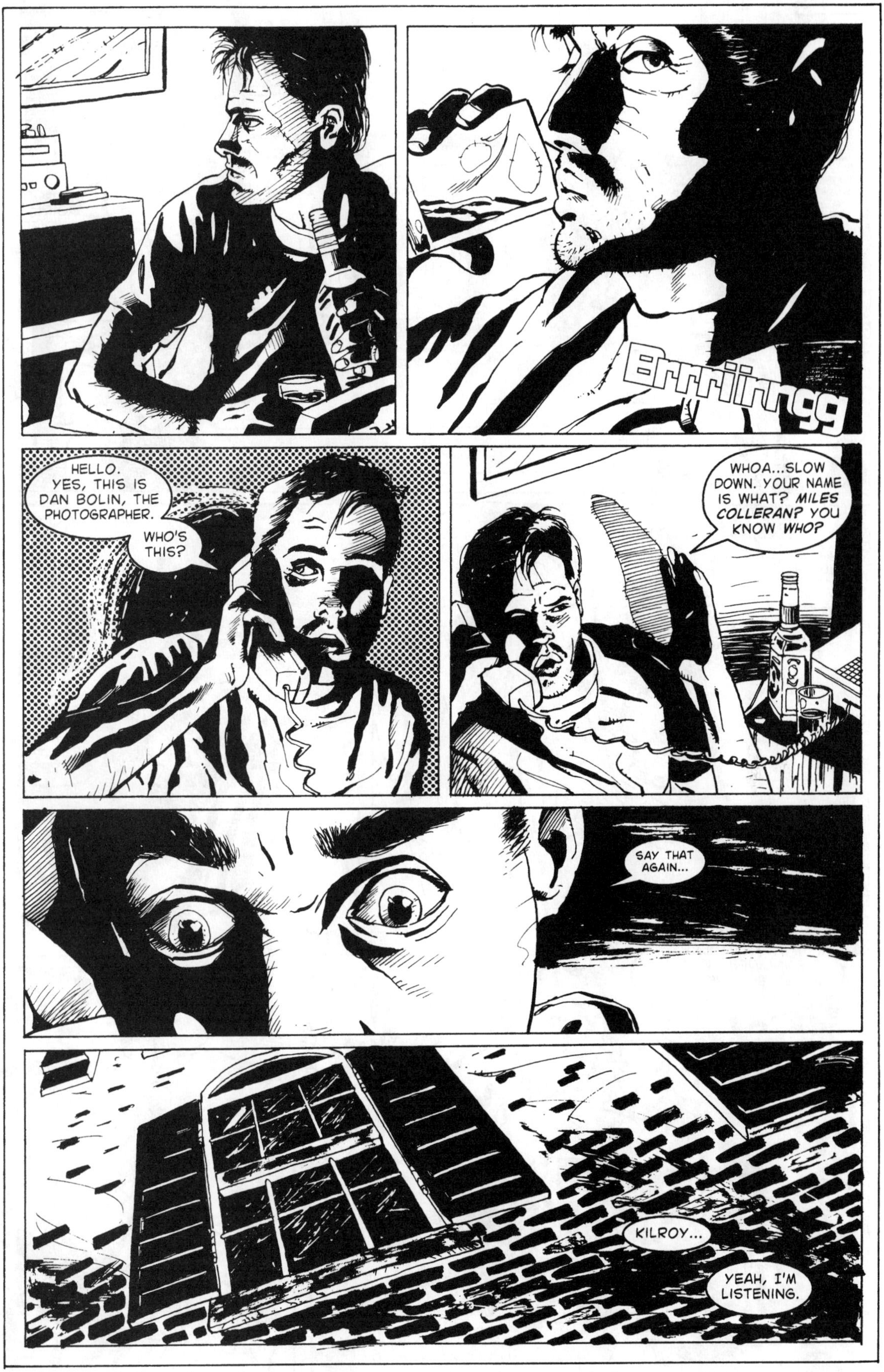
Brrrriirrngg
HELLO. YES, THIS IS DAN BOLIN, THE PHOTOGRAPHER.
WHO'S THIS?
WHOA...SLOW DOWN. YOUR NAME IS WHAT? *MILES COLLERAN?* YOU KNOW *WHO?*
SAY THAT AGAIN...
KILROY...
YEAH, I'M LISTENING.

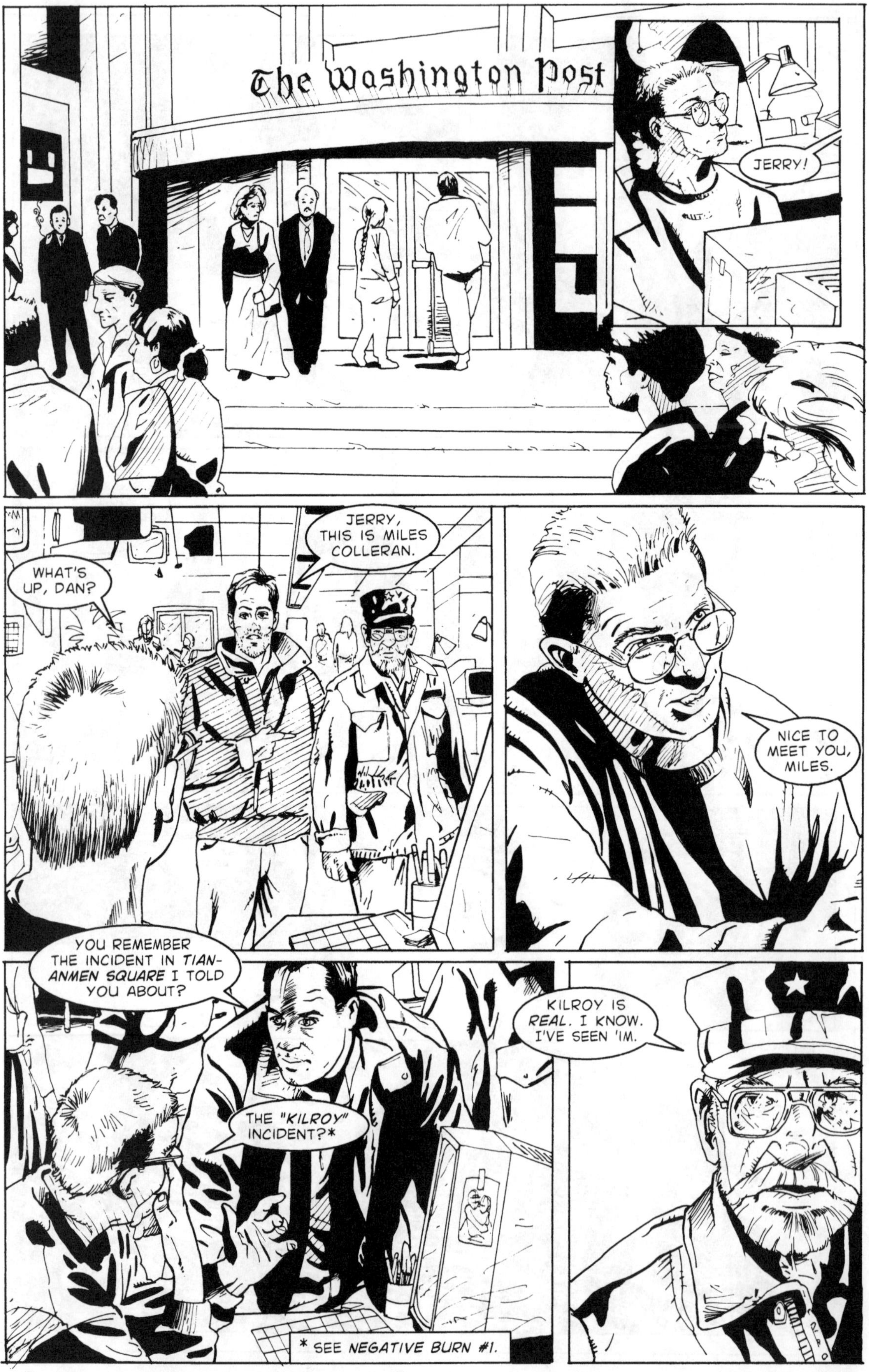
The Washington Post
JERRY!
WHAT'S UP, DAN?
JERRY, THIS IS MILES COLLERAN.
NICE TO MEET YOU, MILES.
YOU REMEMBER THE INCIDENT IN TIAN-ANMEN SQUARE I TOLD YOU ABOUT?
THE "KILROY" INCIDENT?*
KILROY IS REAL. I KNOW. I'VE SEEN 'IM.
* SEE NEGATIVE BURN #1.

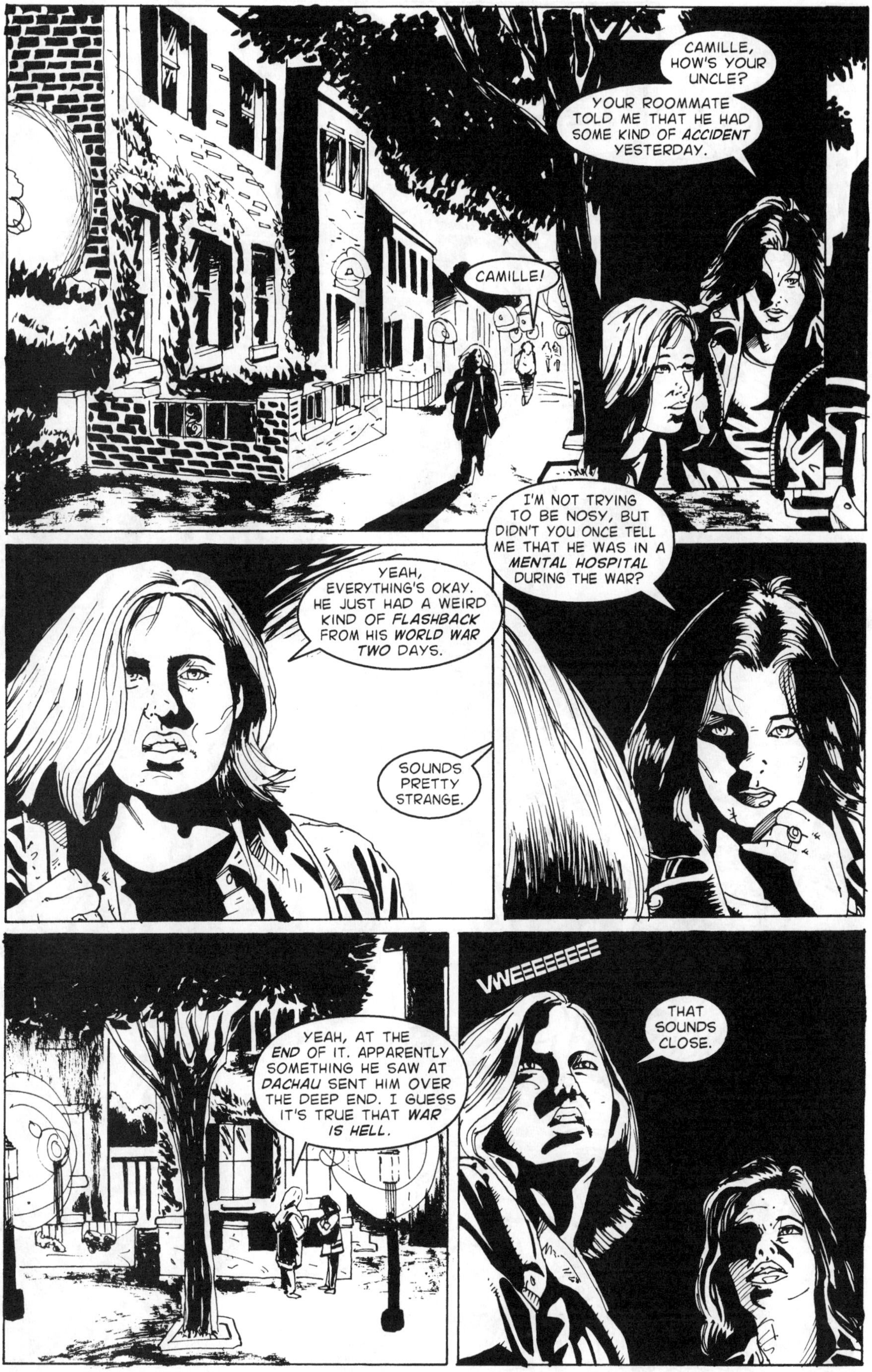
CAMILLE!
CAMILLE, HOW'S YOUR UNCLE?
YOUR ROOMMATE TOLD ME THAT HE HAD SOME KIND OF ACCIDENT YESTERDAY.
YEAH, EVERYTHING'S OKAY. HE JUST HAD A WEIRD KIND OF FLASHBACK FROM HIS WORLD WAR TWO DAYS.
I'M NOT TRYING TO BE NOSY, BUT DIDN'T YOU ONCE TELL ME THAT HE WAS IN A MENTAL HOSPITAL DURING THE WAR?
SOUNDS PRETTY STRANGE.
YEAH, AT THE END OF IT. APPARENTLY SOMETHING HE SAW AT DACHAU SENT HIM OVER THE DEEP END. I GUESS IT'S TRUE THAT WAR IS HELL.
VWEEEEEEEE
THAT SOUNDS CLOSE.

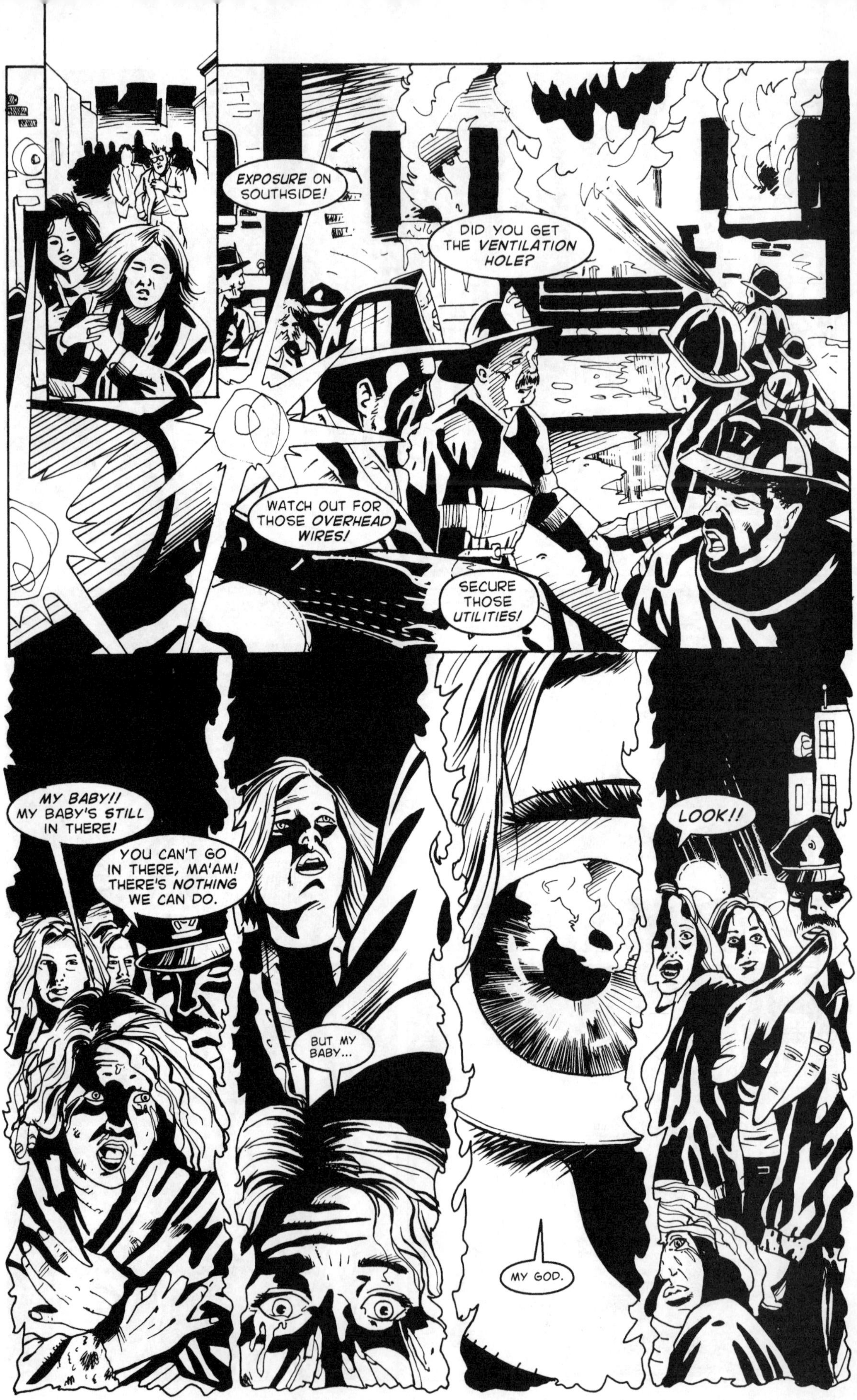
EXPOSURE ON SOUTHSIDE!
DID YOU GET THE VENTILATION HOLE?
WATCH OUT FOR THOSE OVERHEAD WIRES!
SECURE THOSE UTILITIES!
MY BABY!! MY BABY'S STILL IN THERE!
YOU CAN'T GO IN THERE, MA'AM! THERE'S NOTHING WE CAN DO.
BUT MY BABY...
MY GOD.
LOOK!!

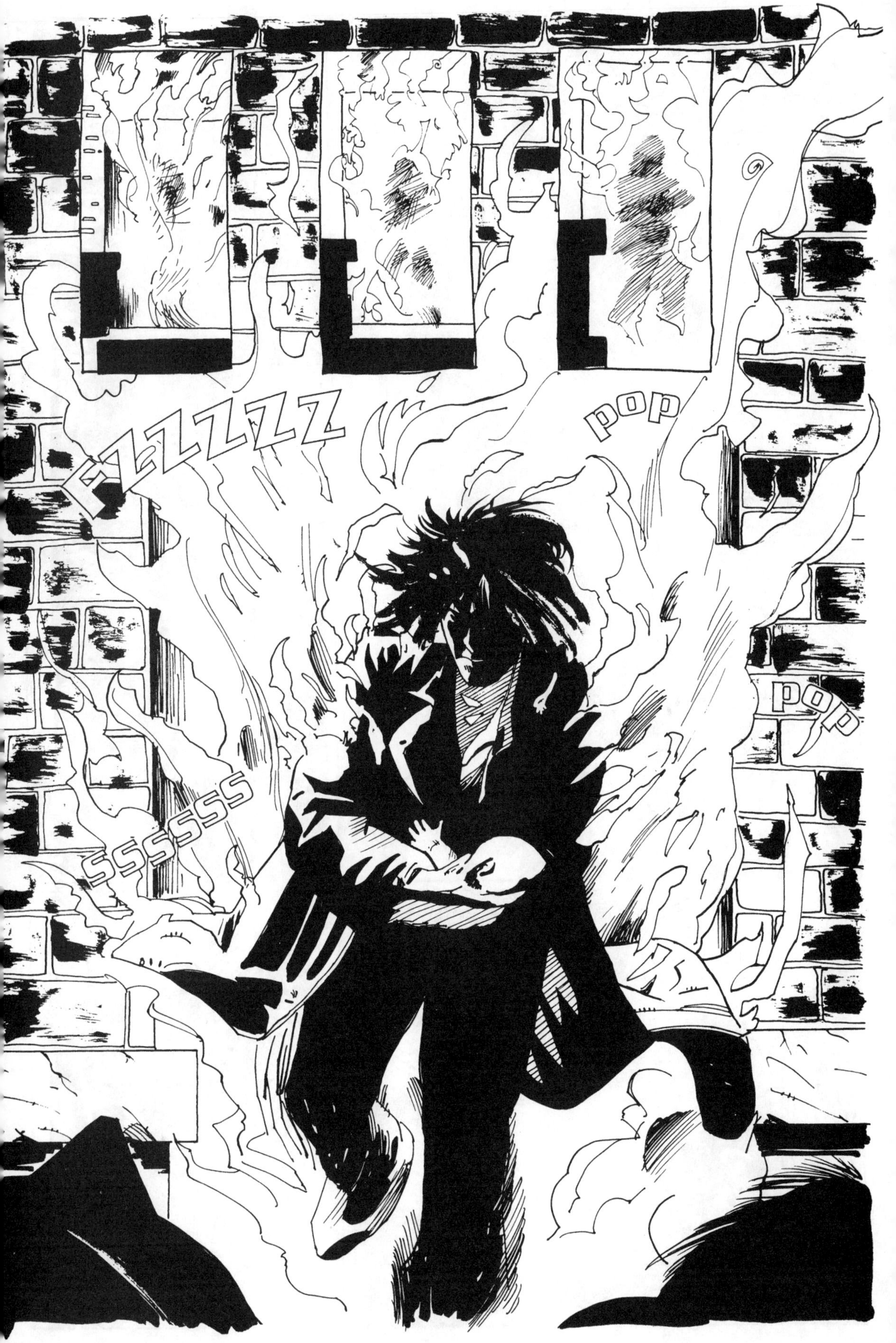
FZZZZZZ
pop
SSSSSSS
pop

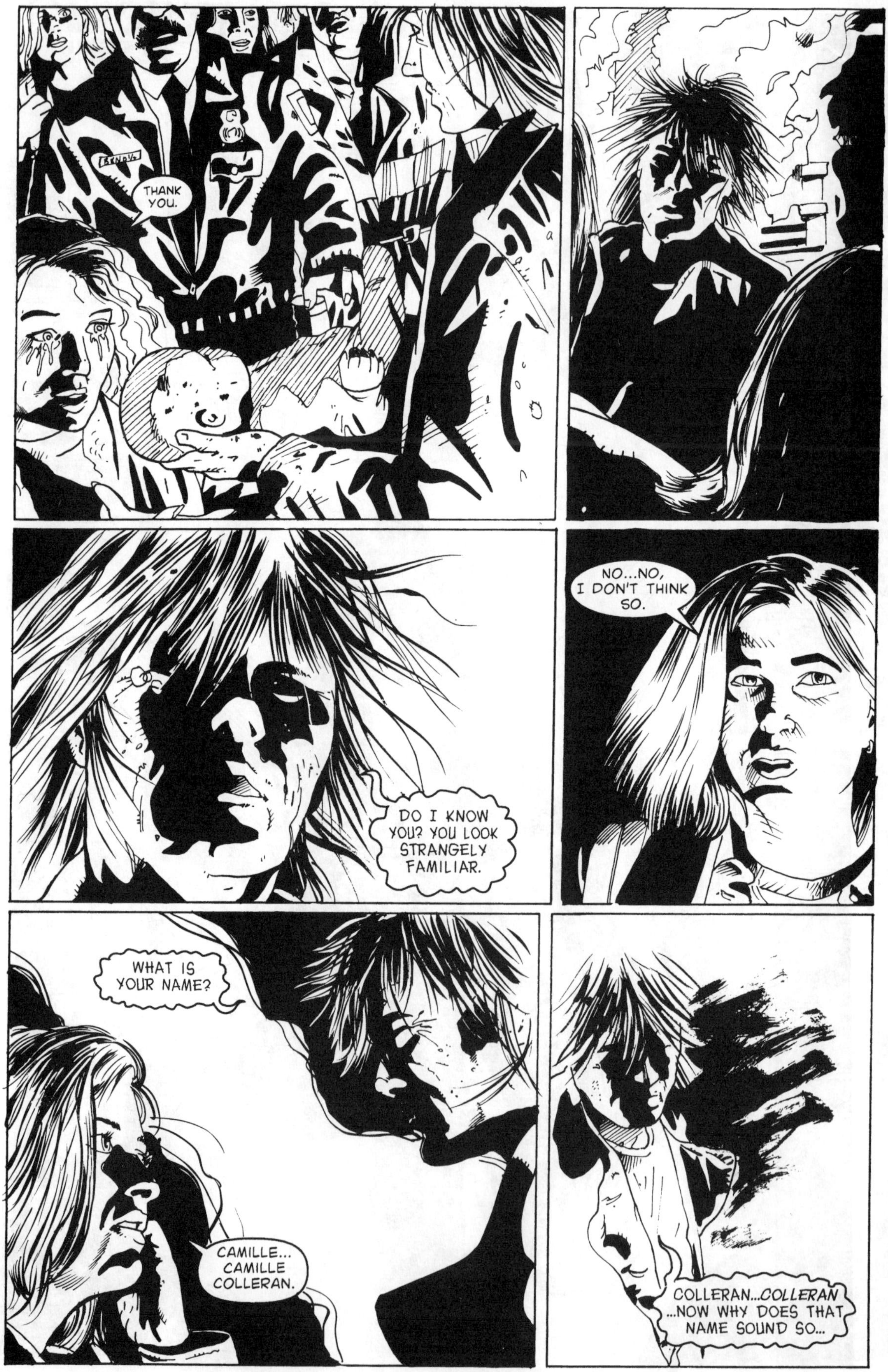
THANK YOU.
DO I KNOW YOU? YOU LOOK STRANGELY FAMILIAR.
NO...NO, I DON'T THINK SO.
WHAT IS YOUR NAME?
CAMILLE... CAMILLE COLLERAN.
COLLERAN...*COLLERAN* ...NOW WHY DOES THAT NAME SOUND SO...

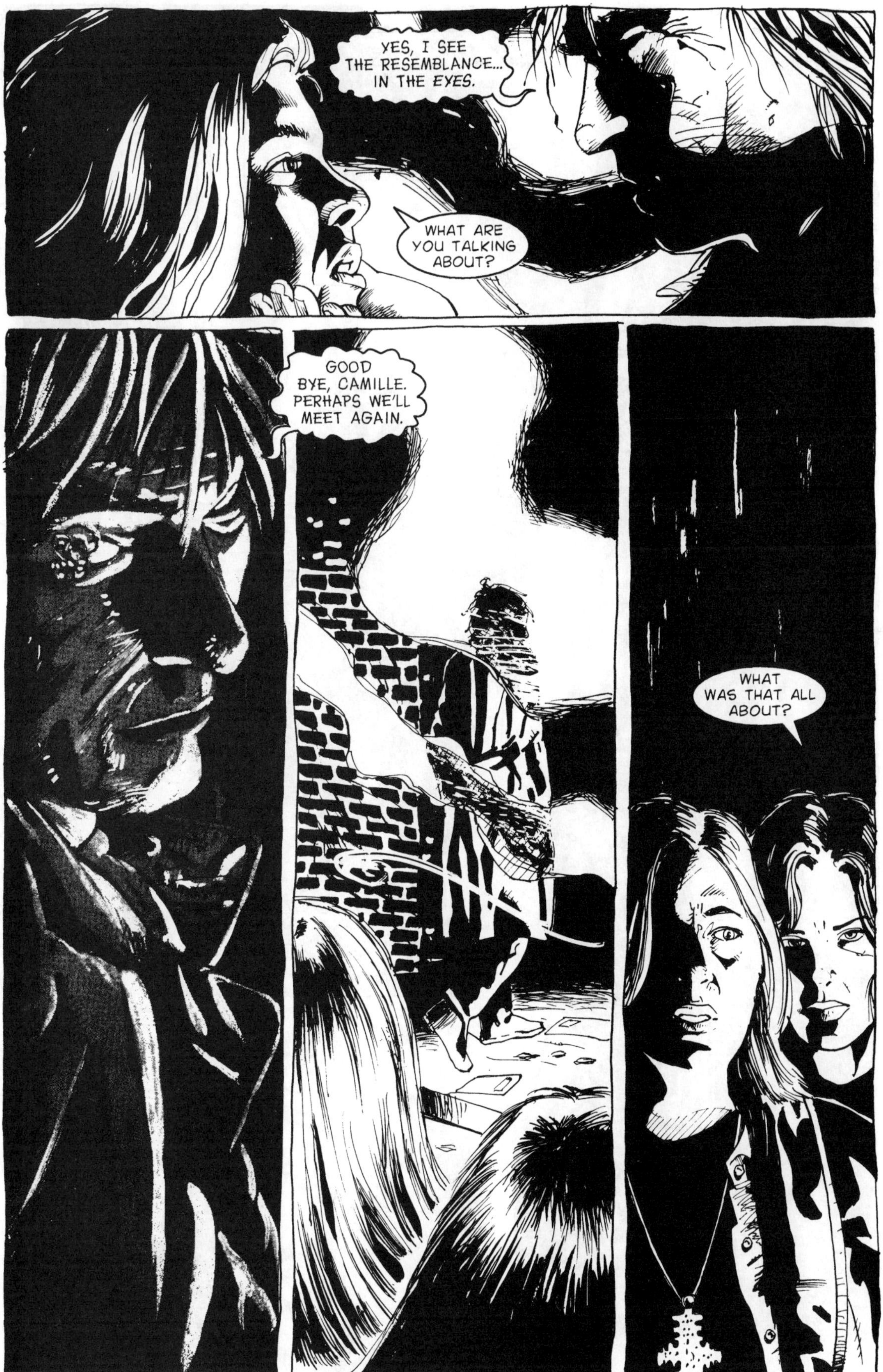
YES, I SEE THE RESEMBLANCE... IN THE EYES.
WHAT ARE YOU TALKING ABOUT?
GOOD BYE, CAMILLE. PERHAPS WE'LL MEET AGAIN.
WHAT WAS THAT ALL ABOUT?

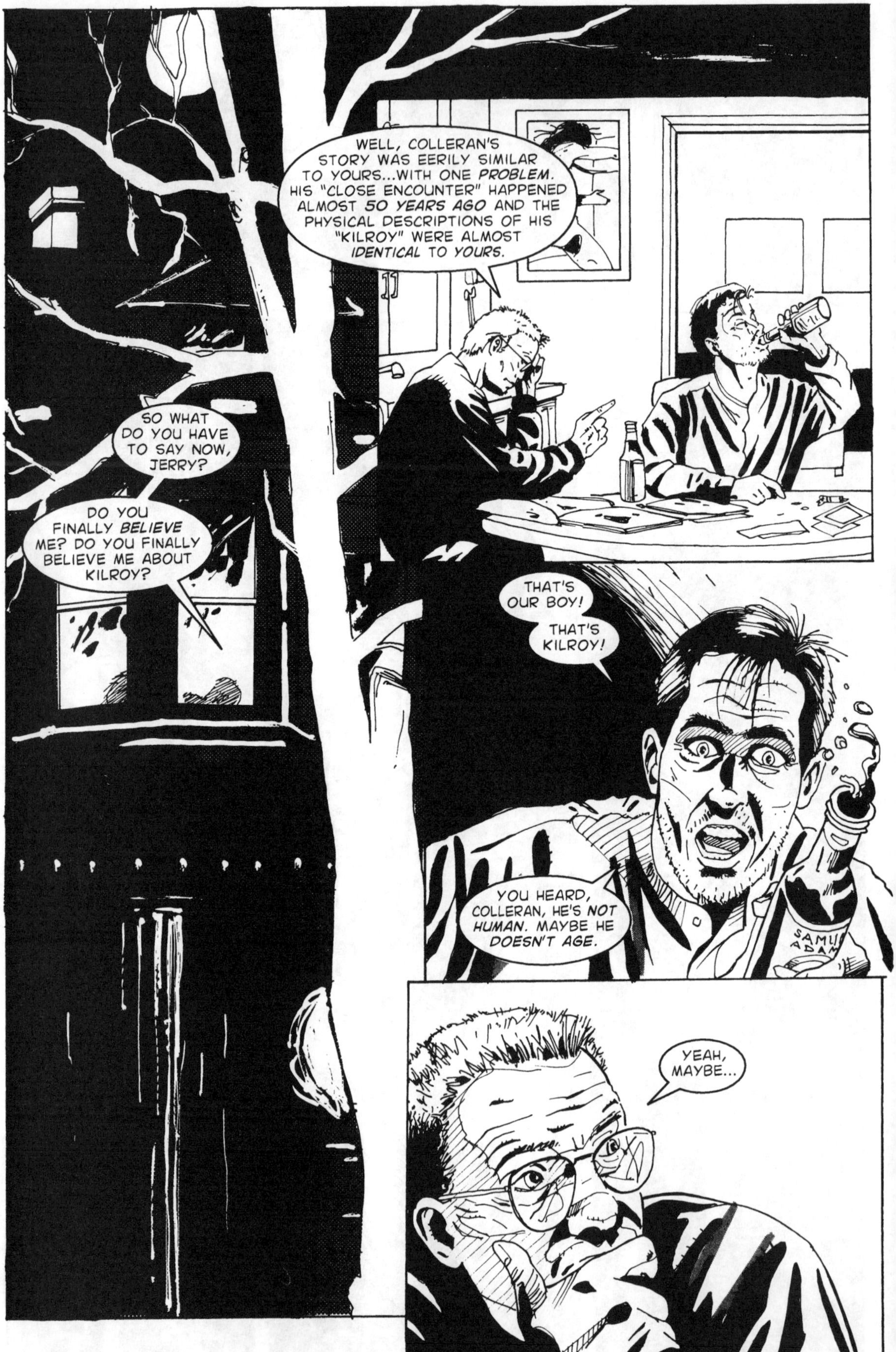
WELL, COLLERAN'S STORY WAS EERILY SIMILAR TO YOURS...WITH ONE PROBLEM. HIS "CLOSE ENCOUNTER" HAPPENED ALMOST 50 YEARS AGO AND THE PHYSICAL DESCRIPTIONS OF HIS "KILROY" WERE ALMOST IDENTICAL TO YOURS.
SO WHAT DO YOU HAVE TO SAY NOW, JERRY?
DO YOU FINALLY BELIEVE ME? DO YOU FINALLY BELIEVE ME ABOUT KILROY?
THAT'S OUR BOY!
THAT'S KILROY!
YOU HEARD, COLLERAN, HE'S NOT HUMAN. MAYBE HE DOESN'T AGE.
YEAH, MAYBE...

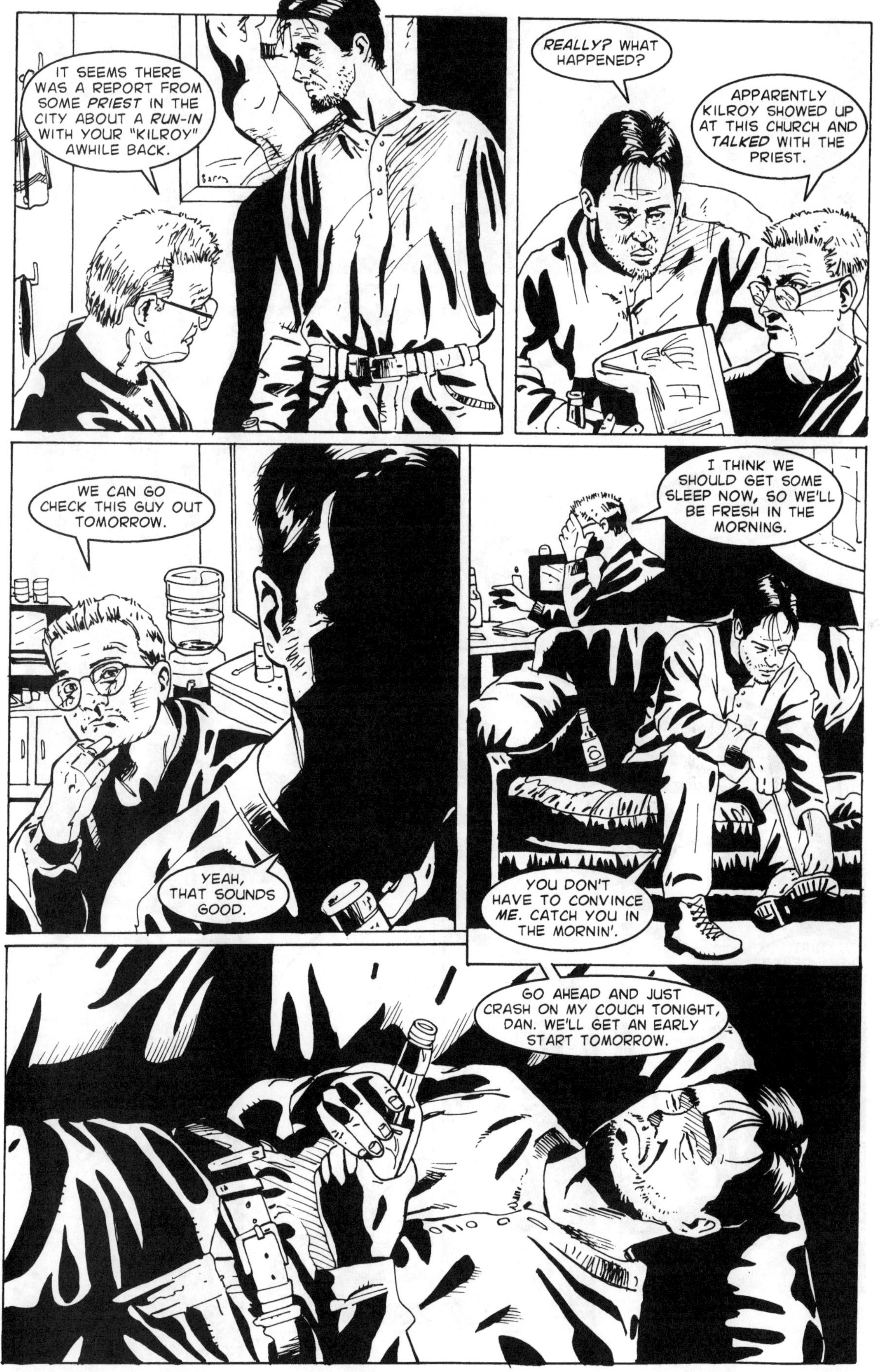
IT SEEMS THERE WAS A REPORT FROM SOME *PRIEST* IN THE CITY ABOUT A *RUN-IN* WITH YOUR "KILROY" AWHILE BACK.
REALLY? WHAT HAPPENED?
APPARENTLY KILROY SHOWED UP AT THIS CHURCH AND *TALKED* WITH THE PRIEST.
WE CAN GO CHECK THIS GUY OUT TOMORROW.
YEAH, THAT SOUNDS GOOD.
I THINK WE SHOULD GET SOME SLEEP NOW, SO WE'LL BE FRESH IN THE MORNING.
YOU DON'T HAVE TO CONVINCE *ME*. CATCH YOU IN THE MORNIN'.
GO AHEAD AND JUST CRASH ON MY COUCH TONIGHT, DAN. WE'LL GET AN EARLY START TOMORROW.

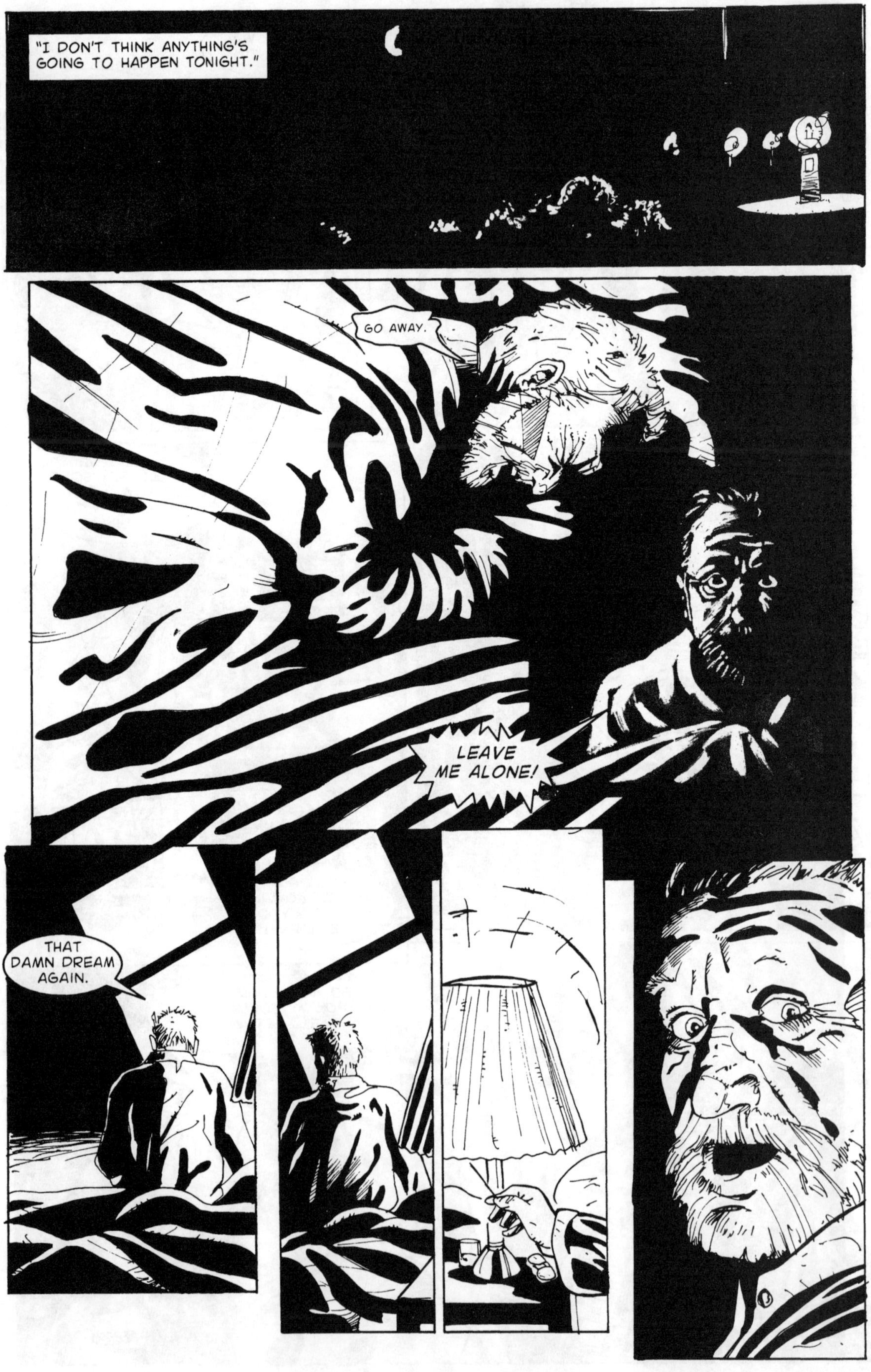
"I DON'T THINK ANYTHING'S GOING TO HAPPEN TONIGHT."
GO AWAY.
LEAVE ME ALONE!
THAT DAMN DREAM AGAIN.

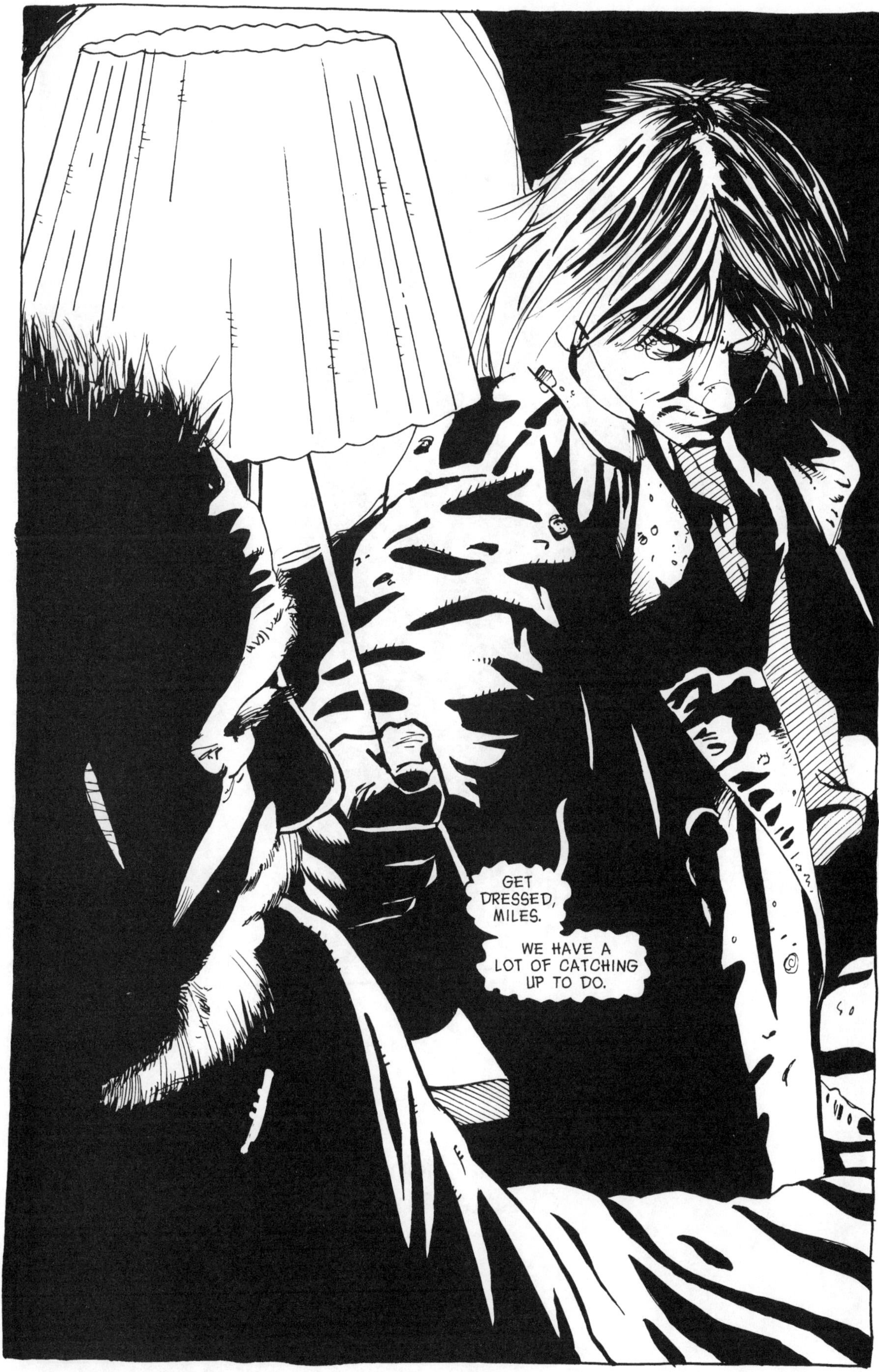
GET DRESSED, MILES.
WE HAVE A LOT OF CATCHING UP TO DO.

"Reflections"
Chapter Three

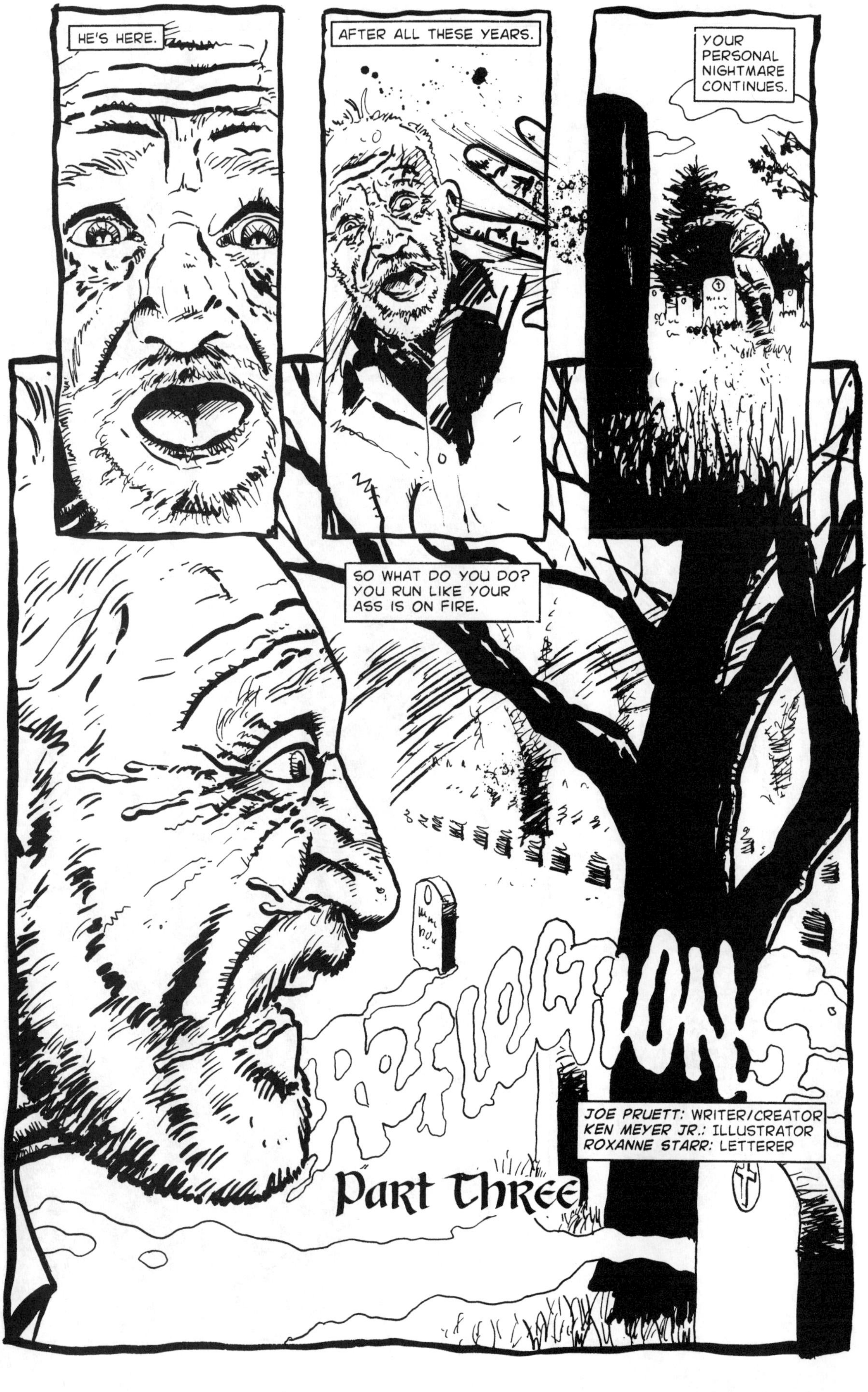
HE'S HERE.
AFTER ALL THESE YEARS.
YOUR PERSONAL NIGHTMARE CONTINUES.
SO WHAT DO YOU DO? YOU RUN LIKE YOUR ASS IS ON FIRE.
REFLECTIONS
Part Three
JOE PRUETT: WRITER/CREATOR
KEN MEYER JR.: ILLUSTRATOR
ROXANNE STARR: LETTERER

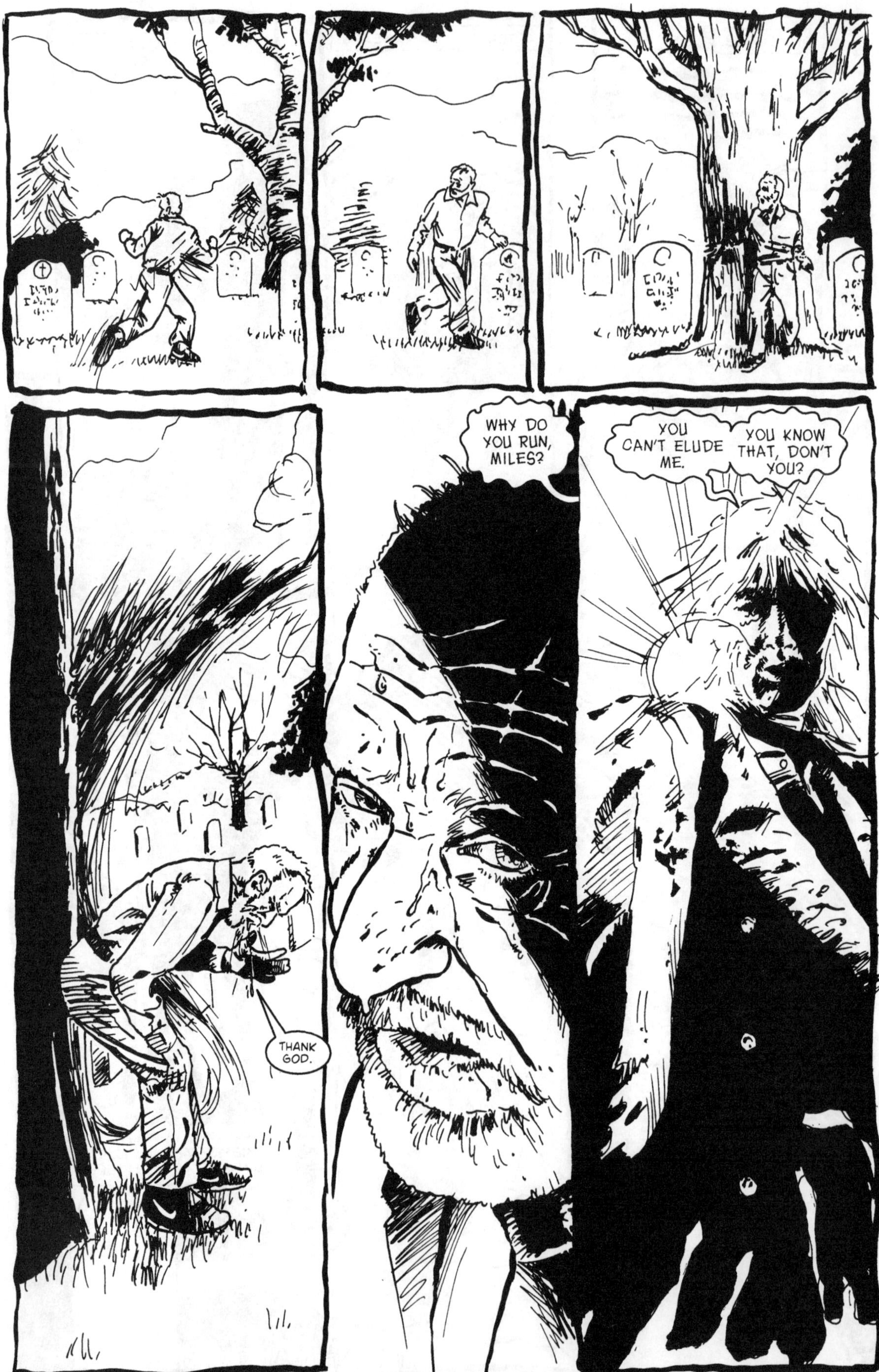
THANK GOD.
WHY DO YOU RUN, MILES?
YOU CAN'T ELUDE ME.
YOU KNOW THAT, DON'T YOU?

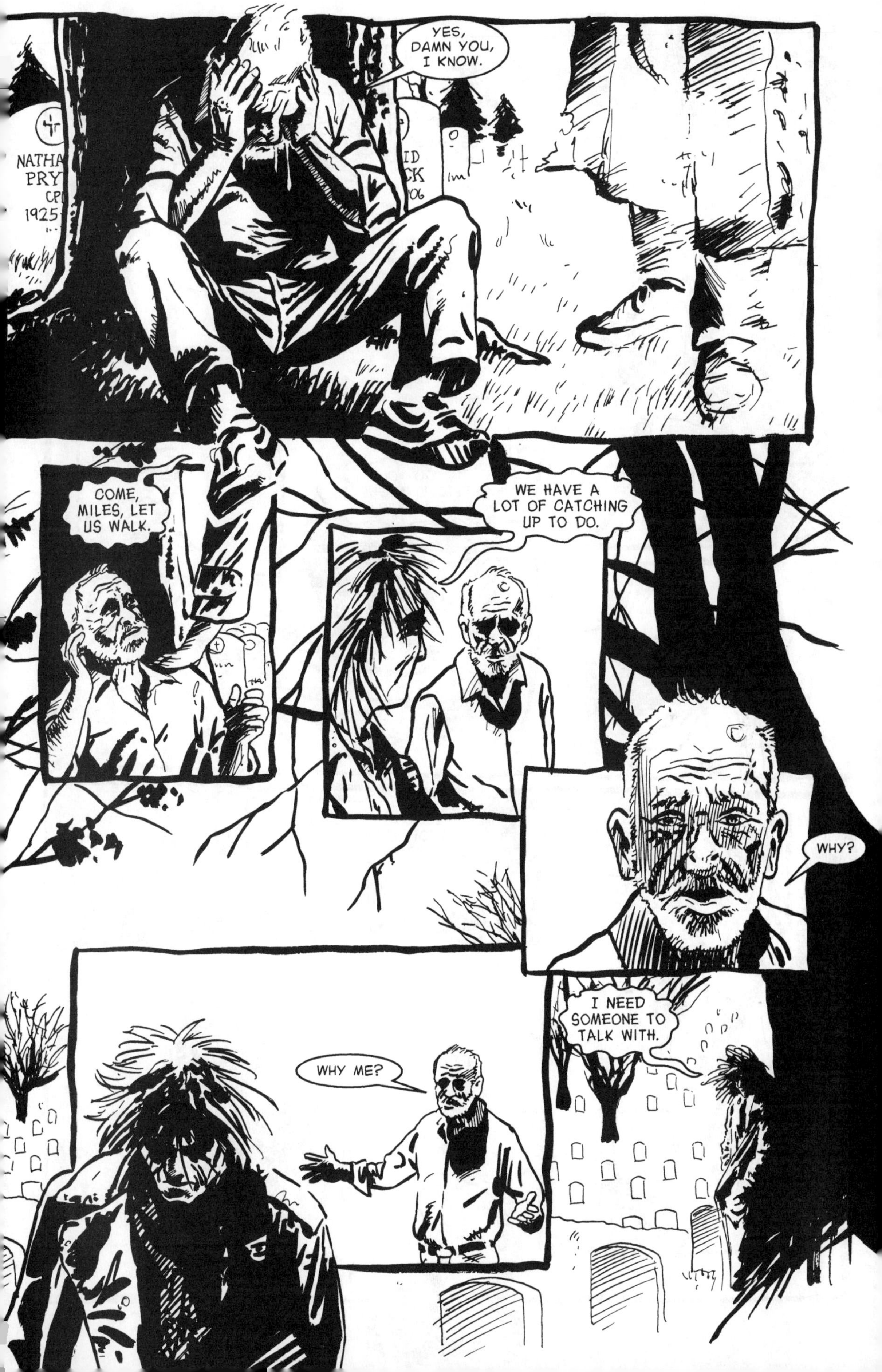
NATHA
PRY
CPL
1925
YES, DAMN YOU, I KNOW.
COME, MILES, LET US WALK.
WE HAVE A LOT OF CATCHING UP TO DO.
WHY?
WHY ME?
I NEED SOMEONE TO TALK WITH.

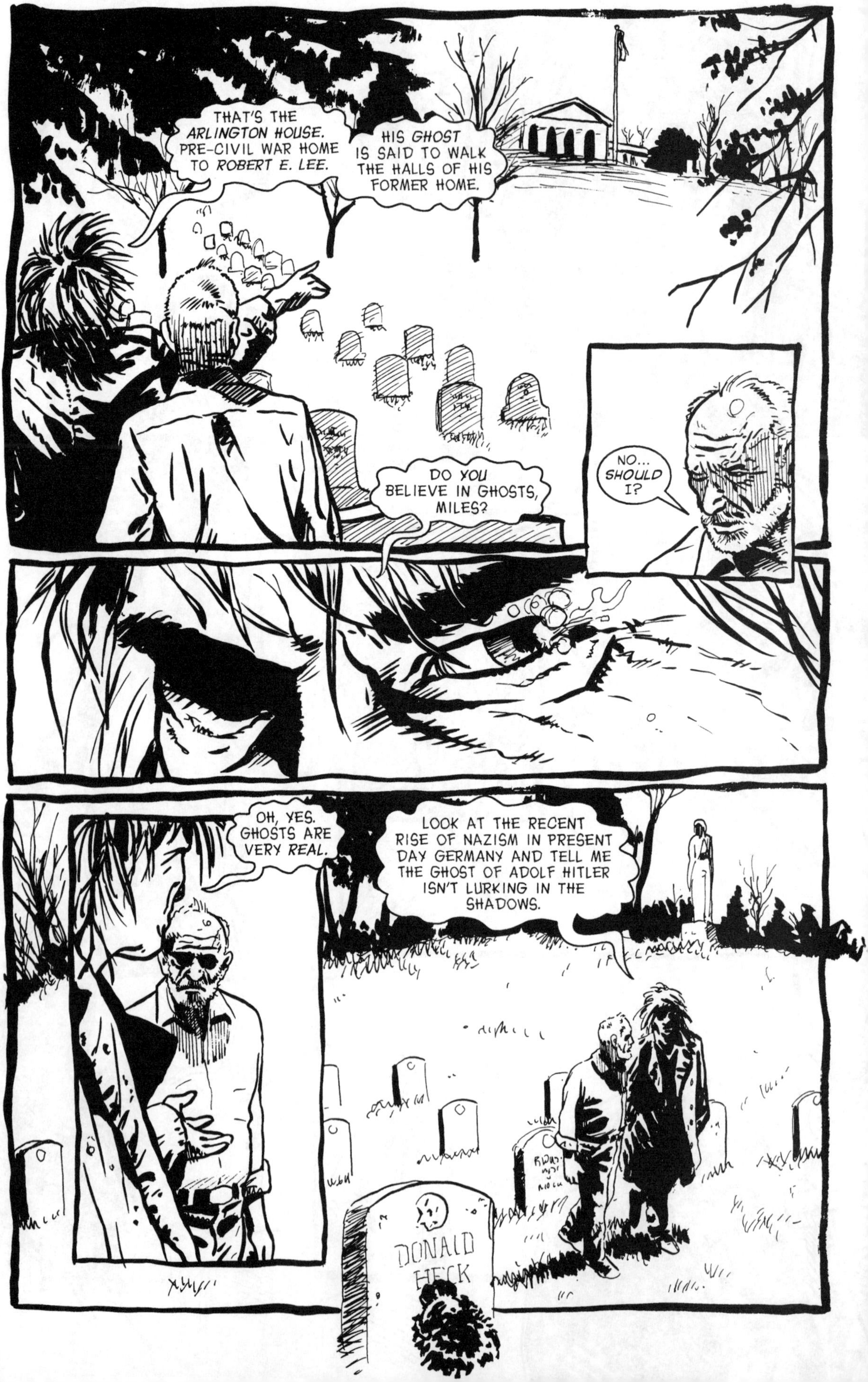
THAT'S THE ARLINGTON HOUSE. PRE-CIVIL WAR HOME TO ROBERT E. LEE.
HIS GHOST IS SAID TO WALK THE HALLS OF HIS FORMER HOME.
DO YOU BELIEVE IN GHOSTS, MILES?
NO... SHOULD I?
OH, YES. GHOSTS ARE VERY REAL.
LOOK AT THE RECENT RISE OF NAZISM IN PRESENT DAY GERMANY AND TELL ME THE GHOST OF ADOLF HITLER ISN'T LURKING IN THE SHADOWS.
DONALD HECK

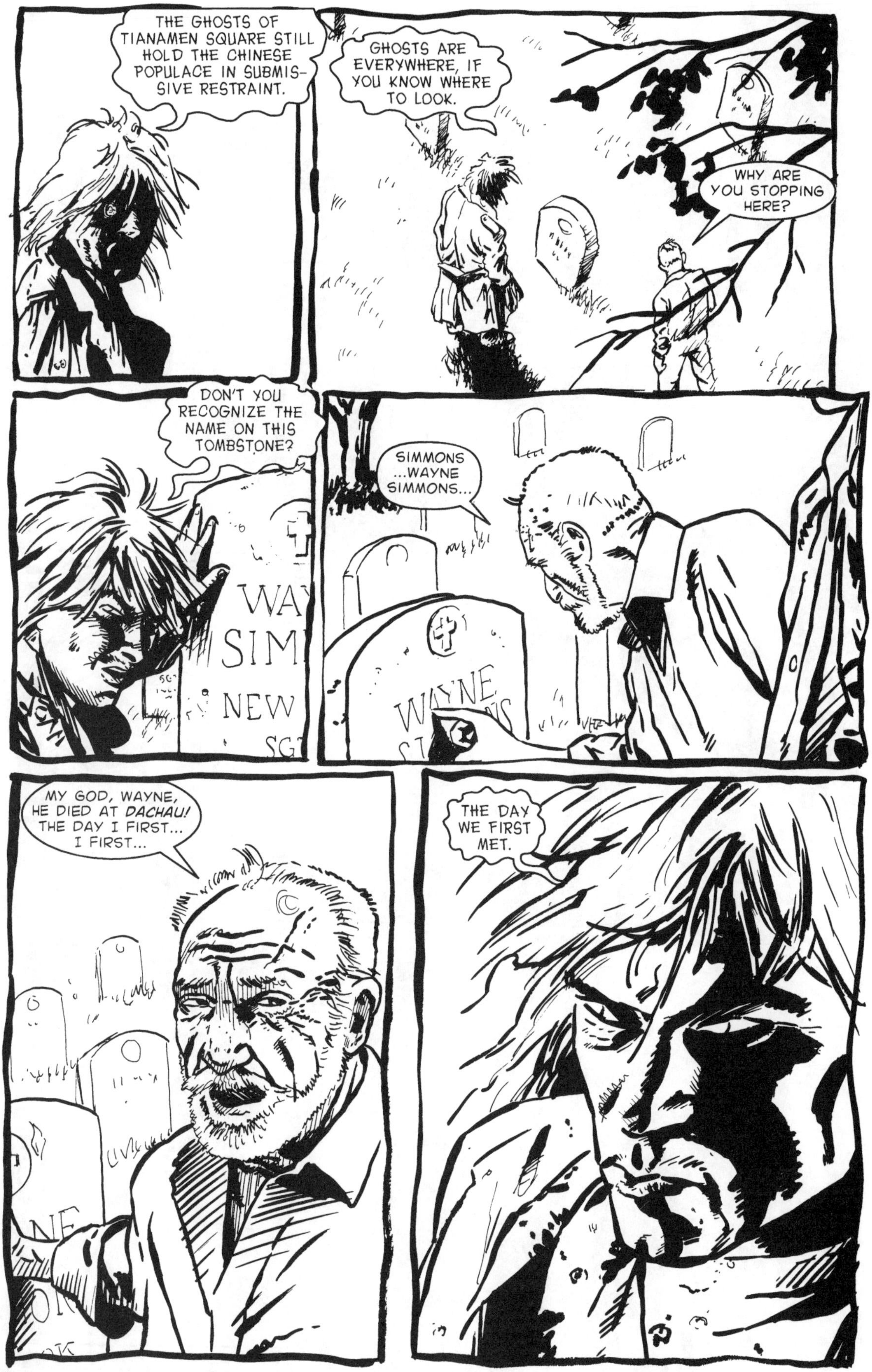
THE GHOSTS OF TIANAMEN SQUARE STILL HOLD THE CHINESE POPULACE IN SUBMIS-SIVE RESTRAINT.
GHOSTS ARE EVERYWHERE, IF YOU KNOW WHERE TO LOOK.
WHY ARE YOU STOPPING HERE?
DON'T YOU RECOGNIZE THE NAME ON THIS TOMBSTONE?
SIMMONS ...WAYNE SIMMONS...
MY GOD, WAYNE, HE DIED AT *DACHAU!* THE DAY I FIRST... I FIRST...
THE DAY WE FIRST MET.

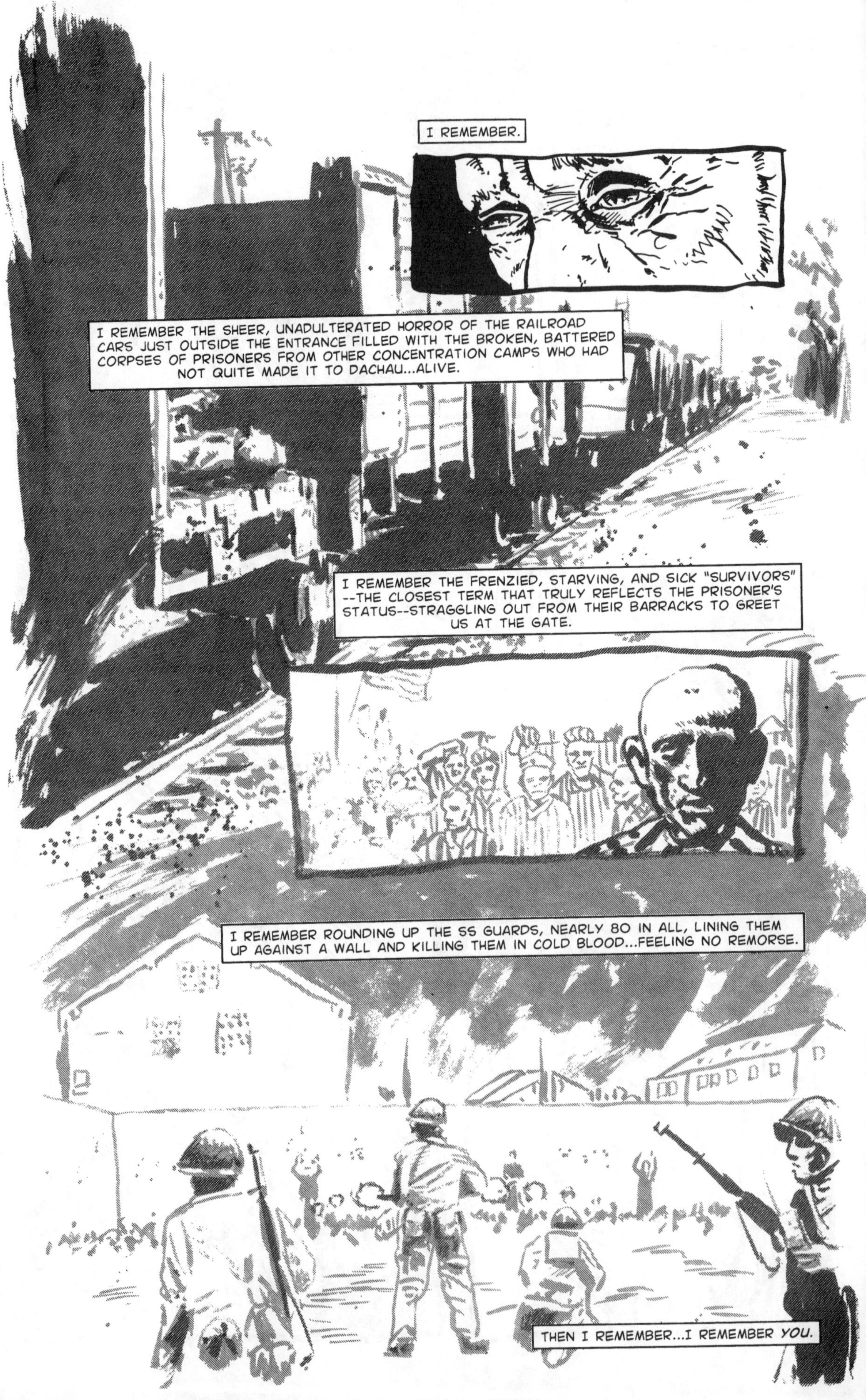
I REMEMBER.
I REMEMBER THE SHEER, UNADULTERATED HORROR OF THE RAILROAD CARS JUST OUTSIDE THE ENTRANCE FILLED WITH THE BROKEN, BATTERED CORPSES OF PRISONERS FROM OTHER CONCENTRATION CAMPS WHO HAD NOT QUITE MADE IT TO DACHAU...ALIVE.
I REMEMBER THE FRENZIED, STARVING, AND SICK "SURVIVORS" --THE CLOSEST TERM THAT TRULY REFLECTS THE PRISONER'S STATUS--STRAGGLING OUT FROM THEIR BARRACKS TO GREET US AT THE GATE.
I REMEMBER ROUNDING UP THE SS GUARDS, NEARLY 80 IN ALL, LINING THEM UP AGAINST A WALL AND KILLING THEM IN COLD BLOOD...FEELING NO REMORSE.
THEN I REMEMBER...I REMEMBER *YOU*.

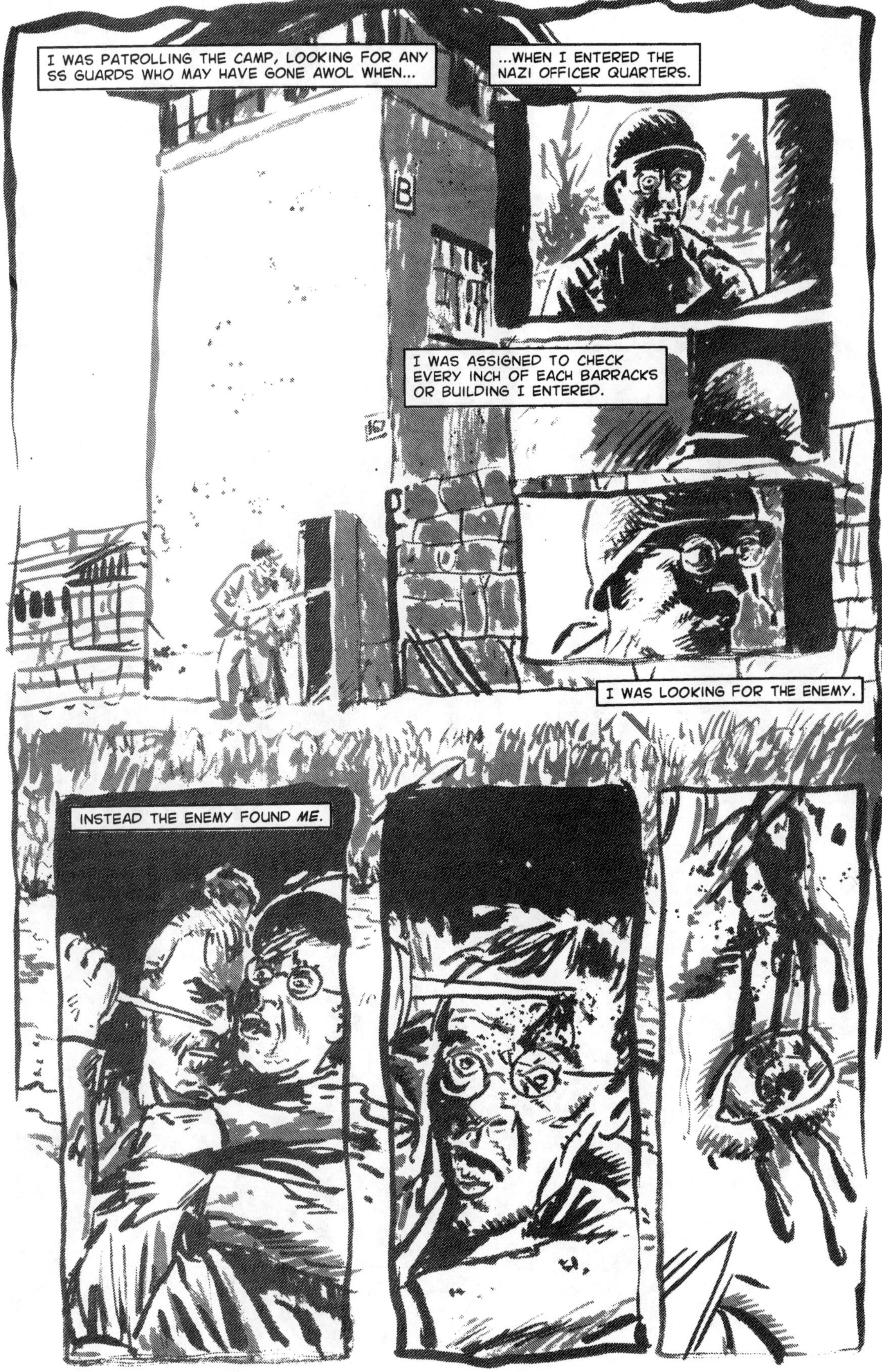
I WAS PATROLLING THE CAMP, LOOKING FOR ANY SS GUARDS WHO MAY HAVE GONE AWOL WHEN...
...WHEN I ENTERED THE NAZI OFFICER QUARTERS.
I WAS ASSIGNED TO CHECK EVERY INCH OF EACH BARRACKS OR BUILDING I ENTERED.
I WAS LOOKING FOR THE ENEMY.
INSTEAD THE ENEMY FOUND *ME*.

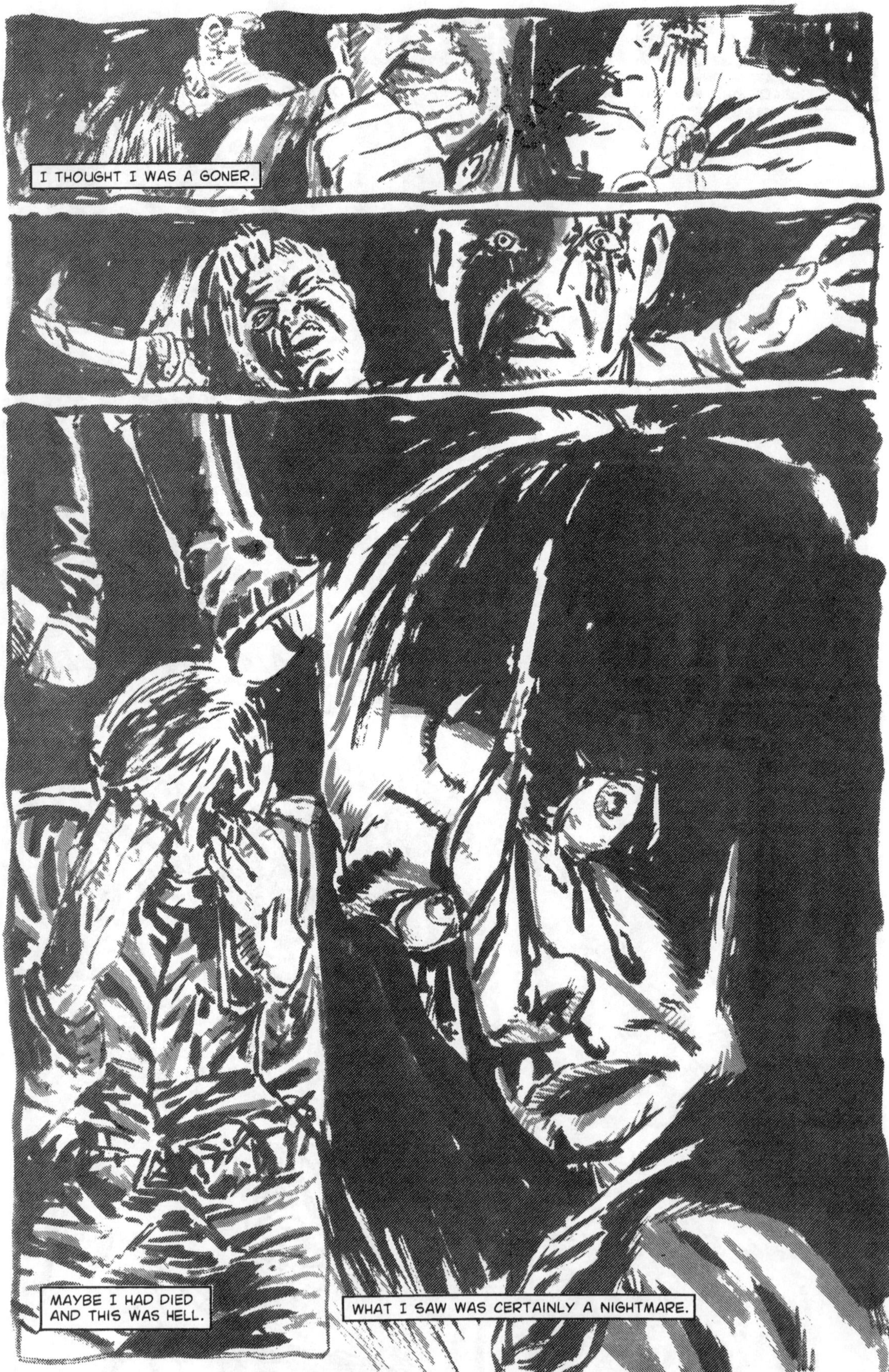
I THOUGHT I WAS A GONER.
MAYBE I HAD DIED AND THIS WAS HELL.
WHAT I SAW WAS CERTAINLY A NIGHTMARE.

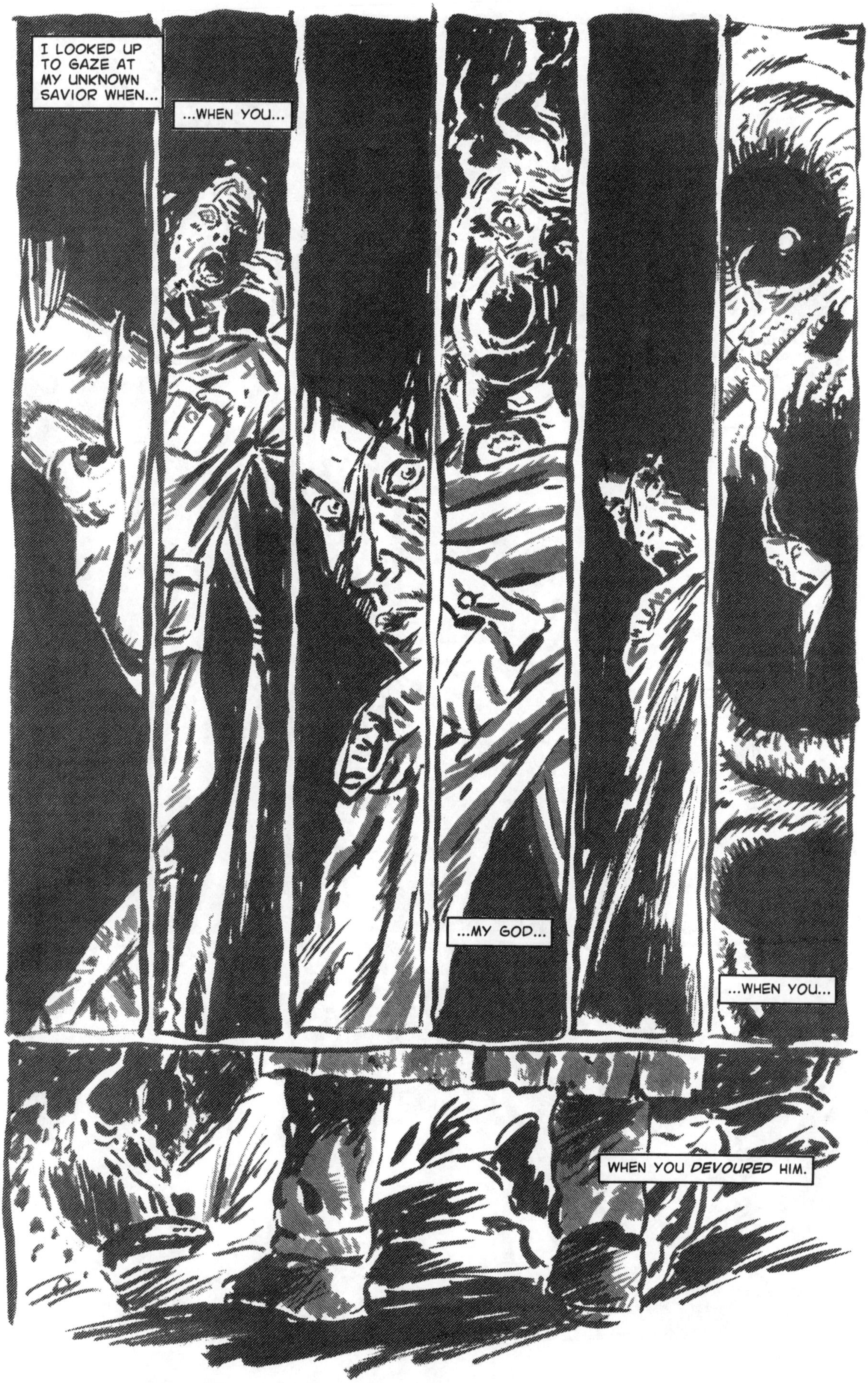
I LOOKED UP TO GAZE AT MY UNKNOWN SAVIOR WHEN...
...WHEN YOU...
...MY GOD...
...WHEN YOU...
WHEN YOU *DEVOURED* HIM.

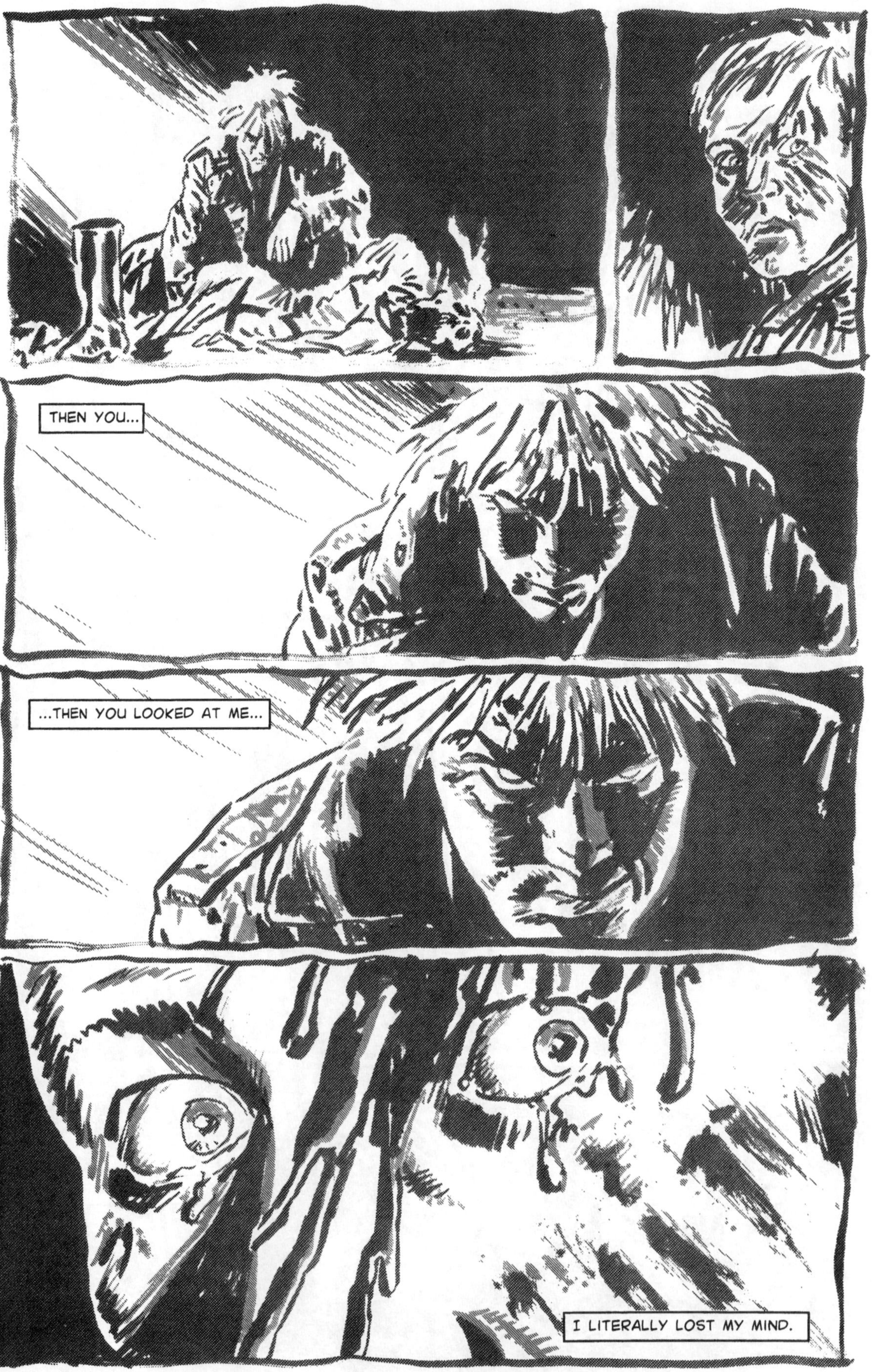
THEN YOU...
...THEN YOU LOOKED AT ME...
I LITERALLY LOST MY MIND.

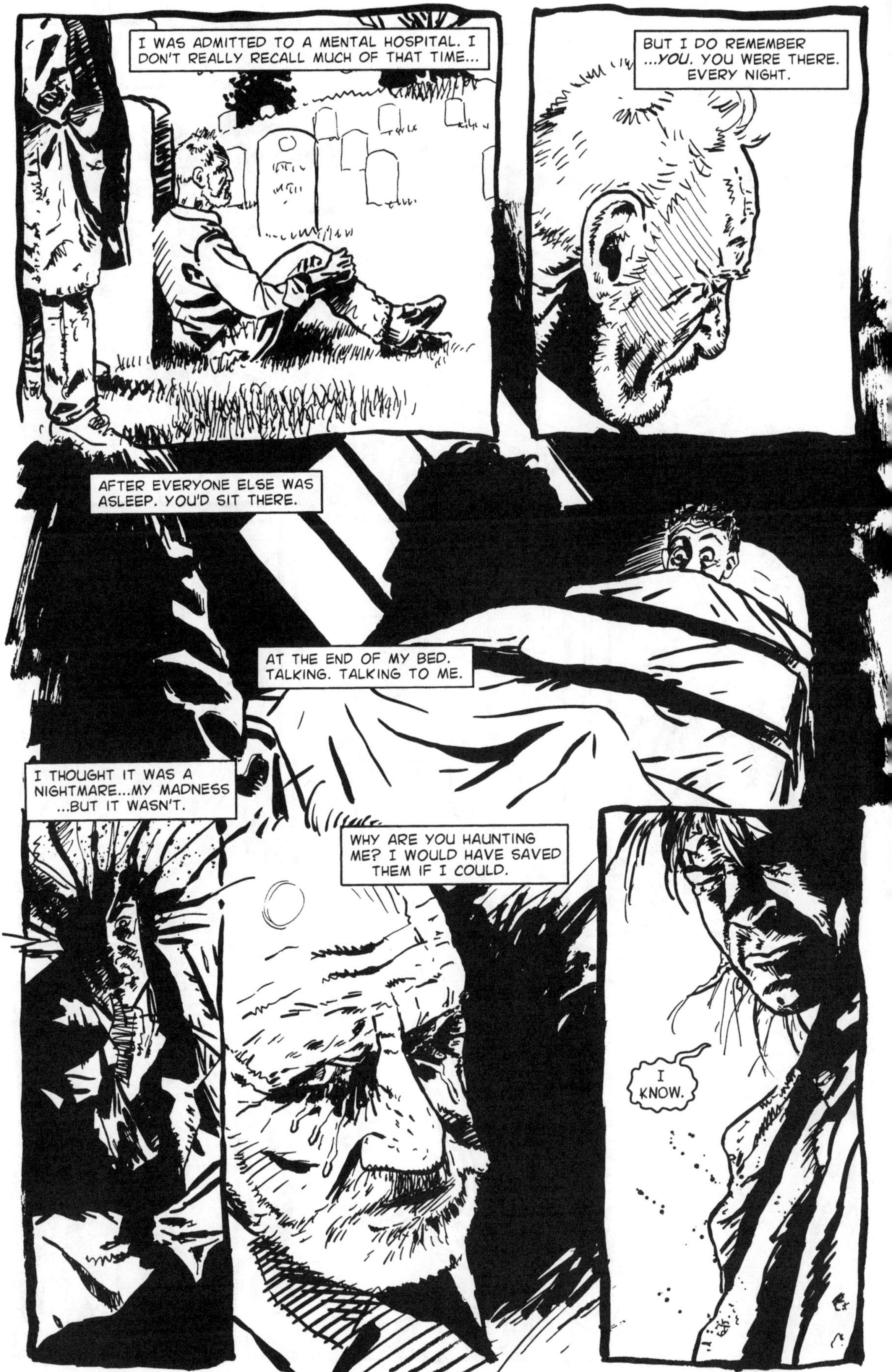
I WAS ADMITTED TO A MENTAL HOSPITAL. I DON'T REALLY RECALL MUCH OF THAT TIME...
BUT I DO REMEMBER ...*YOU*. YOU WERE THERE. EVERY NIGHT.
AFTER EVERYONE ELSE WAS ASLEEP. YOU'D SIT THERE.
AT THE END OF MY BED. TALKING. TALKING TO ME.
I THOUGHT IT WAS A NIGHTMARE...MY MADNESS ...BUT IT WASN'T.
WHY ARE YOU HAUNTING ME? I WOULD HAVE SAVED THEM IF I COULD.
I KNOW.

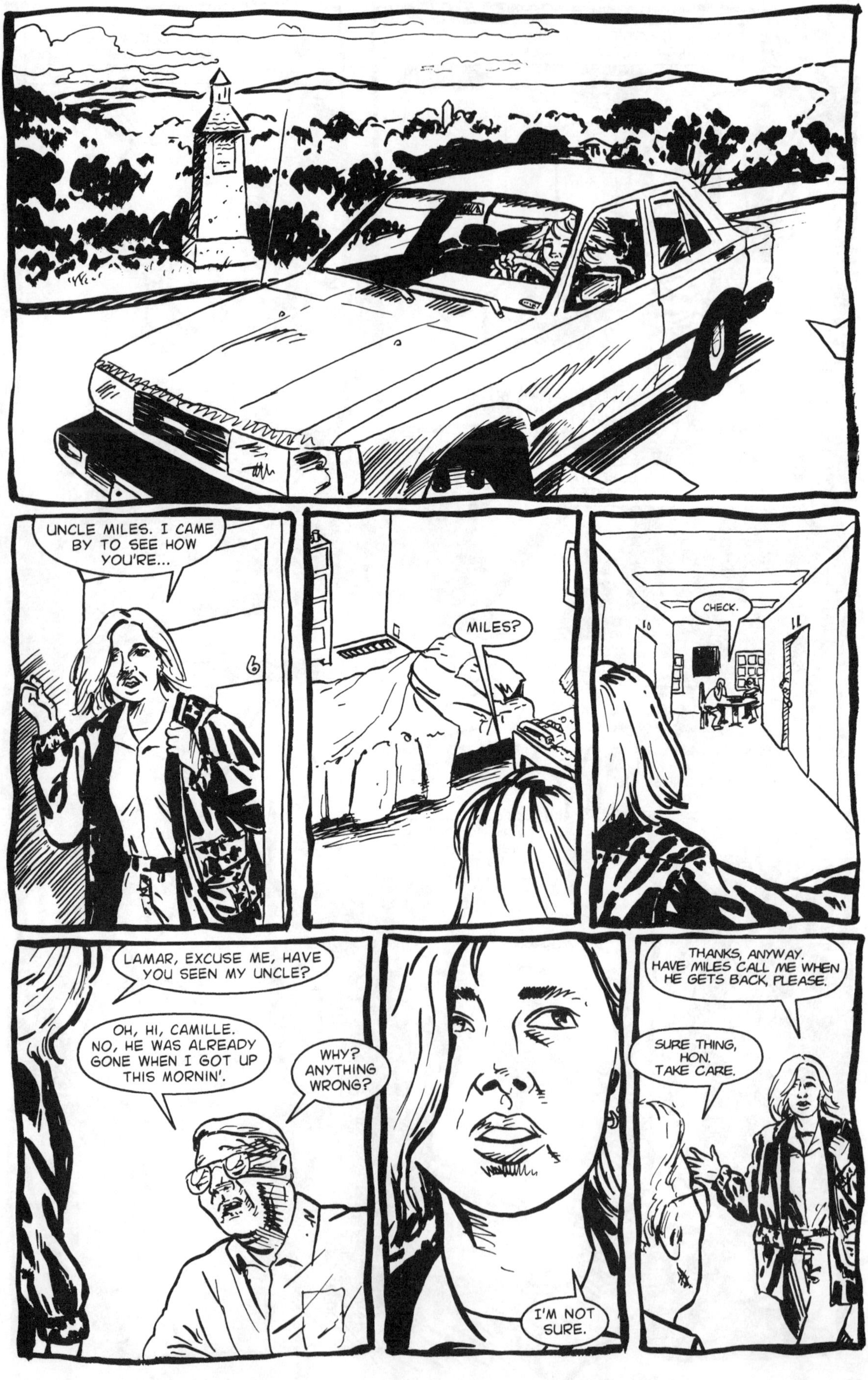
UNCLE MILES. I CAME BY TO SEE HOW YOU'RE...
MILES?
CHECK.
LAMAR, EXCUSE ME, HAVE YOU SEEN MY UNCLE?
OH, HI, CAMILLE. NO, HE WAS ALREADY GONE WHEN I GOT UP THIS MORNIN'.
WHY? ANYTHING WRONG?
I'M NOT SURE.
THANKS, ANYWAY. HAVE MILES CALL ME WHEN HE GETS BACK, PLEASE.
SURE THING, HON. TAKE CARE.

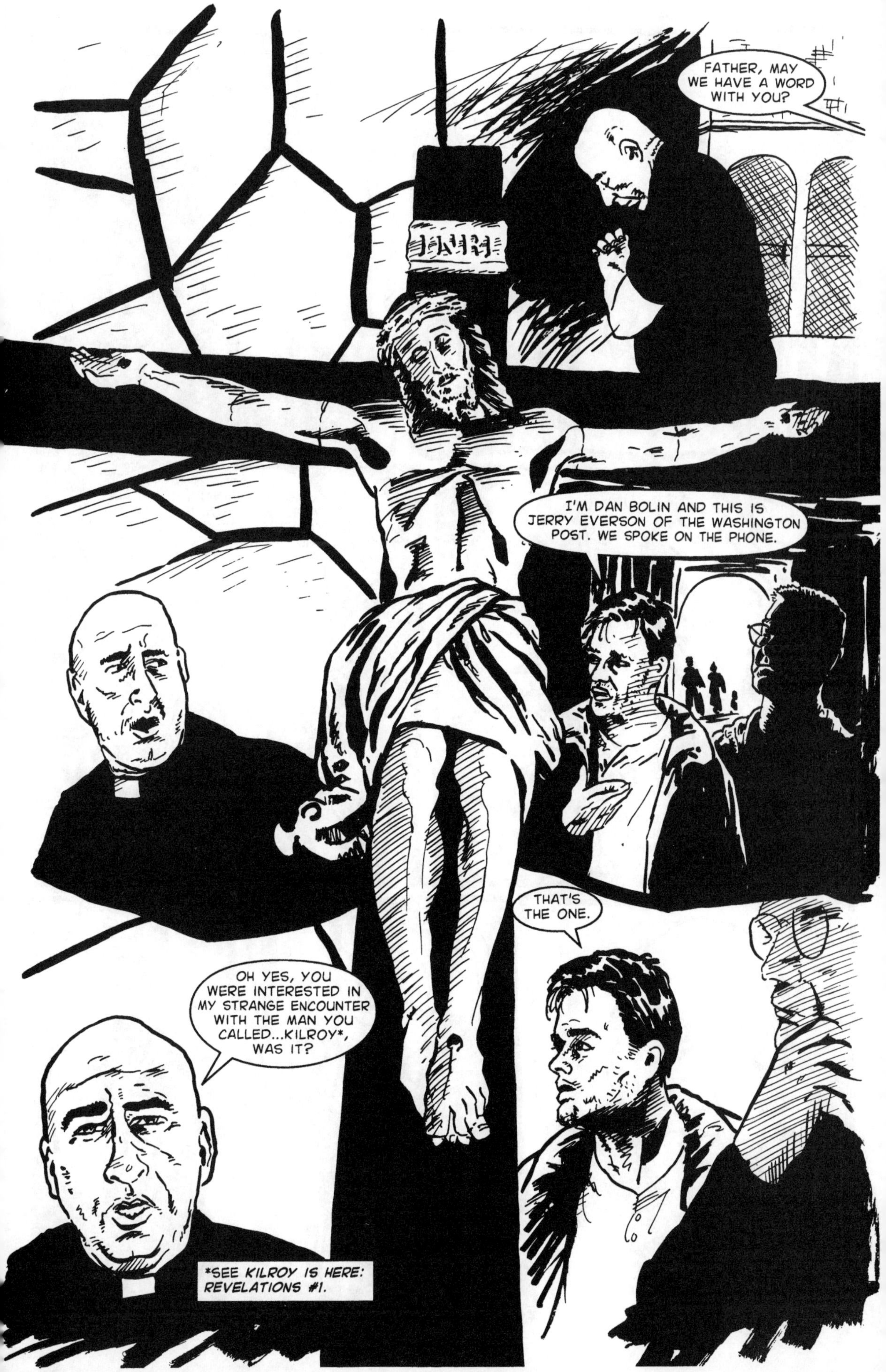
FATHER, MAY WE HAVE A WORD WITH YOU?
I'M DAN BOLIN AND THIS IS JERRY EVERSON OF THE WASHINGTON POST. WE SPOKE ON THE PHONE.
THAT'S THE ONE.
OH YES, YOU WERE INTERESTED IN MY STRANGE ENCOUNTER WITH THE MAN YOU CALLED...KILROY*, WAS IT?
*SEE *KILROY IS HERE: REVELATIONS #1*.

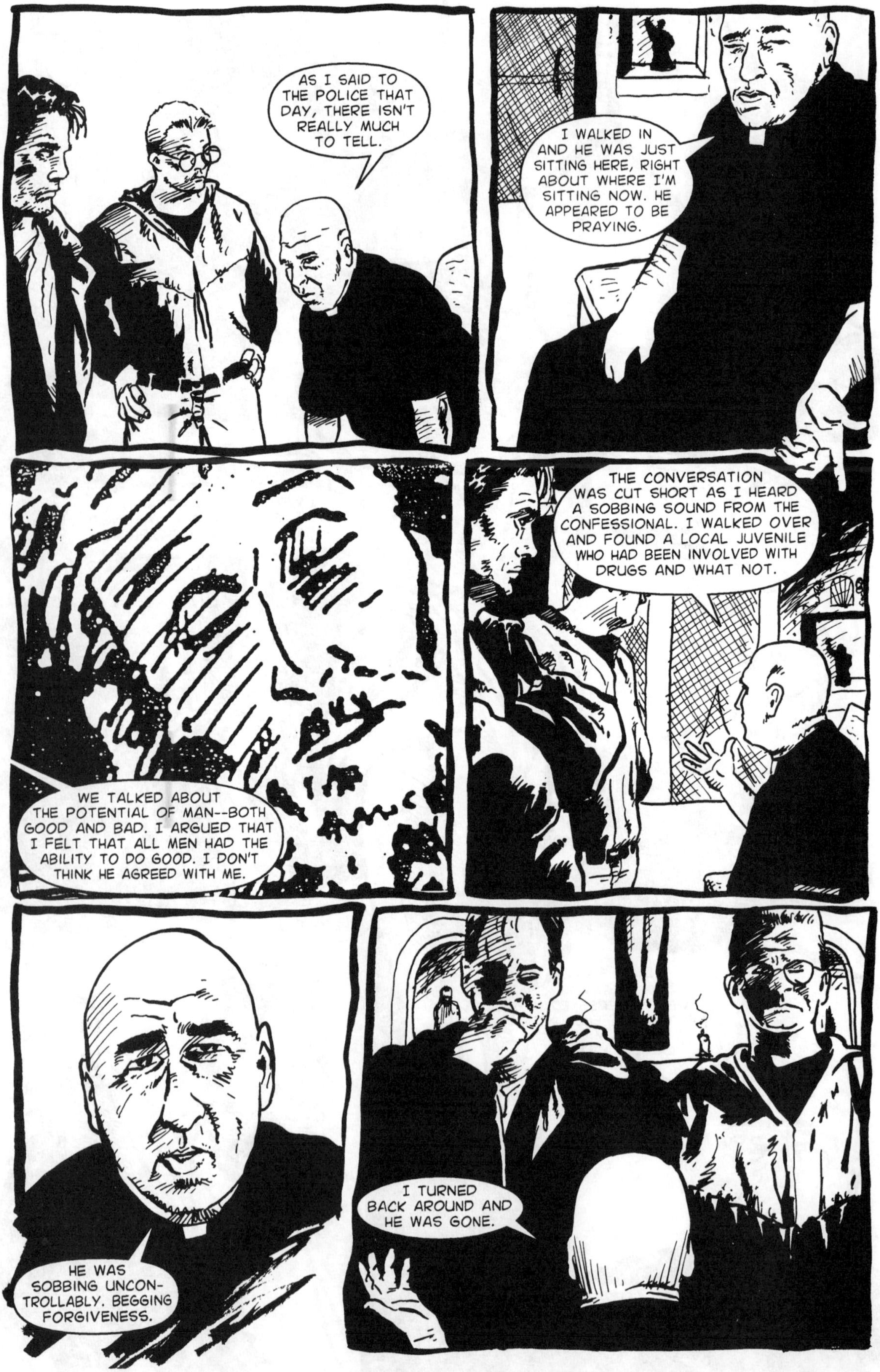
AS I SAID TO THE POLICE THAT DAY, THERE ISN'T REALLY MUCH TO TELL.
I WALKED IN AND HE WAS JUST SITTING HERE, RIGHT ABOUT WHERE I'M SITTING NOW. HE APPEARED TO BE PRAYING.
WE TALKED ABOUT THE POTENTIAL OF MAN--BOTH GOOD AND BAD. I ARGUED THAT I FELT THAT ALL MEN HAD THE ABILITY TO DO GOOD. I DON'T THINK HE AGREED WITH ME.
THE CONVERSATION WAS CUT SHORT AS I HEARD A SOBBING SOUND FROM THE CONFESSIONAL. I WALKED OVER AND FOUND A LOCAL JUVENILE WHO HAD BEEN INVOLVED WITH DRUGS AND WHAT NOT.
HE WAS SOBBING UNCONTROLLABLY. BEGGING FORGIVENESS.
I TURNED BACK AROUND AND HE WAS GONE.

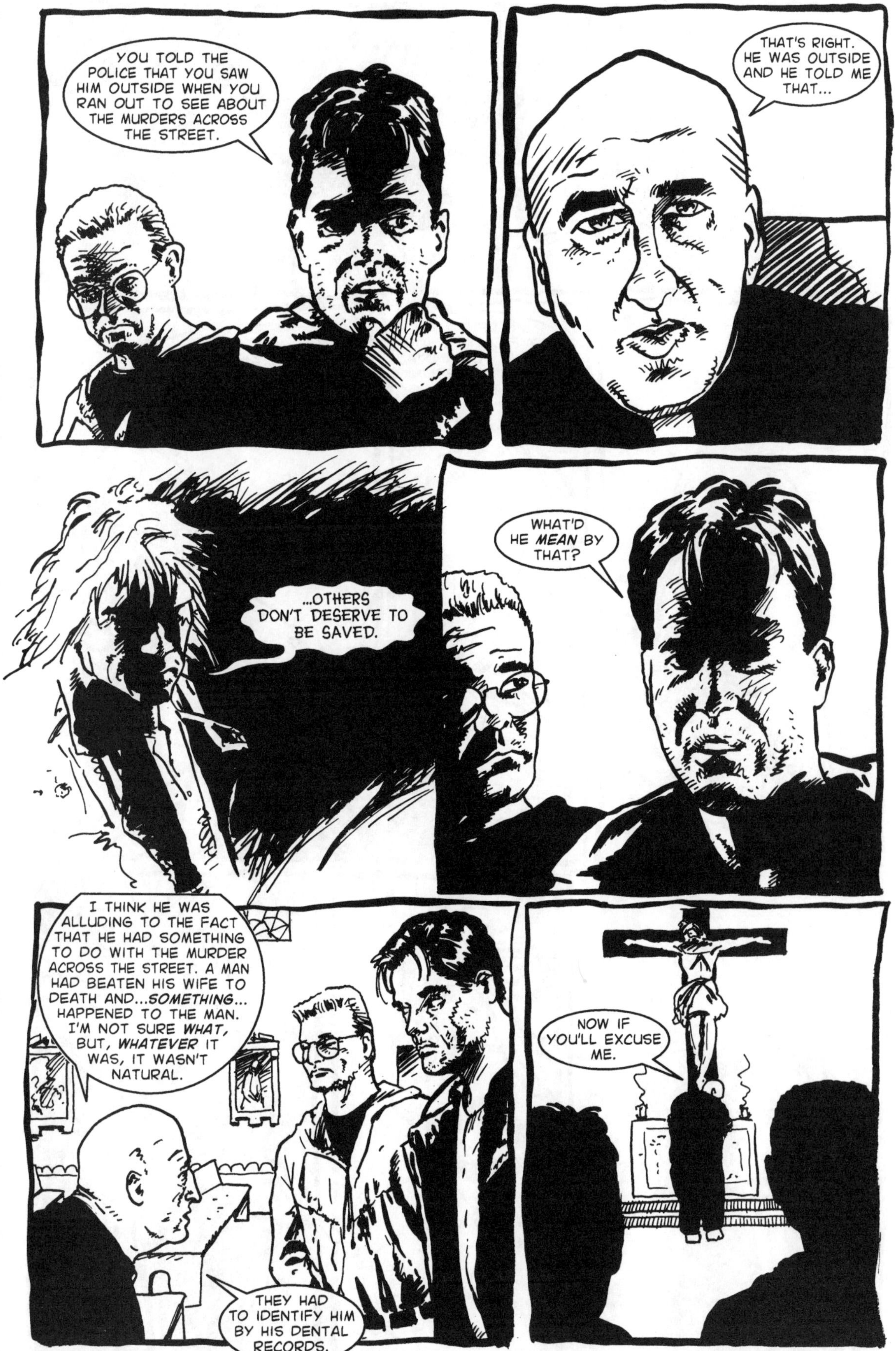
YOU TOLD THE POLICE THAT YOU SAW HIM OUTSIDE WHEN YOU RAN OUT TO SEE ABOUT THE MURDERS ACROSS THE STREET.
THAT'S RIGHT. HE WAS OUTSIDE AND HE TOLD ME THAT...
...OTHERS DON'T DESERVE TO BE SAVED.
WHAT'D HE *MEAN* BY THAT?
I THINK HE WAS ALLUDING TO THE FACT THAT HE HAD SOMETHING TO DO WITH THE MURDER ACROSS THE STREET. A MAN HAD BEATEN HIS WIFE TO DEATH AND...*SOMETHING*... HAPPENED TO THE MAN. I'M NOT SURE *WHAT*, BUT, *WHATEVER* IT WAS, IT WASN'T NATURAL.
THEY HAD TO IDENTIFY HIM BY HIS DENTAL RECORDS.
NOW IF YOU'LL EXCUSE ME.

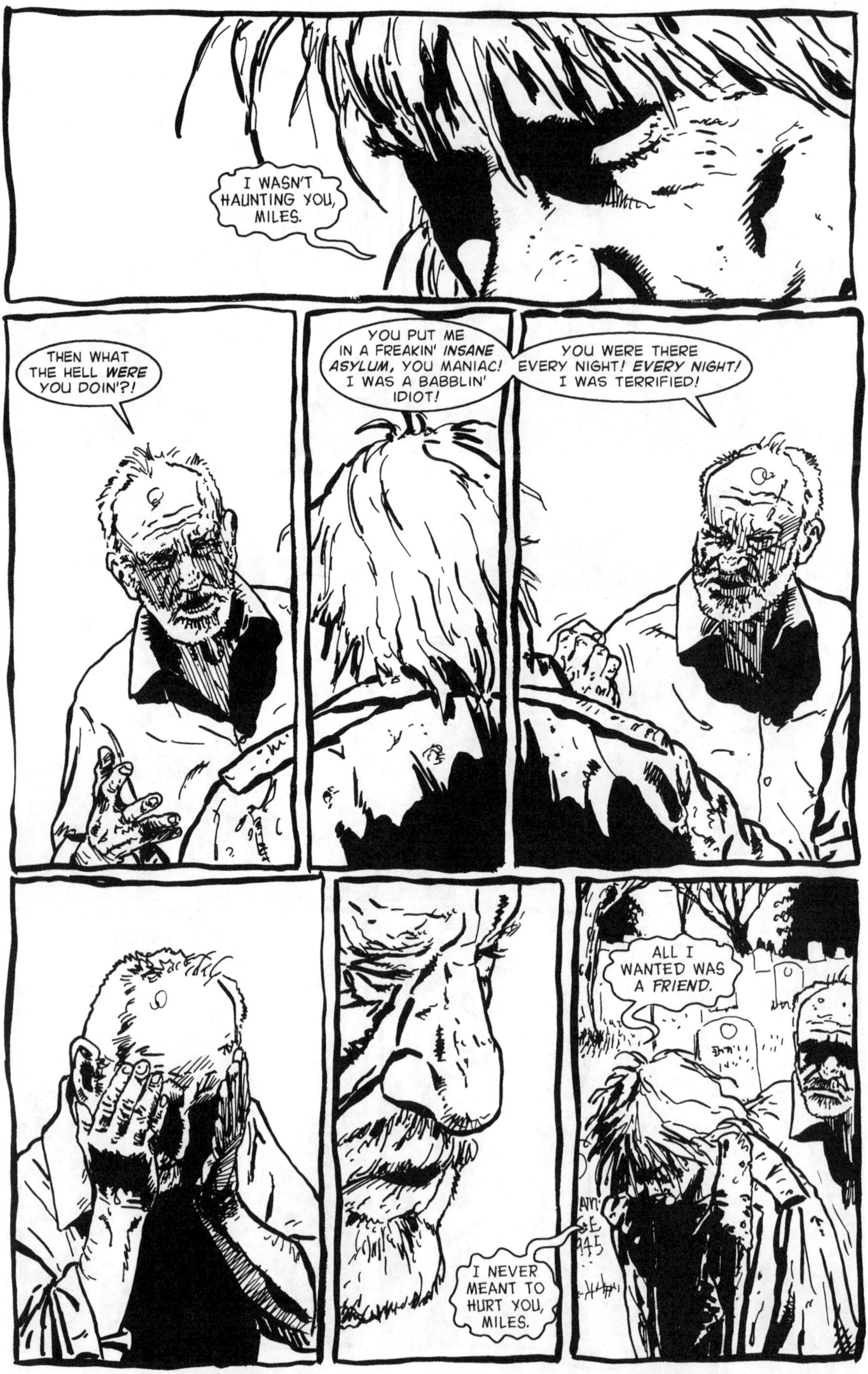

I WASN'T HAUNTING YOU, MILES.
THEN WHAT THE HELL WERE YOU DOIN'?!
YOU PUT ME IN A FREAKIN' INSANE ASYLUM, YOU MANIAC! I WAS A BABBLIN' IDIOT!
YOU WERE THERE EVERY NIGHT! EVERY NIGHT! I WAS TERRIFIED!
I NEVER MEANT TO HURT YOU, MILES.
ALL I WANTED WAS A FRIEND.

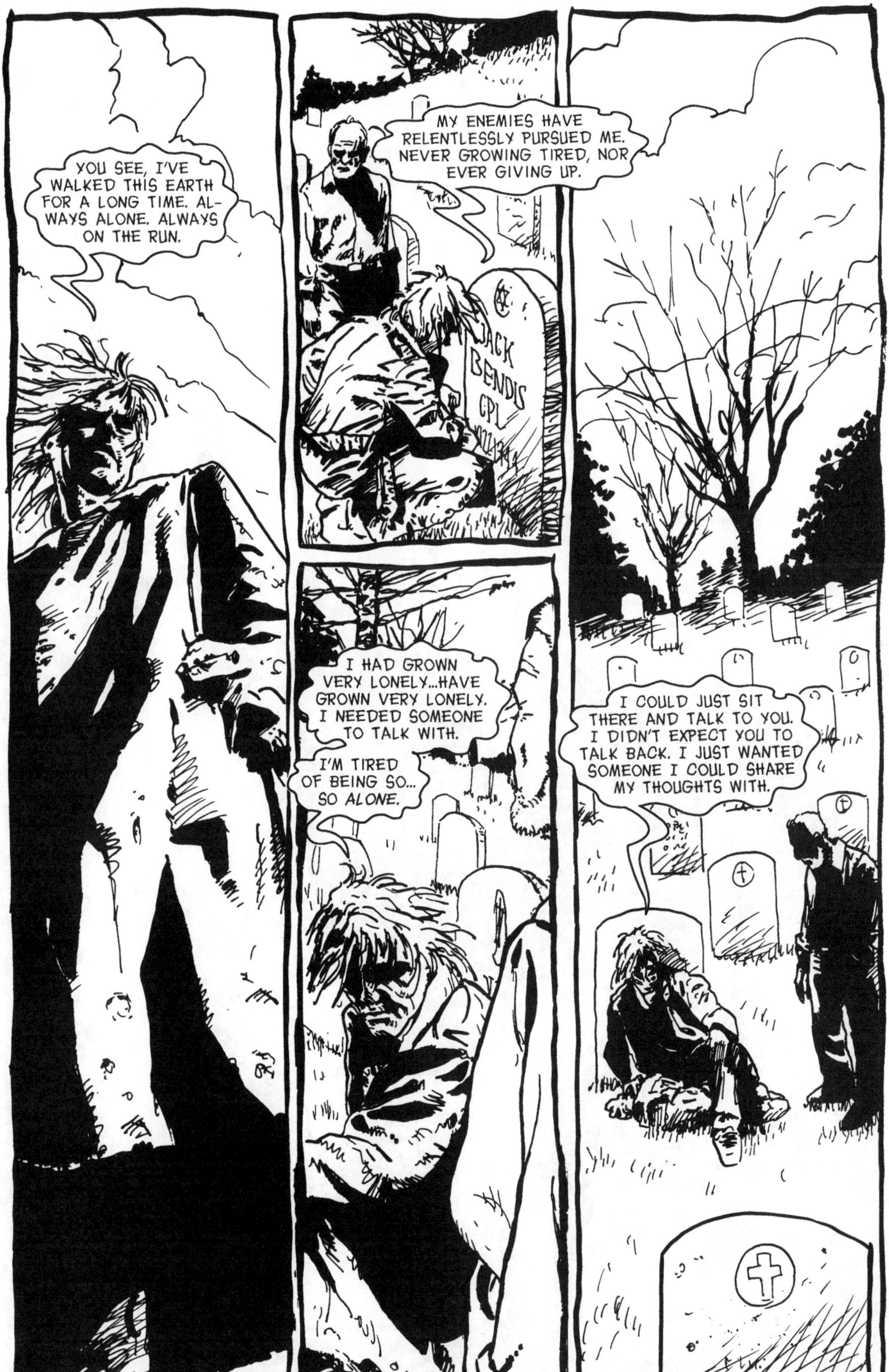
YOU SEE, I'VE WALKED THIS EARTH FOR A LONG TIME. AL-WAYS ALONE. ALWAYS ON THE RUN.
MY ENEMIES HAVE RELENTLESSLY PURSUED ME. NEVER GROWING TIRED, NOR EVER GIVING UP.
JACK BENDIS CPL
I HAD GROWN VERY LONELY...HAVE GROWN VERY LONELY. I NEEDED SOMEONE TO TALK WITH.
I'M TIRED OF BEING SO... SO *ALONE*.
I COULD JUST SIT THERE AND TALK TO YOU. I DIDN'T EXPECT YOU TO TALK BACK. I JUST WANTED SOMEONE I COULD SHARE MY THOUGHTS WITH.

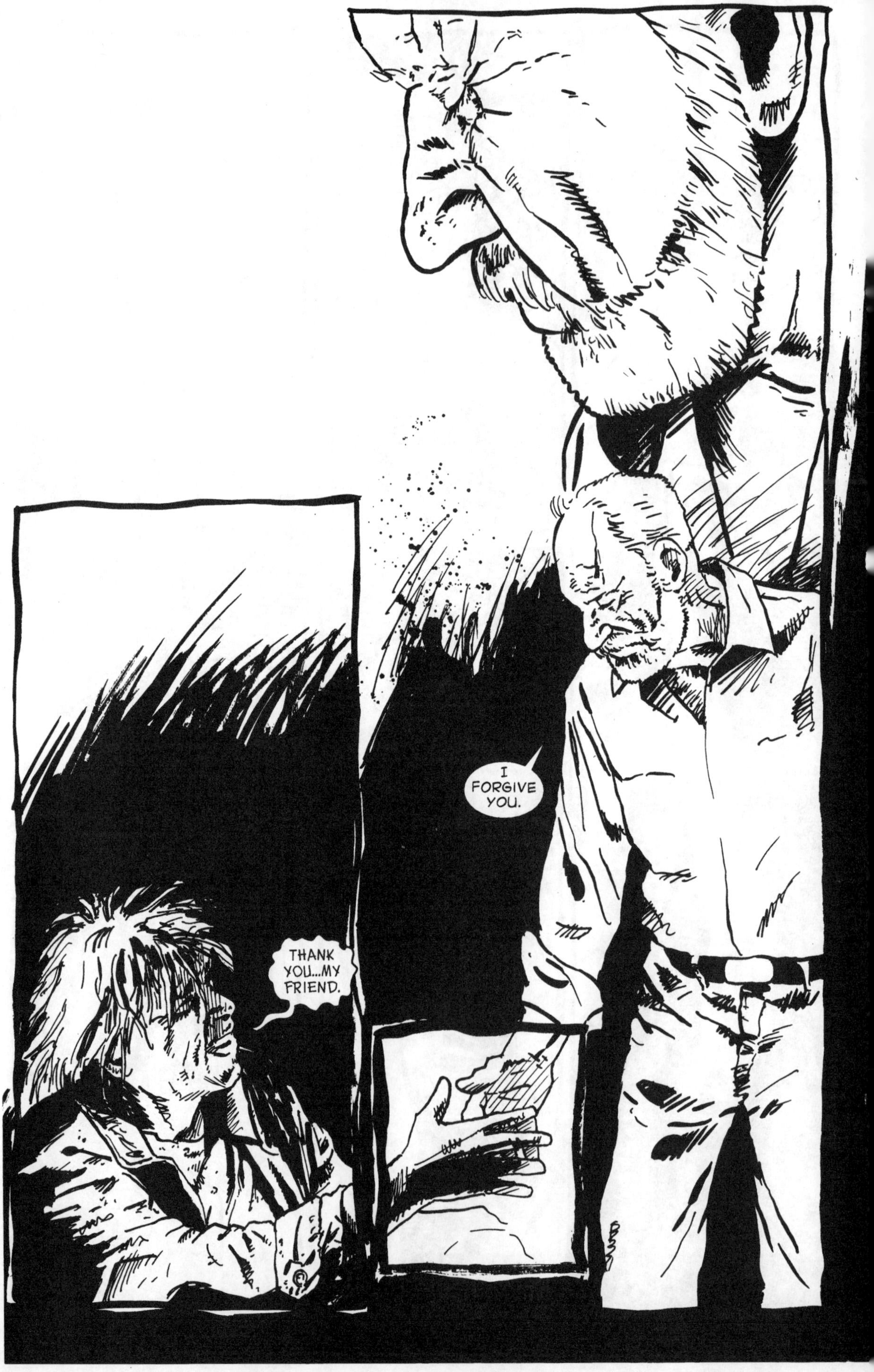
I FORGIVE YOU.
THANK YOU...MY FRIEND.

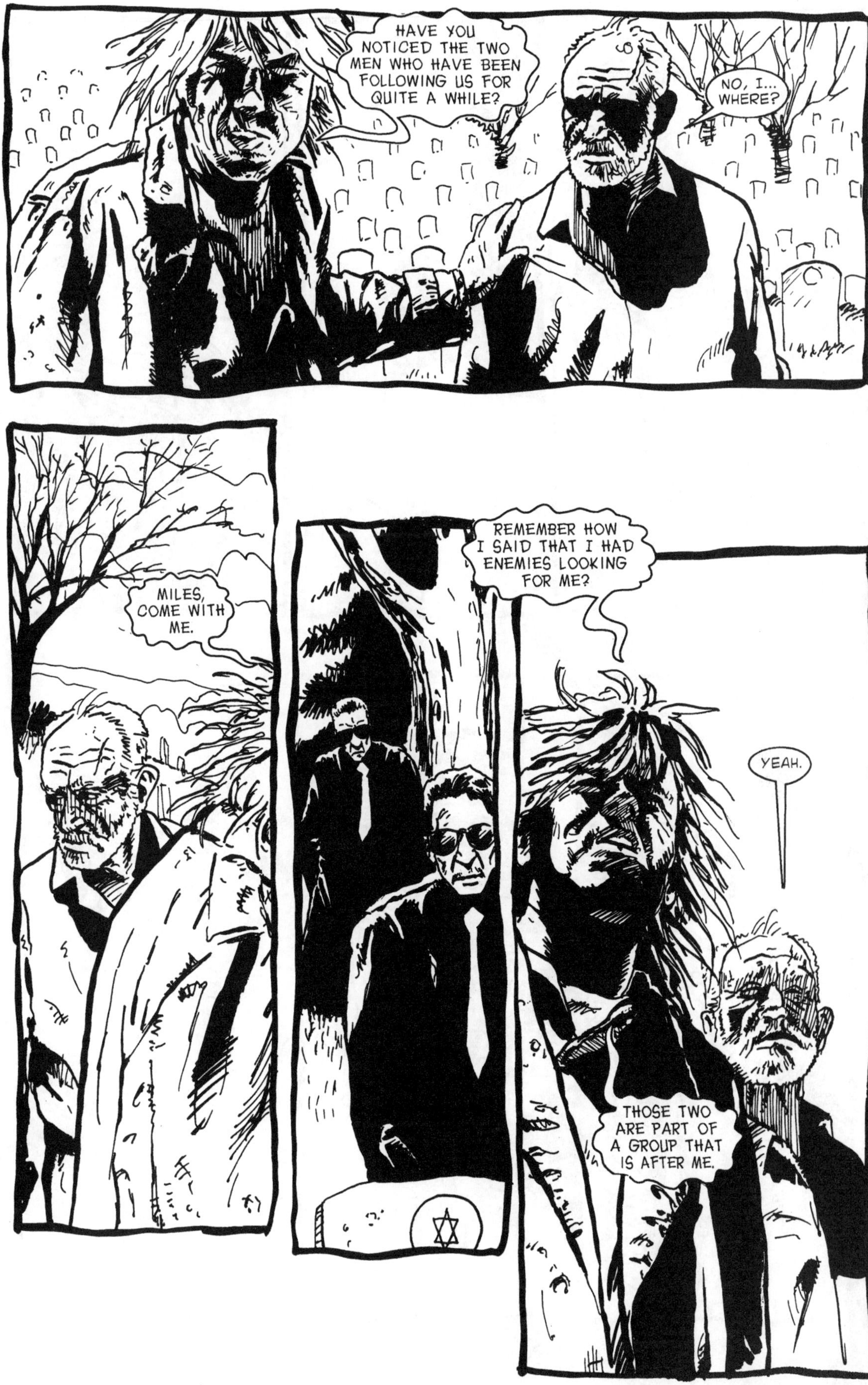
HAVE YOU NOTICED THE TWO MEN WHO HAVE BEEN FOLLOWING US FOR QUITE A WHILE?
NO, I... WHERE?
MILES, COME WITH ME.
REMEMBER HOW I SAID THAT I HAD ENEMIES LOOKING FOR ME?
YEAH.
THOSE TWO ARE PART OF A GROUP THAT IS AFTER ME.

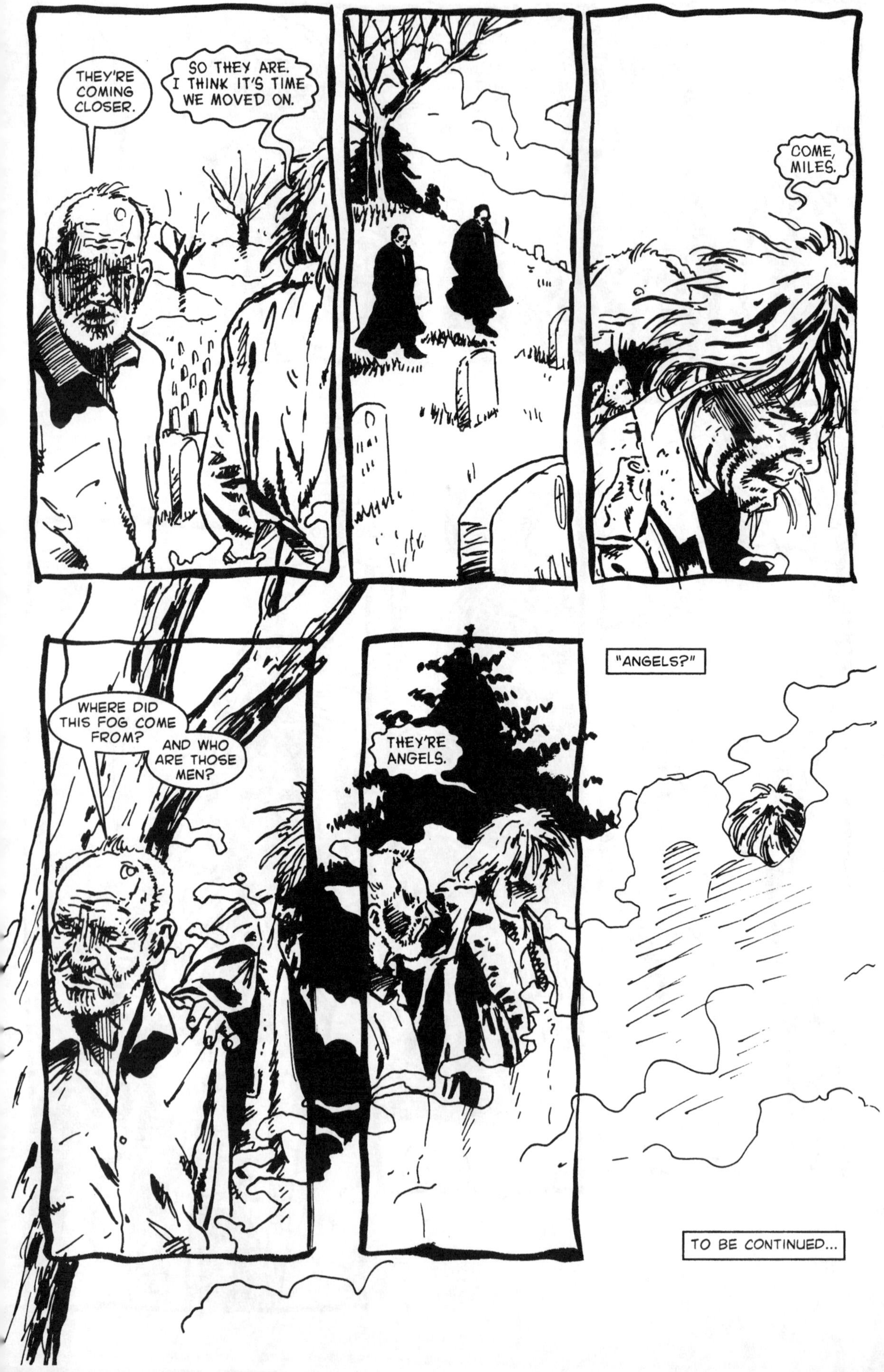
THEY'RE COMING CLOSER.
SO THEY ARE. I THINK IT'S TIME WE MOVED ON.
COME, MILES.
WHERE DID THIS FOG COME FROM?
AND WHO ARE THOSE MEN?
THEY'RE ANGELS.
"ANGELS?"
TO BE CONTINUED...

"Reflections"
Chapter Four

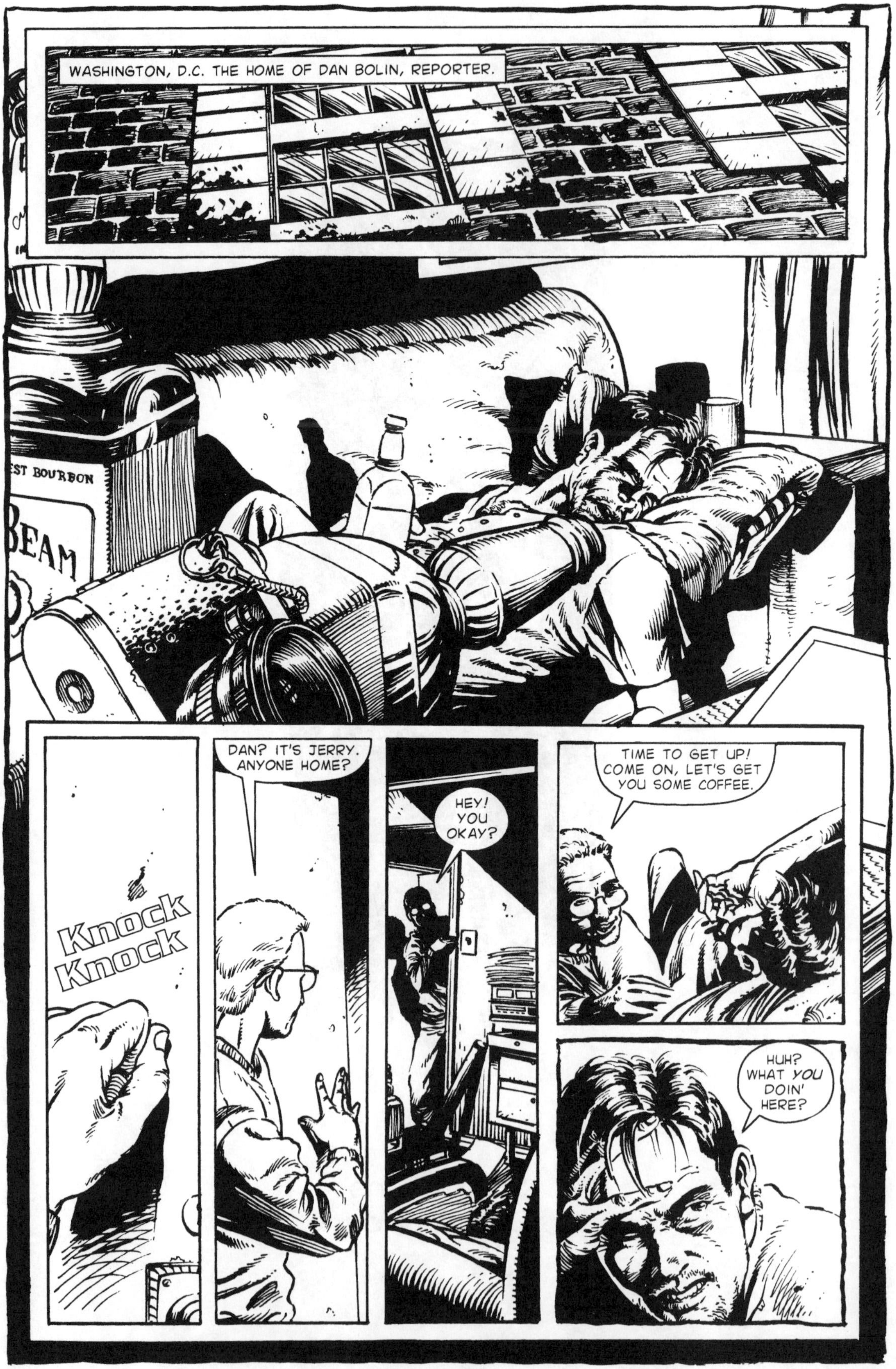
WASHINGTON, D.C. THE HOME OF DAN BOLIN, REPORTER.
EST BOURBON
BEAM
Knock Knock
DAN? IT'S JERRY. ANYONE HOME?
HEY! YOU OKAY?
TIME TO GET UP! COME ON, LET'S GET YOU SOME COFFEE.
HUH? WHAT *YOU* DOIN' HERE?

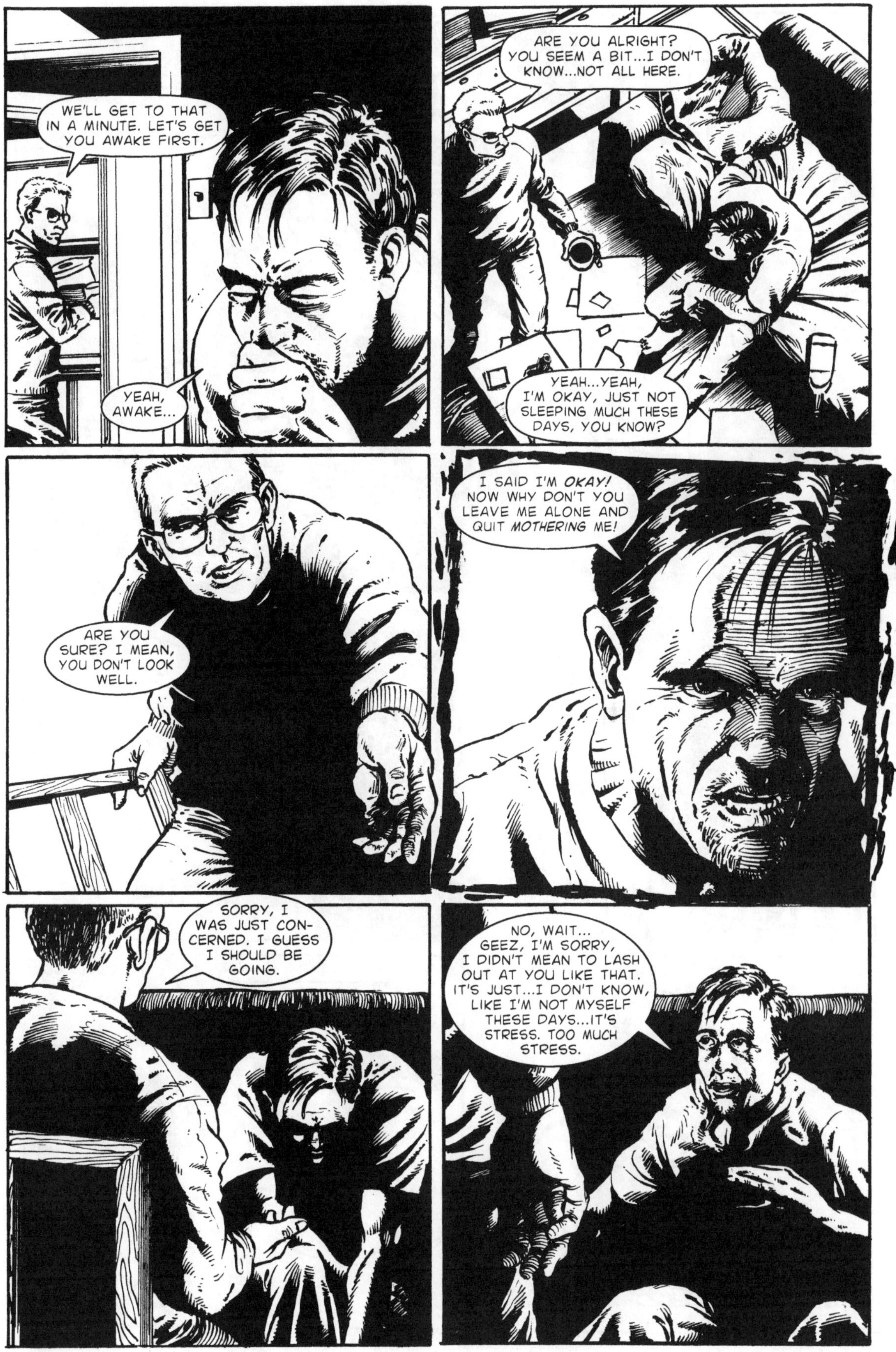
WE'LL GET TO THAT IN A MINUTE. LET'S GET YOU AWAKE FIRST.
YEAH, AWAKE...
ARE YOU ALRIGHT? YOU SEEM A BIT...I DON'T KNOW...NOT ALL HERE.
YEAH...YEAH, I'M OKAY, JUST NOT SLEEPING MUCH THESE DAYS, YOU KNOW?
ARE YOU SURE? I MEAN, YOU DON'T LOOK WELL.
I SAID I'M *OKAY!* NOW WHY DON'T YOU LEAVE ME ALONE AND QUIT *MOTHERING* ME!
SORRY, I WAS JUST CON-CERNED. I GUESS I SHOULD BE GOING.
NO, WAIT... GEEZ, I'M SORRY, I DIDN'T MEAN TO LASH OUT AT YOU LIKE THAT. IT'S JUST...I DON'T KNOW, LIKE I'M NOT MYSELF THESE DAYS...IT'S STRESS. TOO MUCH STRESS.

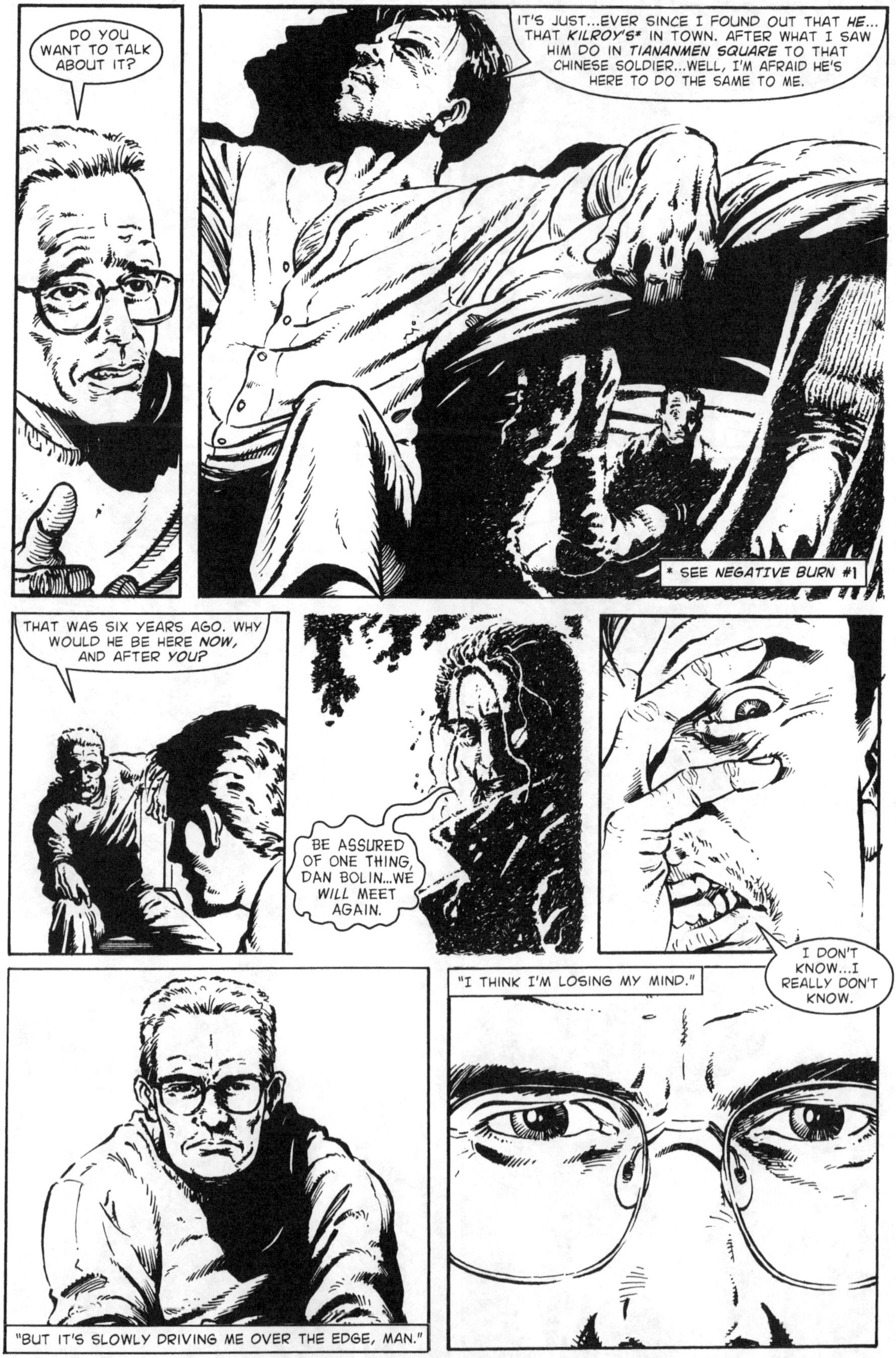
DO YOU WANT TO TALK ABOUT IT?
IT'S JUST...EVER SINCE I FOUND OUT THAT *HE*... THAT *KILROY'S** IN TOWN. AFTER WHAT I SAW HIM DO IN *TIANANMEN SQUARE* TO THAT CHINESE SOLDIER...WELL, I'M AFRAID HE'S HERE TO DO THE SAME TO ME.
* SEE *NEGATIVE BURN #1*
THAT WAS SIX YEARS AGO. WHY WOULD HE BE HERE *NOW*, AND AFTER *YOU*?
BE ASSURED OF ONE THING, DAN BOLIN...WE *WILL* MEET AGAIN.
I DON'T KNOW...I REALLY DON'T KNOW.
"I THINK I'M LOSING MY MIND."
"BUT IT'S SLOWLY DRIVING ME OVER THE EDGE, MAN."

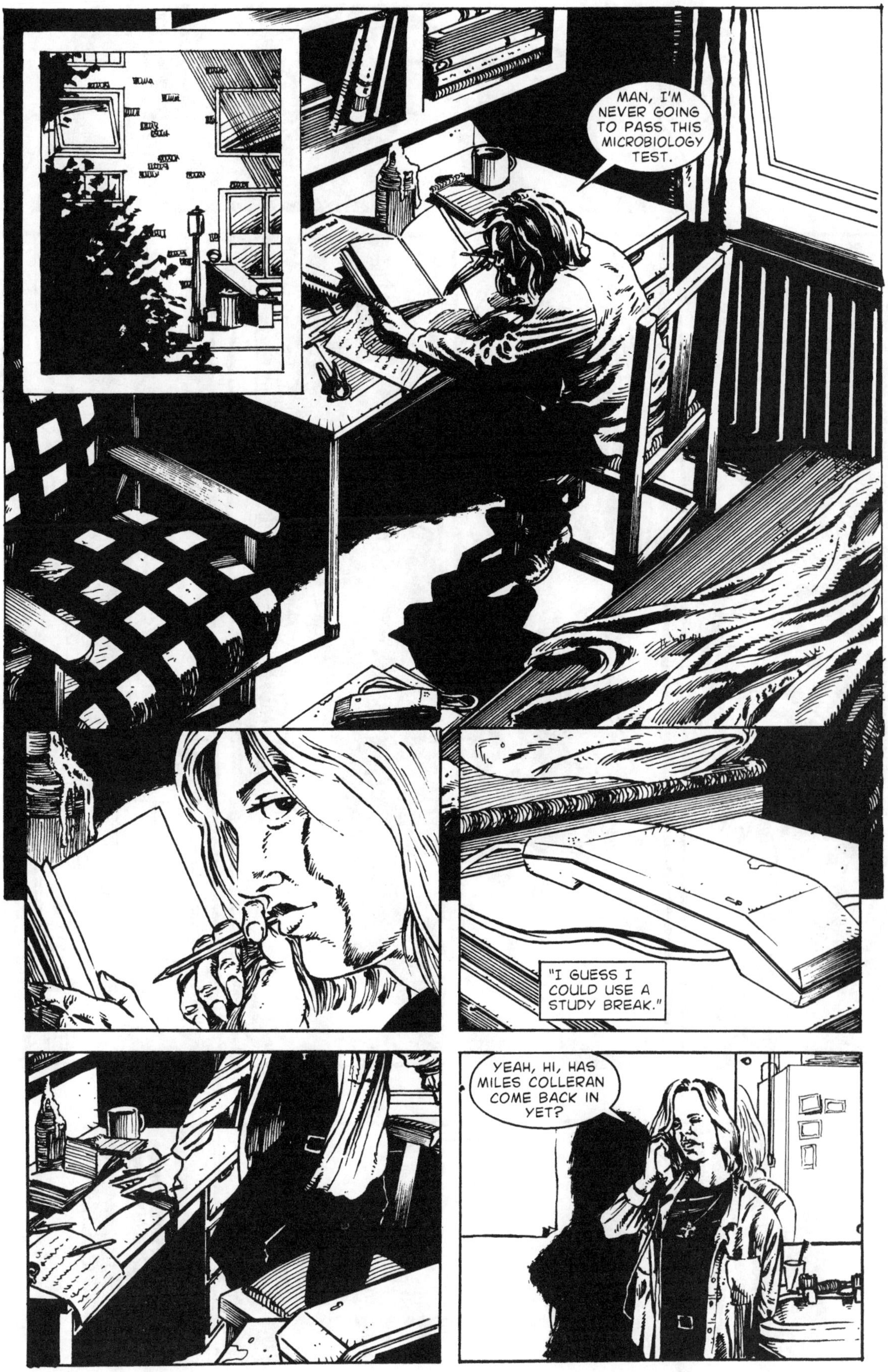
MAN, I'M NEVER GOING TO PASS THIS MICROBIOLOGY TEST.
"I GUESS I COULD USE A STUDY BREAK."
YEAH, HI, HAS MILES COLLERAN COME BACK IN YET?

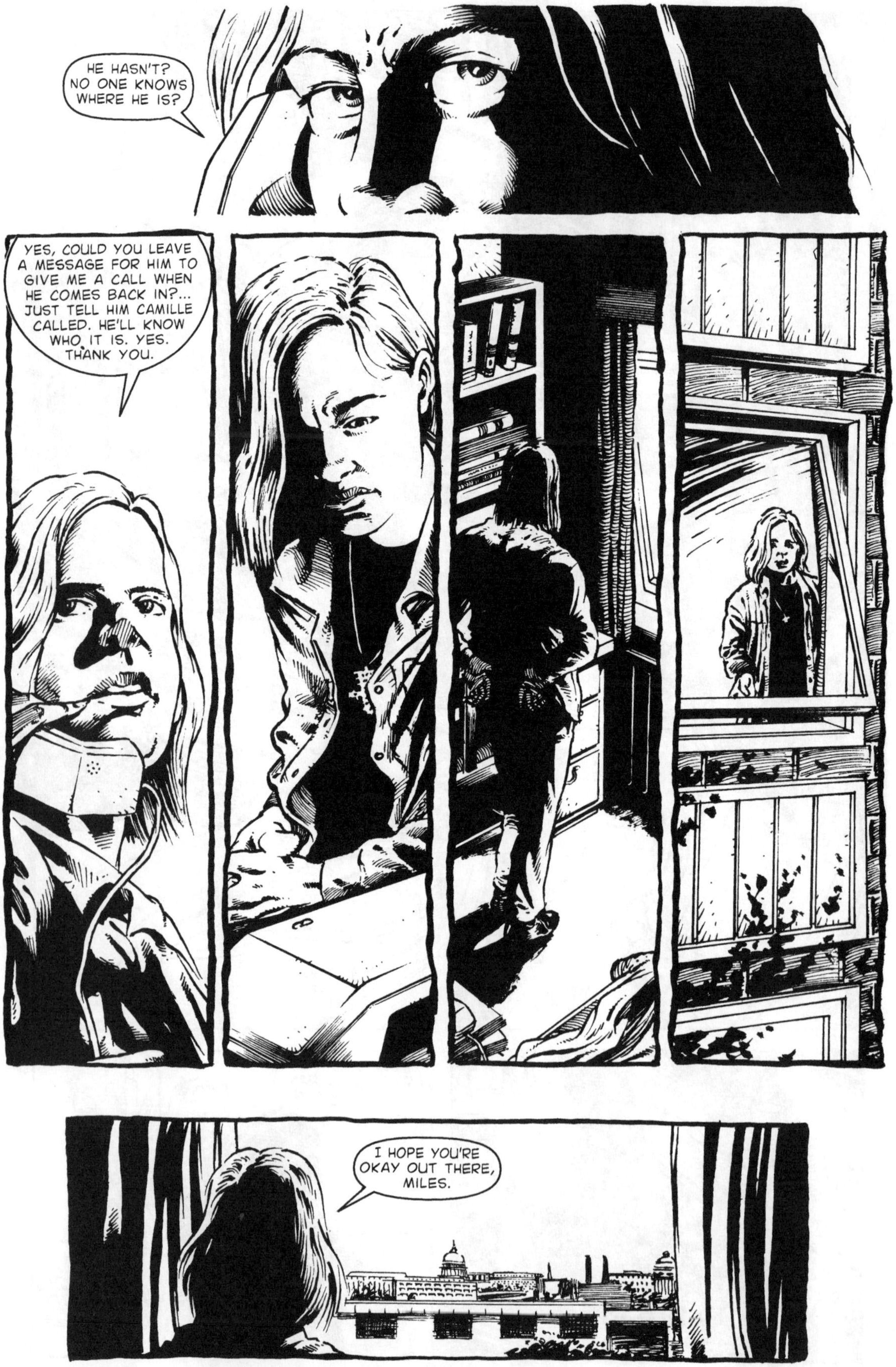
HE HASN'T? NO ONE KNOWS WHERE HE IS?
YES, COULD YOU LEAVE A MESSAGE FOR HIM TO GIVE ME A CALL WHEN HE COMES BACK IN?... JUST TELL HIM CAMILLE CALLED. HE'LL KNOW WHO IT IS. YES. THANK YOU.
I HOPE YOU'RE OKAY OUT THERE, MILES.

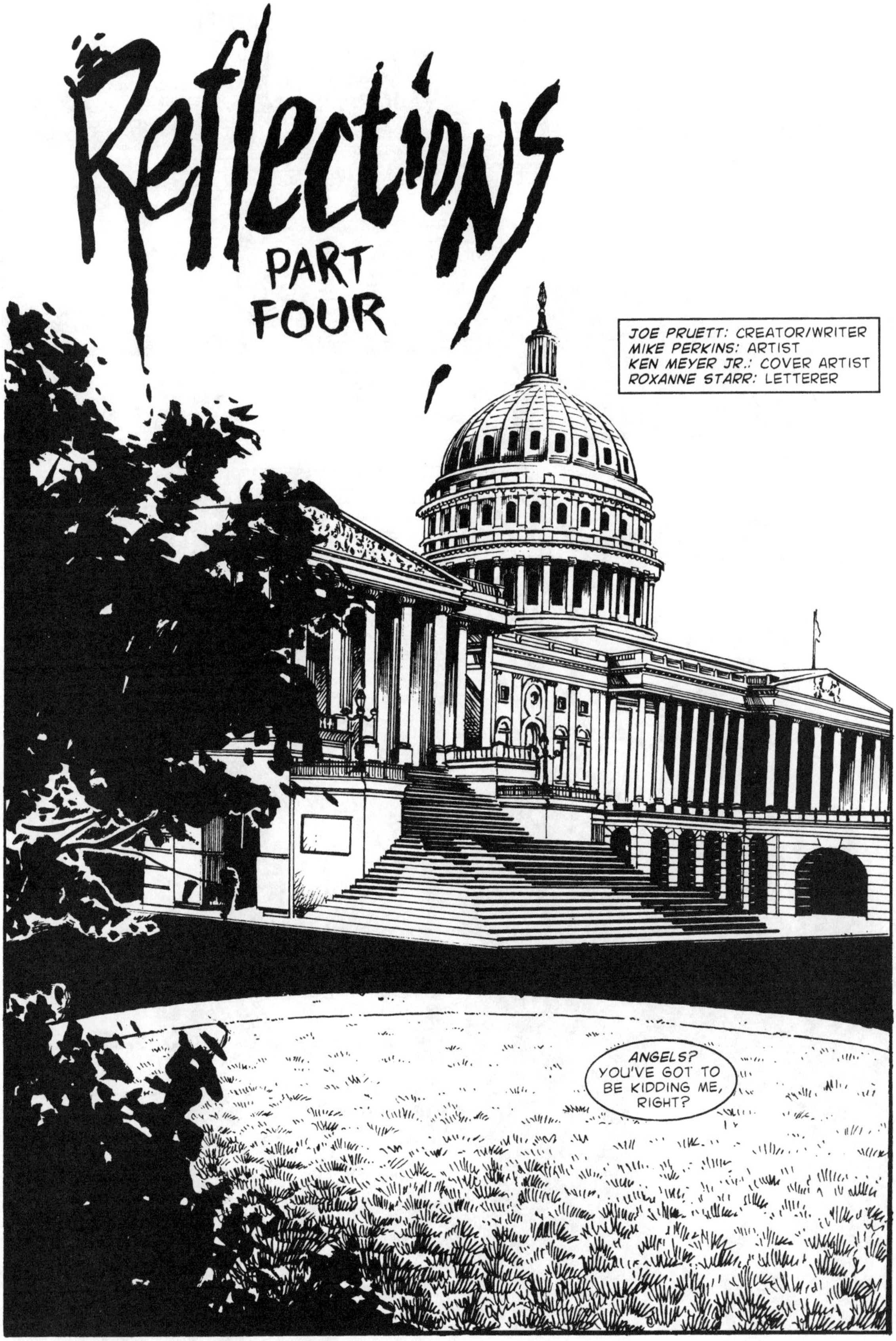
Reflections
PART FOUR
JOE PRUETT: CREATOR/WRITER
MIKE PERKINS: ARTIST
KEN MEYER JR.: COVER ARTIST
ROXANNE STARR: LETTERER
ANGELS? YOU'VE GOT TO BE KIDDING ME, RIGHT?

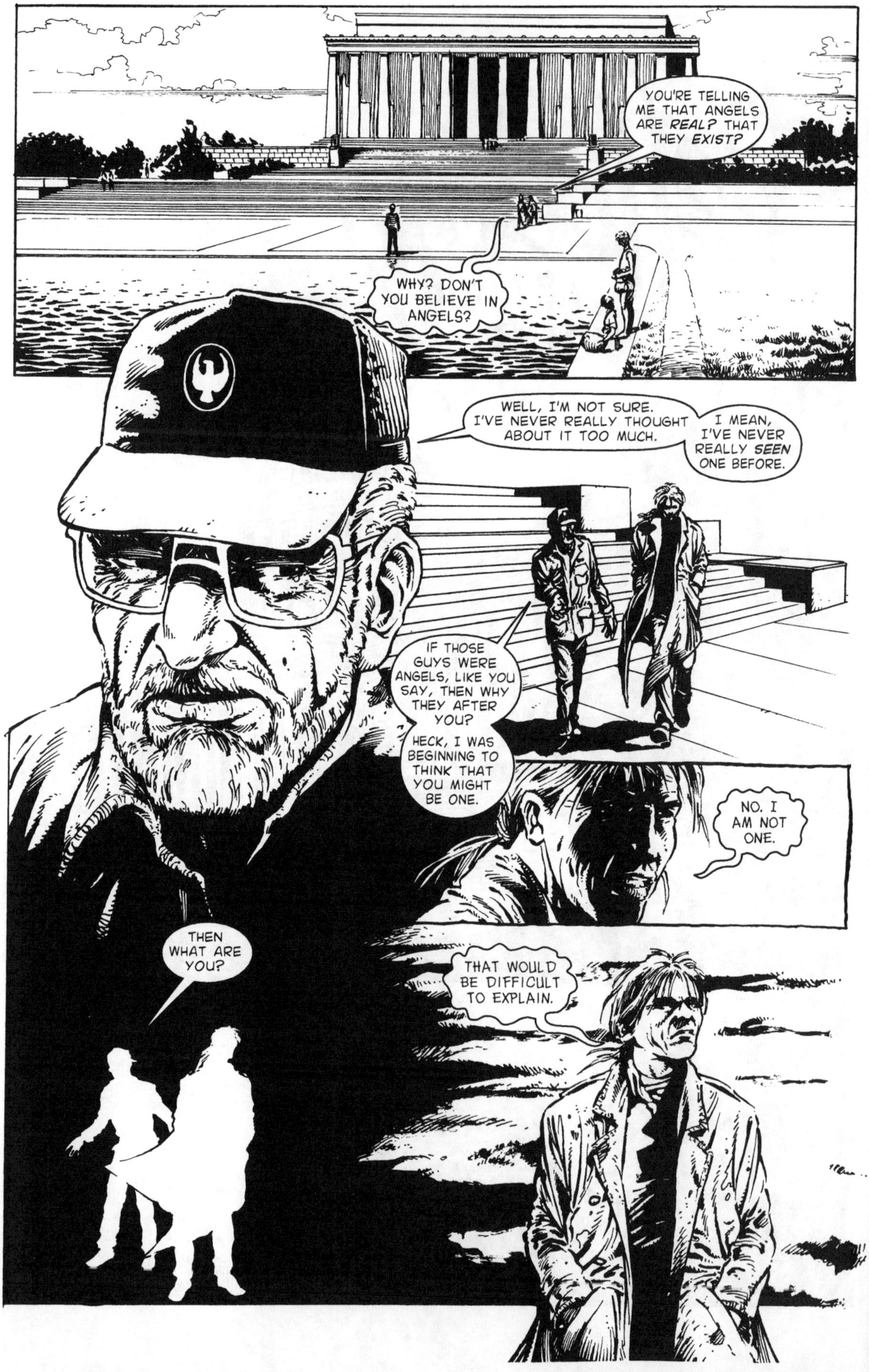
YOU'RE TELLING ME THAT ANGELS ARE *REAL?* THAT THEY *EXIST?*
WHY? DON'T YOU BELIEVE IN ANGELS?
WELL, I'M NOT SURE. I'VE NEVER REALLY THOUGHT ABOUT IT TOO MUCH.
I MEAN, I'VE NEVER REALLY *SEEN* ONE BEFORE.
IF THOSE GUYS WERE ANGELS, LIKE YOU SAY, THEN WHY THEY AFTER YOU?
HECK, I WAS BEGINNING TO THINK THAT YOU MIGHT BE ONE.
NO. I AM NOT ONE.
THEN WHAT ARE YOU?
THAT WOULD BE DIFFICULT TO EXPLAIN.

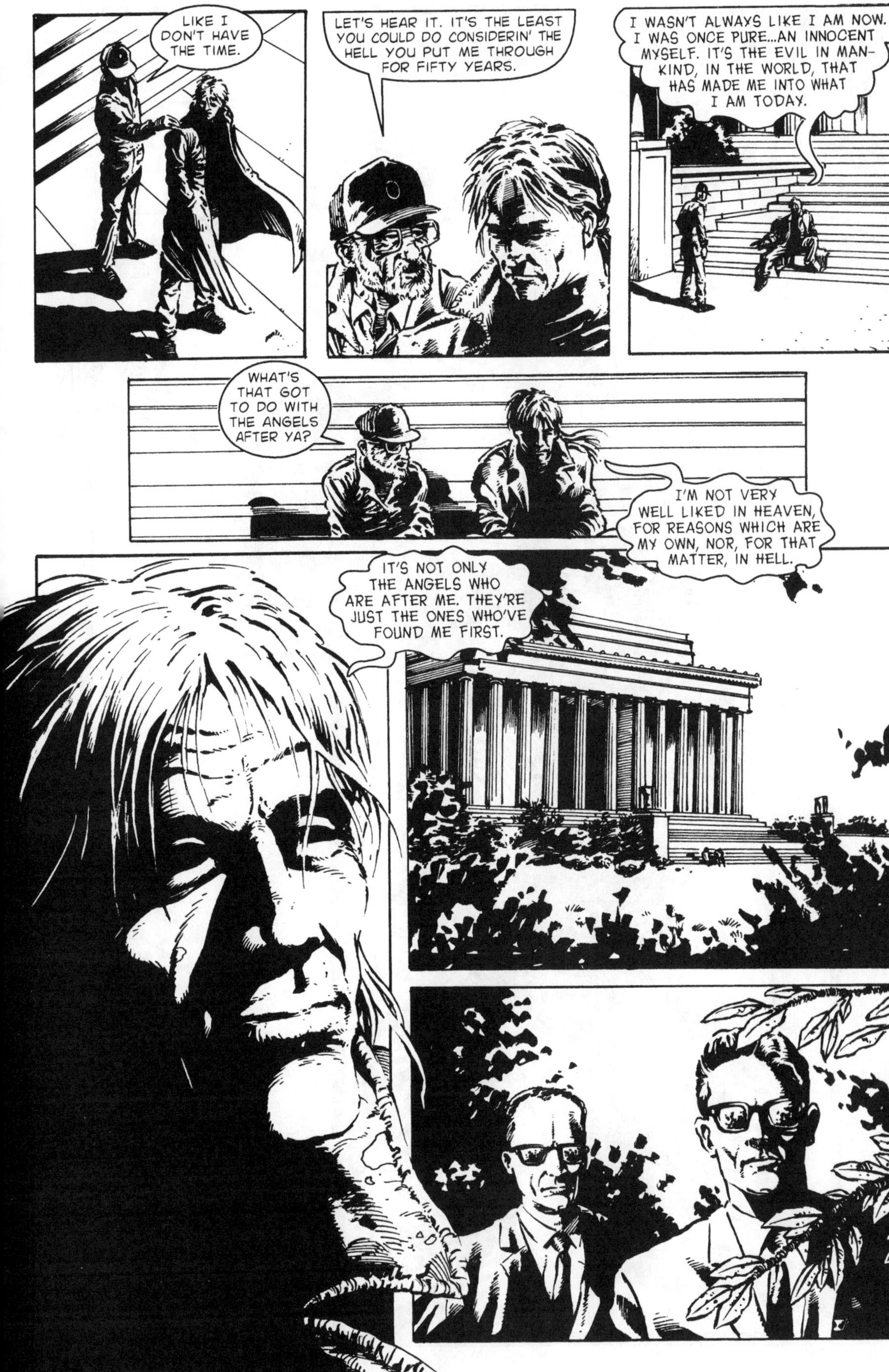
LIKE I DON'T HAVE THE TIME.
LET'S HEAR IT. IT'S THE LEAST YOU COULD DO CONSIDERIN' THE HELL YOU PUT ME THROUGH FOR FIFTY YEARS.
I WASN'T ALWAYS LIKE I AM NOW. I WAS ONCE PURE...AN INNOCENT MYSELF. IT'S THE EVIL IN MAN-KIND, IN THE WORLD, THAT HAS MADE ME INTO WHAT I AM TODAY.
WHAT'S THAT GOT TO DO WITH THE ANGELS AFTER YA?
I'M NOT VERY WELL LIKED IN HEAVEN, FOR REASONS WHICH ARE MY OWN, NOR, FOR THAT MATTER, IN HELL.
IT'S NOT ONLY THE ANGELS WHO ARE AFTER ME. THEY'RE JUST THE ONES WHO'VE FOUND ME FIRST.

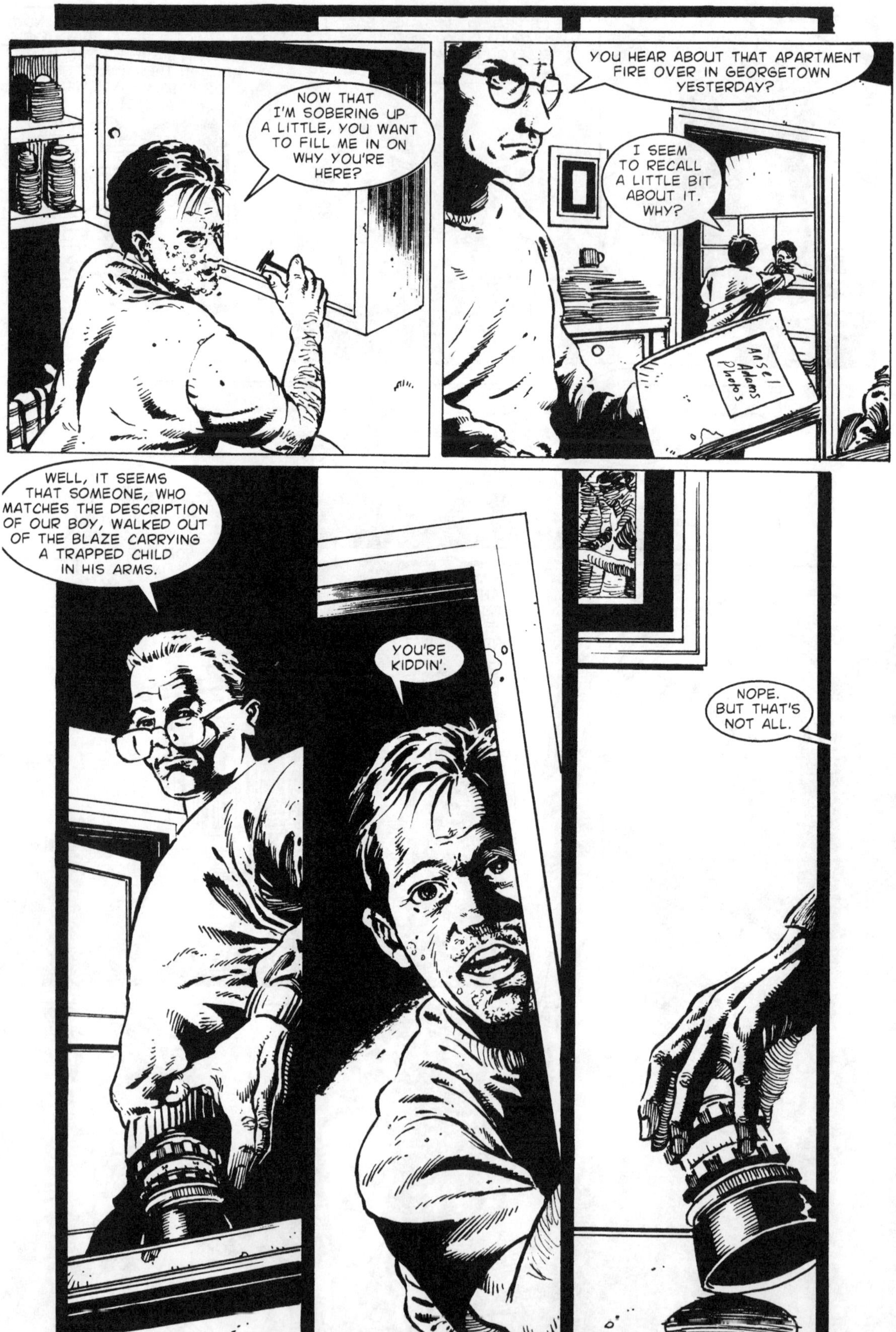
NOW THAT I'M SOBERING UP A LITTLE, YOU WANT TO FILL ME IN ON WHY YOU'RE HERE?
YOU HEAR ABOUT THAT APARTMENT FIRE OVER IN GEORGETOWN YESTERDAY?
I SEEM TO RECALL A LITTLE BIT ABOUT IT. WHY?
Ansel Adams Photos
WELL, IT SEEMS THAT SOMEONE, WHO MATCHES THE DESCRIPTION OF OUR BOY, WALKED OUT OF THE BLAZE CARRYING A TRAPPED CHILD IN HIS ARMS.
YOU'RE KIDDIN'.
NOPE. BUT THAT'S NOT ALL.

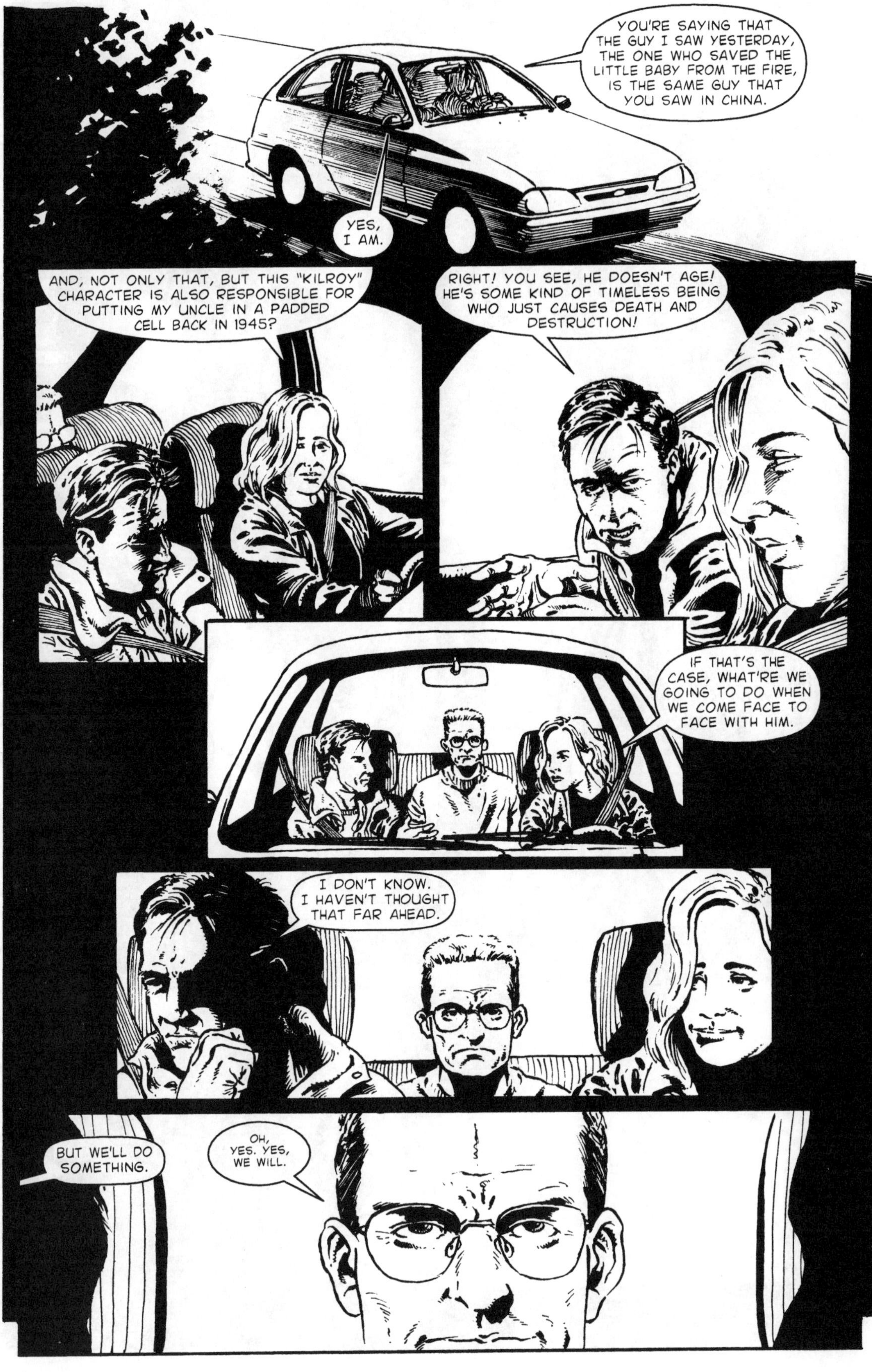
YOU'RE SAYING THAT THE GUY I SAW YESTERDAY, THE ONE WHO SAVED THE LITTLE BABY FROM THE FIRE, IS THE SAME GUY THAT YOU SAW IN CHINA.
YES, I AM.
AND, NOT ONLY THAT, BUT THIS "KILROY" CHARACTER IS ALSO RESPONSIBLE FOR PUTTING MY UNCLE IN A PADDED CELL BACK IN 1945?
RIGHT! YOU SEE, HE DOESN'T AGE! HE'S SOME KIND OF TIMELESS BEING WHO JUST CAUSES DEATH AND DESTRUCTION!
IF THAT'S THE CASE, WHAT'RE WE GOING TO DO WHEN WE COME FACE TO FACE WITH HIM.
I DON'T KNOW. I HAVEN'T THOUGHT THAT FAR AHEAD.
BUT WE'LL DO SOMETHING.
OH, YES. YES, WE WILL.

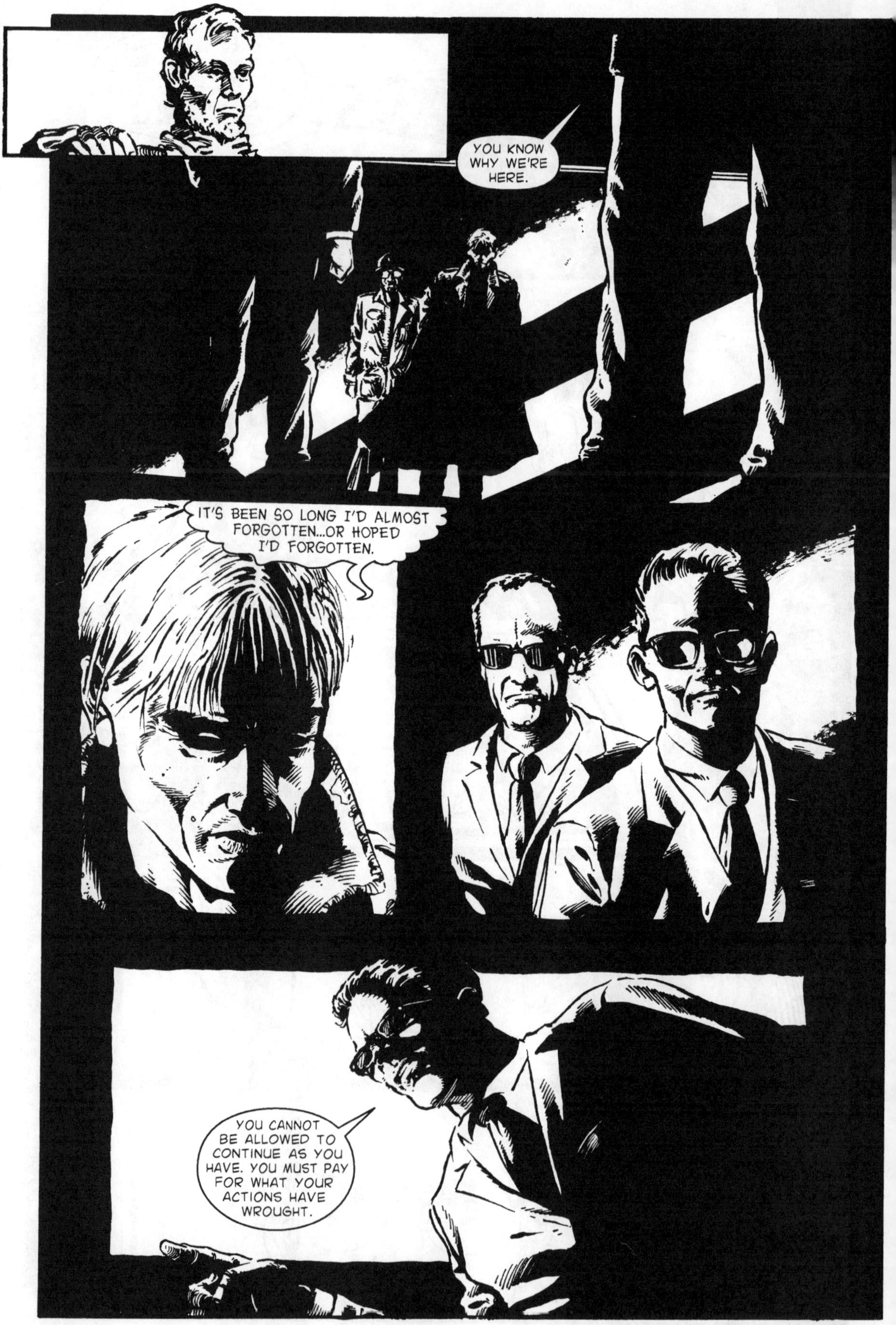
YOU KNOW WHY WE'RE HERE.
IT'S BEEN SO LONG I'D ALMOST FORGOTTEN...OR HOPED I'D FORGOTTEN.
YOU CANNOT BE ALLOWED TO CONTINUE AS YOU HAVE. YOU MUST PAY FOR WHAT YOUR ACTIONS HAVE WROUGHT.

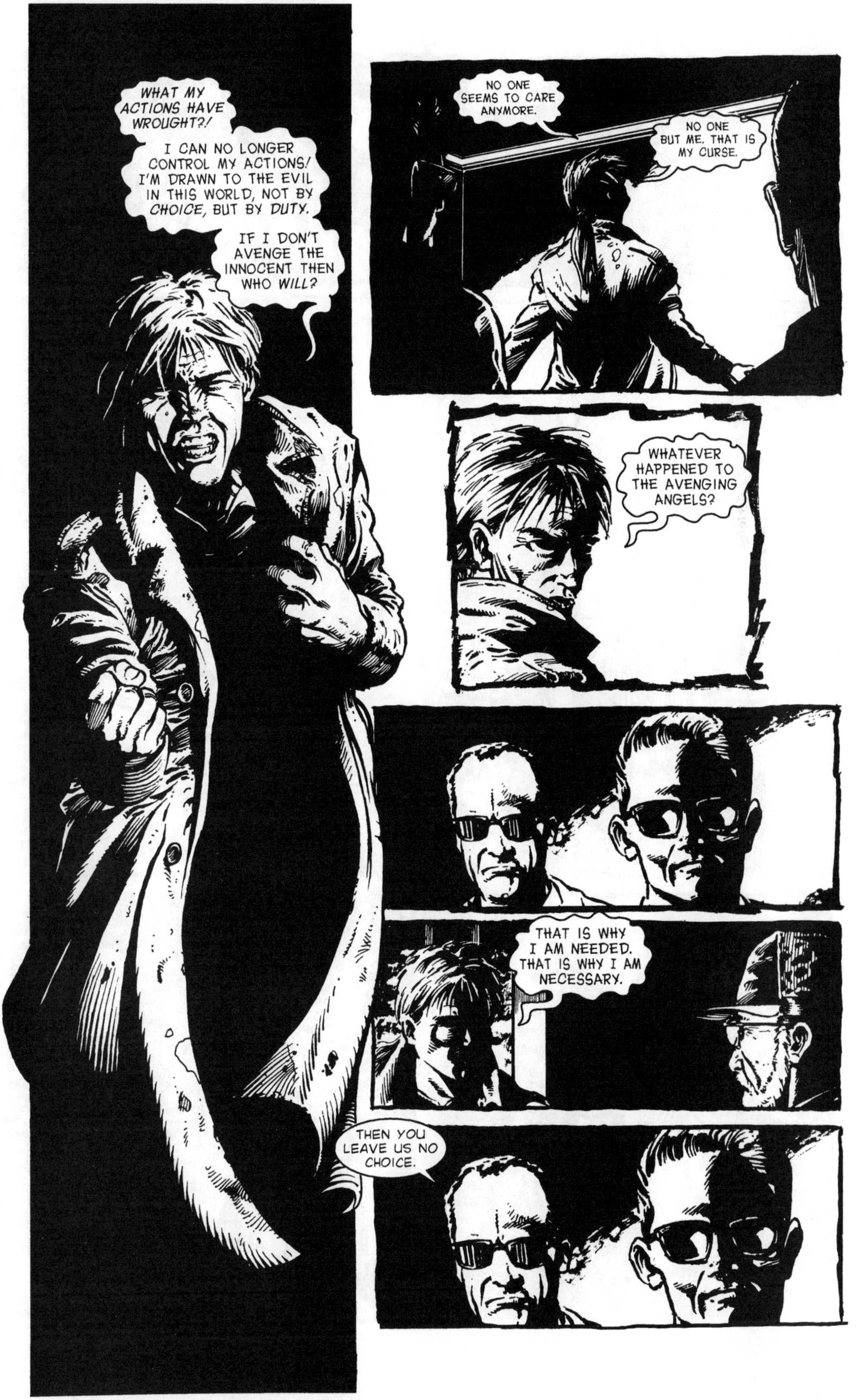
WHAT MY ACTIONS HAVE WROUGHT?!
I CAN NO LONGER CONTROL MY ACTIONS! I'M DRAWN TO THE EVIL IN THIS WORLD, NOT BY *CHOICE*, BUT BY *DUTY*.
IF I DON'T AVENGE THE INNOCENT THEN WHO *WILL*?
NO ONE SEEMS TO CARE ANYMORE.
NO ONE BUT ME. THAT IS MY CURSE.
WHATEVER HAPPENED TO THE AVENGING ANGELS?
THAT IS WHY I AM NEEDED. THAT IS WHY I AM NECESSARY.
THEN YOU LEAVE US NO CHOICE.

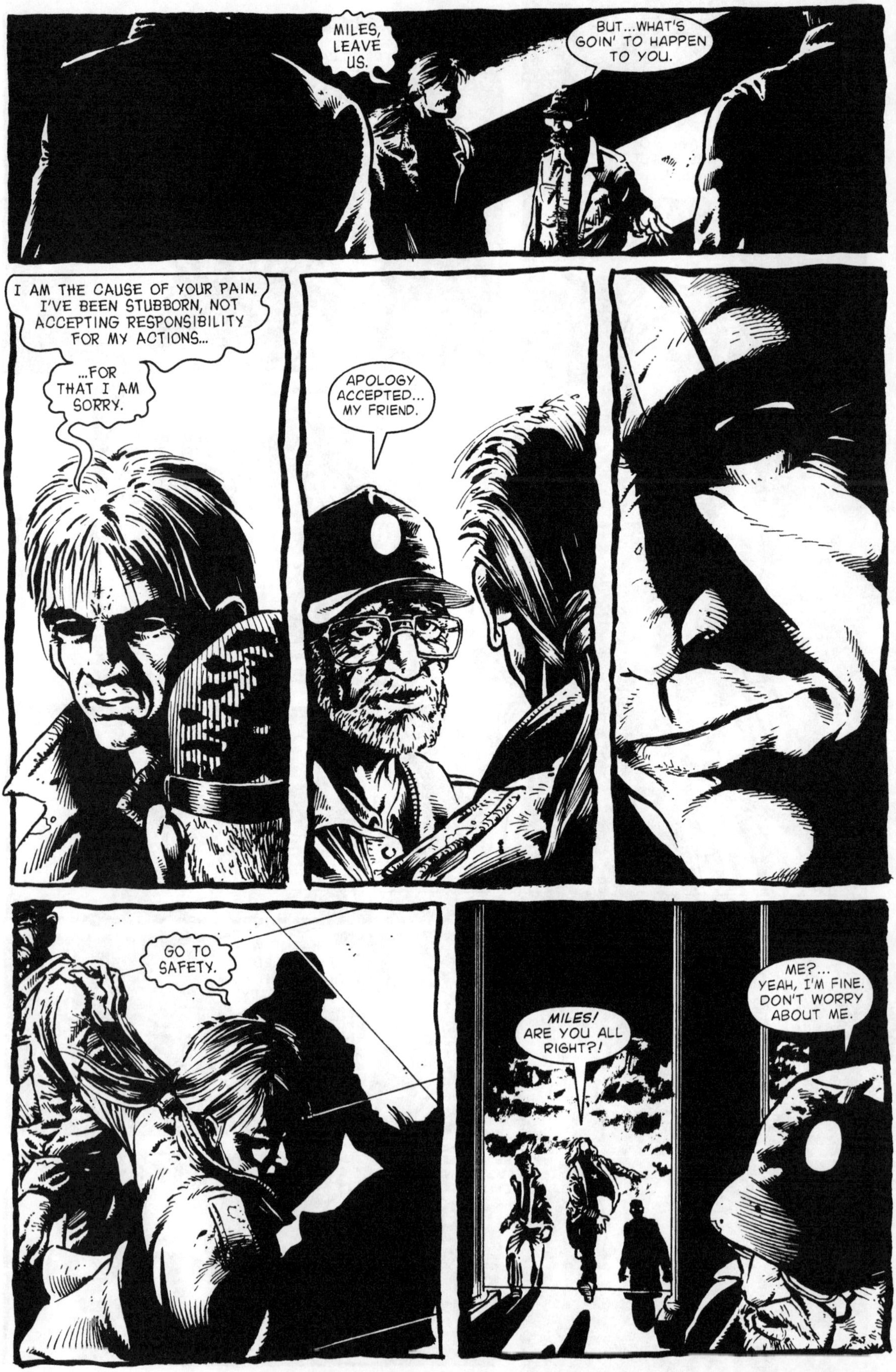
MILES, LEAVE US.
BUT...WHAT'S GOIN' TO HAPPEN TO YOU.
I AM THE CAUSE OF YOUR PAIN. I'VE BEEN STUBBORN, NOT ACCEPTING RESPONSIBILITY FOR MY ACTIONS...
...FOR THAT I AM SORRY.
APOLOGY ACCEPTED... MY FRIEND.
GO TO SAFETY.
MILES! ARE YOU ALL RIGHT?!
ME?... YEAH, I'M FINE. DON'T WORRY ABOUT ME.

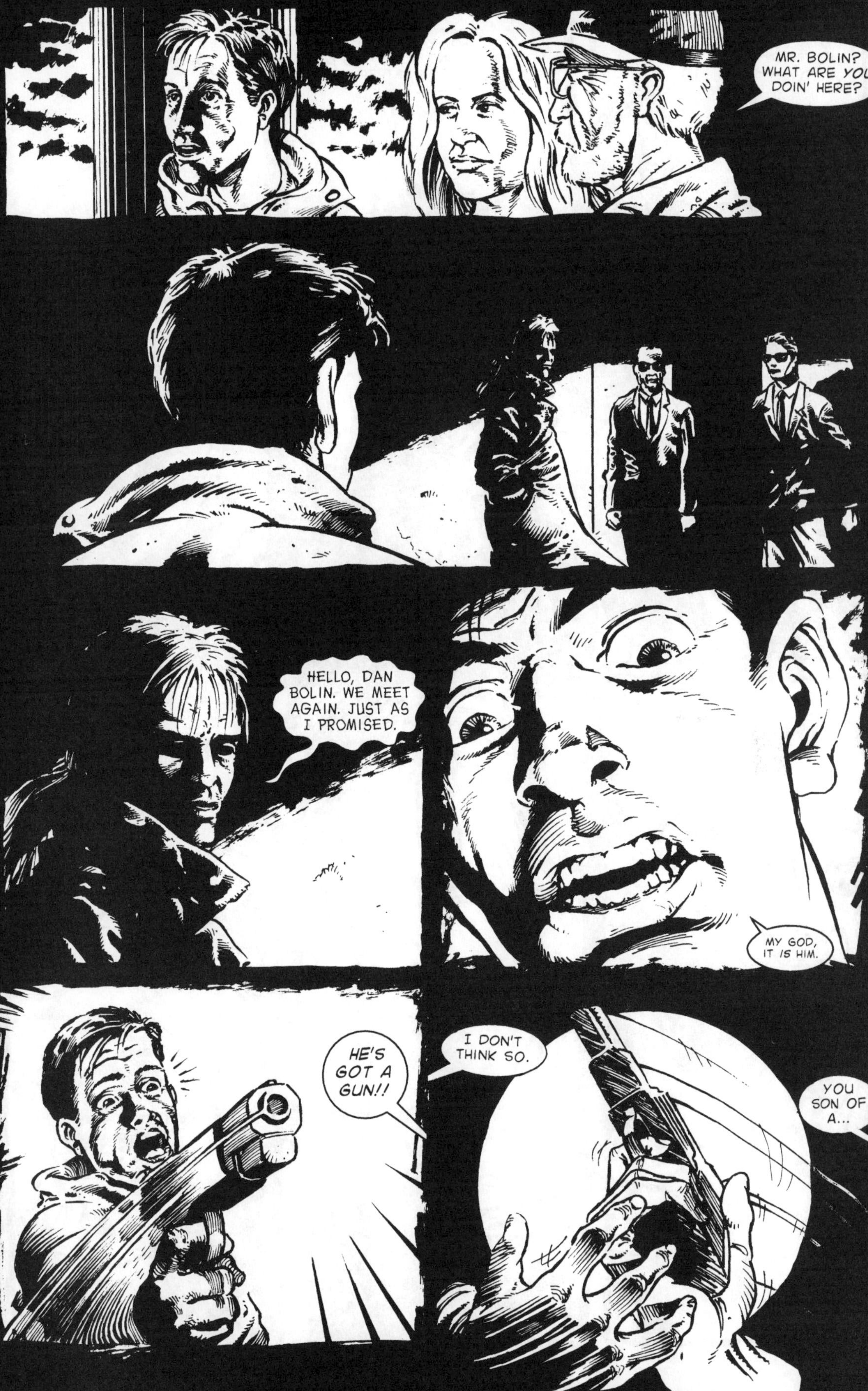
MR. BOLIN? WHAT ARE YOU DOIN' HERE?
HELLO, DAN BOLIN. WE MEET AGAIN. JUST AS I PROMISED.
MY GOD, IT IS HIM.
HE'S GOT A GUN!!
I DON'T THINK SO.
YOU SON OF A...

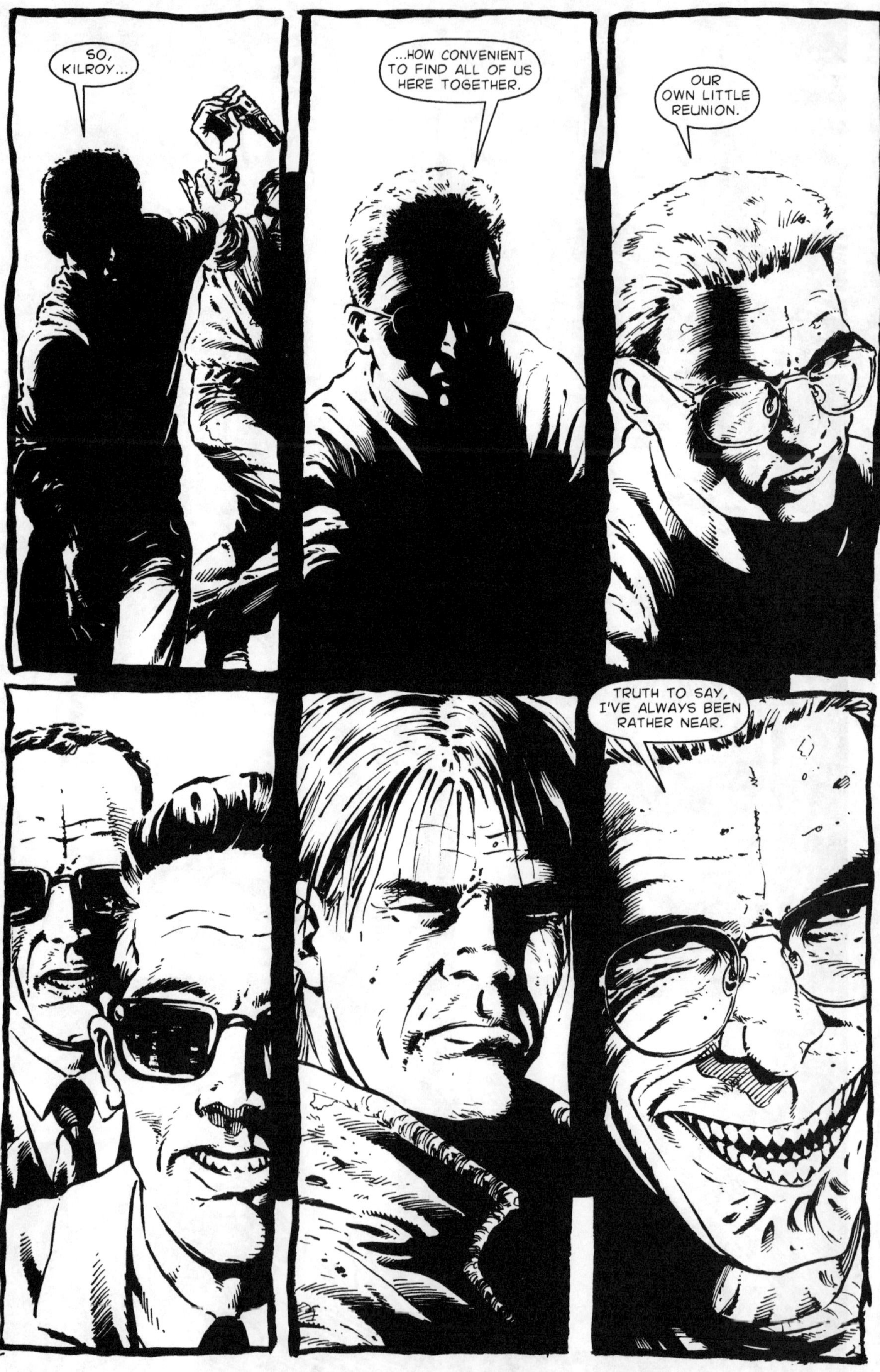
SO, KILROY...
...HOW CONVENIENT TO FIND ALL OF US HERE TOGETHER.
OUR OWN LITTLE REUNION.
TRUTH TO SAY, I'VE ALWAYS BEEN RATHER NEAR.

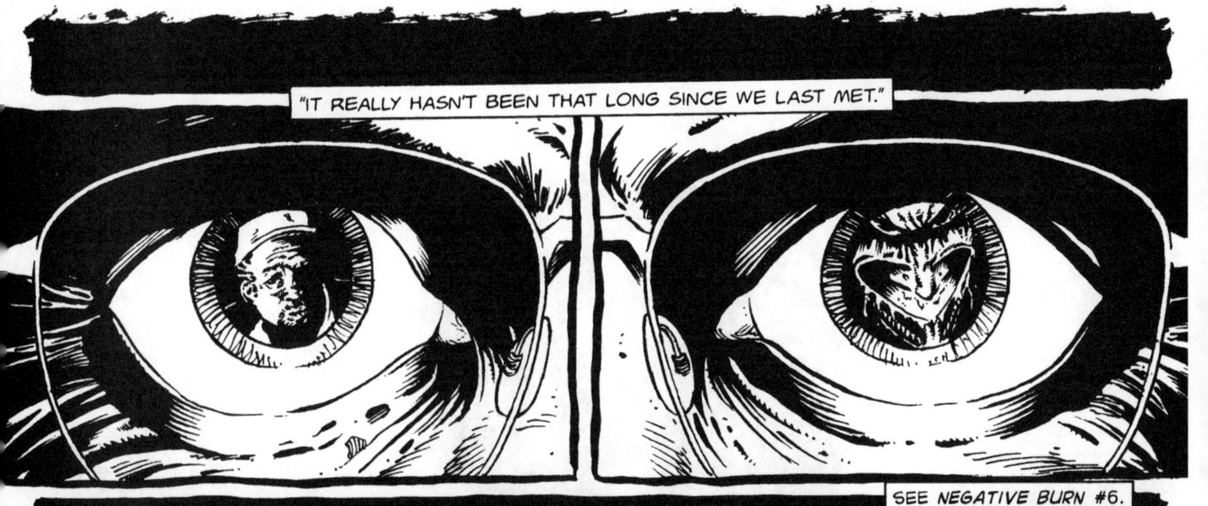
"IT REALLY HASN'T BEEN THAT LONG SINCE WE LAST MET."
SEE *NEGATIVE BURN* #6.

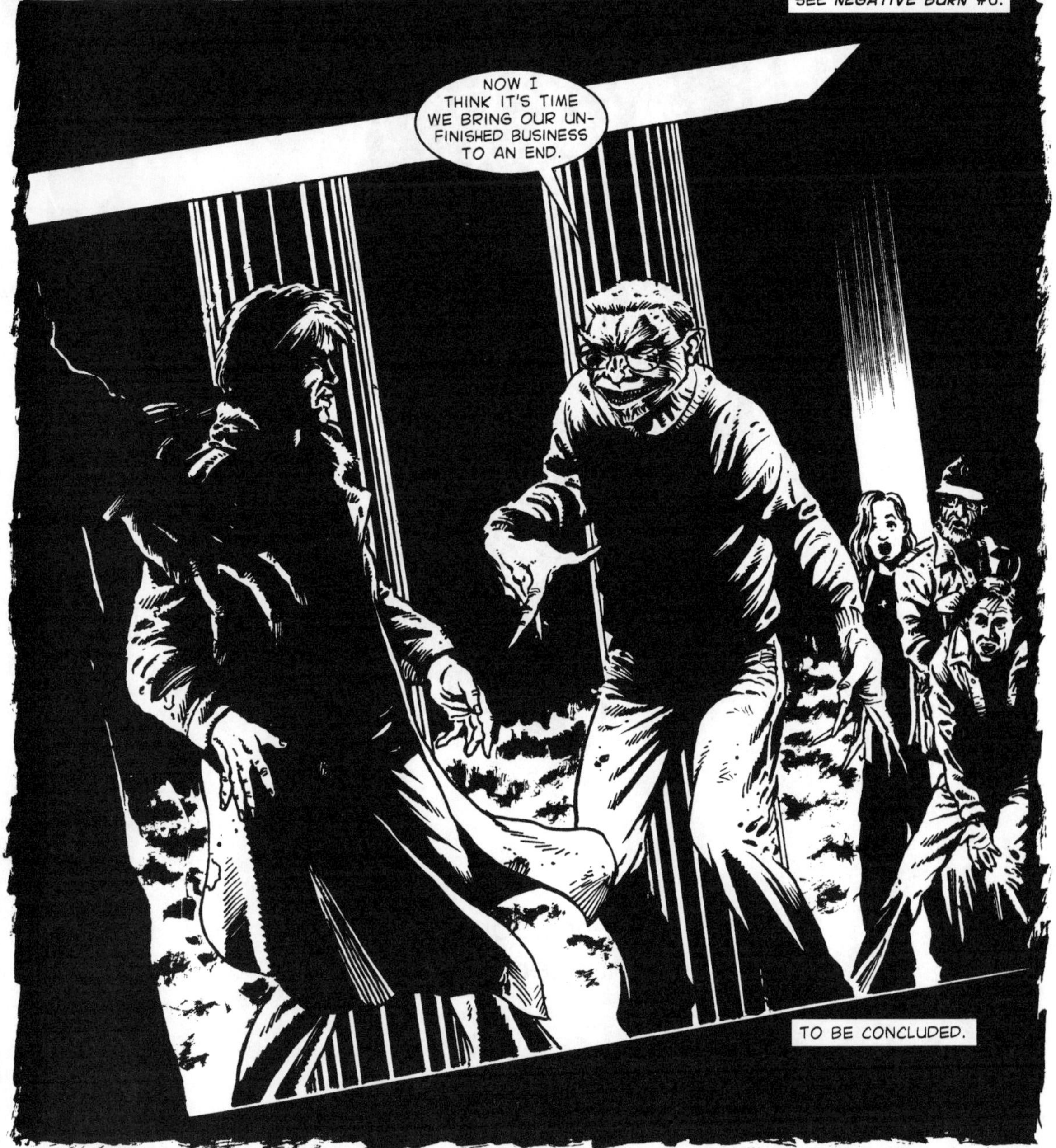
NOW I THINK IT'S TIME WE BRING OUR UN-FINISHED BUSINESS TO AN END.
TO BE CONCLUDED.

"Reflections"
Chapter Five

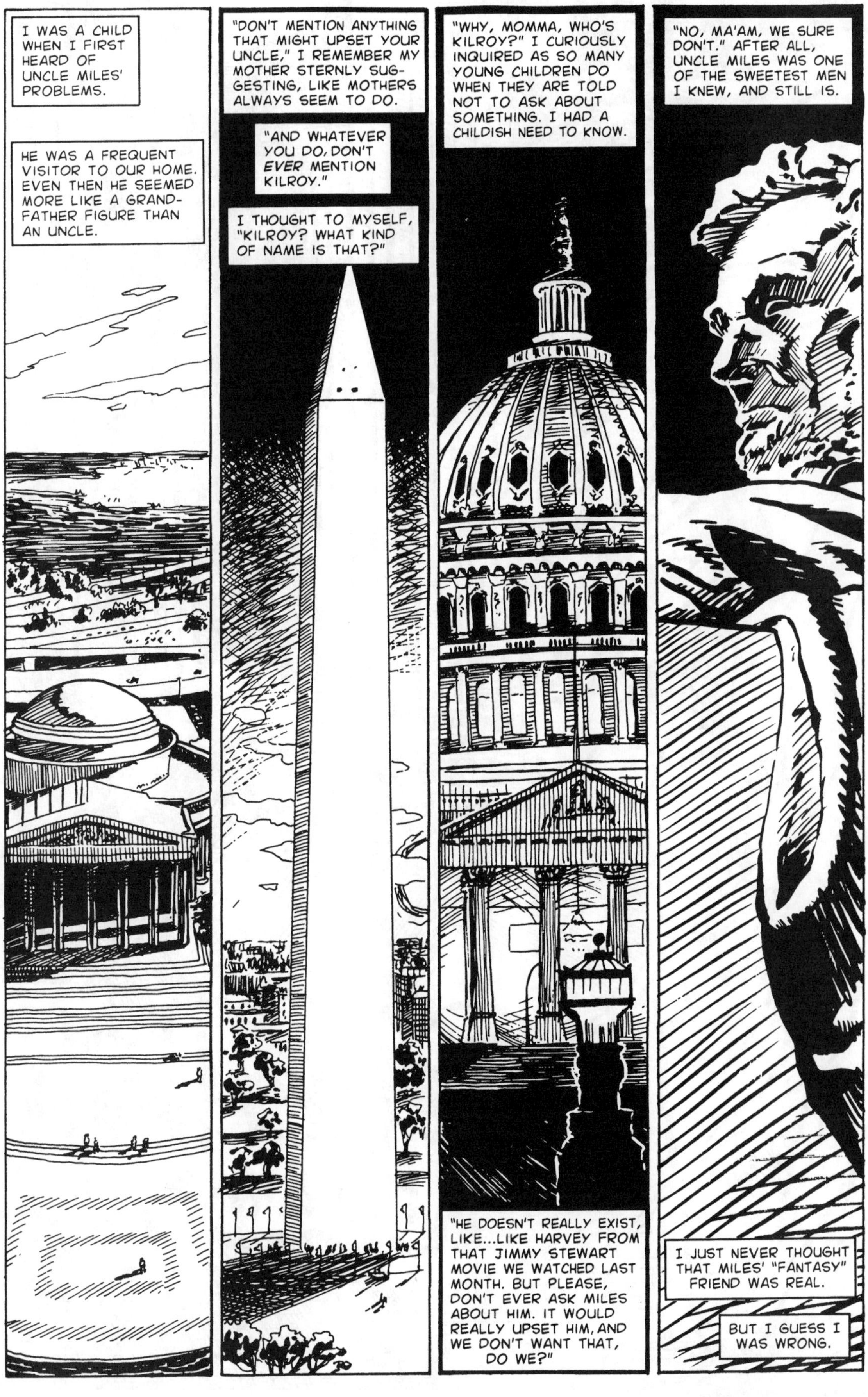
I WAS A CHILD WHEN I FIRST HEARD OF UNCLE MILES' PROBLEMS.
HE WAS A FREQUENT VISITOR TO OUR HOME. EVEN THEN HE SEEMED MORE LIKE A GRAND-FATHER FIGURE THAN AN UNCLE.
"DON'T MENTION ANYTHING THAT MIGHT UPSET YOUR UNCLE," I REMEMBER MY MOTHER STERNLY SUG-GESTING, LIKE MOTHERS ALWAYS SEEM TO DO.
"AND WHATEVER YOU DO, DON'T *EVER* MENTION KILROY."
I THOUGHT TO MYSELF, "KILROY? WHAT KIND OF NAME IS THAT?"
"WHY, MOMMA, WHO'S KILROY?" I CURIOUSLY INQUIRED AS SO MANY YOUNG CHILDREN DO WHEN THEY ARE TOLD NOT TO ASK ABOUT SOMETHING. I HAD A CHILDISH NEED TO KNOW.
"HE DOESN'T REALLY EXIST, LIKE...LIKE HARVEY FROM THAT JIMMY STEWART MOVIE WE WATCHED LAST MONTH. BUT PLEASE, DON'T EVER ASK MILES ABOUT HIM. IT WOULD REALLY UPSET HIM, AND WE DON'T WANT THAT, DO WE?"
"NO, MA'AM, WE SURE DON'T." AFTER ALL, UNCLE MILES WAS ONE OF THE SWEETEST MEN I KNEW, AND STILL IS.
I JUST NEVER THOUGHT THAT MILES' "FANTASY" FRIEND WAS REAL.
BUT I GUESS I WAS WRONG.

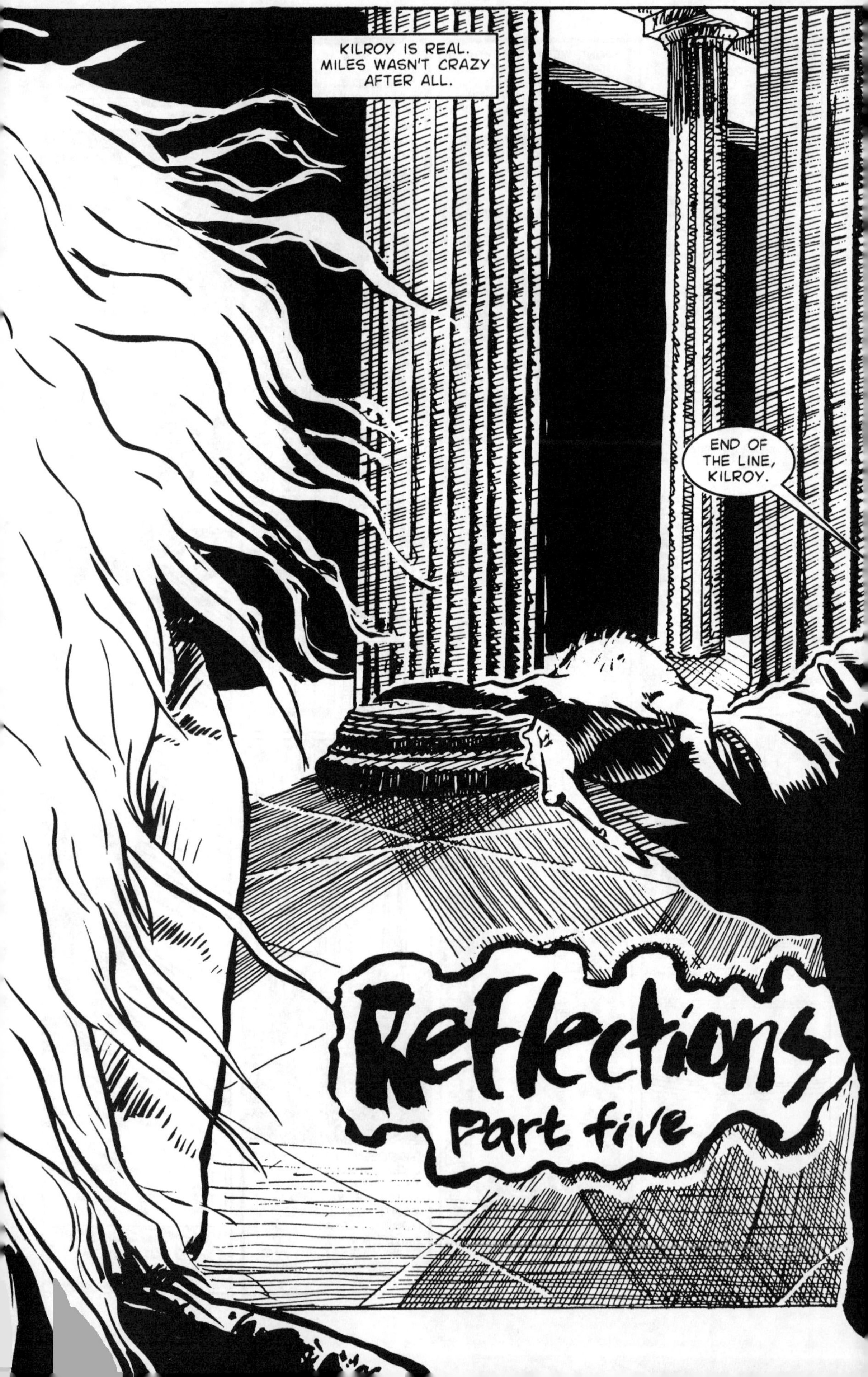
KILROY IS REAL. MILES WASN'T CRAZY AFTER ALL.
END OF THE LINE, KILROY.
Reflections
Part five

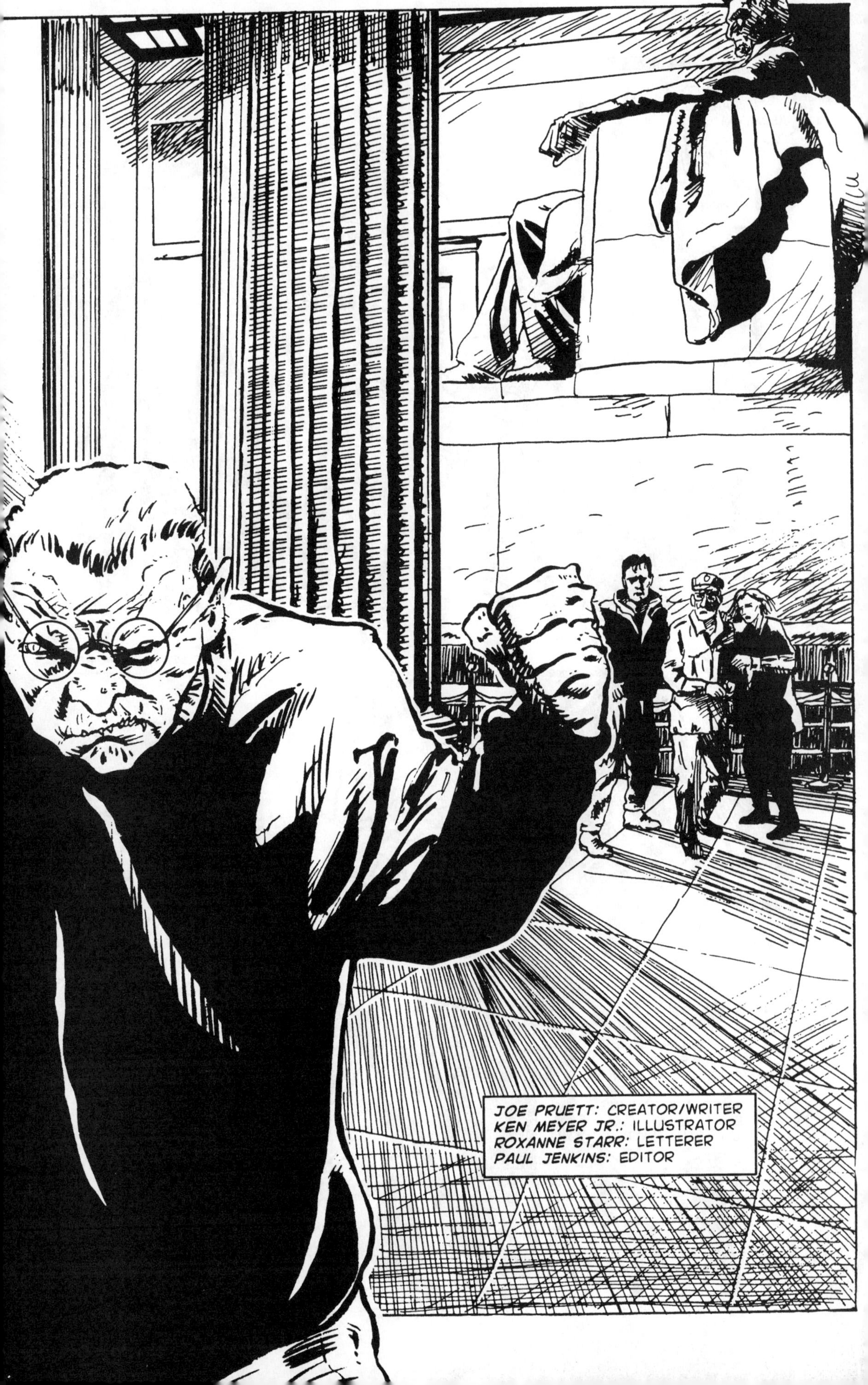
JOE PRUETT: CREATOR/WRITER
KEN MEYER JR.: ILLUSTRATOR
ROXANNE STARR: LETTERER
PAUL JENKINS: EDITOR

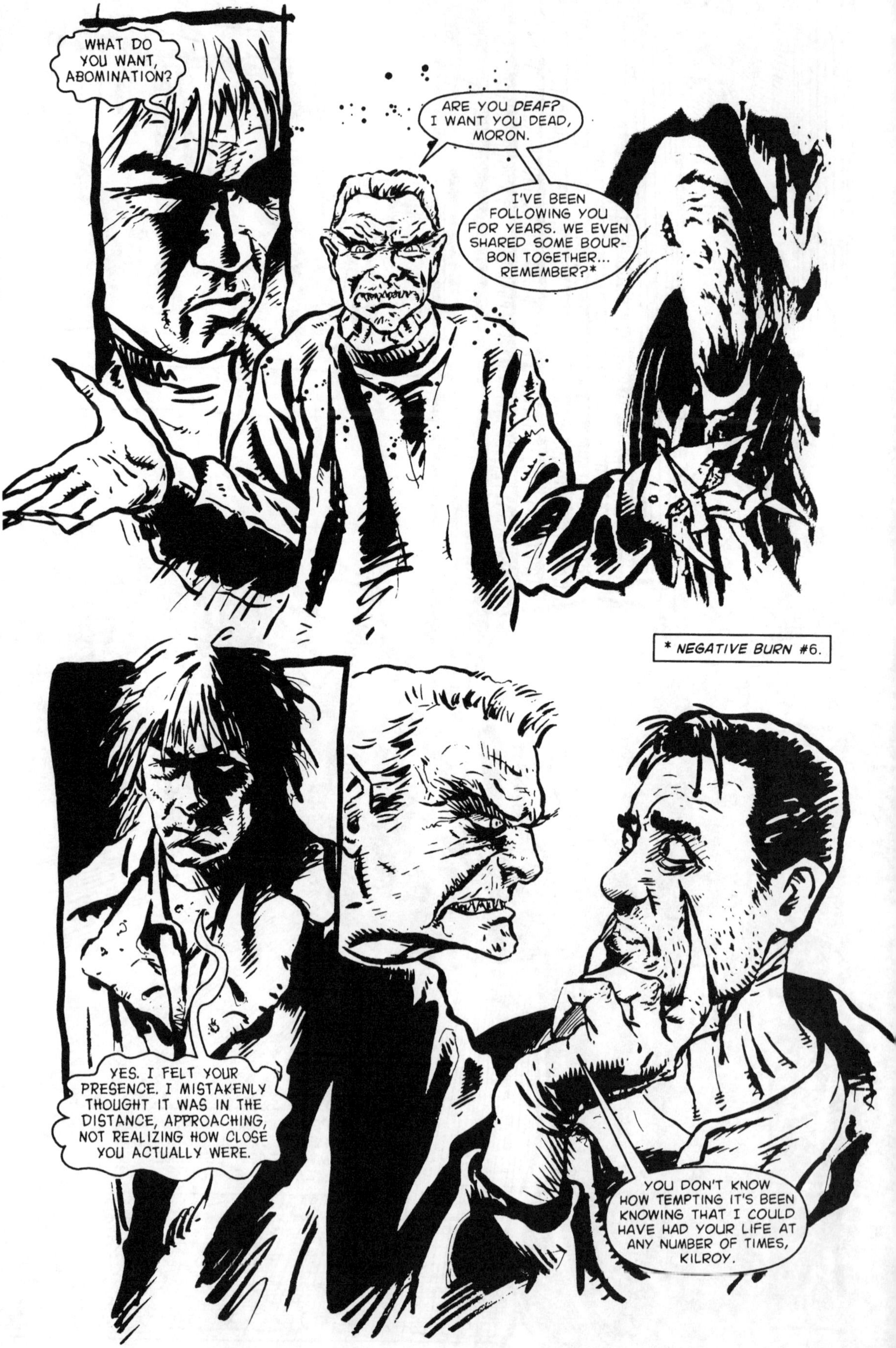
WHAT DO YOU WANT, ABOMINATION?
ARE YOU *DEAF?* I WANT YOU DEAD, MORON.
I'VE BEEN FOLLOWING YOU FOR YEARS. WE EVEN SHARED SOME BOURBON TOGETHER... REMEMBER?*
* *NEGATIVE BURN* #6.
YES. I FELT YOUR PRESENCE. I MISTAKENLY THOUGHT IT WAS IN THE DISTANCE, APPROACHING, NOT REALIZING HOW CLOSE YOU ACTUALLY WERE.
YOU DON'T KNOW HOW TEMPTING IT'S BEEN KNOWING THAT I COULD HAVE HAD YOUR LIFE AT ANY NUMBER OF TIMES, KILROY.

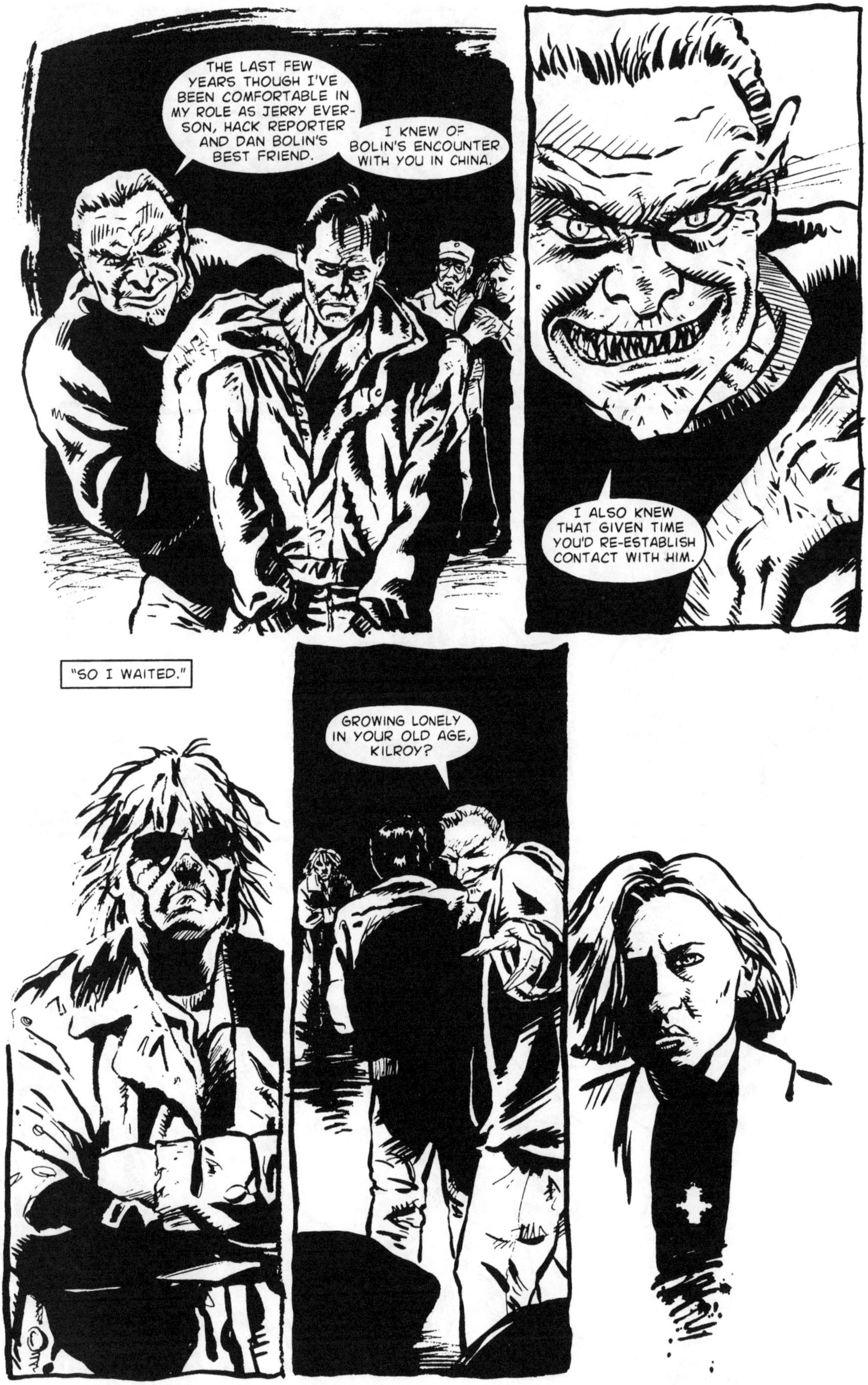
THE LAST FEW YEARS THOUGH I'VE BEEN COMFORTABLE IN MY ROLE AS JERRY EVERSON, HACK REPORTER AND DAN BOLIN'S BEST FRIEND.
I KNEW OF BOLIN'S ENCOUNTER WITH YOU IN CHINA.
I ALSO KNEW THAT GIVEN TIME YOU'D RE-ESTABLISH CONTACT WITH HIM.
"SO I WAITED."
GROWING LONELY IN YOUR OLD AGE, KILROY?

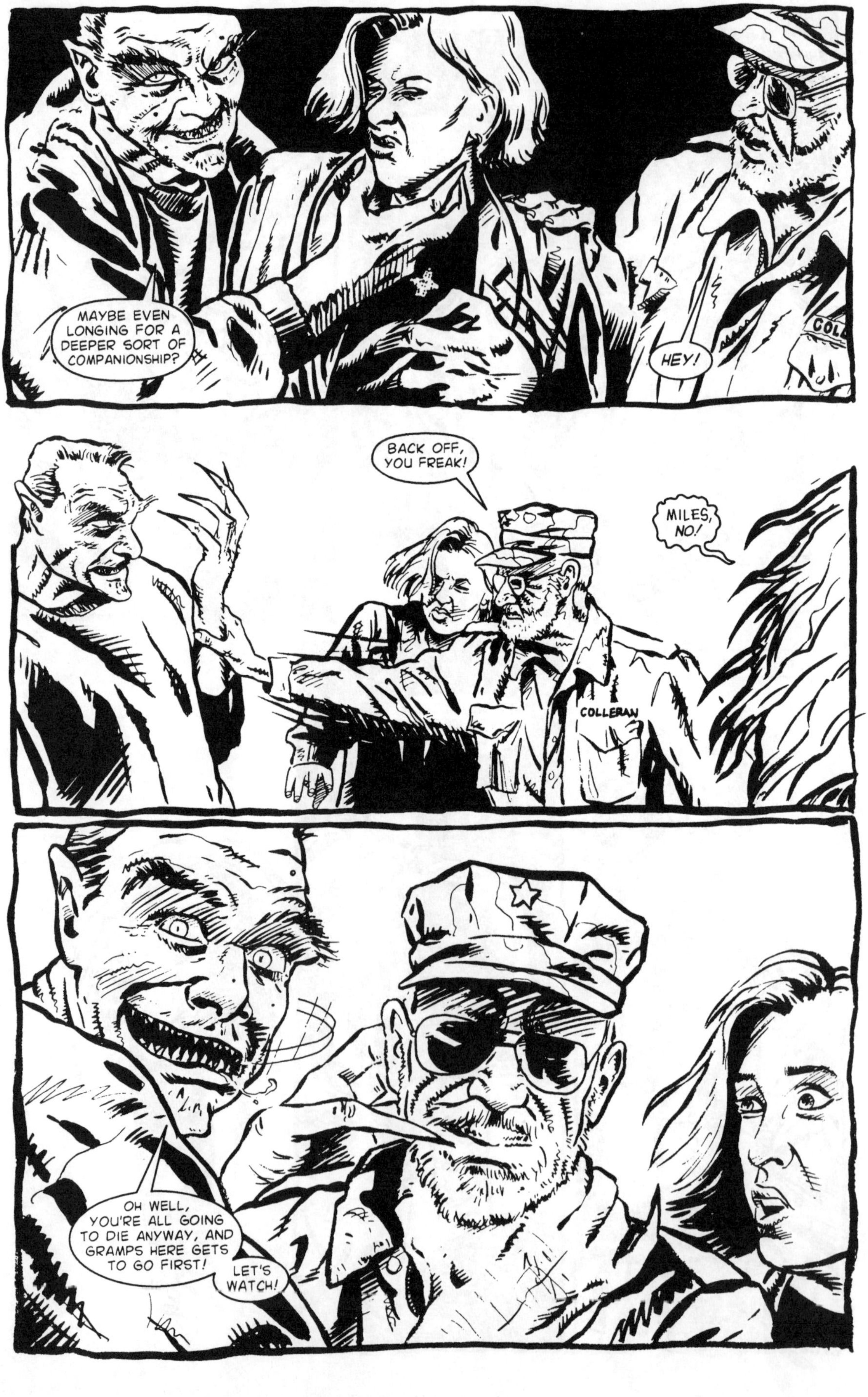
MAYBE EVEN LONGING FOR A DEEPER SORT OF COMPANIONSHIP?
HEY!
COLL
BACK OFF, YOU FREAK!
MILES, NO!
COLLERAN
OH WELL, YOU'RE ALL GOING TO DIE ANYWAY, AND GRAMPS HERE GETS TO GO FIRST!
LET'S WATCH!

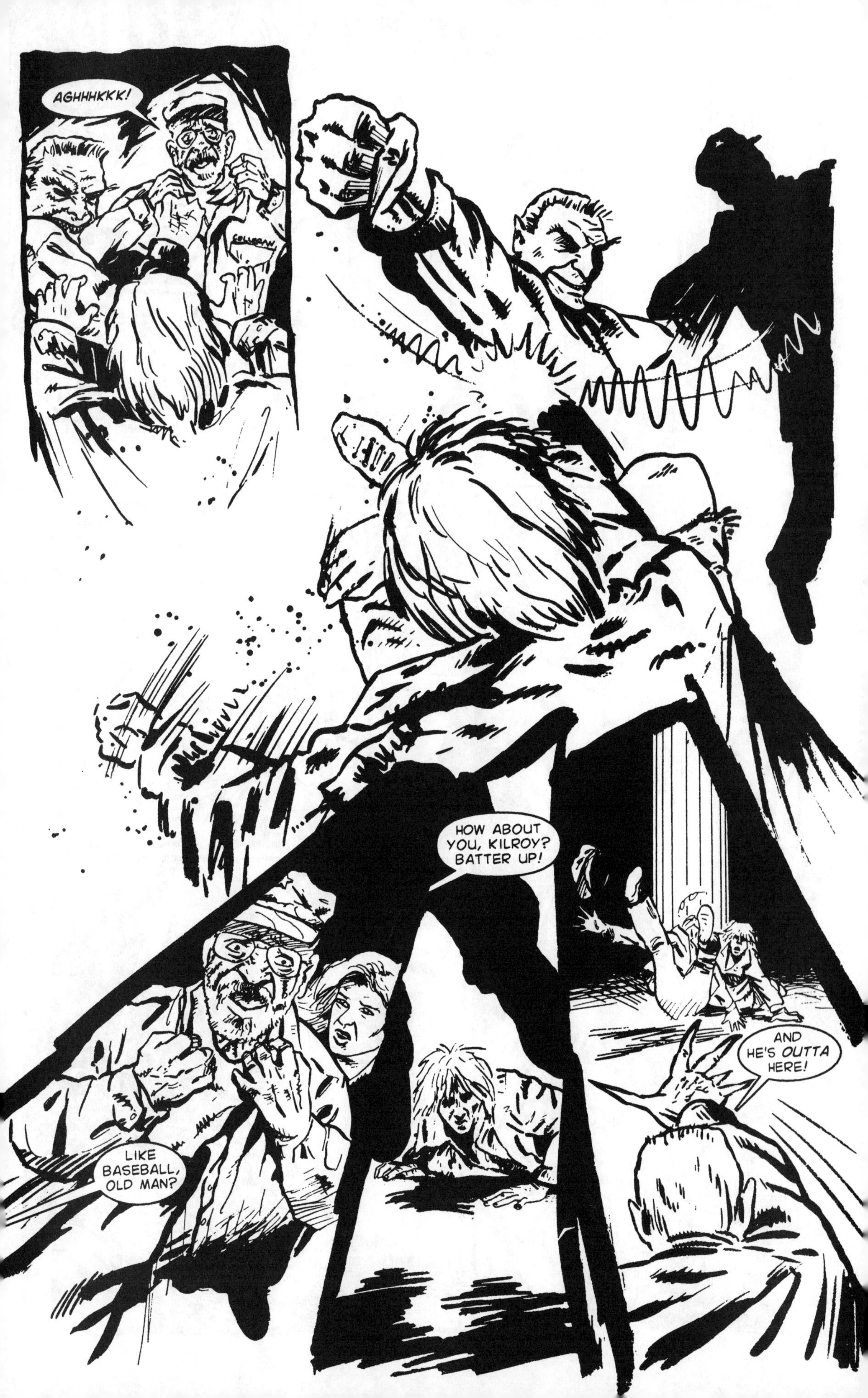
AGHHHKKK!
HOW ABOUT YOU, KILROY? BATTER UP!
LIKE BASEBALL, OLD MAN?
AND HE'S OUTTA HERE!

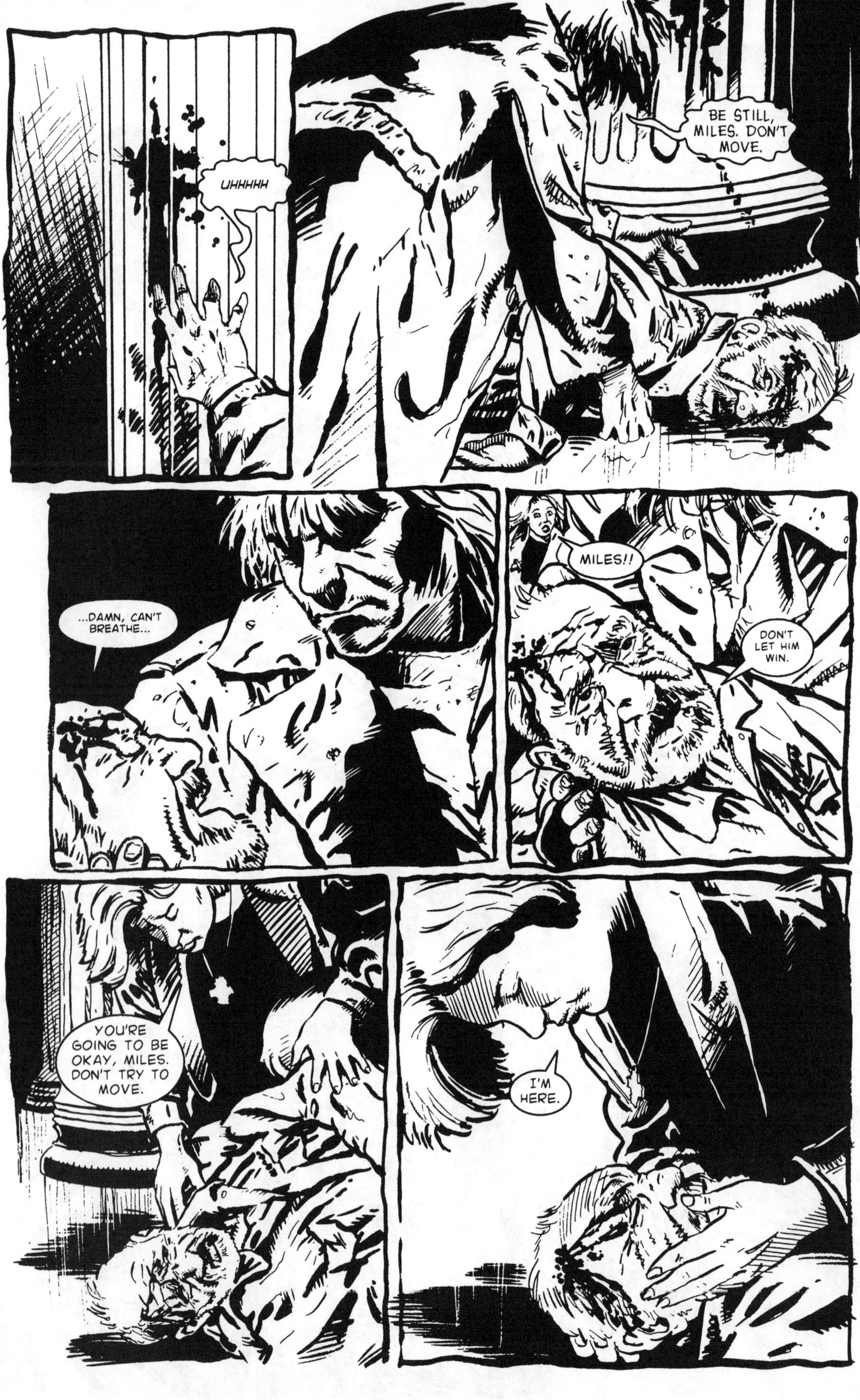
UHHHHH
BE STILL, MILES. DON'T MOVE.
...DAMN, CAN'T BREATHE...
MILES!!
DON'T LET HIM WIN.
YOU'RE GOING TO BE OKAY, MILES. DON'T TRY TO MOVE.
I'M HERE.

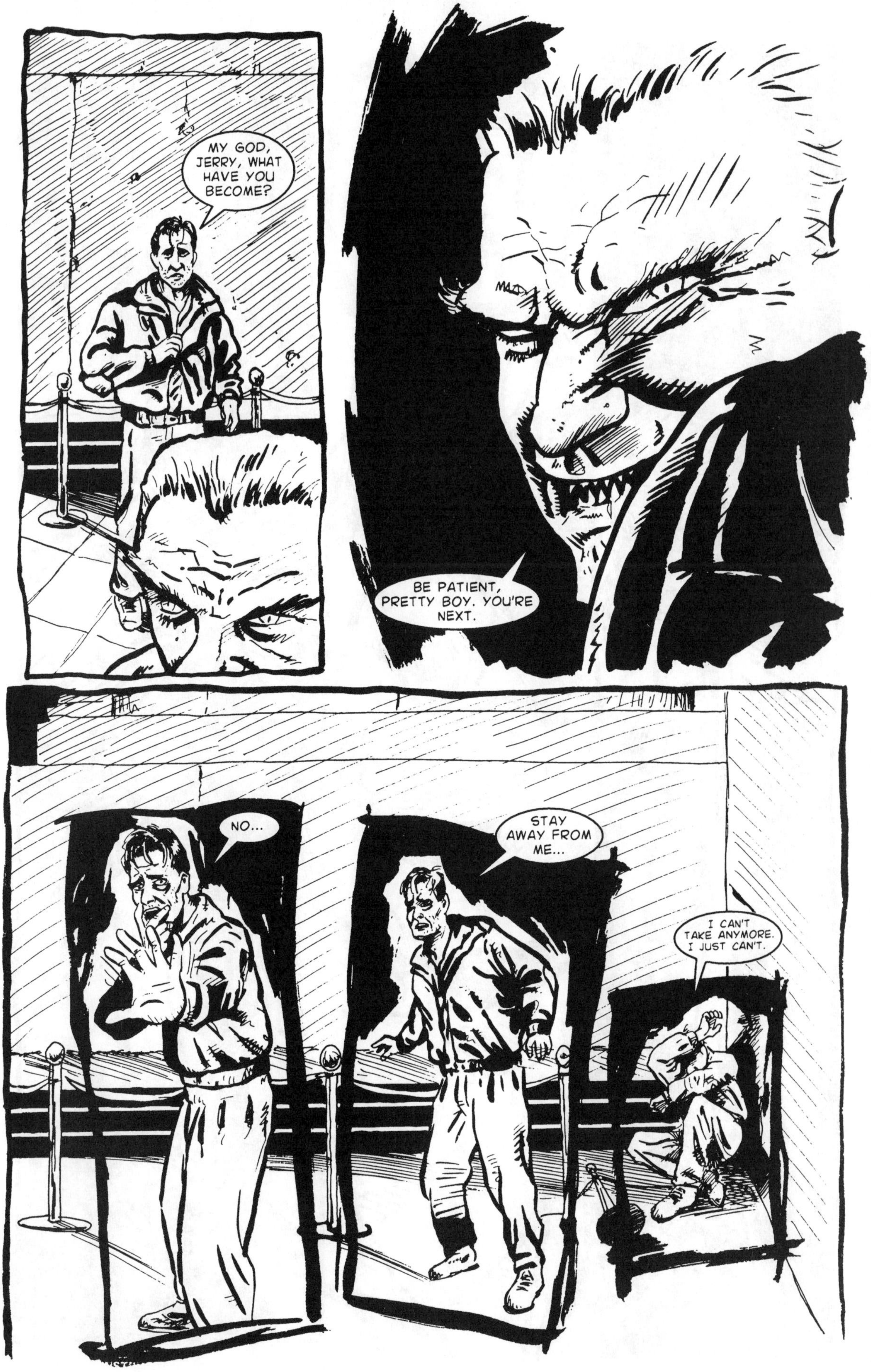
MY GOD, JERRY, WHAT HAVE YOU BECOME?
BE PATIENT, PRETTY BOY. YOU'RE NEXT.
NO...
STAY AWAY FROM ME...
I CAN'T TAKE ANYMORE. I JUST CAN'T.

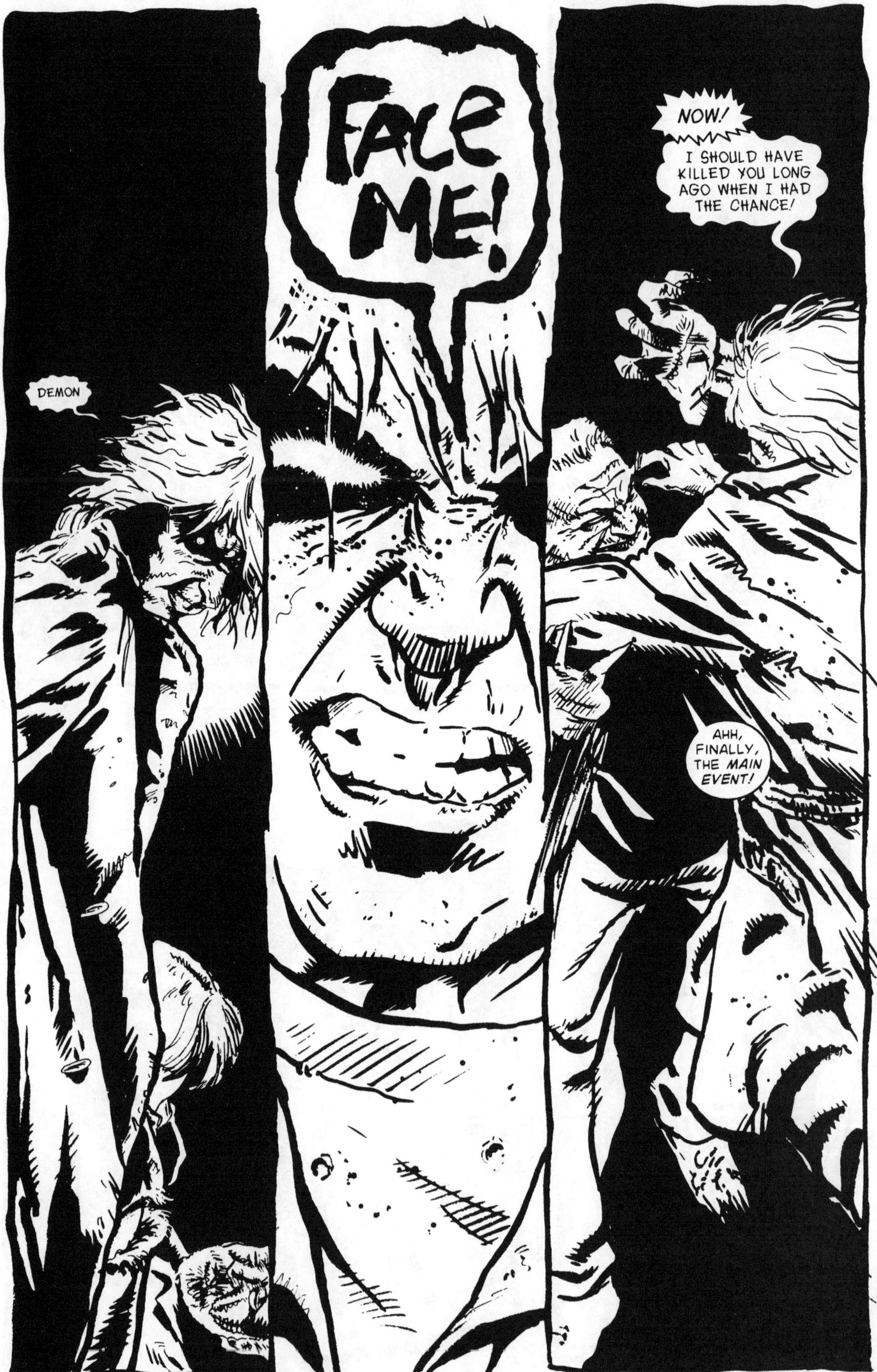
DEMON
FACE ME!
NOW!
I SHOULD HAVE KILLED YOU LONG AGO WHEN I HAD THE CHANCE!
AHH, FINALLY, THE MAIN EVENT!

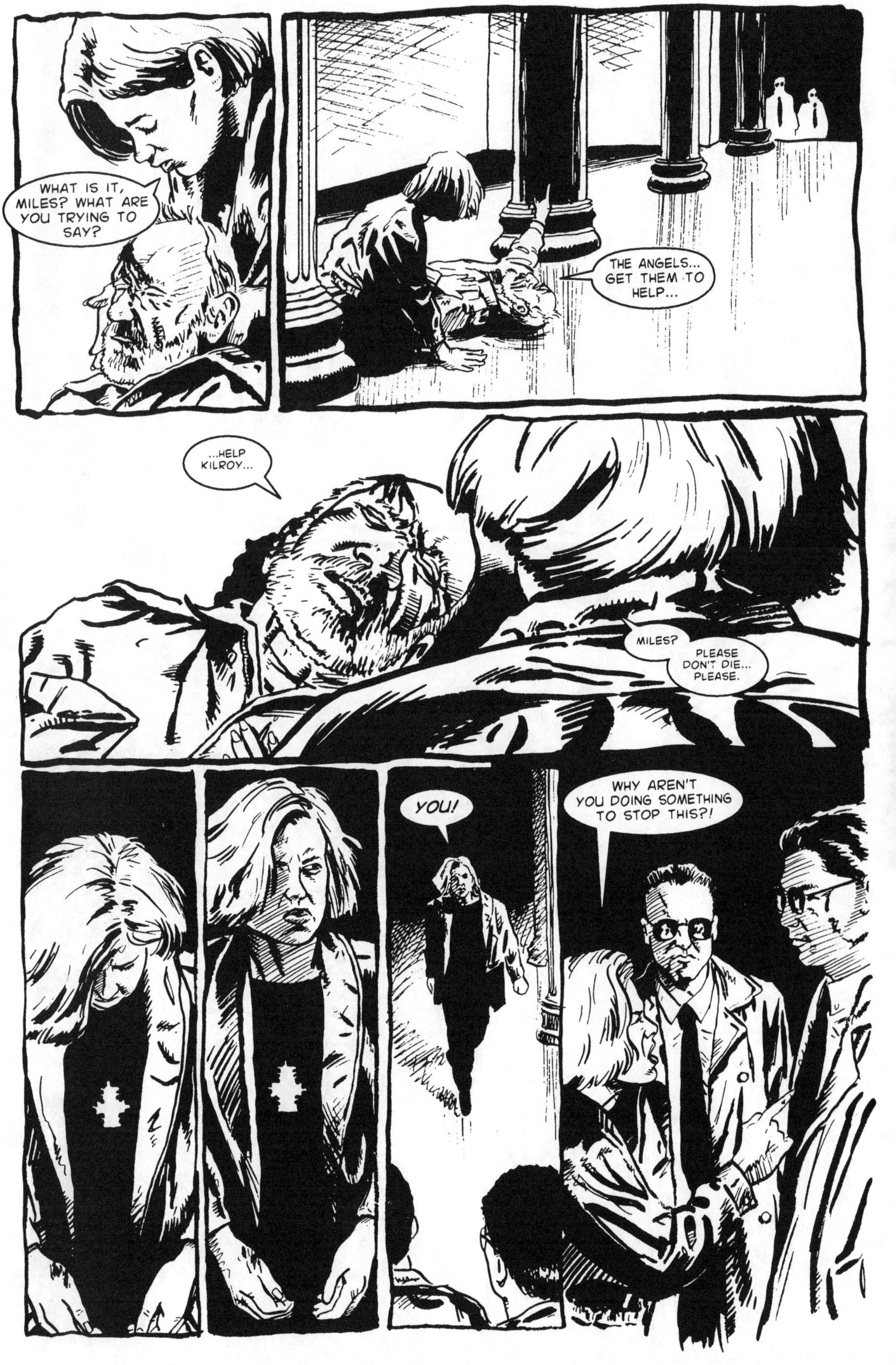
WHAT IS IT, MILES? WHAT ARE YOU TRYING TO SAY?
THE ANGELS... GET THEM TO HELP...
...HELP KILROY...
MILES?
PLEASE DON'T DIE... PLEASE.
YOU!
WHY AREN'T YOU DOING SOMETHING TO STOP THIS?!

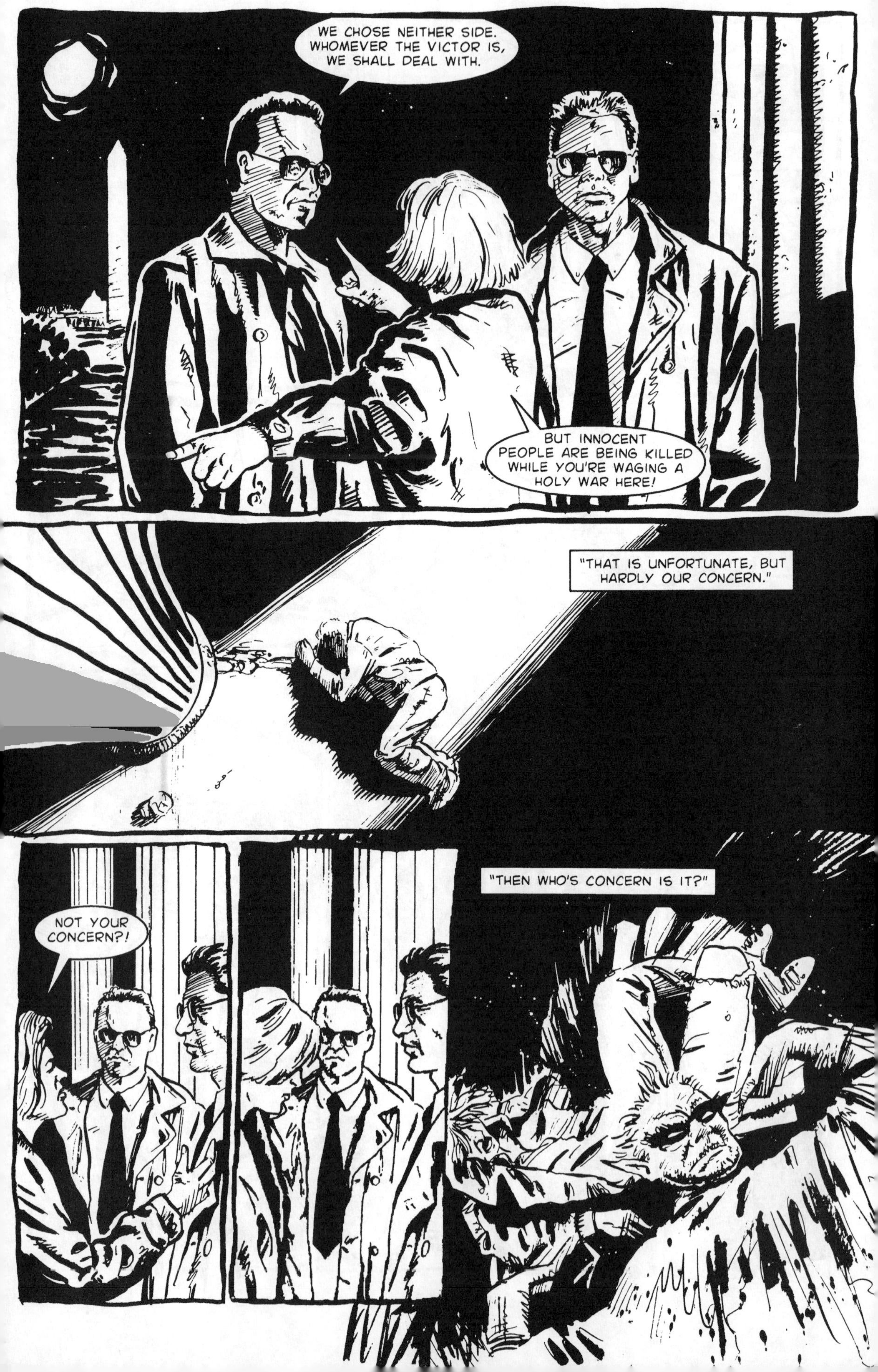
WE CHOSE NEITHER SIDE. WHOMEVER THE VICTOR IS, WE SHALL DEAL WITH.
BUT INNOCENT PEOPLE ARE BEING KILLED WHILE YOU'RE WAGING A HOLY WAR HERE!
"THAT IS UNFORTUNATE, BUT HARDLY OUR CONCERN."
NOT YOUR CONCERN?!
"THEN WHO'S CONCERN IS IT?"

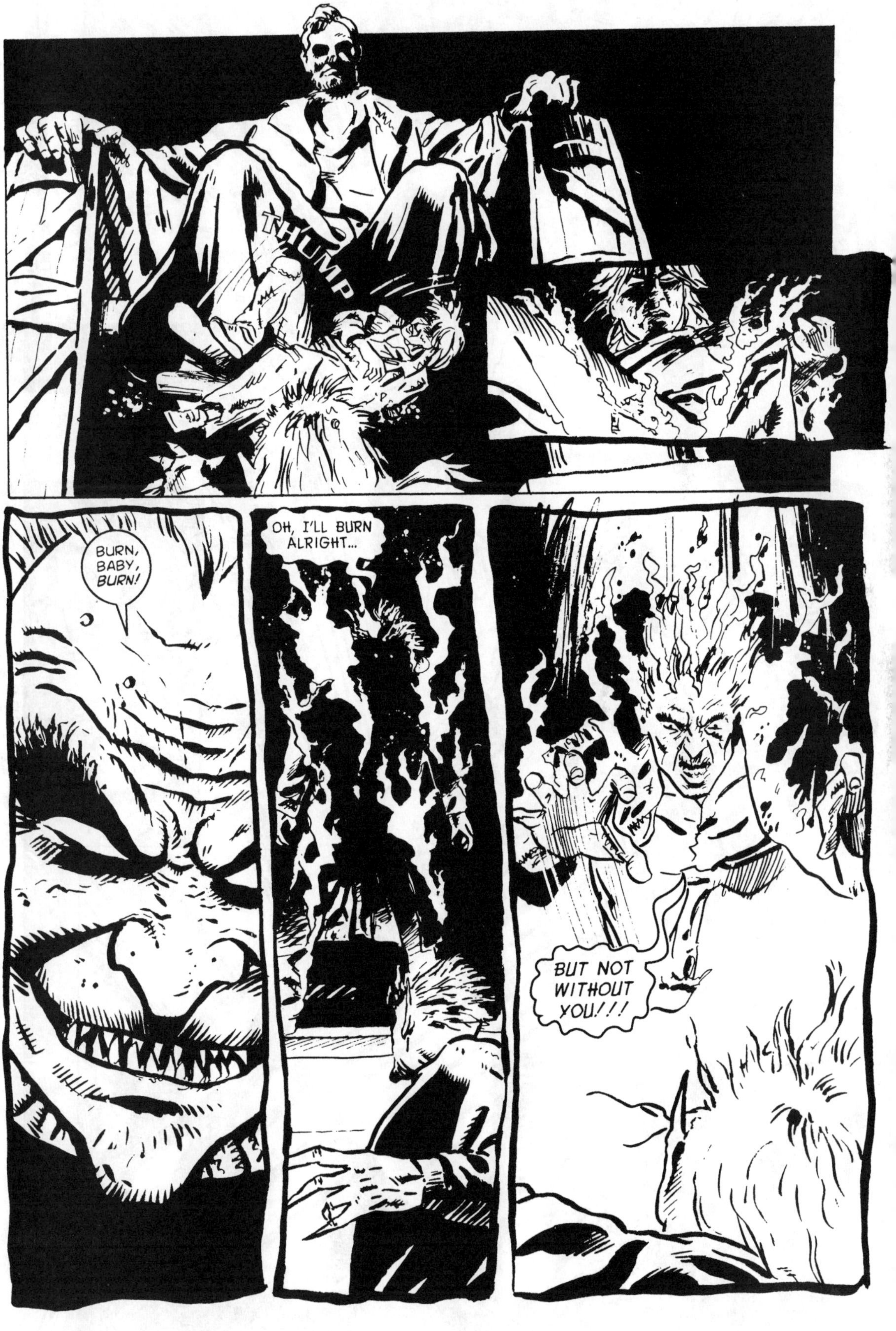
THUMP
BURN, BABY, BURN!
OH, I'LL BURN ALRIGHT...
BUT NOT WITHOUT YOU!!!

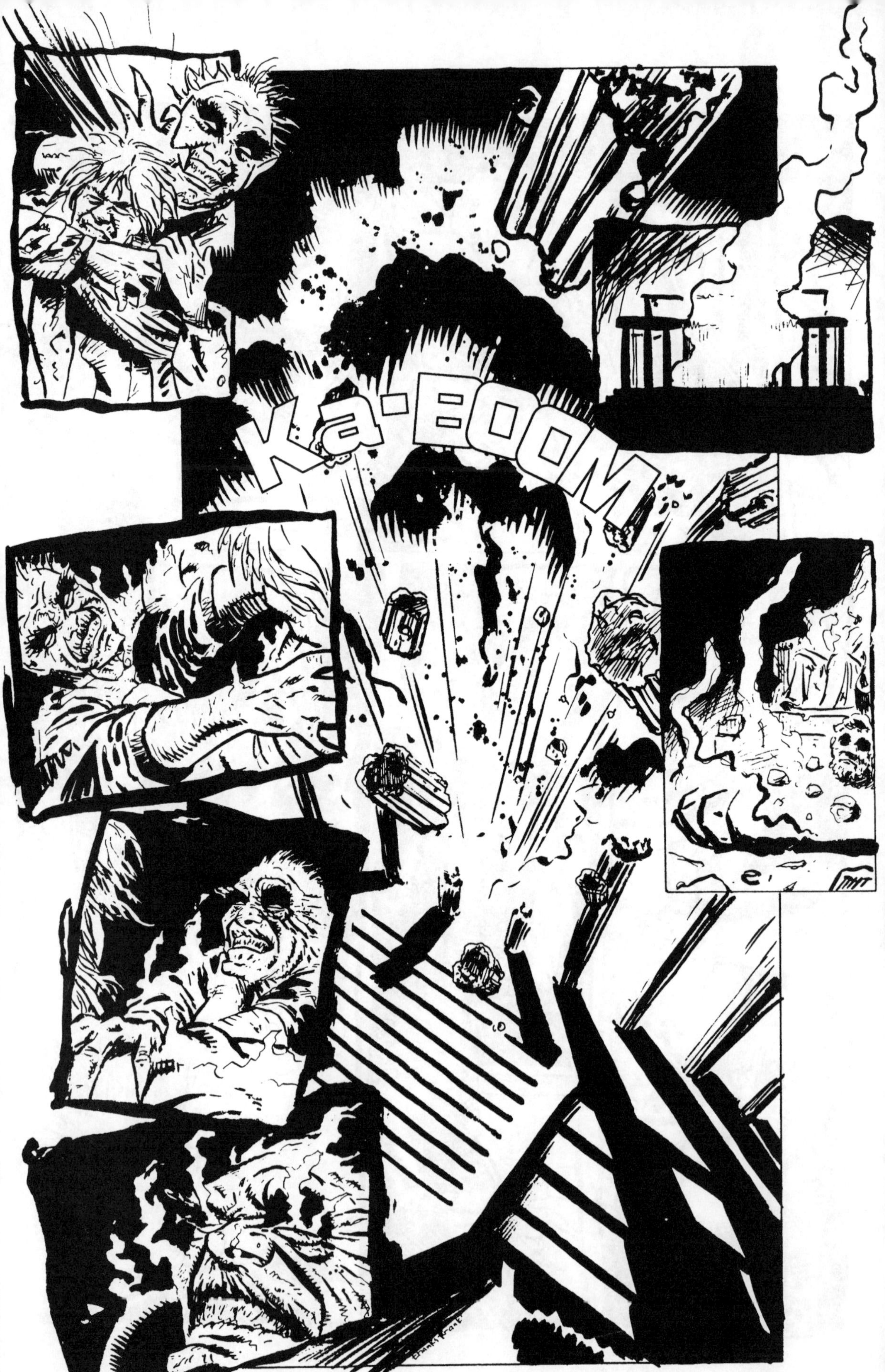
KA-BOOM

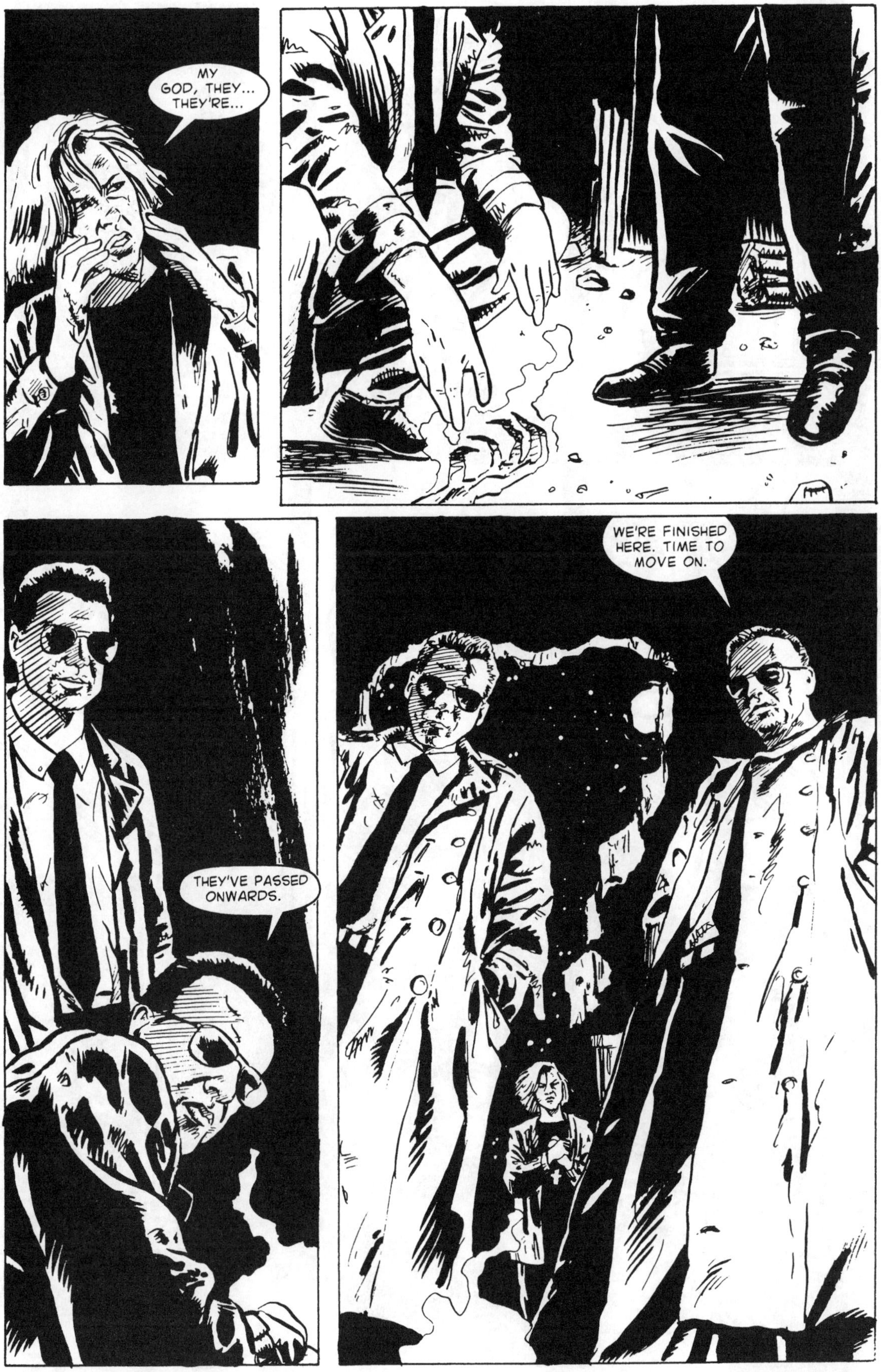
MY GOD, THEY... THEY'RE...
THEY'VE PASSED ONWARDS.
WE'RE FINISHED HERE. TIME TO MOVE ON.

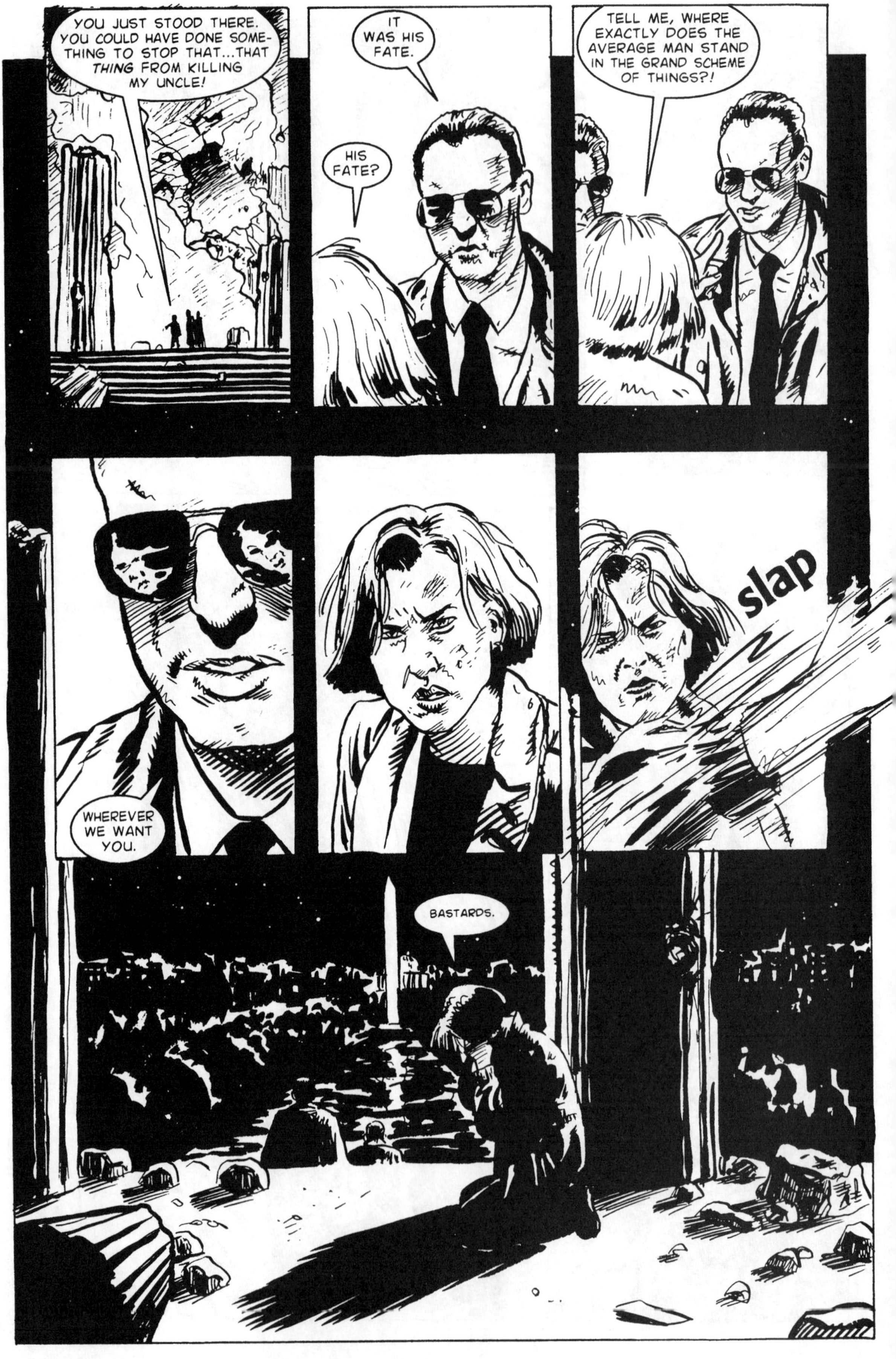
YOU JUST STOOD THERE. YOU COULD HAVE DONE SOME-THING TO STOP THAT...THAT *THING* FROM KILLING MY UNCLE!
IT WAS HIS FATE.
HIS FATE?
TELL ME, WHERE EXACTLY DOES THE AVERAGE MAN STAND IN THE GRAND SCHEME OF THINGS?!
WHEREVER WE WANT YOU.
slap
BASTARDS.

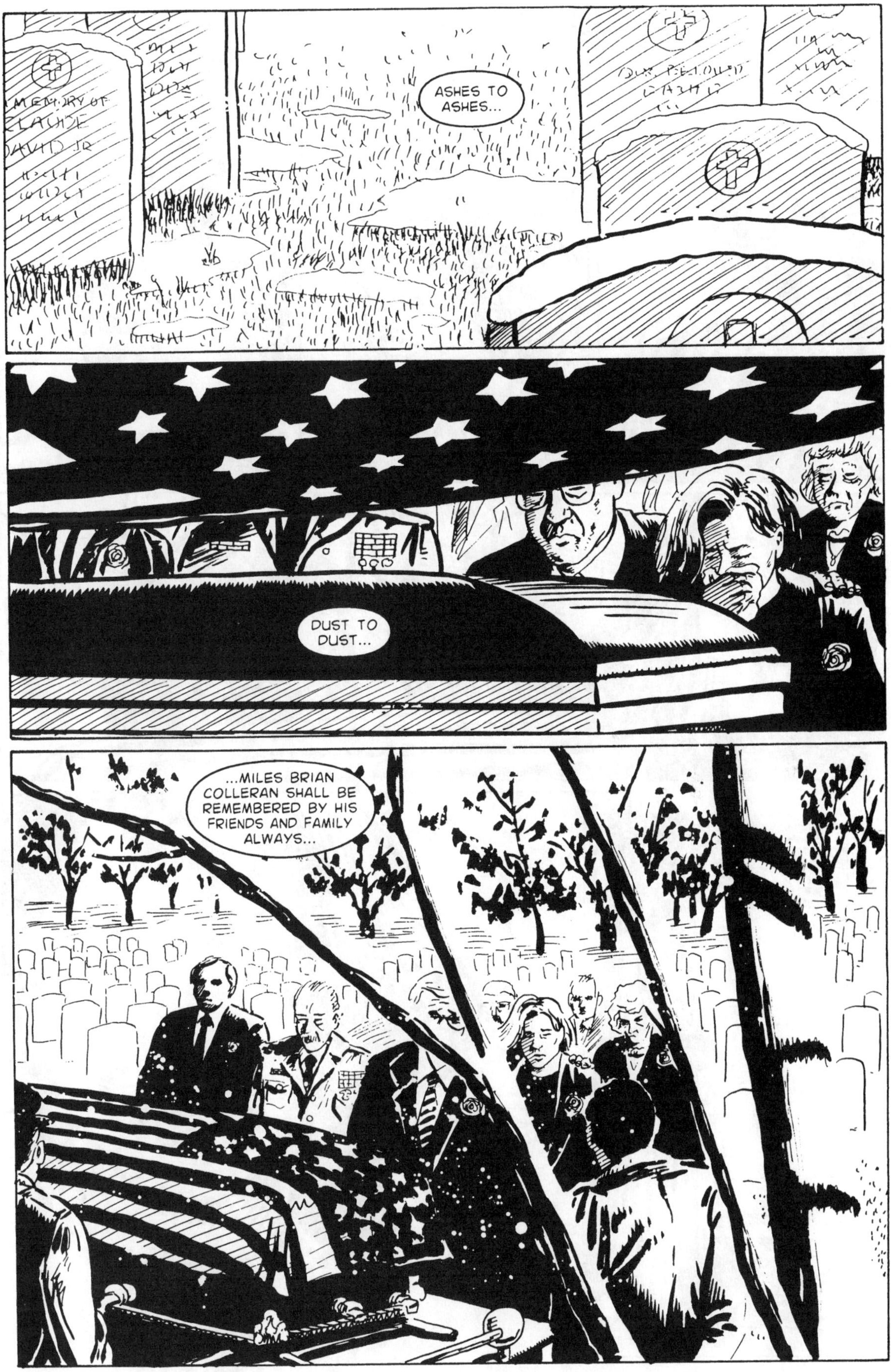
ASHES TO ASHES...
DUST TO DUST...
...MILES BRIAN COLLERAN SHALL BE REMEMBERED BY HIS FRIENDS AND FAMILY ALWAYS...

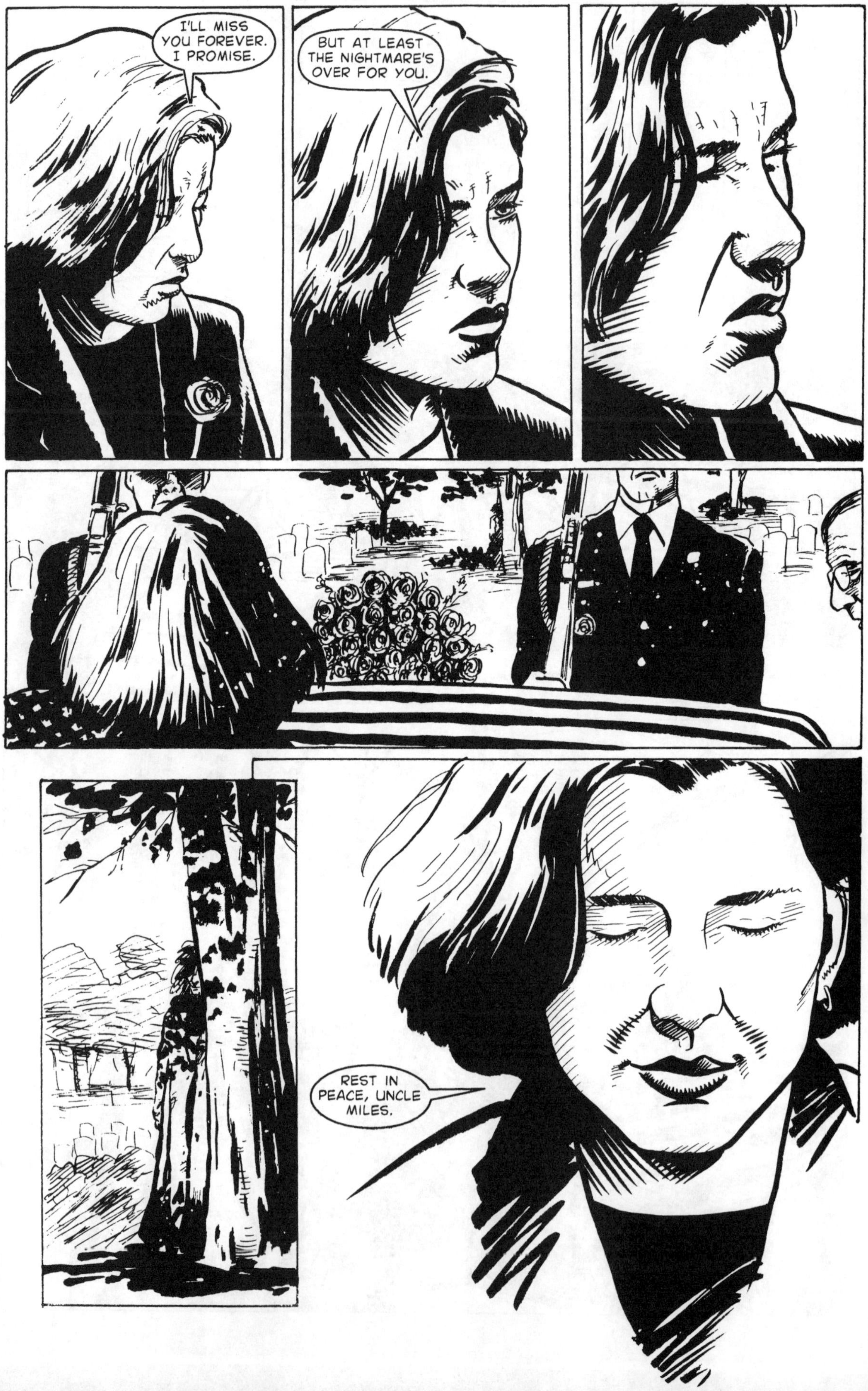
I'LL MISS YOU FOREVER. I PROMISE.
BUT AT LEAST THE NIGHTMARE'S OVER FOR YOU.
REST IN PEACE, UNCLE MILES.

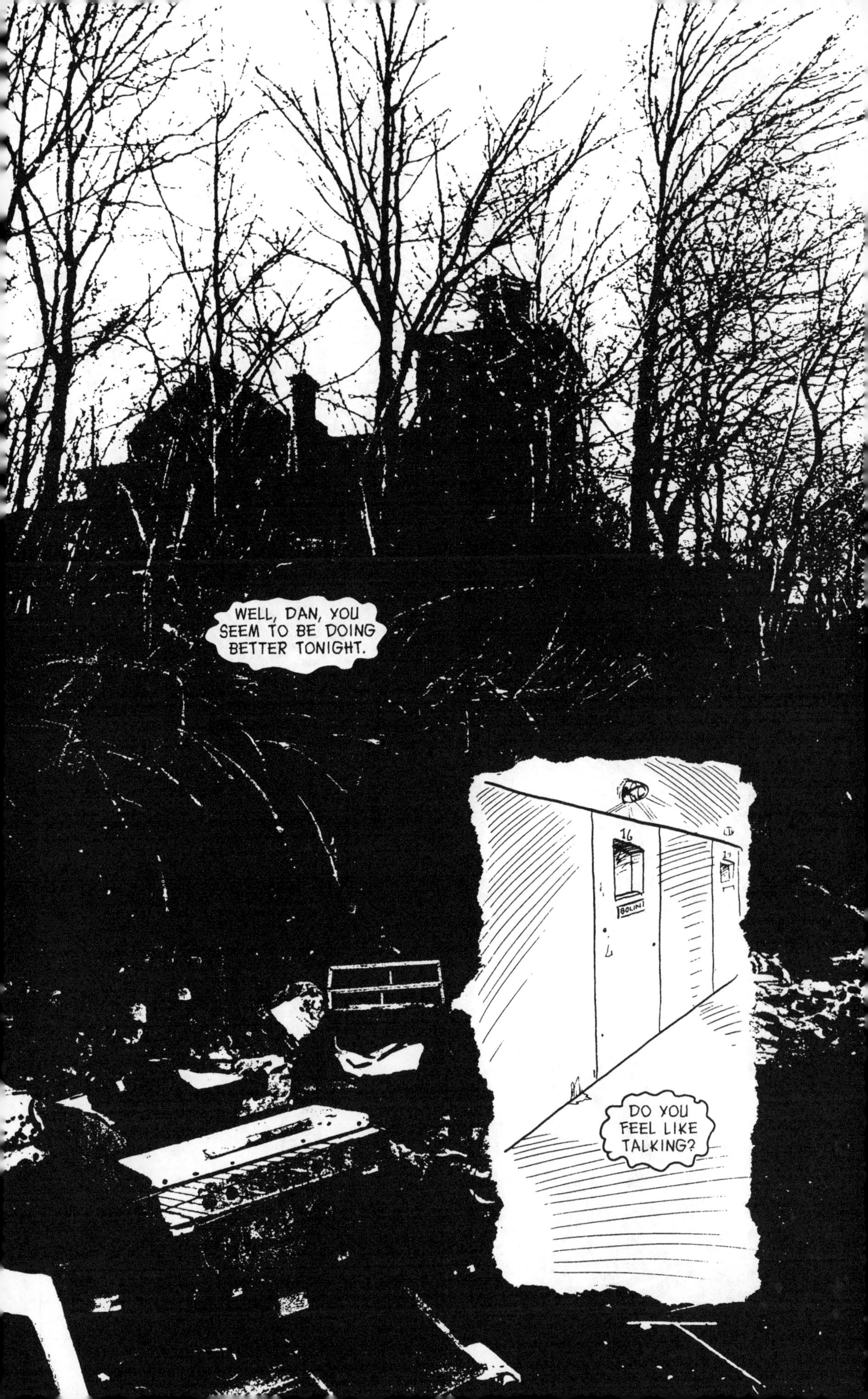
WELL, DAN, YOU SEEM TO BE DOING BETTER TONIGHT.
16
BOLINI
DO YOU FEEL LIKE TALKING?

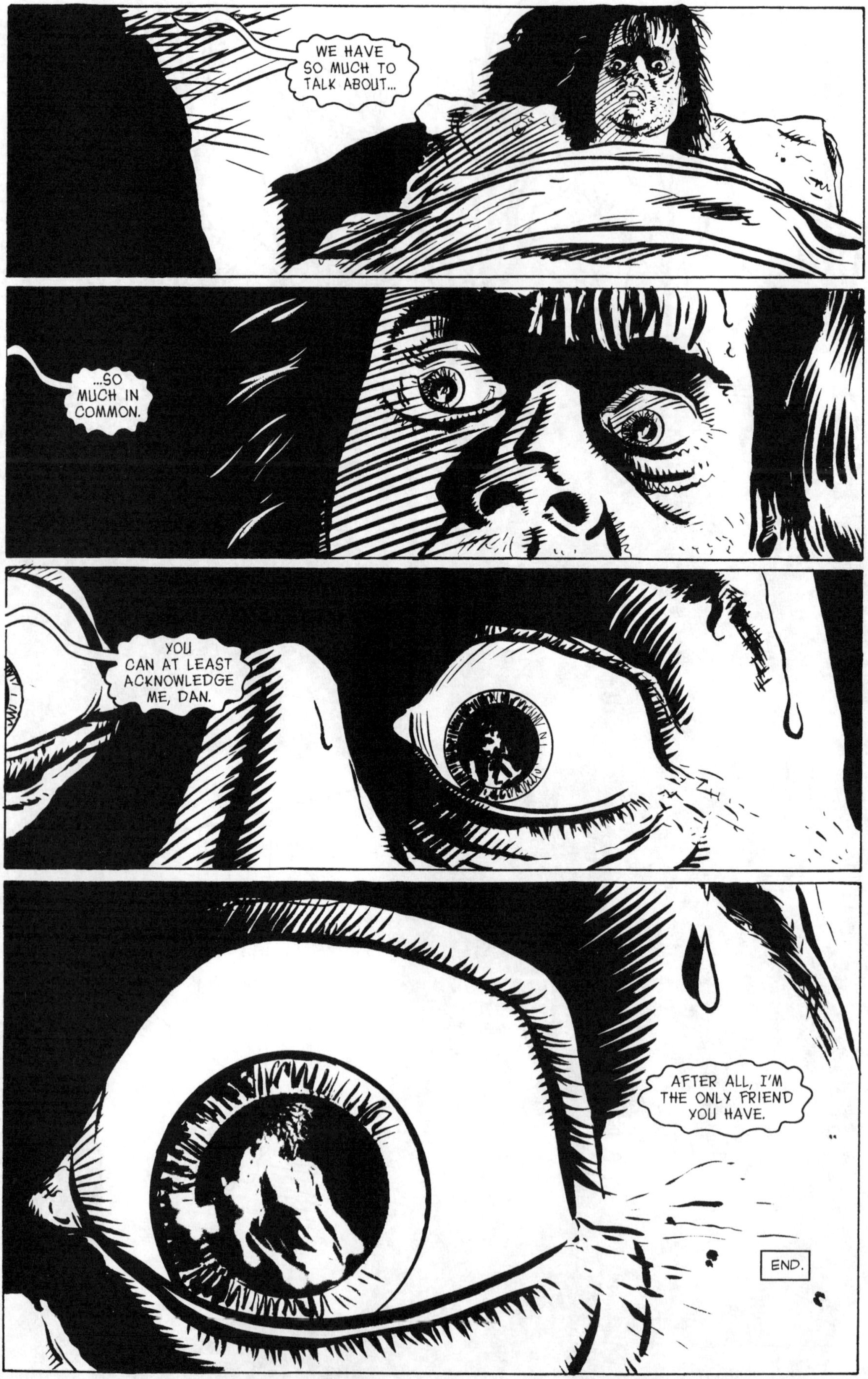
WE HAVE SO MUCH TO TALK ABOUT...
...SO MUCH IN COMMON.
YOU CAN AT LEAST ACKNOWLEDGE ME, DAN.
AFTER ALL, I'M THE ONLY FRIEND YOU HAVE.
END.

"Pride, Prejudice and Persecution"
Chapter One

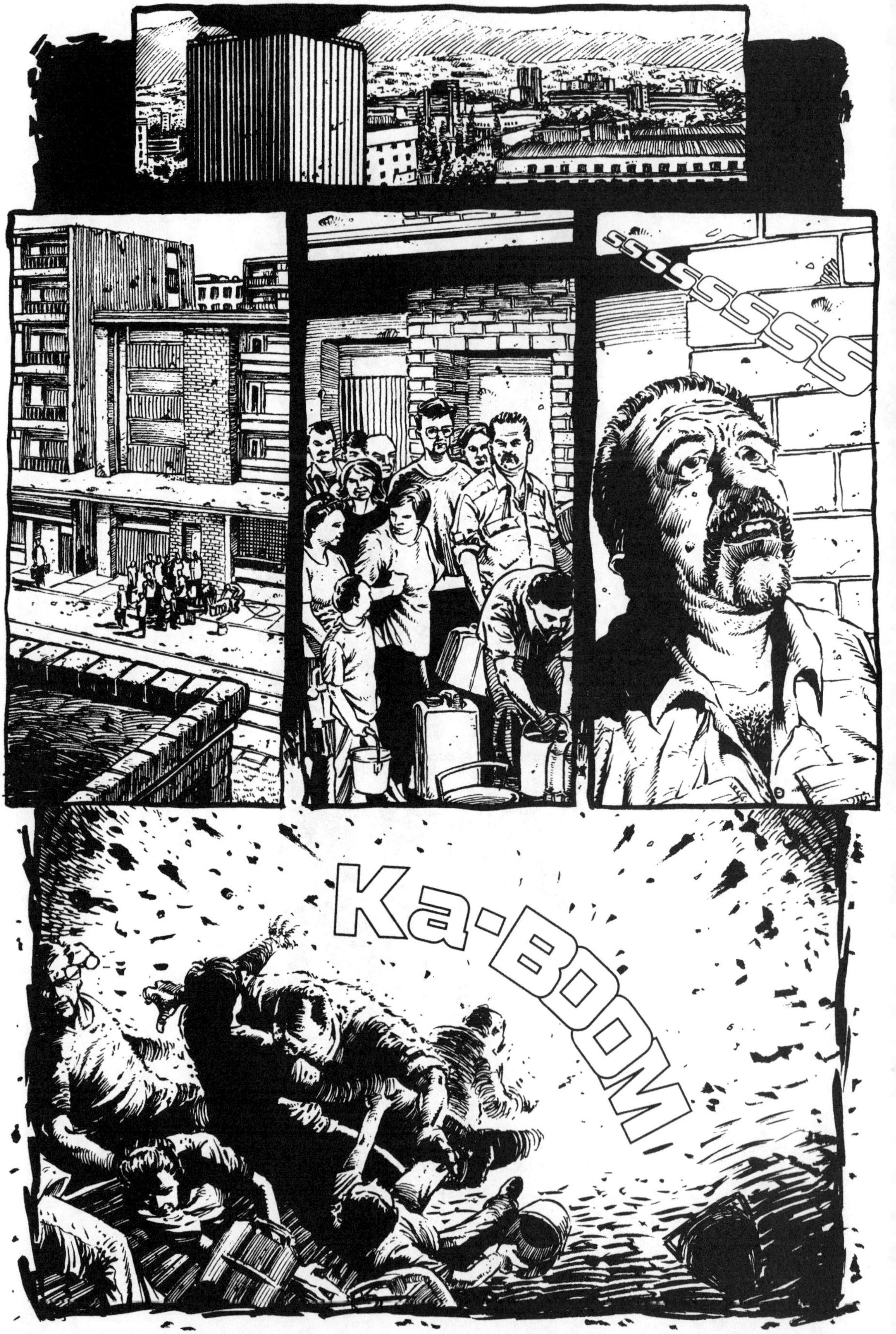
sssSSSSS
Ka-BOOM

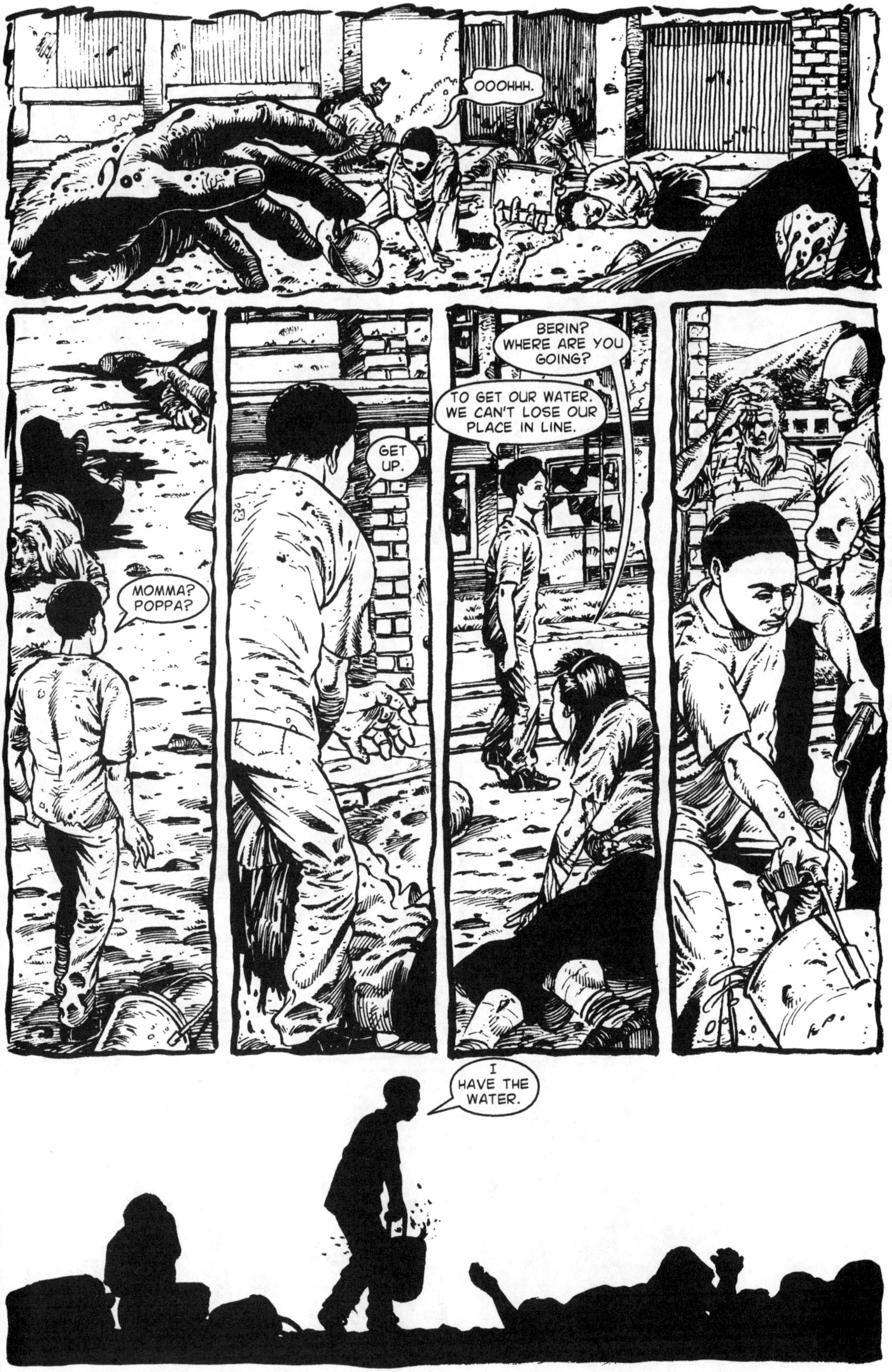
OOOHHH.
MOMMA? POPPA?
GET UP.
BERIN? WHERE ARE YOU GOING?
TO GET OUR WATER. WE CAN'T LOSE OUR PLACE IN LINE.
I HAVE THE WATER.

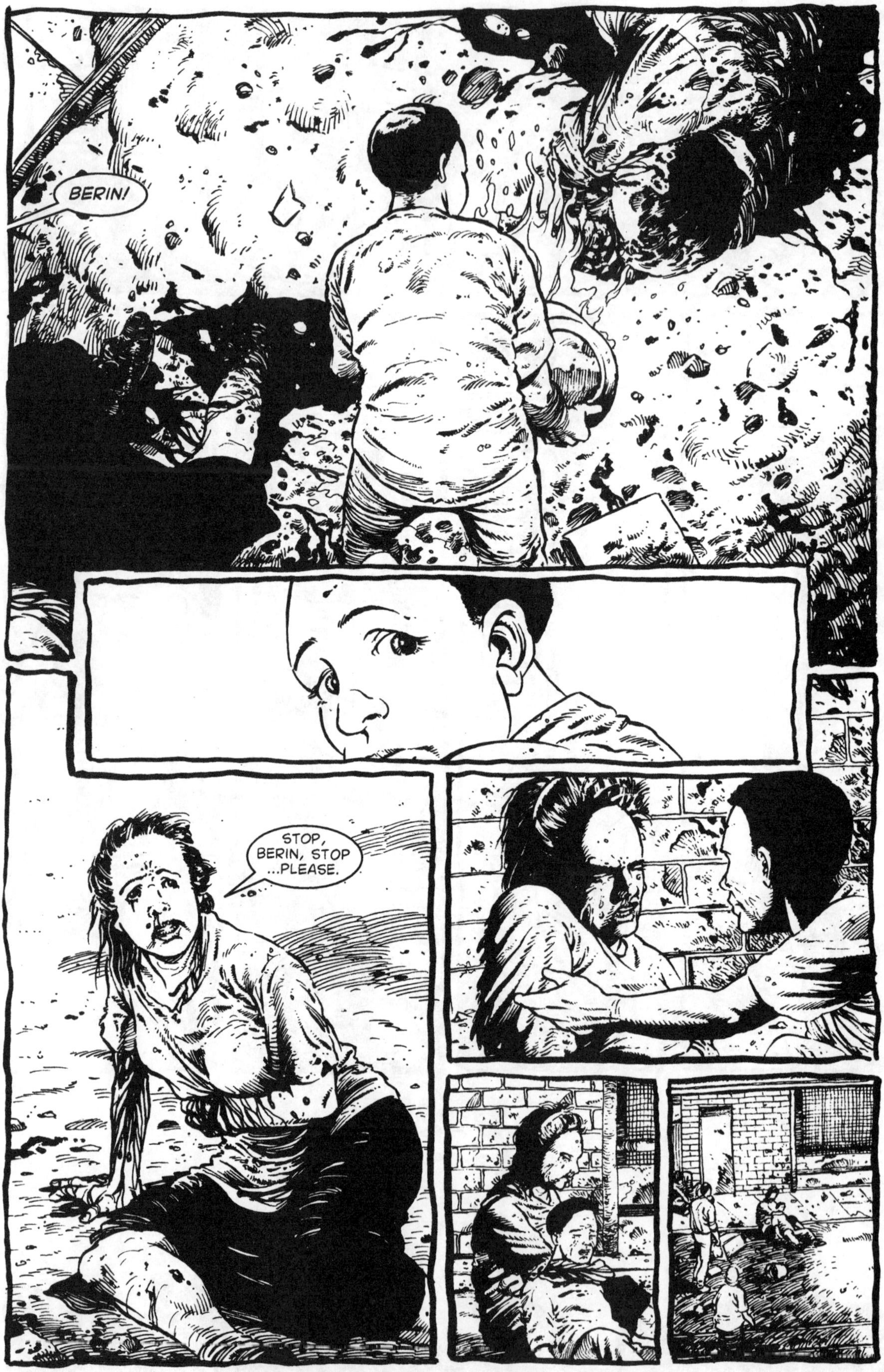
BERIN!
STOP, BERIN, STOP ...PLEASE.

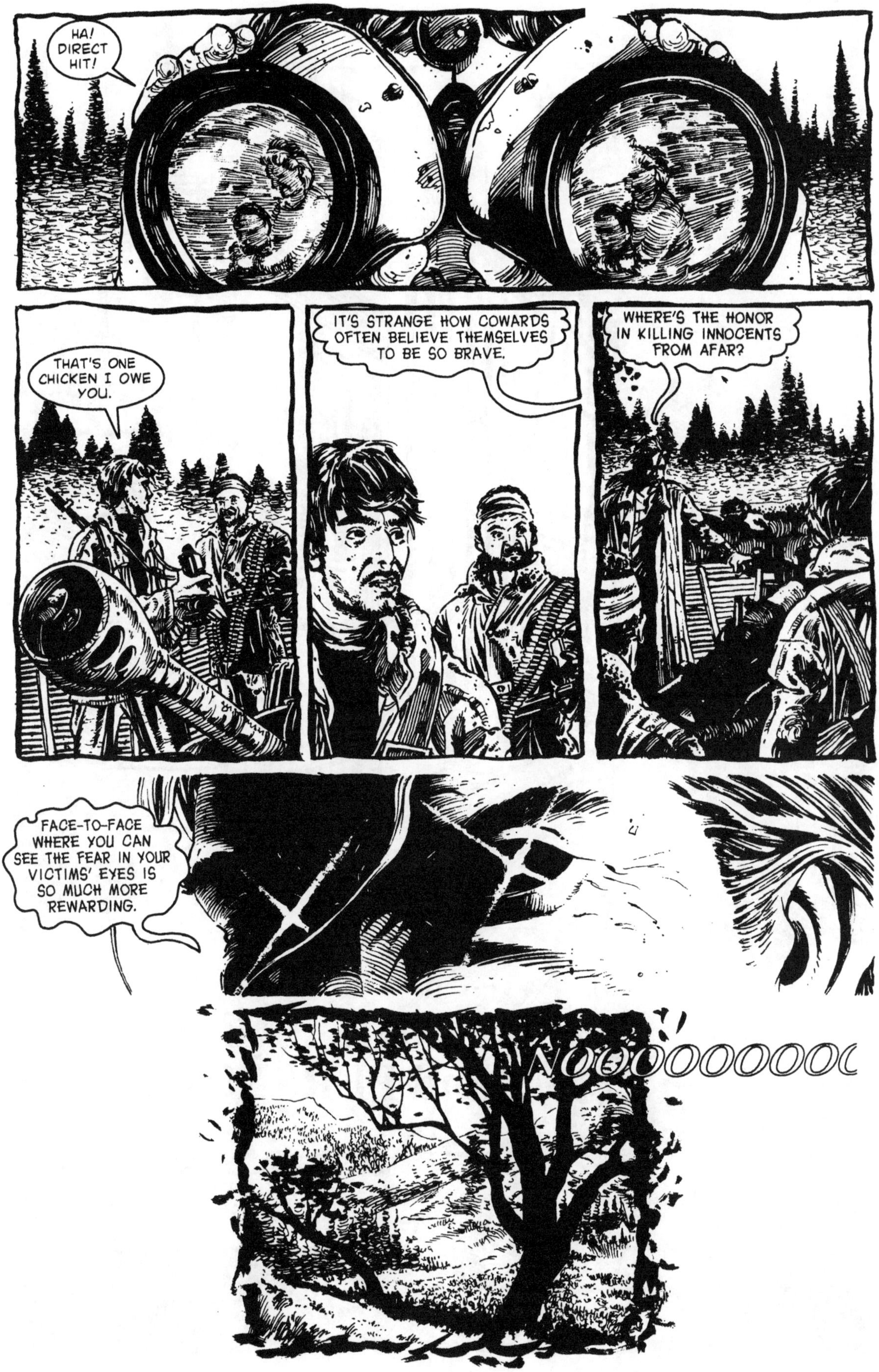
HA! DIRECT HIT!
THAT'S ONE CHICKEN I OWE YOU.
IT'S STRANGE HOW COWARDS OFTEN BELIEVE THEMSELVES TO BE SO BRAVE.
WHERE'S THE HONOR IN KILLING INNOCENTS FROM AFAR?
FACE-TO-FACE WHERE YOU CAN SEE THE FEAR IN YOUR VICTIMS' EYES IS SO MUCH MORE REWARDING.
NOOOOOOOOOC

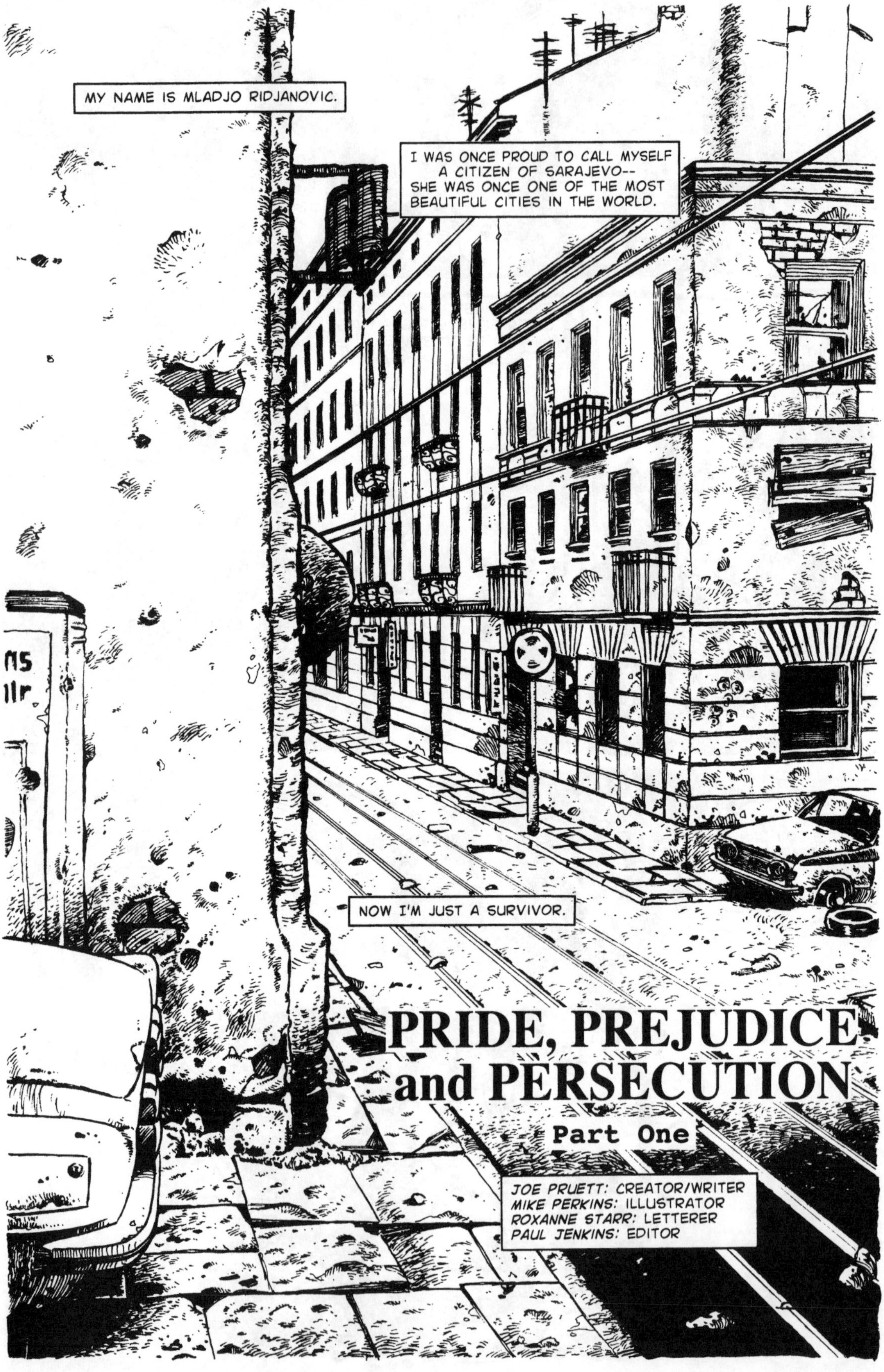
MY NAME IS MLADJO RIDJANOVIC.
I WAS ONCE PROUD TO CALL MYSELF A CITIZEN OF SARAJEVO-- SHE WAS ONCE ONE OF THE MOST BEAUTIFUL CITIES IN THE WORLD.
NOW I'M JUST A SURVIVOR.
PRIDE, PREJUDICE and PERSECUTION
Part One
JOE PRUETT: CREATOR/WRITER
MIKE PERKINS: ILLUSTRATOR
ROXANNE STARR: LETTERER
PAUL JENKINS: EDITOR

It's funny how it's
the little things
you miss the most.

I've forgotten
what it's like to
take a shower;
to receive letters
through the mail;
to be irritated
by a television
commercial.

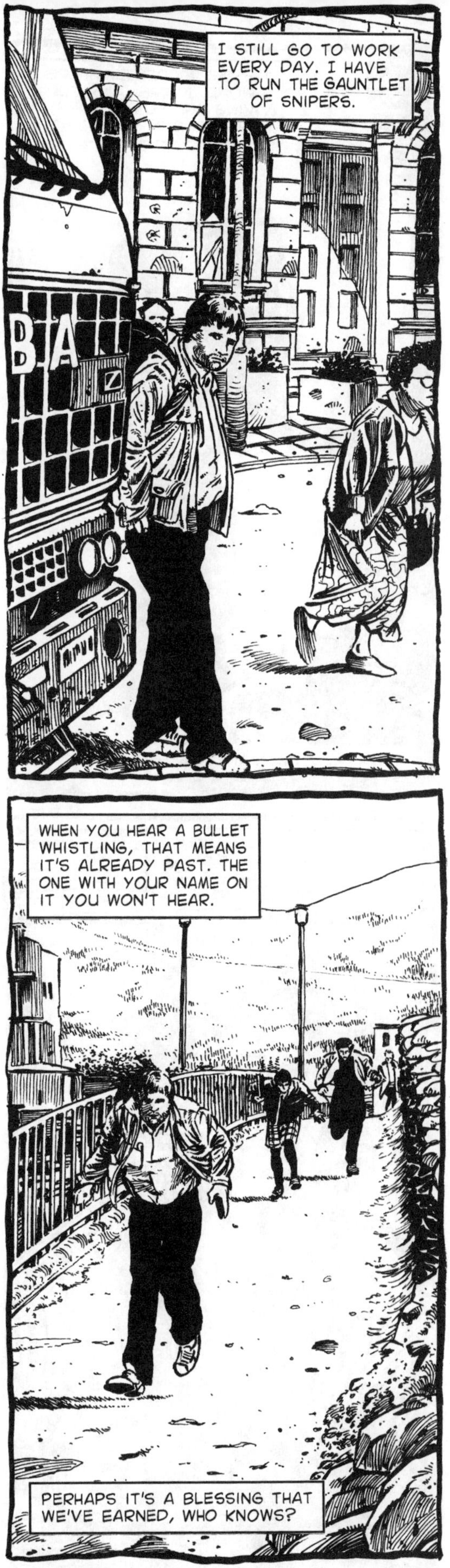
I STILL GO TO WORK EVERY DAY. I HAVE TO RUN THE GAUNTLET OF SNIPERS.
BA
WHEN YOU HEAR A BULLET WHISTLING, THAT MEANS IT'S ALREADY PAST. THE ONE WITH YOUR NAME ON IT YOU WON'T HEAR.
PERHAPS IT'S A BLESSING THAT WE'VE EARNED, WHO KNOWS?

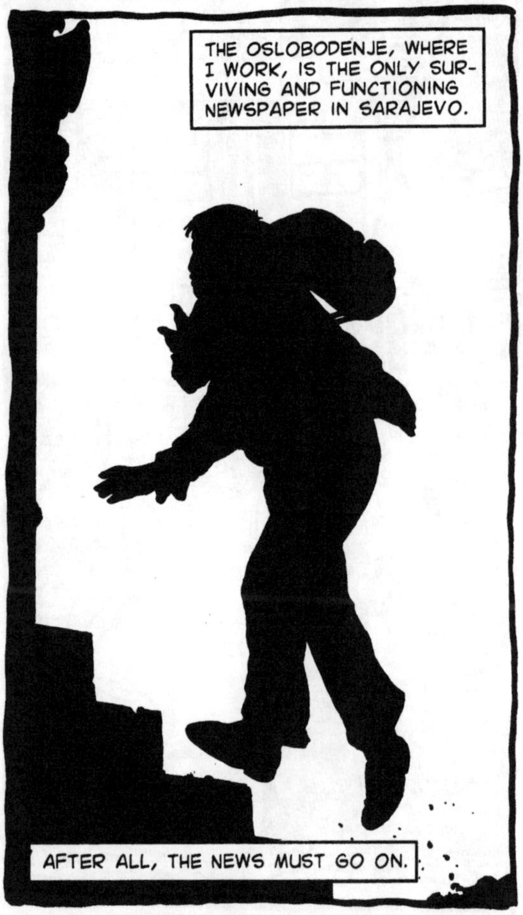
THE OSLOBODENJE, WHERE I WORK, IS THE ONLY SURVIVING AND FUNCTIONING NEWSPAPER IN SARAJEVO.
AFTER ALL, THE NEWS MUST GO ON.

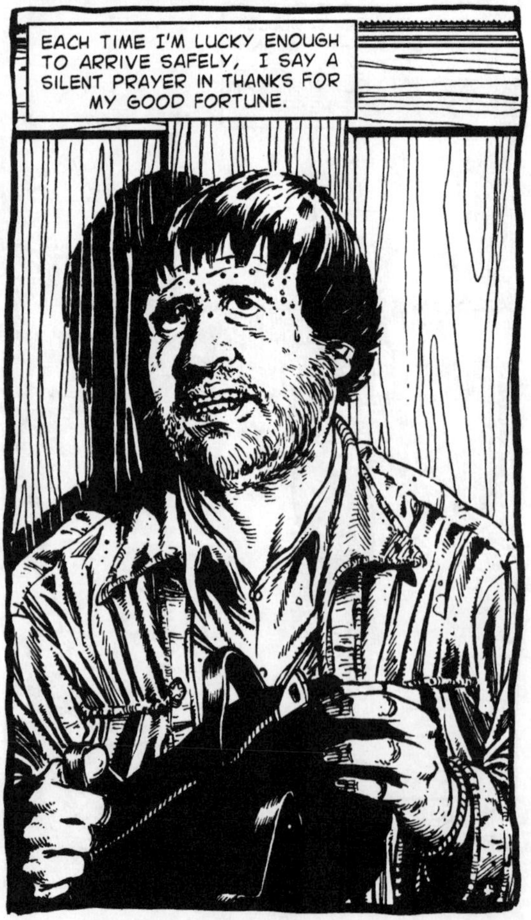
EACH TIME I'M LUCKY ENOUGH TO ARRIVE SAFELY, I SAY A SILENT PRAYER IN THANKS FOR MY GOOD FORTUNE.

It's then that I realize that there's no such thing as good fortune anymore.

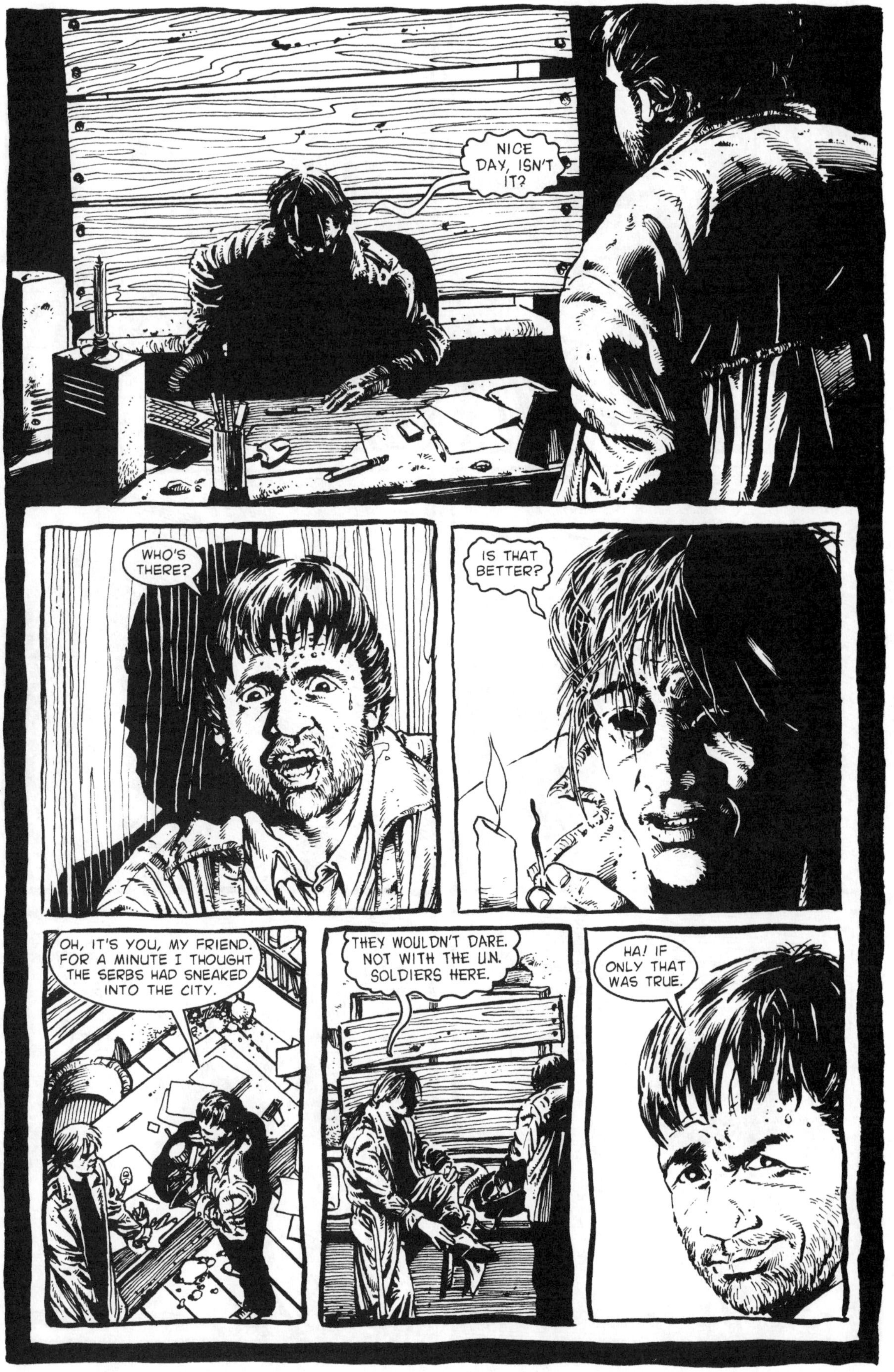
NICE DAY, ISN'T IT?
WHO'S THERE?
IS THAT BETTER?
OH, IT'S YOU, MY FRIEND. FOR A MINUTE I THOUGHT THE SERBS HAD SNEAKED INTO THE CITY.
THEY WOULDN'T DARE. NOT WITH THE U.N. SOLDIERS HERE.
HA! IF ONLY THAT WAS TRUE.

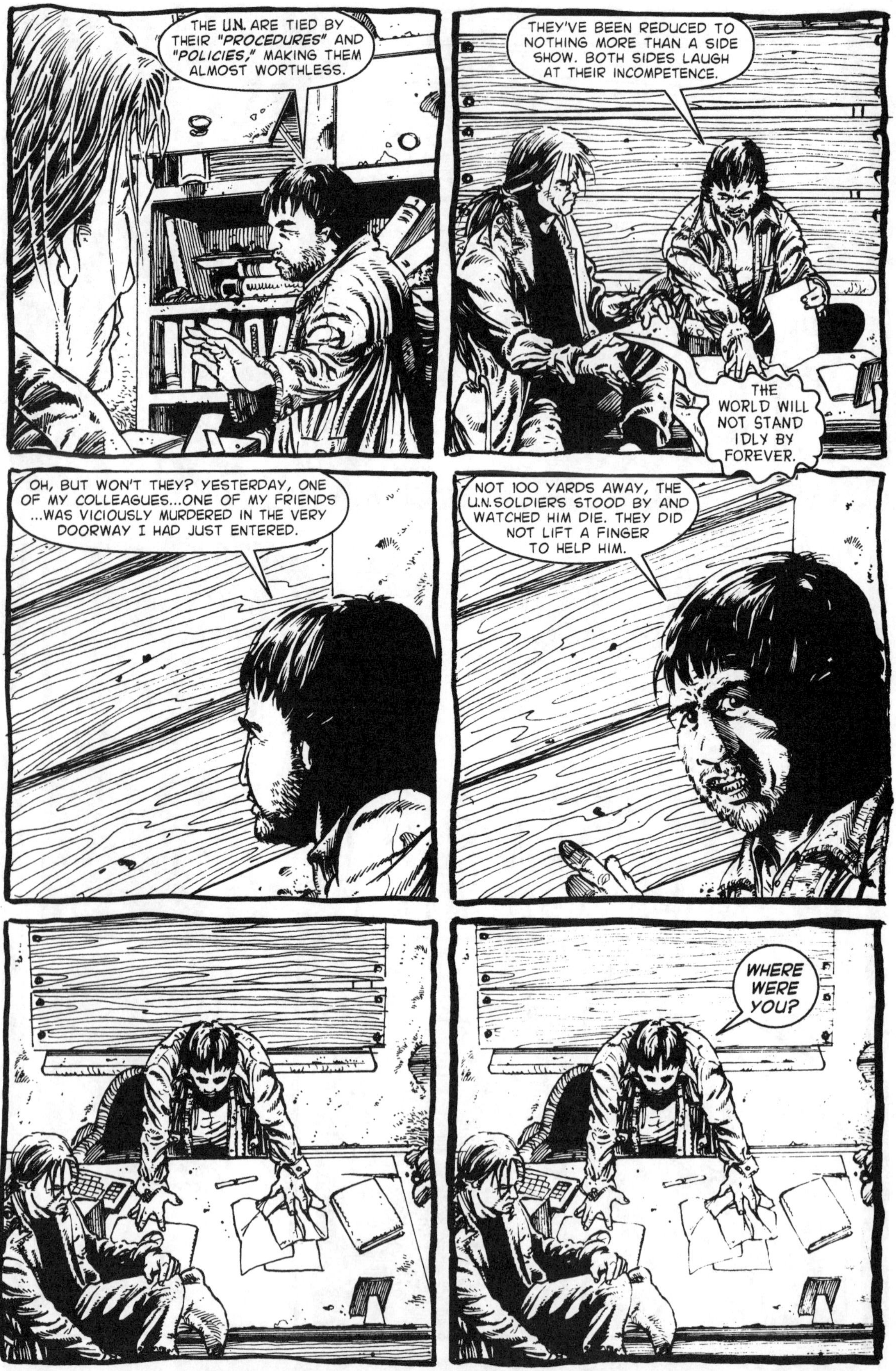
THE U.N. ARE TIED BY THEIR "PROCEDURES" AND "POLICIES," MAKING THEM ALMOST WORTHLESS.
THEY'VE BEEN REDUCED TO NOTHING MORE THAN A SIDE SHOW. BOTH SIDES LAUGH AT THEIR INCOMPETENCE.
THE WORLD WILL NOT STAND IDLY BY FOREVER.
OH, BUT WON'T THEY? YESTERDAY, ONE OF MY COLLEAGUES...ONE OF MY FRIENDS ...WAS VICIOUSLY MURDERED IN THE VERY DOORWAY I HAD JUST ENTERED.
NOT 100 YARDS AWAY, THE U.N. SOLDIERS STOOD BY AND WATCHED HIM DIE. THEY DID NOT LIFT A FINGER TO HELP HIM.
WHERE WERE YOU?

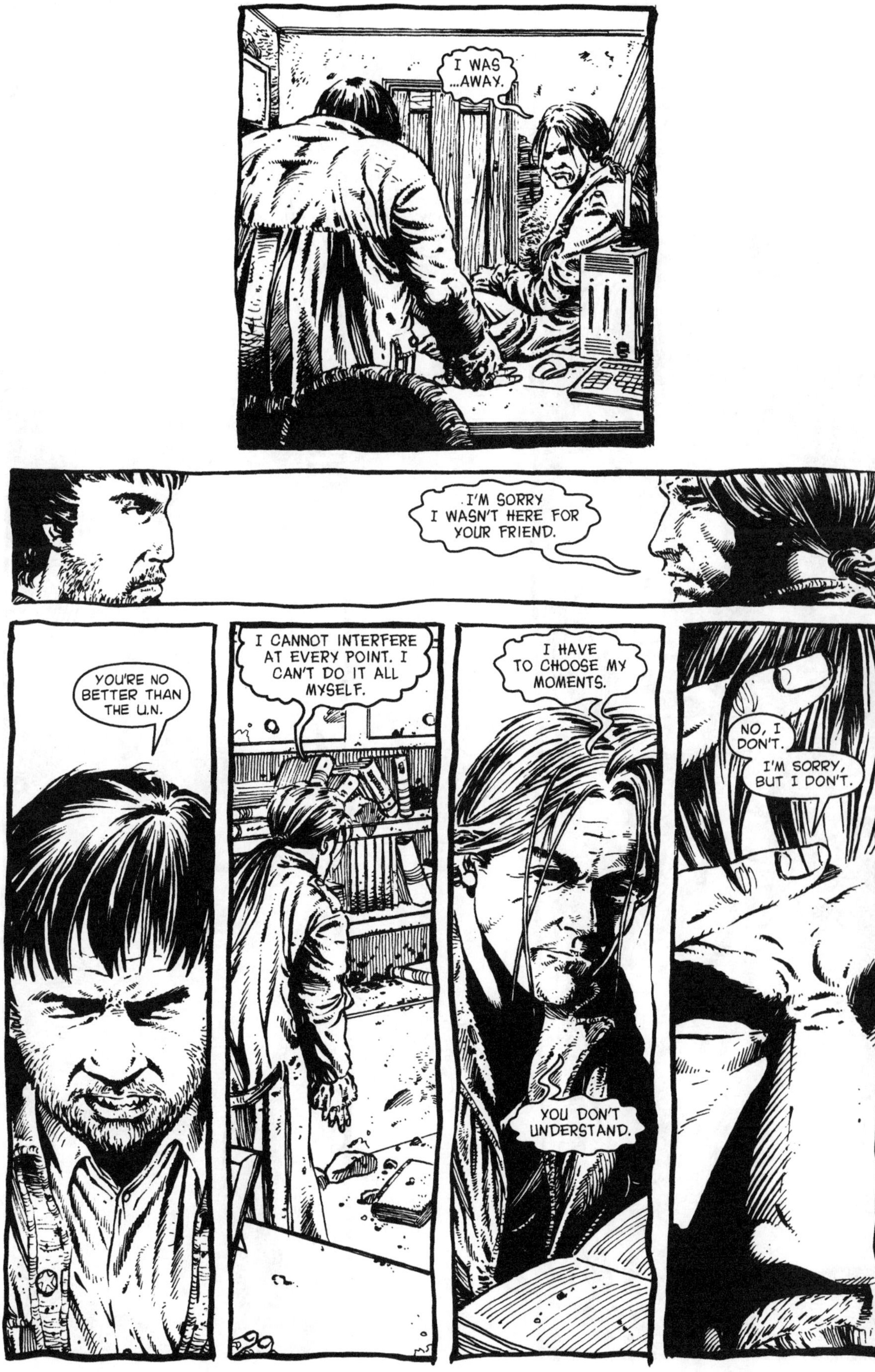
I WAS ...AWAY.
I'M SORRY I WASN'T HERE FOR YOUR FRIEND.
YOU'RE NO BETTER THAN THE U.N.
I CANNOT INTERFERE AT EVERY POINT. I CAN'T DO IT ALL MYSELF.
I HAVE TO CHOOSE MY MOMENTS.
YOU DON'T UNDERSTAND.
NO, I DON'T.
I'M SORRY, BUT I DON'T.

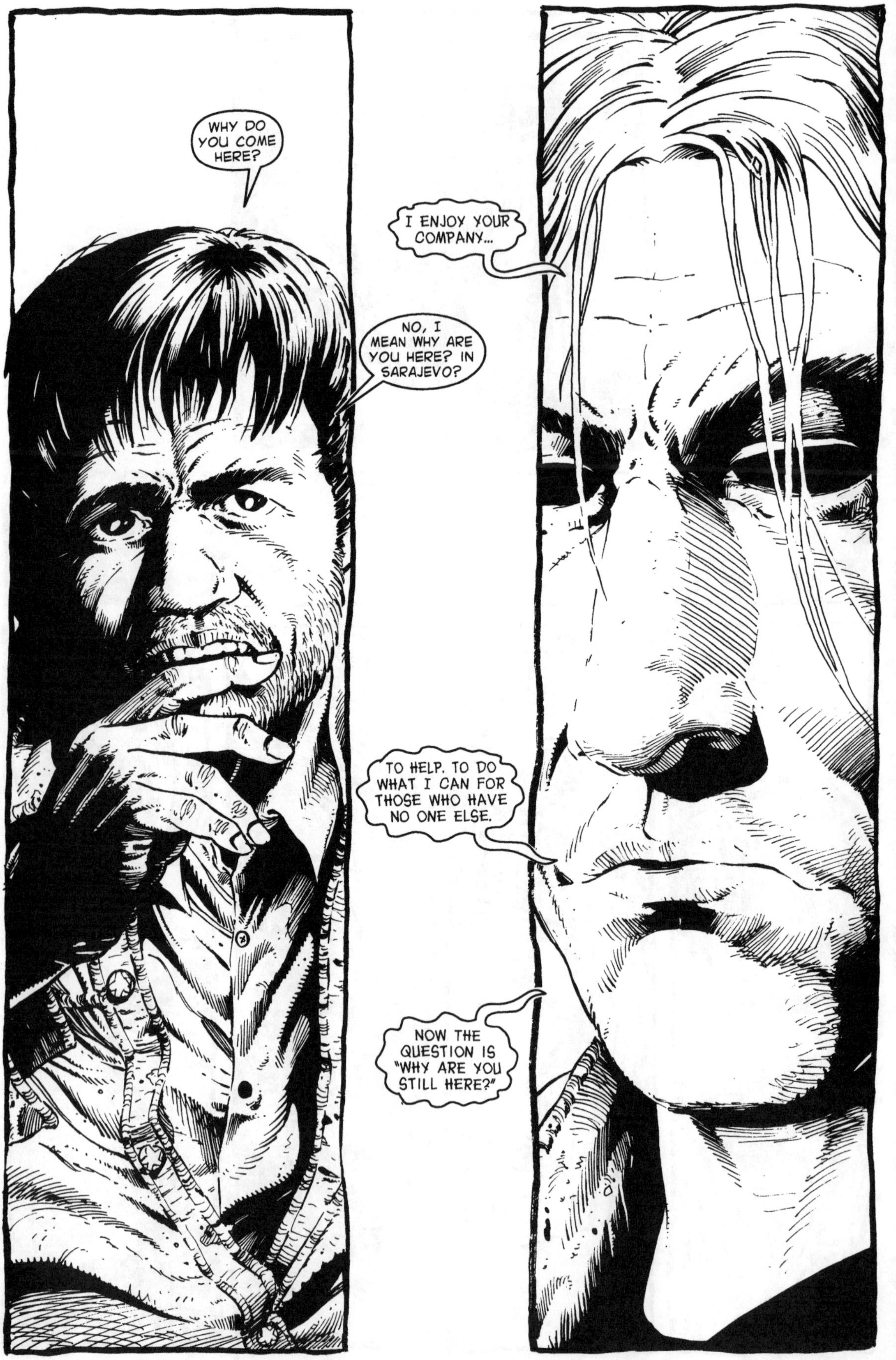
WHY DO YOU COME HERE?
I ENJOY YOUR COMPANY...
NO, I MEAN WHY ARE YOU HERE? IN SARAJEVO?
TO HELP. TO DO WHAT I CAN FOR THOSE WHO HAVE NO ONE ELSE.
NOW THE QUESTION IS "WHY ARE YOU STILL HERE?"

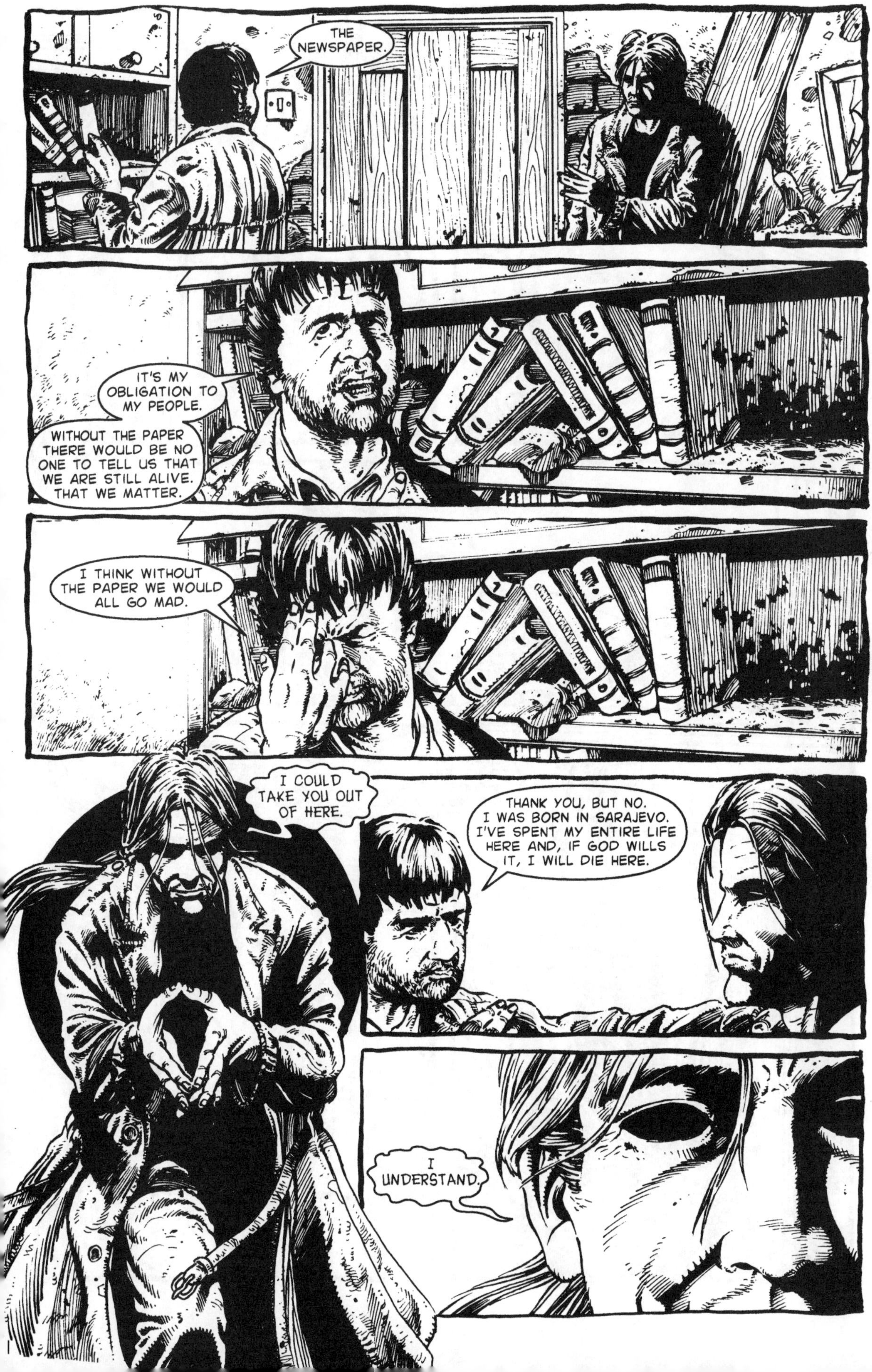
THE NEWSPAPER.
IT'S MY OBLIGATION TO MY PEOPLE.
WITHOUT THE PAPER THERE WOULD BE NO ONE TO TELL US THAT WE ARE STILL ALIVE. THAT WE MATTER.
I THINK WITHOUT THE PAPER WE WOULD ALL GO MAD.
I COULD TAKE YOU OUT OF HERE.
THANK YOU, BUT NO. I WAS BORN IN SARAJEVO. I'VE SPENT MY ENTIRE LIFE HERE AND, IF GOD WILLS IT, I WILL DIE HERE.
I UNDERSTAND.

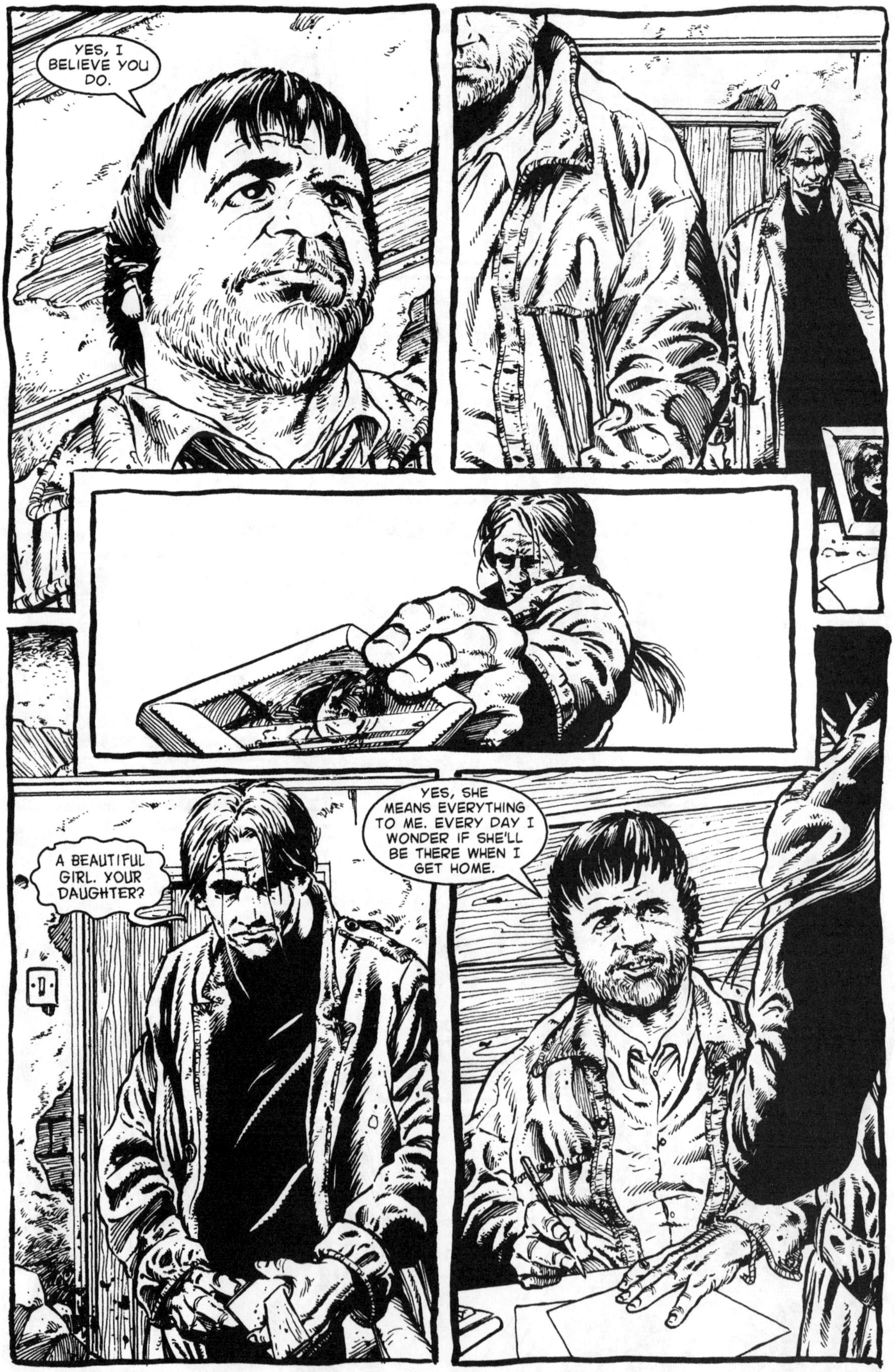
YES, I BELIEVE YOU DO.
A BEAUTIFUL GIRL. YOUR DAUGHTER?
YES, SHE MEANS EVERYTHING TO ME. EVERY DAY I WONDER IF SHE'LL BE THERE WHEN I GET HOME.

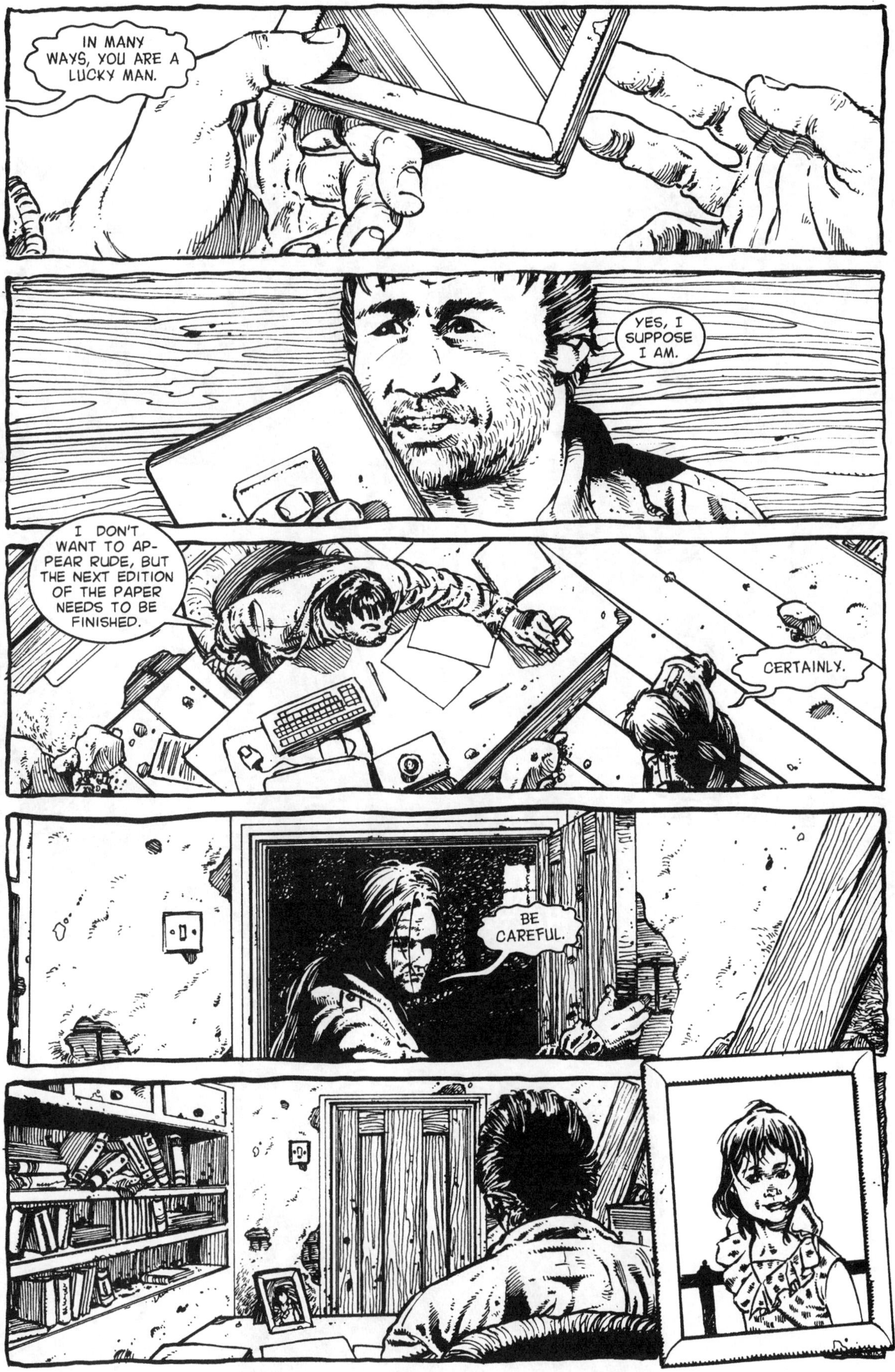
IN MANY WAYS, YOU ARE A LUCKY MAN.
YES, I SUPPOSE I AM.
I DON'T WANT TO AP-PEAR RUDE, BUT THE NEXT EDITION OF THE PAPER NEEDS TO BE FINISHED.
CERTAINLY.
BE CAREFUL.

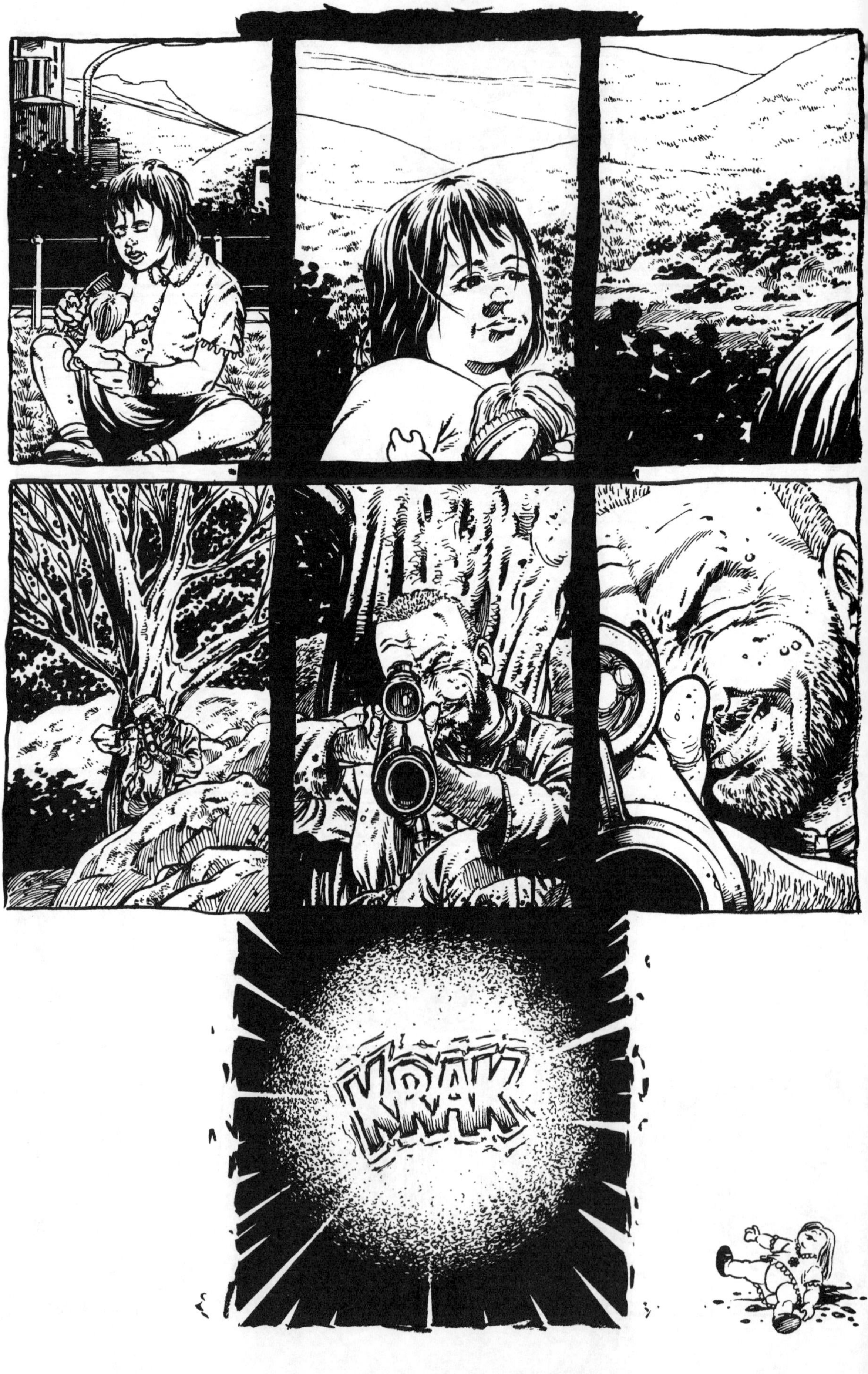
KRAK

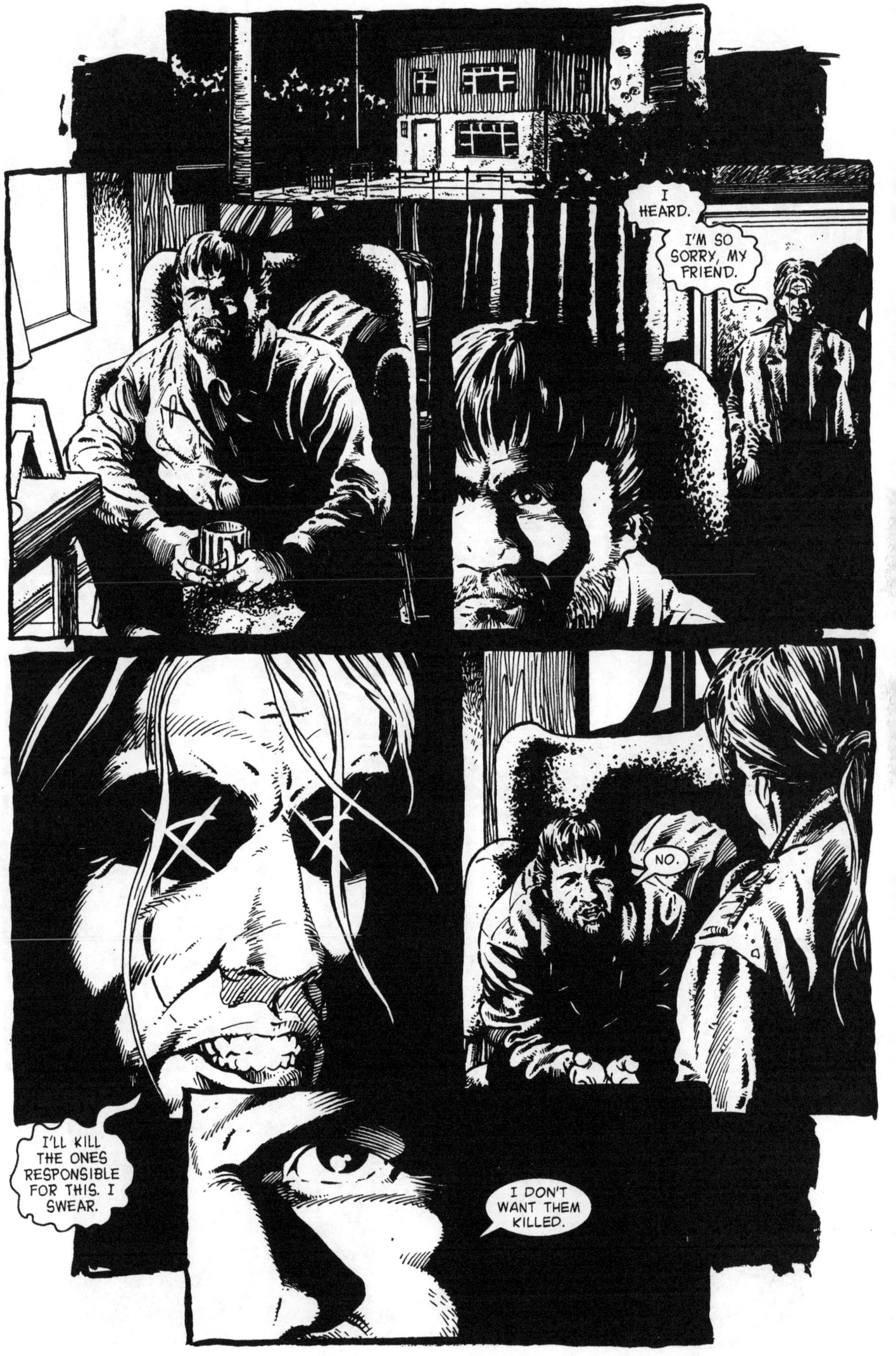
I HEARD.
I'M SO SORRY, MY FRIEND.
NO.
I'LL KILL THE ONES RESPONSIBLE FOR THIS. I SWEAR.
I DON'T WANT THEM KILLED.

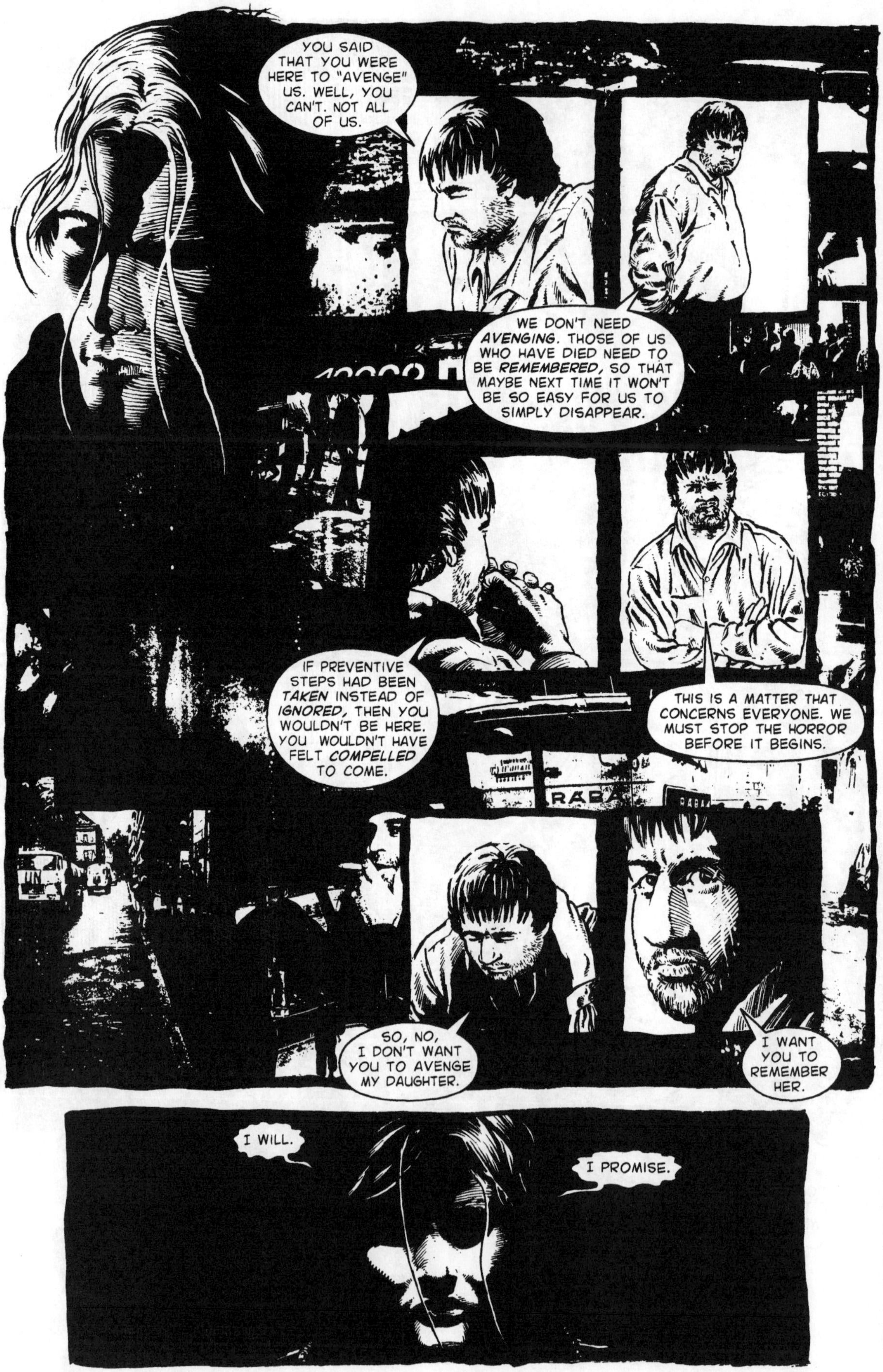

YOU SAID THAT YOU WERE HERE TO "AVENGE" US. WELL, YOU CAN'T. NOT ALL OF US.
WE DON'T NEED AVENGING. THOSE OF US WHO HAVE DIED NEED TO BE REMEMBERED, SO THAT MAYBE NEXT TIME IT WON'T BE SO EASY FOR US TO SIMPLY DISAPPEAR.
IF PREVENTIVE STEPS HAD BEEN TAKEN INSTEAD OF IGNORED, THEN YOU WOULDN'T BE HERE. YOU WOULDN'T HAVE FELT COMPELLED TO COME.
THIS IS A MATTER THAT CONCERNS EVERYONE. WE MUST STOP THE HORROR BEFORE IT BEGINS.
SO, NO, I DON'T WANT YOU TO AVENGE MY DAUGHTER.
I WANT YOU TO REMEMBER HER.
I WILL.
I PROMISE.

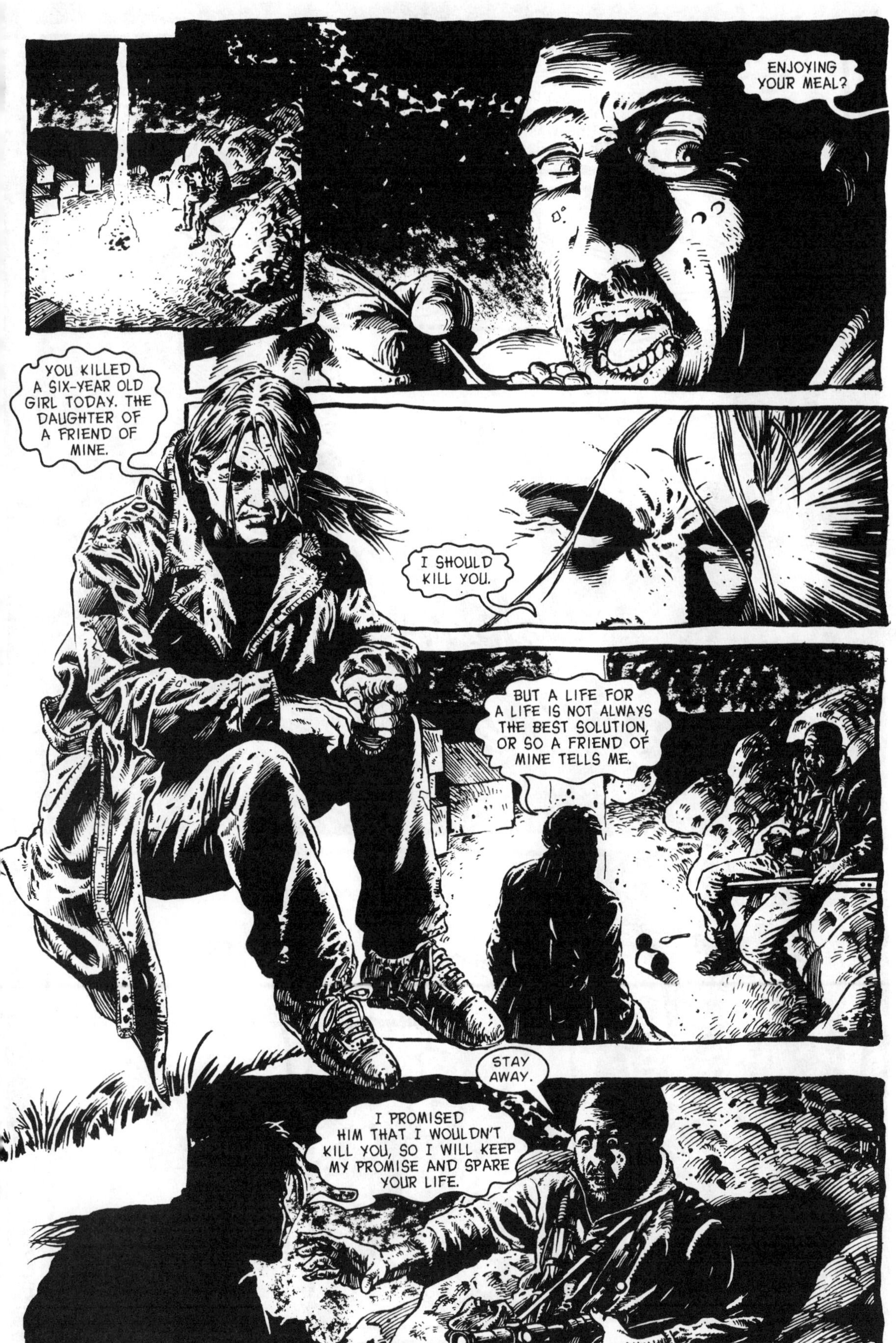
ENJOYING YOUR MEAL?
YOU KILLED A SIX-YEAR OLD GIRL TODAY. THE DAUGHTER OF A FRIEND OF MINE.
I SHOULD KILL YOU.
BUT A LIFE FOR A LIFE IS NOT ALWAYS THE BEST SOLUTION, OR SO A FRIEND OF MINE TELLS ME.
STAY AWAY.
I PROMISED HIM THAT I WOULDN'T KILL YOU, SO I WILL KEEP MY PROMISE AND SPARE YOUR LIFE.

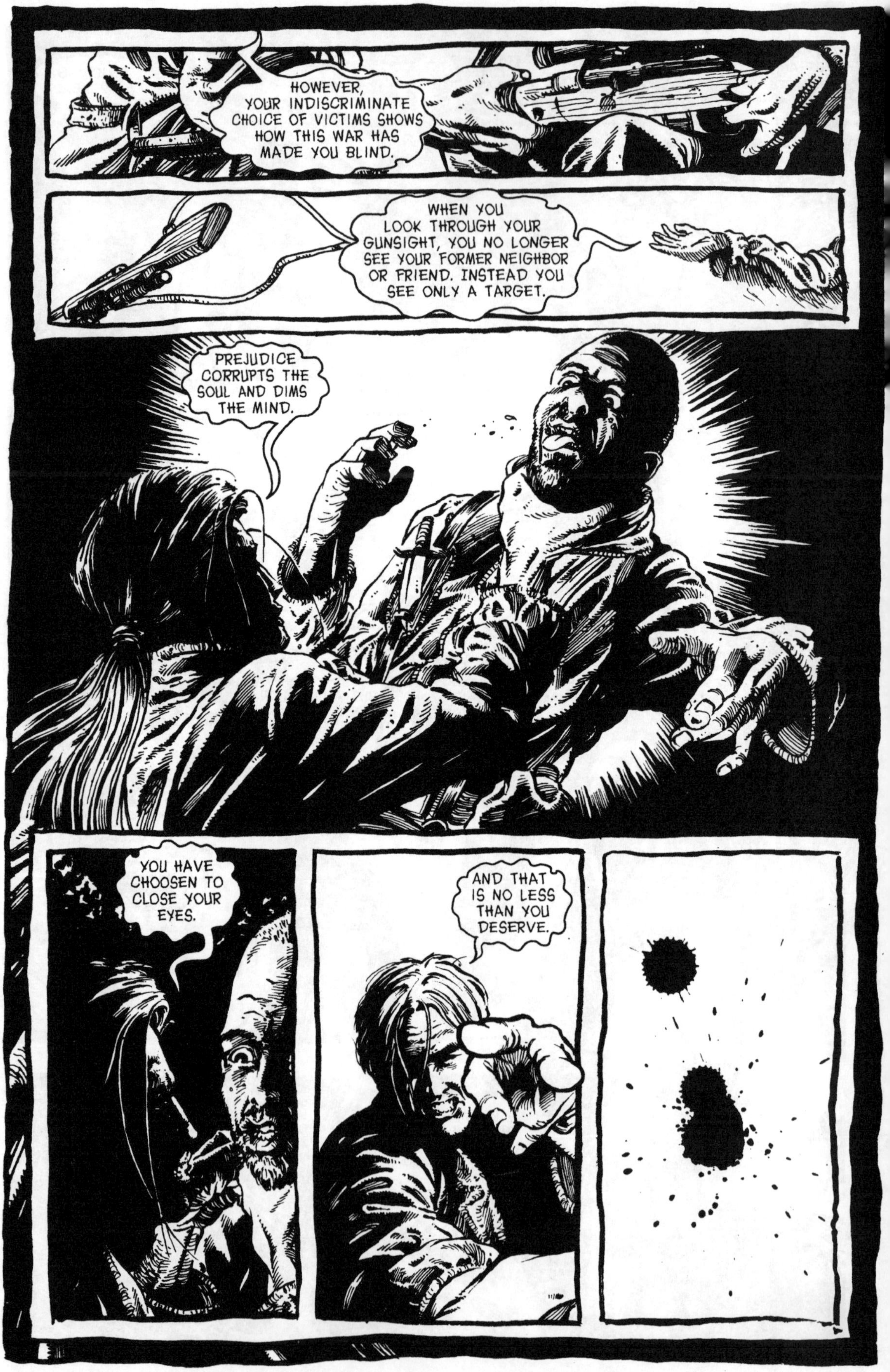
HOWEVER, YOUR INDISCRIMINATE CHOICE OF VICTIMS SHOWS HOW THIS WAR HAS MADE YOU BLIND.
WHEN YOU LOOK THROUGH YOUR GUNSIGHT, YOU NO LONGER SEE YOUR FORMER NEIGHBOR OR FRIEND. INSTEAD YOU SEE ONLY A TARGET.
PREJUDICE CORRUPTS THE SOUL AND DIMS THE MIND.
YOU HAVE CHOOSEN TO CLOSE YOUR EYES.
AND THAT IS NO LESS THAN YOU DESERVE.

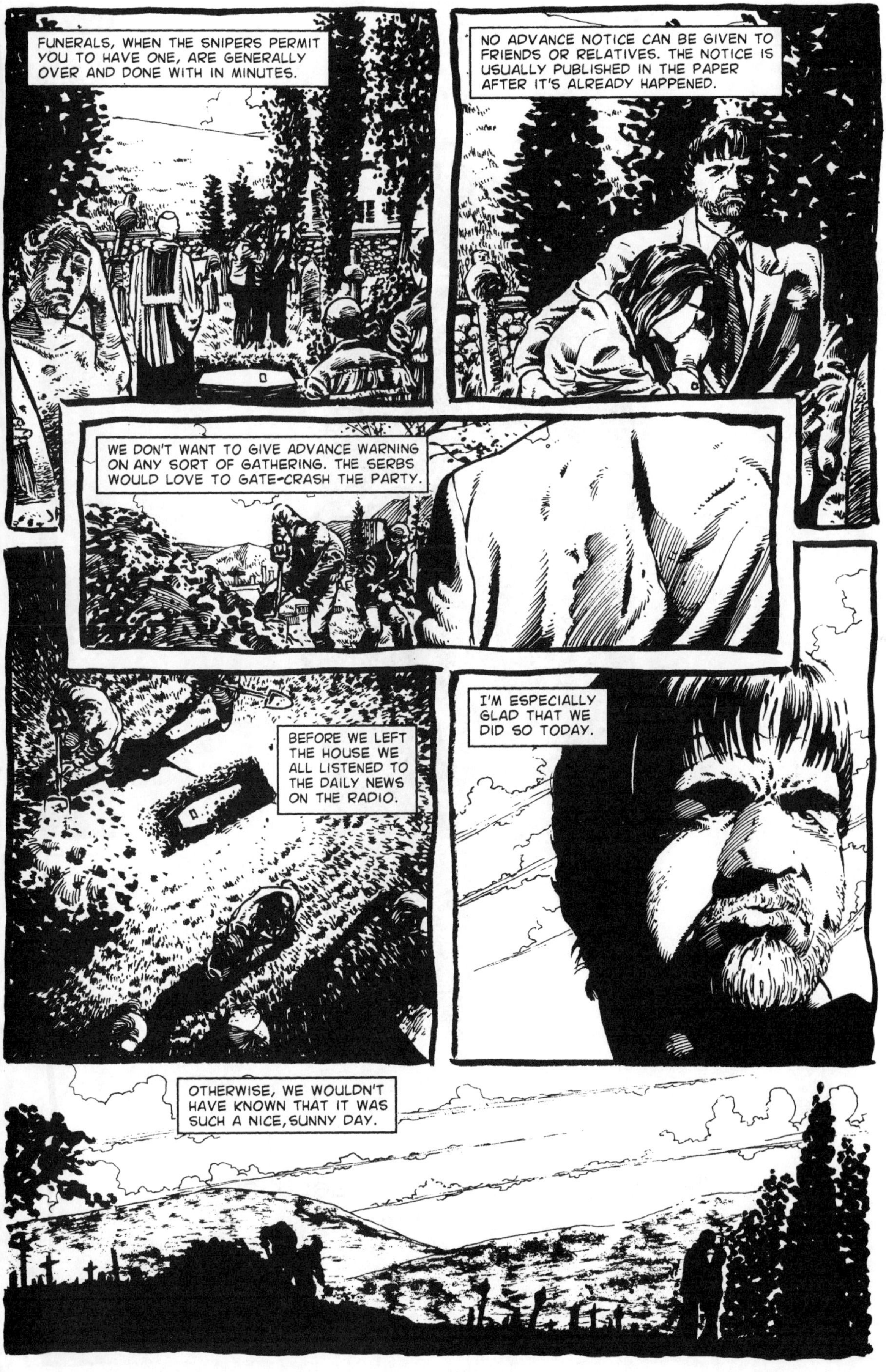
FUNERALS, WHEN THE SNIPERS PERMIT YOU TO HAVE ONE, ARE GENERALLY OVER AND DONE WITH IN MINUTES.
NO ADVANCE NOTICE CAN BE GIVEN TO FRIENDS OR RELATIVES. THE NOTICE IS USUALLY PUBLISHED IN THE PAPER AFTER IT'S ALREADY HAPPENED.
WE DON'T WANT TO GIVE ADVANCE WARNING ON ANY SORT OF GATHERING. THE SERBS WOULD LOVE TO GATE-CRASH THE PARTY.
BEFORE WE LEFT THE HOUSE WE ALL LISTENED TO THE DAILY NEWS ON THE RADIO.
I'M ESPECIALLY GLAD THAT WE DID SO TODAY.
OTHERWISE, WE WOULDN'T HAVE KNOWN THAT IT WAS SUCH A NICE, SUNNY DAY.

"Pride, Prejudice and Persecution"
Chapter Two

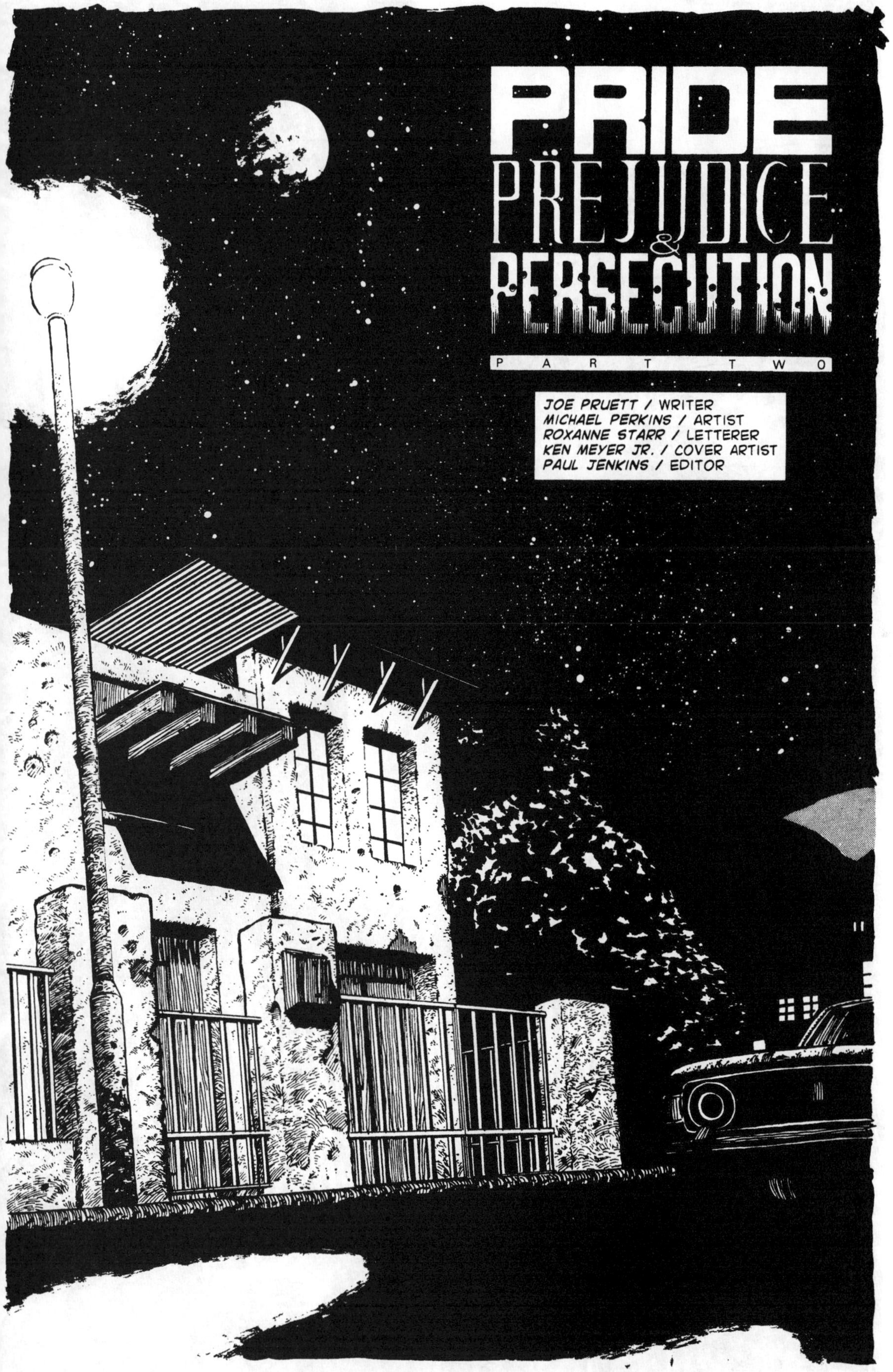
PRIDE PREJUDICE & PERSECUTION
PART TWO
JOE PRUETT / WRITER
MICHAEL PERKINS / ARTIST
ROXANNE STARR / LETTERER
KEN MEYER JR. / COVER ARTIST
PAUL JENKINS / EDITOR

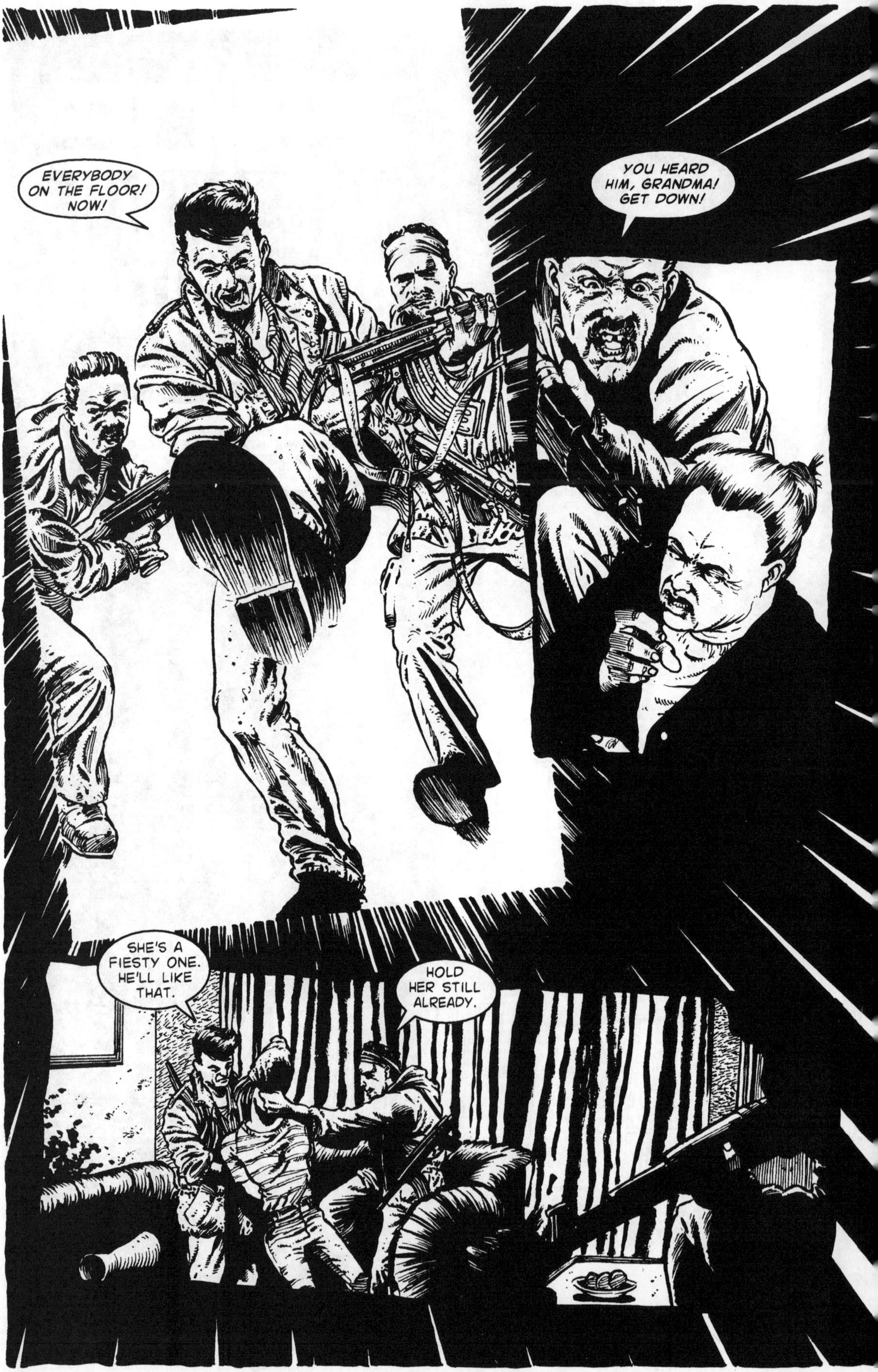
EVERYBODY ON THE FLOOR! NOW!
YOU HEARD HIM, GRANDMA! GET DOWN!
SHE'S A FIESTY ONE. HE'LL LIKE THAT.
HOLD HER STILL ALREADY.

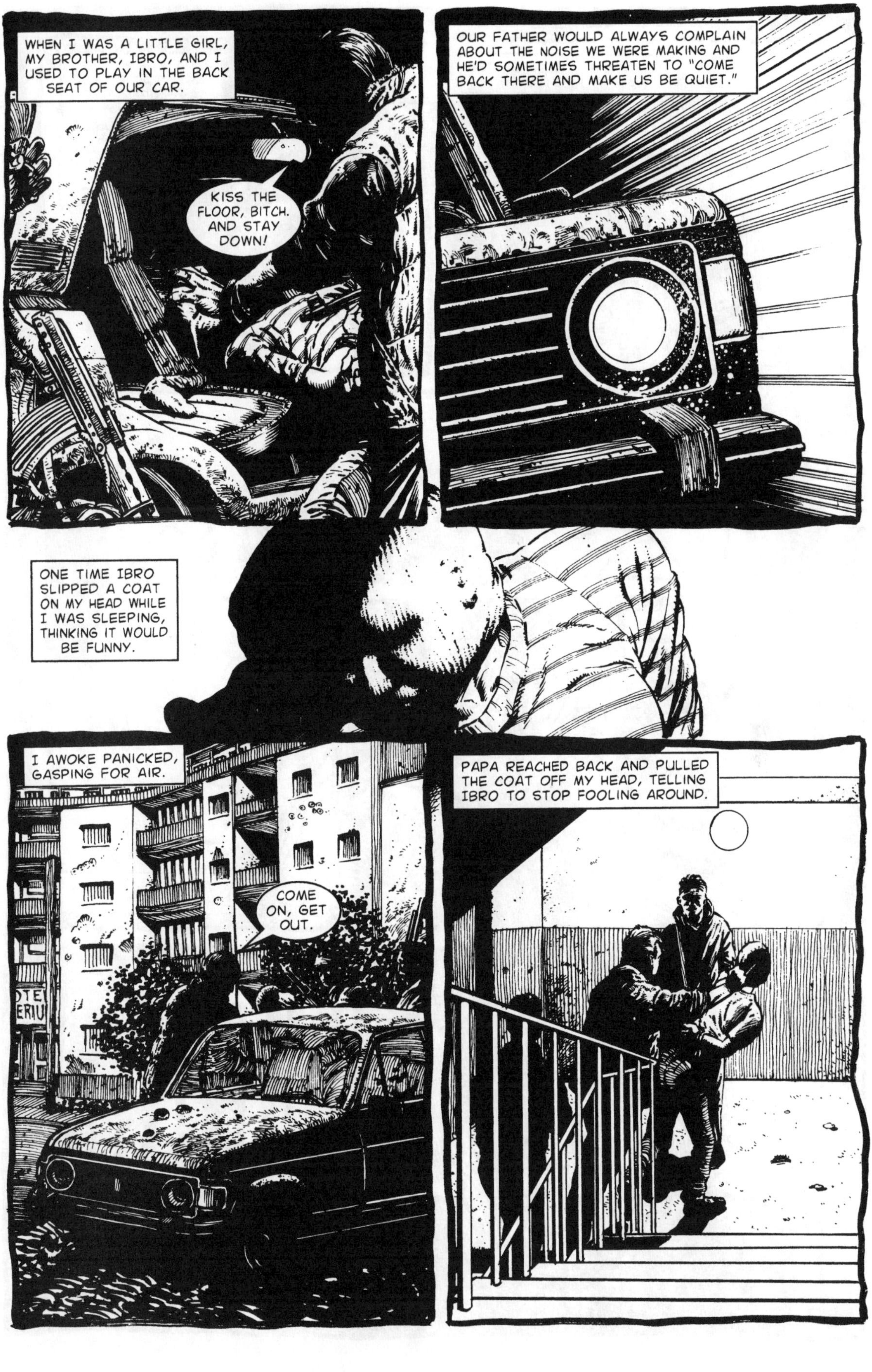
WHEN I WAS A LITTLE GIRL, MY BROTHER, IBRO, AND I USED TO PLAY IN THE BACK SEAT OF OUR CAR.
KISS THE FLOOR, BITCH. AND STAY DOWN!
OUR FATHER WOULD ALWAYS COMPLAIN ABOUT THE NOISE WE WERE MAKING AND HE'D SOMETIMES THREATEN TO "COME BACK THERE AND MAKE US BE QUIET."
ONE TIME IBRO SLIPPED A COAT ON MY HEAD WHILE I WAS SLEEPING, THINKING IT WOULD BE FUNNY.
I AWOKE PANICKED, GASPING FOR AIR.
COME ON, GET OUT.
PAPA REACHED BACK AND PULLED THE COAT OFF MY HEAD, TELLING IBRO TO STOP FOOLING AROUND.

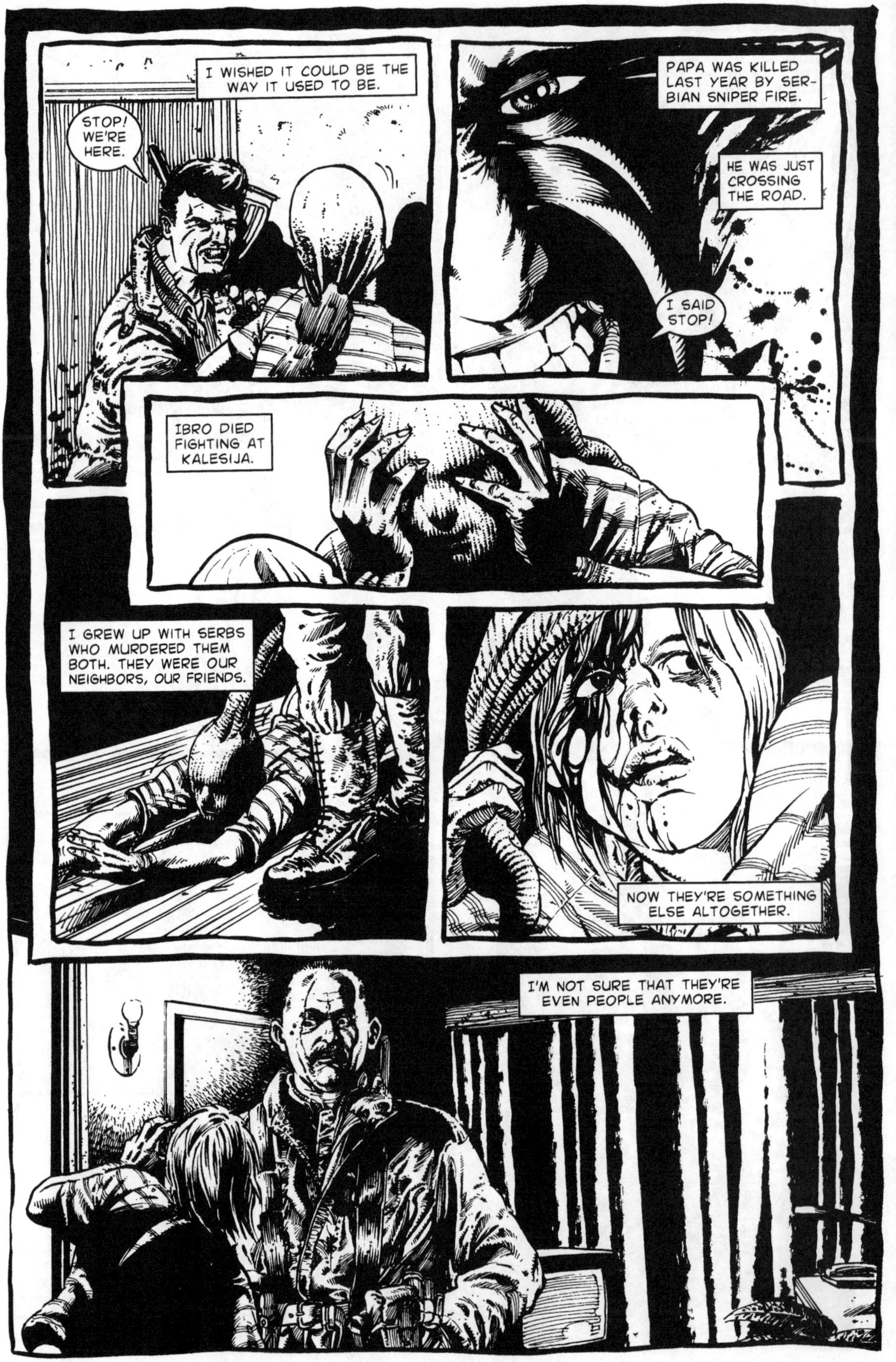
I WISHED IT COULD BE THE WAY IT USED TO BE.
STOP! WE'RE HERE.
PAPA WAS KILLED LAST YEAR BY SER-BIAN SNIPER FIRE.
HE WAS JUST CROSSING THE ROAD.
I SAID STOP!
IBRO DIED FIGHTING AT KALESIJA.
I GREW UP WITH SERBS WHO MURDERED THEM BOTH. THEY WERE OUR NEIGHBORS, OUR FRIENDS.
NOW THEY'RE SOMETHING ELSE ALTOGETHER.
I'M NOT SURE THAT THEY'RE EVEN PEOPLE ANYMORE.

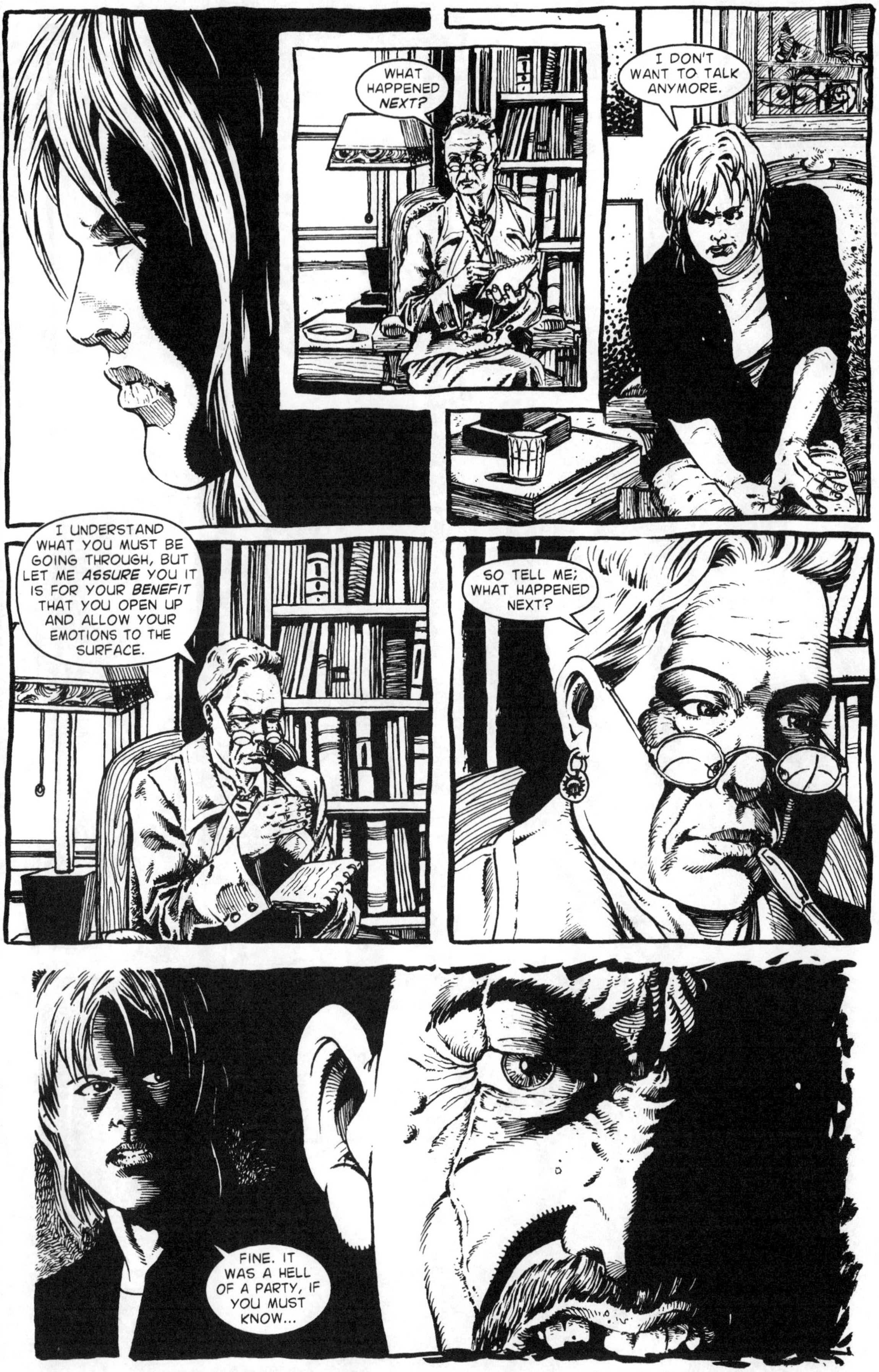
WHAT HAPPENED NEXT?
I DON'T WANT TO TALK ANYMORE.
I UNDERSTAND WHAT YOU MUST BE GOING THROUGH, BUT LET ME ASSURE YOU IT IS FOR YOUR BENEFIT THAT YOU OPEN UP AND ALLOW YOUR EMOTIONS TO THE SURFACE.
SO TELL ME; WHAT HAPPENED NEXT?
FINE. IT WAS A HELL OF A PARTY, IF YOU MUST KNOW...

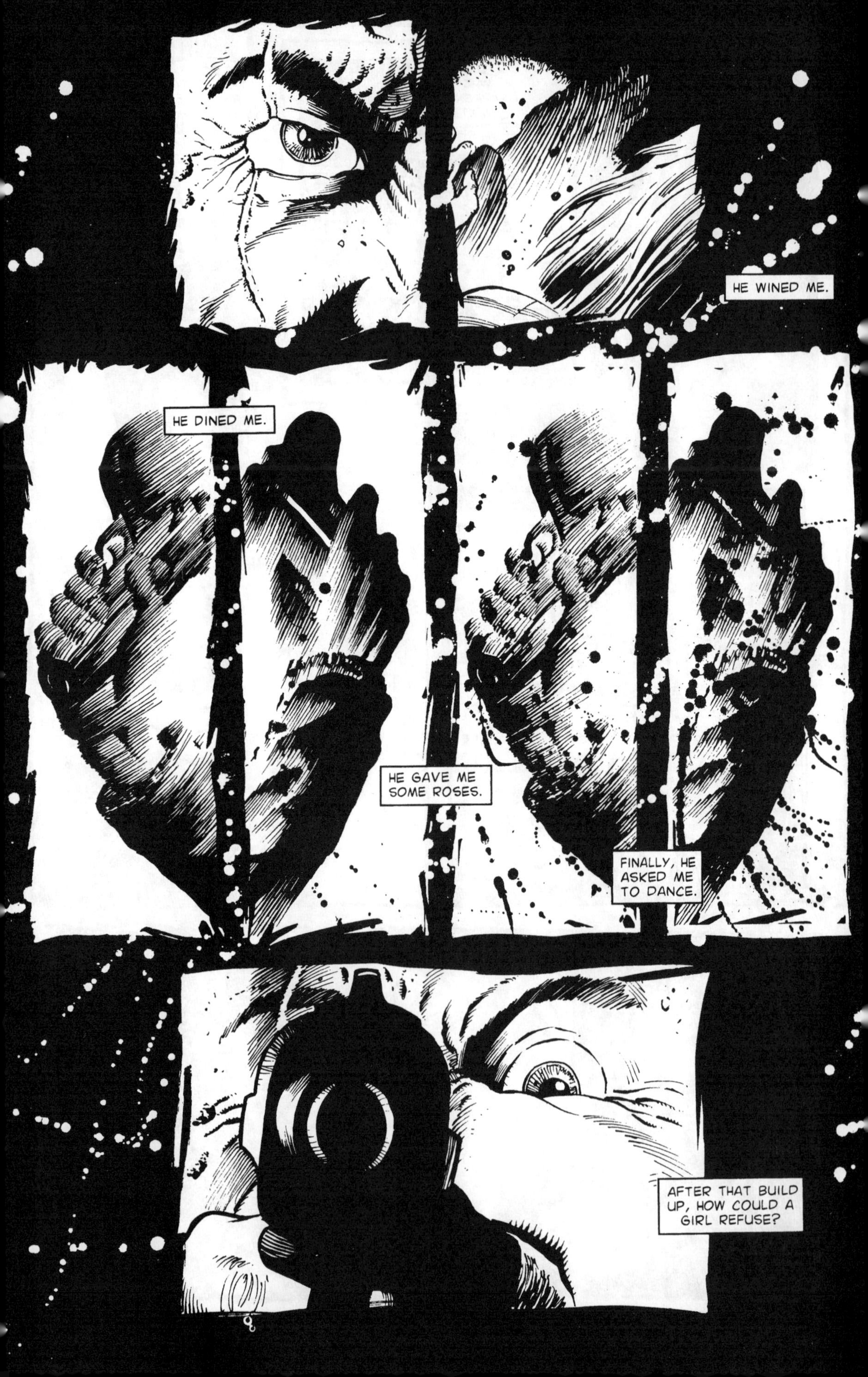
HE WINED ME.
HE DINED ME.
HE GAVE ME SOME ROSES.
FINALLY, HE ASKED ME TO DANCE.
AFTER THAT BUILD UP, HOW COULD A GIRL REFUSE?

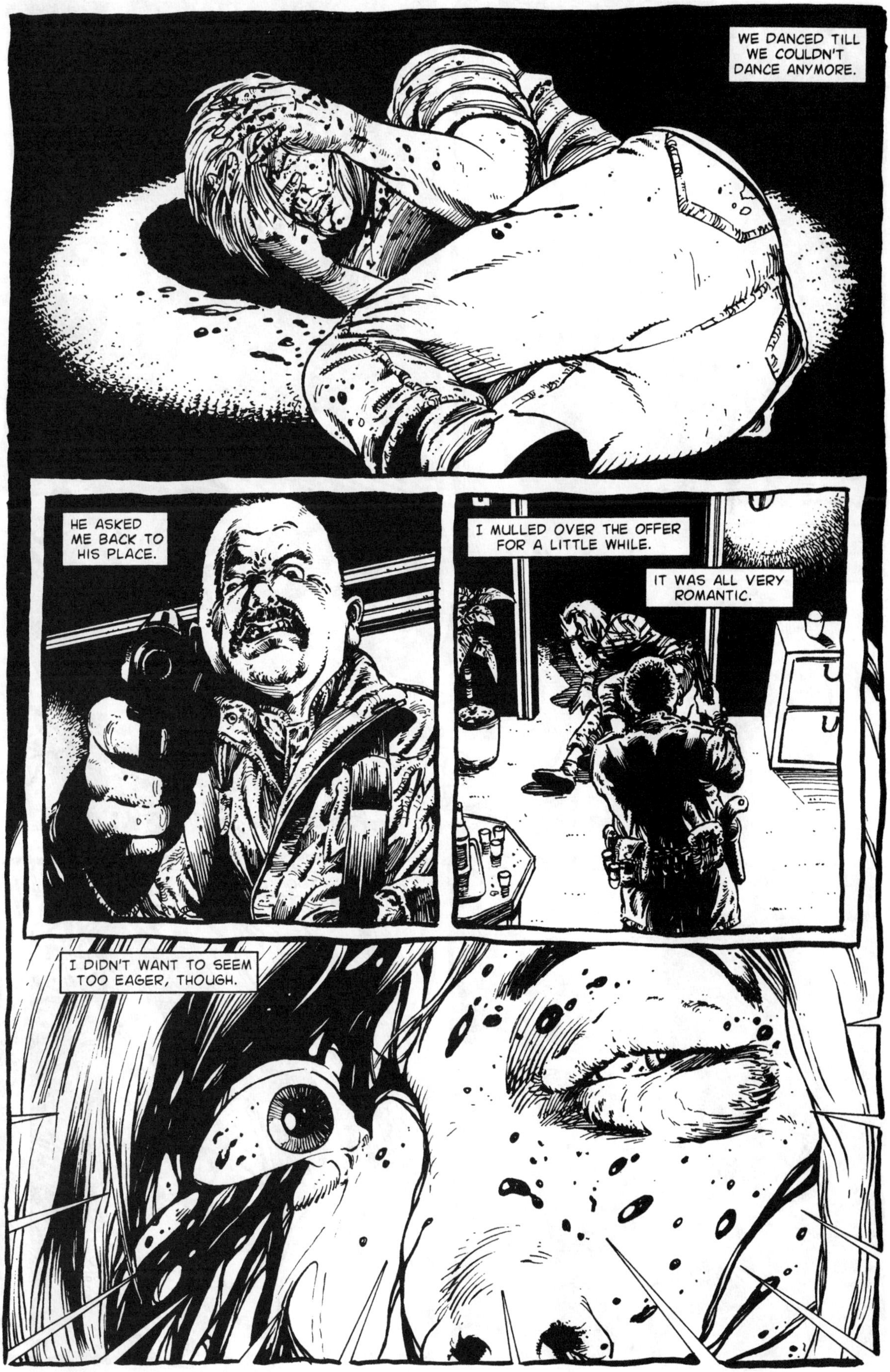

WE DANCED TILL WE COULDN'T DANCE ANYMORE.
HE ASKED ME BACK TO HIS PLACE.
I MULLED OVER THE OFFER FOR A LITTLE WHILE.
IT WAS ALL VERY ROMANTIC.
I DIDN'T WANT TO SEEM TOO EAGER, THOUGH.

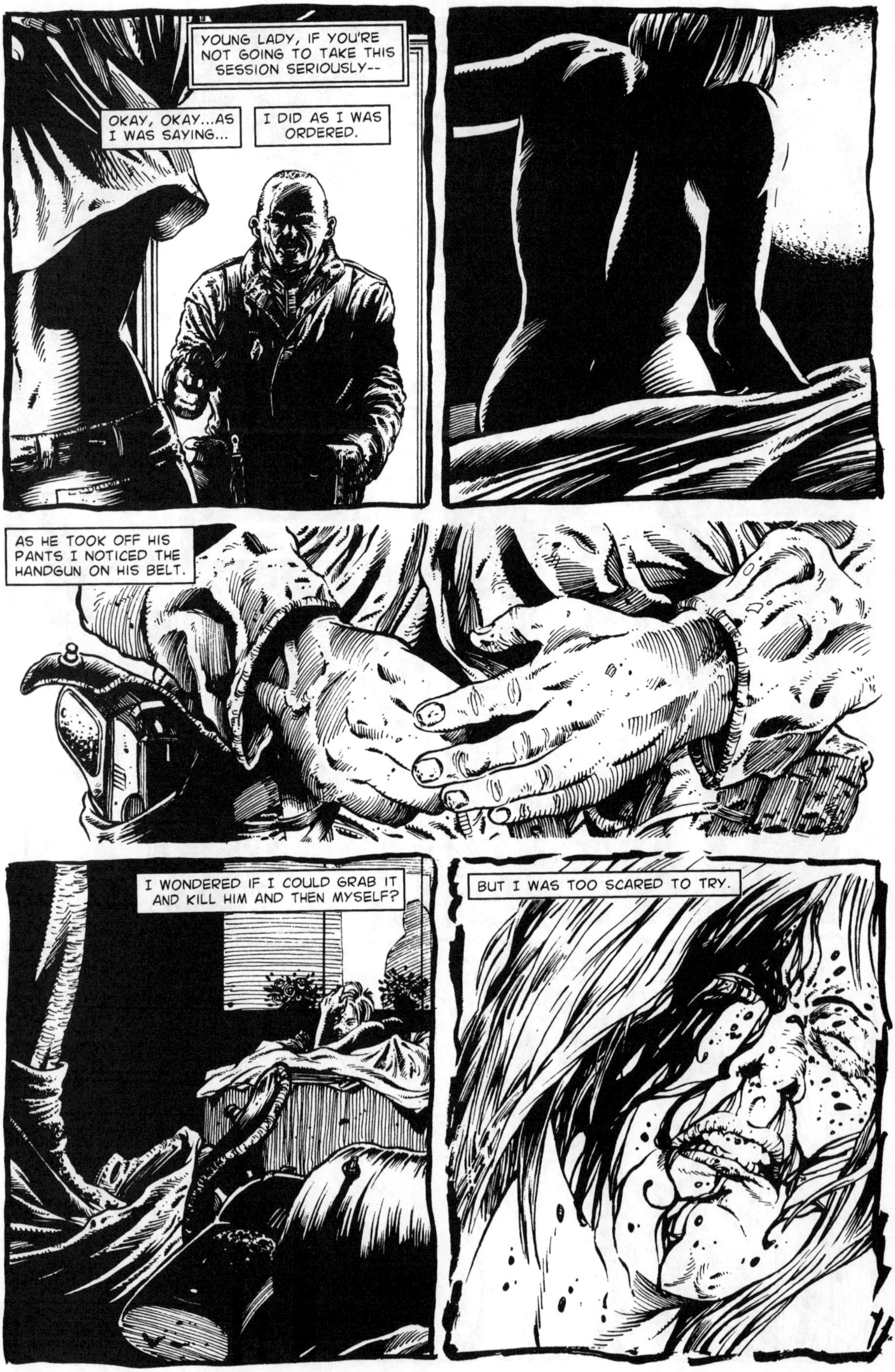
YOUNG LADY, IF YOU'RE NOT GOING TO TAKE THIS SESSION SERIOUSLY--
OKAY, OKAY...AS I WAS SAYING...
I DID AS I WAS ORDERED.
AS HE TOOK OFF HIS PANTS I NOTICED THE HANDGUN ON HIS BELT.
I WONDERED IF I COULD GRAB IT AND KILL HIM AND THEN MYSELF?
BUT I WAS TOO SCARED TO TRY.

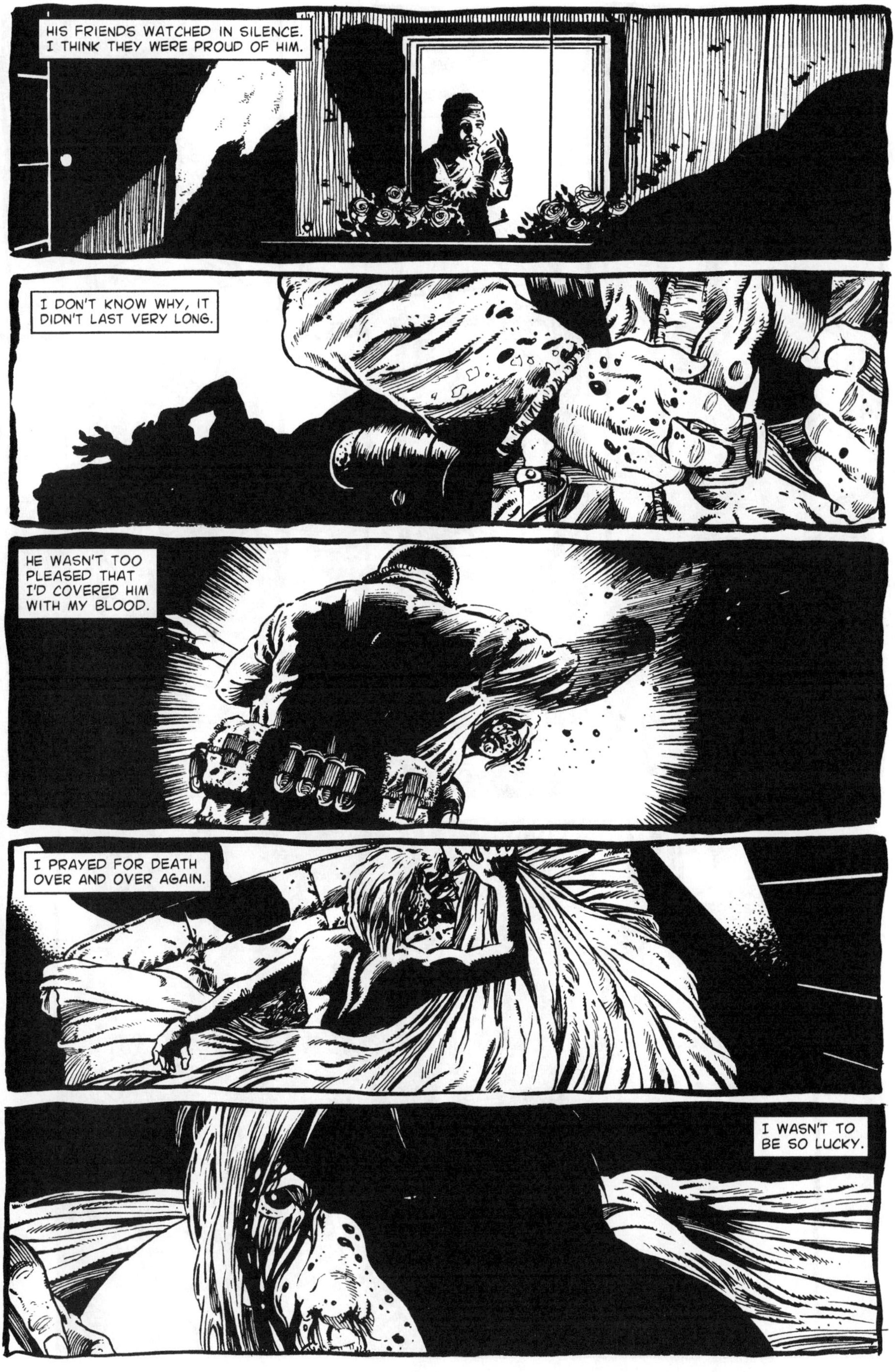
HIS FRIENDS WATCHED IN SILENCE. I THINK THEY WERE PROUD OF HIM.
I DON'T KNOW WHY, IT DIDN'T LAST VERY LONG.
HE WASN'T TOO PLEASED THAT I'D COVERED HIM WITH MY BLOOD.
I PRAYED FOR DEATH OVER AND OVER AGAIN.
I WASN'T TO BE SO LUCKY.

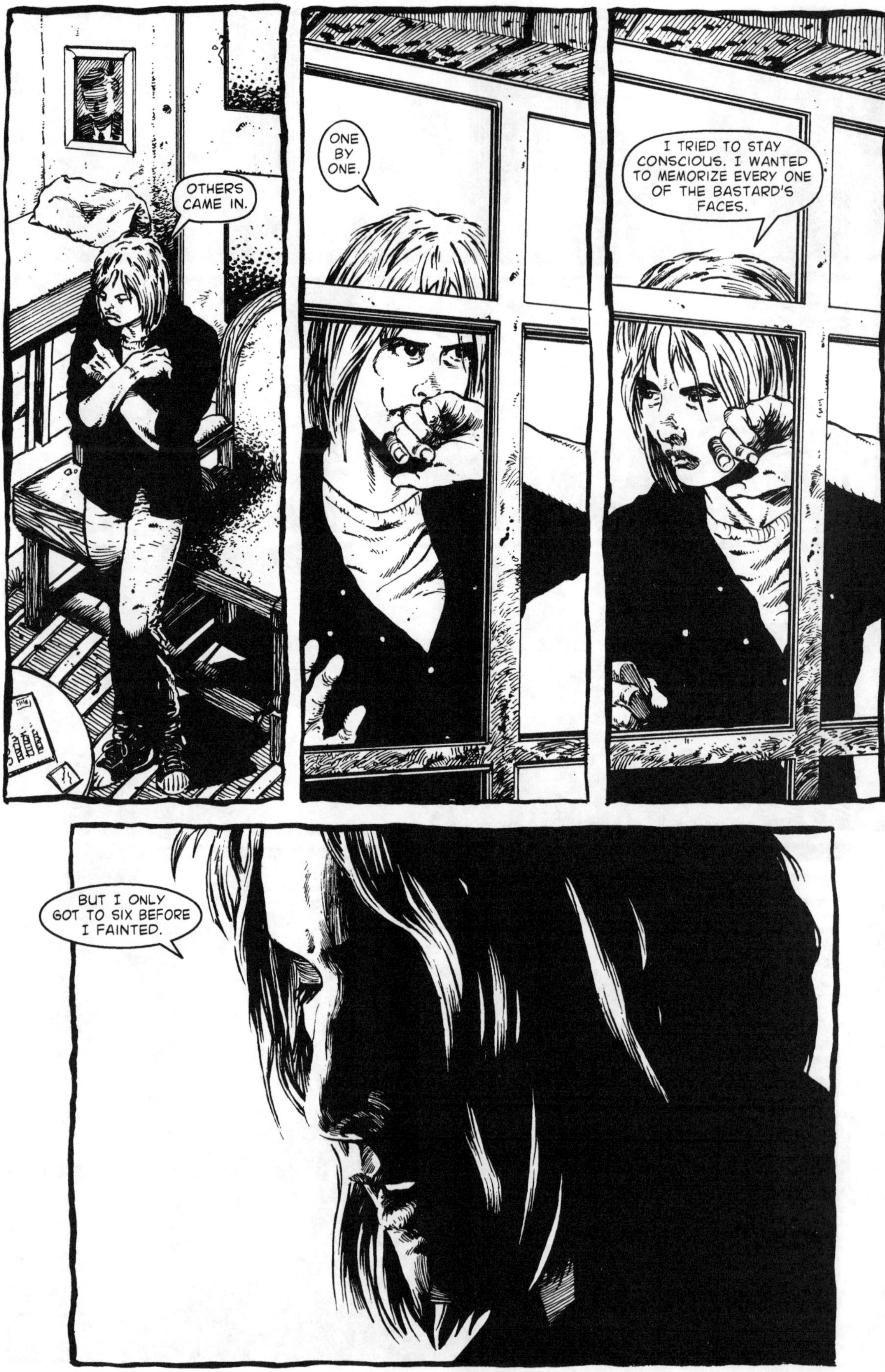
OTHERS CAME IN.
ONE BY ONE.
I TRIED TO STAY CONSCIOUS. I WANTED TO MEMORIZE EVERY ONE OF THE BASTARD'S FACES.
BUT I ONLY GOT TO SIX BEFORE I FAINTED.

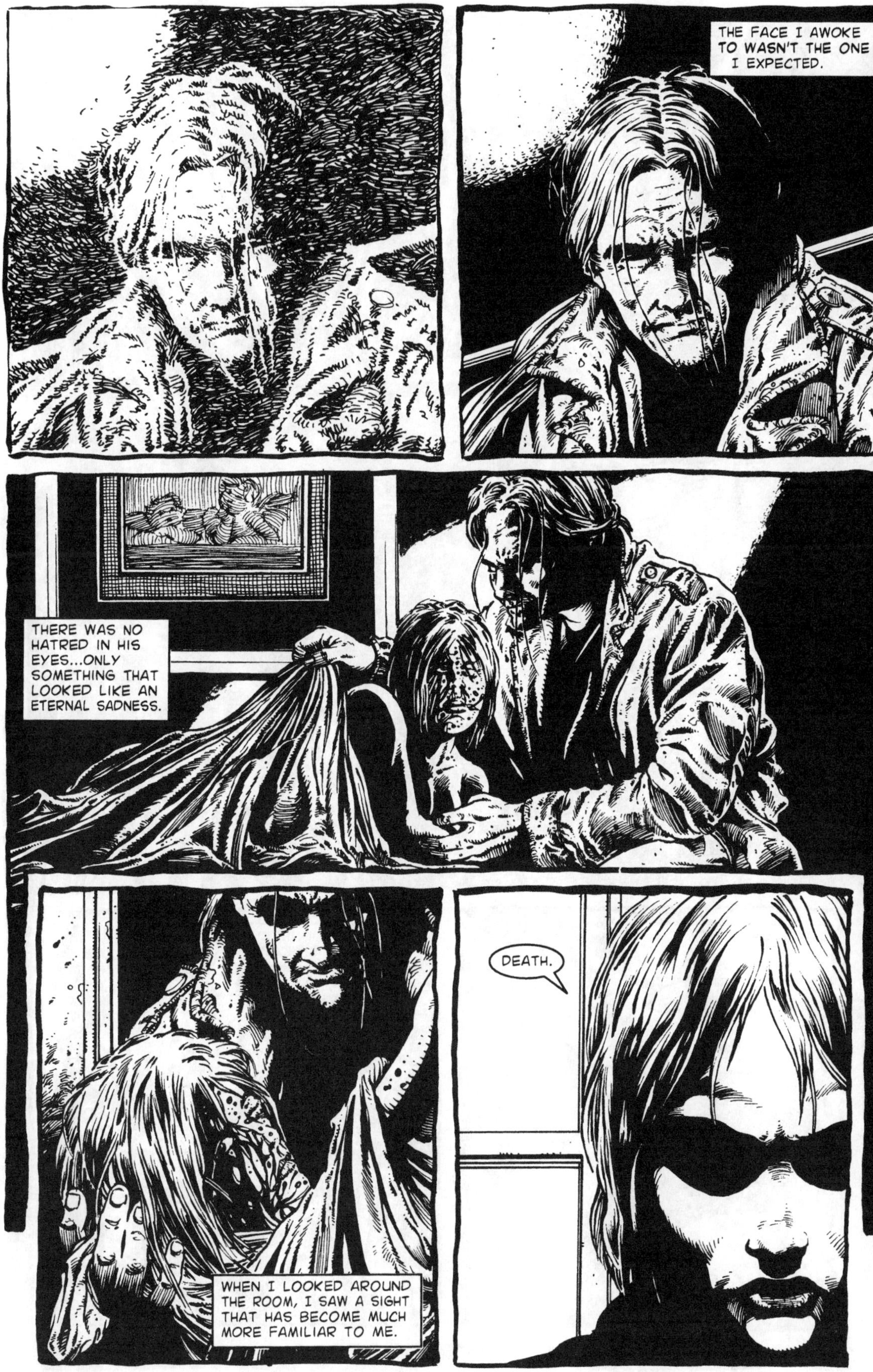
THE FACE I AWOKE TO WASN'T THE ONE I EXPECTED.
THERE WAS NO HATRED IN HIS EYES...ONLY SOMETHING THAT LOOKED LIKE AN ETERNAL SADNESS.
WHEN I LOOKED AROUND THE ROOM, I SAW A SIGHT THAT HAS BECOME MUCH MORE FAMILIAR TO ME.
DEATH.

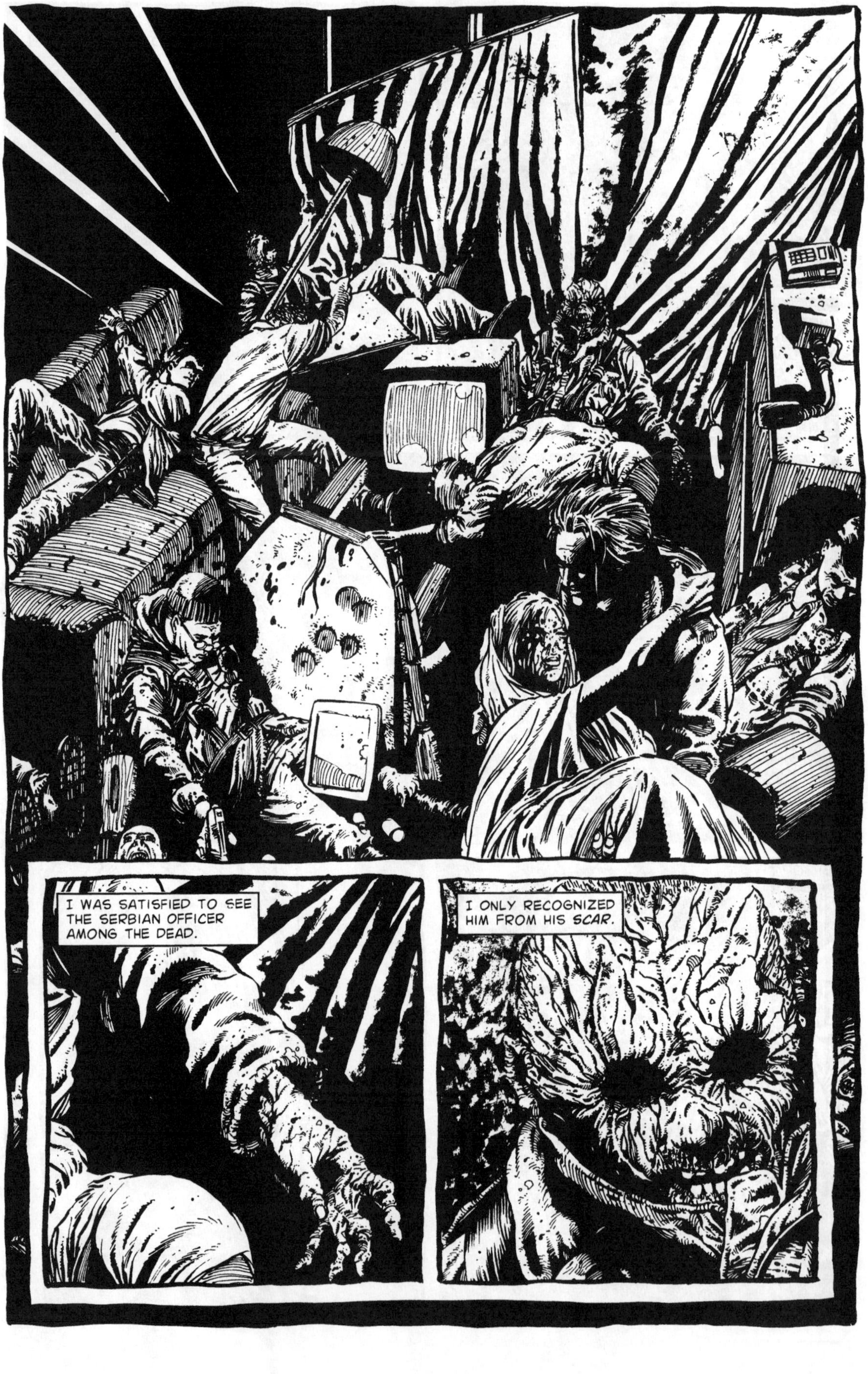
I WAS SATISFIED TO SEE THE SERBIAN OFFICER AMONG THE DEAD.
I ONLY RECOGNIZED HIM FROM HIS *SCAR*.

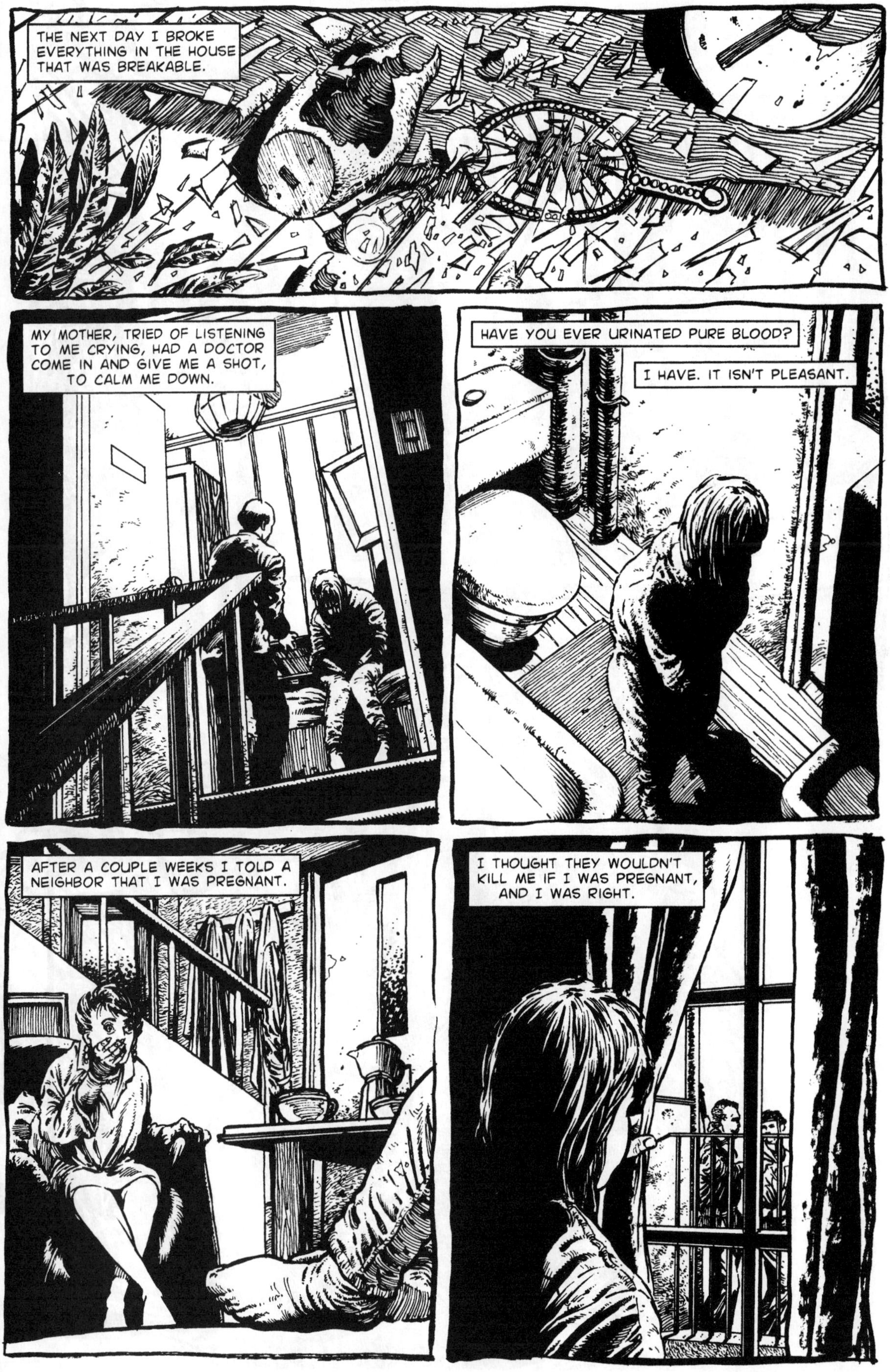
THE NEXT DAY I BROKE EVERYTHING IN THE HOUSE THAT WAS BREAKABLE.
MY MOTHER, TRIED OF LISTENING TO ME CRYING, HAD A DOCTOR COME IN AND GIVE ME A SHOT, TO CALM ME DOWN.
HAVE YOU EVER URINATED PURE BLOOD?
I HAVE. IT ISN'T PLEASANT.
AFTER A COUPLE WEEKS I TOLD A NEIGHBOR THAT I WAS PREGNANT.
I THOUGHT THEY WOULDN'T KILL ME IF I WAS PREGNANT, AND I WAS RIGHT.

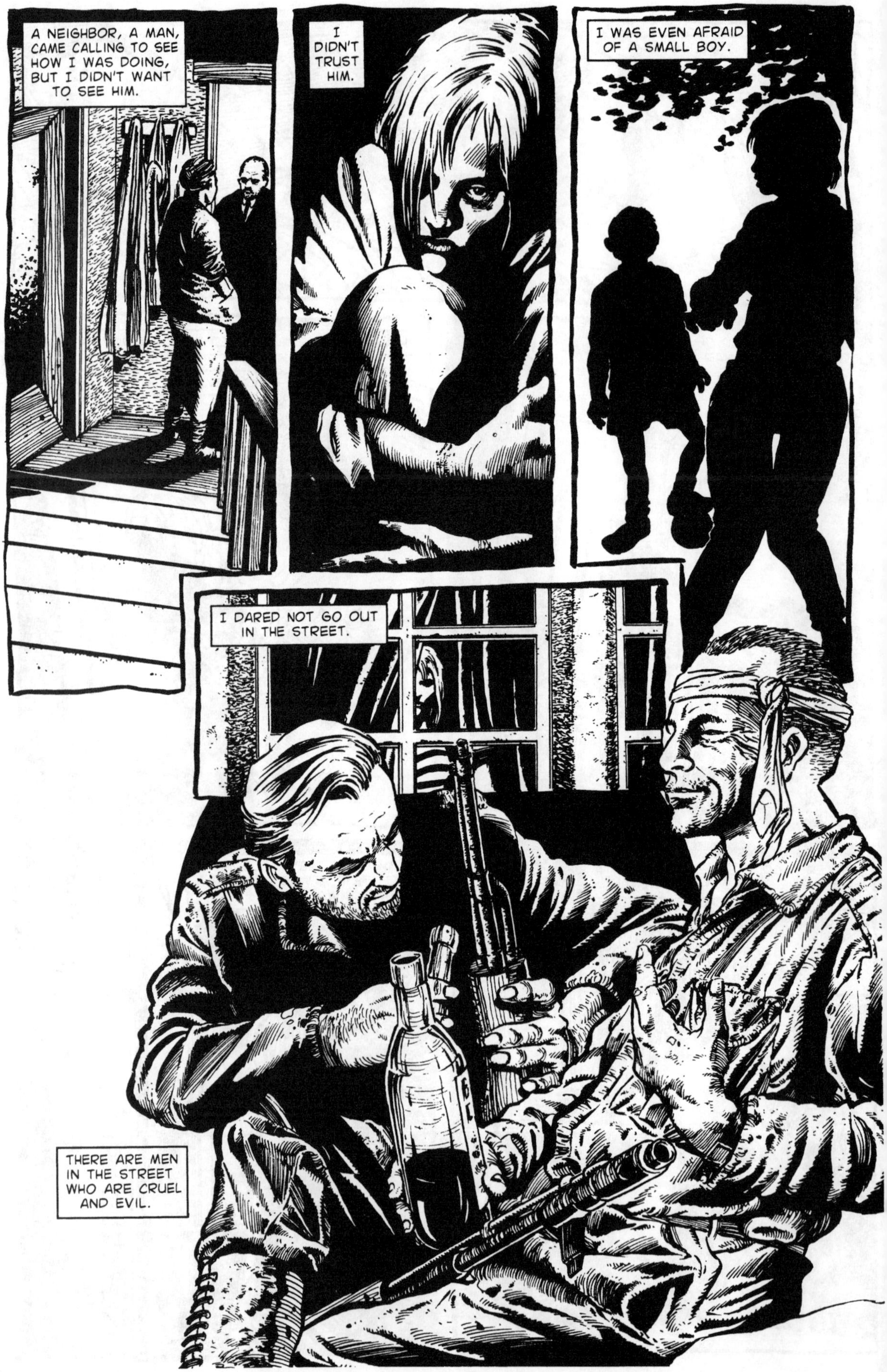
A NEIGHBOR, A MAN, CAME CALLING TO SEE HOW I WAS DOING, BUT I DIDN'T WANT TO SEE HIM.
I DIDN'T TRUST HIM.
I WAS EVEN AFRAID OF A SMALL BOY.
I DARED NOT GO OUT IN THE STREET.
THERE ARE MEN IN THE STREET WHO ARE CRUEL AND EVIL.

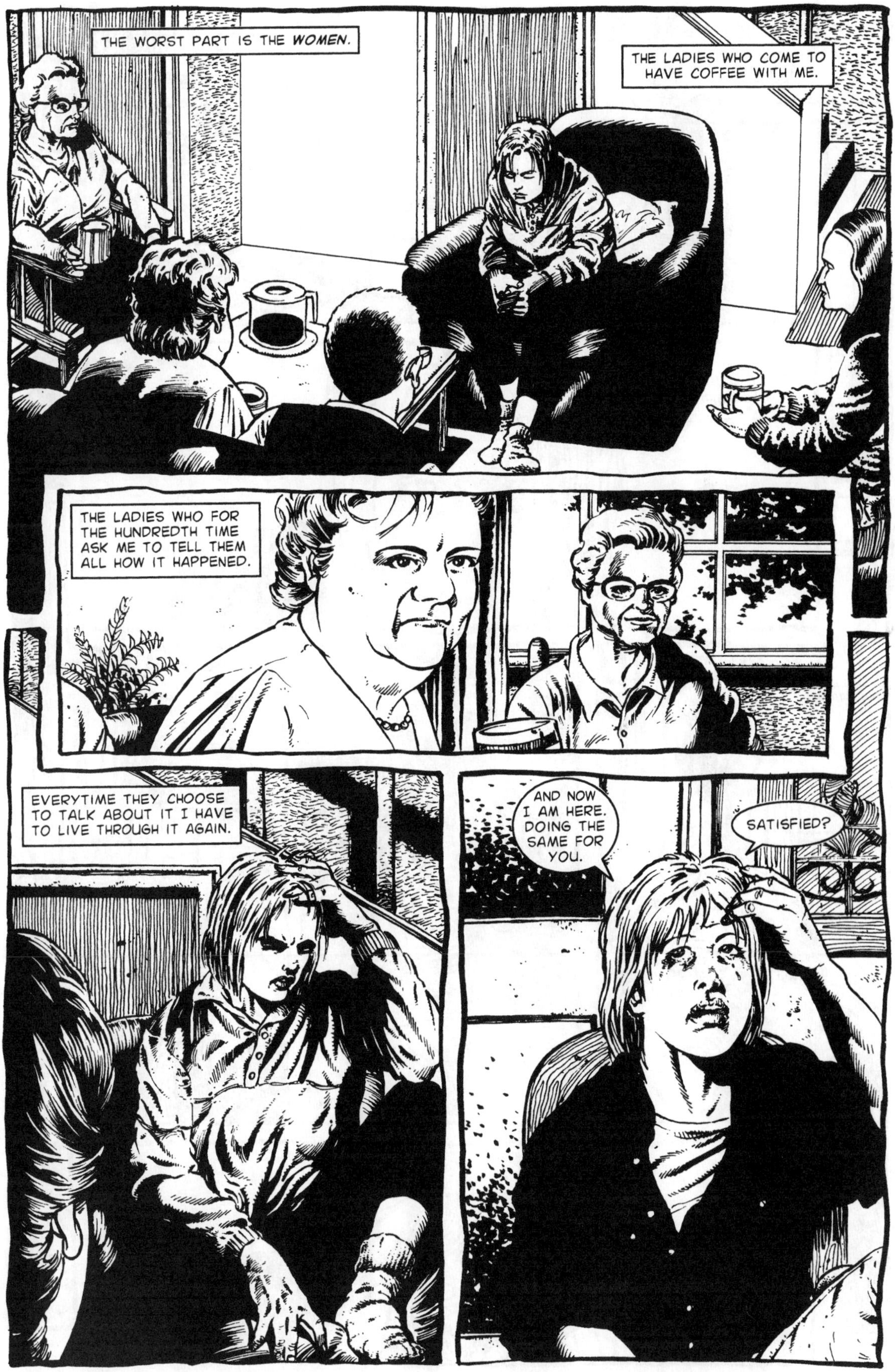
THE WORST PART IS THE *WOMEN*.
THE LADIES WHO COME TO HAVE COFFEE WITH ME.
THE LADIES WHO FOR THE HUNDREDTH TIME ASK ME TO TELL THEM ALL HOW IT HAPPENED.
EVERYTIME THEY CHOOSE TO TALK ABOUT IT I HAVE TO LIVE THROUGH IT AGAIN.
AND NOW I AM HERE. DOING THE SAME FOR YOU.
SATISFIED?

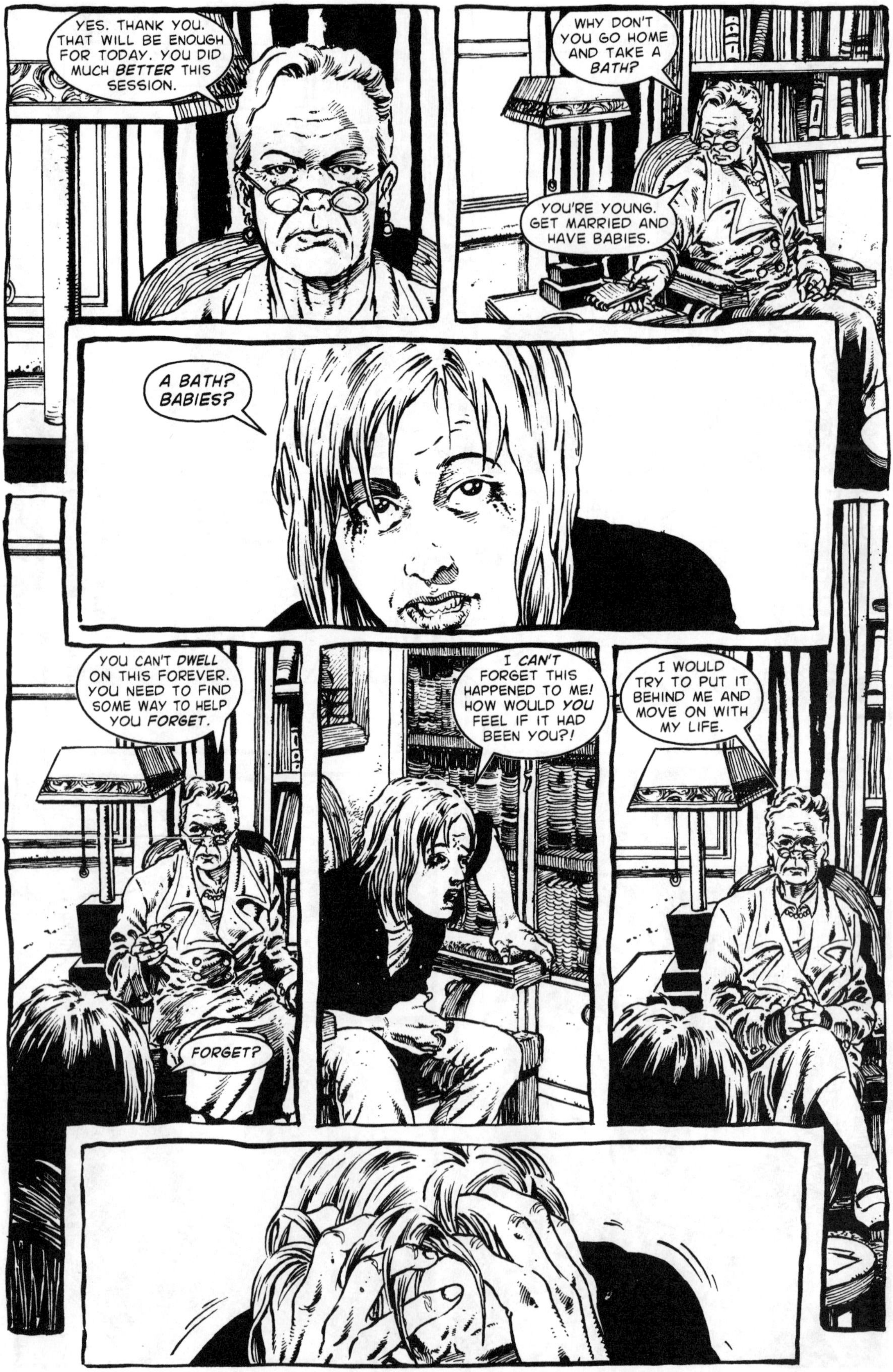
YES. THANK YOU. THAT WILL BE ENOUGH FOR TODAY. YOU DID MUCH BETTER THIS SESSION.
WHY DON'T YOU GO HOME AND TAKE A BATH?
YOU'RE YOUNG. GET MARRIED AND HAVE BABIES.
A BATH? BABIES?
YOU CAN'T DWELL ON THIS FOREVER. YOU NEED TO FIND SOME WAY TO HELP YOU FORGET.
FORGET?
I CAN'T FORGET THIS HAPPENED TO ME! HOW WOULD YOU FEEL IF IT HAD BEEN YOU?!
I WOULD TRY TO PUT IT BEHIND ME AND MOVE ON WITH MY LIFE.

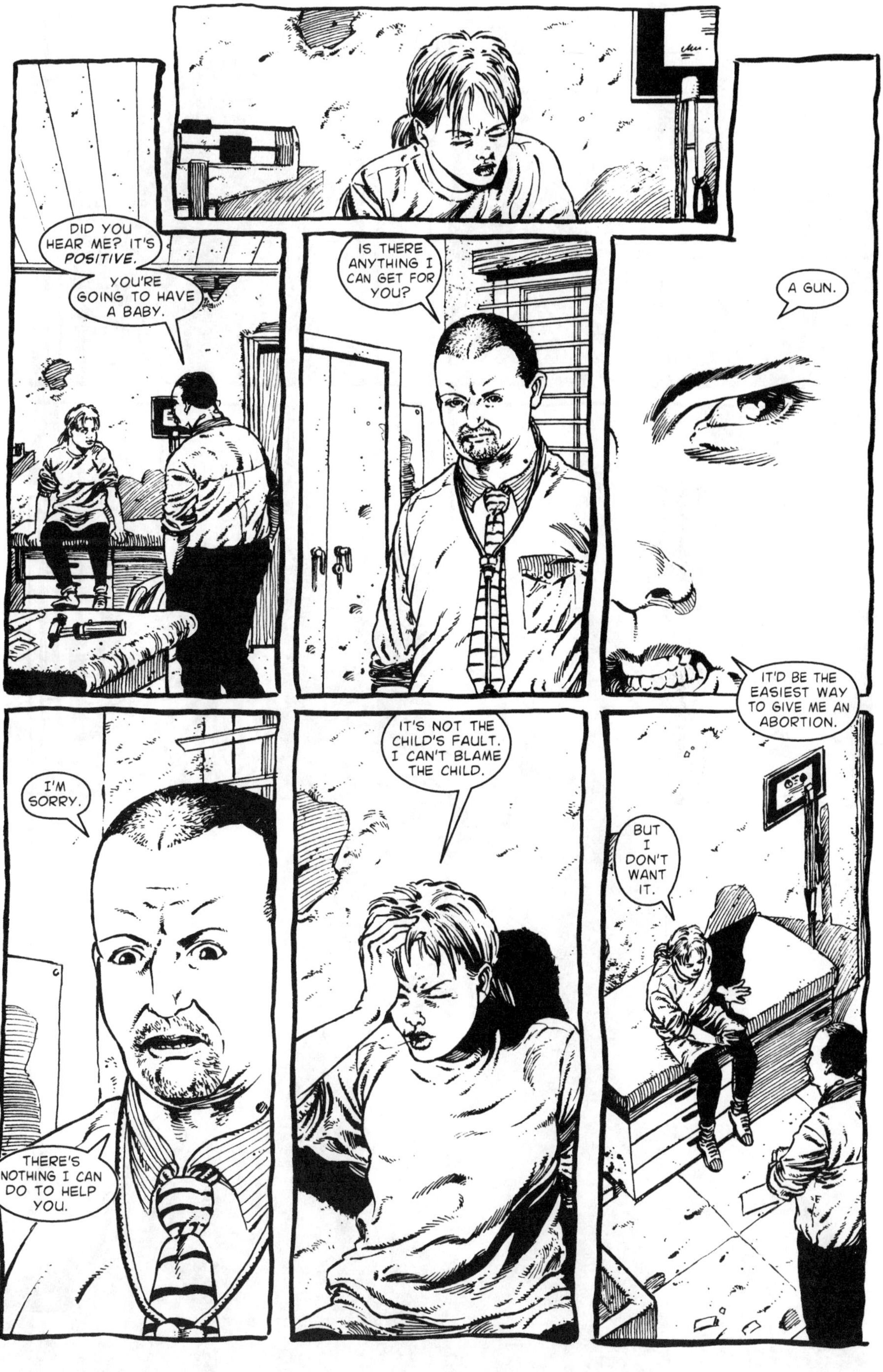
DID YOU HEAR ME? IT'S *POSITIVE.*
YOU'RE GOING TO HAVE A BABY.
IS THERE ANYTHING I CAN GET FOR YOU?
A GUN.
IT'D BE THE EASIEST WAY TO GIVE ME AN ABORTION.
I'M SORRY.
THERE'S NOTHING I CAN DO TO HELP YOU.
IT'S NOT THE CHILD'S FAULT. I CAN'T BLAME THE CHILD.
BUT I DON'T WANT IT.

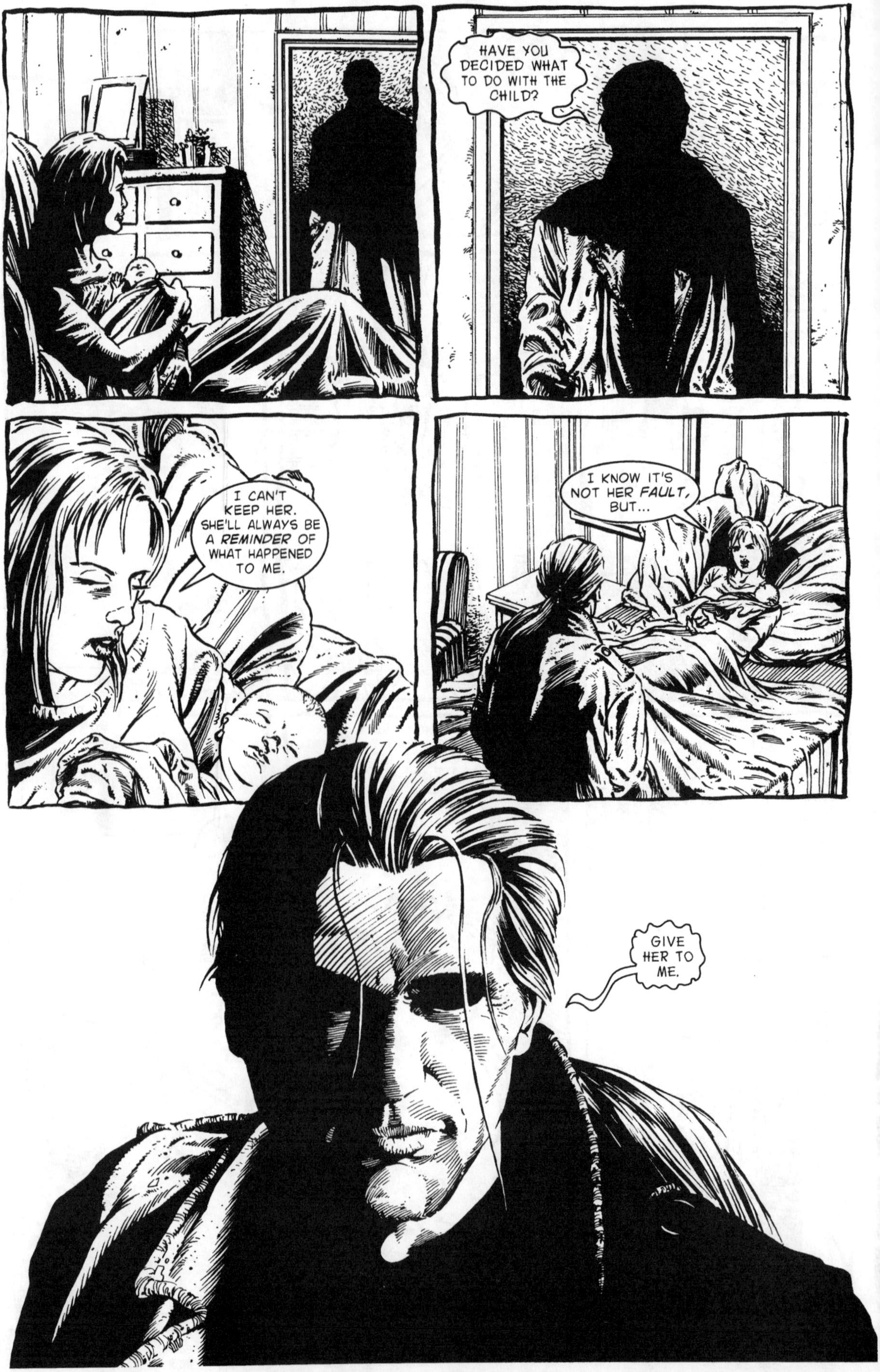
HAVE YOU DECIDED WHAT TO DO WITH THE CHILD?
I CAN'T KEEP HER. SHE'LL ALWAYS BE A *REMINDER* OF WHAT HAPPENED TO ME.
I KNOW IT'S NOT HER *FAULT*, BUT...
GIVE HER TO ME.

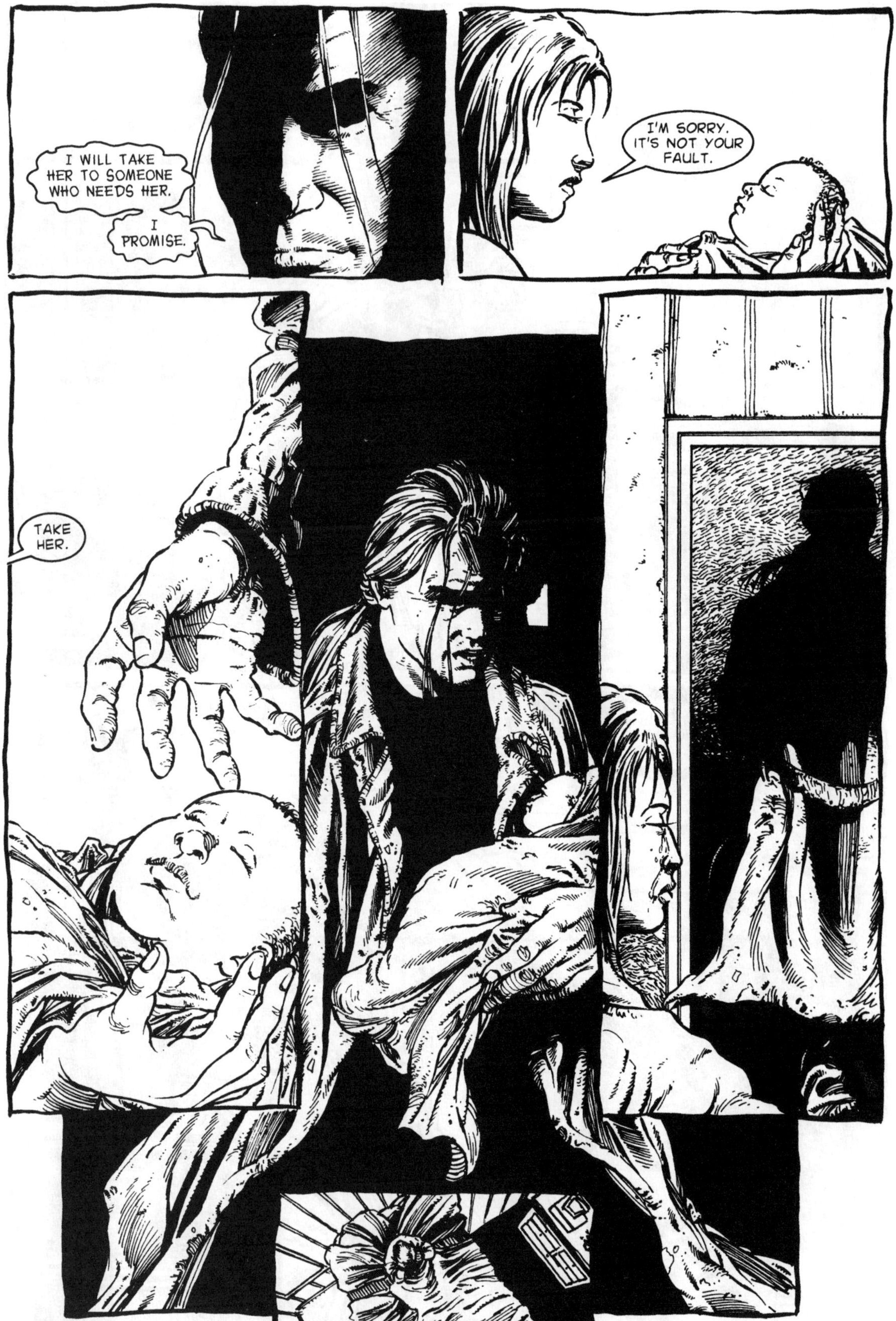
I WILL TAKE HER TO SOMEONE WHO NEEDS HER.
I PROMISE.
I'M SORRY. IT'S NOT YOUR FAULT.
TAKE HER.

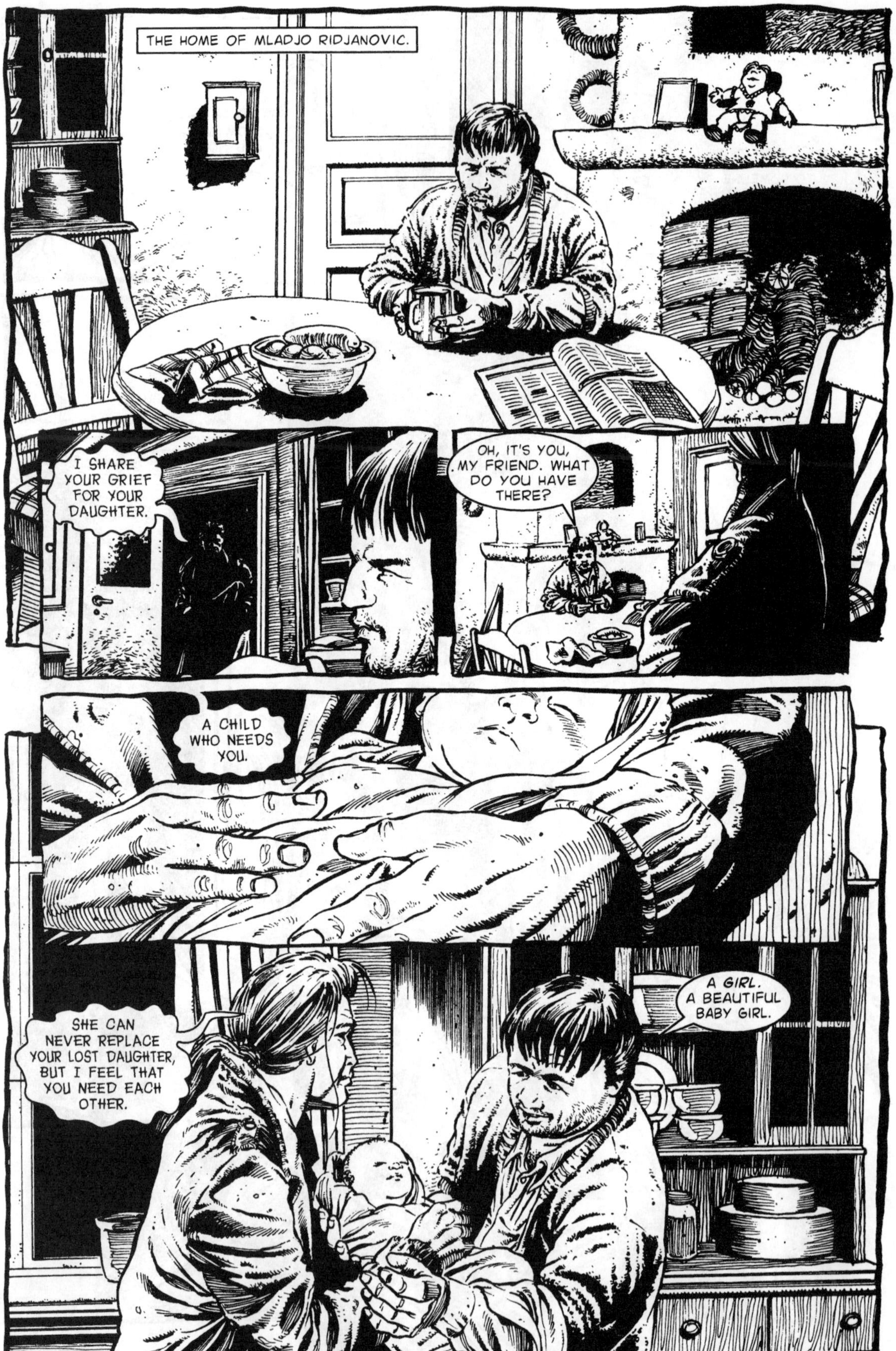
THE HOME OF MLADJO RIDJANOVIC.
I SHARE YOUR GRIEF FOR YOUR DAUGHTER.
OH, IT'S YOU, MY FRIEND. WHAT DO YOU HAVE THERE?
A CHILD WHO NEEDS YOU.
SHE CAN NEVER REPLACE YOUR LOST DAUGHTER, BUT I FEEL THAT YOU NEED EACH OTHER.
A GIRL. A BEAUTIFUL BABY GIRL.

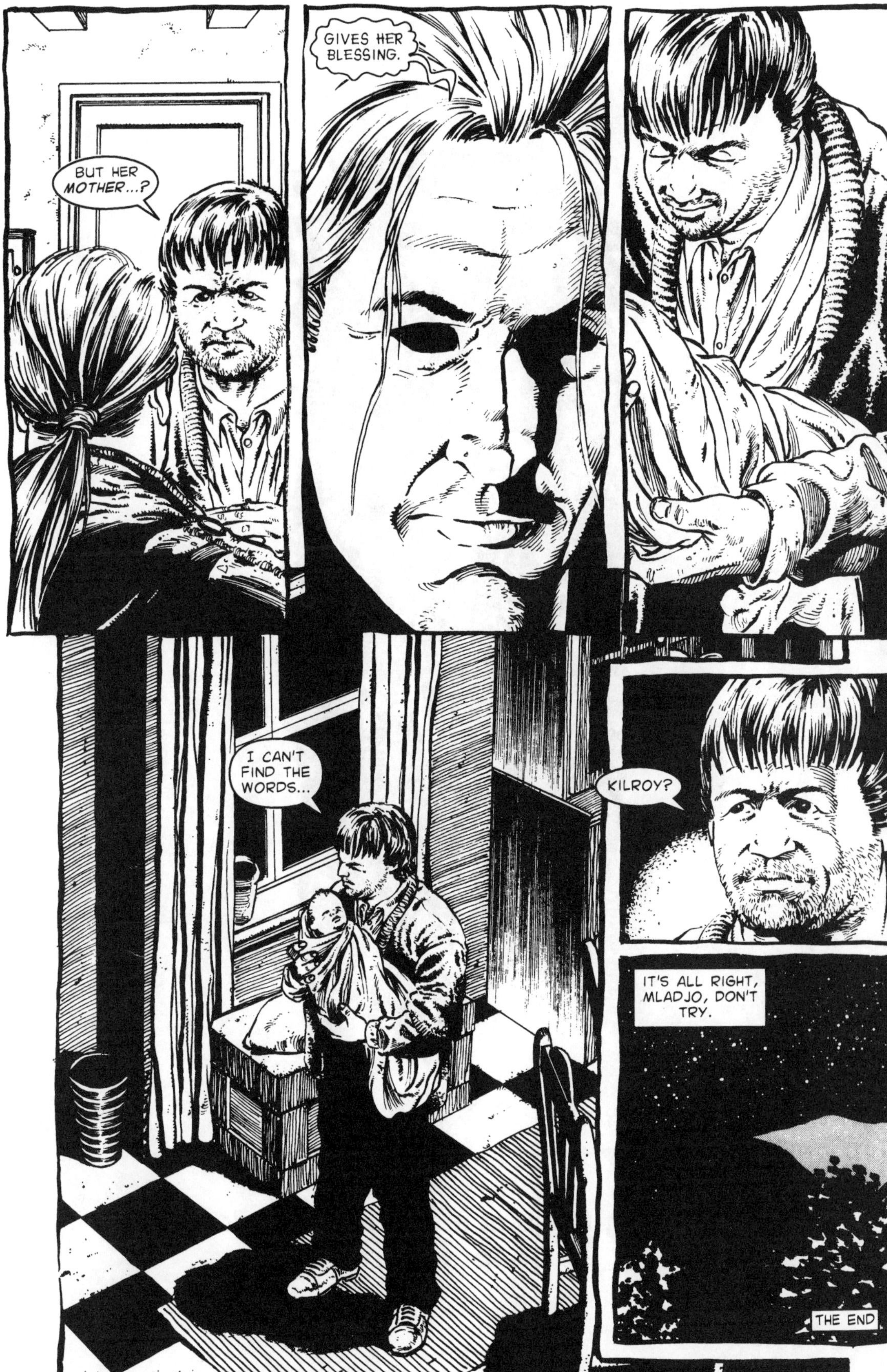
BUT HER MOTHER...?
GIVES HER BLESSING.
I CAN'T FIND THE WORDS...
KILROY?
IT'S ALL RIGHT, MLADJO, DON'T TRY.
THE END

"Pride, Prejudice and Persecution"
Chapter Three

HELL HAS FROZEN OVER.

THE BLOOD-DRENCHED BATTLEFIELDS HAVE BECOME A FROZEN TUNDRA THAT DOESN'T DISCRIMINATE AMONG THE RIGHT OR THE WRONG, THE LIVING NOR THE DEAD.

IT ATTACKS BOTH SIDES WITHOUT COMPASSION OR REMORSE WITH ITS BITTER, BONE-NUMBING WRATH.

NEITHER SIDE OF THIS MINDLESS, ABOMINATION CALLED WAR SEEM TO NOTICE THE CHANGING SEASONS.

THE BATTLES CONTINUE TO RAGE AND THE BLOOD CONTINUES TO DRIP INTO THE NEWLY, FALLEN SNOW.

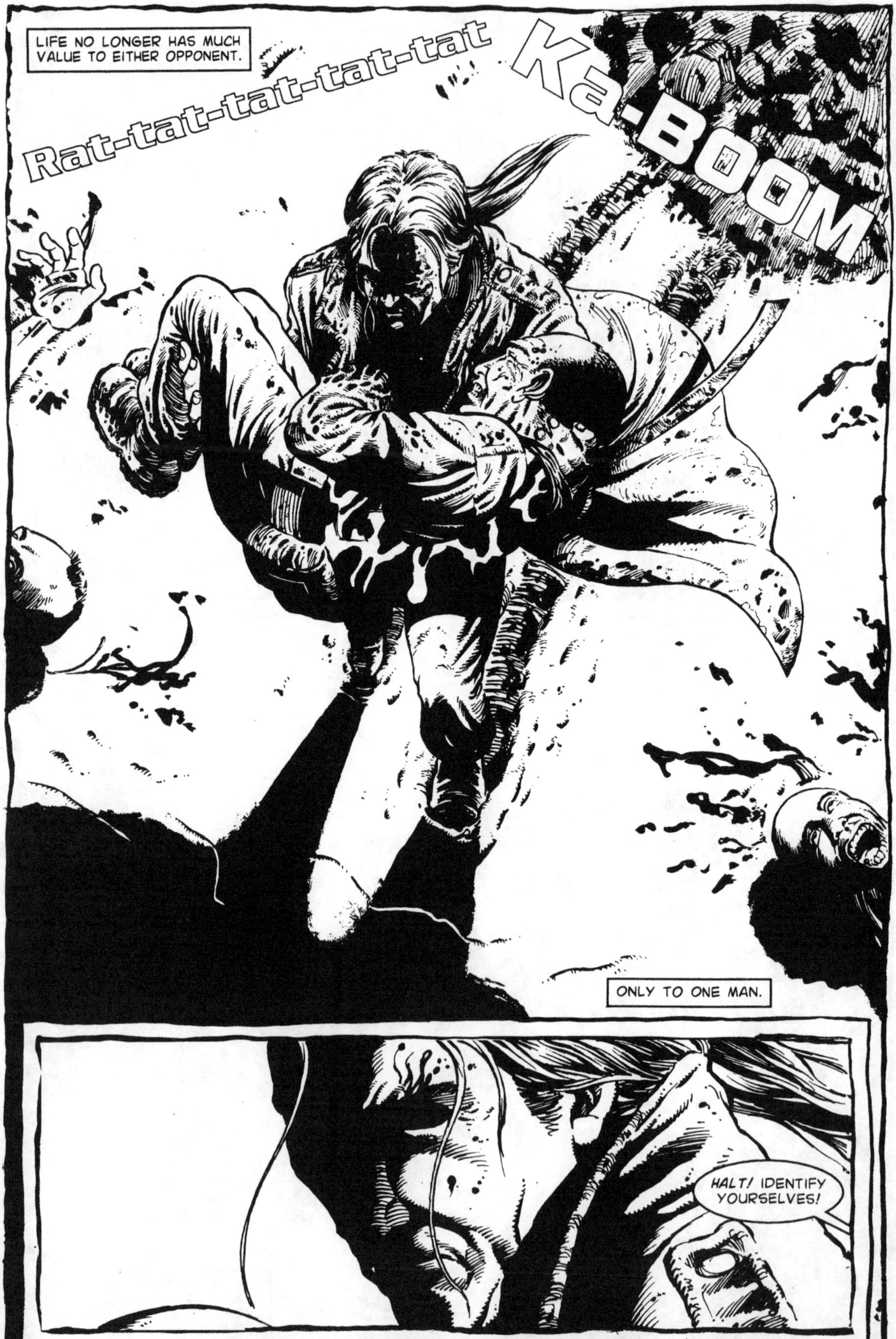
LIFE NO LONGER HAS MUCH VALUE TO EITHER OPPONENT.
Rat-tat-tat-tat-tat
Ka-BOOM
ONLY TO ONE MAN.
HALT! IDENTIFY YOURSELVES!

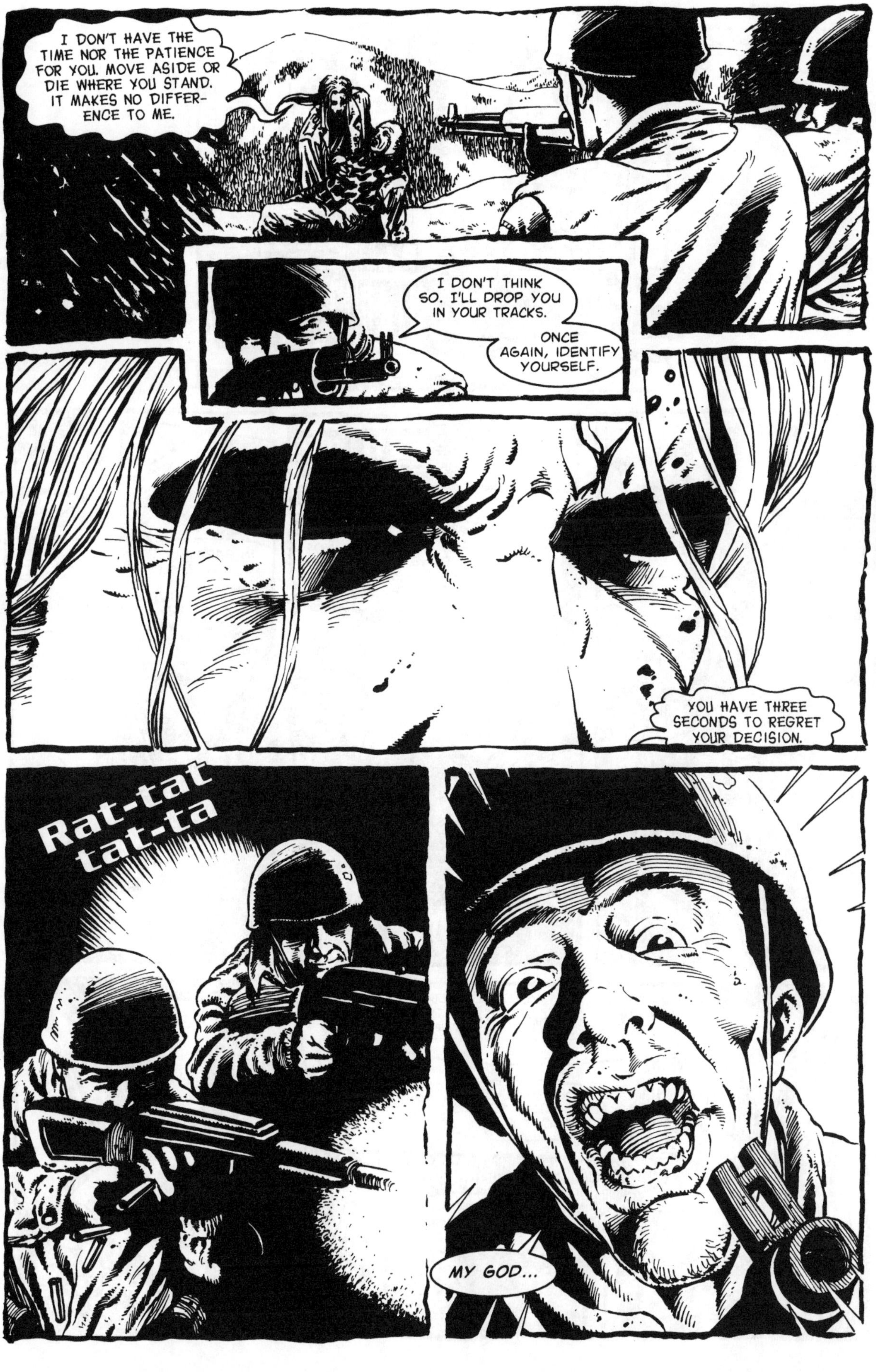
I DON'T HAVE THE TIME NOR THE PATIENCE FOR YOU. MOVE ASIDE OR DIE WHERE YOU STAND. IT MAKES NO DIFFERENCE TO ME.
I DON'T THINK SO. I'LL DROP YOU IN YOUR TRACKS.
ONCE AGAIN, IDENTIFY YOURSELF.
YOU HAVE THREE SECONDS TO REGRET YOUR DECISION.
Rat-tat tat-ta
MY GOD...

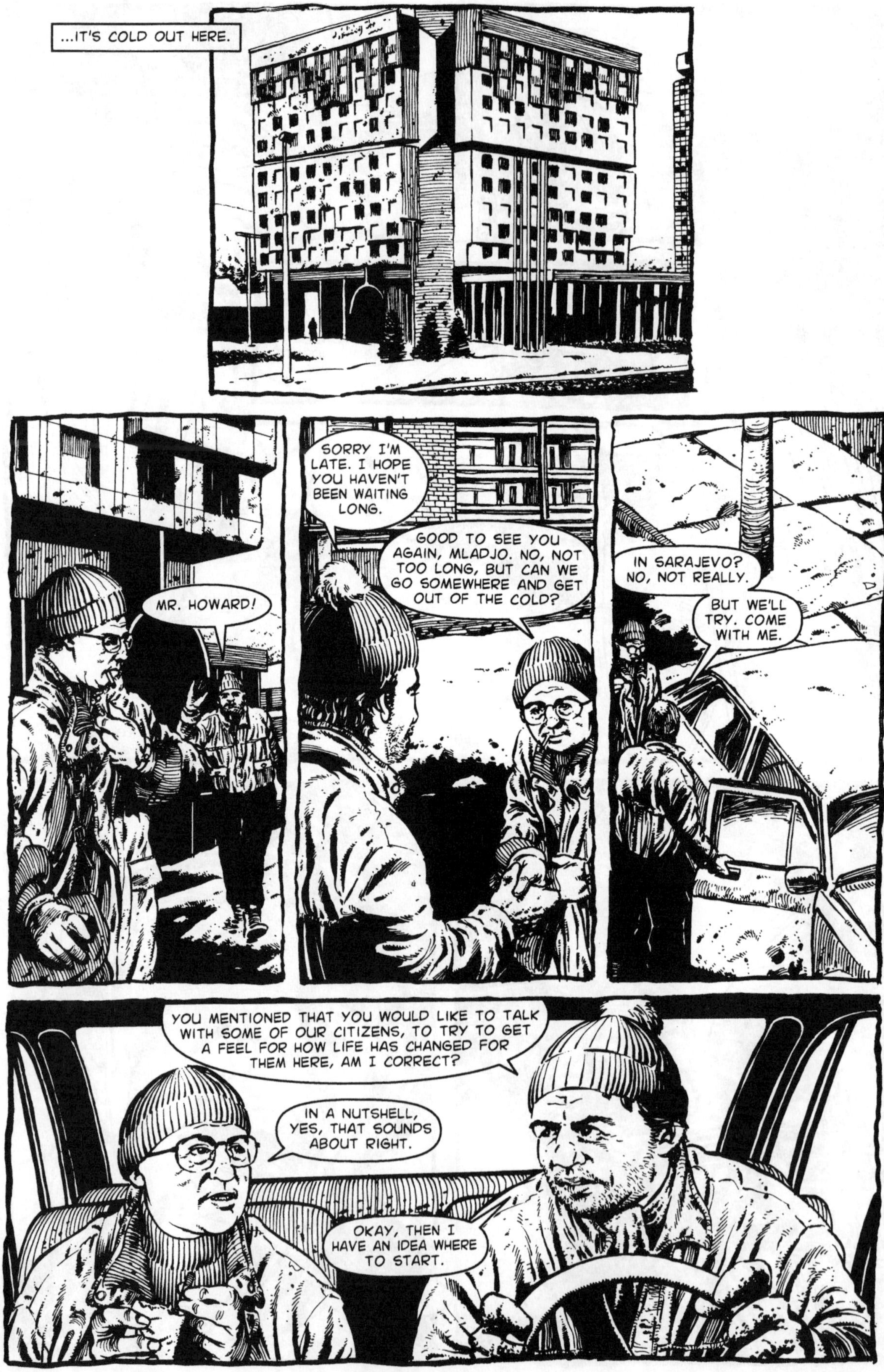
...IT'S COLD OUT HERE.
MR. HOWARD!
SORRY I'M LATE. I HOPE YOU HAVEN'T BEEN WAITING LONG.
GOOD TO SEE YOU AGAIN, MLADJO. NO, NOT TOO LONG, BUT CAN WE GO SOMEWHERE AND GET OUT OF THE COLD?
IN SARAJEVO? NO, NOT REALLY.
BUT WE'LL TRY. COME WITH ME.
YOU MENTIONED THAT YOU WOULD LIKE TO TALK WITH SOME OF OUR CITIZENS, TO TRY TO GET A FEEL FOR HOW LIFE HAS CHANGED FOR THEM HERE, AM I CORRECT?
IN A NUTSHELL, YES, THAT SOUNDS ABOUT RIGHT.
OKAY, THEN I HAVE AN IDEA WHERE TO START.

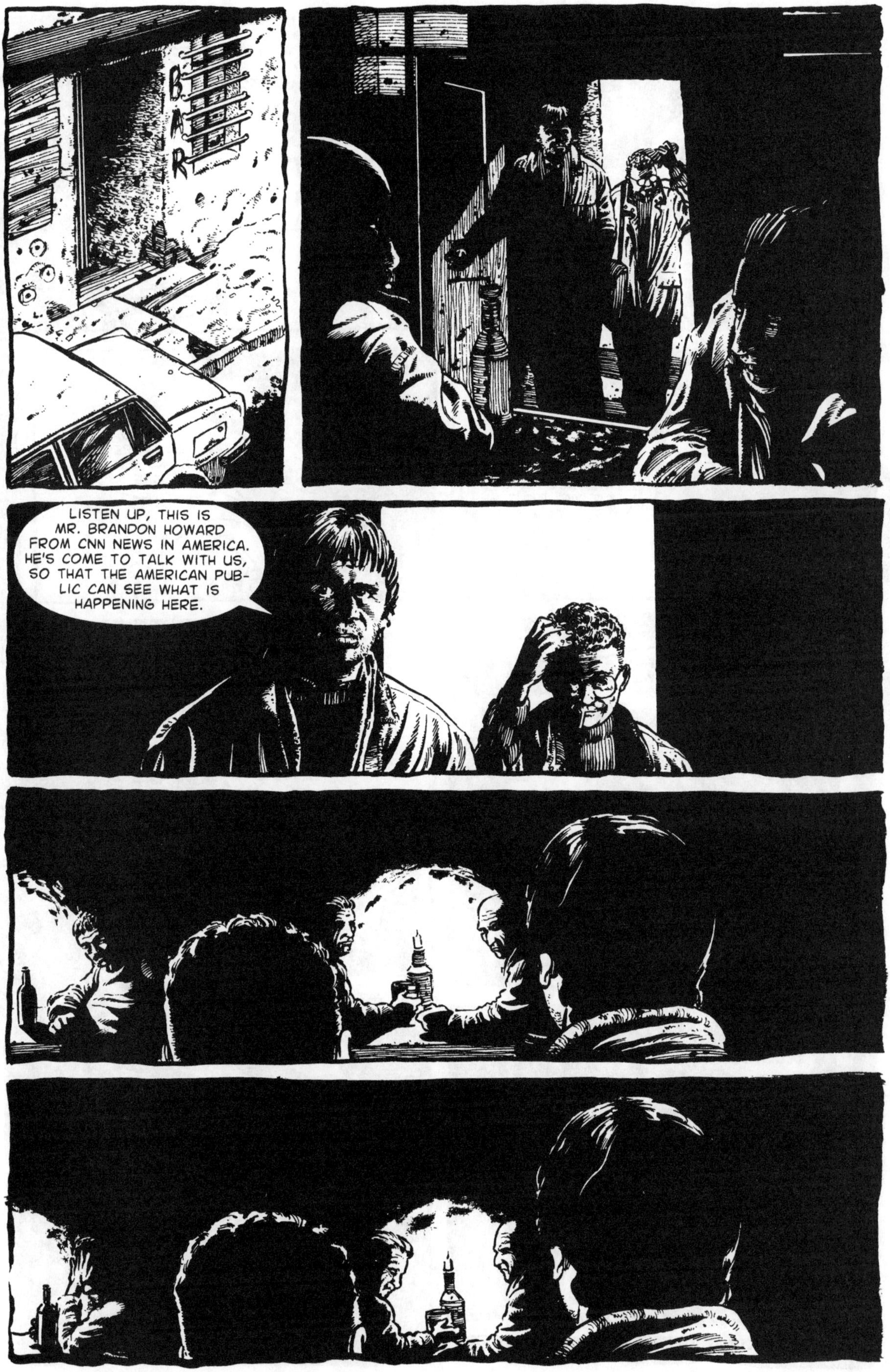
BAR
LISTEN UP, THIS IS MR. BRANDON HOWARD FROM CNN NEWS IN AMERICA. HE'S COME TO TALK WITH US, SO THAT THE AMERICAN PUBLIC CAN SEE WHAT IS HAPPENING HERE.

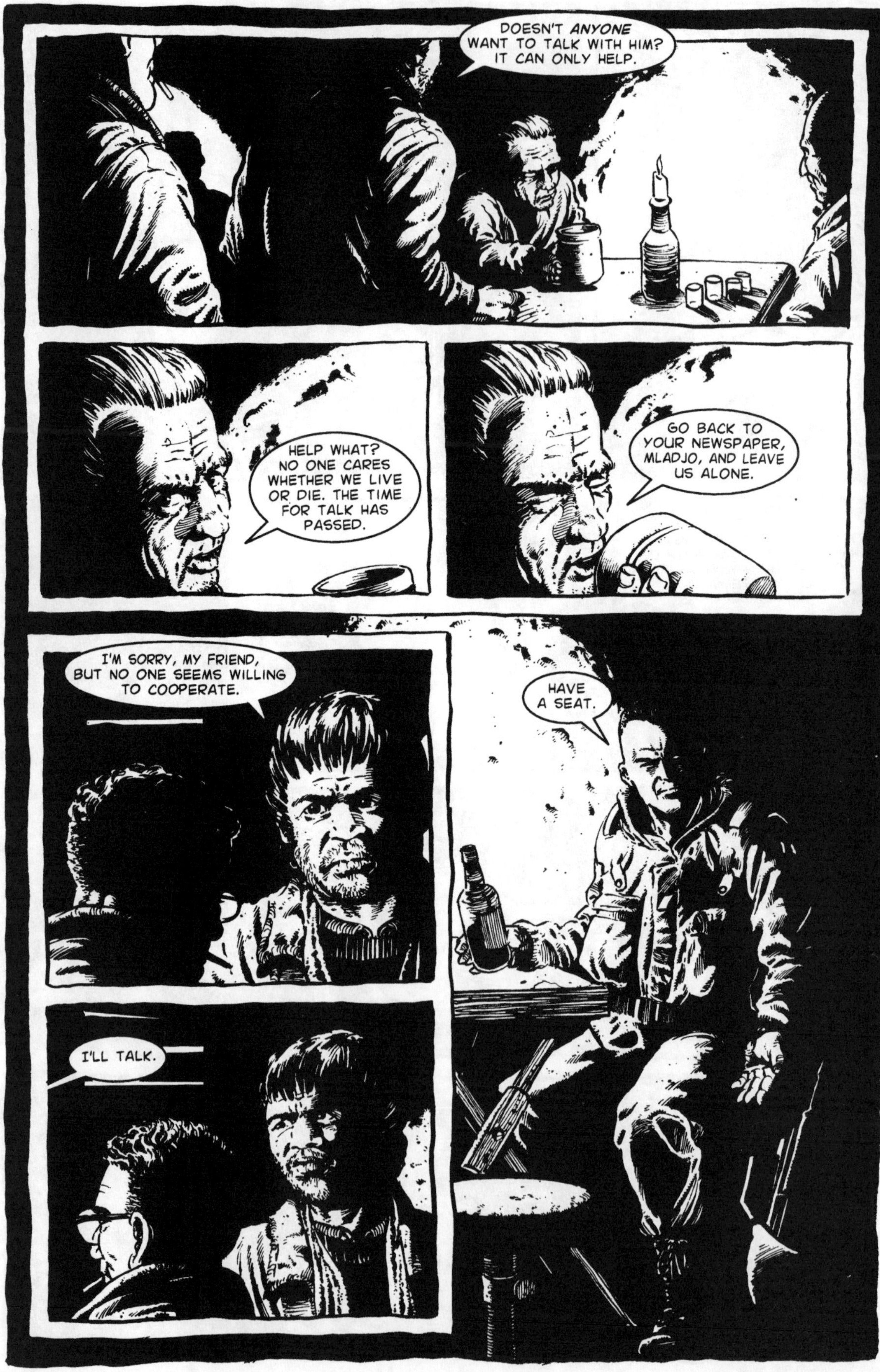
DOESN'T ANYONE WANT TO TALK WITH HIM? IT CAN ONLY HELP.
HELP WHAT? NO ONE CARES WHETHER WE LIVE OR DIE. THE TIME FOR TALK HAS PASSED.
GO BACK TO YOUR NEWSPAPER, MLADJO, AND LEAVE US ALONE.
I'M SORRY, MY FRIEND, BUT NO ONE SEEMS WILLING TO COOPERATE.
I'LL TALK.
HAVE A SEAT.

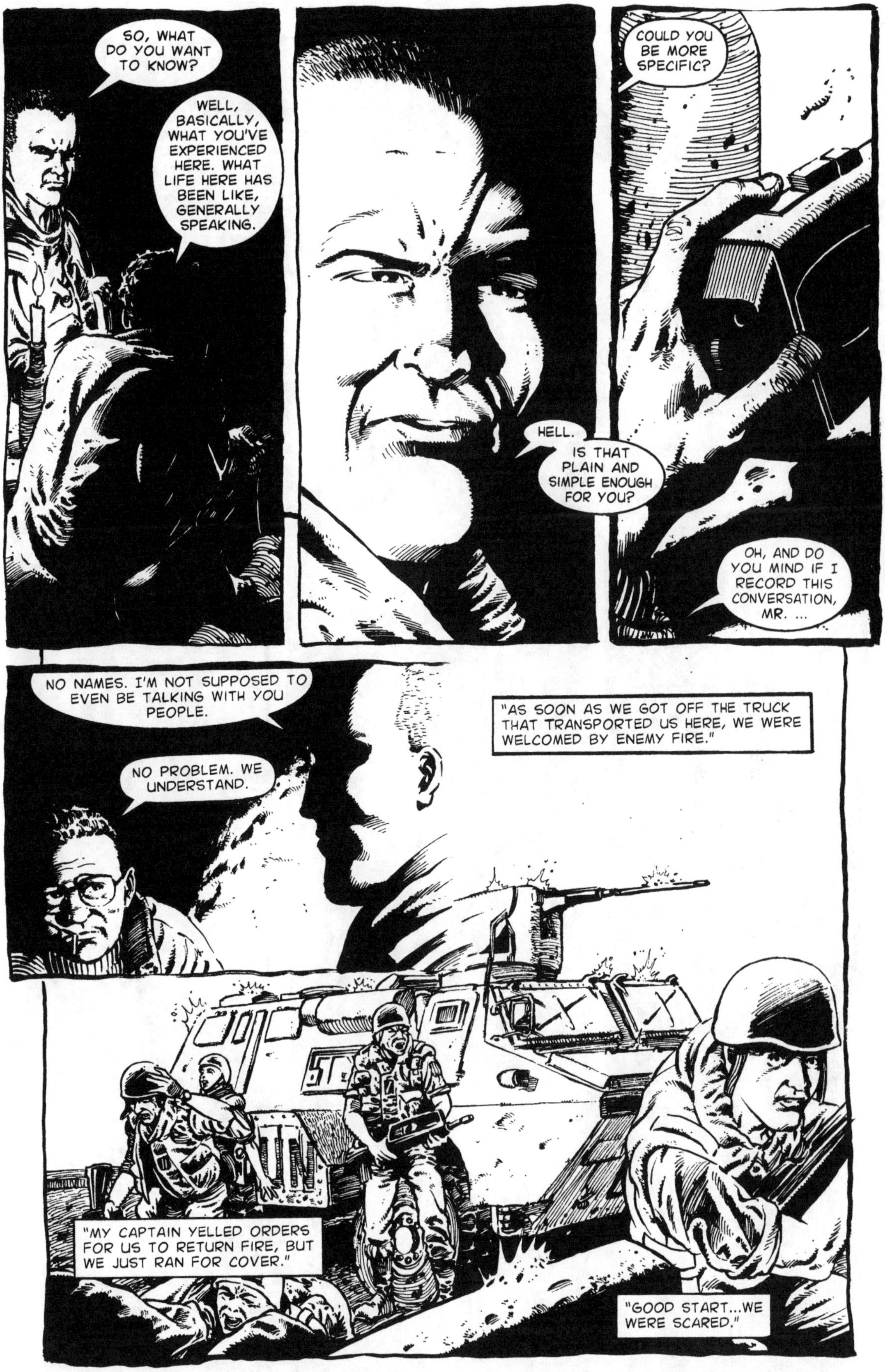

SO, WHAT DO YOU WANT TO KNOW?
WELL, BASICALLY, WHAT YOU'VE EXPERIENCED HERE. WHAT LIFE HERE HAS BEEN LIKE, GENERALLY SPEAKING.
HELL. IS THAT PLAIN AND SIMPLE ENOUGH FOR YOU?
COULD YOU BE MORE SPECIFIC?
OH, AND DO YOU MIND IF I RECORD THIS CONVERSATION, MR. ...
NO NAMES. I'M NOT SUPPOSED TO EVEN BE TALKING WITH YOU PEOPLE.
NO PROBLEM. WE UNDERSTAND.
"AS SOON AS WE GOT OFF THE TRUCK THAT TRANSPORTED US HERE, WE WERE WELCOMED BY ENEMY FIRE."
"MY CAPTAIN YELLED ORDERS FOR US TO RETURN FIRE, BUT WE JUST RAN FOR COVER."
"GOOD START...WE WERE SCARED."

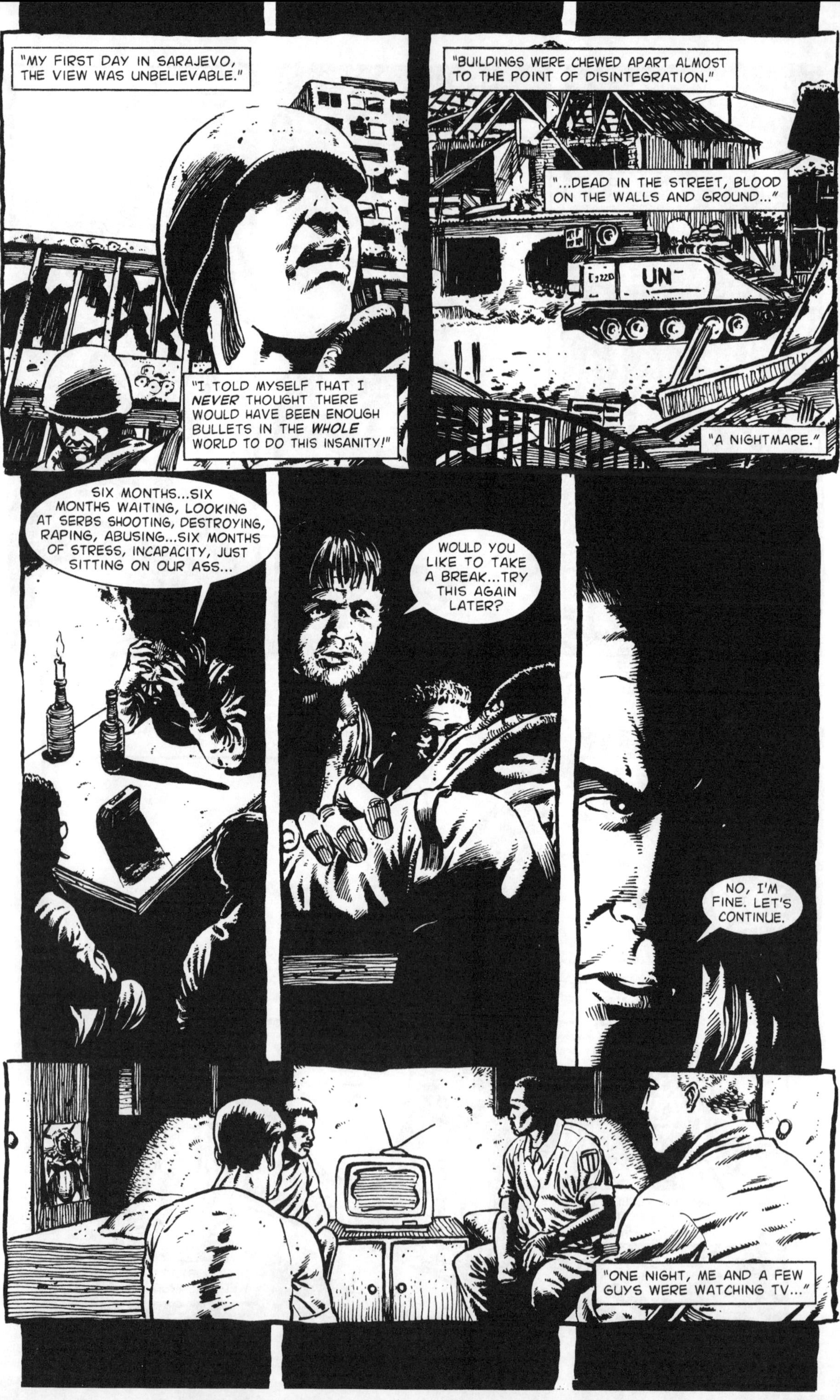

"MY FIRST DAY IN SARAJEVO, THE VIEW WAS UNBELIEVABLE."
"I TOLD MYSELF THAT I NEVER THOUGHT THERE WOULD HAVE BEEN ENOUGH BULLETS IN THE WHOLE WORLD TO DO THIS INSANITY!"
"BUILDINGS WERE CHEWED APART ALMOST TO THE POINT OF DISINTEGRATION."
"...DEAD IN THE STREET, BLOOD ON THE WALLS AND GROUND..."
UN
"A NIGHTMARE."
SIX MONTHS...SIX MONTHS WAITING, LOOKING AT SERBS SHOOTING, DESTROYING, RAPING, ABUSING...SIX MONTHS OF STRESS, INCAPACITY, JUST SITTING ON OUR ASS...
WOULD YOU LIKE TO TAKE A BREAK...TRY THIS AGAIN LATER?
NO, I'M FINE. LET'S CONTINUE.
"ONE NIGHT, ME AND A FEW GUYS WERE WATCHING TV..."

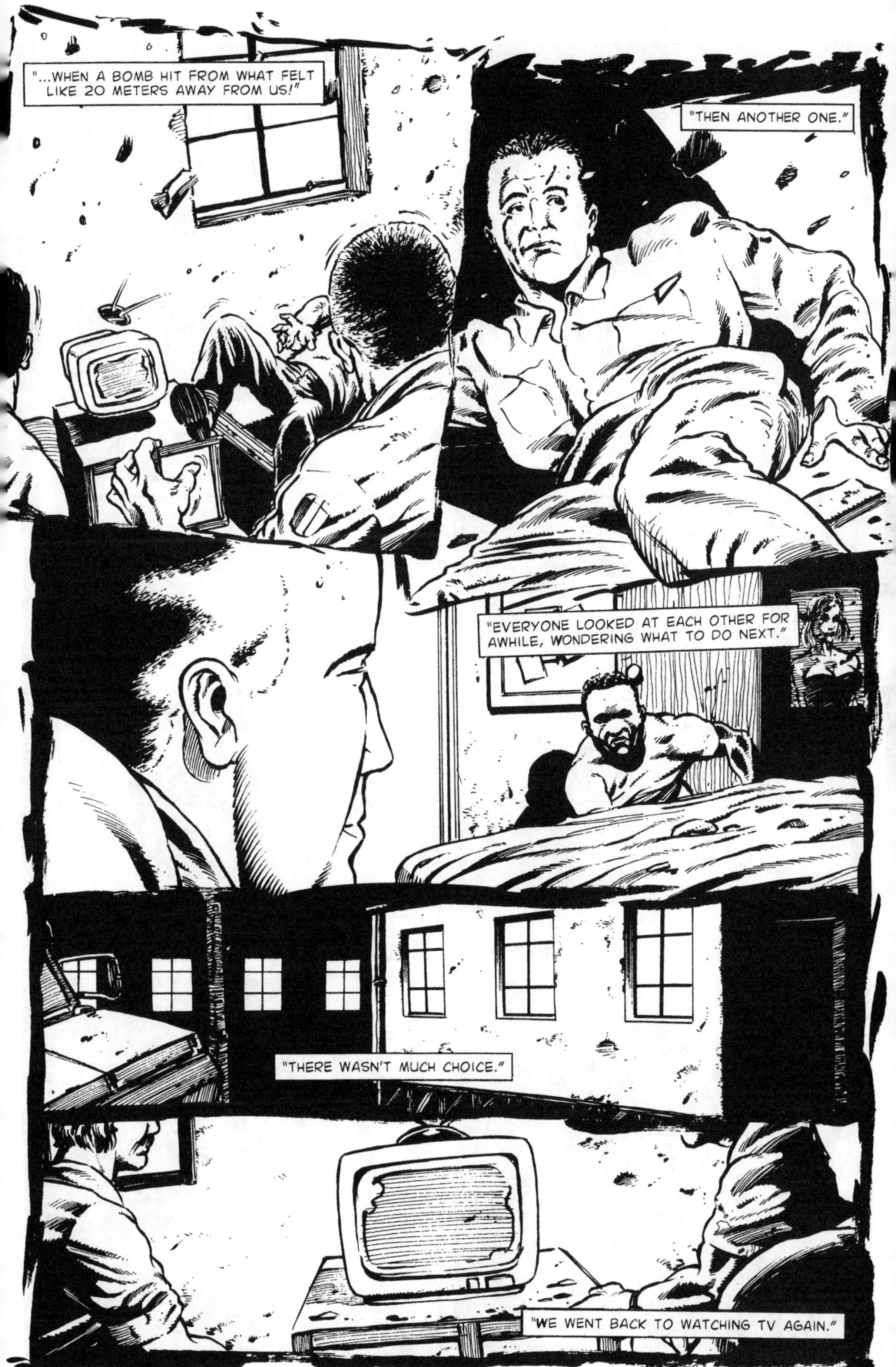
"...WHEN A BOMB HIT FROM WHAT FELT LIKE 20 METERS AWAY FROM US!"
"THEN ANOTHER ONE."
"EVERYONE LOOKED AT EACH OTHER FOR AWHILE, WONDERING WHAT TO DO NEXT."
"THERE WASN'T MUCH CHOICE."
"WE WENT BACK TO WATCHING TV AGAIN."

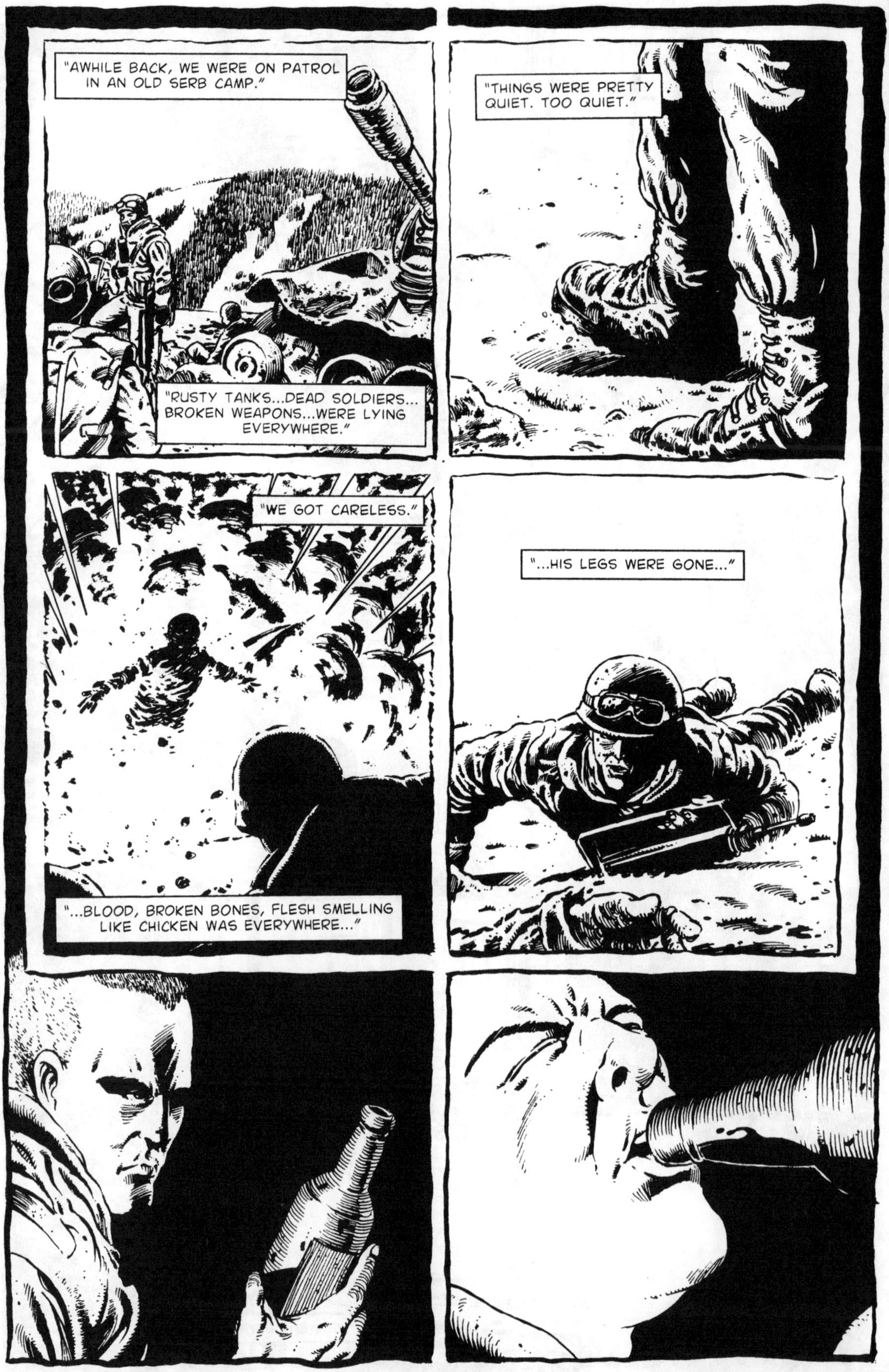
"AWHILE BACK, WE WERE ON PATROL IN AN OLD SERB CAMP."
"RUSTY TANKS...DEAD SOLDIERS... BROKEN WEAPONS...WERE LYING EVERYWHERE."
"THINGS WERE PRETTY QUIET. TOO QUIET."
"WE GOT CARELESS."
"...BLOOD, BROKEN BONES, FLESH SMELLING LIKE CHICKEN WAS EVERYWHERE..."
"...HIS LEGS WERE GONE..."

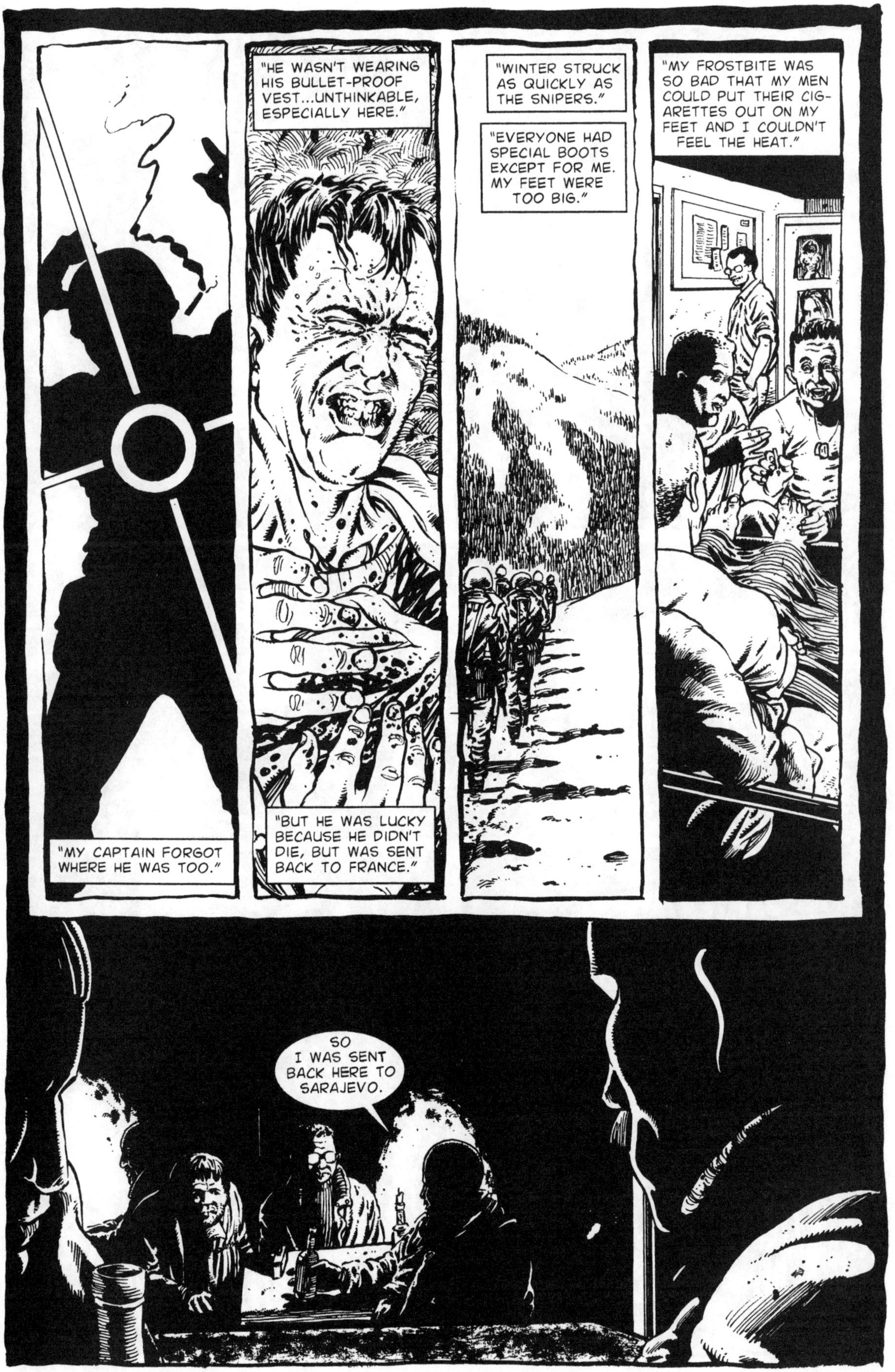
"MY CAPTAIN FORGOT WHERE HE WAS TOO."
"HE WASN'T WEARING HIS BULLET-PROOF VEST...UNTHINKABLE, ESPECIALLY HERE."
"BUT HE WAS LUCKY BECAUSE HE DIDN'T DIE, BUT WAS SENT BACK TO FRANCE."
"WINTER STRUCK AS QUICKLY AS THE SNIPERS."
"EVERYONE HAD SPECIAL BOOTS EXCEPT FOR ME. MY FEET WERE TOO BIG."
"MY FROSTBITE WAS SO BAD THAT MY MEN COULD PUT THEIR CIG-ARETTES OUT ON MY FEET AND I COULDN'T FEEL THE HEAT."
SO I WAS SENT BACK HERE TO SARAJEVO.

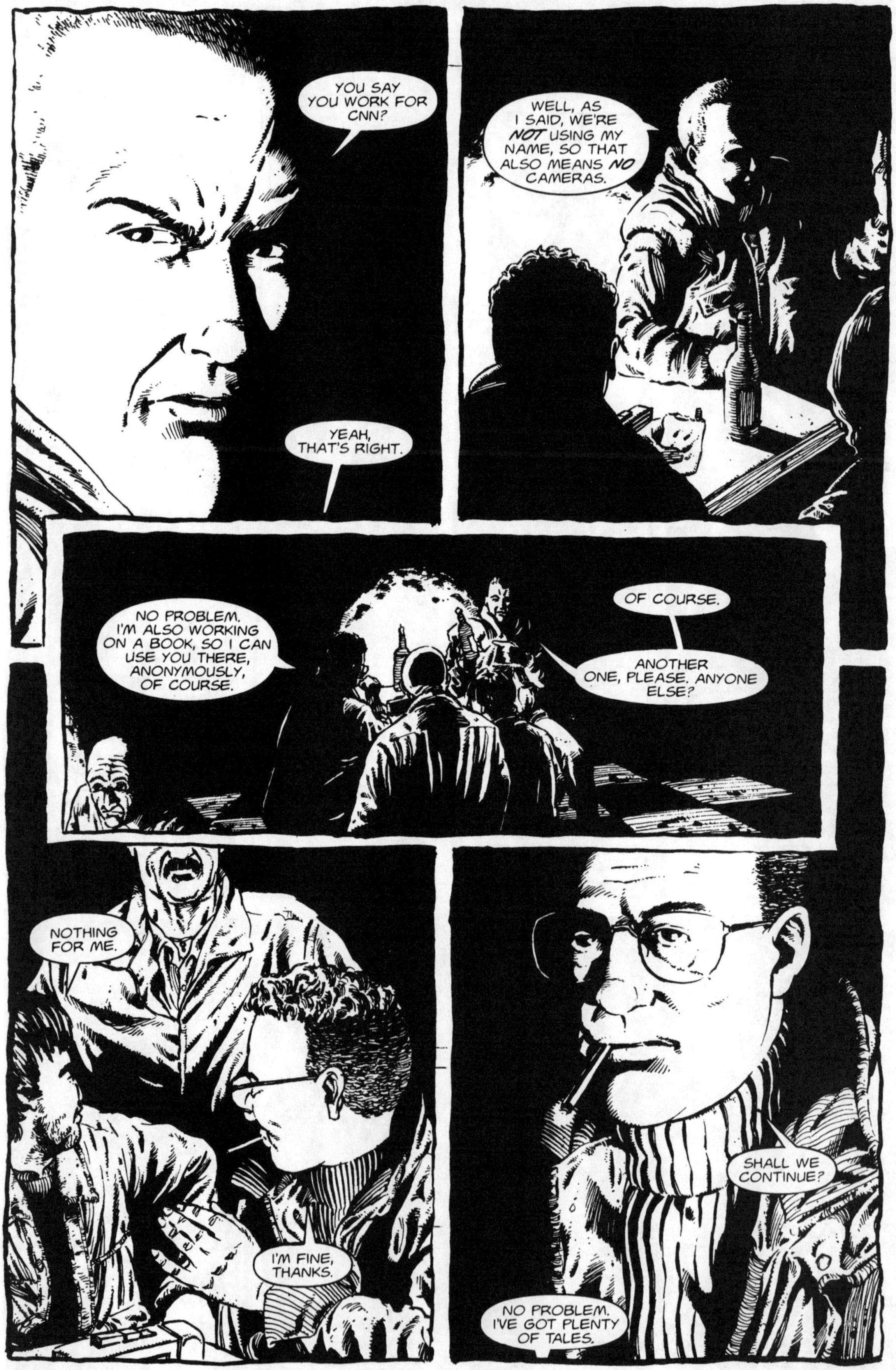
YOU SAY YOU WORK FOR CNN?
YEAH, THAT'S RIGHT.
WELL, AS I SAID, WE'RE *NOT* USING MY NAME, SO THAT ALSO MEANS *NO* CAMERAS.
NO PROBLEM. I'M ALSO WORKING ON A BOOK, SO I CAN USE YOU THERE, ANONYMOUSLY, OF COURSE.
OF COURSE.
ANOTHER ONE, PLEASE. ANYONE ELSE?
NOTHING FOR ME.
I'M FINE, THANKS.
SHALL WE CONTINUE?
NO PROBLEM. I'VE GOT PLENTY OF TALES.

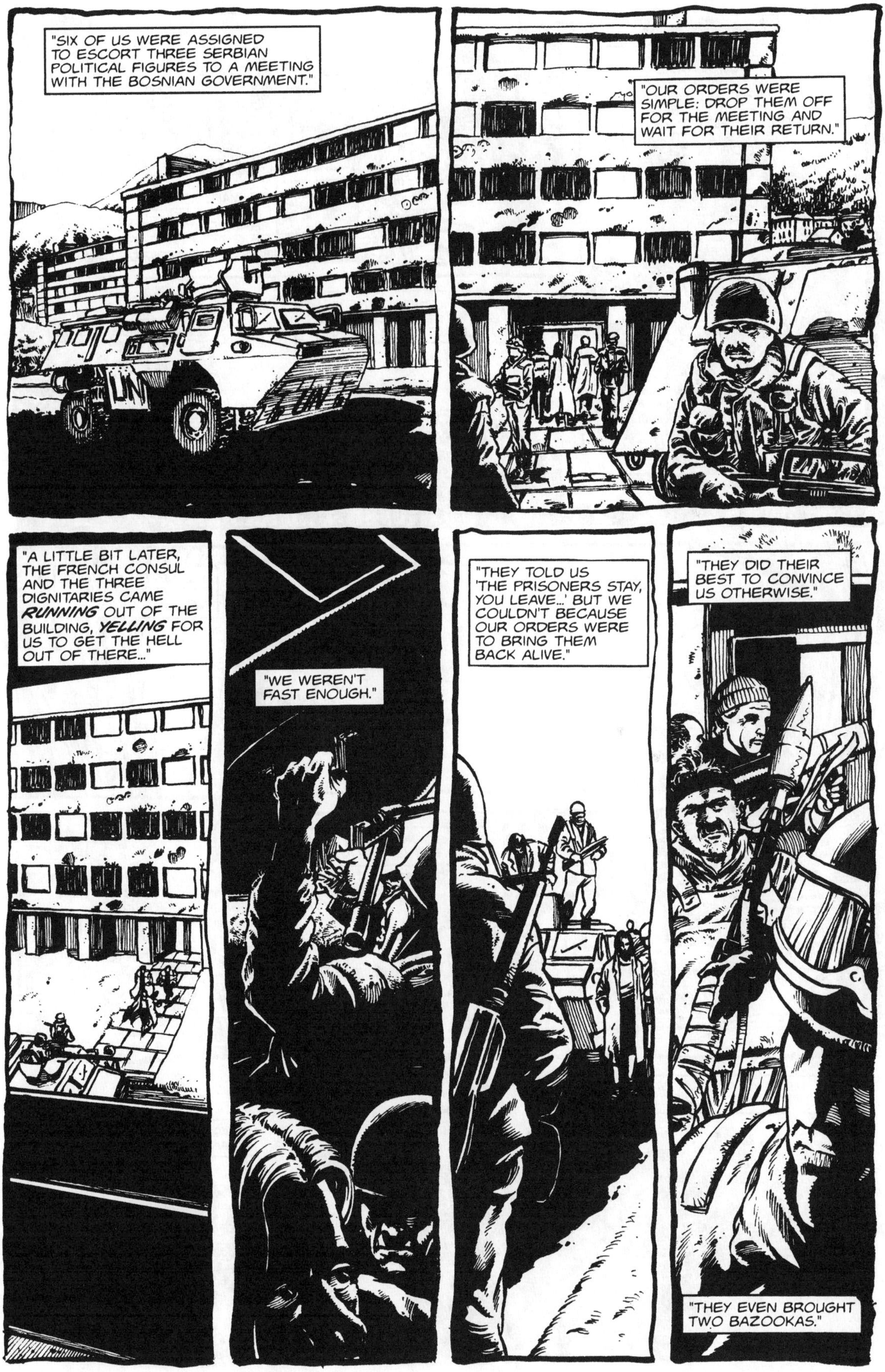
"SIX OF US WERE ASSIGNED TO ESCORT THREE SERBIAN POLITICAL FIGURES TO A MEETING WITH THE BOSNIAN GOVERNMENT."
UN
UN
"OUR ORDERS WERE SIMPLE: DROP THEM OFF FOR THE MEETING AND WAIT FOR THEIR RETURN."
"A LITTLE BIT LATER, THE FRENCH CONSUL AND THE THREE DIGNITARIES CAME ***RUNNING*** OUT OF THE BUILDING, ***YELLING*** FOR US TO GET THE HELL OUT OF THERE..."
"WE WEREN'T FAST ENOUGH."
"THEY TOLD US 'THE PRISONERS STAY, YOU LEAVE...' BUT WE COULDN'T BECAUSE OUR ORDERS WERE TO BRING THEM BACK ALIVE."
"THEY DID THEIR BEST TO CONVINCE US OTHERWISE."
"THEY EVEN BROUGHT TWO BAZOOKAS."

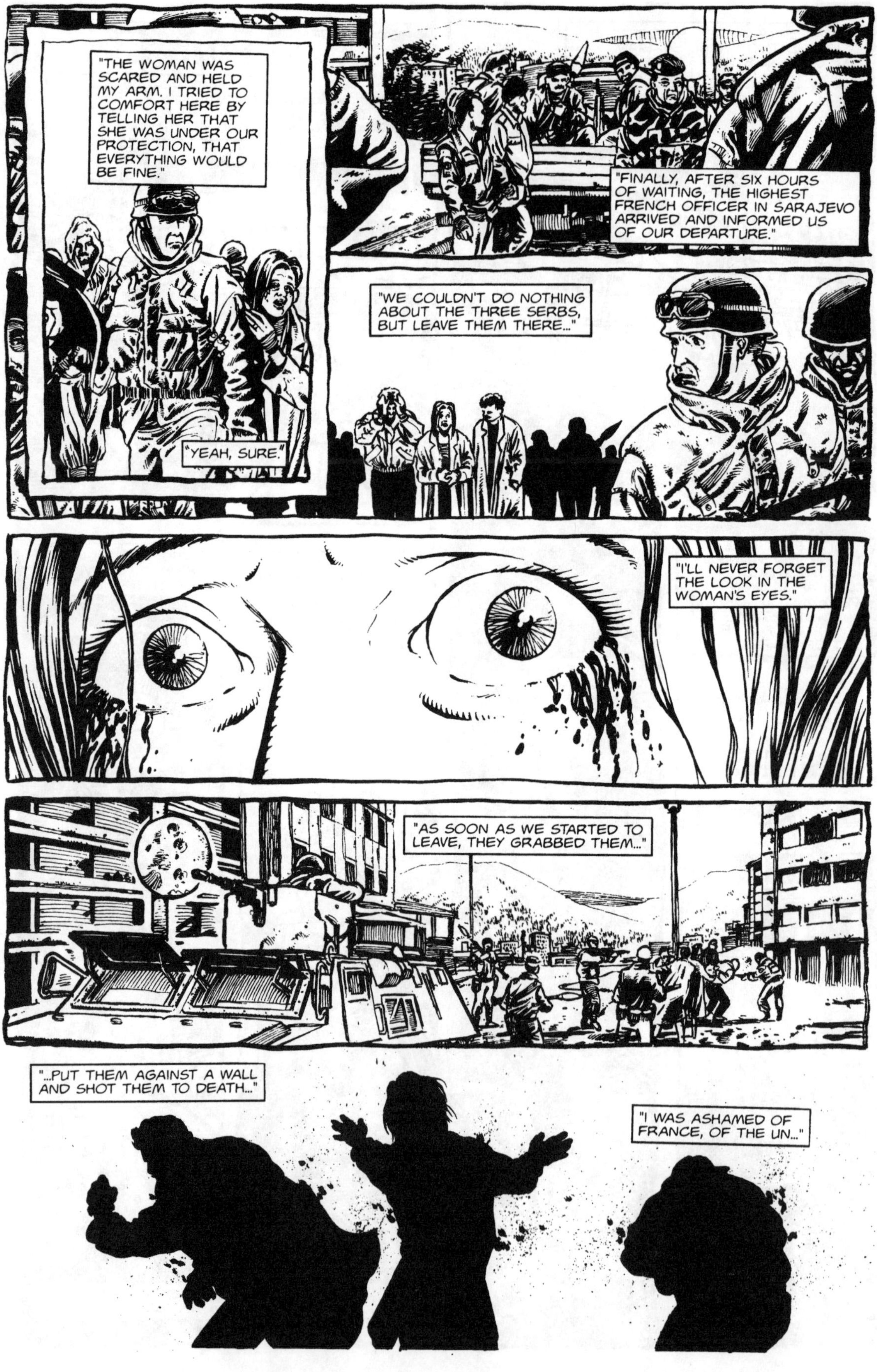
"THE WOMAN WAS SCARED AND HELD MY ARM. I TRIED TO COMFORT HERE BY TELLING HER THAT SHE WAS UNDER OUR PROTECTION, THAT EVERYTHING WOULD BE FINE."
"YEAH, SURE."
"FINALLY, AFTER SIX HOURS OF WAITING, THE HIGHEST FRENCH OFFICER IN SARAJEVO ARRIVED AND INFORMED US OF OUR DEPARTURE."
"WE COULDN'T DO NOTHING ABOUT THE THREE SERBS, BUT LEAVE THEM THERE..."
"I'LL NEVER FORGET THE LOOK IN THE WOMAN'S EYES."
"AS SOON AS WE STARTED TO LEAVE, THEY GRABBED THEM..."
"...PUT THEM AGAINST A WALL AND SHOT THEM TO DEATH..."
"I WAS ASHAMED OF FRANCE, OF THE UN..."

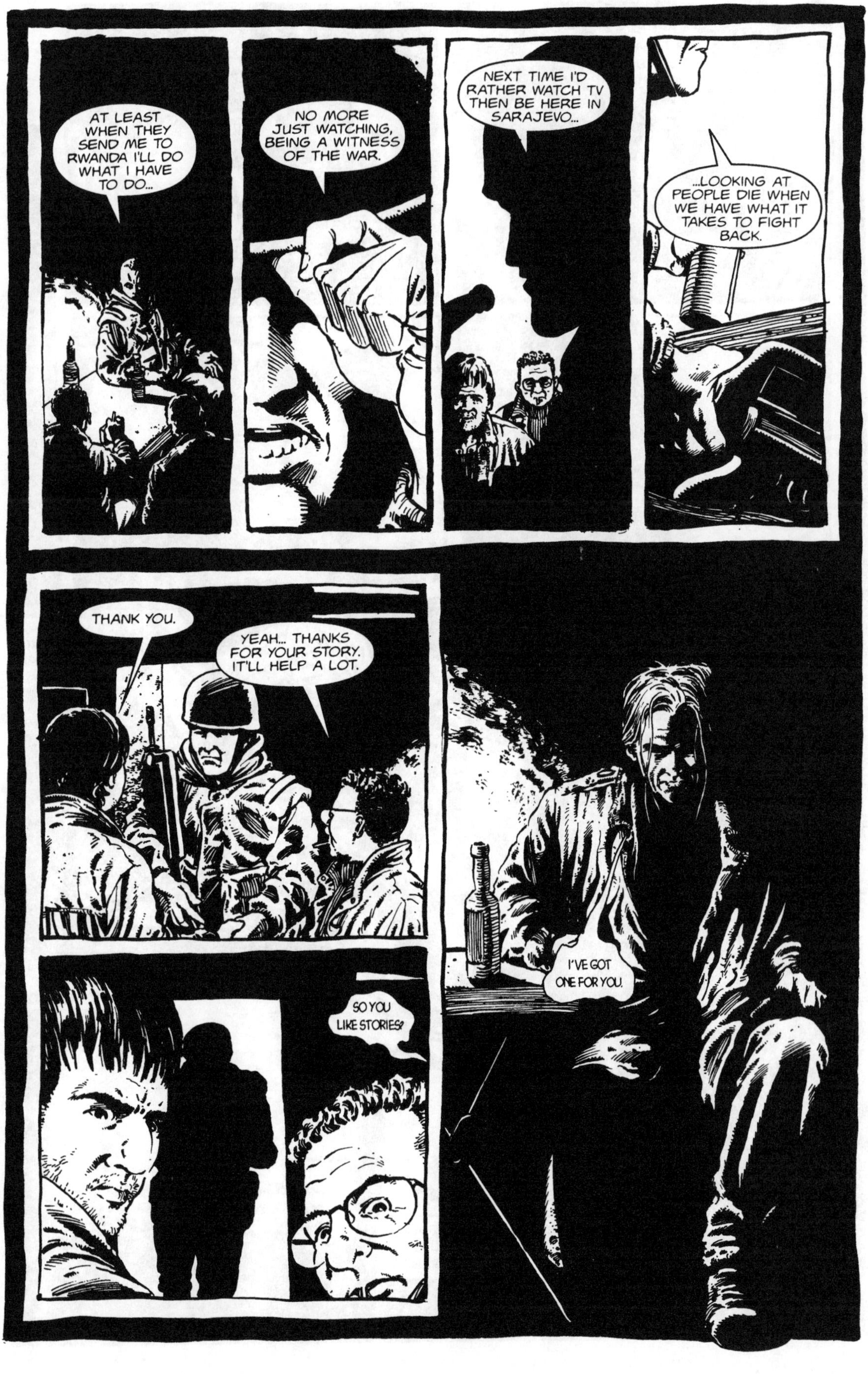
AT LEAST WHEN THEY SEND ME TO RWANDA I'LL DO WHAT I HAVE TO DO...
NO MORE JUST WATCHING, BEING A WITNESS OF THE WAR.
NEXT TIME I'D RATHER WATCH TV THEN BE HERE IN SARAJEVO...
...LOOKING AT PEOPLE DIE WHEN WE HAVE WHAT IT TAKES TO FIGHT BACK.
THANK YOU.
YEAH... THANKS FOR YOUR STORY. IT'LL HELP A LOT.
I'VE GOT ONE FOR YOU.
SO YOU LIKE STORIES?

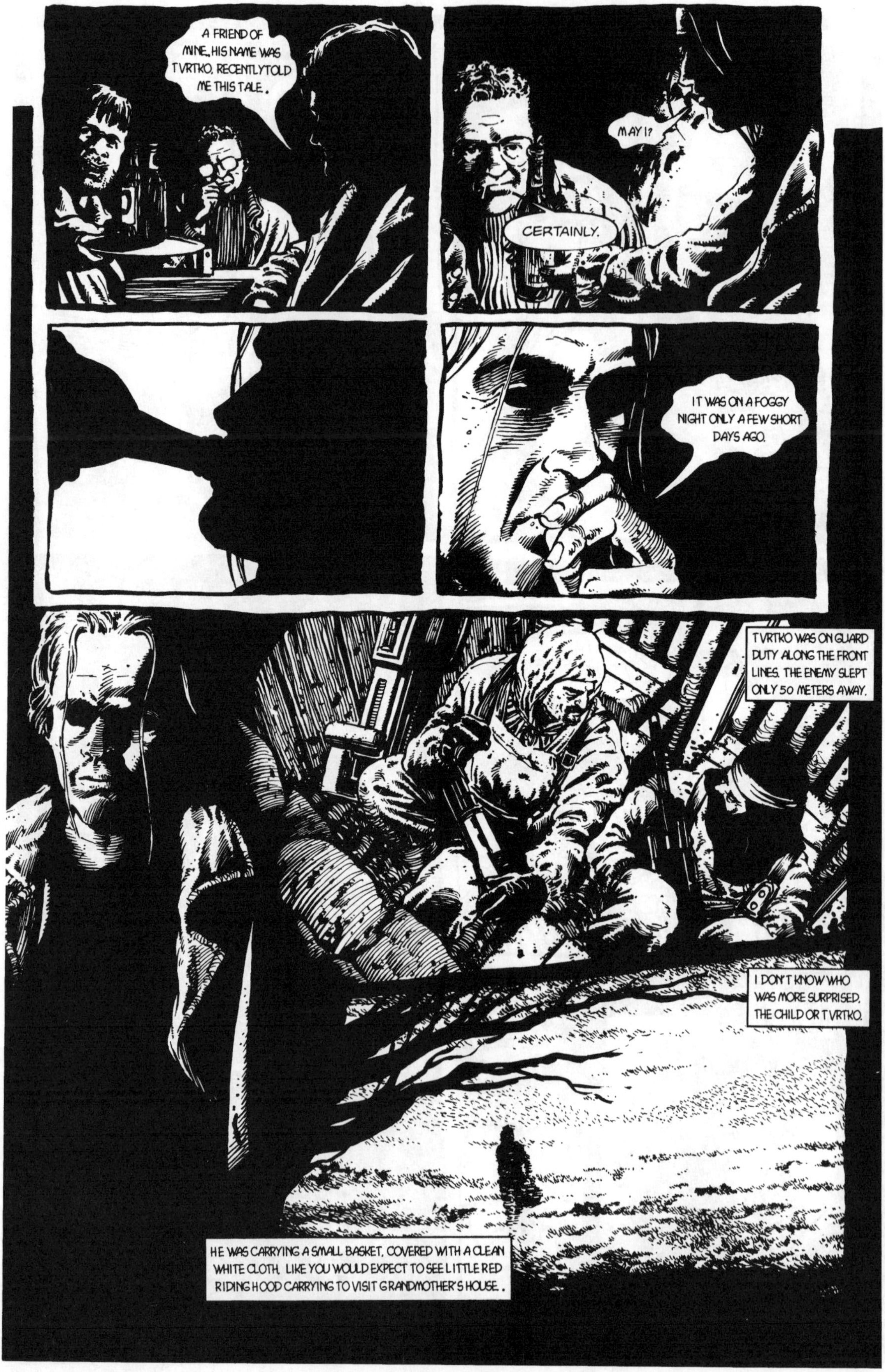
A FRIEND OF MINE, HIS NAME WAS TVRTKO, RECENTLY TOLD ME THIS TALE.
MAY I?
CERTAINLY.
IT WAS ON A FOGGY NIGHT ONLY A FEW SHORT DAYS AGO.
TVRTKO WAS ON GUARD DUTY ALONG THE FRONT LINES. THE ENEMY SLEPT ONLY 50 METERS AWAY.
I DON'T KNOW WHO WAS MORE SURPRISED, THE CHILD OR TVRTKO.
HE WAS CARRYING A SMALL BASKET, COVERED WITH A CLEAN WHITE CLOTH, LIKE YOU WOULD EXPECT TO SEE LITTLE RED RIDING HOOD CARRYING TO VISIT GRANDMOTHER'S HOUSE.

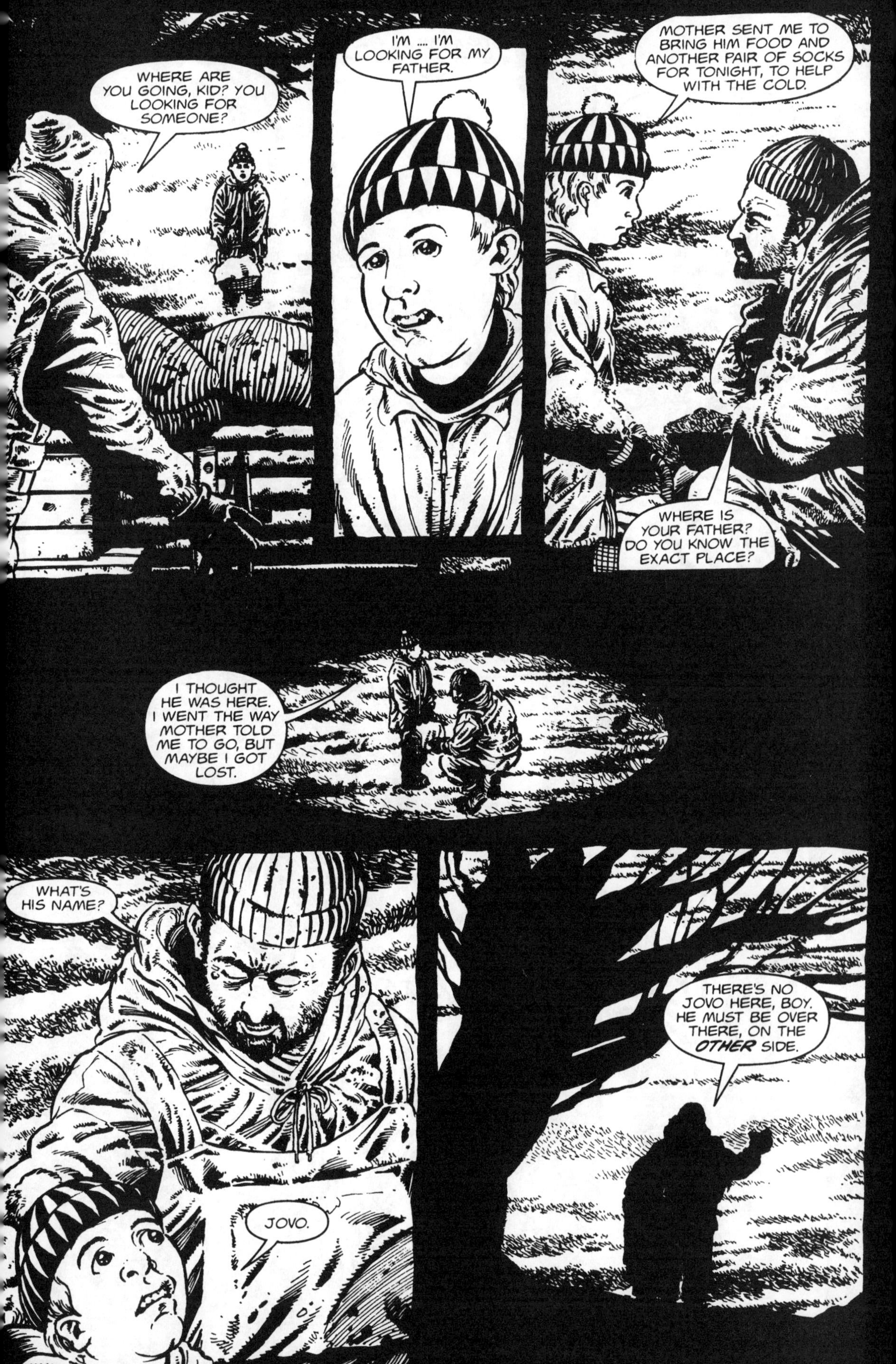
WHERE ARE YOU GOING, KID? YOU LOOKING FOR SOMEONE?
I'M .... I'M LOOKING FOR MY FATHER.
MOTHER SENT ME TO BRING HIM FOOD AND ANOTHER PAIR OF SOCKS FOR TONIGHT, TO HELP WITH THE COLD.
WHERE IS YOUR FATHER? DO YOU KNOW THE EXACT PLACE?
I THOUGHT HE WAS HERE. I WENT THE WAY MOTHER TOLD ME TO GO, BUT MAYBE I GOT LOST.
WHAT'S HIS NAME?
JOVO.
THERE'S NO JOVO HERE, BOY. HE MUST BE OVER THERE, ON THE OTHER SIDE.

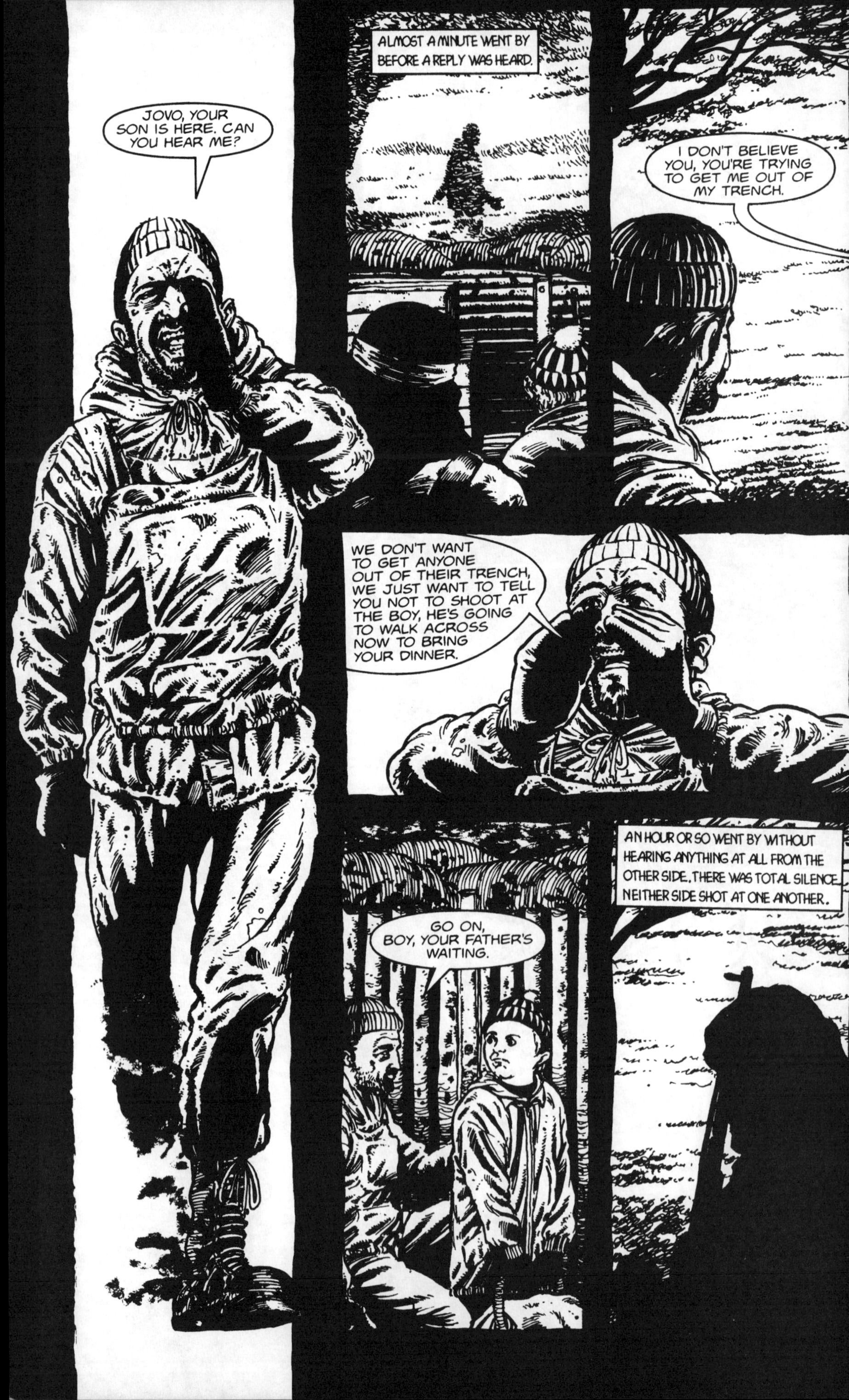
JOVO, YOUR SON IS HERE. CAN YOU HEAR ME?
ALMOST A MINUTE WENT BY BEFORE A REPLY WAS HEARD.
I DON'T BELIEVE YOU, YOU'RE TRYING TO GET ME OUT OF MY TRENCH.
WE DON'T WANT TO GET ANYONE OUT OF THEIR TRENCH, WE JUST WANT TO TELL YOU NOT TO SHOOT AT THE BOY, HE'S GOING TO WALK ACROSS NOW TO BRING YOUR DINNER.
GO ON, BOY, YOUR FATHER'S WAITING.
AN HOUR OR SO WENT BY WITHOUT HEARING ANYTHING AT ALL FROM THE OTHER SIDE. THERE WAS TOTAL SILENCE NEITHER SIDE SHOT AT ONE ANOTHER.

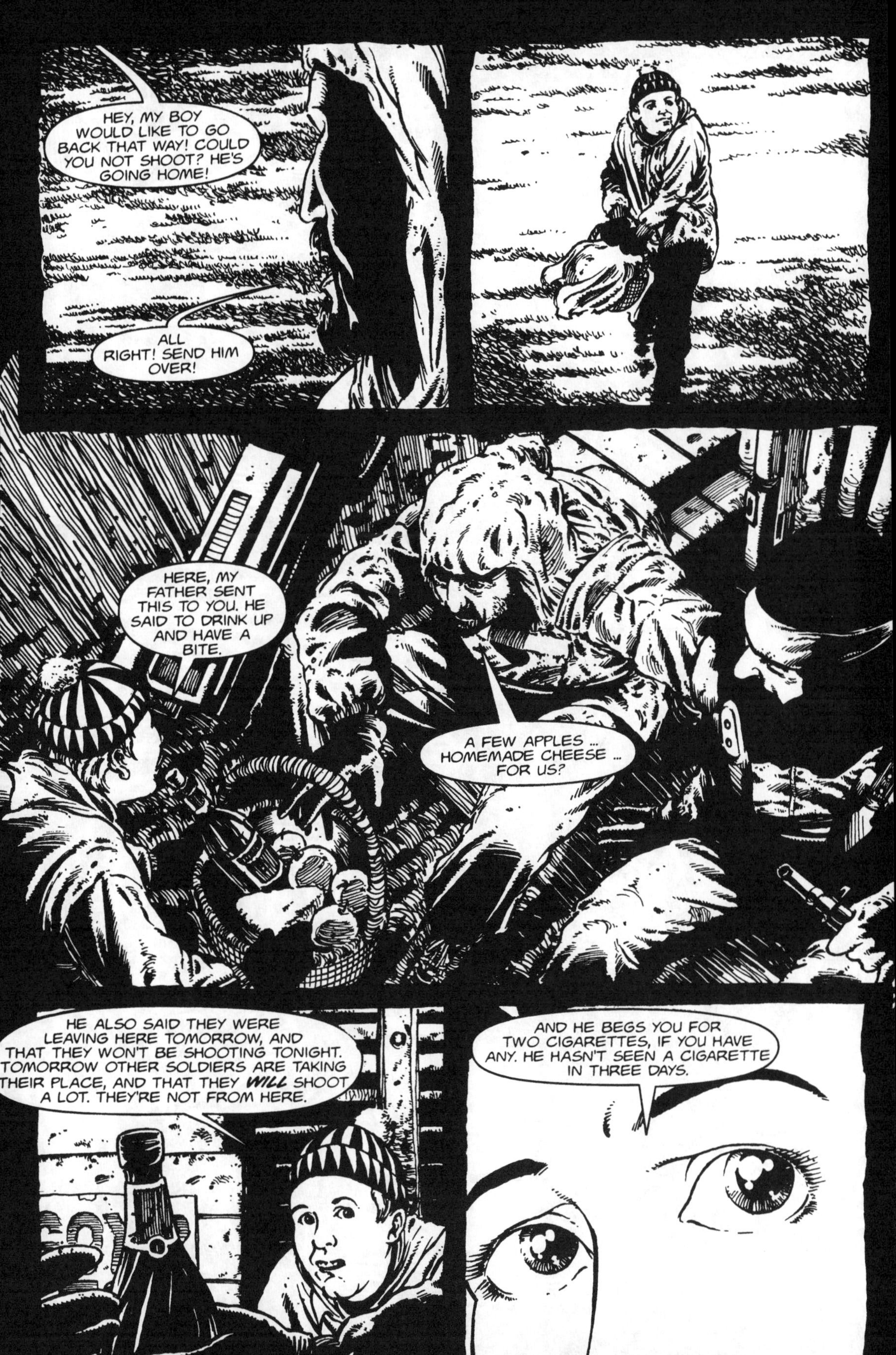
HEY, MY BOY WOULD LIKE TO GO BACK THAT WAY! COULD YOU NOT SHOOT? HE'S GOING HOME!
ALL RIGHT! SEND HIM OVER!
HERE, MY FATHER SENT THIS TO YOU. HE SAID TO DRINK UP AND HAVE A BITE.
A FEW APPLES ... HOMEMADE CHEESE ... FOR US?
HE ALSO SAID THEY WERE LEAVING HERE TOMORROW, AND THAT THEY WON'T BE SHOOTING TONIGHT. TOMORROW OTHER SOLDIERS ARE TAKING THEIR PLACE, AND THAT THEY WILL SHOOT A LOT. THEY'RE NOT FROM HERE.
AND HE BEGS YOU FOR TWO CIGARETTES, IF YOU HAVE ANY. HE HASN'T SEEN A CIGARETTE IN THREE DAYS.

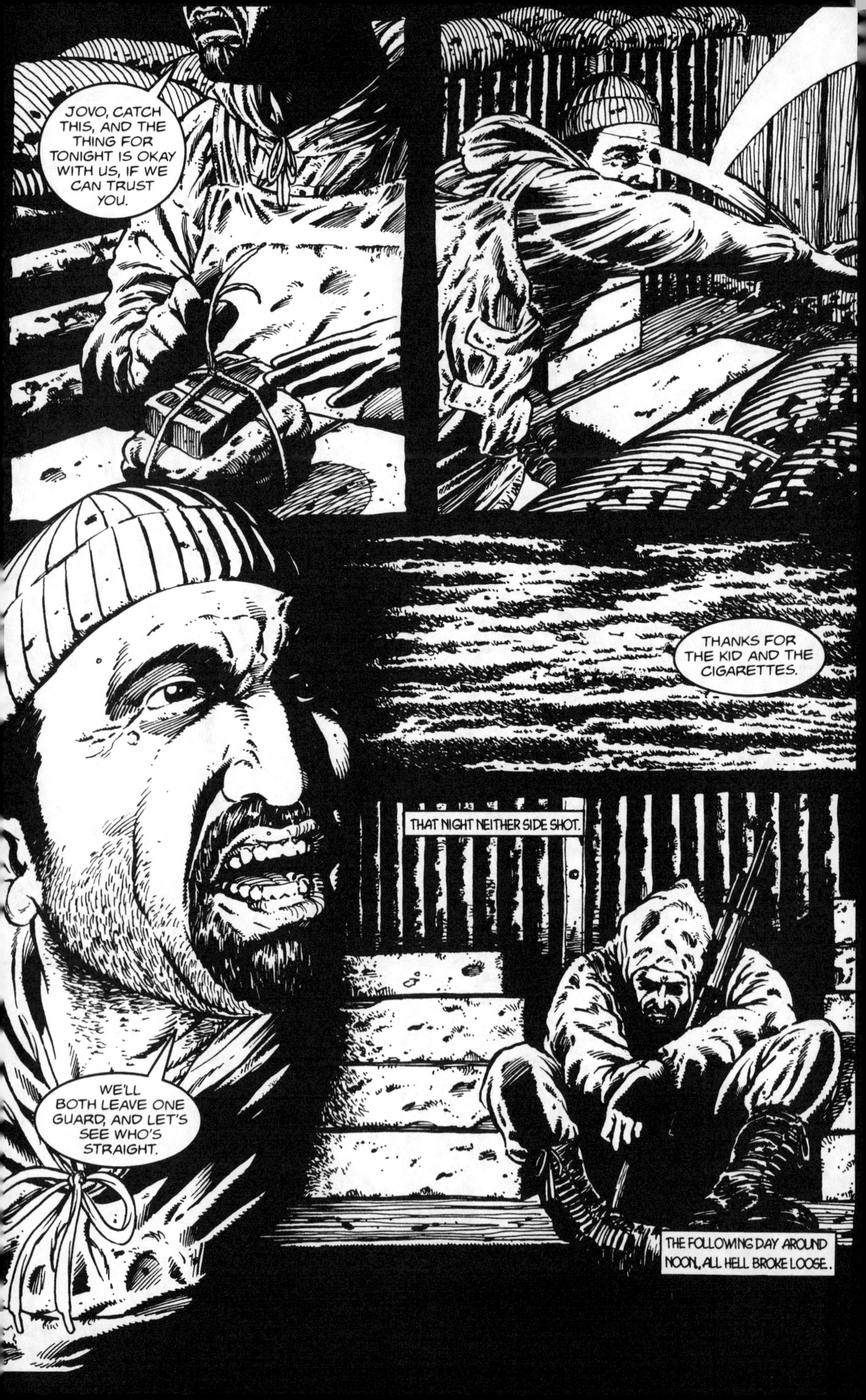
JOVO, CATCH THIS, AND THE THING FOR TONIGHT IS OKAY WITH US, IF WE CAN TRUST YOU.
THANKS FOR THE KID AND THE CIGARETTES.
WE'LL BOTH LEAVE ONE GUARD, AND LET'S SEE WHO'S STRAIGHT.
THAT NIGHT NEITHER SIDE SHOT.
THE FOLLOWING DAY AROUND NOON, ALL HELL BROKE LOOSE.

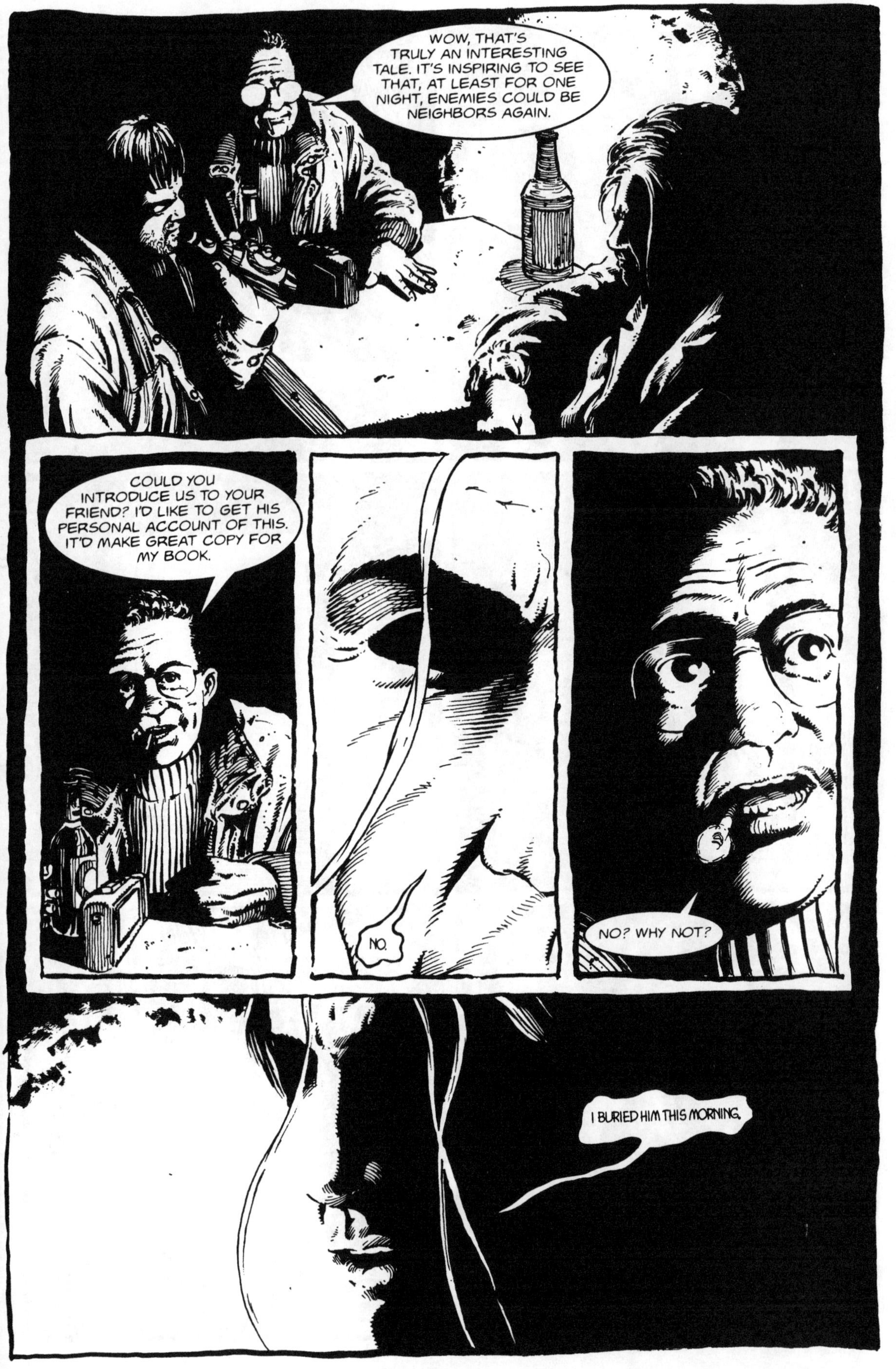
WOW, THAT'S TRULY AN INTERESTING TALE. IT'S INSPIRING TO SEE THAT, AT LEAST FOR ONE NIGHT, ENEMIES COULD BE NEIGHBORS AGAIN.
COULD YOU INTRODUCE US TO YOUR FRIEND? I'D LIKE TO GET HIS PERSONAL ACCOUNT OF THIS. IT'D MAKE GREAT COPY FOR MY BOOK.
NO.
NO? WHY NOT?
I BURIED HIM THIS MORNING.

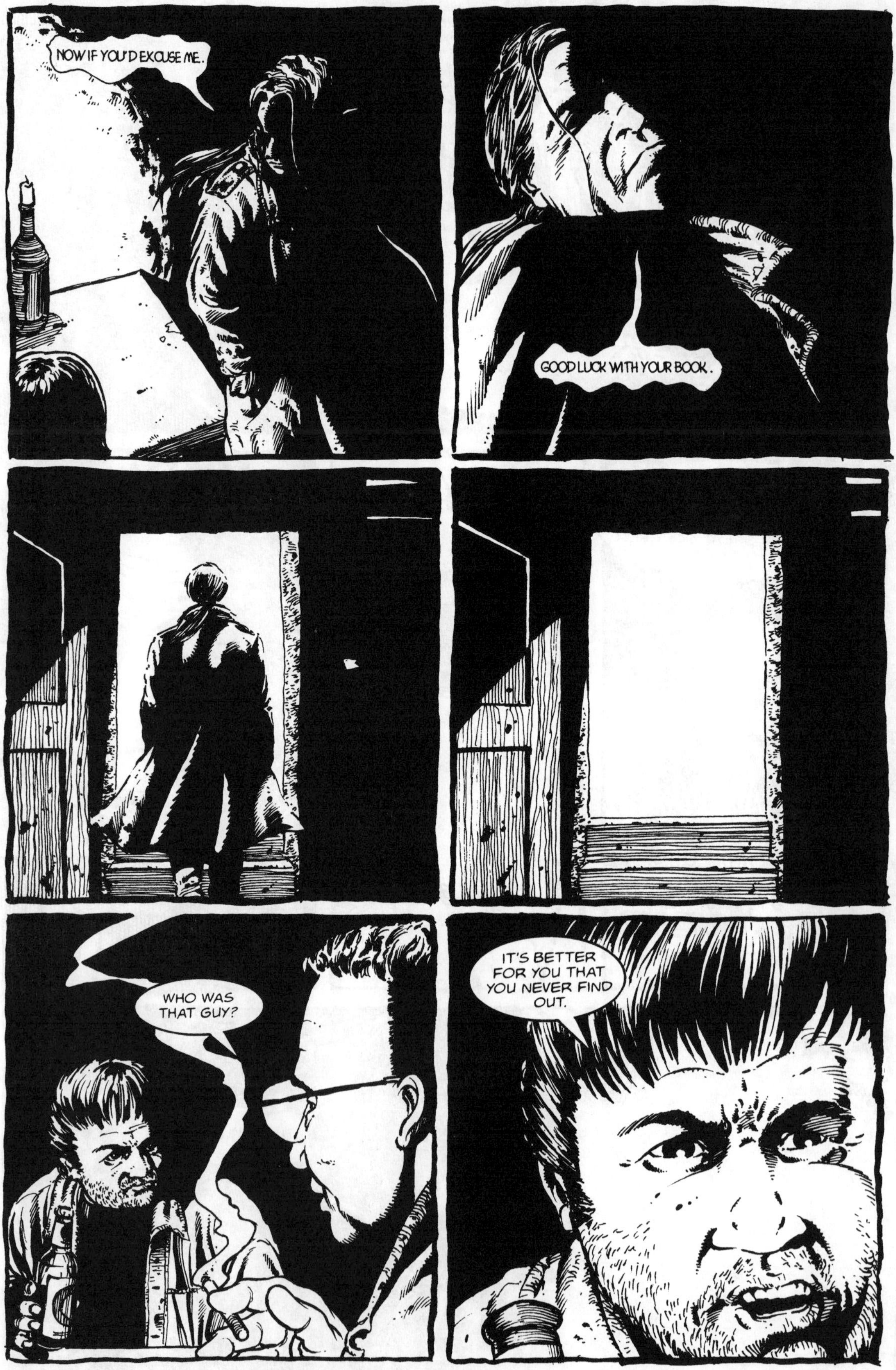
NOW IF YOU'D EXCUSE ME.
GOOD LUCK WITH YOUR BOOK.
WHO WAS THAT GUY?
IT'S BETTER FOR YOU THAT YOU NEVER FIND OUT.

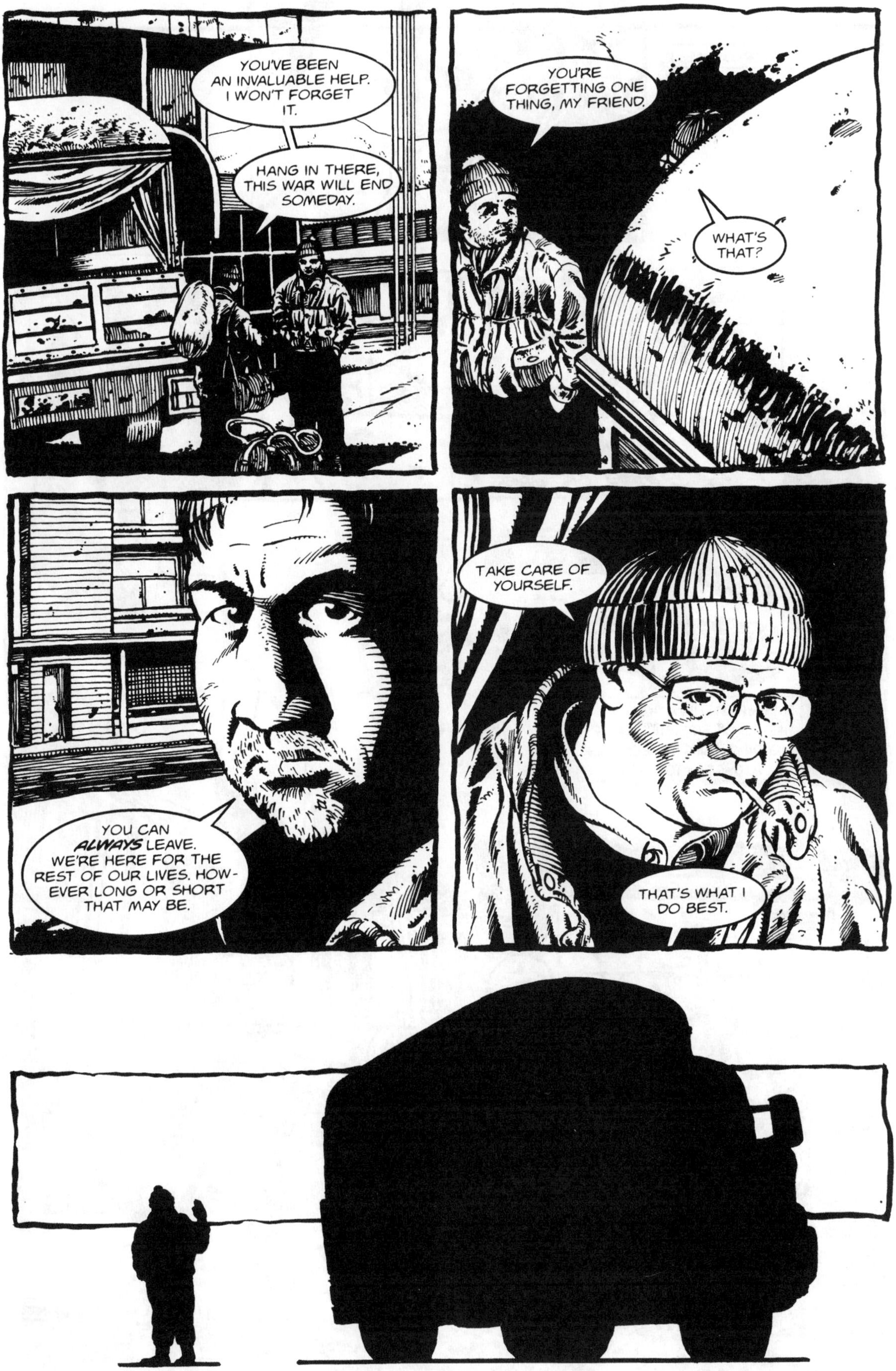
YOU'VE BEEN AN INVALUABLE HELP. I WON'T FORGET IT.
HANG IN THERE, THIS WAR WILL END SOMEDAY.
YOU'RE FORGETTING ONE THING, MY FRIEND.
WHAT'S THAT?
YOU CAN ALWAYS LEAVE. WE'RE HERE FOR THE REST OF OUR LIVES. HOW-EVER LONG OR SHORT THAT MAY BE.
TAKE CARE OF YOURSELF.
THAT'S WHAT I DO BEST.

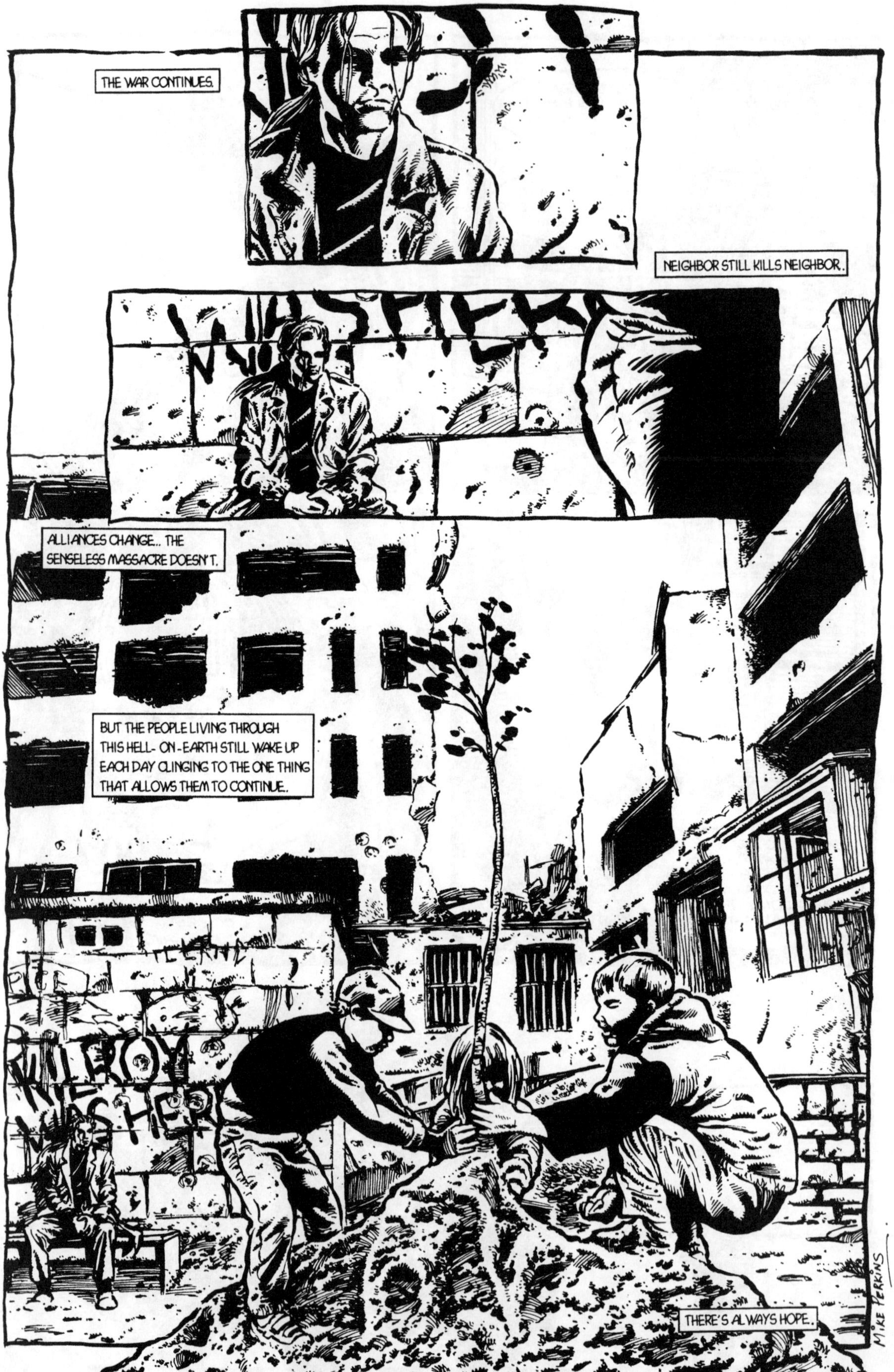
THE WAR CONTINUES.
NEIGHBOR STILL KILLS NEIGHBOR.
ALLIANCES CHANGE... THE SENSELESS MASSACRE DOESN'T.
BUT THE PEOPLE LIVING THROUGH THIS HELL-ON-EARTH STILL WAKE UP EACH DAY CLINGING TO THE ONE THING THAT ALLOWS THEM TO CONTINUE.
THERE'S ALWAYS HOPE.
MIKE PERKINS

"Stalked"

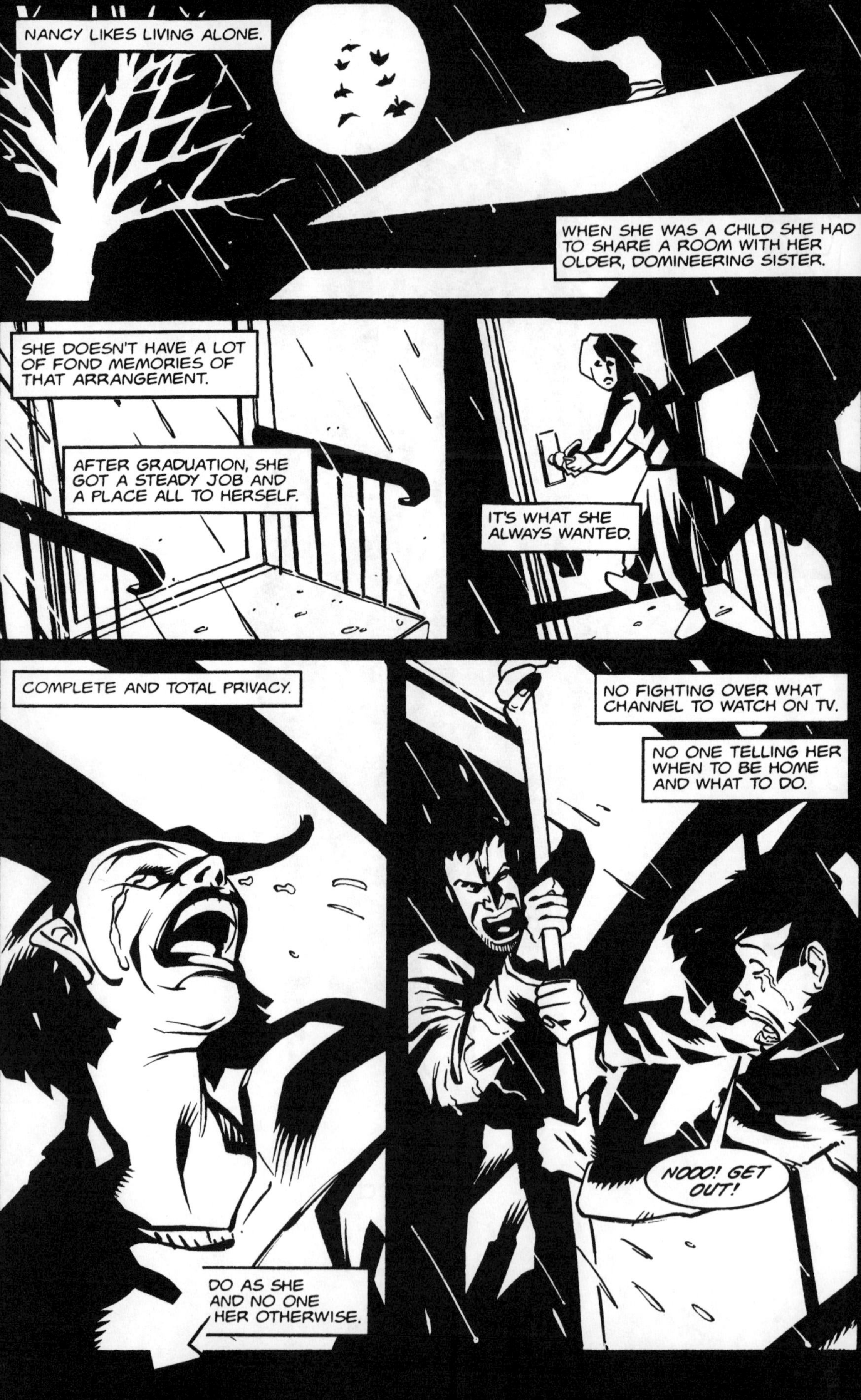

NANCY LIKES LIVING ALONE.
WHEN SHE WAS A CHILD SHE HAD TO SHARE A ROOM WITH HER OLDER, DOMINEERING SISTER.
SHE DOESN'T HAVE A LOT OF FOND MEMORIES OF THAT ARRANGEMENT.
AFTER GRADUATION, SHE GOT A STEADY JOB AND A PLACE ALL TO HERSELF.
IT'S WHAT SHE ALWAYS WANTED.
COMPLETE AND TOTAL PRIVACY.
NO FIGHTING OVER WHAT CHANNEL TO WATCH ON TV.
NO ONE TELLING HER WHEN TO BE HOME AND WHAT TO DO.
NOOO! GET OUT!
DO AS SHE
AND NO ONE
HER OTHERWISE.

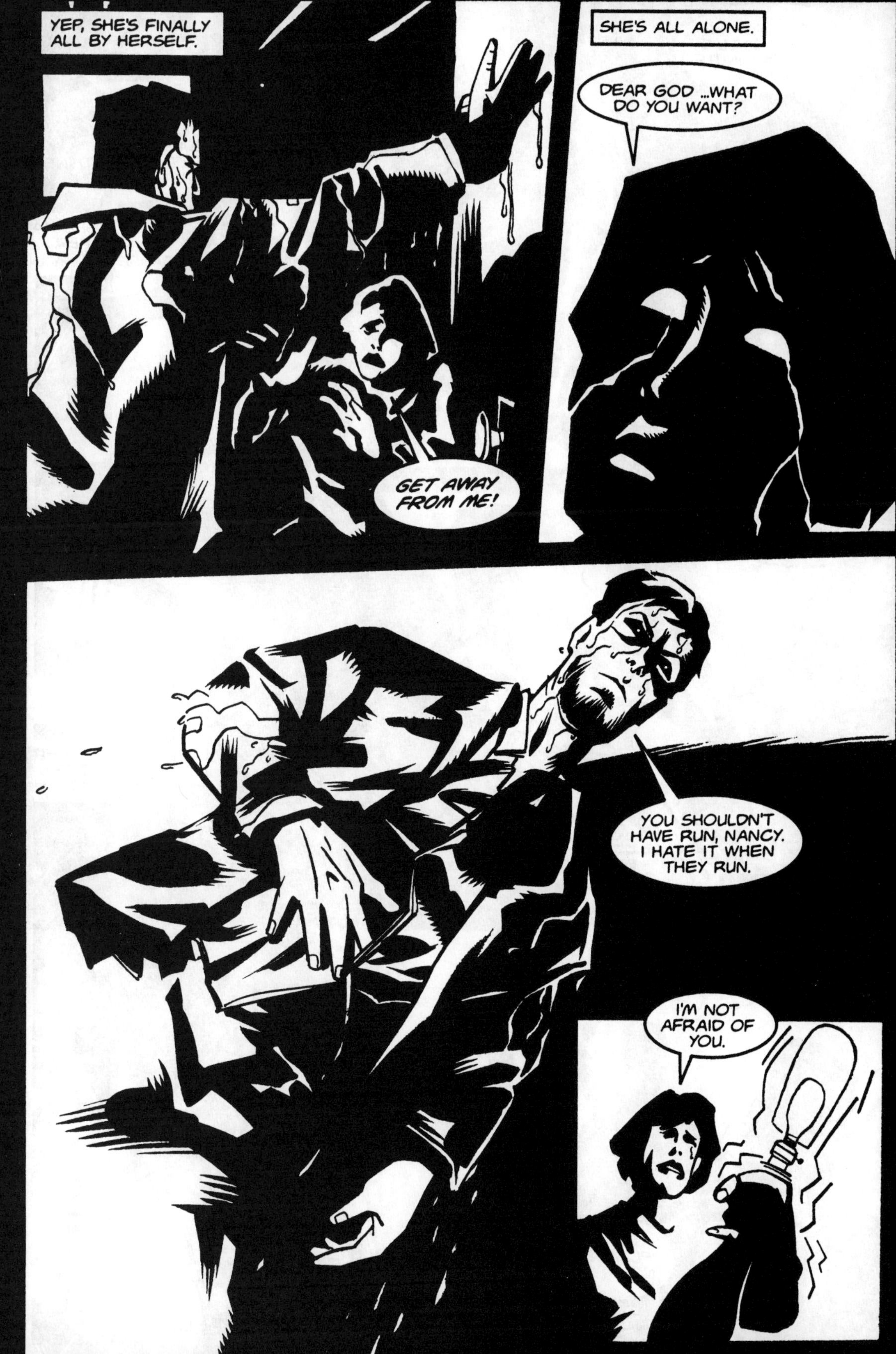
YEP, SHE'S FINALLY ALL BY HERSELF.
GET AWAY FROM ME!
SHE'S ALL ALONE.
DEAR GOD ...WHAT DO YOU WANT?
YOU SHOULDN'T HAVE RUN, NANCY. I HATE IT WHEN THEY RUN.
I'M NOT AFRAID OF YOU.

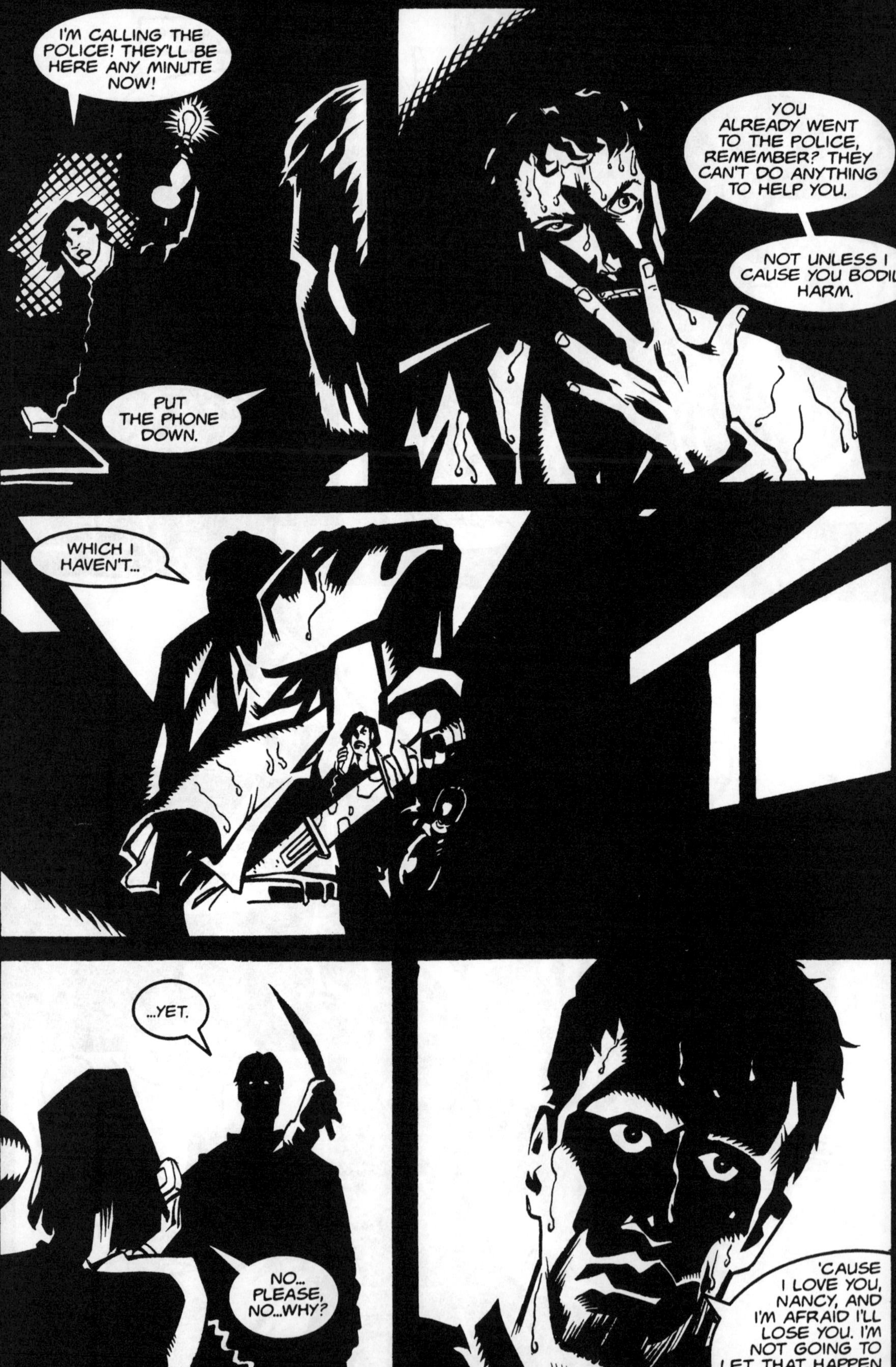
I'M CALLING THE POLICE! THEY'LL BE HERE ANY MINUTE NOW!
PUT THE PHONE DOWN.
YOU ALREADY WENT TO THE POLICE, REMEMBER? THEY CAN'T DO ANYTHING TO HELP YOU.
NOT UNLESS I CAUSE YOU BODILY HARM.
WHICH I HAVEN'T...
...YET.
NO... PLEASE, NO...WHY?
'CAUSE I LOVE YOU, NANCY, AND I'M AFRAID I'LL LOSE YOU. I'M NOT GOING TO LET THAT HAPPEN AGAIN. EVER.

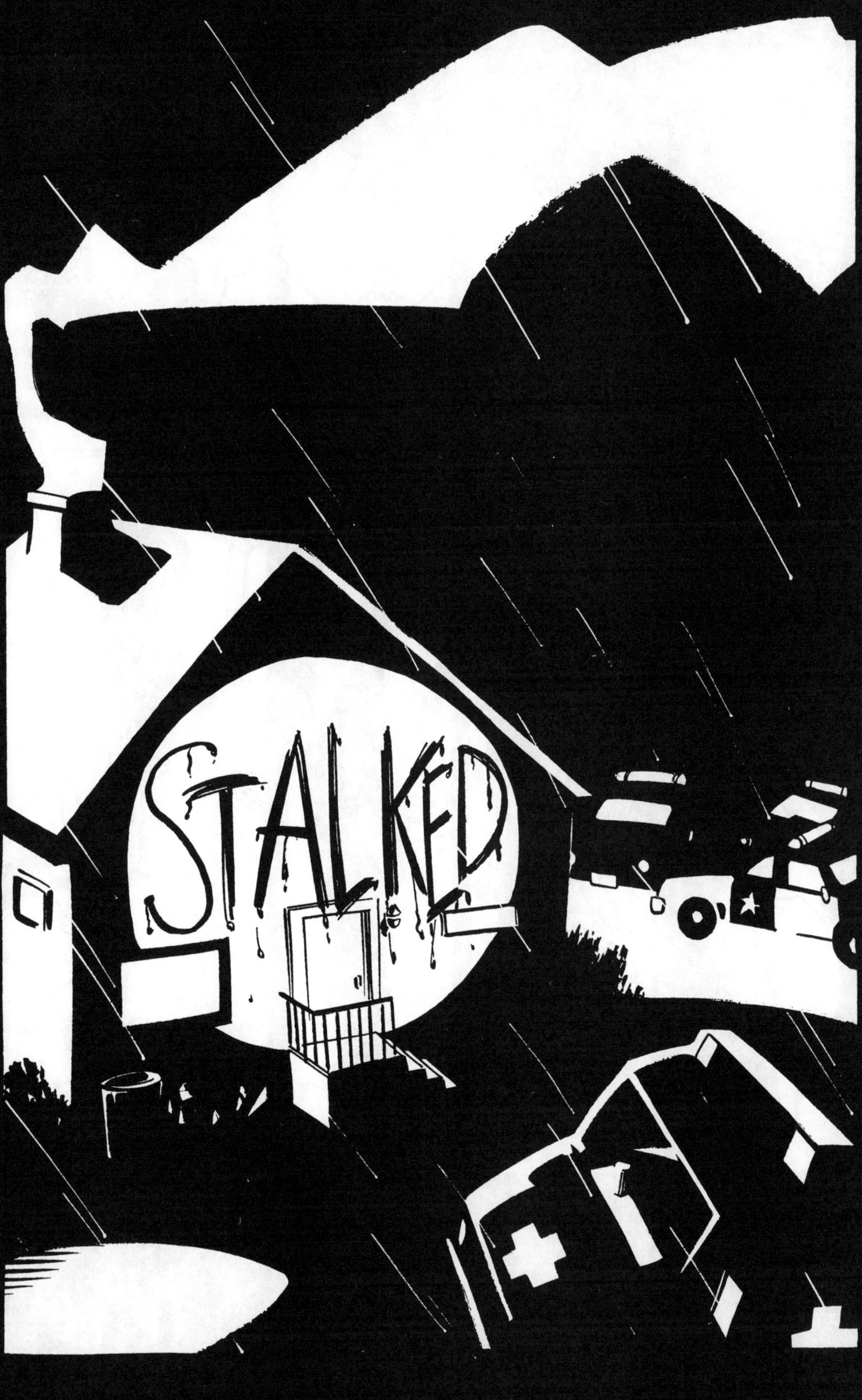
STALKED

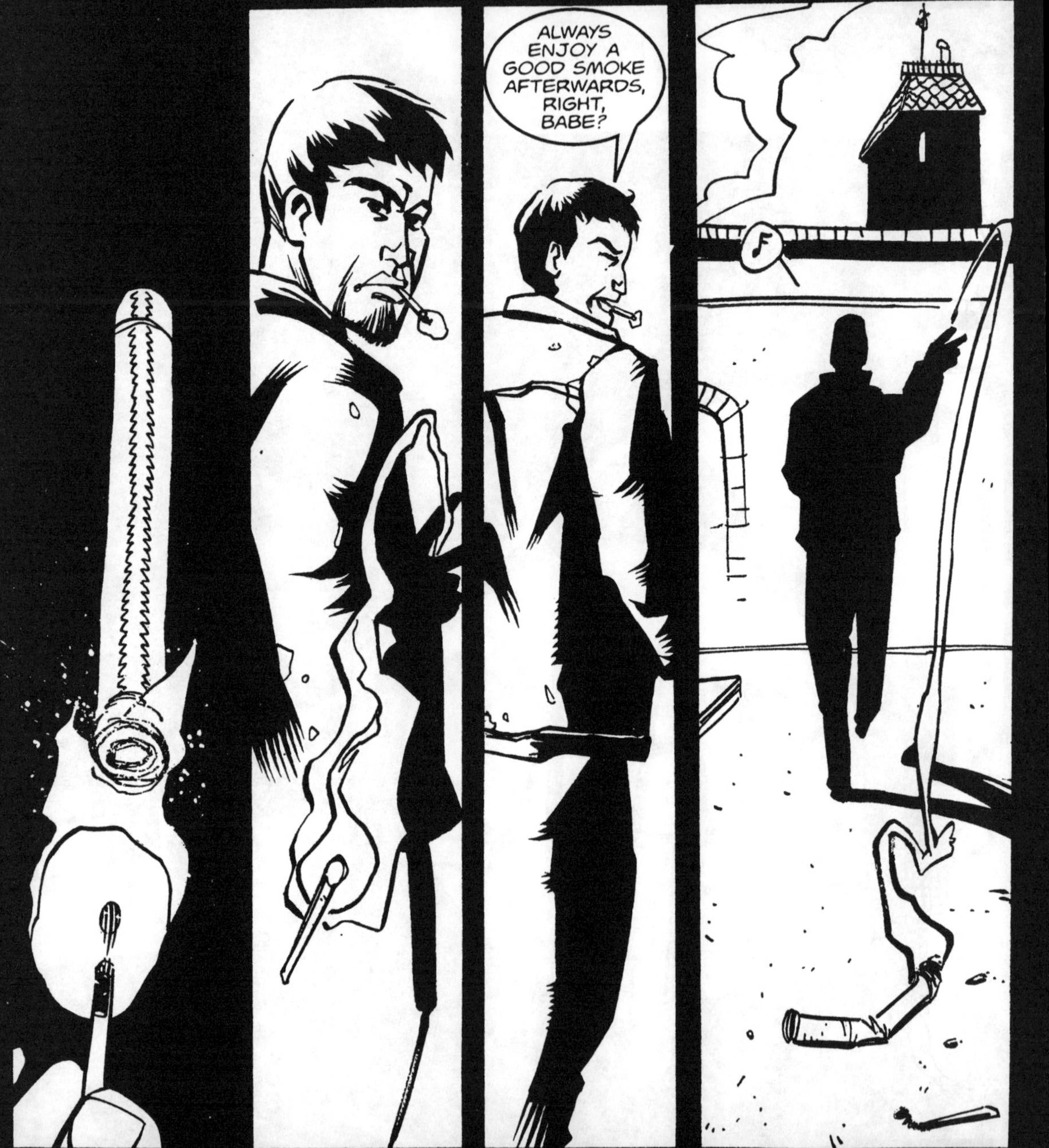
ALWAYS ENJOY A GOOD SMOKE AFTERWARDS, RIGHT, BABE?

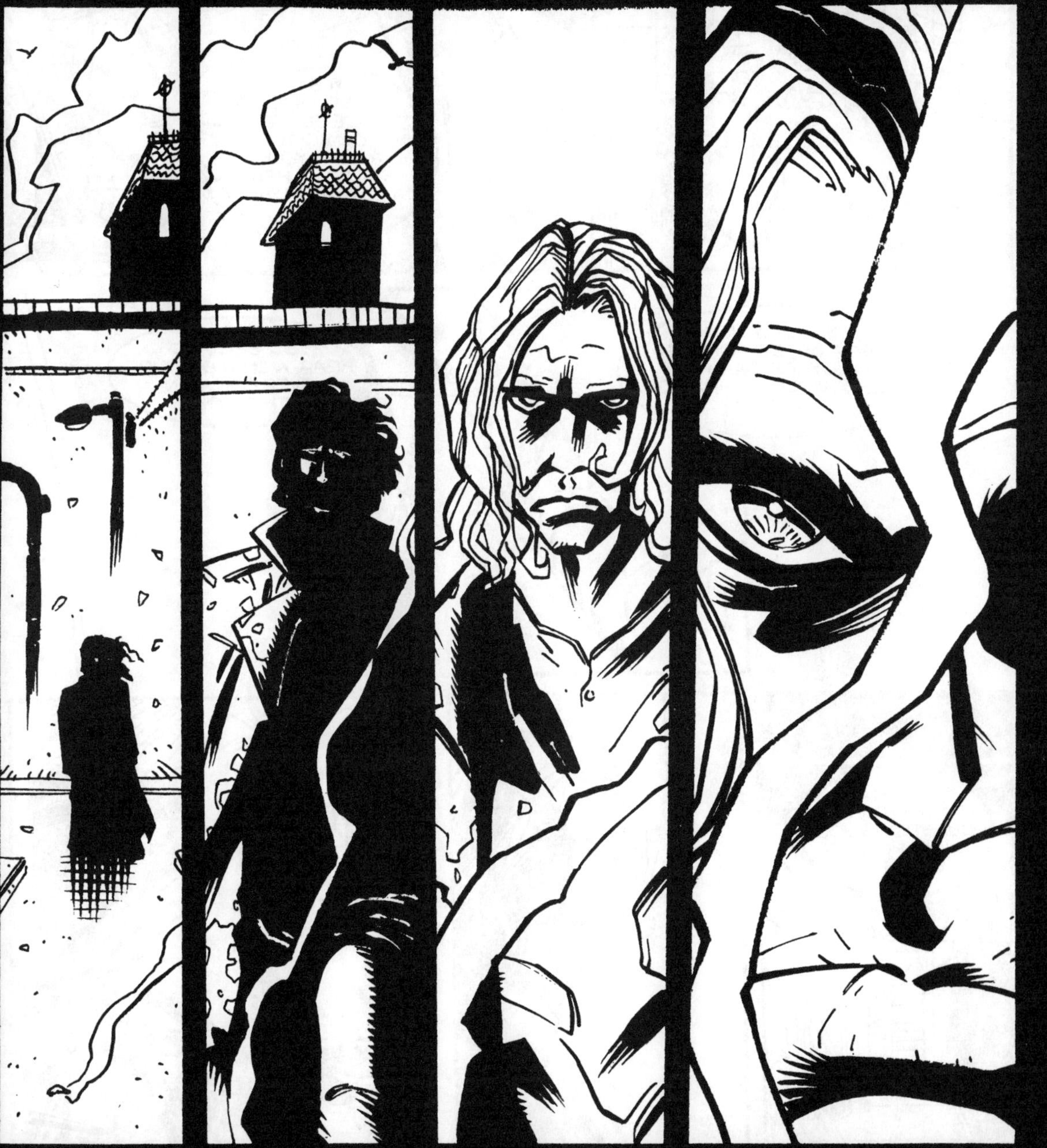

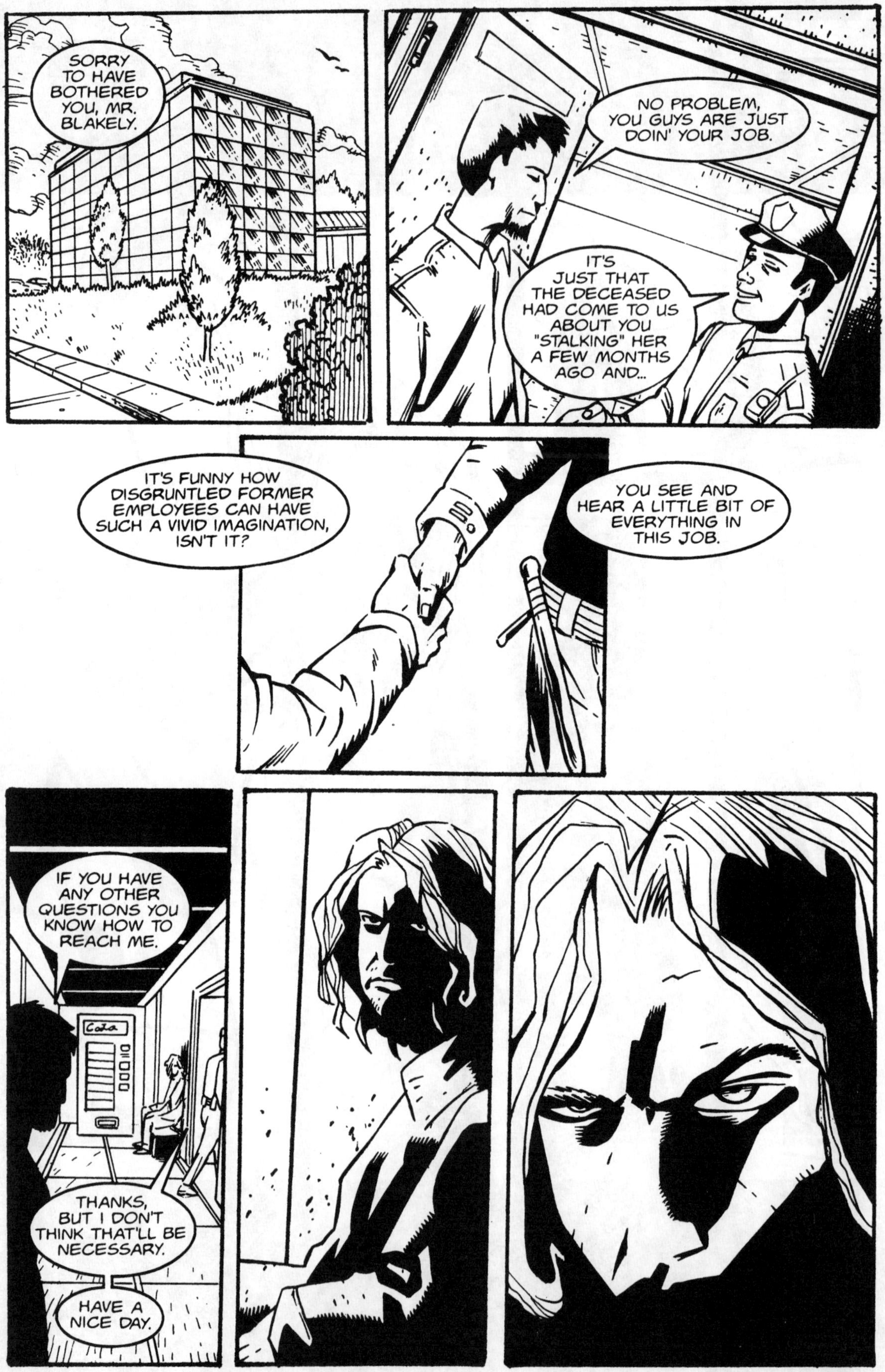
SORRY TO HAVE BOTHERED YOU, MR. BLAKELY.
NO PROBLEM, YOU GUYS ARE JUST DOIN' YOUR JOB.
IT'S JUST THAT THE DECEASED HAD COME TO US ABOUT YOU "STALKING" HER A FEW MONTHS AGO AND...
IT'S FUNNY HOW DISGRUNTLED FORMER EMPLOYEES CAN HAVE SUCH A VIVID IMAGINATION, ISN'T IT?
YOU SEE AND HEAR A LITTLE BIT OF EVERYTHING IN THIS JOB.
IF YOU HAVE ANY OTHER QUESTIONS YOU KNOW HOW TO REACH ME.
THANKS, BUT I DON'T THINK THAT'LL BE NECESSARY.
HAVE A NICE DAY.

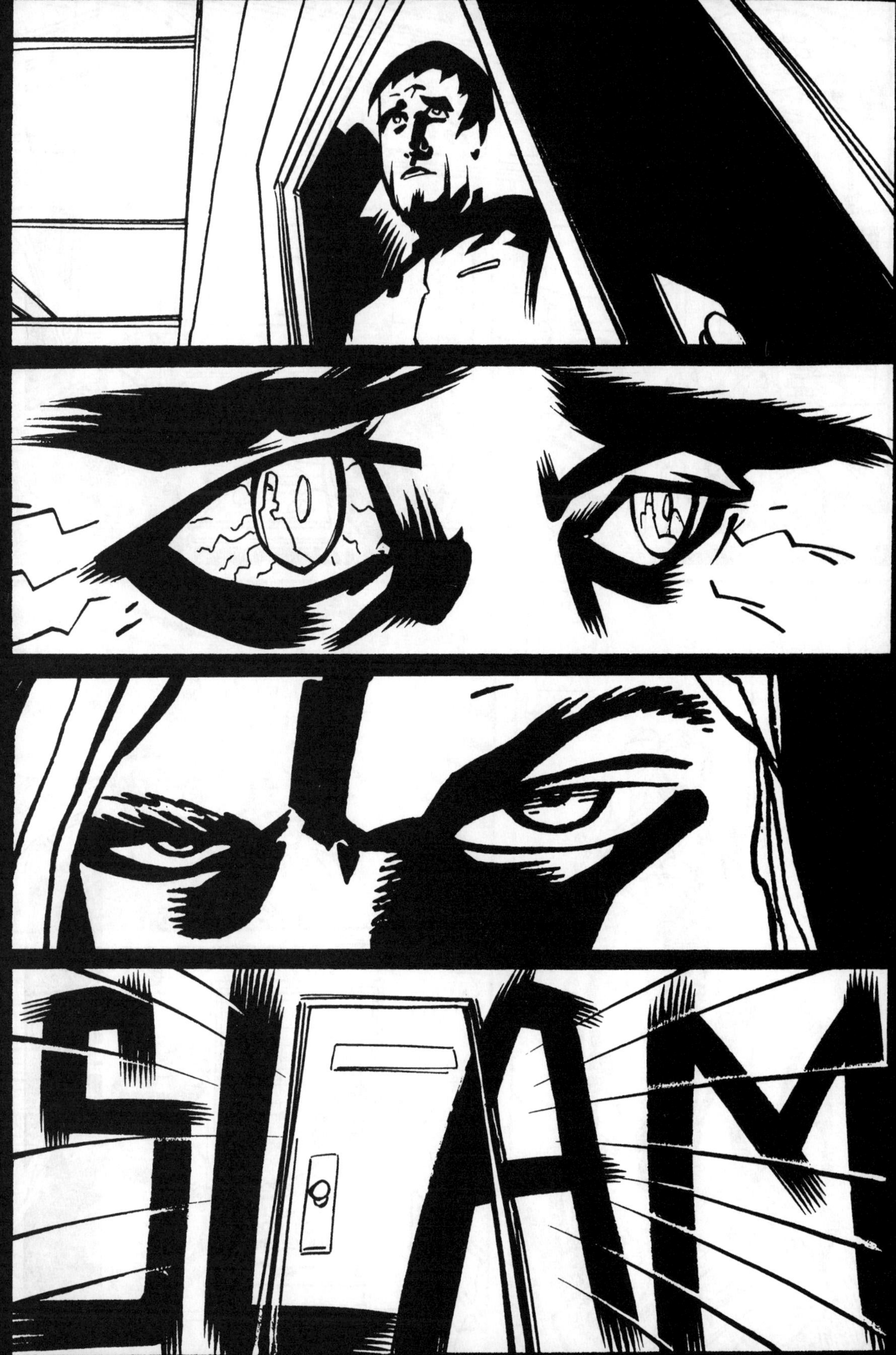
SLAM

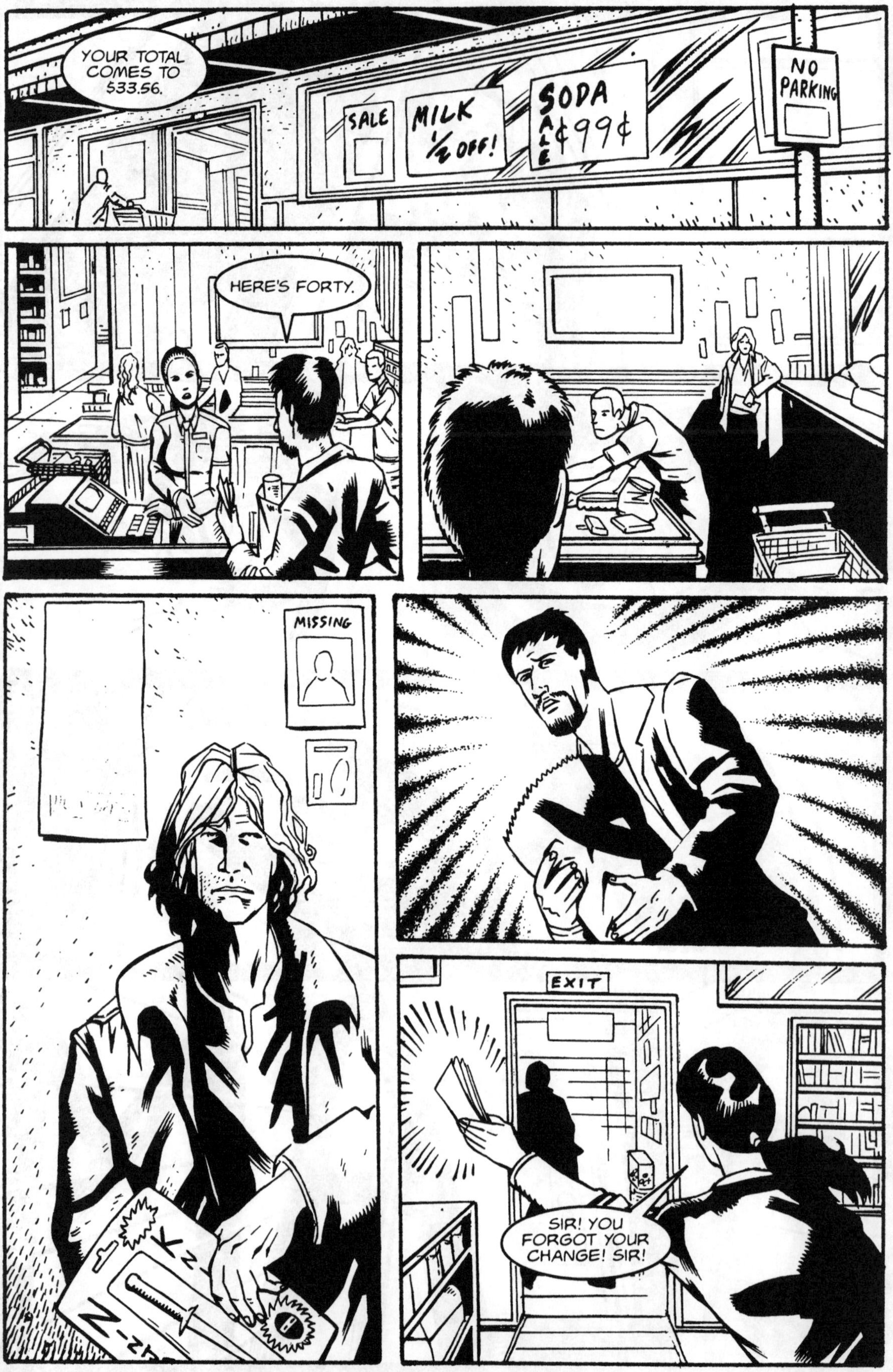
YOUR TOTAL COMES TO $33.56.
SALE
MILK 1/2 OFF!
SODA SALE ¢99¢
NO PARKING
HERE'S FORTY.
MISSING
EXIT
SIR! YOU FORGOT YOUR CHANGE! SIR!

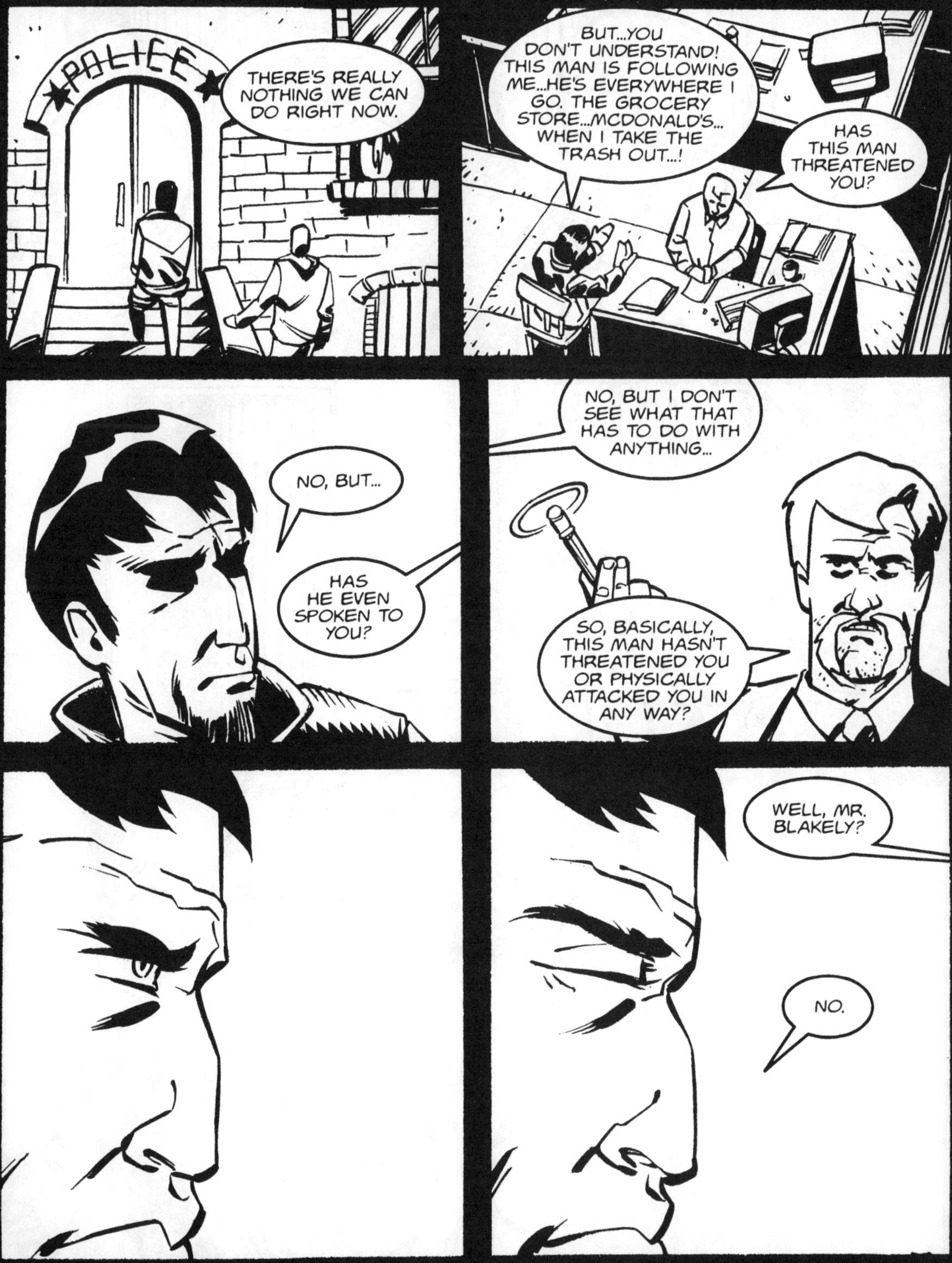
POLICE
THERE'S REALLY NOTHING WE CAN DO RIGHT NOW.
BUT...YOU DON'T UNDERSTAND! THIS MAN IS FOLLOWING ME...HE'S EVERYWHERE I GO. THE GROCERY STORE...MCDONALD'S... WHEN I TAKE THE TRASH OUT...!
HAS THIS MAN THREATENED YOU?
NO, BUT...
HAS HE EVEN SPOKEN TO YOU?
NO, BUT I DON'T SEE WHAT THAT HAS TO DO WITH ANYTHING...
SO, BASICALLY, THIS MAN HASN'T THREATENED YOU OR PHYSICALLY ATTACKED YOU IN ANY WAY?
WELL, MR. BLAKELY?
NO.

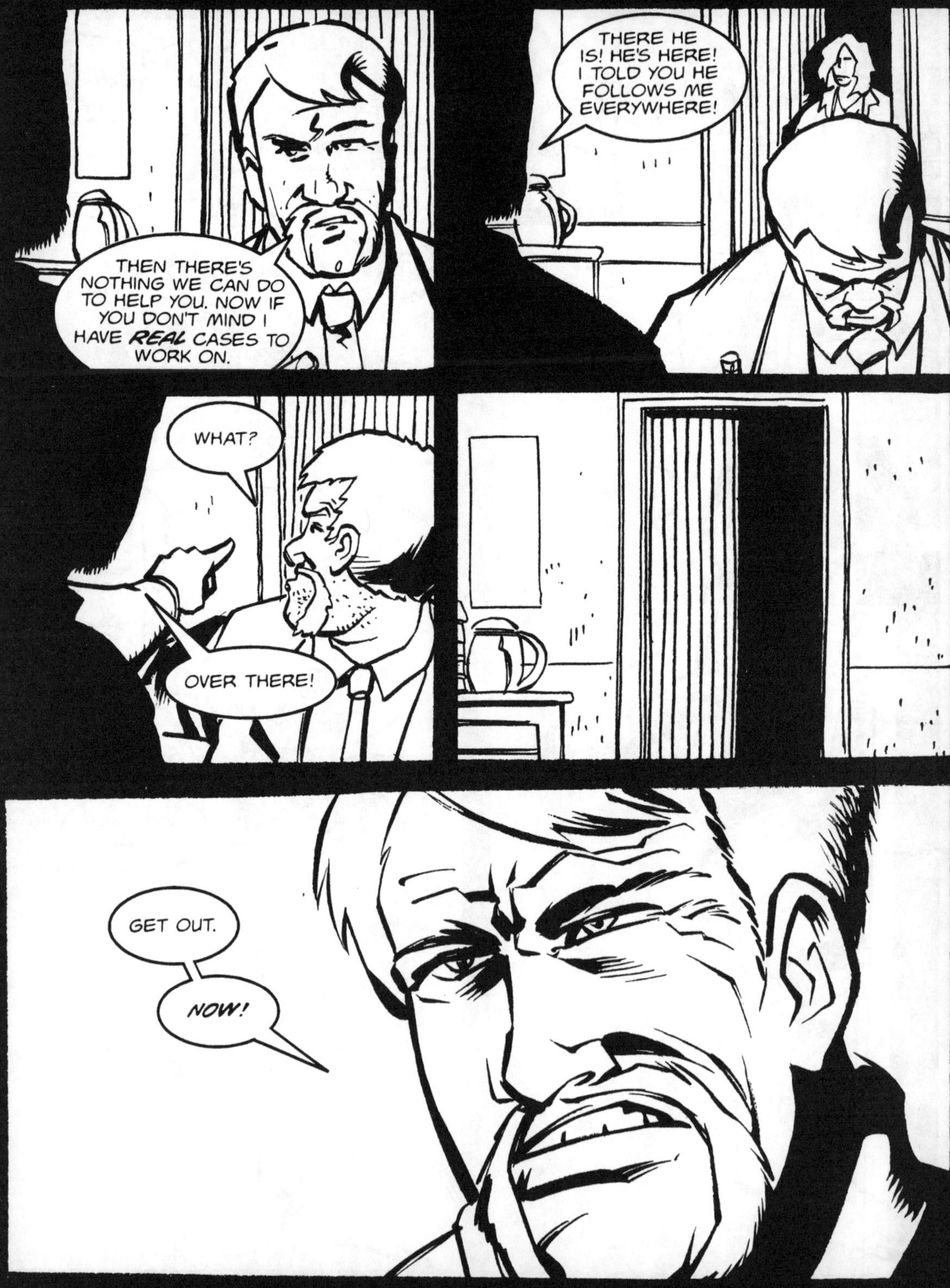
THEN THERE'S NOTHING WE CAN DO TO HELP YOU. NOW IF YOU DON'T MIND I HAVE REAL CASES TO WORK ON.
THERE HE IS! HE'S HERE! I TOLD YOU HE FOLLOWS ME EVERYWHERE!
WHAT?
OVER THERE!
GET OUT.
NOW!

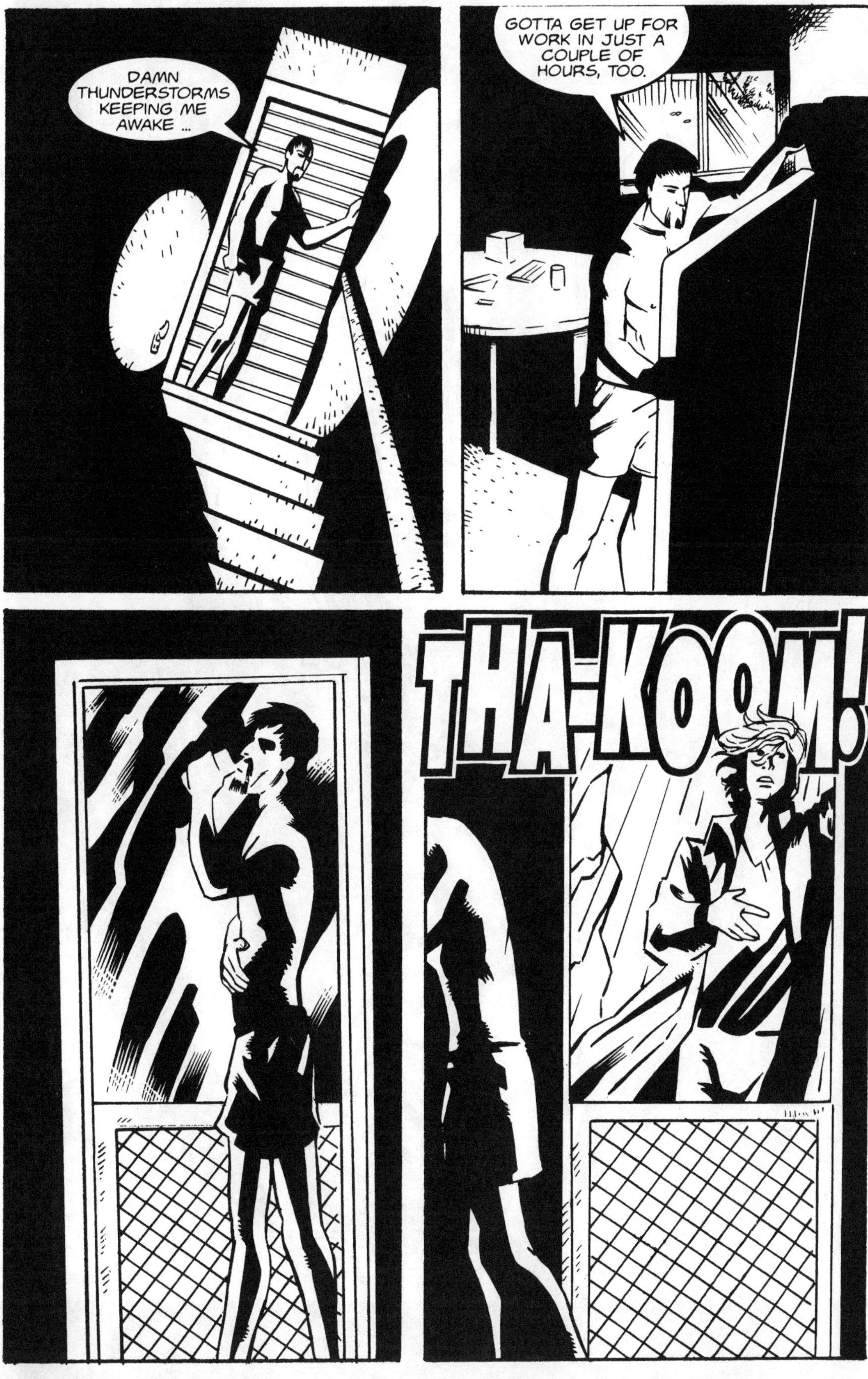
DAMN THUNDERSTORMS KEEPING ME AWAKE ...
GOTTA GET UP FOR WORK IN JUST A COUPLE OF HOURS, TOO.
THA-KOOM!

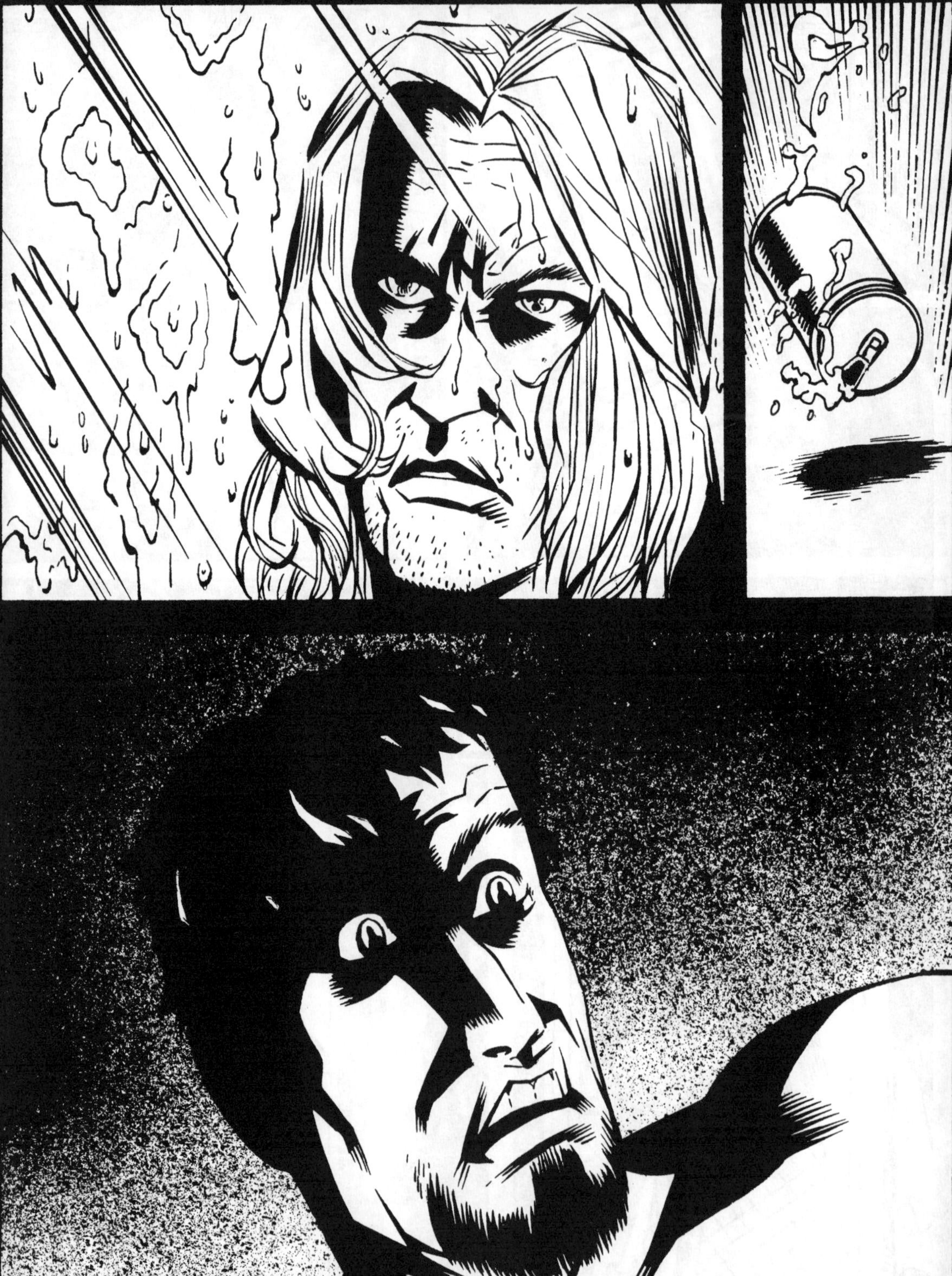

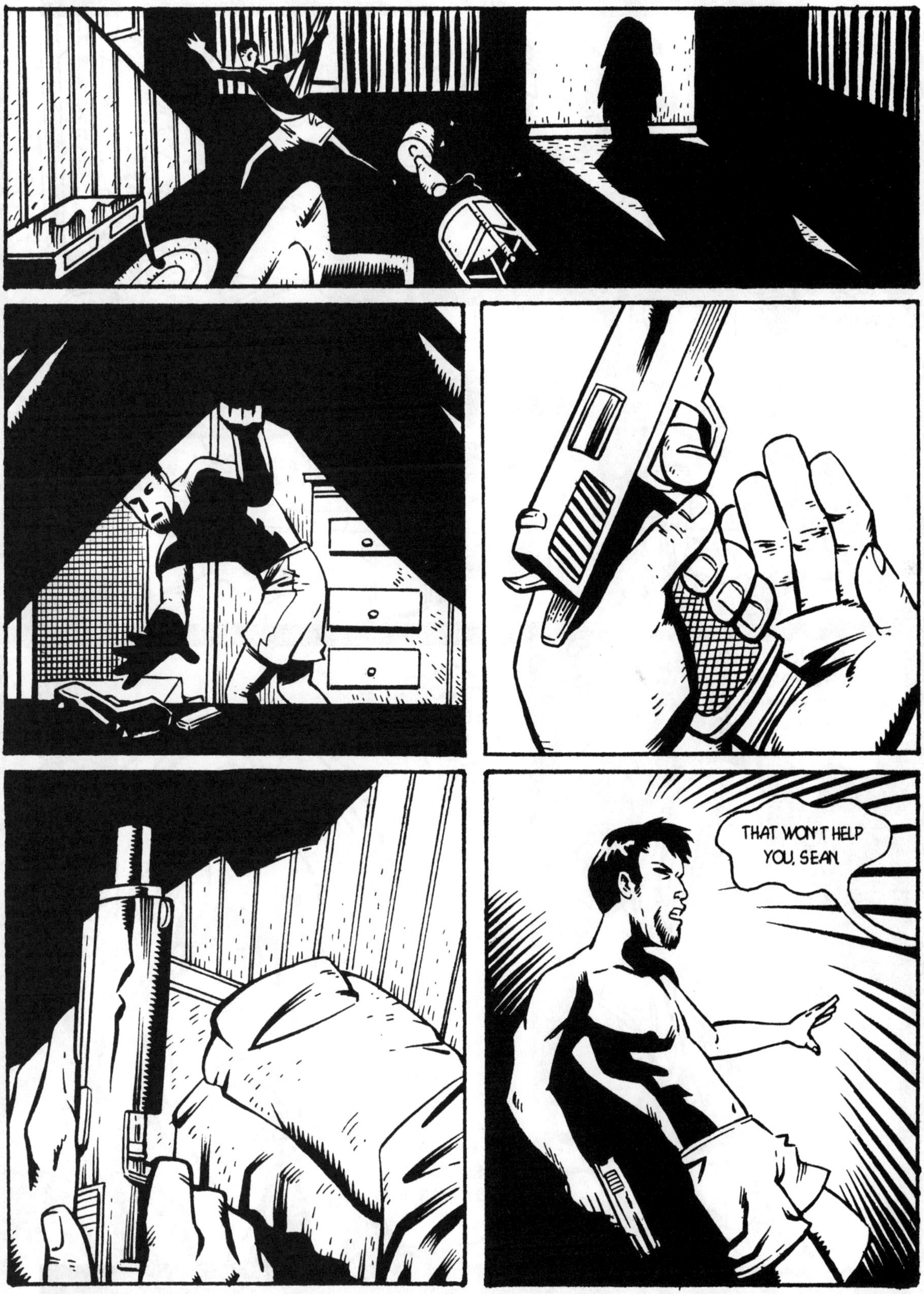
THAT WON'T HELP YOU, SEAN.

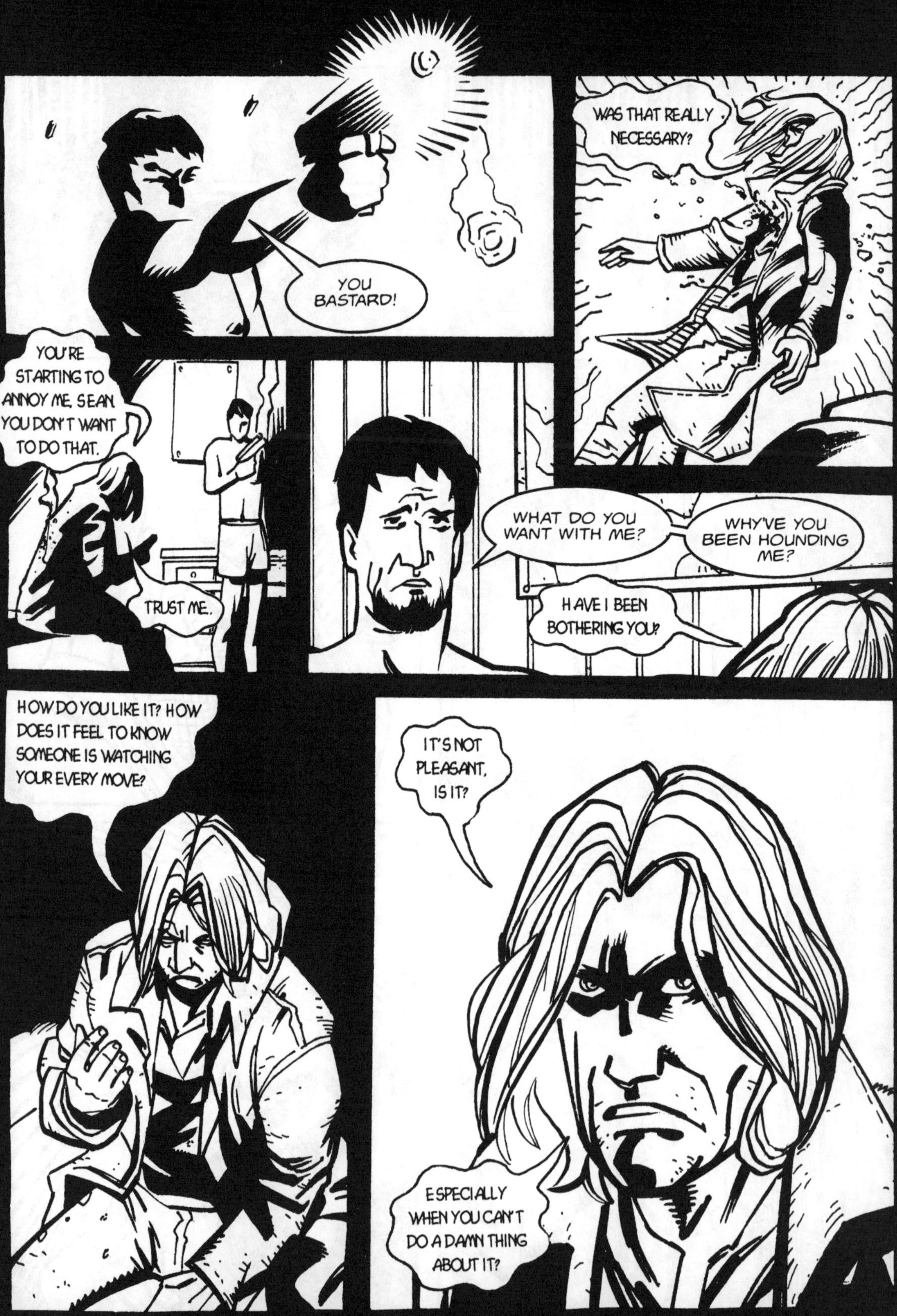
YOU BASTARD!
WAS THAT REALLY NECESSARY?
YOU'RE STARTING TO ANNOY ME, SEAN. YOU DON'T WANT TO DO THAT.
TRUST ME.
WHAT DO YOU WANT WITH ME?
WHY'VE YOU BEEN HOUNDING ME?
HAVE I BEEN BOTHERING YOU?
HOW DO YOU LIKE IT? HOW DOES IT FEEL TO KNOW SOMEONE IS WATCHING YOUR EVERY MOVE?
IT'S NOT PLEASANT, IS IT?
ESPECIALLY WHEN YOU CAN'T DO A DAMN THING ABOUT IT?

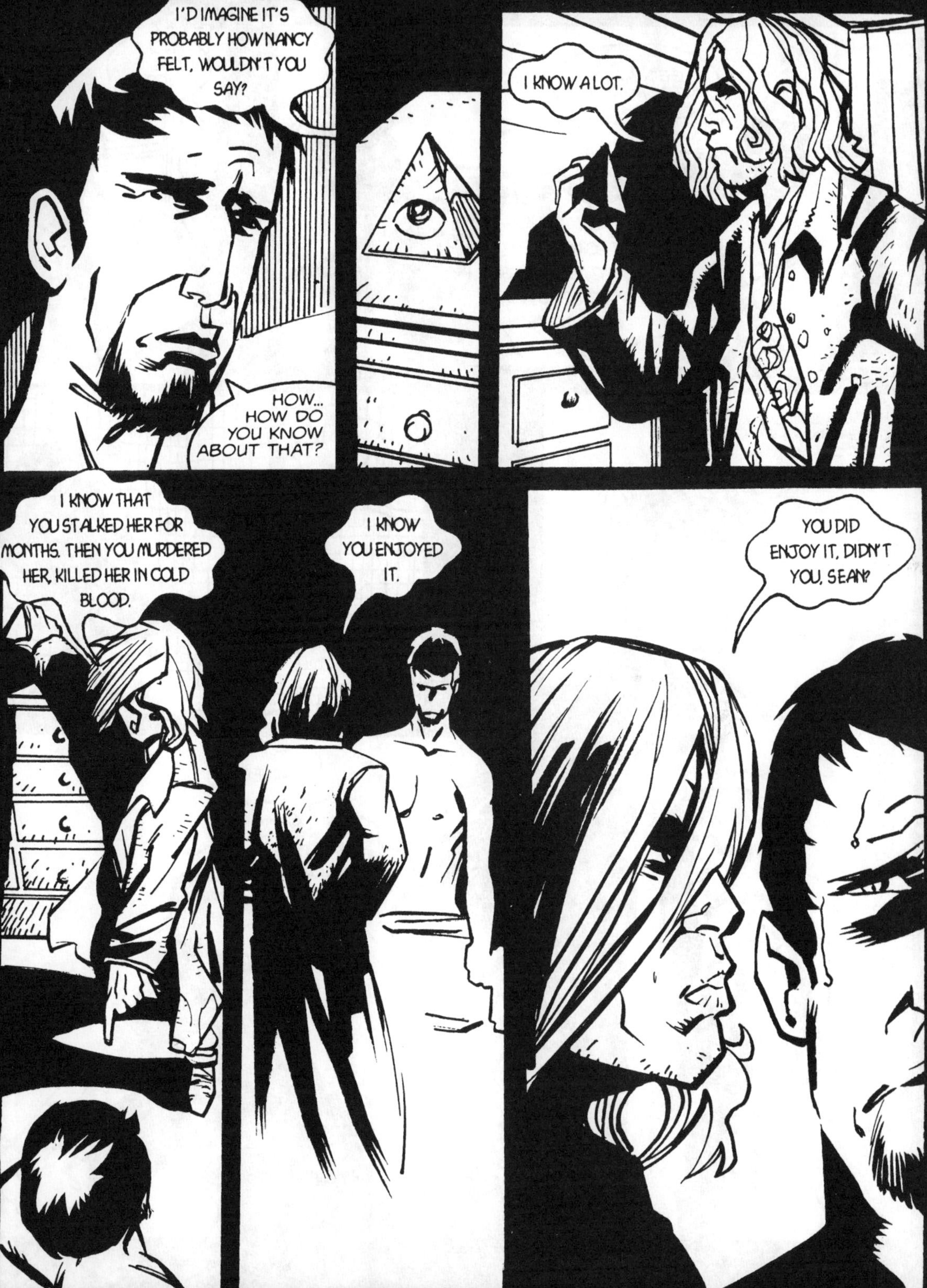
I'D IMAGINE IT'S PROBABLY HOW NANCY FELT, WOULDN'T YOU SAY?
HOW... HOW DO YOU KNOW ABOUT THAT?
I KNOW A LOT.
I KNOW THAT YOU STALKED HER FOR MONTHS. THEN YOU MURDERED HER, KILLED HER IN COLD BLOOD.
I KNOW YOU ENJOYED IT.
YOU DID ENJOY IT, DIDN'T YOU, SEAN?

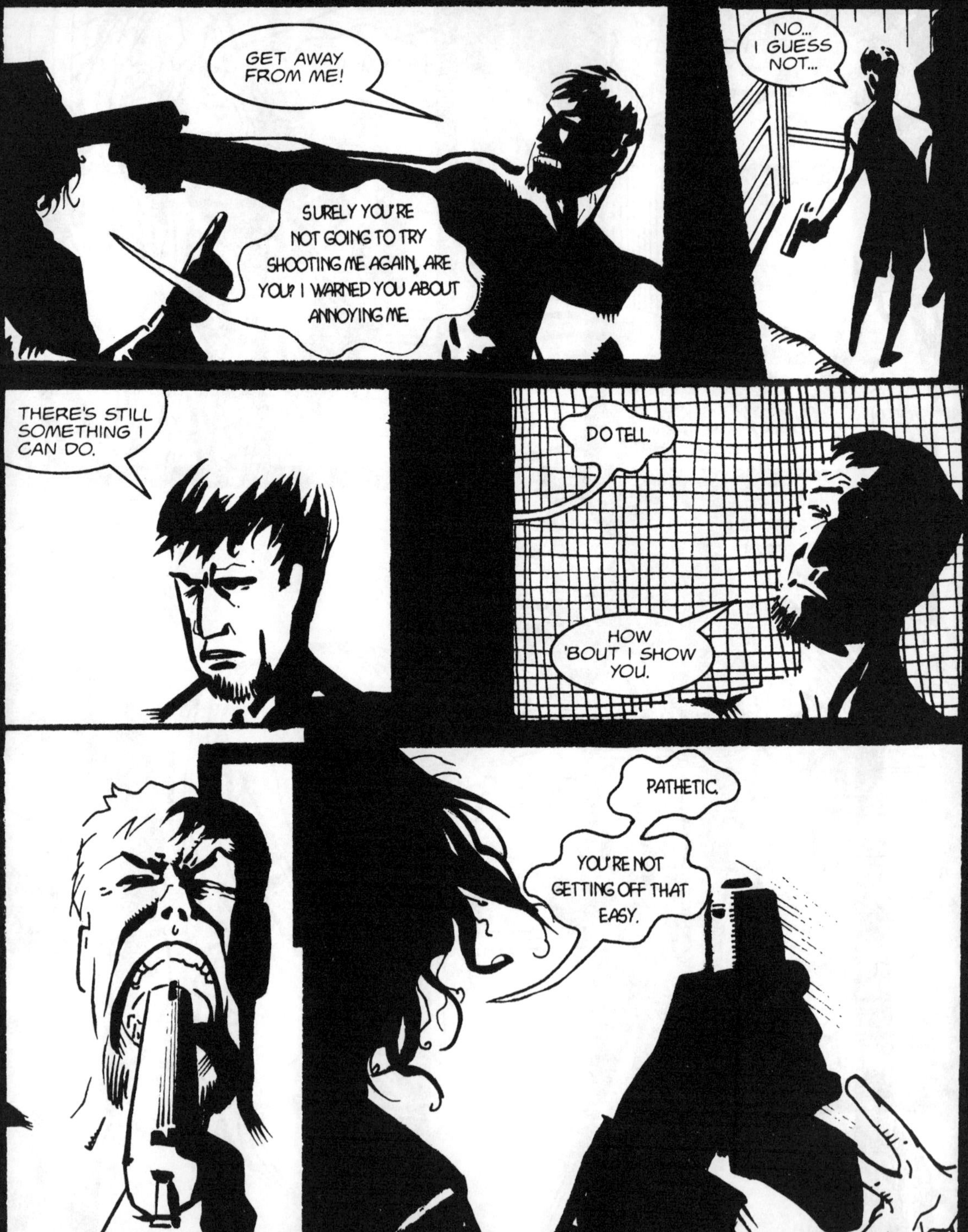
GET AWAY FROM ME!
SURELY YOU'RE NOT GOING TO TRY SHOOTING ME AGAIN, ARE YOU? I WARNED YOU ABOUT ANNOYING ME
NO... I GUESS NOT...
THERE'S STILL SOMETHING I CAN DO.
DO TELL.
HOW 'BOUT I SHOW YOU.
PATHETIC.
YOU'RE NOT GETTING OFF THAT EASY.

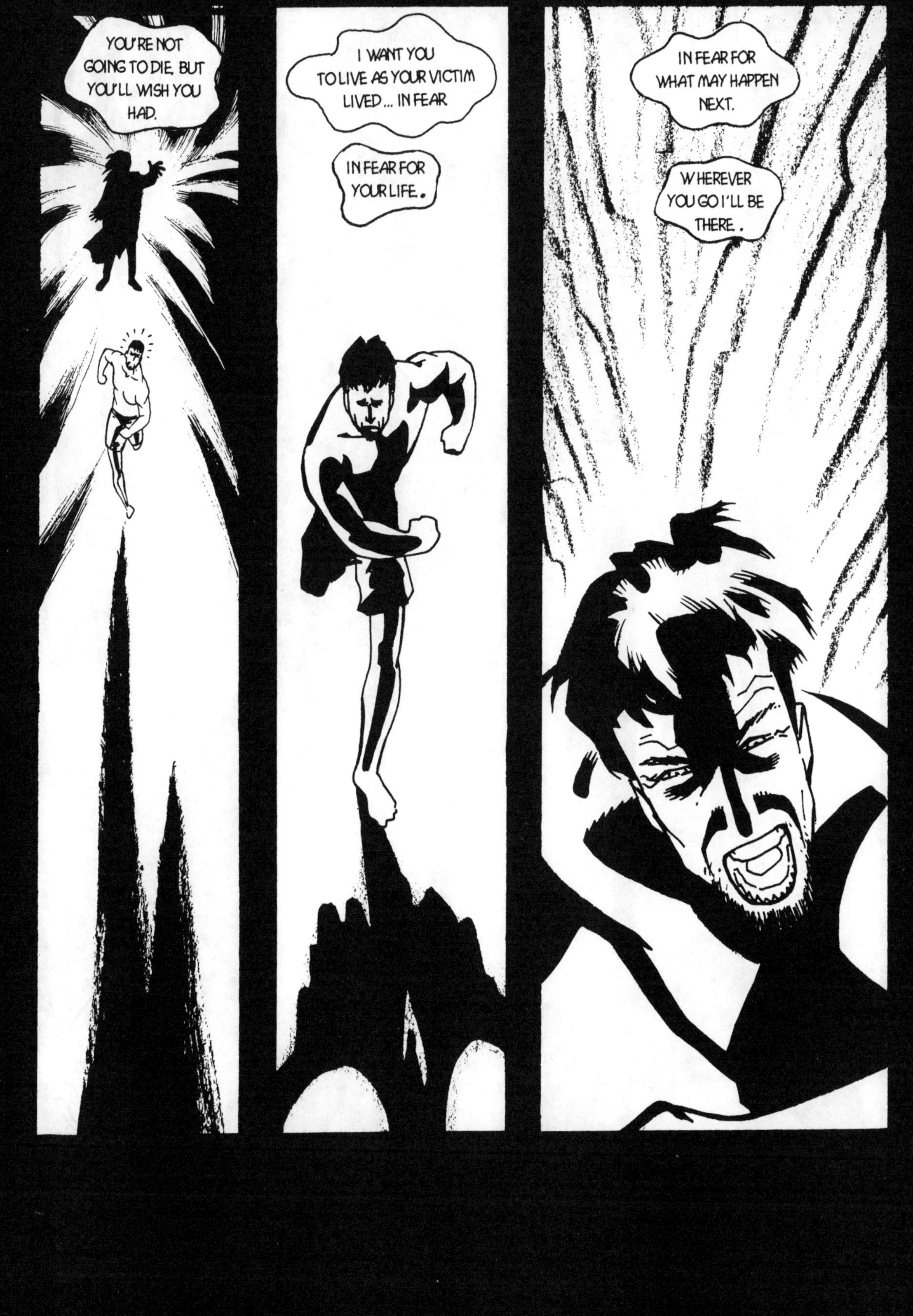
YOU'RE NOT GOING TO DIE, BUT YOU'LL WISH YOU HAD.
I WANT YOU TO LIVE AS YOUR VICTIM LIVED... IN FEAR
IN FEAR FOR YOUR LIFE.
IN FEAR FOR WHAT MAY HAPPEN NEXT.
WHEREVER YOU GO I'LL BE THERE.

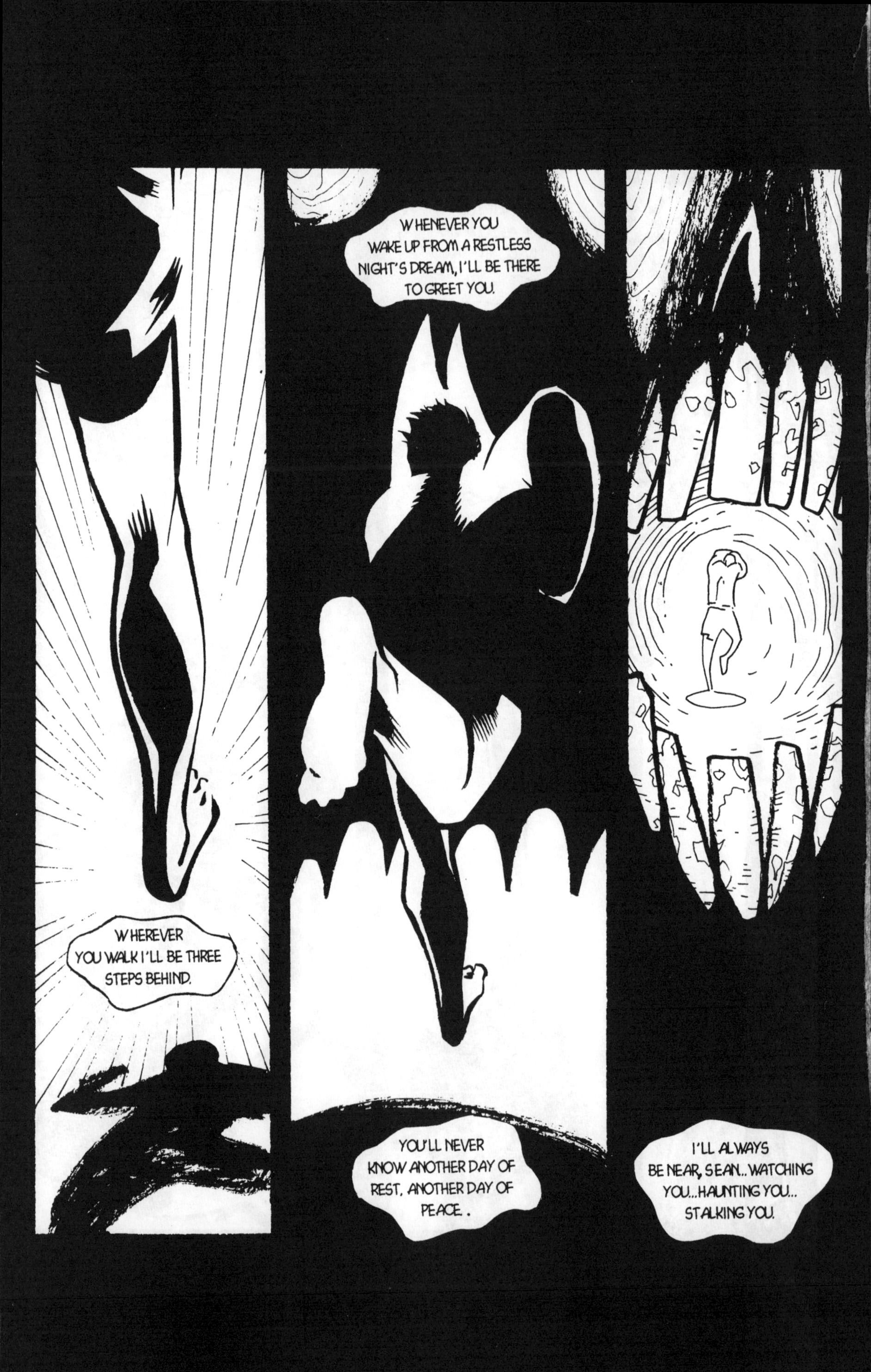
WHEREVER YOU WALK I'LL BE THREE STEPS BEHIND.
WHENEVER YOU WAKE UP FROM A RESTLESS NIGHT'S DREAM, I'LL BE THERE TO GREET YOU.
YOU'LL NEVER KNOW ANOTHER DAY OF REST, ANOTHER DAY OF PEACE.
I'LL ALWAYS BE NEAR, SEAN.. WATCHING YOU... HAUNTING YOU... STALKING YOU.

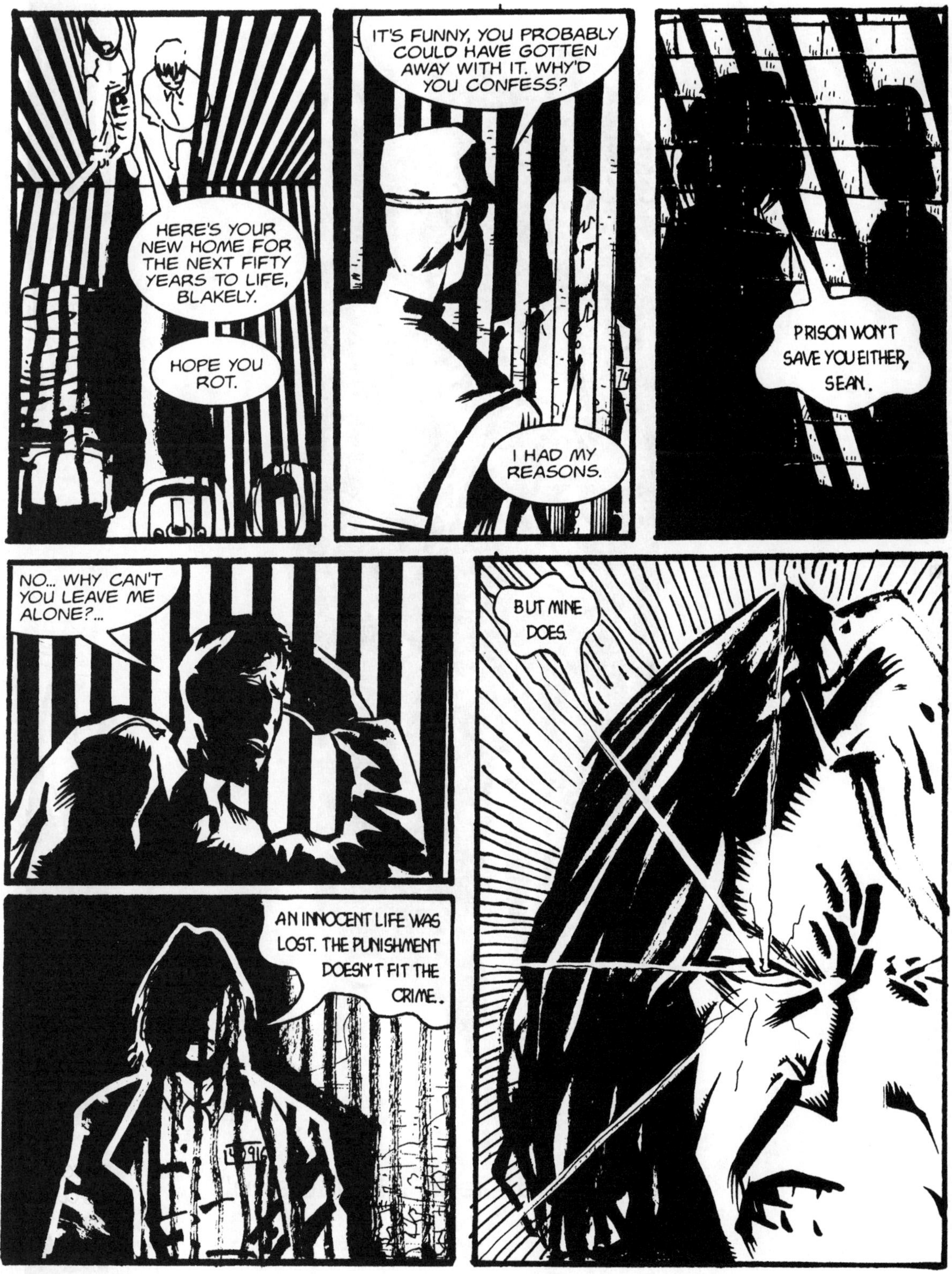
HERE'S YOUR NEW HOME FOR THE NEXT FIFTY YEARS TO LIFE, BLAKELY.
HOPE YOU ROT.
IT'S FUNNY, YOU PROBABLY COULD HAVE GOTTEN AWAY WITH IT. WHY'D YOU CONFESS?
I HAD MY REASONS.
PRISON WON'T SAVE YOU EITHER, SEAN.
NO... WHY CAN'T YOU LEAVE ME ALONE?...
AN INNOCENT LIFE WAS LOST. THE PUNISHMENT DOESN'T FIT THE CRIME..
BUT MINE DOES.

"To Live and Die in Mogadishu"

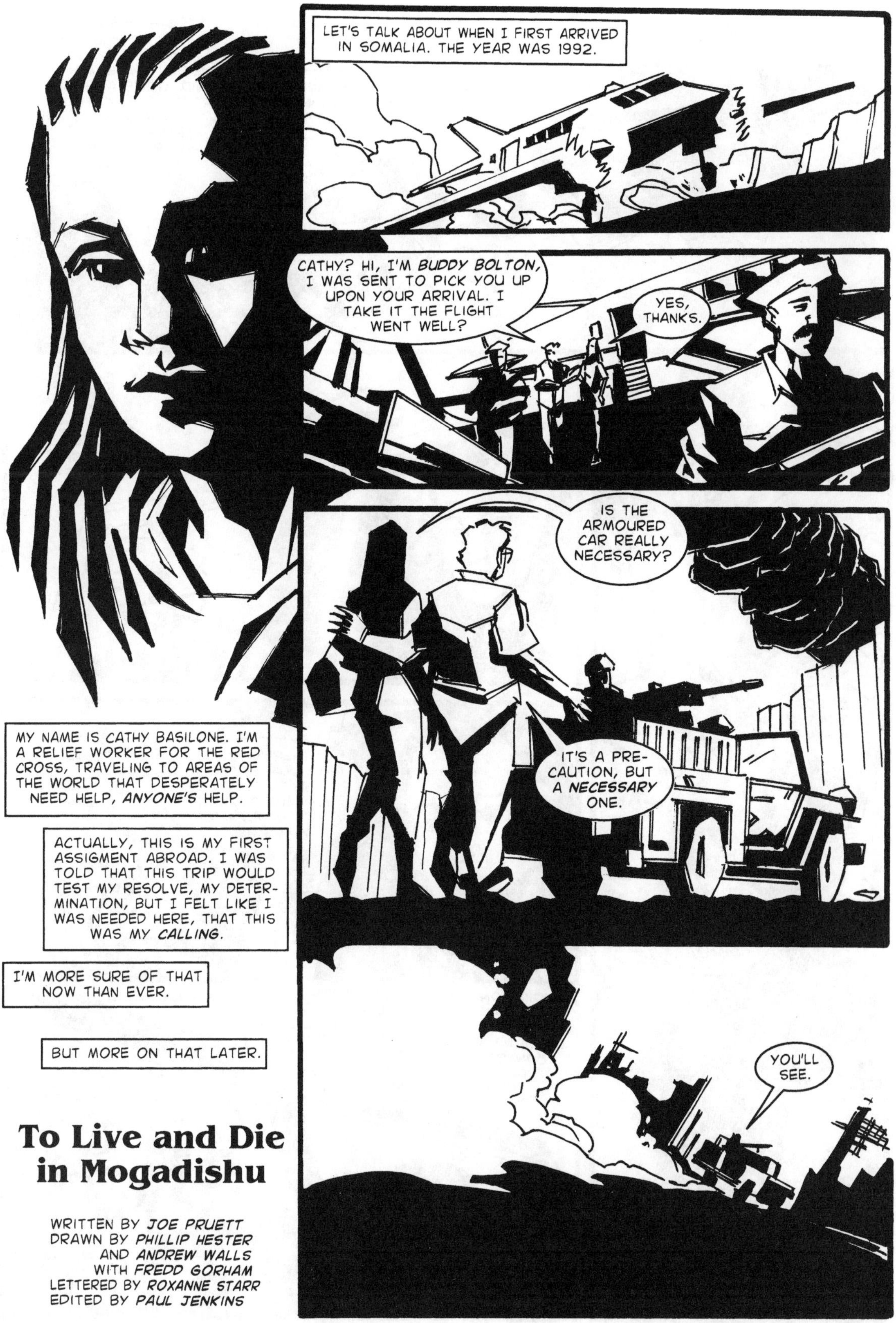

MY NAME IS CATHY BASILONE. I'M A RELIEF WORKER FOR THE RED CROSS, TRAVELING TO AREAS OF THE WORLD THAT DESPERATELY NEED HELP, *ANYONE'S* HELP.
ACTUALLY, THIS IS MY FIRST ASSIGMENT ABROAD. I WAS TOLD THAT THIS TRIP WOULD TEST MY RESOLVE, MY DETERMINATION, BUT I FELT LIKE I WAS NEEDED HERE, THAT THIS WAS MY *CALLING*.
I'M MORE SURE OF THAT NOW THAN EVER.
BUT MORE ON THAT LATER.
LET'S TALK ABOUT WHEN I FIRST ARRIVED IN SOMALIA. THE YEAR WAS 1992.
CATHY? HI, I'M *BUDDY BOLTON,* I WAS SENT TO PICK YOU UP UPON YOUR ARRIVAL. I TAKE IT THE FLIGHT WENT WELL?
YES, THANKS.
IS THE ARMOURED CAR REALLY NECESSARY?
IT'S A PRECAUTION, BUT A *NECESSARY* ONE.
YOU'LL SEE.

To Live and Die in Mogadishu

WRITTEN BY *JOE PRUETT*
DRAWN BY *PHILLIP HESTER*
AND *ANDREW WALLS*
WITH *FREDD GORHAM*
LETTERED BY *ROXANNE STARR*
EDITED BY *PAUL JENKINS*

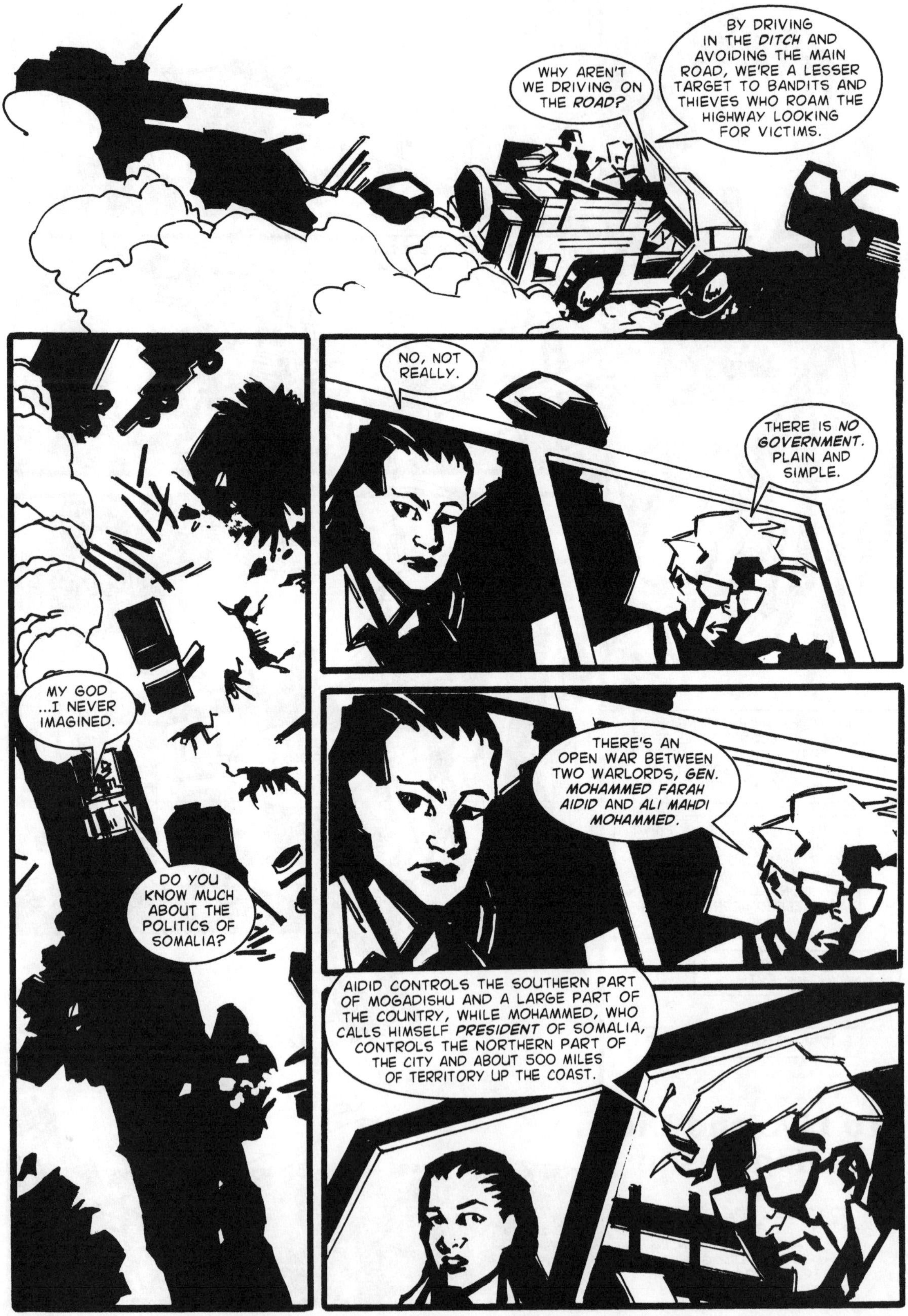
WHY AREN'T WE DRIVING ON THE *ROAD?*
BY DRIVING IN THE *DITCH* AND AVOIDING THE MAIN ROAD, WE'RE A LESSER TARGET TO BANDITS AND THIEVES WHO ROAM THE HIGHWAY LOOKING FOR VICTIMS.
MY GOD ...I NEVER IMAGINED.
DO YOU KNOW MUCH ABOUT THE POLITICS OF SOMALIA?
NO, NOT REALLY.
THERE IS *NO GOVERNMENT*. PLAIN AND SIMPLE.
THERE'S AN OPEN WAR BETWEEN TWO WARLORDS, *GEN. MOHAMMED FARAH AIDID* AND *ALI MAHDI MOHAMMED*.
AIDID CONTROLS THE SOUTHERN PART OF MOGADISHU AND A LARGE PART OF THE COUNTRY, WHILE MOHAMMED, WHO CALLS HIMSELF *PRESIDENT* OF SOMALIA, CONTROLS THE NORTHERN PART OF THE CITY AND ABOUT 500 MILES OF TERRITORY UP THE COAST.

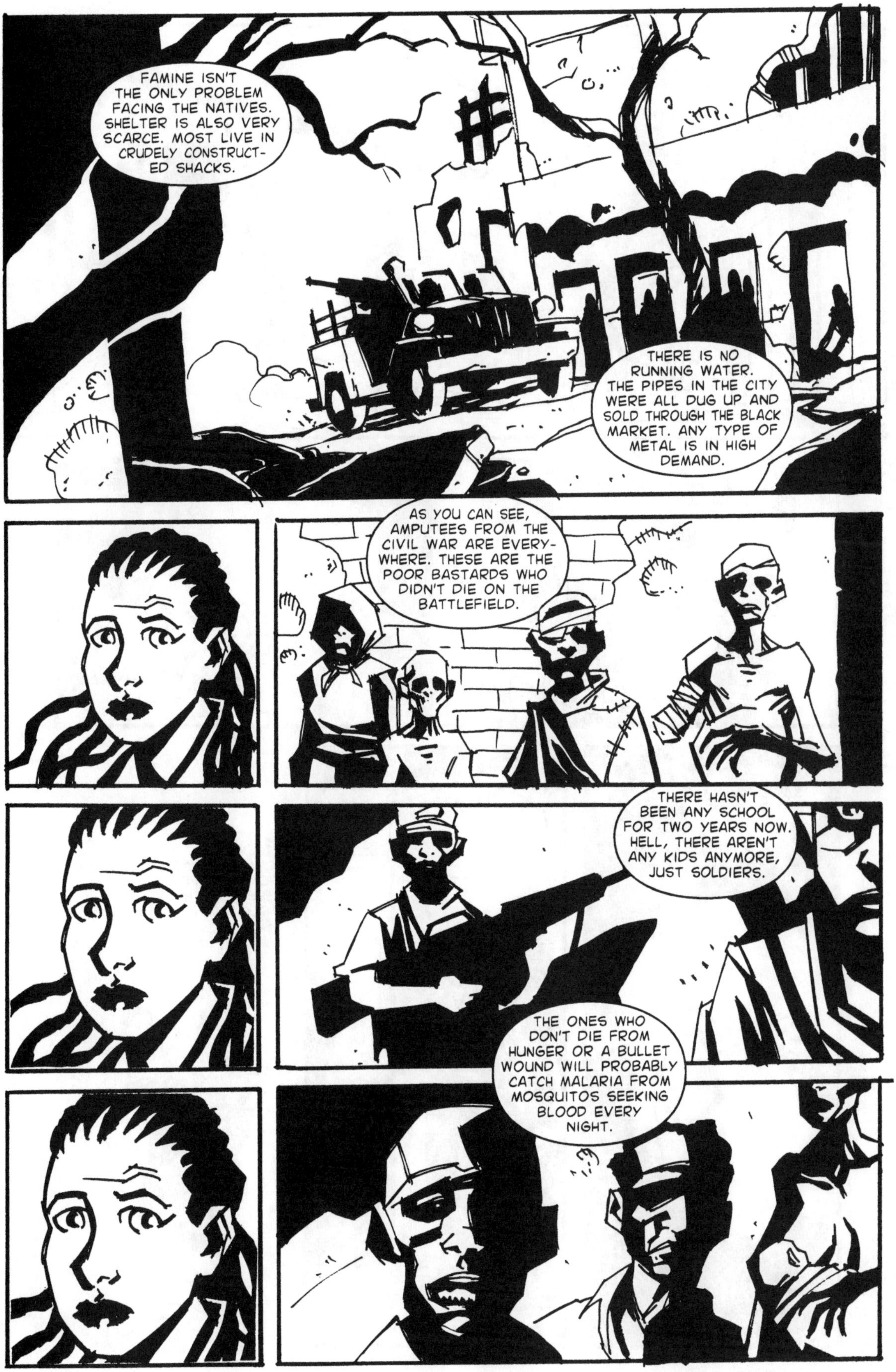
FAMINE ISN'T THE ONLY PROBLEM FACING THE NATIVES. SHELTER IS ALSO VERY SCARCE. MOST LIVE IN CRUDELY CONSTRUCTED SHACKS.
THERE IS NO RUNNING WATER. THE PIPES IN THE CITY WERE ALL DUG UP AND SOLD THROUGH THE BLACK MARKET. ANY TYPE OF METAL IS IN HIGH DEMAND.
AS YOU CAN SEE, AMPUTEES FROM THE CIVIL WAR ARE EVERYWHERE. THESE ARE THE POOR BASTARDS WHO DIDN'T DIE ON THE BATTLEFIELD.
THERE HASN'T BEEN ANY SCHOOL FOR TWO YEARS NOW. HELL, THERE AREN'T ANY KIDS ANYMORE, JUST SOLDIERS.
THE ONES WHO DON'T DIE FROM HUNGER OR A BULLET WOUND WILL PROBABLY CATCH MALARIA FROM MOSQUITOS SEEKING BLOOD EVERY NIGHT.

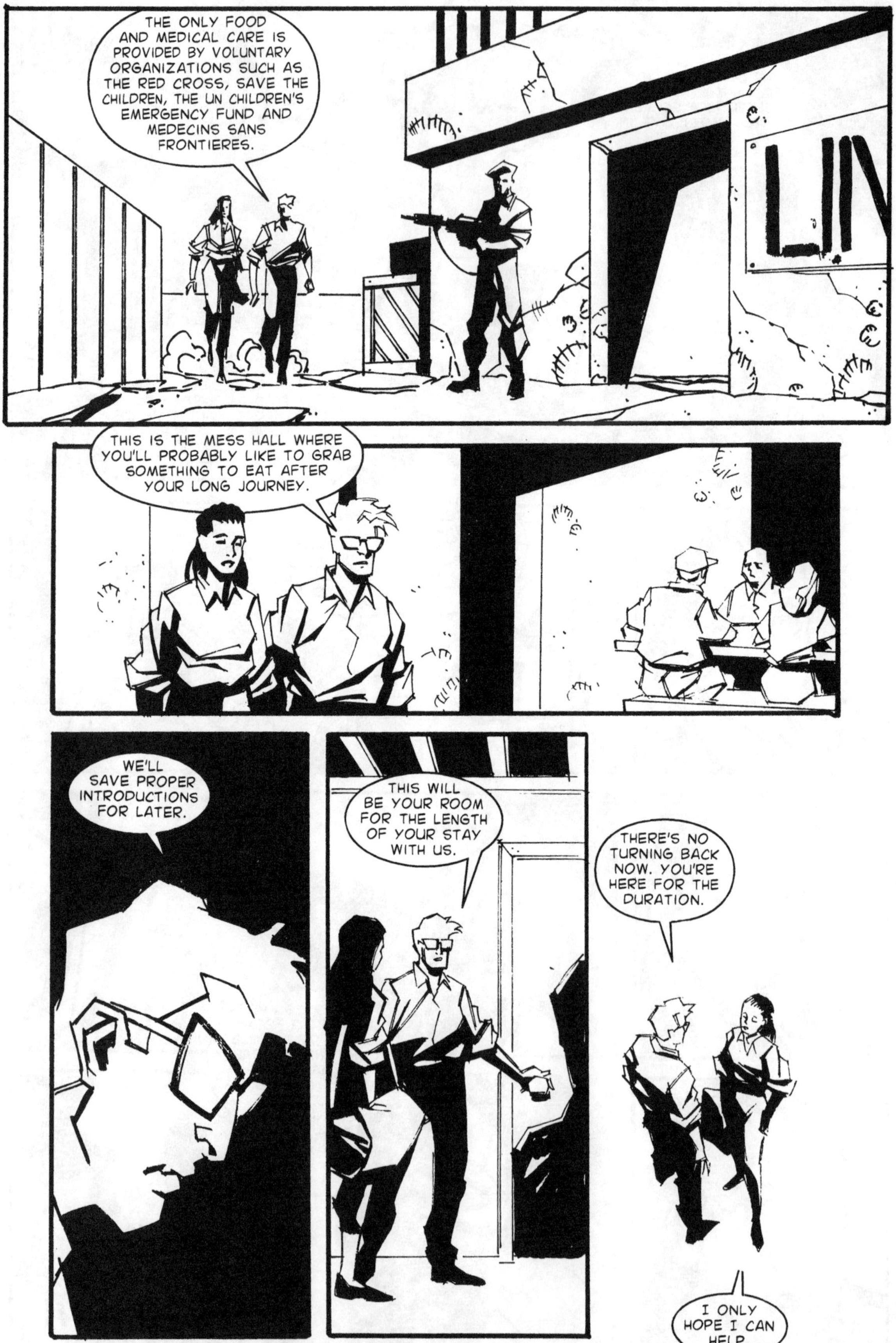
THE ONLY FOOD AND MEDICAL CARE IS PROVIDED BY VOLUNTARY ORGANIZATIONS SUCH AS THE RED CROSS, SAVE THE CHILDREN, THE UN CHILDREN'S EMERGENCY FUND AND MEDECINS SANS FRONTIERES.
THIS IS THE MESS HALL WHERE YOU'LL PROBABLY LIKE TO GRAB SOMETHING TO EAT AFTER YOUR LONG JOURNEY.
WE'LL SAVE PROPER INTRODUCTIONS FOR LATER.
THIS WILL BE YOUR ROOM FOR THE LENGTH OF YOUR STAY WITH US.
THERE'S NO TURNING BACK NOW. YOU'RE HERE FOR THE DURATION.
I ONLY HOPE I CAN HELP.

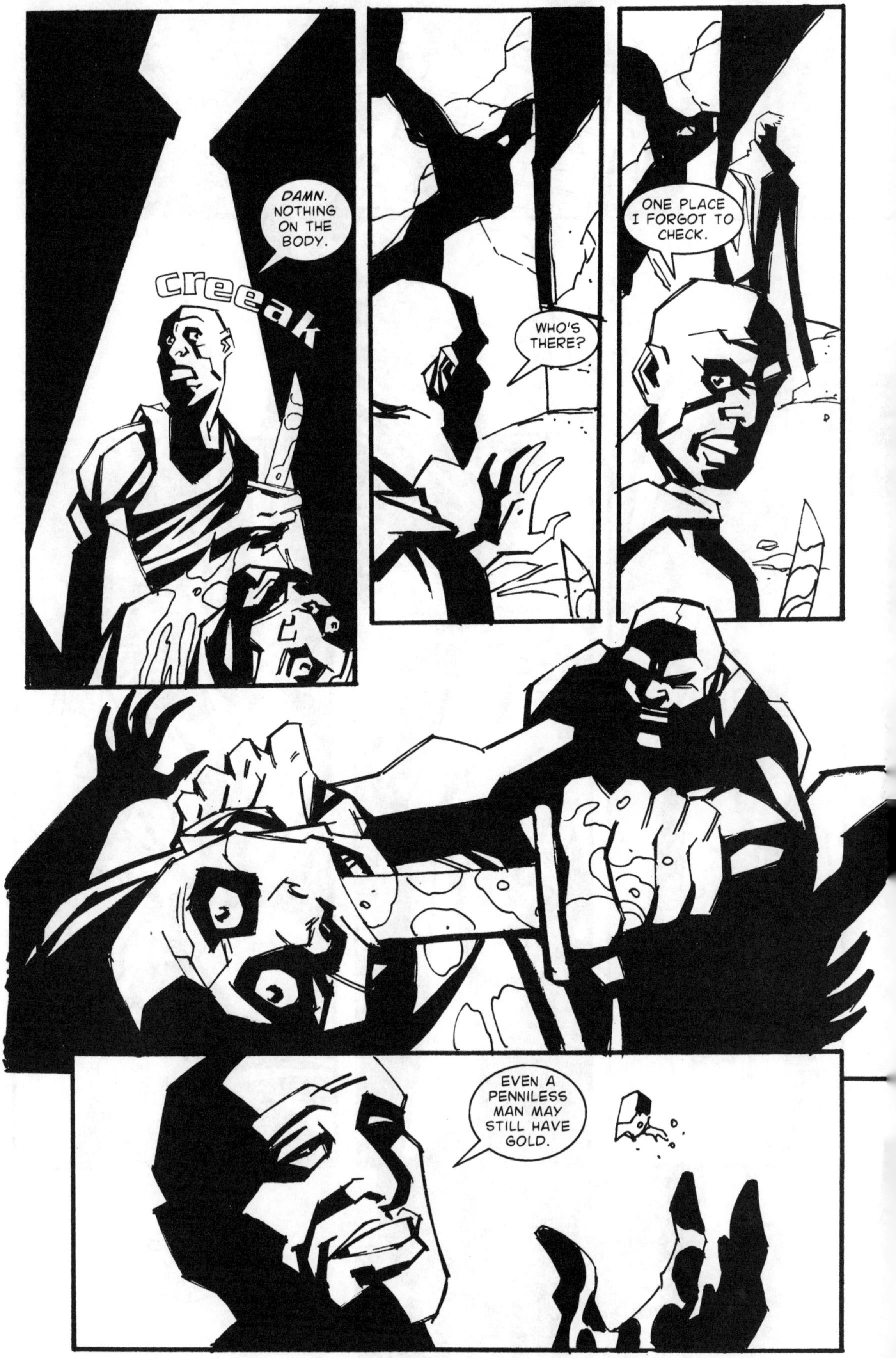
DAMN. NOTHING ON THE BODY.
creeak
WHO'S THERE?
ONE PLACE I FORGOT TO CHECK.
EVEN A PENNILESS MAN MAY STILL HAVE GOLD.

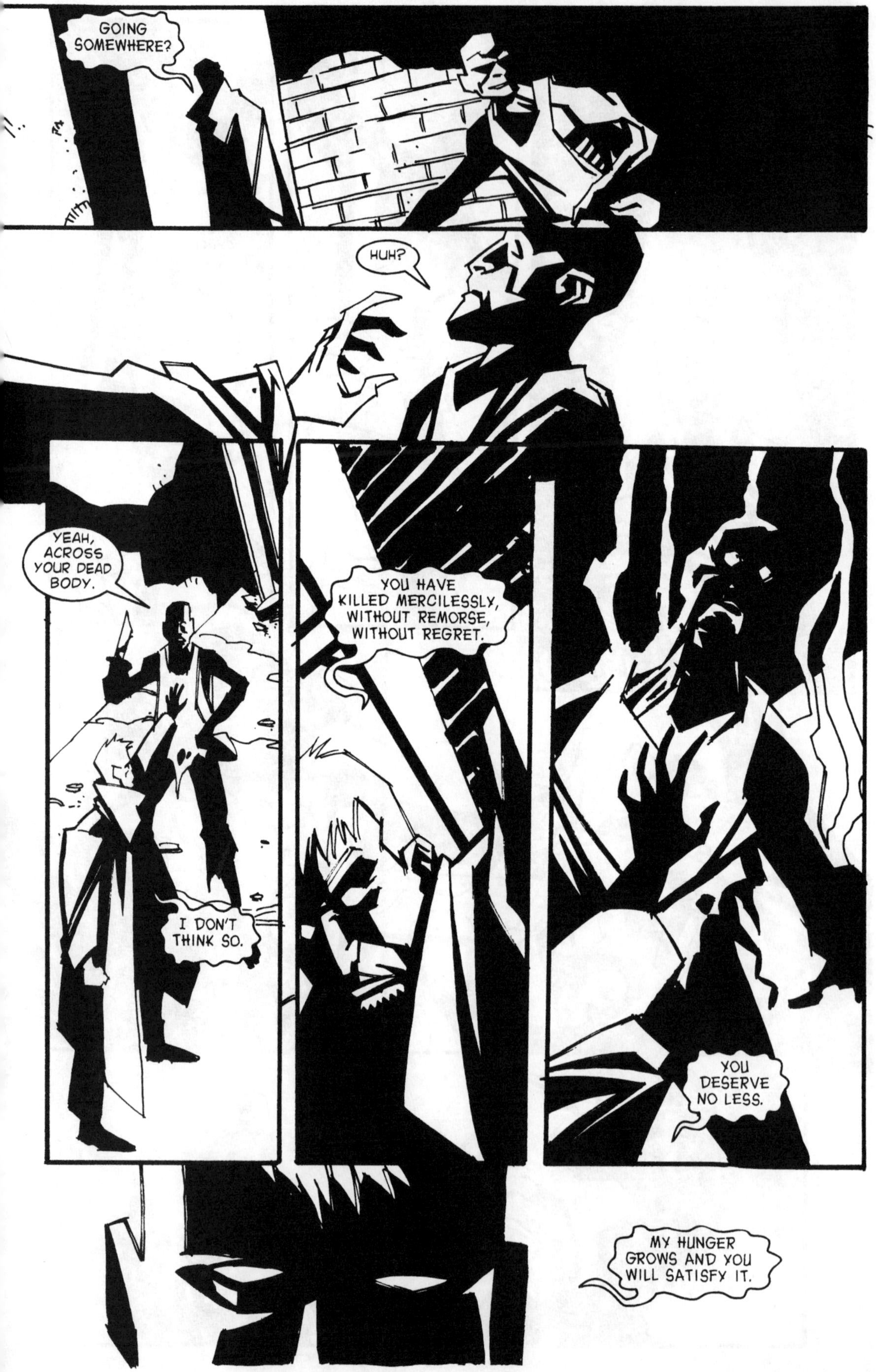
GOING SOMEWHERE?
HUH?
YEAH, ACROSS YOUR DEAD BODY.
I DON'T THINK SO.
YOU HAVE KILLED MERCILESSLY, WITHOUT REMORSE, WITHOUT REGRET.
YOU DESERVE NO LESS.
MY HUNGER GROWS AND YOU WILL SATISFY IT.

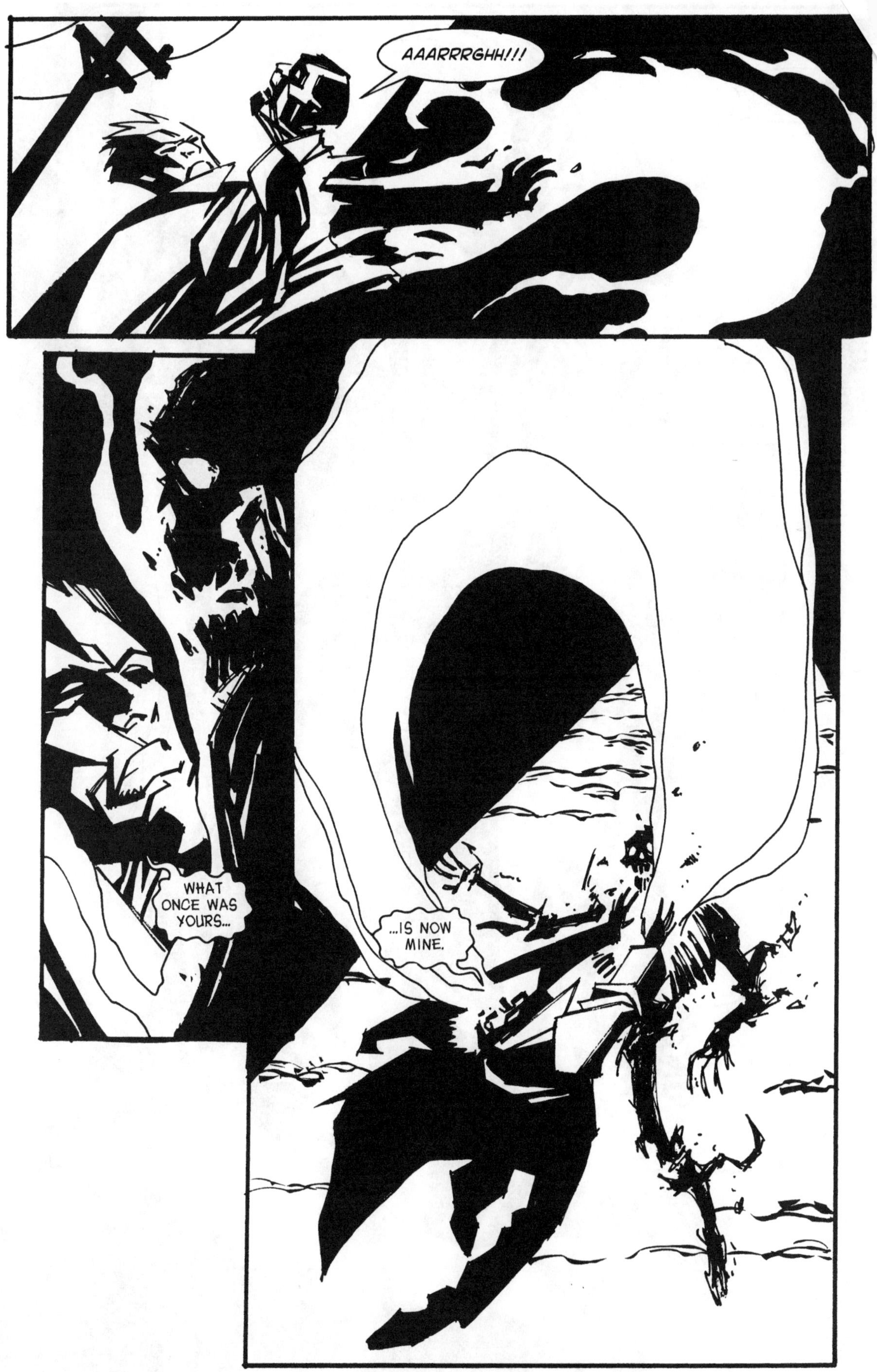
AAARRRGHH!!!
WHAT ONCE WAS YOURS...
...IS NOW MINE.

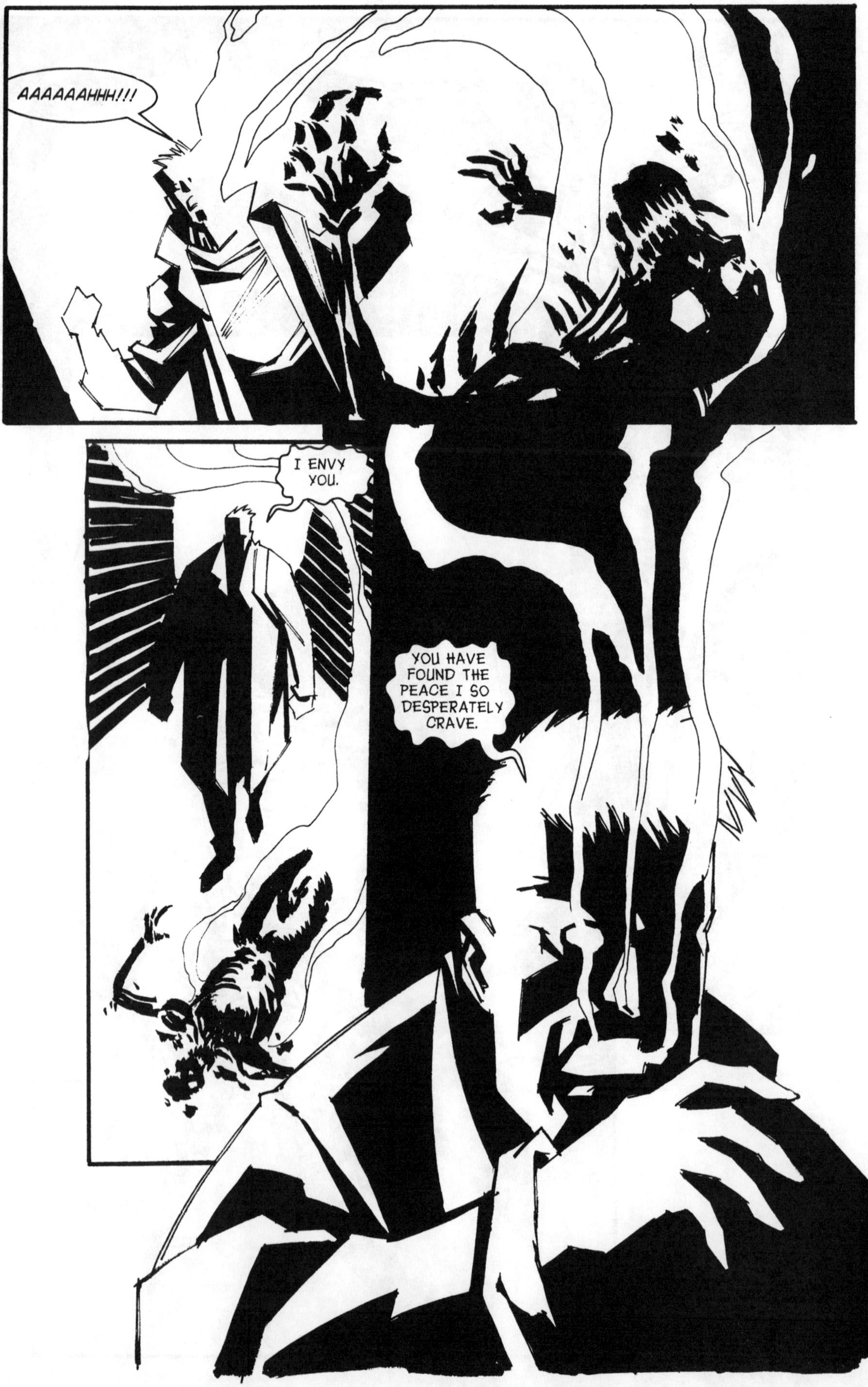
AAAAAAHHH!!!
I ENVY YOU.
YOU HAVE FOUND THE PEACE I SO DESPERATELY CRAVE.

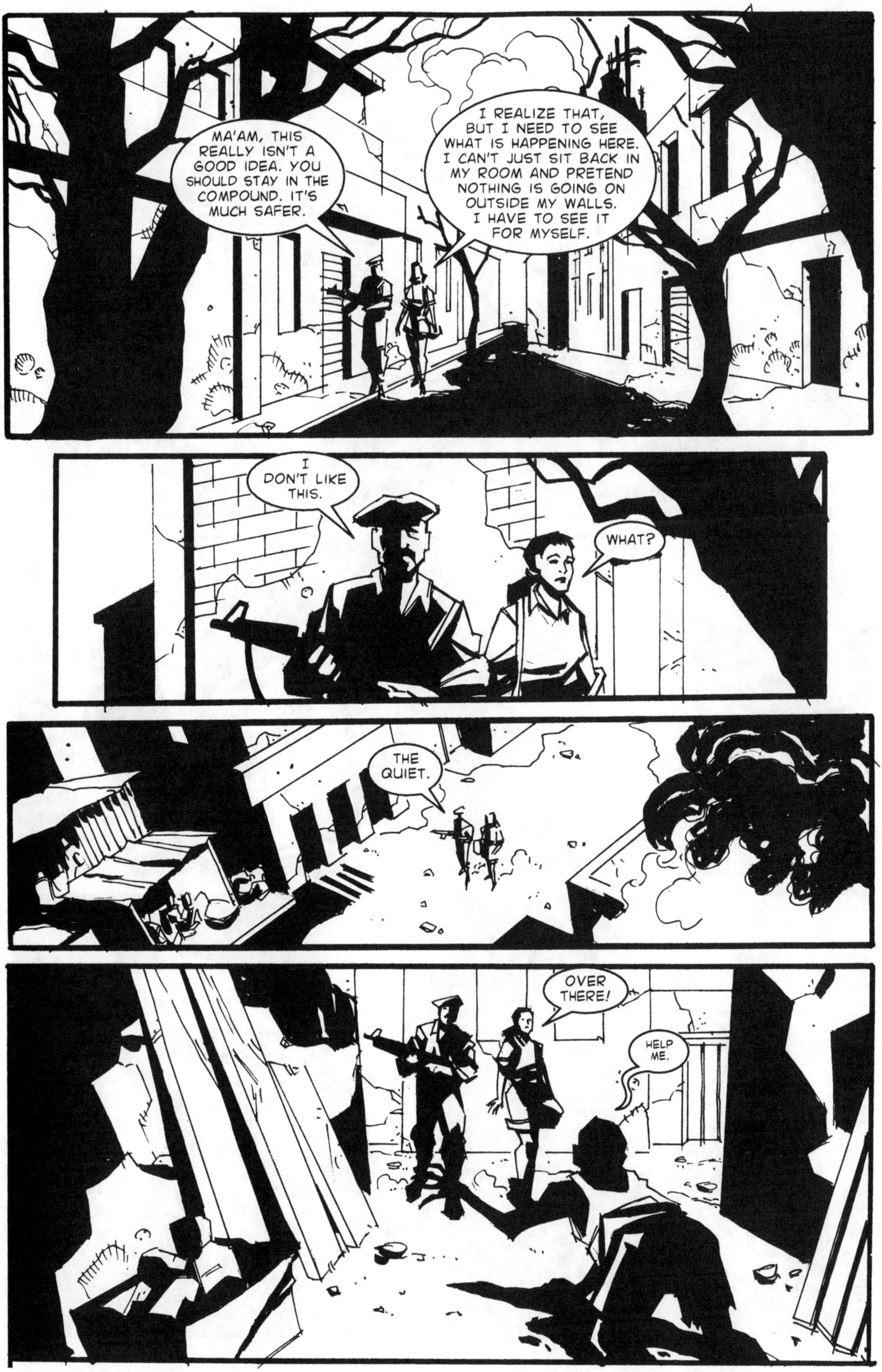
MA'AM, THIS REALLY ISN'T A GOOD IDEA. YOU SHOULD STAY IN THE COMPOUND. IT'S MUCH SAFER.
I REALIZE THAT, BUT I NEED TO SEE WHAT IS HAPPENING HERE. I CAN'T JUST SIT BACK IN MY ROOM AND PRETEND NOTHING IS GOING ON OUTSIDE MY WALLS. I HAVE TO SEE IT FOR MYSELF.
I DON'T LIKE THIS.
WHAT?
THE QUIET.
OVER THERE!
HELP ME.

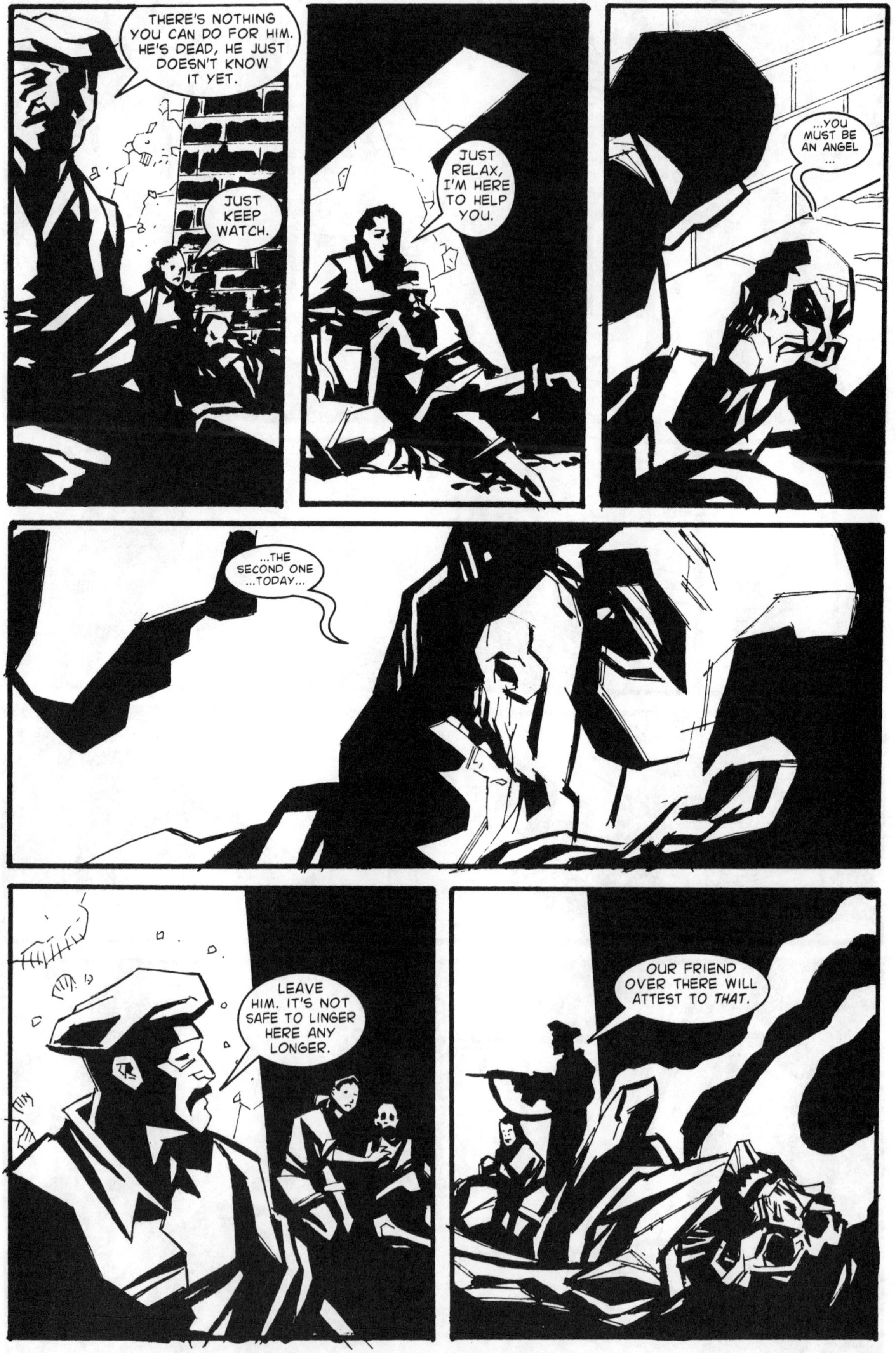
THERE'S NOTHING YOU CAN DO FOR HIM. HE'S DEAD, HE JUST DOESN'T KNOW IT YET.
JUST KEEP WATCH.
JUST RELAX, I'M HERE TO HELP YOU.
...YOU MUST BE AN ANGEL ...
...THE SECOND ONE ...TODAY...
LEAVE HIM. IT'S NOT SAFE TO LINGER HERE ANY LONGER.
OUR FRIEND OVER THERE WILL ATTEST TO *THAT*.

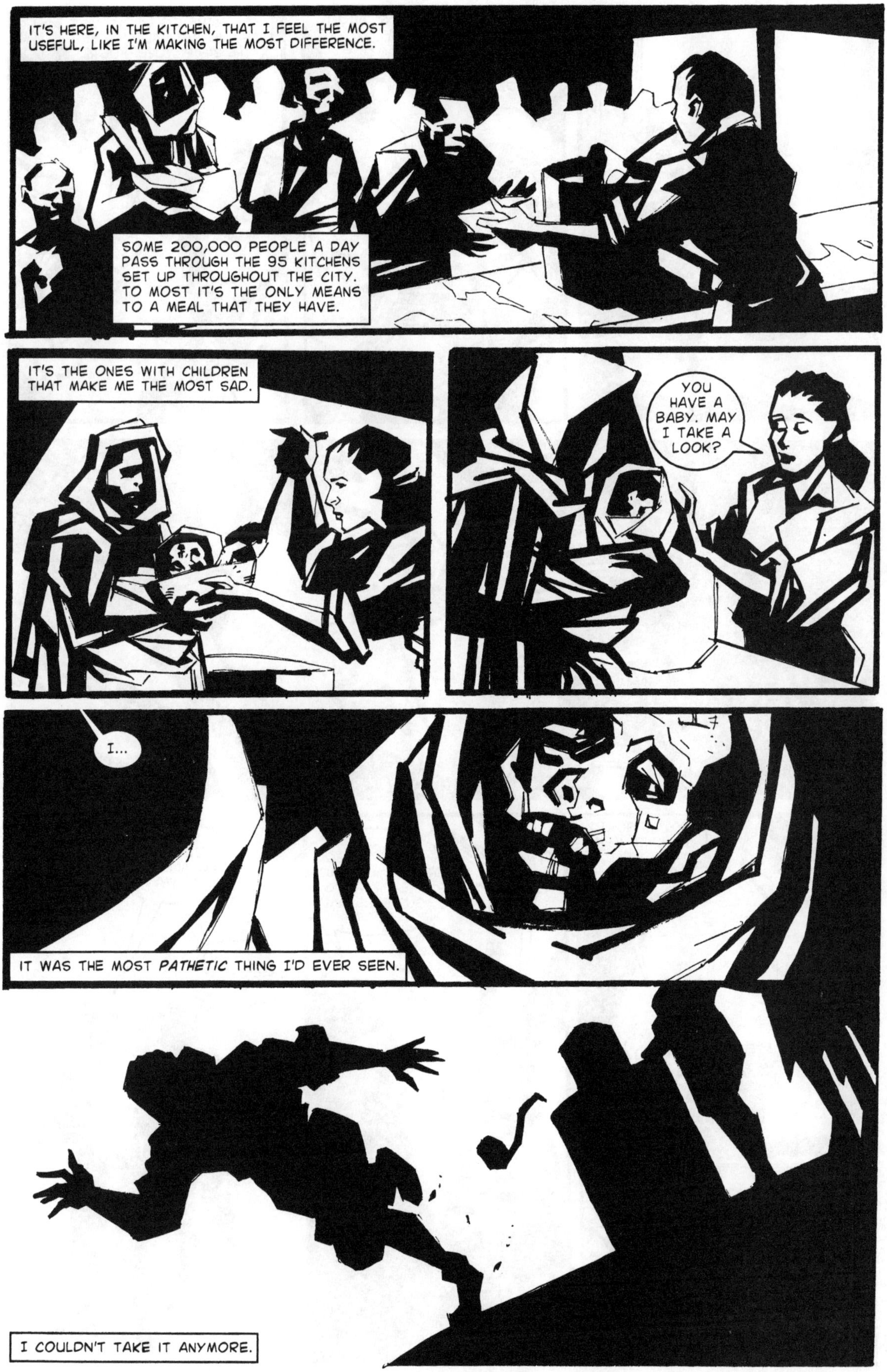
IT'S HERE, IN THE KITCHEN, THAT I FEEL THE MOST USEFUL, LIKE I'M MAKING THE MOST DIFFERENCE.
SOME 200,000 PEOPLE A DAY PASS THROUGH THE 95 KITCHENS SET UP THROUGHOUT THE CITY. TO MOST IT'S THE ONLY MEANS TO A MEAL THAT THEY HAVE.
IT'S THE ONES WITH CHILDREN THAT MAKE ME THE MOST SAD.
YOU HAVE A BABY. MAY I TAKE A LOOK?
I...
IT WAS THE MOST *PATHETIC* THING I'D EVER SEEN.
I COULDN'T TAKE IT ANYMORE.

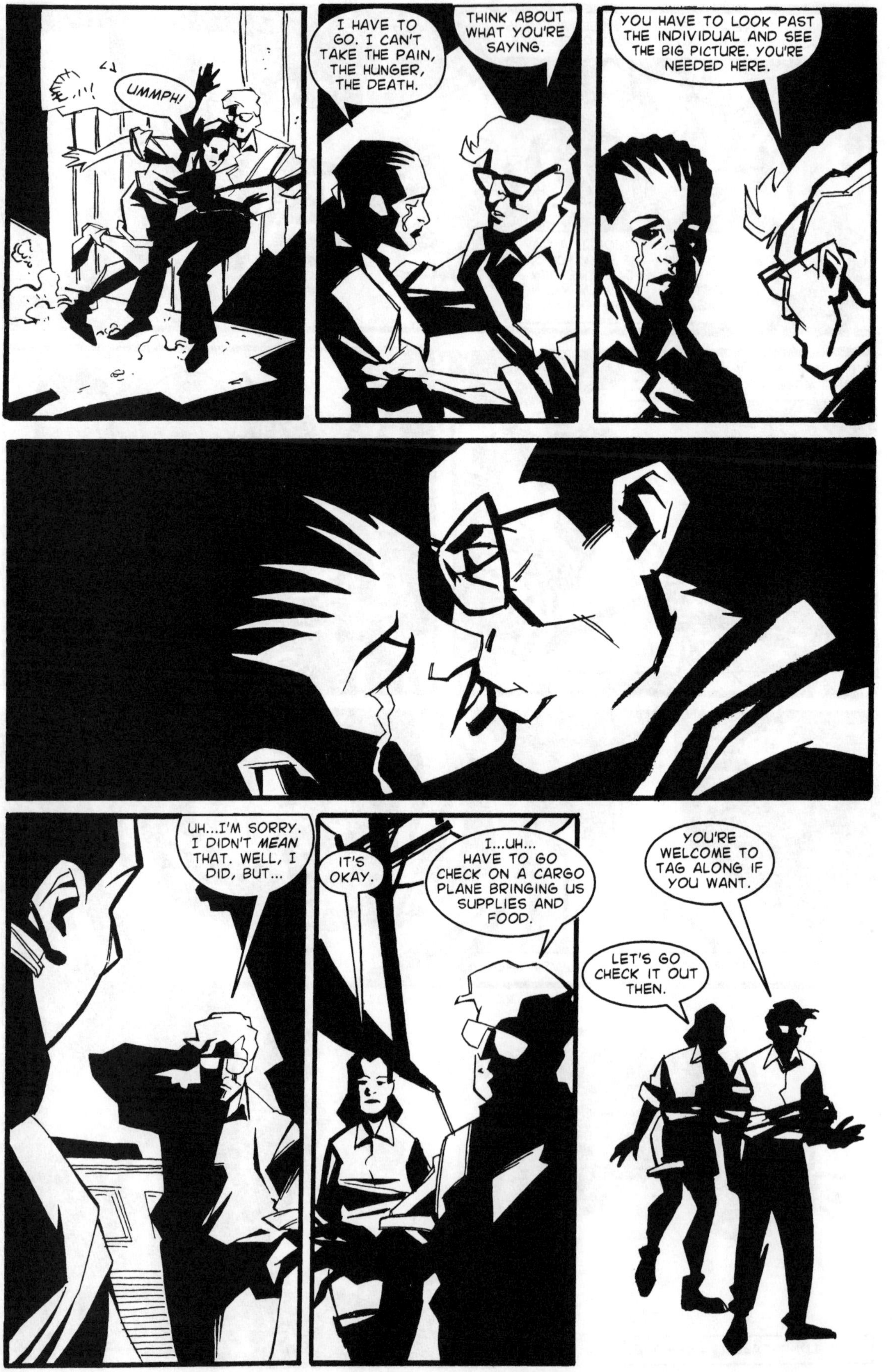
UMMPH!
I HAVE TO GO. I CAN'T TAKE THE PAIN, THE HUNGER, THE DEATH.
THINK ABOUT WHAT YOU'RE SAYING.
YOU HAVE TO LOOK PAST THE INDIVIDUAL AND SEE THE BIG PICTURE. YOU'RE NEEDED HERE.
UH...I'M SORRY. I DIDN'T *MEAN* THAT. WELL, I DID, BUT...
IT'S OKAY.
I...UH... HAVE TO GO CHECK ON A CARGO PLANE BRINGING US SUPPLIES AND FOOD.
YOU'RE WELCOME TO TAG ALONG IF YOU WANT.
LET'S GO CHECK IT OUT THEN.

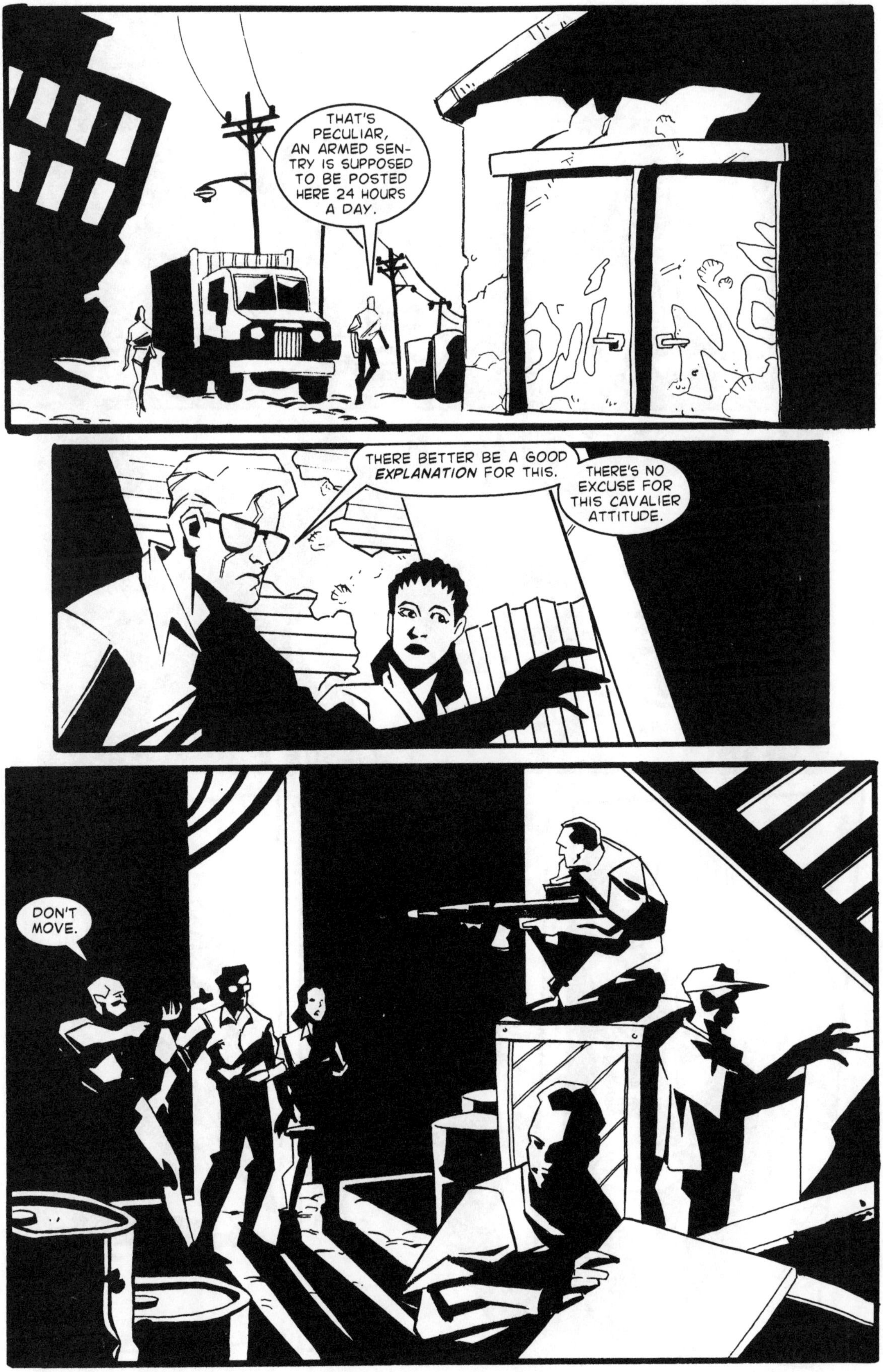
THAT'S PECULIAR, AN ARMED SENTRY IS SUPPOSED TO BE POSTED HERE 24 HOURS A DAY.
THERE BETTER BE A GOOD *EXPLANATION* FOR THIS.
THERE'S NO EXCUSE FOR THIS CAVALIER ATTITUDE.
DON'T MOVE.

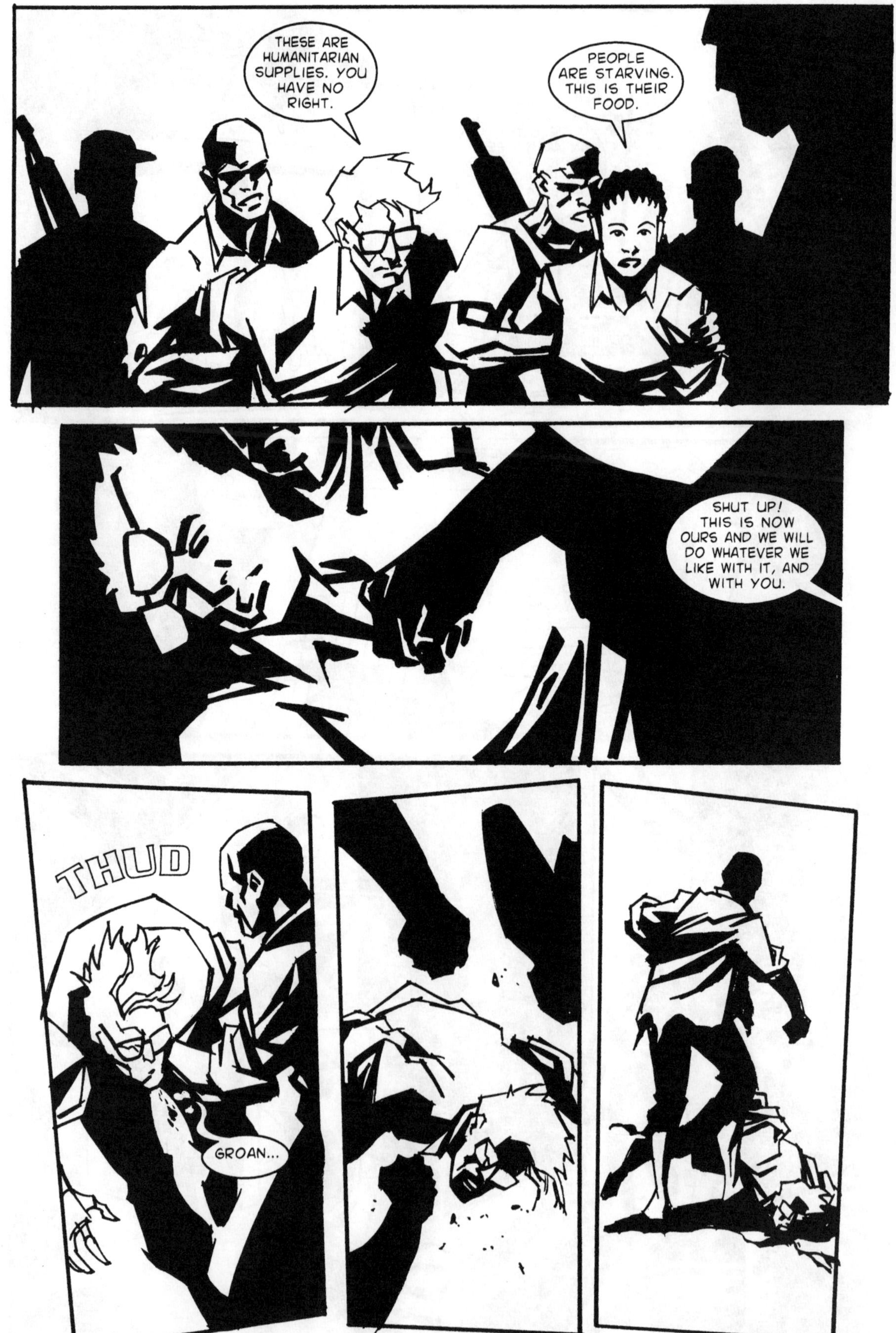
THESE ARE HUMANITARIAN SUPPLIES. YOU HAVE NO RIGHT.
PEOPLE ARE STARVING. THIS IS THEIR FOOD.
SHUT UP! THIS IS NOW OURS AND WE WILL DO WHATEVER WE LIKE WITH IT, AND WITH YOU.
THUD
GROAN...

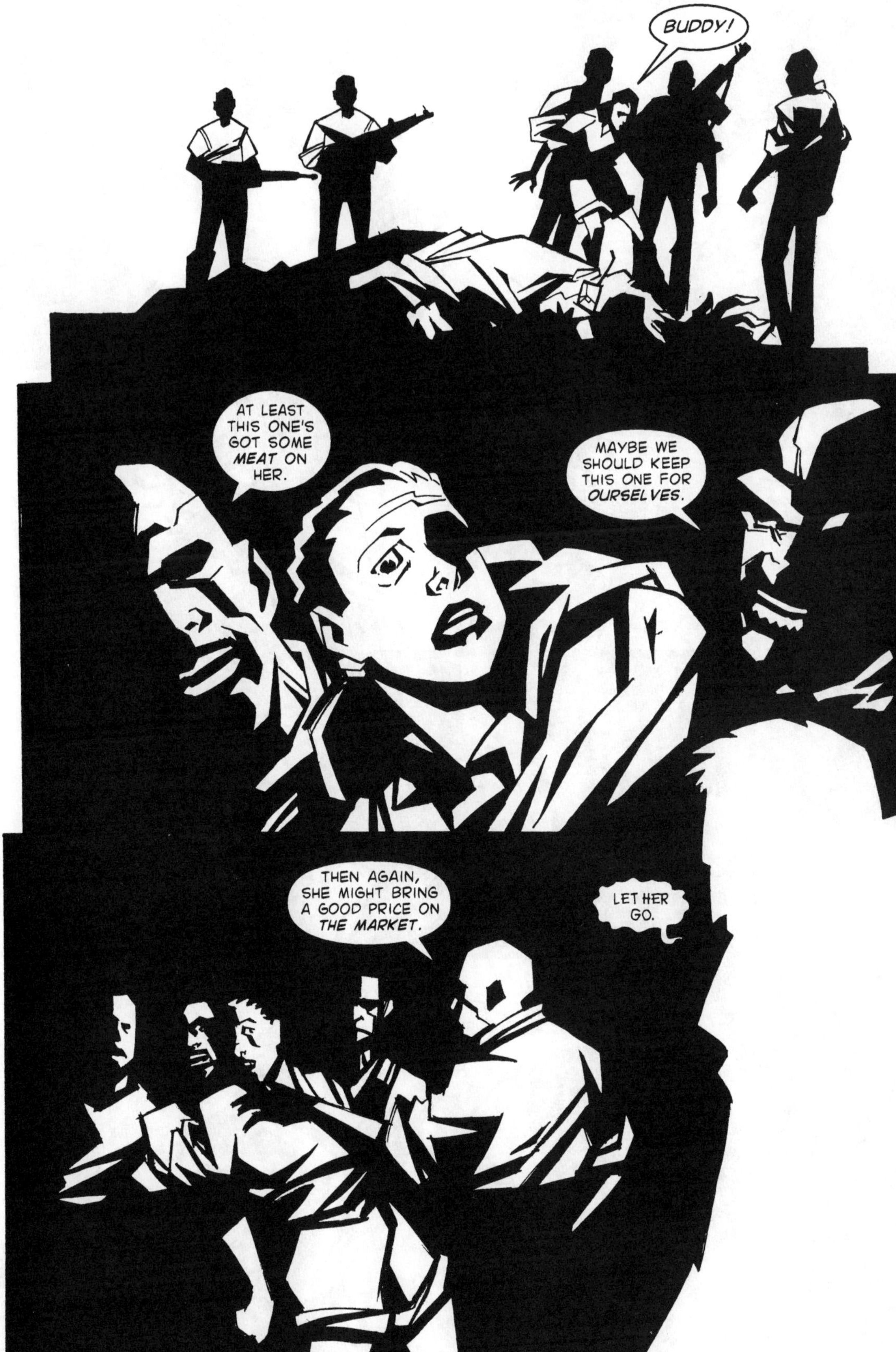
BUDDY!
AT LEAST THIS ONE'S GOT SOME MEAT ON HER.
MAYBE WE SHOULD KEEP THIS ONE FOR OURSELVES.
THEN AGAIN, SHE MIGHT BRING A GOOD PRICE ON THE MARKET.
LET HER GO.

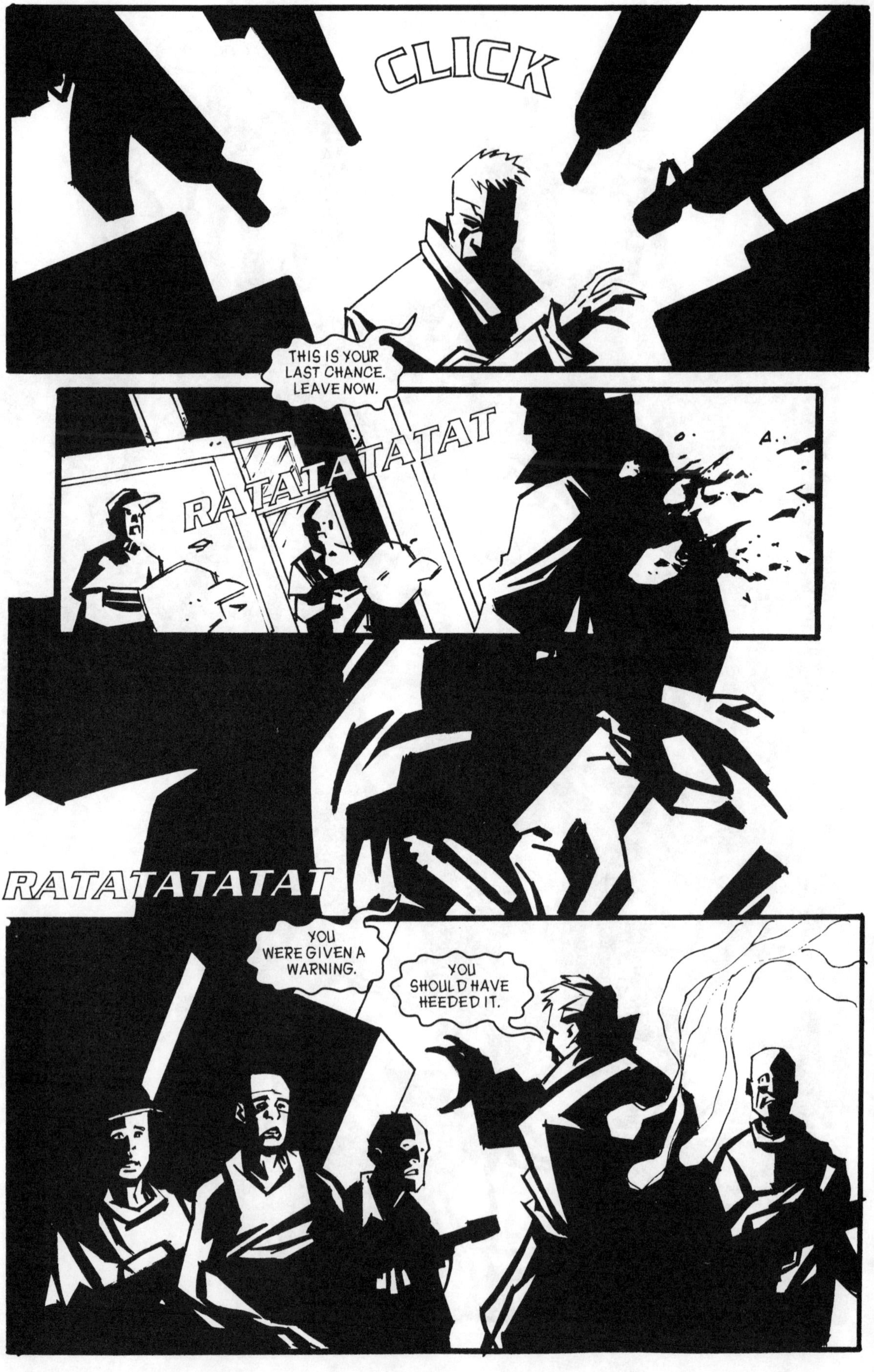
CLICK
THIS IS YOUR LAST CHANCE. LEAVE NOW.
RATATATATATAT
RATATATATATAT
YOU WERE GIVEN A WARNING.
YOU SHOULD HAVE HEEDED IT.

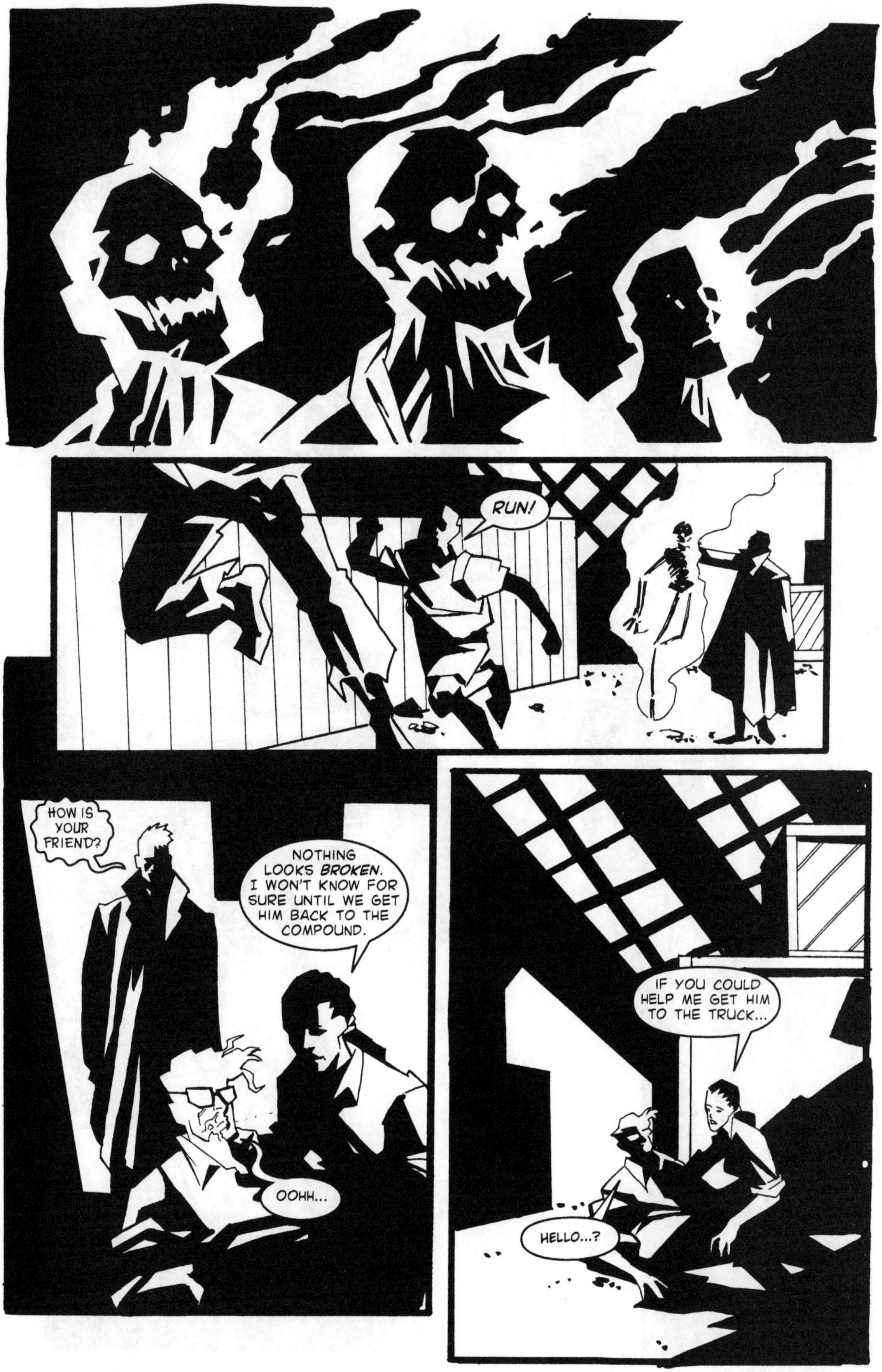
RUN!
HOW IS YOUR FRIEND?
NOTHING LOOKS *BROKEN*. I WON'T KNOW FOR SURE UNTIL WE GET HIM BACK TO THE COMPOUND.
OOHH...
IF YOU COULD HELP ME GET HIM TO THE TRUCK...
HELLO...?

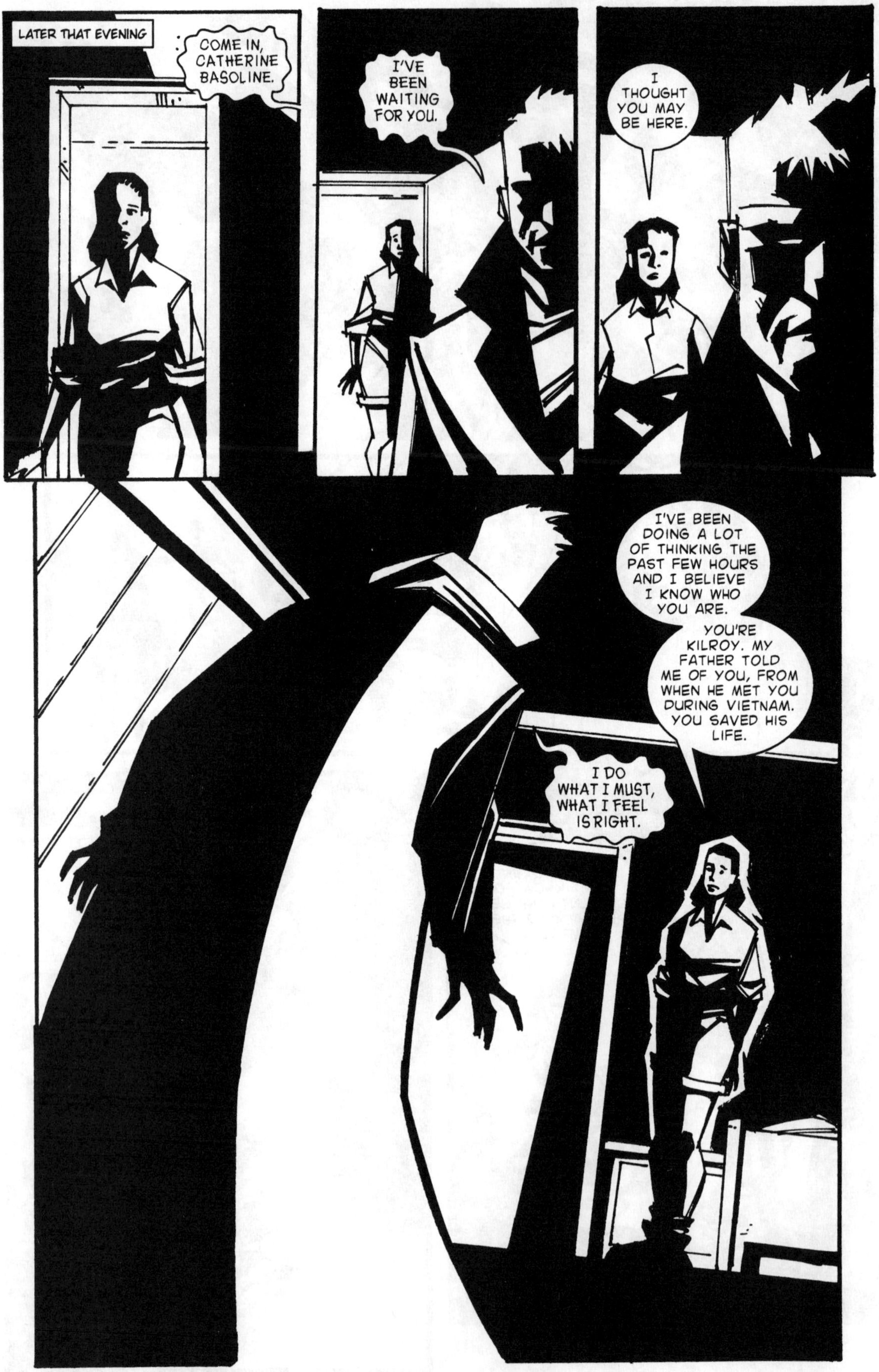
LATER THAT EVENING
COME IN, CATHERINE BASOLINE.
I'VE BEEN WAITING FOR YOU.
I THOUGHT YOU MAY BE HERE.
I'VE BEEN DOING A LOT OF THINKING THE PAST FEW HOURS AND I BELIEVE I KNOW WHO YOU ARE.
YOU'RE KILROY. MY FATHER TOLD ME OF YOU, FROM WHEN HE MET YOU DURING VIETNAM. YOU SAVED HIS LIFE.
I DO WHAT I MUST, WHAT I FEEL IS RIGHT.

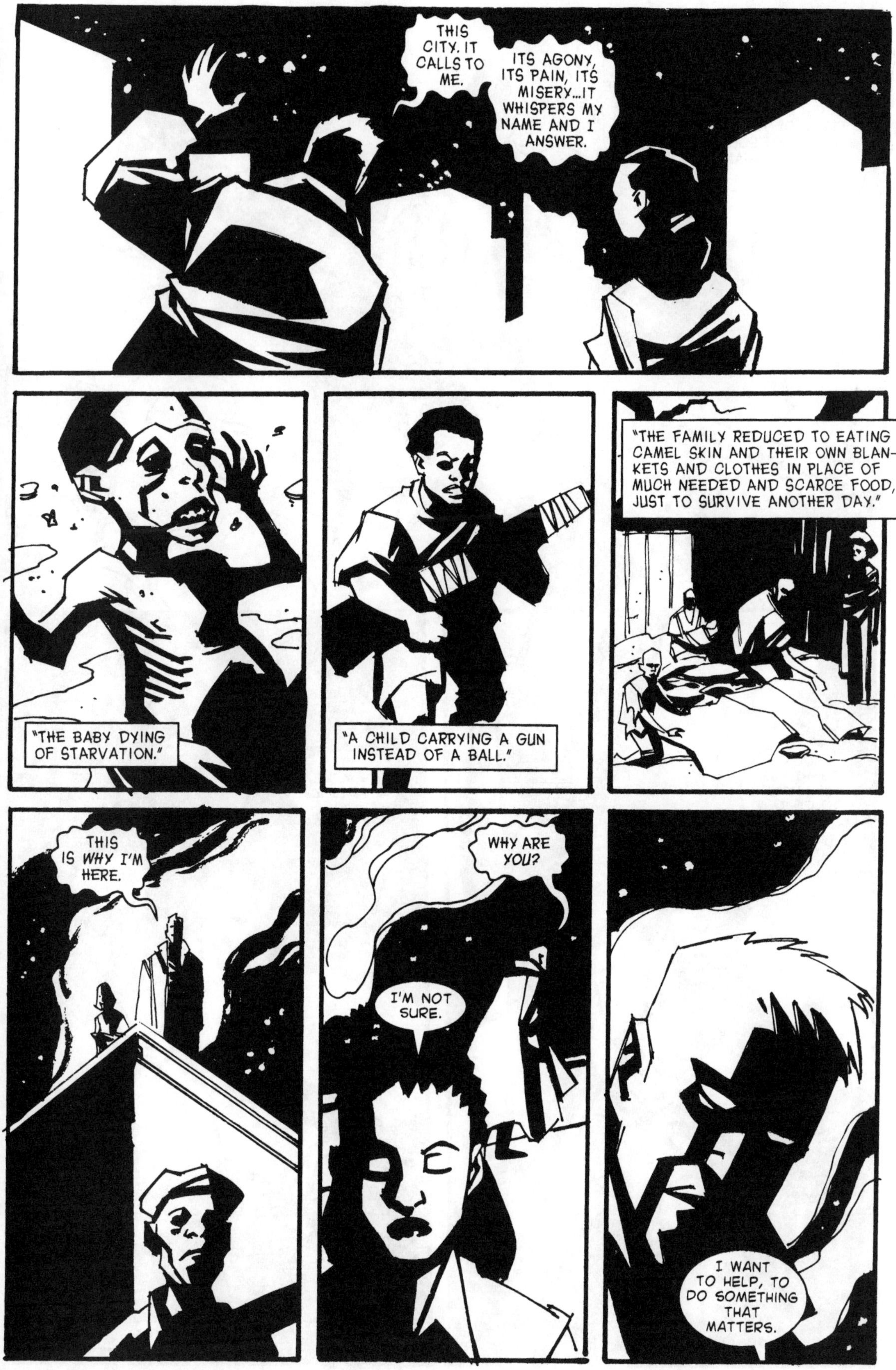
THIS CITY. IT CALLS TO ME.
ITS AGONY, ITS PAIN, ITS MISERY...IT WHISPERS MY NAME AND I ANSWER.
"THE BABY DYING OF STARVATION."
"A CHILD CARRYING A GUN INSTEAD OF A BALL."
"THE FAMILY REDUCED TO EATING CAMEL SKIN AND THEIR OWN BLANKETS AND CLOTHES IN PLACE OF MUCH NEEDED AND SCARCE FOOD, JUST TO SURVIVE ANOTHER DAY."
THIS IS *WHY* I'M HERE.
WHY ARE *YOU*?
I'M NOT SURE.
I WANT TO HELP, TO DO SOMETHING THAT MATTERS.

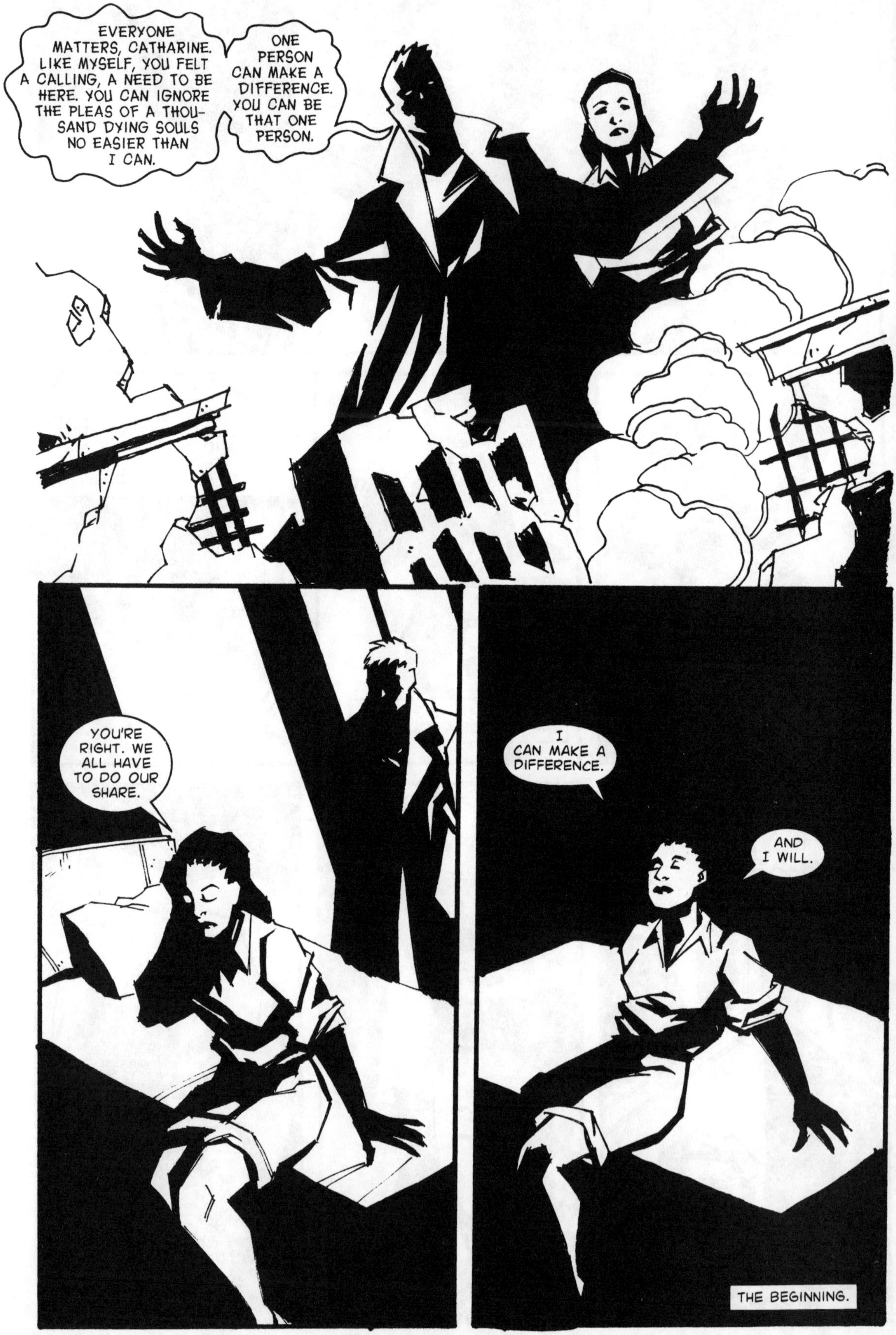
EVERYONE MATTERS, CATHARINE. LIKE MYSELF, YOU FELT A CALLING, A NEED TO BE HERE. YOU CAN IGNORE THE PLEAS OF A THOU-SAND DYING SOULS NO EASIER THAN I CAN.
ONE PERSON CAN MAKE A DIFFERENCE. YOU CAN BE THAT ONE PERSON.
YOU'RE RIGHT. WE ALL HAVE TO DO OUR SHARE.
I CAN MAKE A DIFFERENCE.
AND I WILL.
THE BEGINNING.

"Revelations"

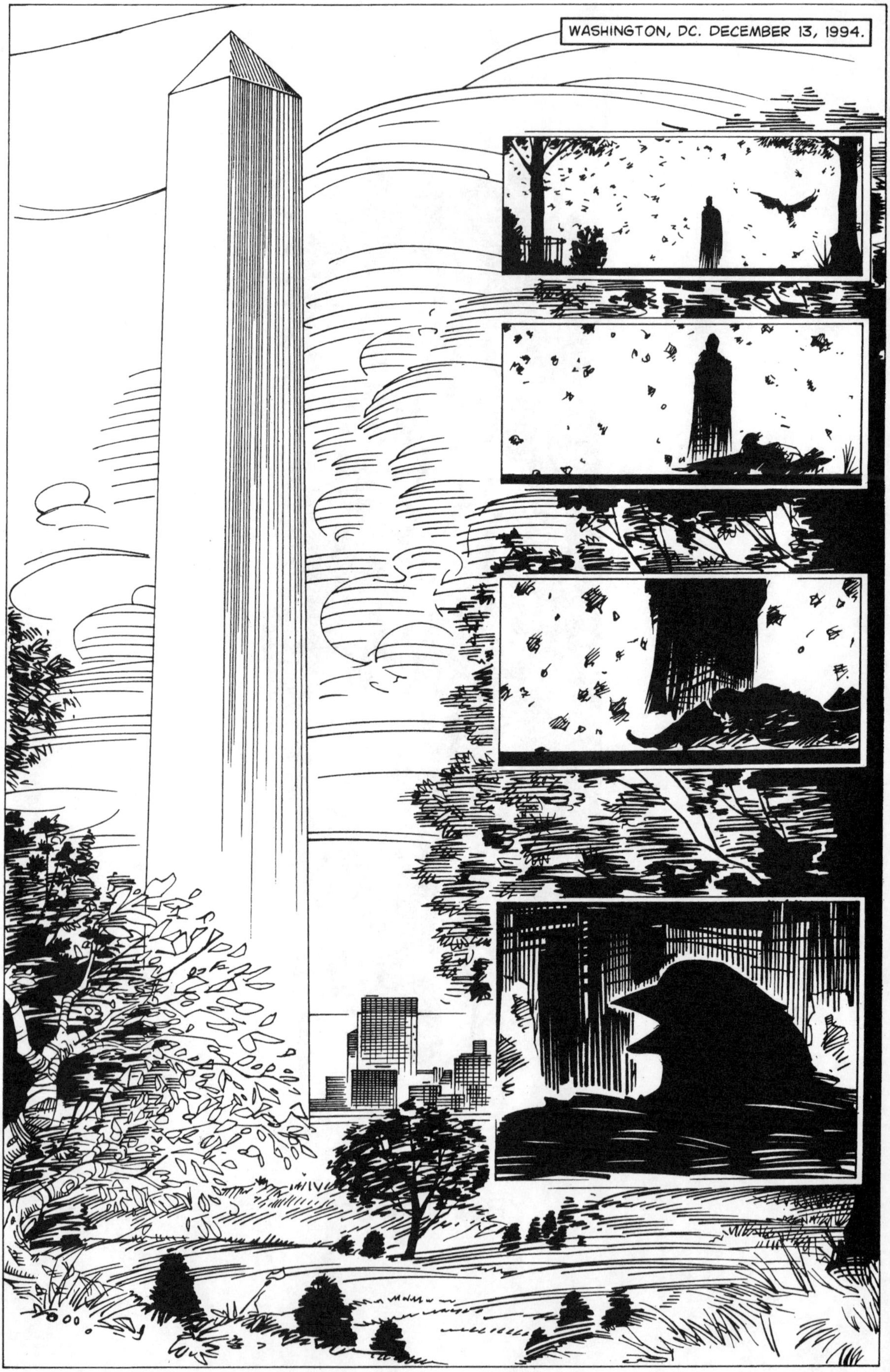
WASHINGTON, DC. DECEMBER 13, 1994.

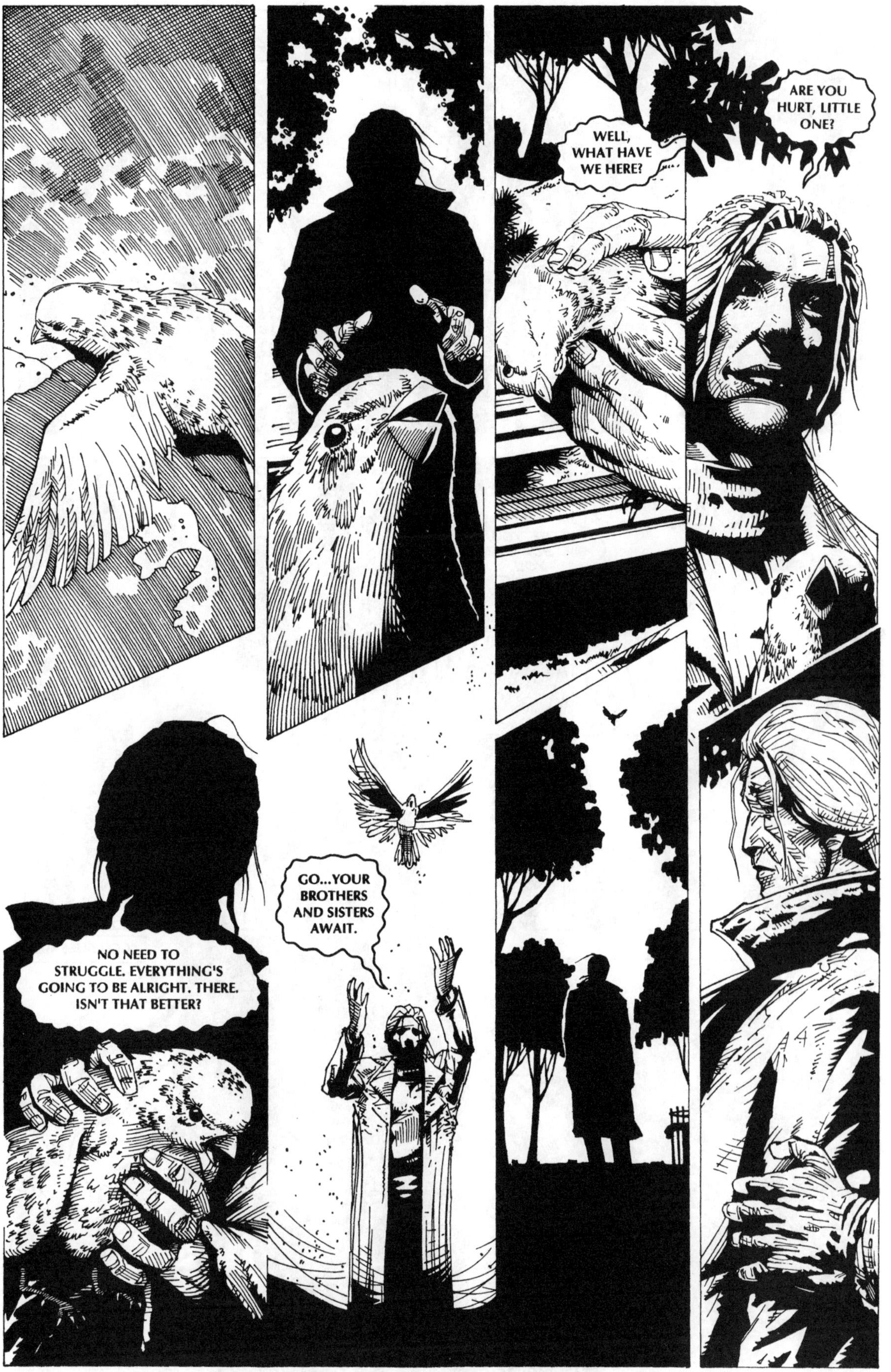
WELL, WHAT HAVE WE HERE?
ARE YOU HURT, LITTLE ONE?
NO NEED TO STRUGGLE. EVERYTHING'S GOING TO BE ALRIGHT. THERE. ISN'T THAT BETTER?
GO...YOUR BROTHERS AND SISTERS AWAIT.

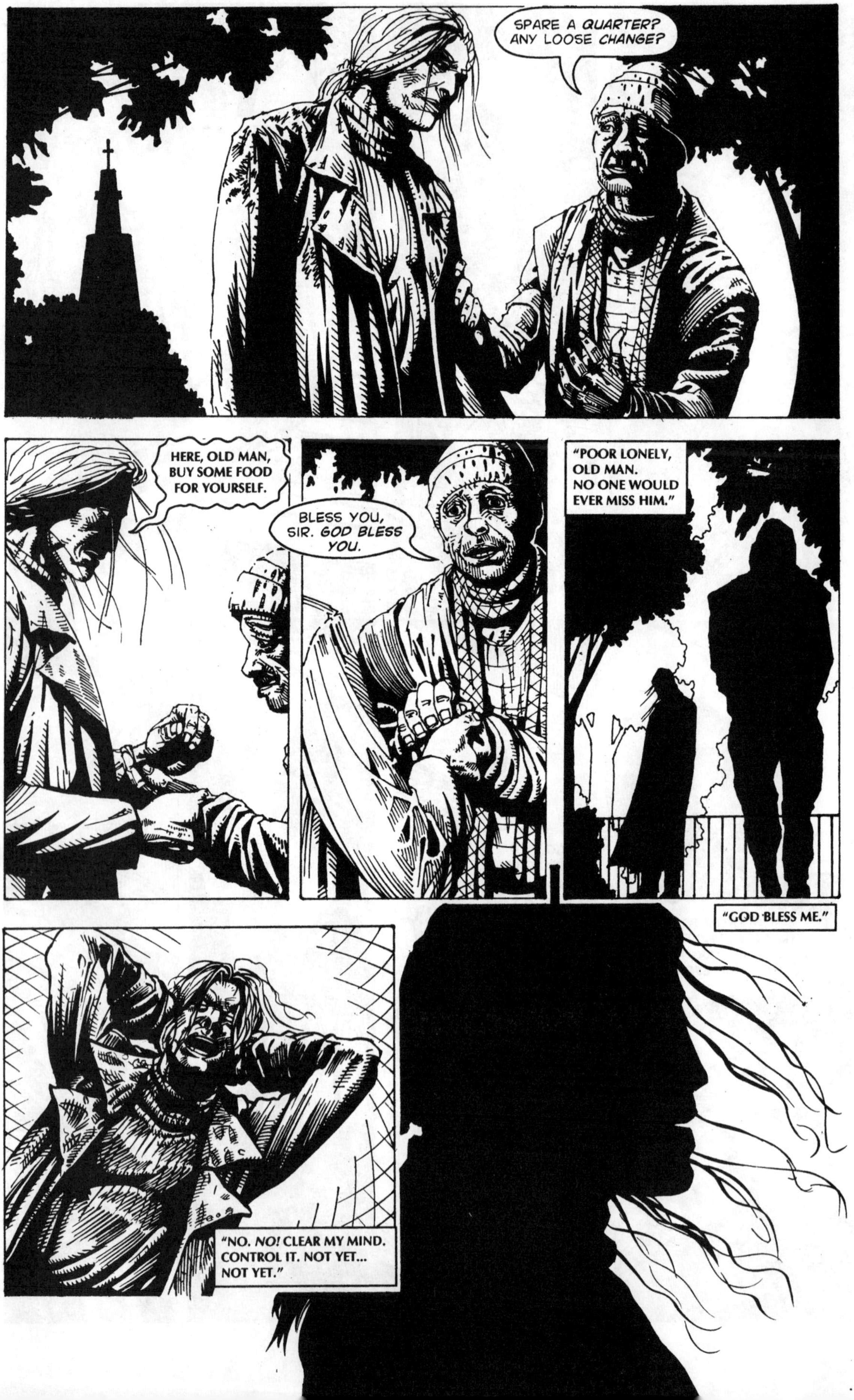
SPARE A QUARTER? ANY LOOSE CHANGE?
HERE, OLD MAN, BUY SOME FOOD FOR YOURSELF.
BLESS YOU, SIR. GOD BLESS YOU.
"POOR LONELY, OLD MAN. NO ONE WOULD EVER MISS HIM."
"GOD BLESS ME."
"NO. NO! CLEAR MY MIND. CONTROL IT. NOT YET... NOT YET."

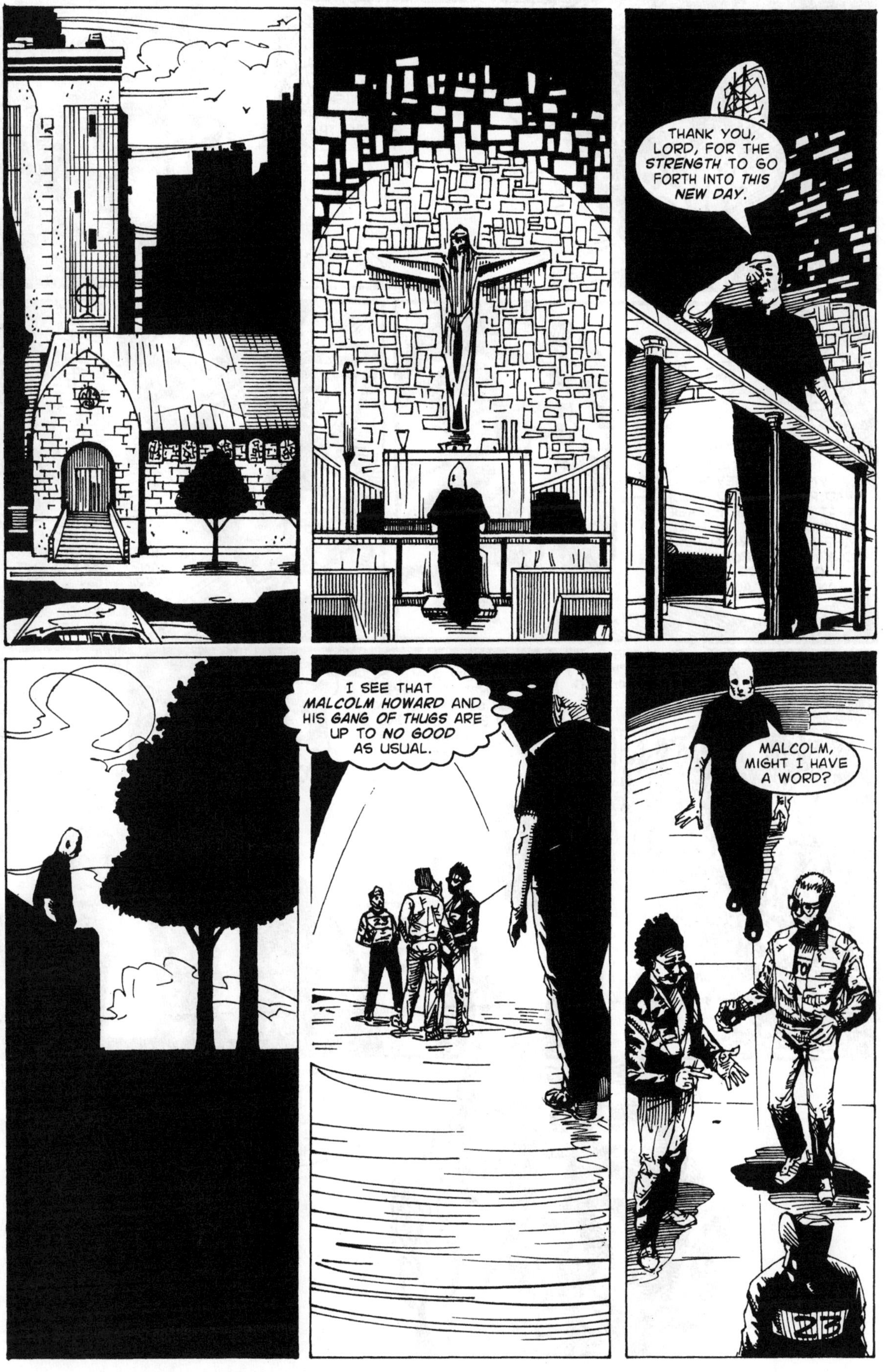
THANK YOU, LORD, FOR THE STRENGTH TO GO FORTH INTO THIS NEW DAY.
I SEE THAT MALCOLM HOWARD AND HIS GANG OF THUGS ARE UP TO NO GOOD AS USUAL.
MALCOLM, MIGHT I HAVE A WORD?

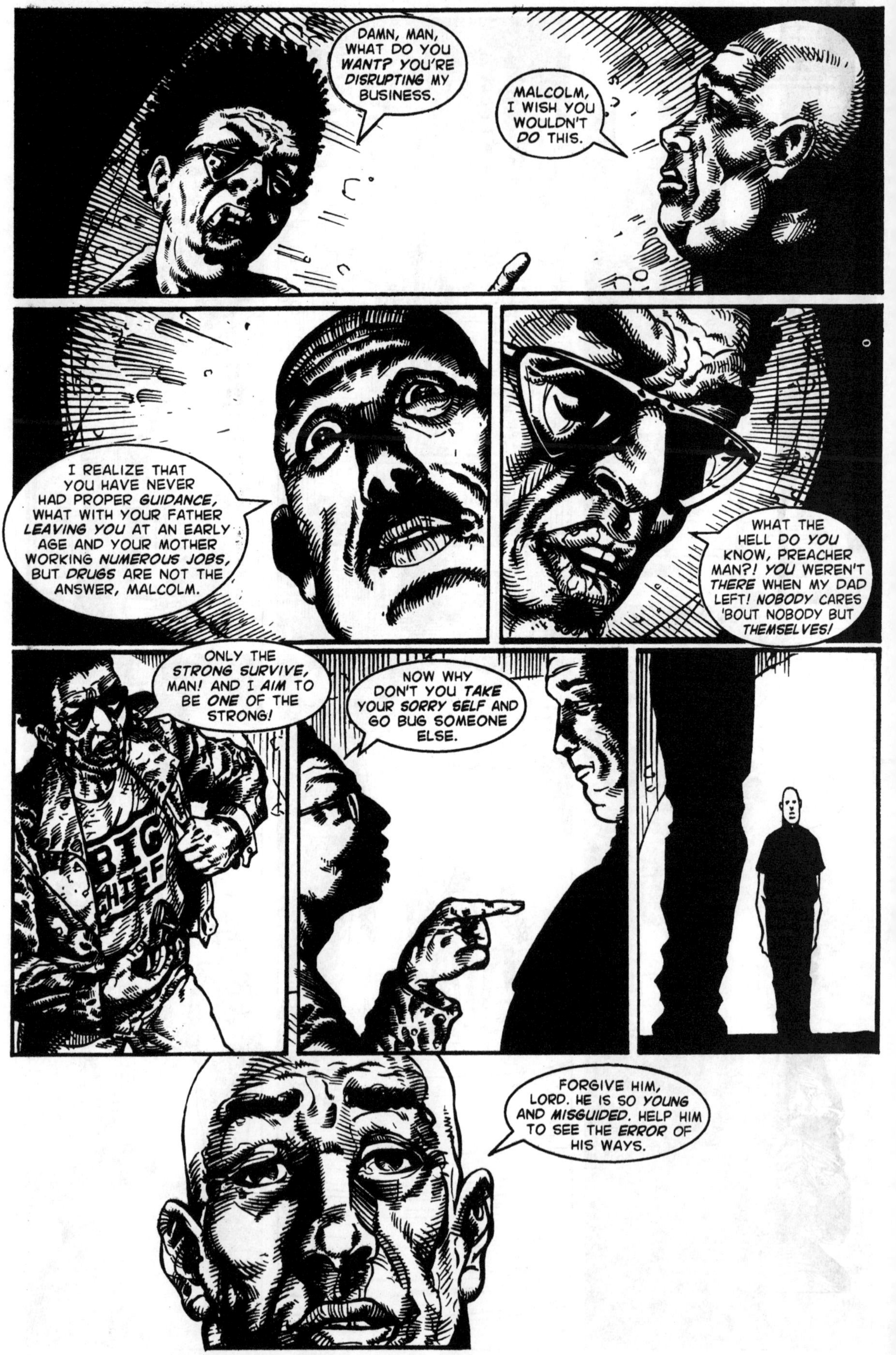

DAMN, MAN, WHAT DO YOU WANT? YOU'RE DISRUPTING MY BUSINESS.
MALCOLM, I WISH YOU WOULDN'T DO THIS.
I REALIZE THAT YOU HAVE NEVER HAD PROPER GUIDANCE, WHAT WITH YOUR FATHER LEAVING YOU AT AN EARLY AGE AND YOUR MOTHER WORKING NUMEROUS JOBS, BUT DRUGS ARE NOT THE ANSWER, MALCOLM.
WHAT THE HELL DO YOU KNOW, PREACHER MAN?! YOU WEREN'T THERE WHEN MY DAD LEFT! NOBODY CARES 'BOUT NOBODY BUT THEMSELVES!
ONLY THE STRONG SURVIVE, MAN! AND I AIM TO BE ONE OF THE STRONG!
BIG CHIEF
NOW WHY DON'T YOU TAKE YOUR SORRY SELF AND GO BUG SOMEONE ELSE.
FORGIVE HIM, LORD. HE IS SO YOUNG AND MISGUIDED. HELP HIM TO SEE THE ERROR OF HIS WAYS.

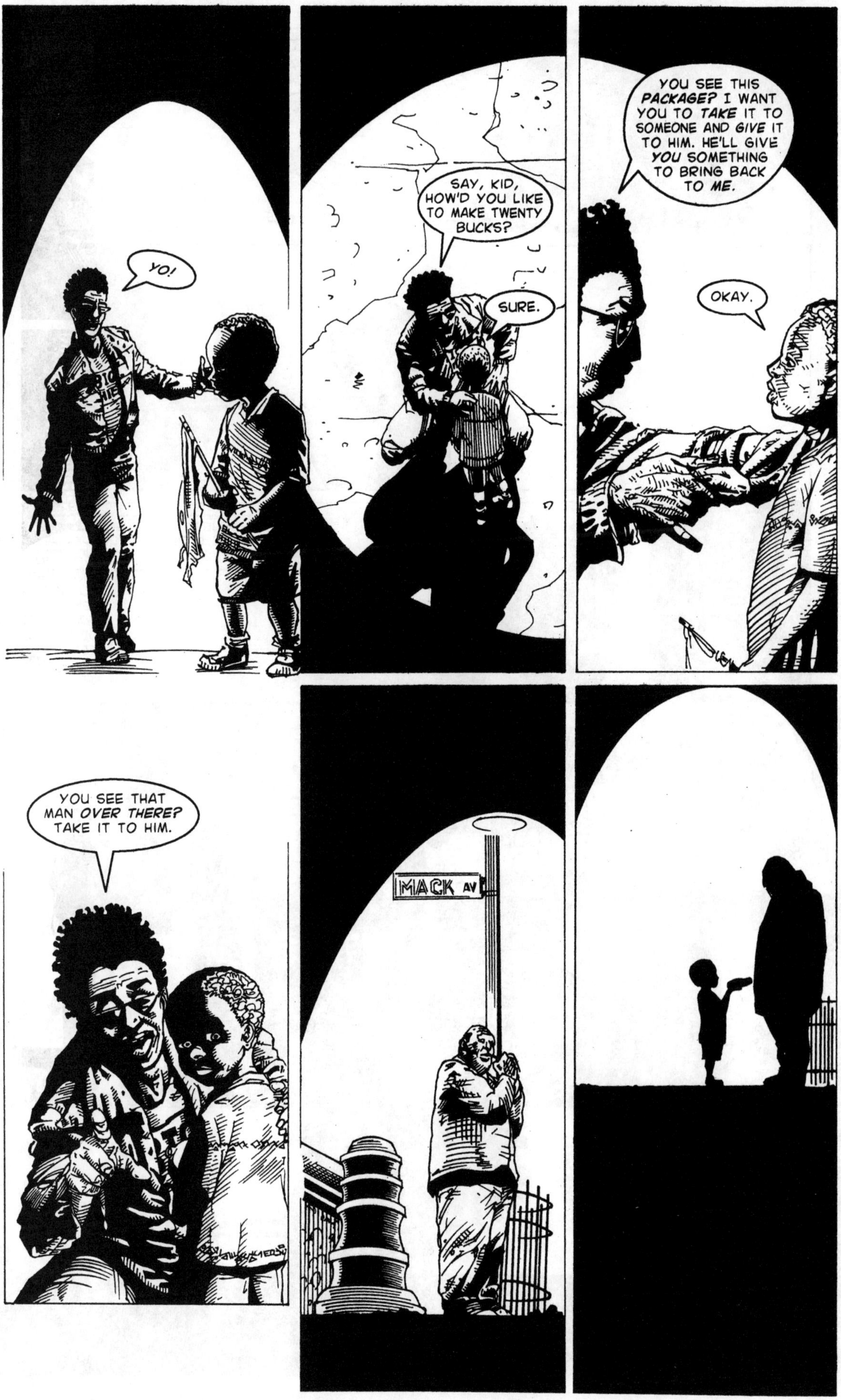

YO!
SAY, KID, HOW'D YOU LIKE TO MAKE TWENTY BUCKS?
SURE.
YOU SEE THIS PACKAGE? I WANT YOU TO TAKE IT TO SOMEONE AND GIVE IT TO HIM. HE'LL GIVE YOU SOMETHING TO BRING BACK TO ME.
OKAY.
YOU SEE THAT MAN OVER THERE? TAKE IT TO HIM.
MACK AV

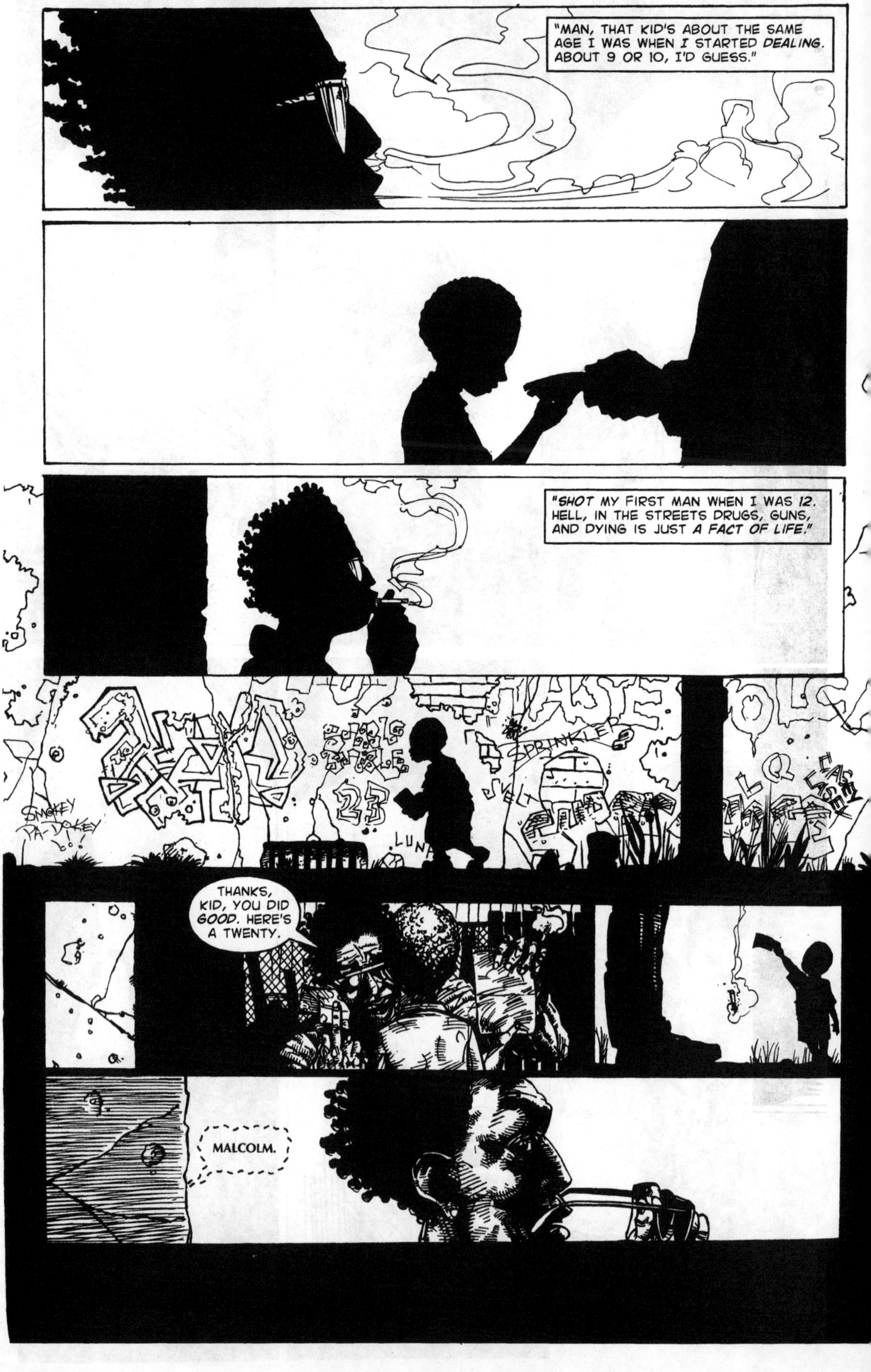
"MAN, THAT KID'S ABOUT THE SAME AGE I WAS WHEN I STARTED DEALING. ABOUT 9 OR 10, I'D GUESS."
"SHOT MY FIRST MAN WHEN I WAS 12. HELL, IN THE STREETS DRUGS, GUNS, AND DYING IS JUST A FACT OF LIFE."
SMOKEY PA-DOKEY
23
LUNA
SPRINKLER
CASEY
CASEY
THANKS, KID, YOU DID GOOD. HERE'S A TWENTY.
MALCOLM.

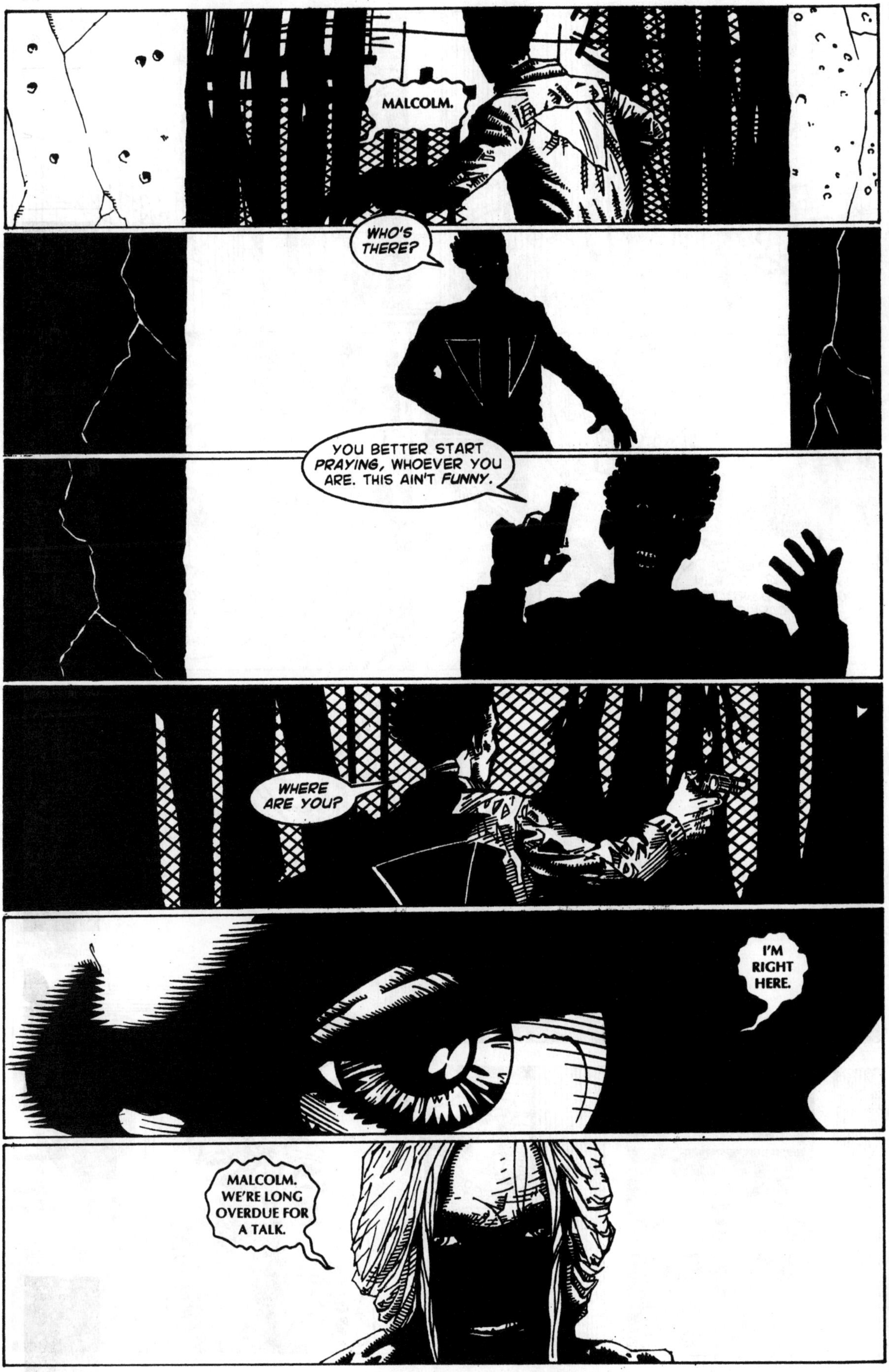
MALCOLM.
WHO'S THERE?
YOU BETTER START PRAYING, WHOEVER YOU ARE. THIS AIN'T FUNNY.
WHERE ARE YOU?
I'M RIGHT HERE.
MALCOLM. WE'RE LONG OVERDUE FOR A TALK.

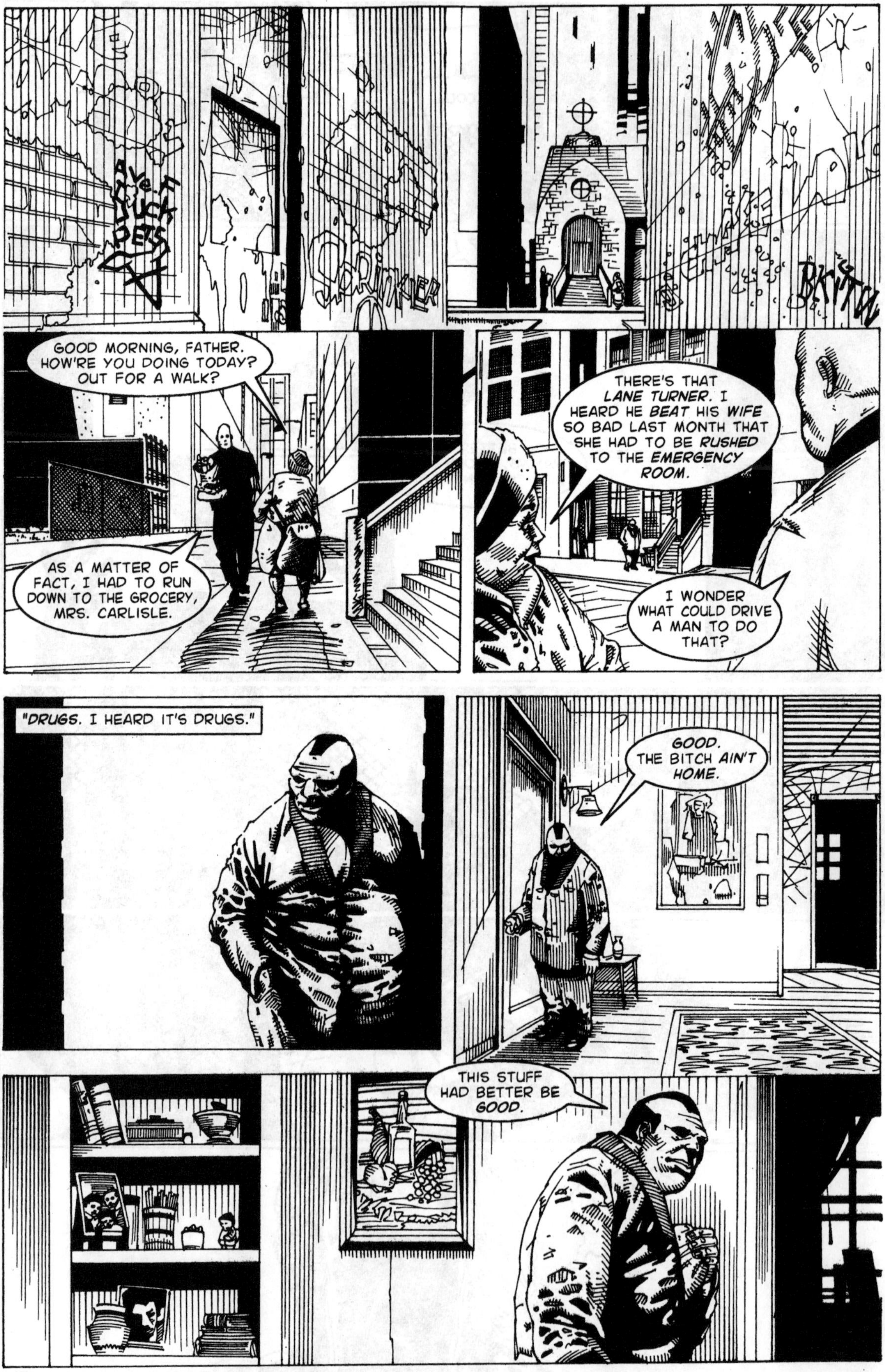
GOOD MORNING, FATHER. HOW'RE YOU DOING TODAY? OUT FOR A WALK?
AS A MATTER OF FACT, I HAD TO RUN DOWN TO THE GROCERY, MRS. CARLISLE.
THERE'S THAT *LANE TURNER*. I HEARD HE *BEAT* HIS *WIFE* SO BAD LAST MONTH THAT SHE HAD TO BE *RUSHED* TO THE *EMERGENCY ROOM*.
I WONDER WHAT COULD DRIVE A MAN TO DO THAT?
"*DRUGS*. I HEARD IT'S DRUGS."
GOOD. THE BITCH *AIN'T HOME*.
THIS STUFF HAD BETTER BE *GOOD*.

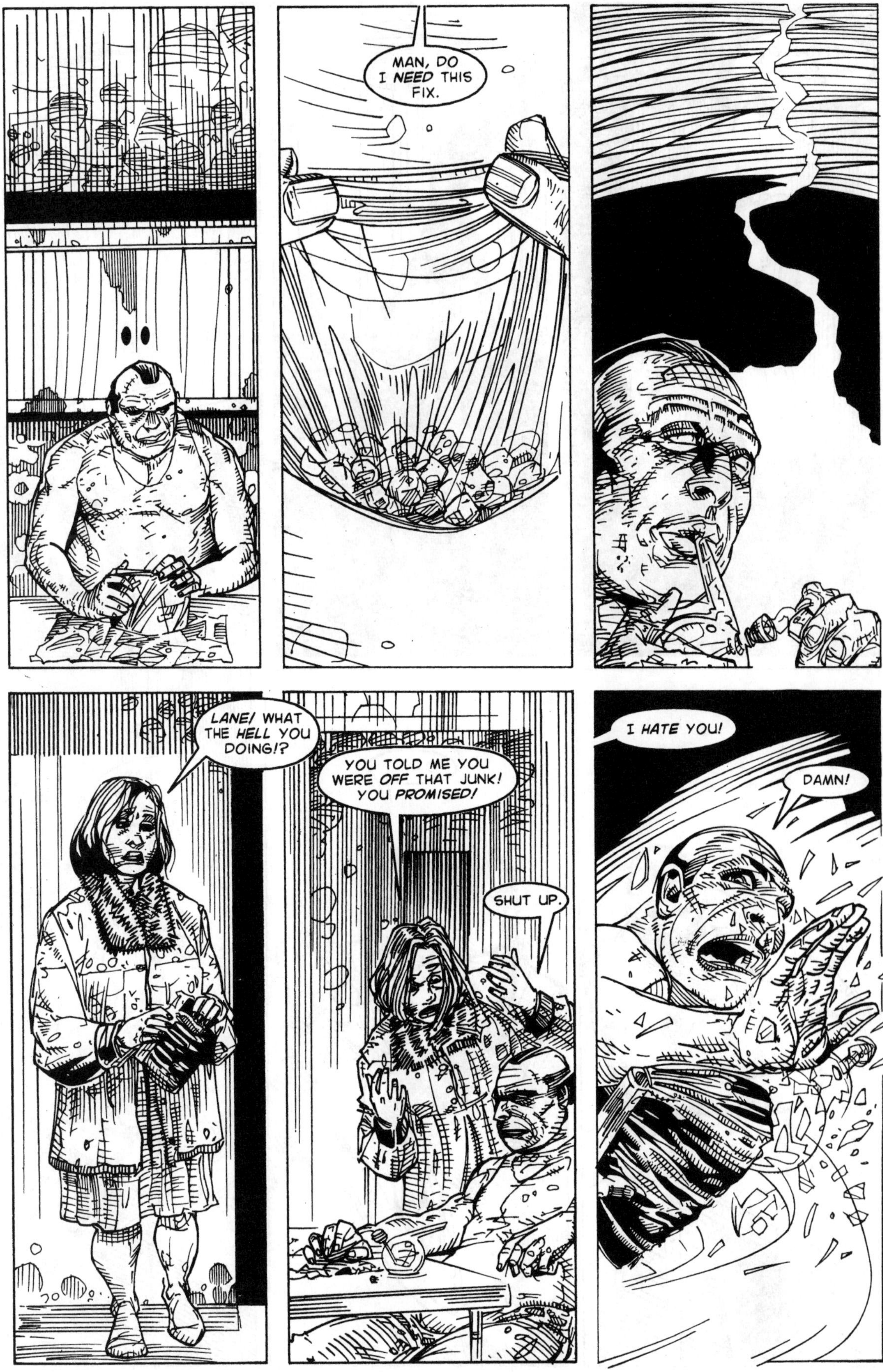
MAN, DO I NEED THIS FIX.
LANE! WHAT THE HELL YOU DOING!?
YOU TOLD ME YOU WERE OFF THAT JUNK! YOU PROMISED!
SHUT UP.
I HATE YOU!
DAMN!

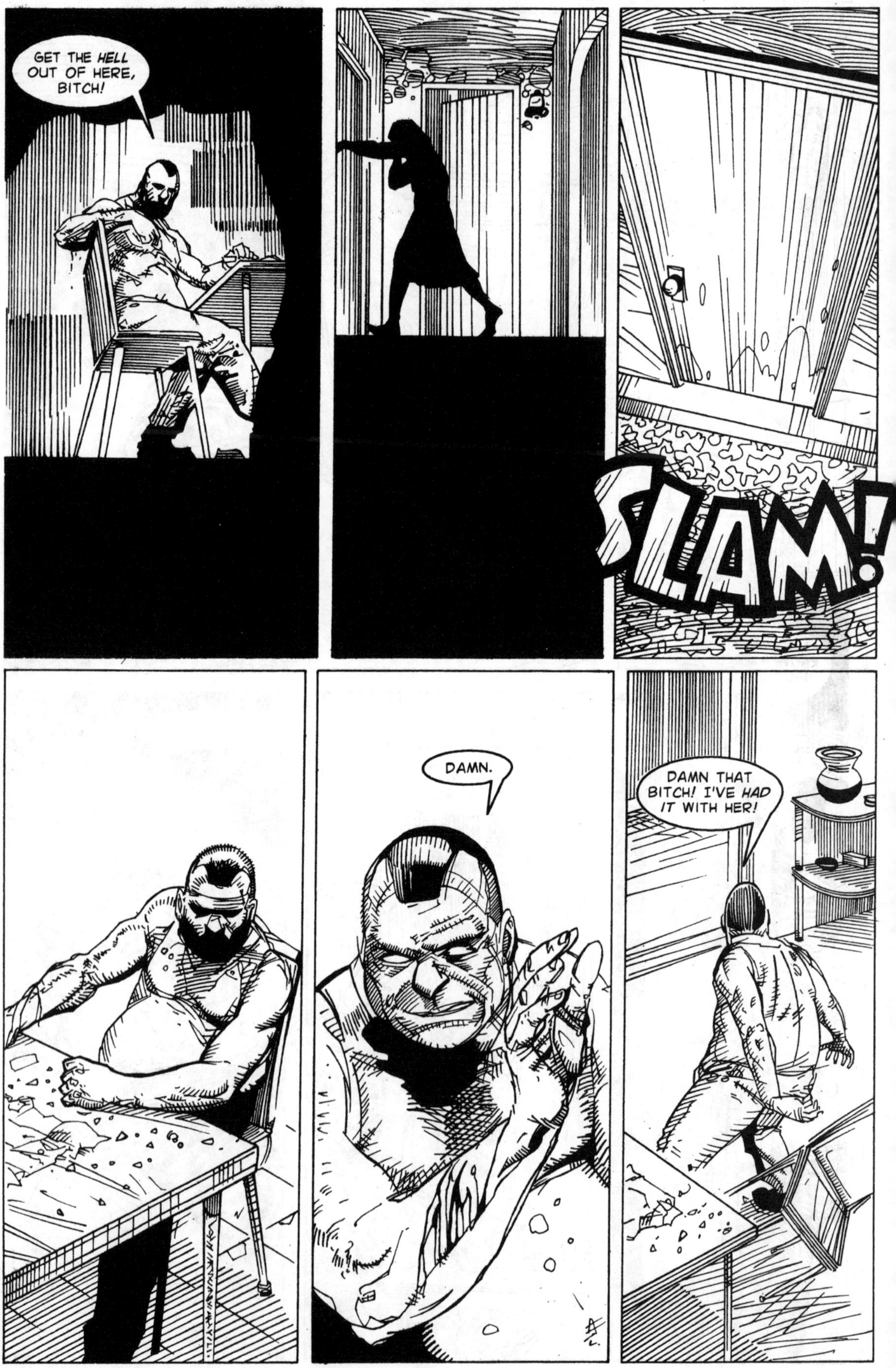
GET THE HELL OUT OF HERE, BITCH!
SLAM!
DAMN.
DAMN THAT BITCH! I'VE HAD IT WITH HER!

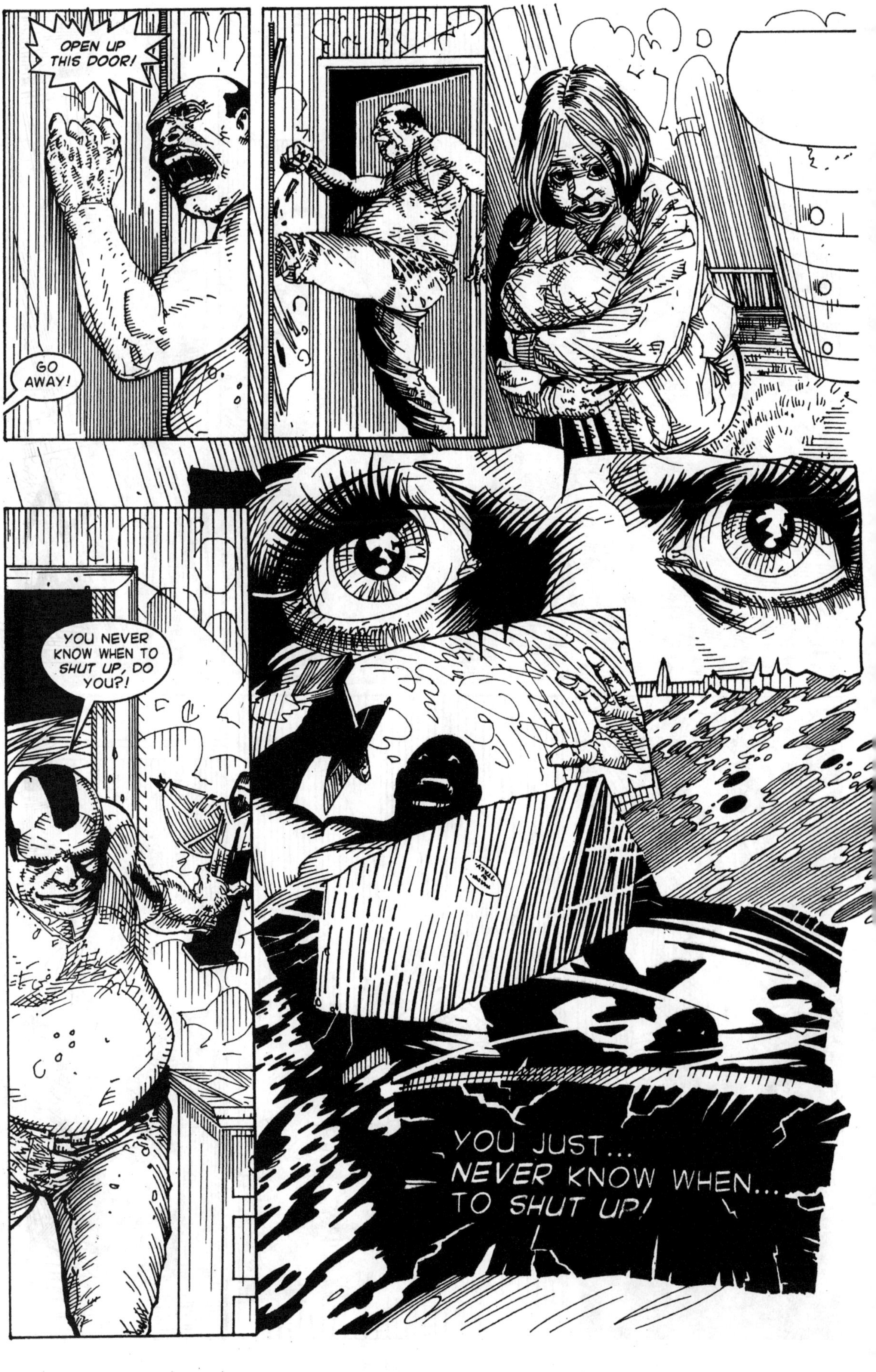
OPEN UP THIS DOOR!
GO AWAY!
YOU NEVER KNOW WHEN TO SHUT UP, DO YOU?!
YOU JUST... NEVER KNOW WHEN... TO SHUT UP!

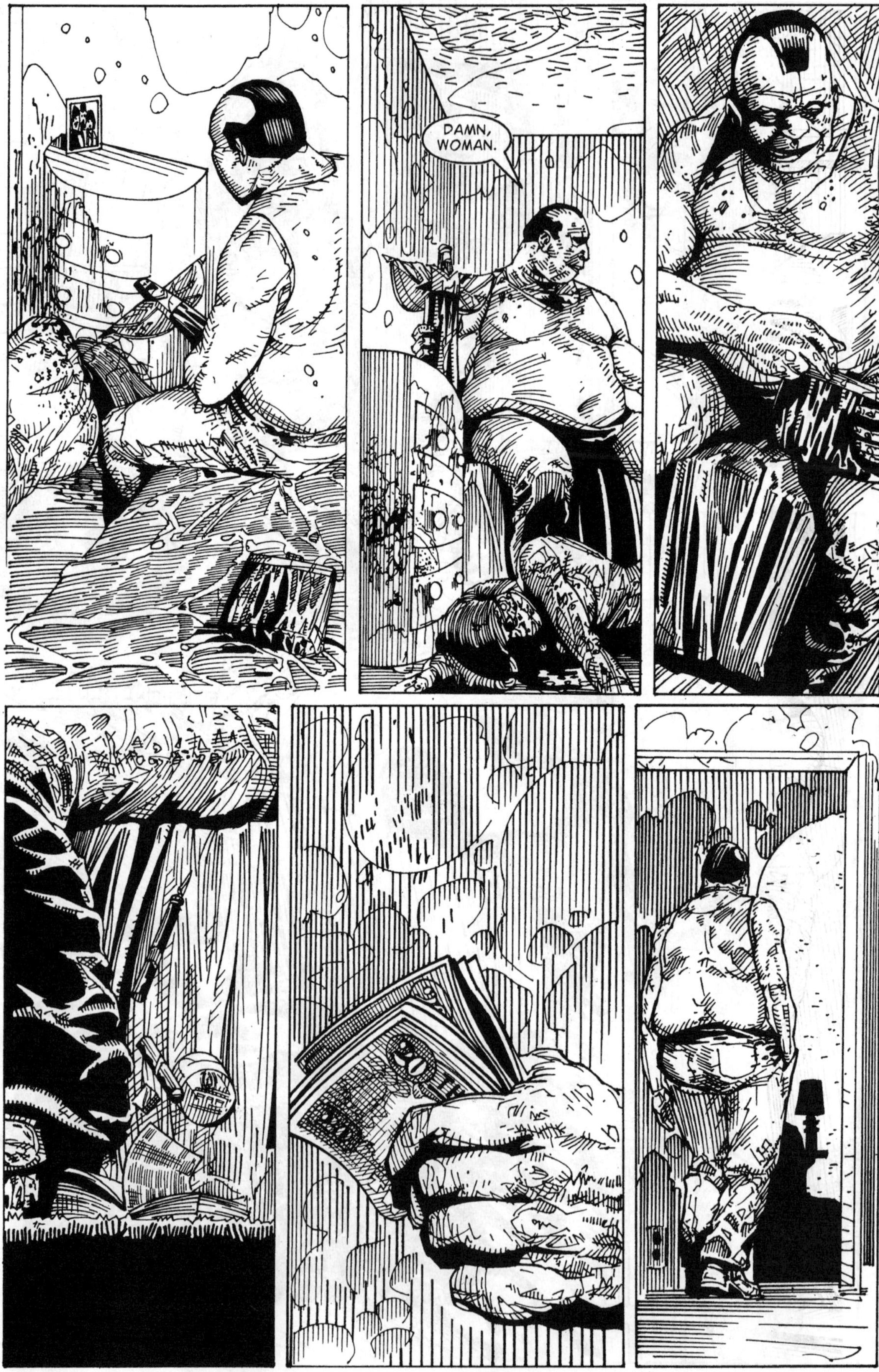
DAMN, WOMAN.

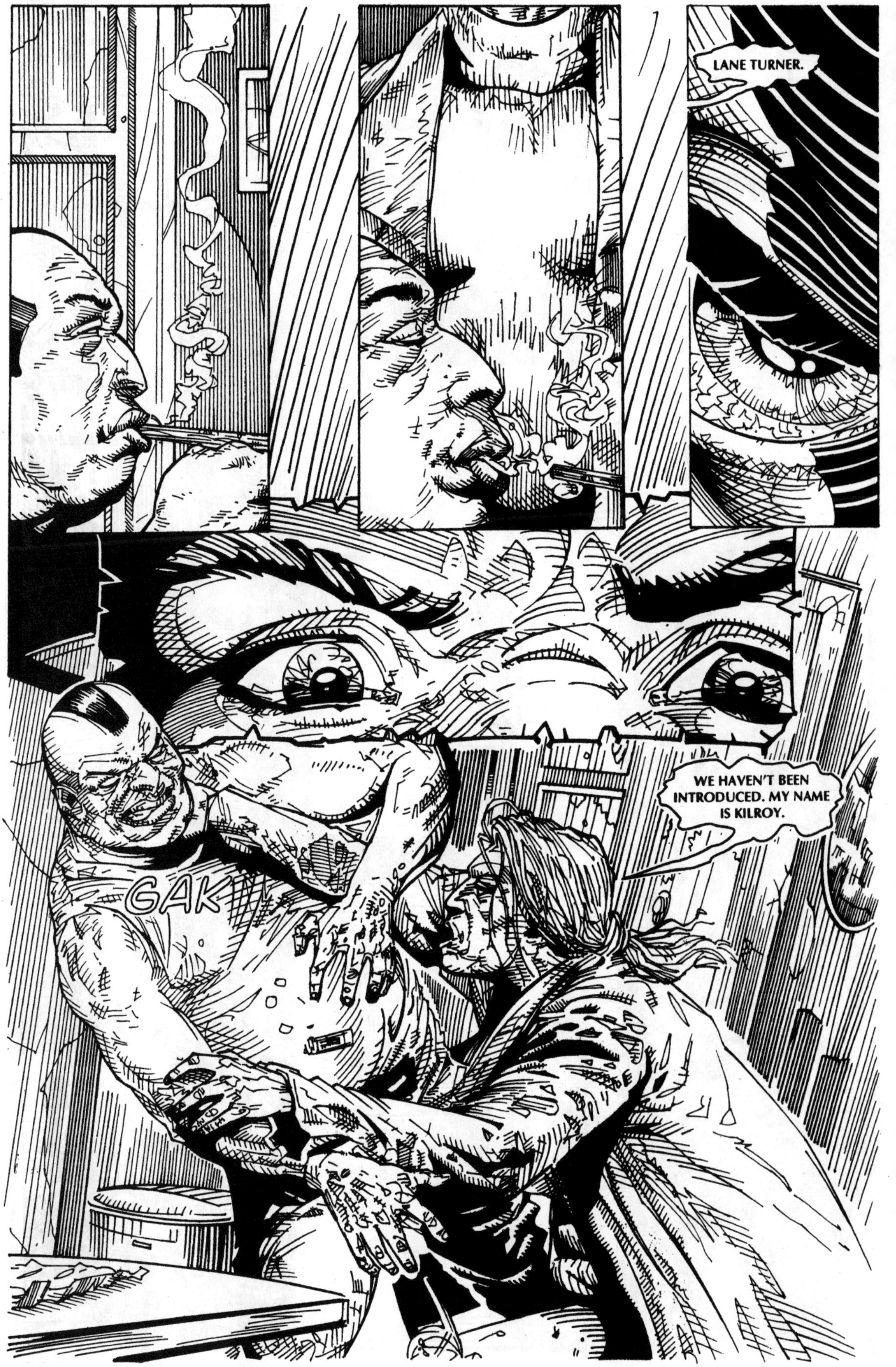
LANE TURNER.
GAK
WE HAVEN'T BEEN INTRODUCED. MY NAME IS KILROY.

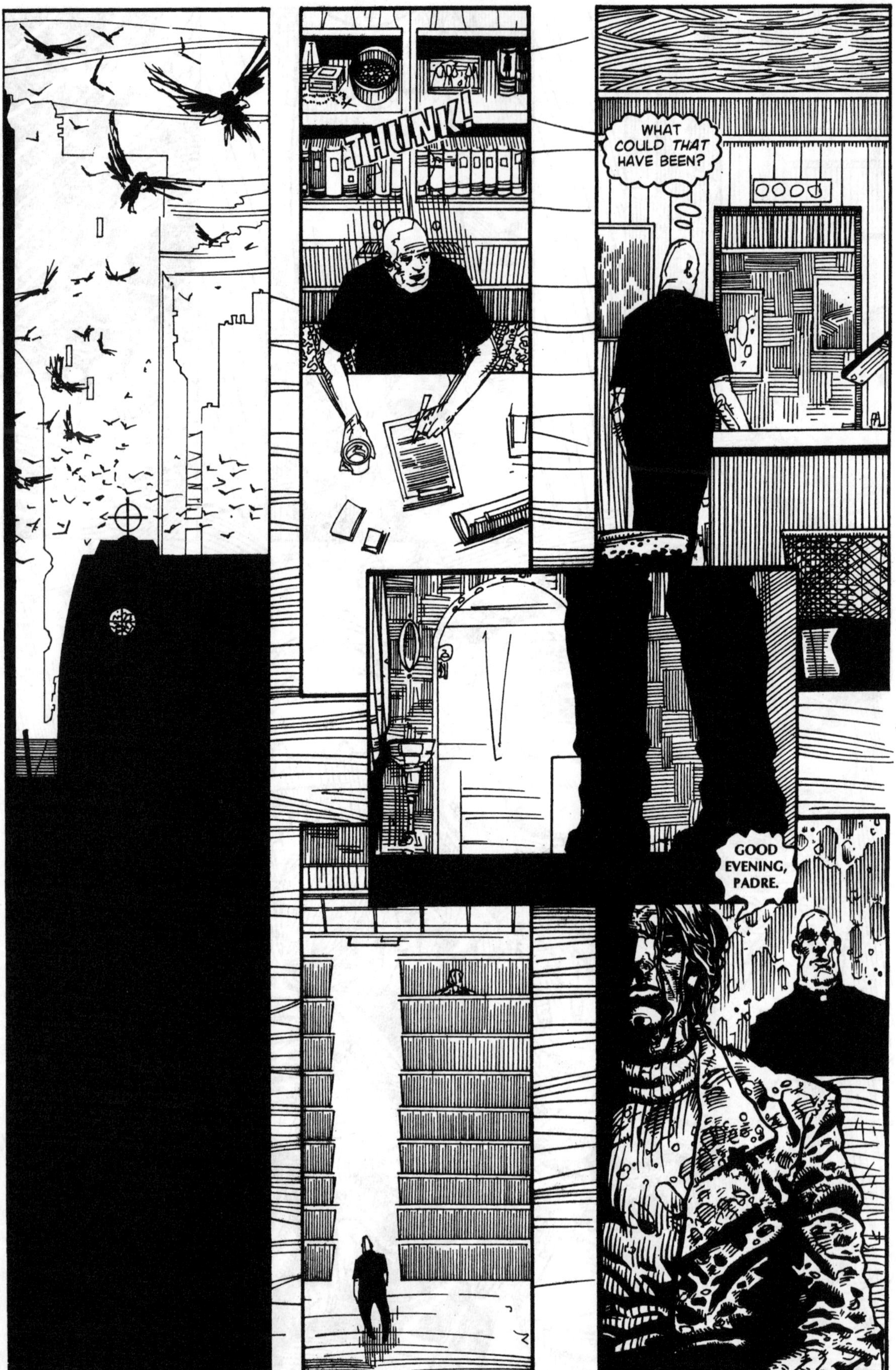
THUNK!
WHAT COULD THAT HAVE BEEN?
GOOD EVENING, PADRE.

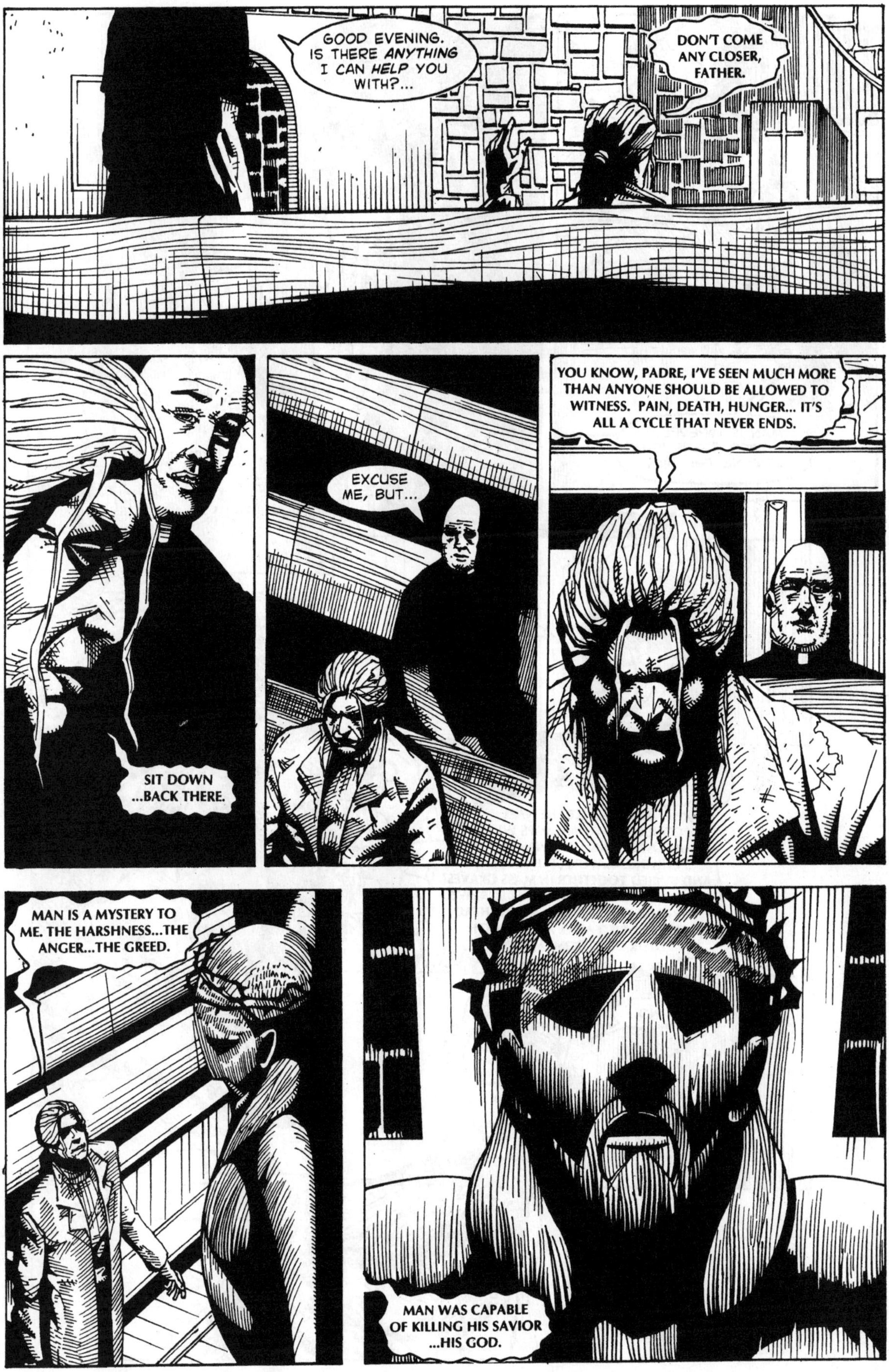
GOOD EVENING. IS THERE ANYTHING I CAN HELP YOU WITH?...
DON'T COME ANY CLOSER, FATHER.
SIT DOWN ...BACK THERE.
EXCUSE ME, BUT...
YOU KNOW, PADRE, I'VE SEEN MUCH MORE THAN ANYONE SHOULD BE ALLOWED TO WITNESS. PAIN, DEATH, HUNGER... IT'S ALL A CYCLE THAT NEVER ENDS.
MAN IS A MYSTERY TO ME. THE HARSHNESS...THE ANGER...THE GREED.
MAN WAS CAPABLE OF KILLING HIS SAVIOR ...HIS GOD.

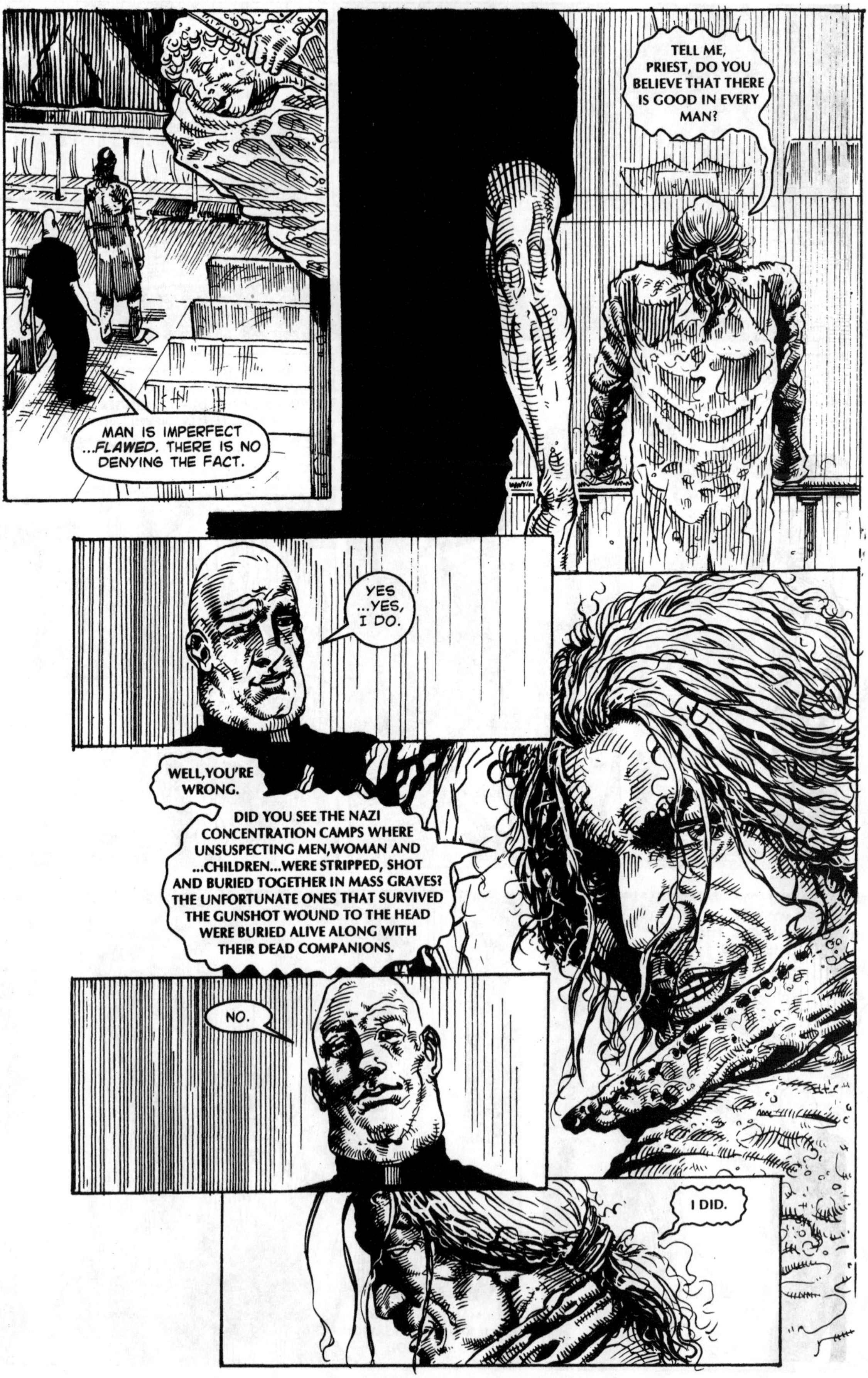
MAN IS IMPERFECT ...FLAWED. THERE IS NO DENYING THE FACT.
TELL ME, PRIEST, DO YOU BELIEVE THAT THERE IS GOOD IN EVERY MAN?
YES ...YES, I DO.
WELL, YOU'RE WRONG.
DID YOU SEE THE NAZI CONCENTRATION CAMPS WHERE UNSUSPECTING MEN, WOMAN AND ...CHILDREN...WERE STRIPPED, SHOT AND BURIED TOGETHER IN MASS GRAVES? THE UNFORTUNATE ONES THAT SURVIVED THE GUNSHOT WOUND TO THE HEAD WERE BURIED ALIVE ALONG WITH THEIR DEAD COMPANIONS.
NO.
I DID.

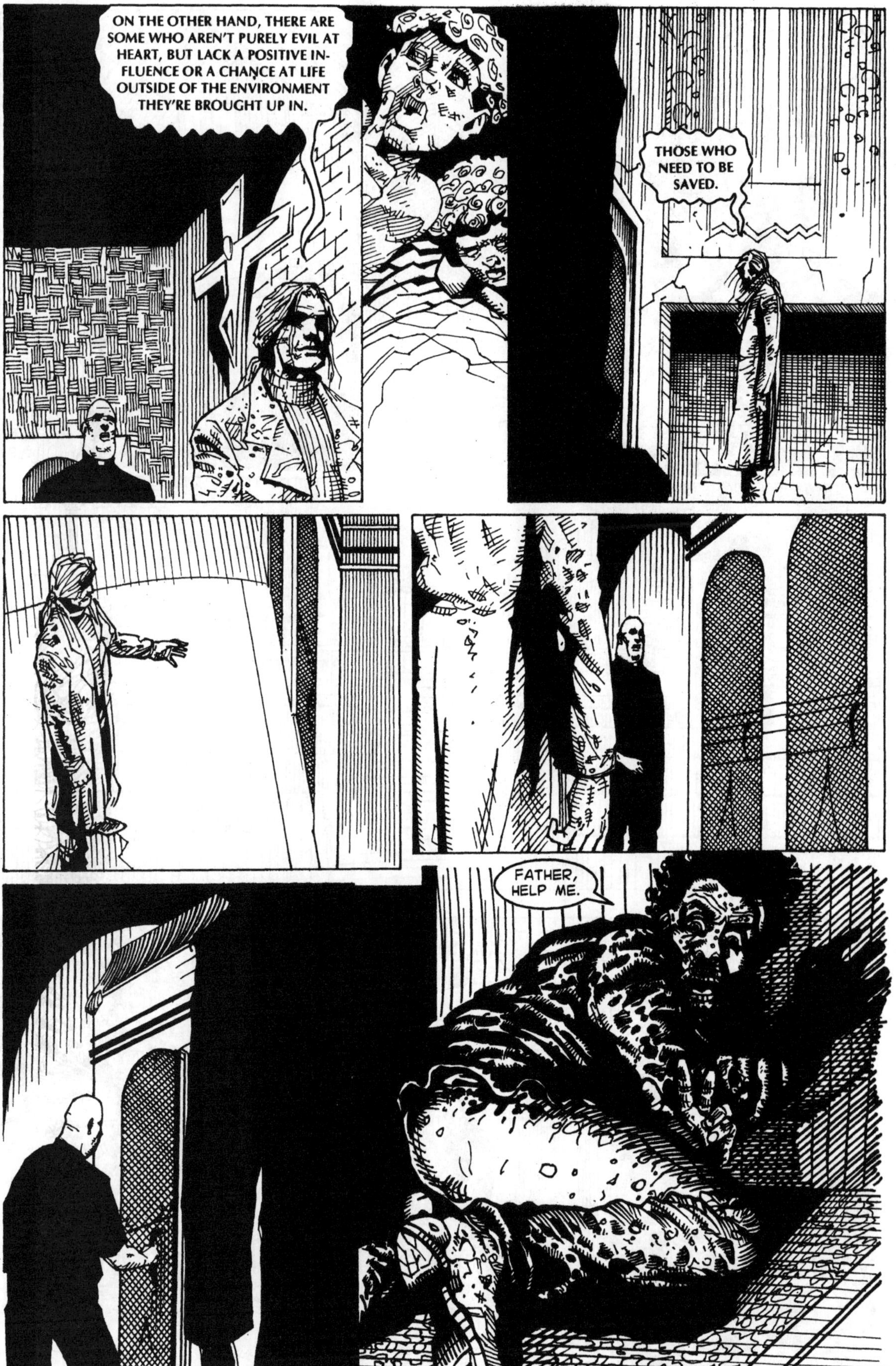
ON THE OTHER HAND, THERE ARE SOME WHO AREN'T PURELY EVIL AT HEART, BUT LACK A POSITIVE INFLUENCE OR A CHANCE AT LIFE OUTSIDE OF THE ENVIRONMENT THEY'RE BROUGHT UP IN.
THOSE WHO NEED TO BE SAVED.
FATHER, HELP ME.

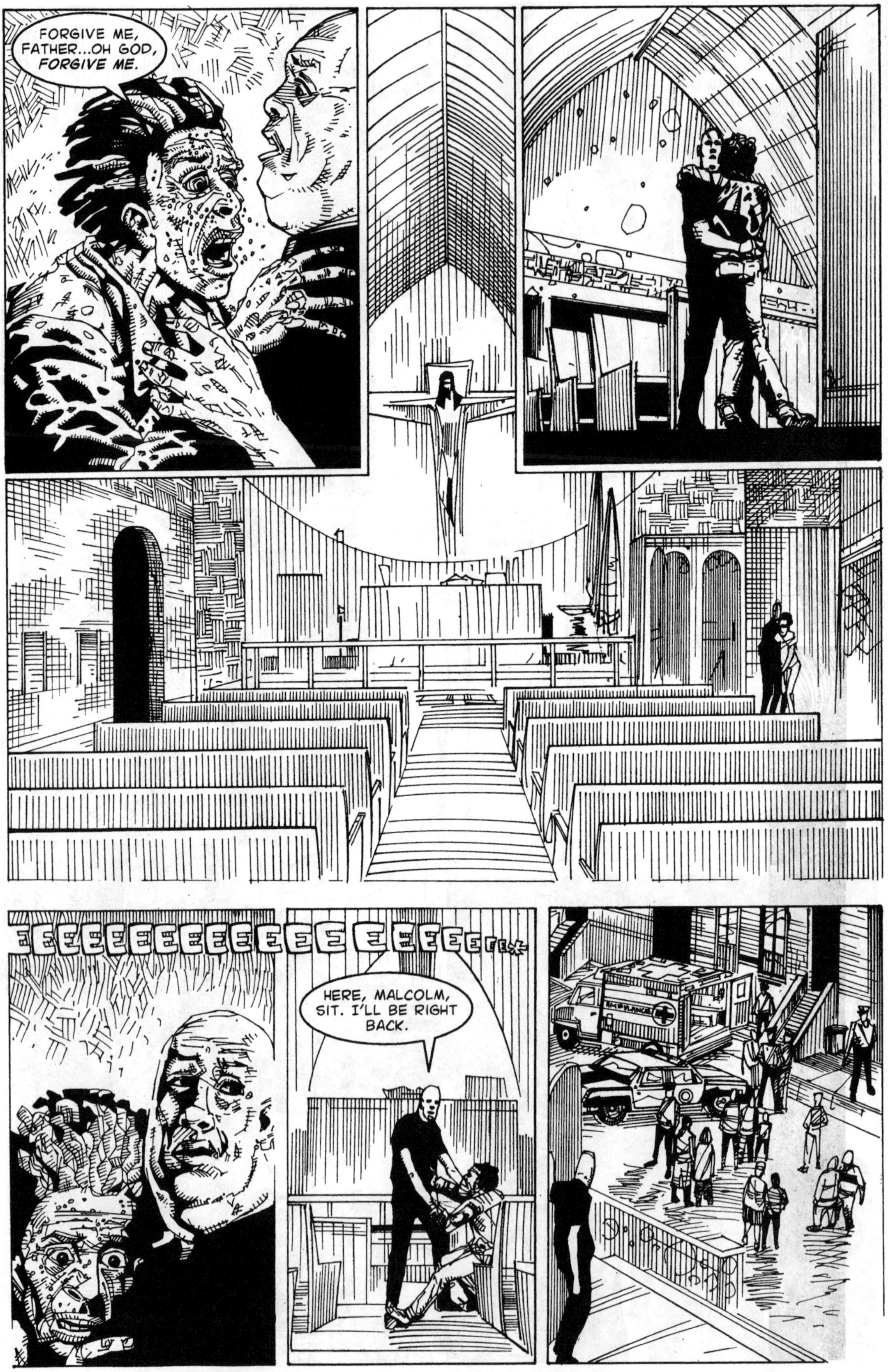

FORGIVE ME, FATHER...OH GOD, *FORGIVE ME.*
EEEEEEEEEEEEEEEEEEEEeeee*
HERE, MALCOLM, SIT. I'LL BE RIGHT BACK.

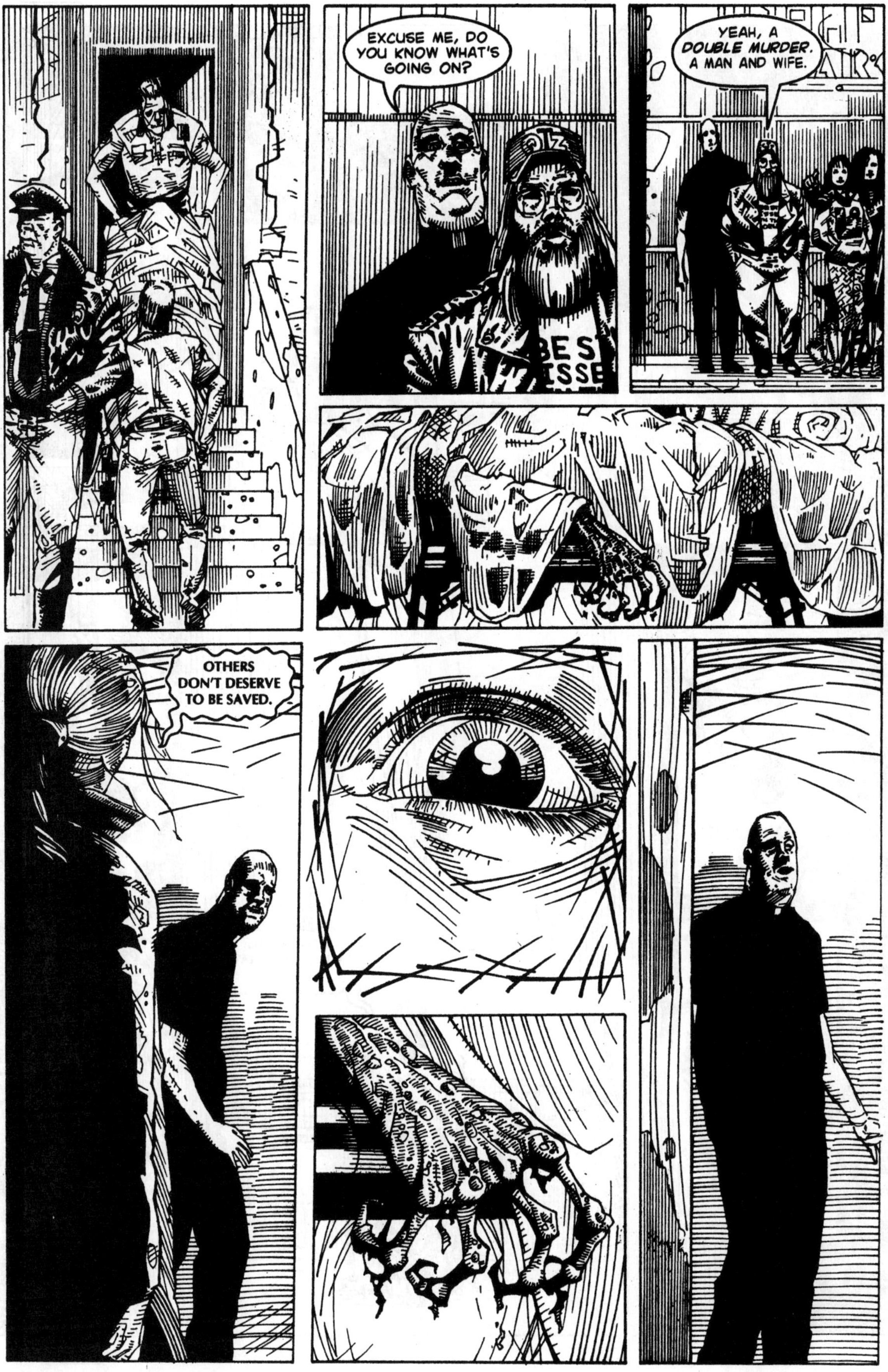
EXCUSE ME, DO YOU KNOW WHAT'S GOING ON?
YEAH, A DOUBLE MURDER. A MAN AND WIFE.
OTHERS DON'T DESERVE TO BE SAVED.

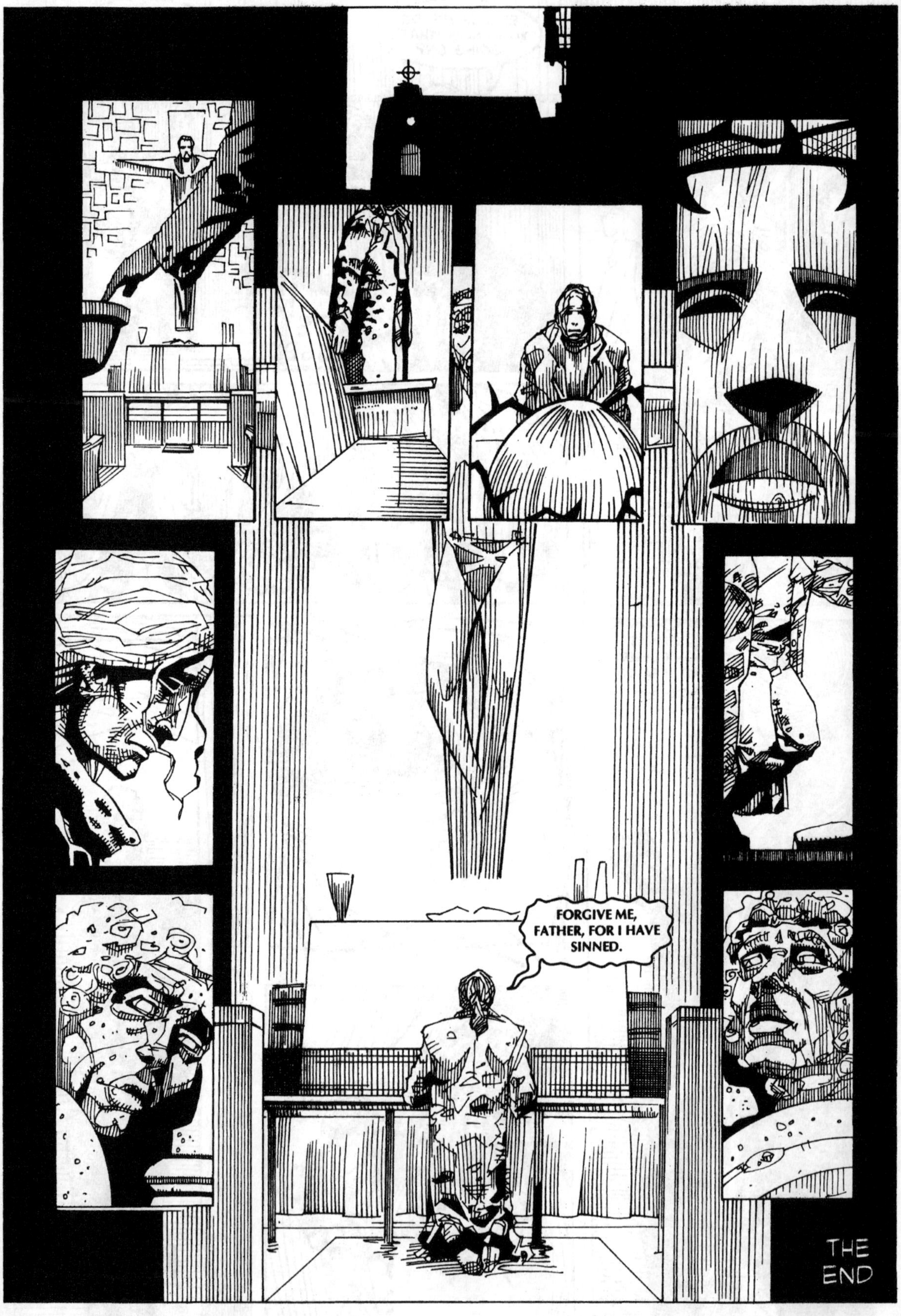
FORGIVE ME, FATHER, FOR I HAVE SINNED.
THE END

"Sympathy for the Devil"

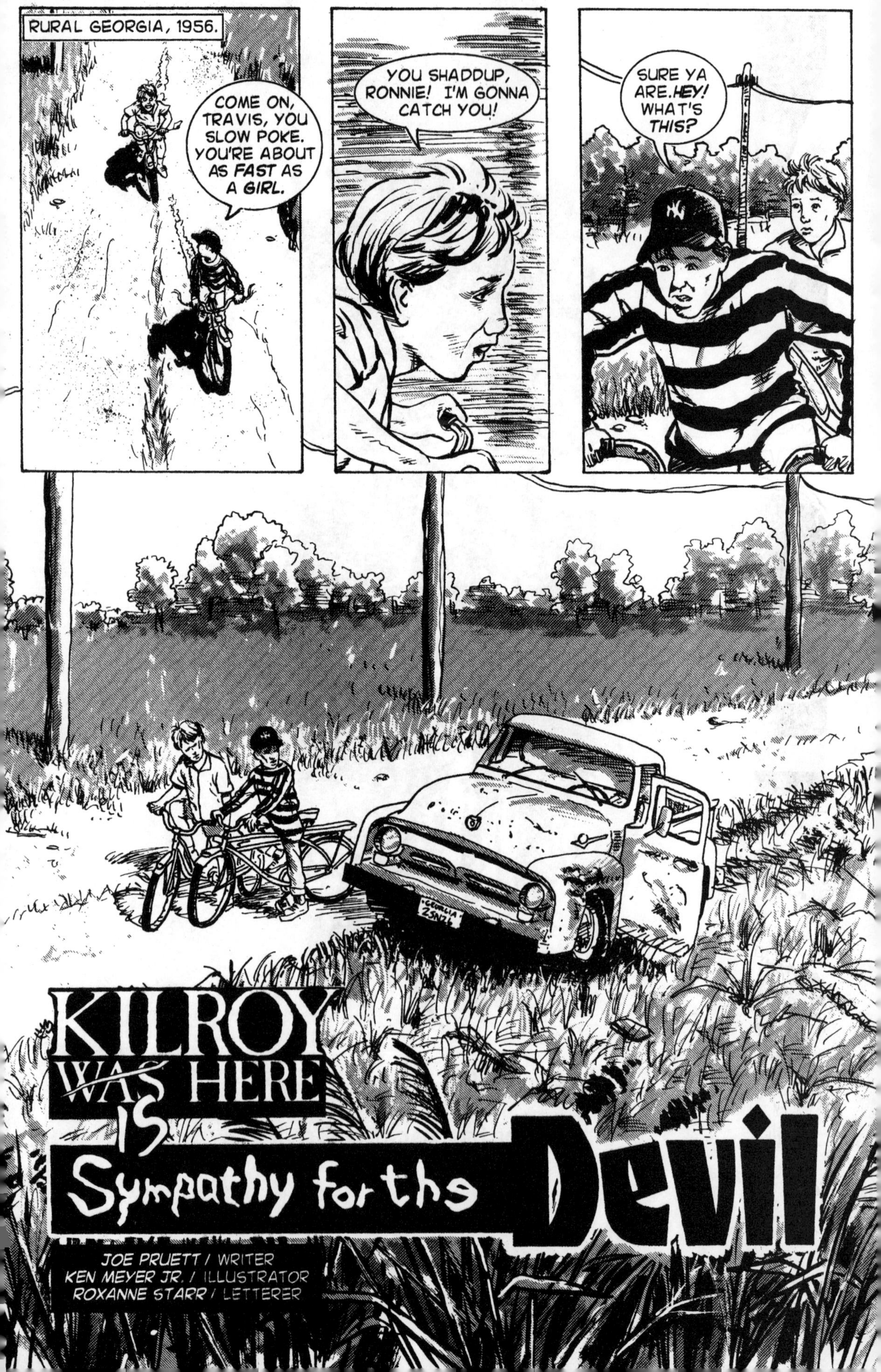
RURAL GEORGIA, 1956.
COME ON, TRAVIS, YOU SLOW POKE. YOU'RE ABOUT AS FAST AS A GIRL.
YOU SHADDUP, RONNIE! I'M GONNA CATCH YOU!
SURE YA ARE. HEY! WHAT'S THIS?
GEORGIA
KILROY WAS HERE IS Sympathy for the Devil
JOE PRUETT / WRITER
KEN MEYER JR. / ILLUSTRATOR
ROXANNE STARR / LETTERER

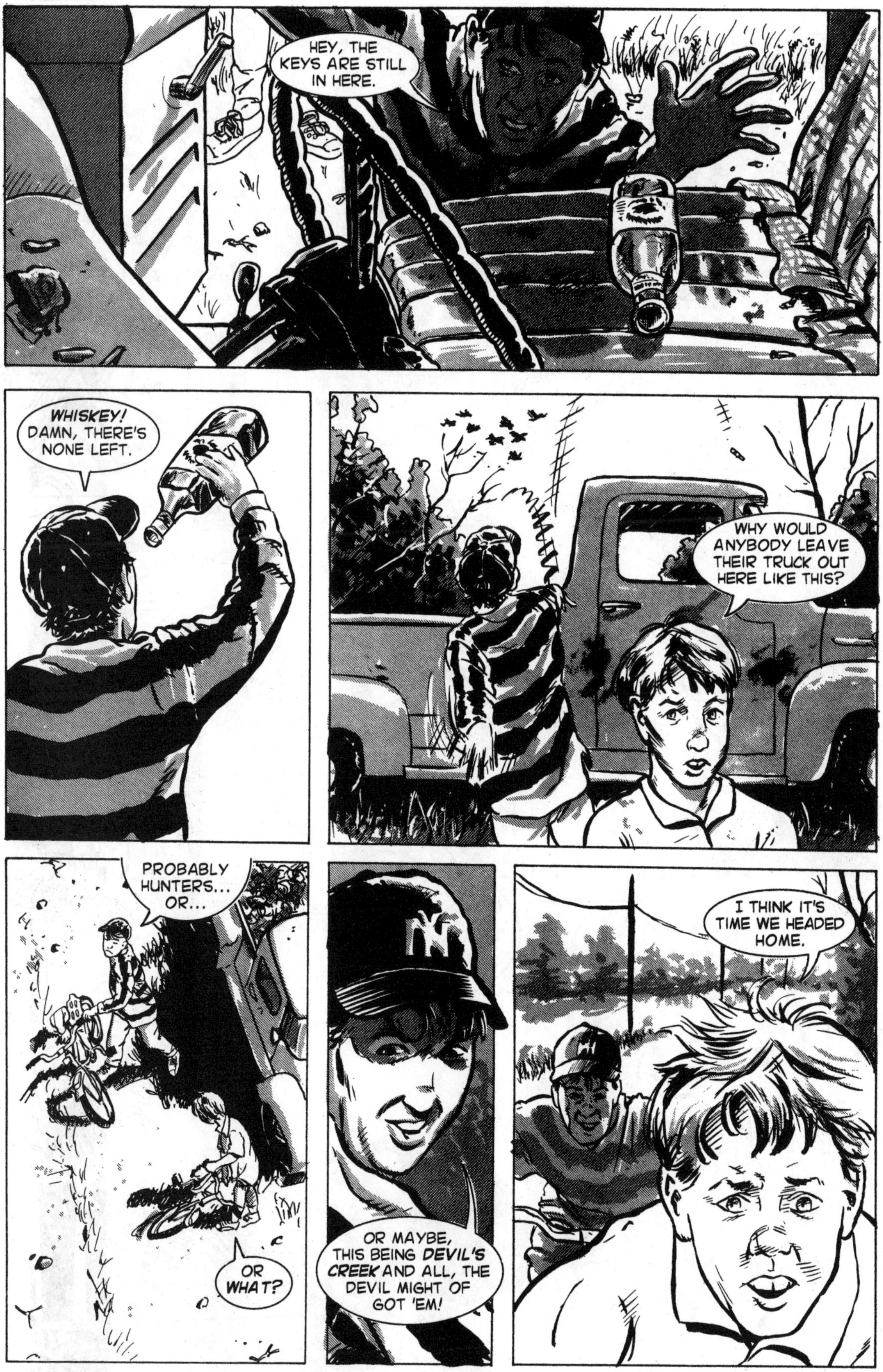
HEY, THE KEYS ARE STILL IN HERE.
WHISKEY! DAMN, THERE'S NONE LEFT.
WHY WOULD ANYBODY LEAVE THEIR TRUCK OUT HERE LIKE THIS?
PROBABLY HUNTERS... OR...
OR WHAT?
OR MAYBE, THIS BEING DEVIL'S CREEK AND ALL, THE DEVIL MIGHT OF GOT 'EM!
I THINK IT'S TIME WE HEADED HOME.

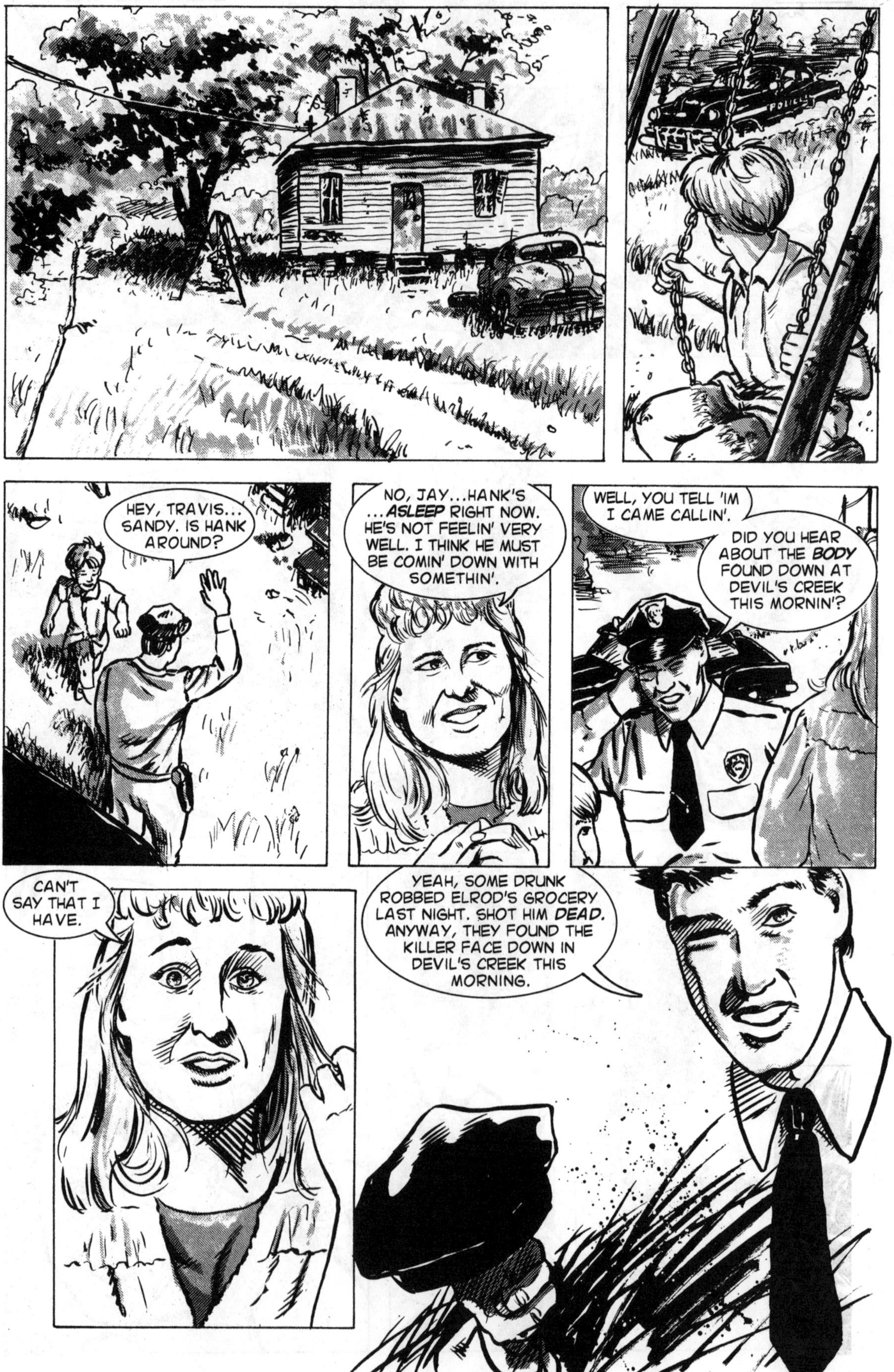
HEY, TRAVIS... SANDY. IS HANK AROUND?
NO, JAY...HANK'S ...ASLEEP RIGHT NOW. HE'S NOT FEELIN' VERY WELL. I THINK HE MUST BE COMIN' DOWN WITH SOMETHIN'.
WELL, YOU TELL 'IM I CAME CALLIN'.
DID YOU HEAR ABOUT THE BODY FOUND DOWN AT DEVIL'S CREEK THIS MORNIN'?
CAN'T SAY THAT I HAVE.
YEAH, SOME DRUNK ROBBED ELROD'S GROCERY LAST NIGHT. SHOT HIM DEAD. ANYWAY, THEY FOUND THE KILLER FACE DOWN IN DEVIL'S CREEK THIS MORNING.
POLICE

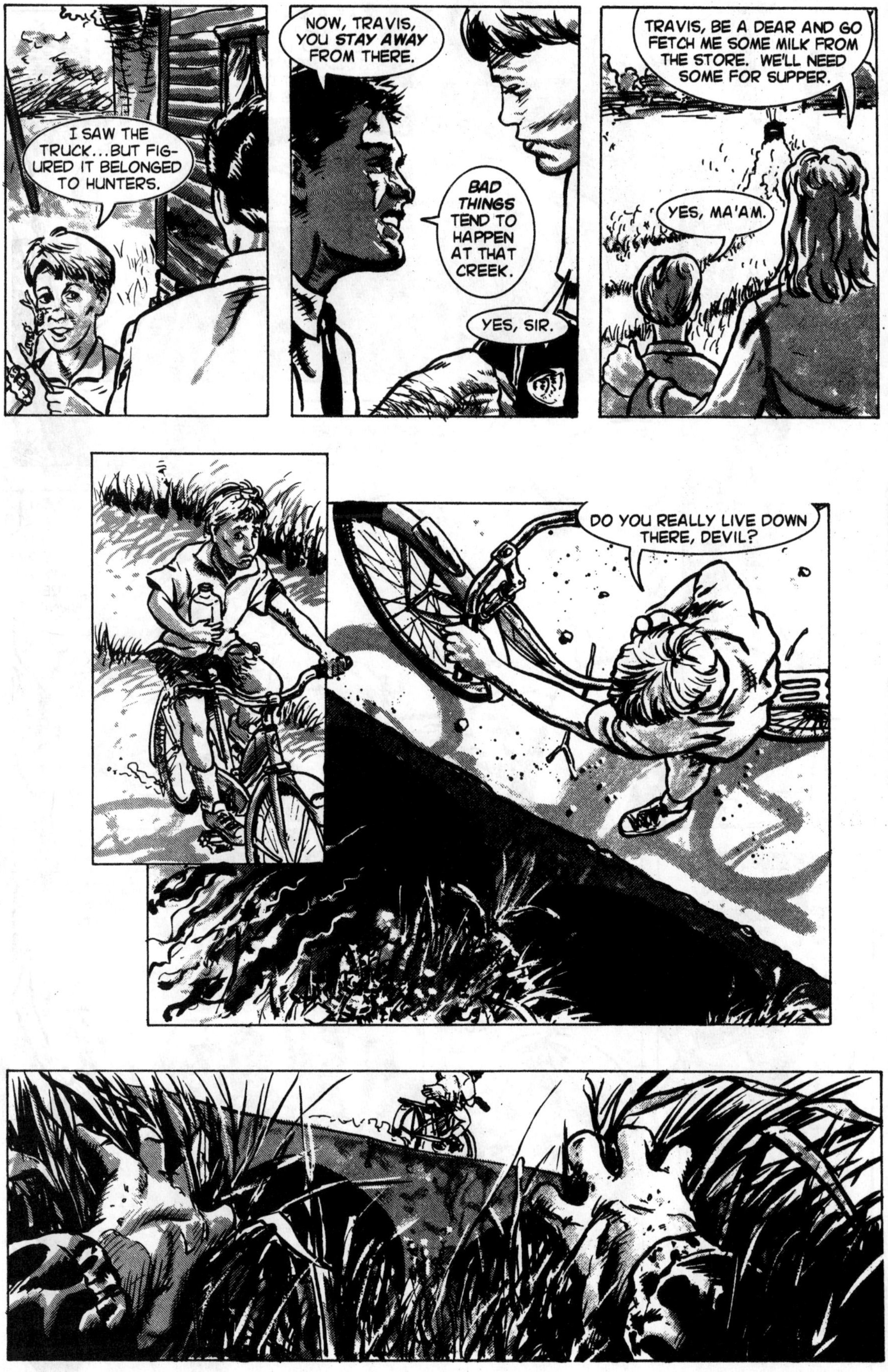
I SAW THE TRUCK...BUT FIGURED IT BELONGED TO HUNTERS.
NOW, TRAVIS, YOU STAY AWAY FROM THERE.
BAD THINGS TEND TO HAPPEN AT THAT CREEK.
YES, SIR.
TRAVIS, BE A DEAR AND GO FETCH ME SOME MILK FROM THE STORE. WE'LL NEED SOME FOR SUPPER.
YES, MA'AM.
DO YOU REALLY LIVE DOWN THERE, DEVIL?

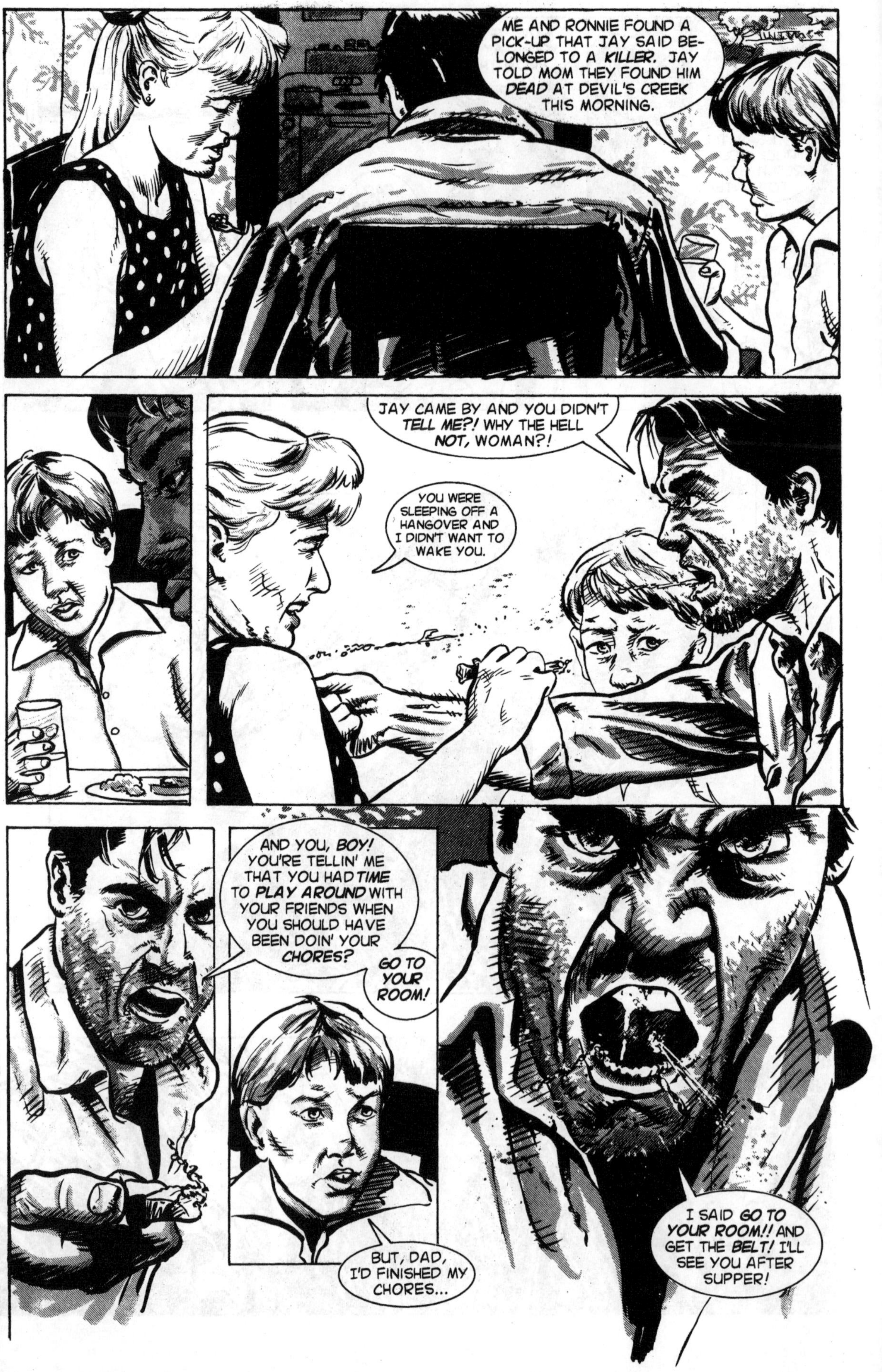
ME AND RONNIE FOUND A PICK-UP THAT JAY SAID BE-LONGED TO A KILLER. JAY TOLD MOM THEY FOUND HIM DEAD AT DEVIL'S CREEK THIS MORNING.
JAY CAME BY AND YOU DIDN'T TELL ME?! WHY THE HELL NOT, WOMAN?!
YOU WERE SLEEPING OFF A HANGOVER AND I DIDN'T WANT TO WAKE YOU.
AND YOU, BOY! YOU'RE TELLIN' ME THAT YOU HAD TIME TO PLAY AROUND WITH YOUR FRIENDS WHEN YOU SHOULD HAVE BEEN DOIN' YOUR CHORES?
GO TO YOUR ROOM!
BUT, DAD, I'D FINISHED MY CHORES...
I SAID GO TO YOUR ROOM!! AND GET THE BELT! I'LL SEE YOU AFTER SUPPER!

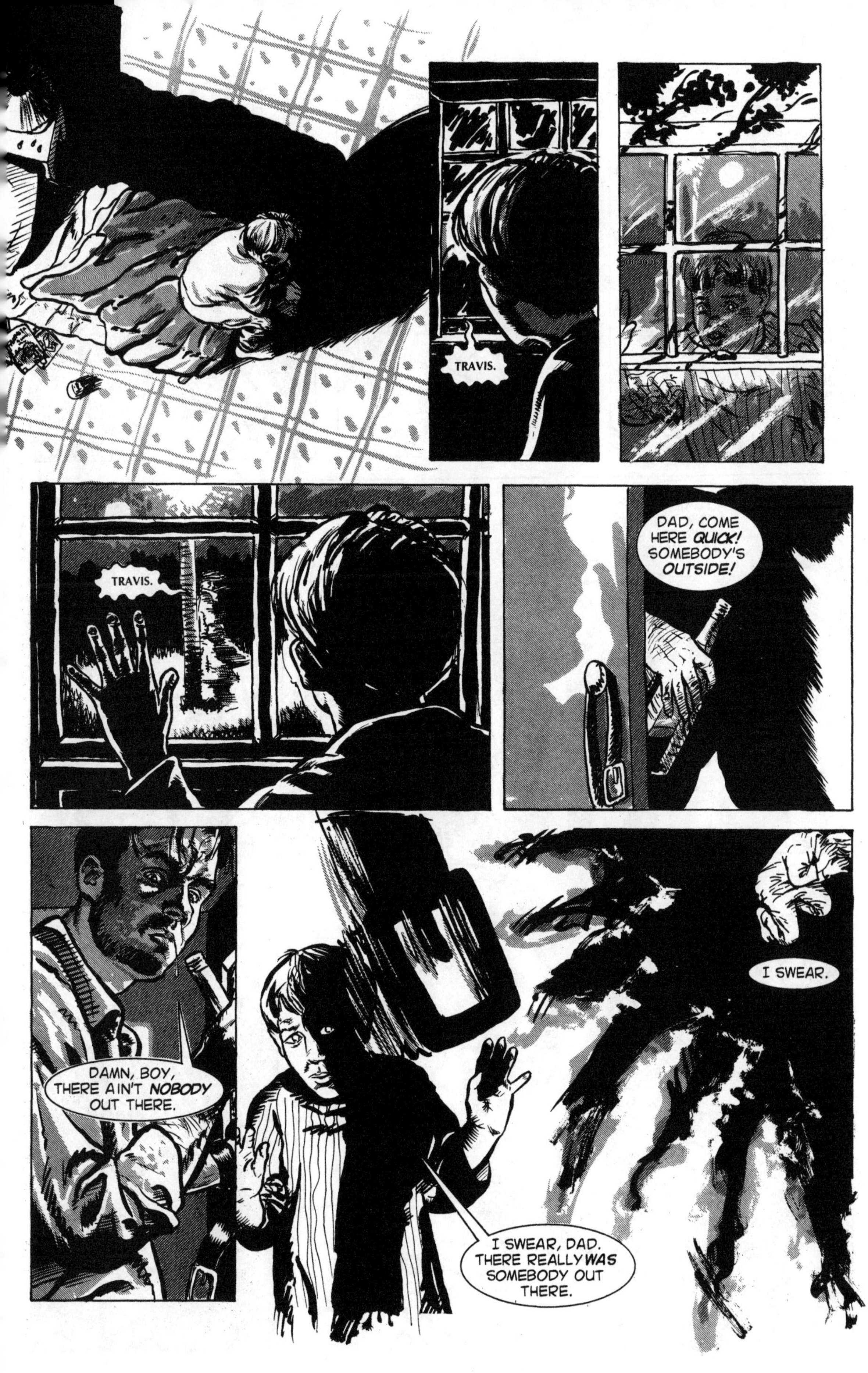
TRAVIS.
TRAVIS.
DAD, COME HERE QUICK! SOMEBODY'S OUTSIDE!
DAMN, BOY, THERE AIN'T NOBODY OUT THERE.
I SWEAR, DAD. THERE REALLY WAS SOMEBODY OUT THERE.
I SWEAR.

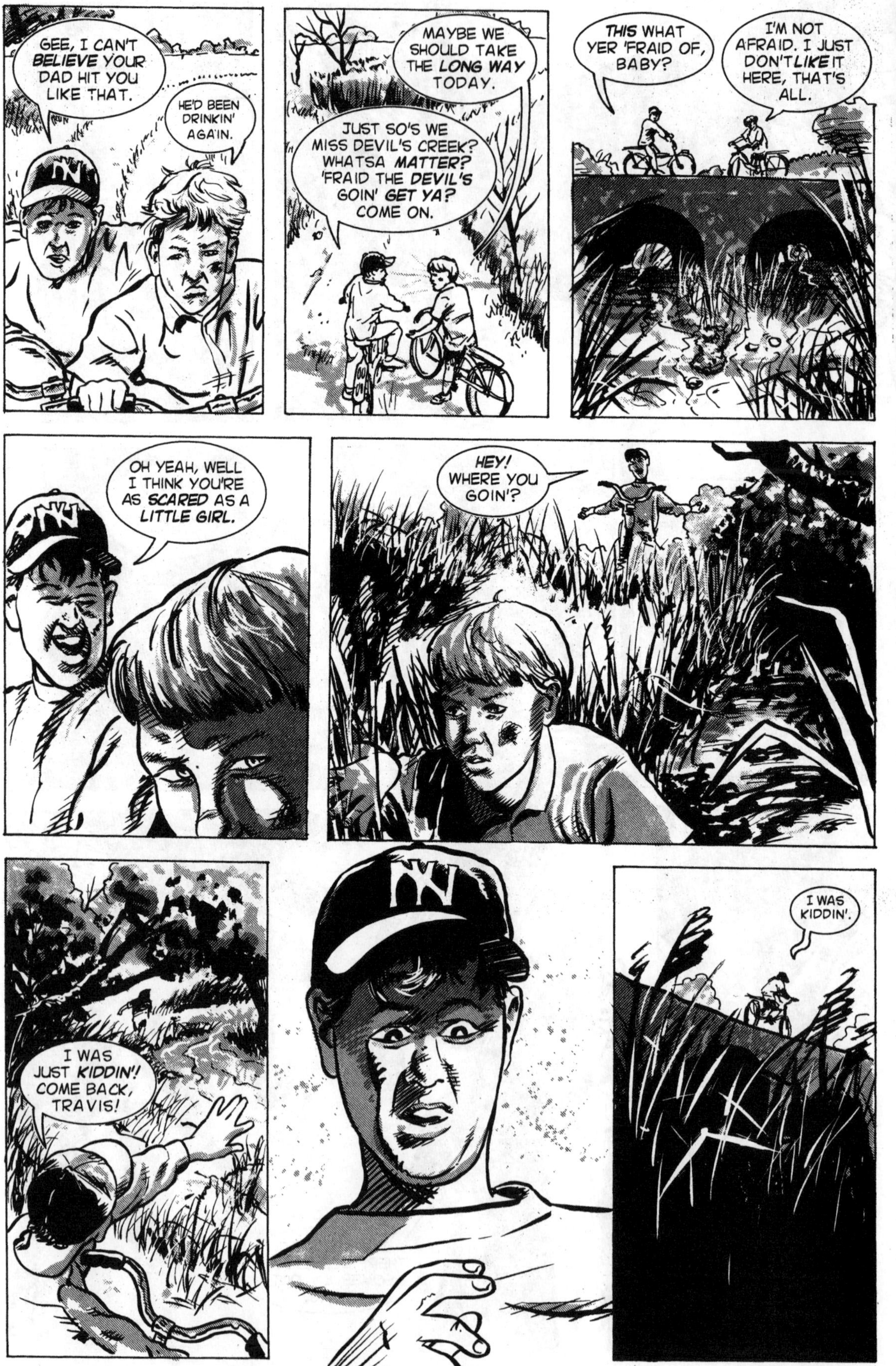
GEE, I CAN'T BELIEVE YOUR DAD HIT YOU LIKE THAT.
HE'D BEEN DRINKIN' AGAIN.
MAYBE WE SHOULD TAKE THE LONG WAY TODAY.
JUST SO'S WE MISS DEVIL'S CREEK? WHATSA MATTER? 'FRAID THE DEVIL'S GOIN' GET YA? COME ON.
THIS WHAT YER 'FRAID OF, BABY?
I'M NOT AFRAID. I JUST DON'T LIKE IT HERE, THAT'S ALL.
OH YEAH, WELL I THINK YOU'RE AS SCARED AS A LITTLE GIRL.
HEY! WHERE YOU GOIN'?
I WAS JUST KIDDIN'! COME BACK, TRAVIS!
I WAS KIDDIN'.

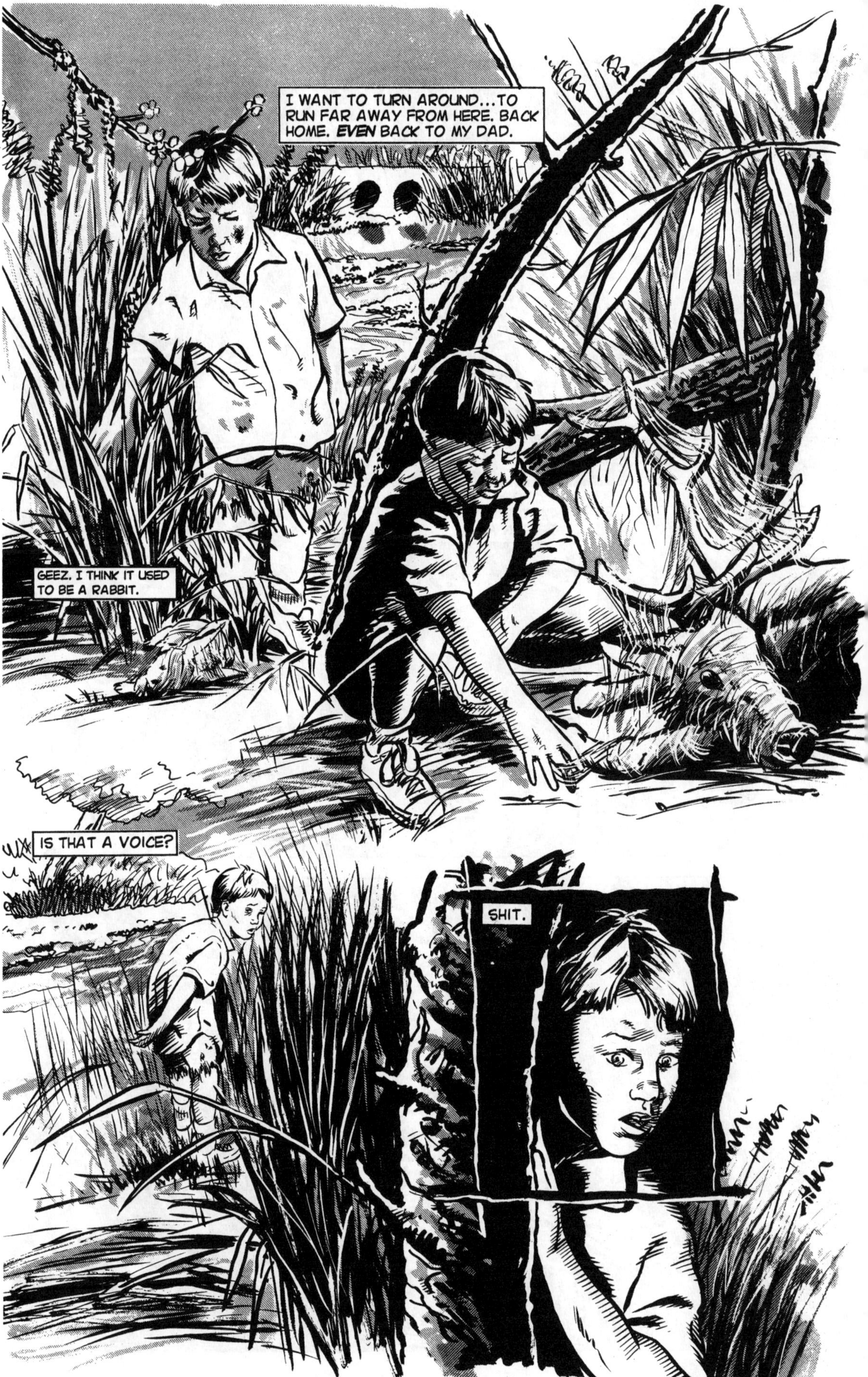
I WANT TO TURN AROUND...TO RUN FAR AWAY FROM HERE. BACK HOME. EVEN BACK TO MY DAD.
GEEZ. I THINK IT USED TO BE A RABBIT.
IS THAT A VOICE?
SHIT.

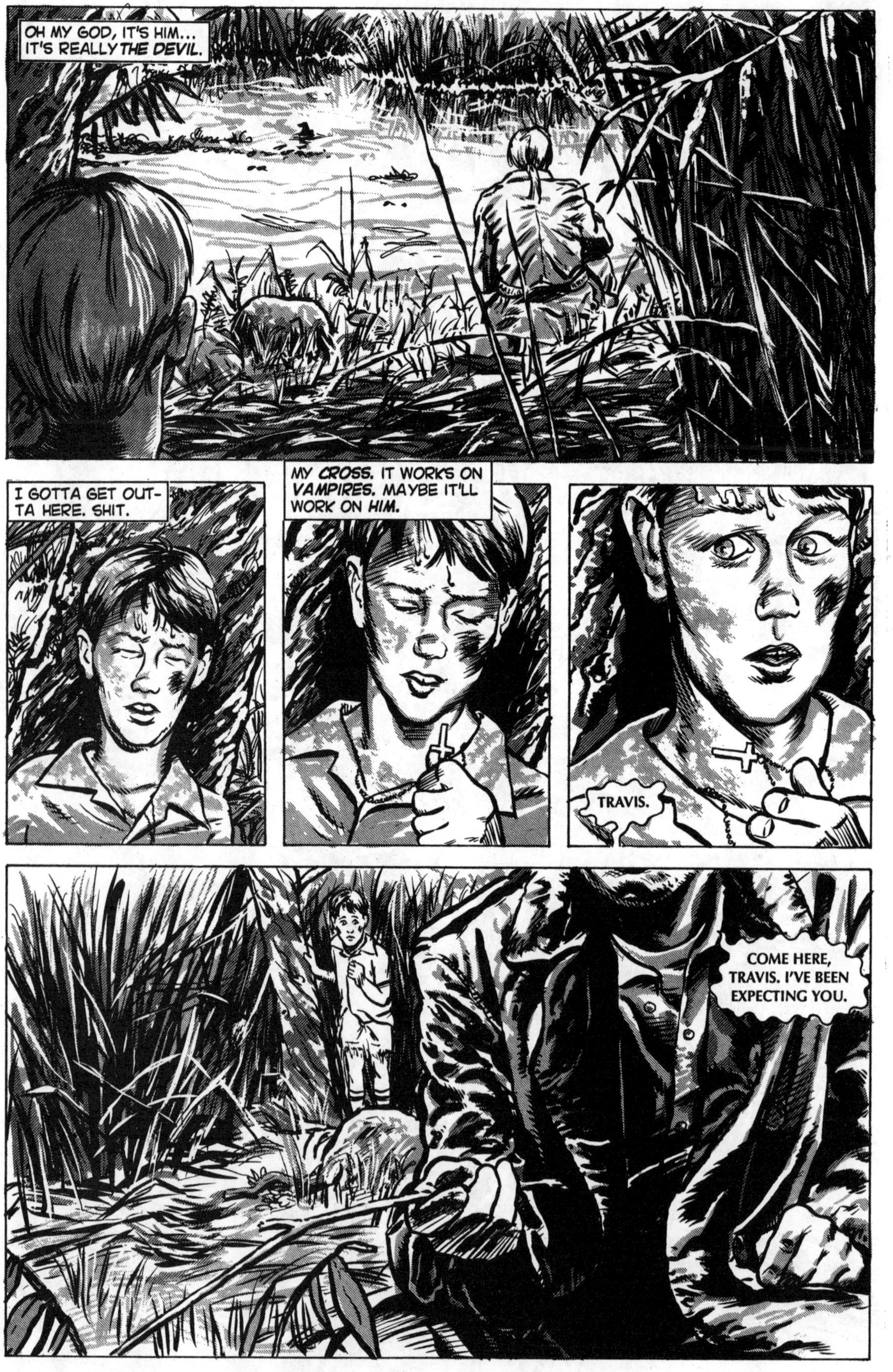
OH MY GOD, IT'S HIM... IT'S REALLY THE DEVIL.
I GOTTA GET OUT-TA HERE. SHIT.
MY CROSS. IT WORKS ON VAMPIRES. MAYBE IT'LL WORK ON HIM.
TRAVIS.
COME HERE, TRAVIS. I'VE BEEN EXPECTING YOU.

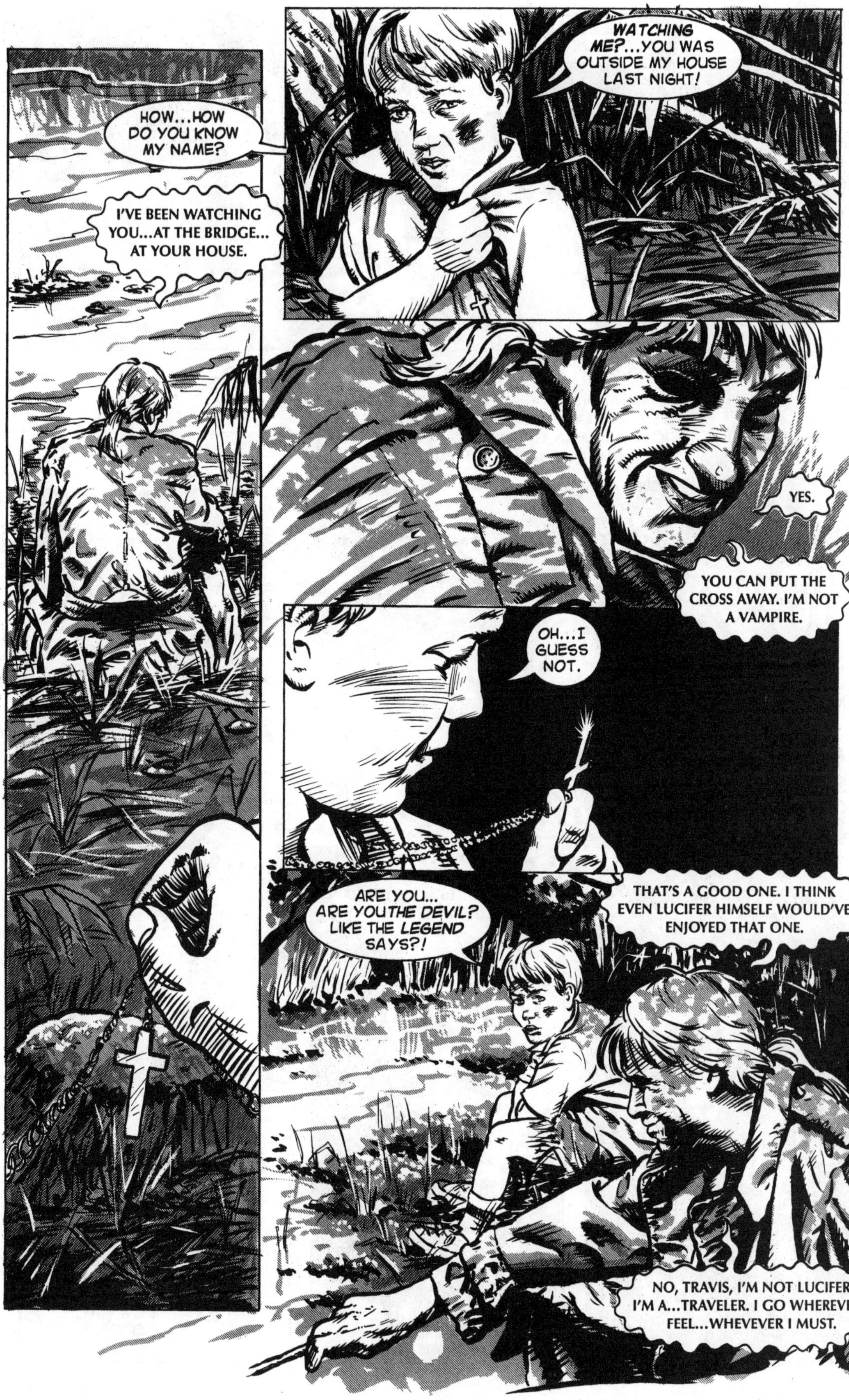
WATCHING ME?...YOU WAS OUTSIDE MY HOUSE LAST NIGHT!
HOW...HOW DO YOU KNOW MY NAME?
I'VE BEEN WATCHING YOU...AT THE BRIDGE... AT YOUR HOUSE.
YES.
YOU CAN PUT THE CROSS AWAY. I'M NOT A VAMPIRE.
OH...I GUESS NOT.
ARE YOU... ARE YOU THE DEVIL? LIKE THE LEGEND SAYS?!
THAT'S A GOOD ONE. I THINK EVEN LUCIFER HIMSELF WOULD'VE ENJOYED THAT ONE.
NO, TRAVIS, I'M NOT LUCIFER. I'M A...TRAVELER. I GO WHEREVER I FEEL...WHEVEVER I MUST.

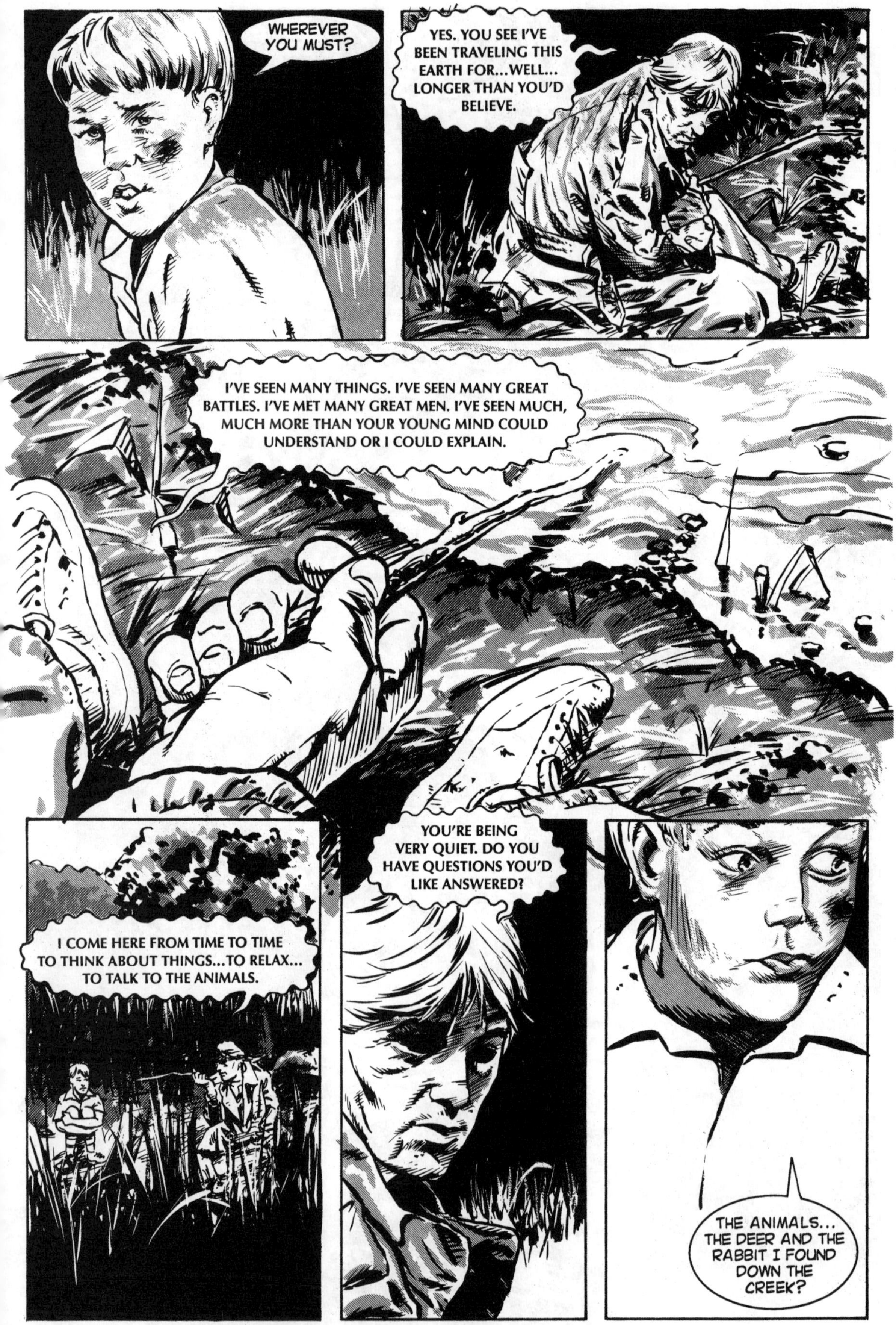
WHEREVER YOU MUST?
YES. YOU SEE I'VE BEEN TRAVELING THIS EARTH FOR...WELL... LONGER THAN YOU'D BELIEVE.
I'VE SEEN MANY THINGS. I'VE SEEN MANY GREAT BATTLES. I'VE MET MANY GREAT MEN. I'VE SEEN MUCH, MUCH MORE THAN YOUR YOUNG MIND COULD UNDERSTAND OR I COULD EXPLAIN.
I COME HERE FROM TIME TO TIME TO THINK ABOUT THINGS...TO RELAX... TO TALK TO THE ANIMALS.
YOU'RE BEING VERY QUIET. DO YOU HAVE QUESTIONS YOU'D LIKE ANSWERED?
THE ANIMALS... THE DEER AND THE RABBIT I FOUND DOWN THE CREEK?

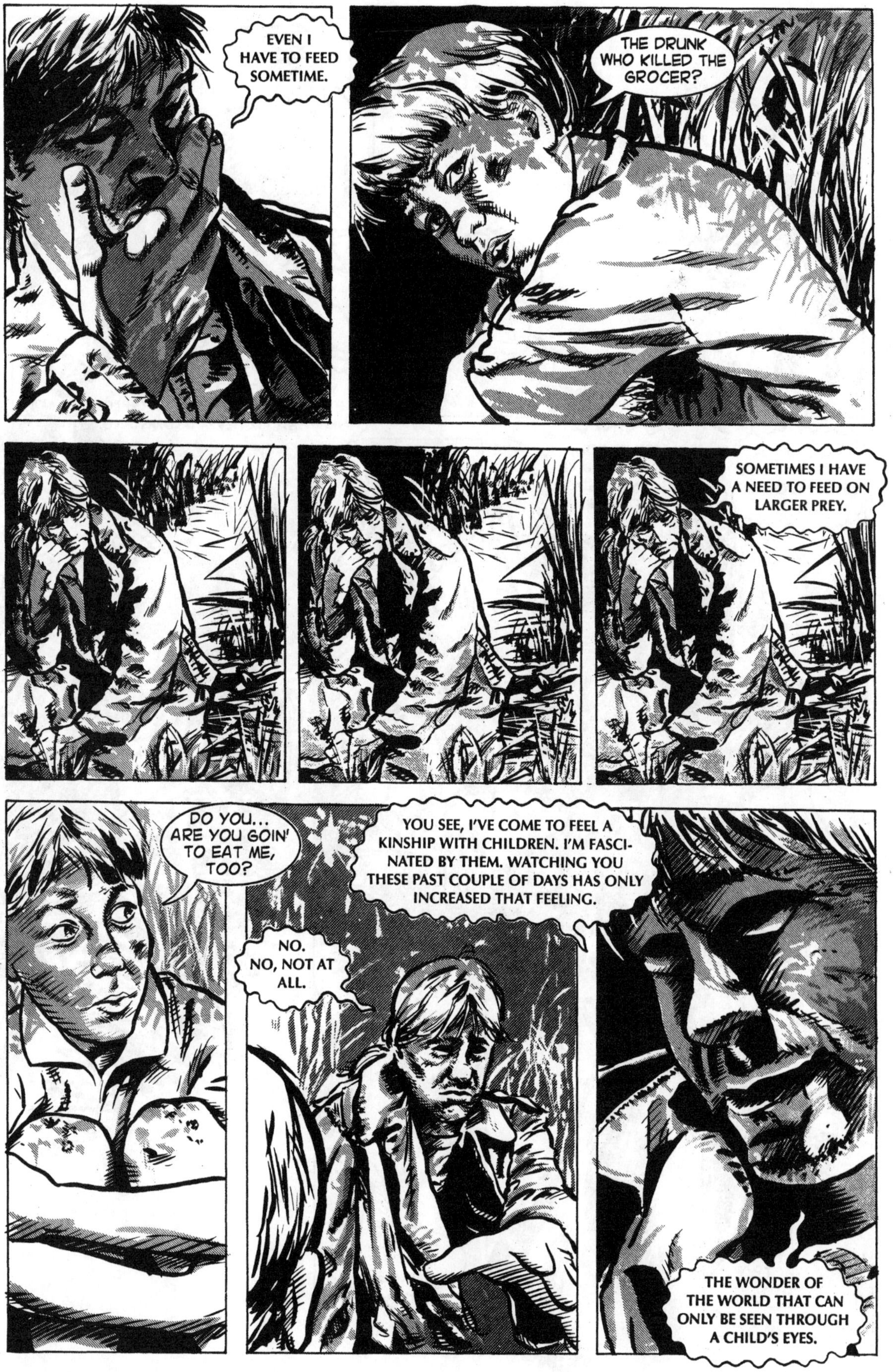
EVEN I HAVE TO FEED SOMETIME.
THE DRUNK WHO KILLED THE GROCER?
SOMETIMES I HAVE A NEED TO FEED ON LARGER PREY.
DO YOU... ARE YOU GOIN' TO EAT ME, TOO?
NO. NO, NOT AT ALL.
YOU SEE, I'VE COME TO FEEL A KINSHIP WITH CHILDREN. I'M FASCINATED BY THEM. WATCHING YOU THESE PAST COUPLE OF DAYS HAS ONLY INCREASED THAT FEELING.
THE WONDER OF THE WORLD THAT CAN ONLY BE SEEN THROUGH A CHILD'S EYES.

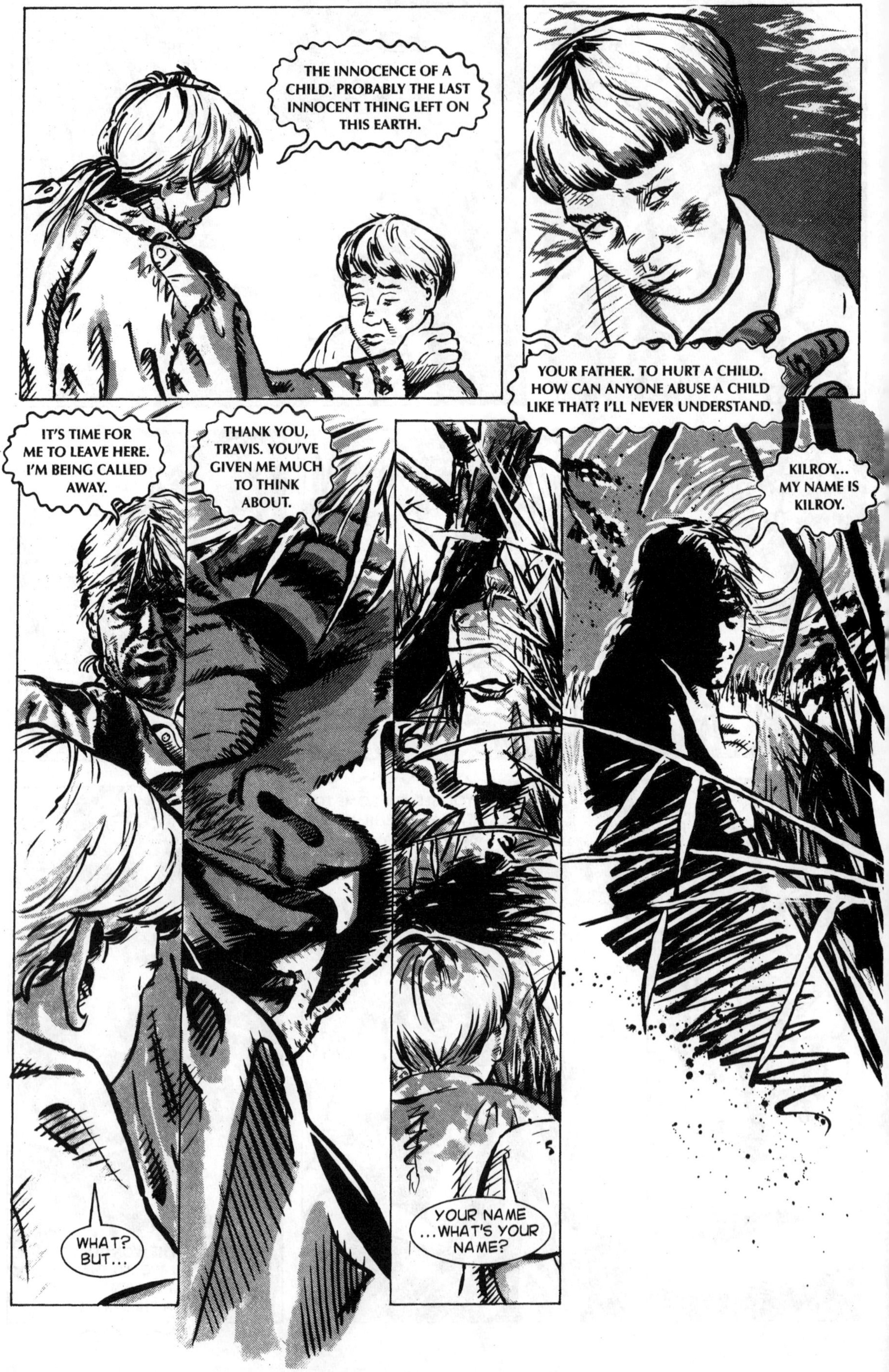
THE INNOCENCE OF A CHILD. PROBABLY THE LAST INNOCENT THING LEFT ON THIS EARTH.
YOUR FATHER. TO HURT A CHILD. HOW CAN ANYONE ABUSE A CHILD LIKE THAT? I'LL NEVER UNDERSTAND.
IT'S TIME FOR ME TO LEAVE HERE. I'M BEING CALLED AWAY.
WHAT? BUT...
THANK YOU, TRAVIS. YOU'VE GIVEN ME MUCH TO THINK ABOUT.
YOUR NAME ...WHAT'S YOUR NAME?
KILROY... MY NAME IS KILROY.

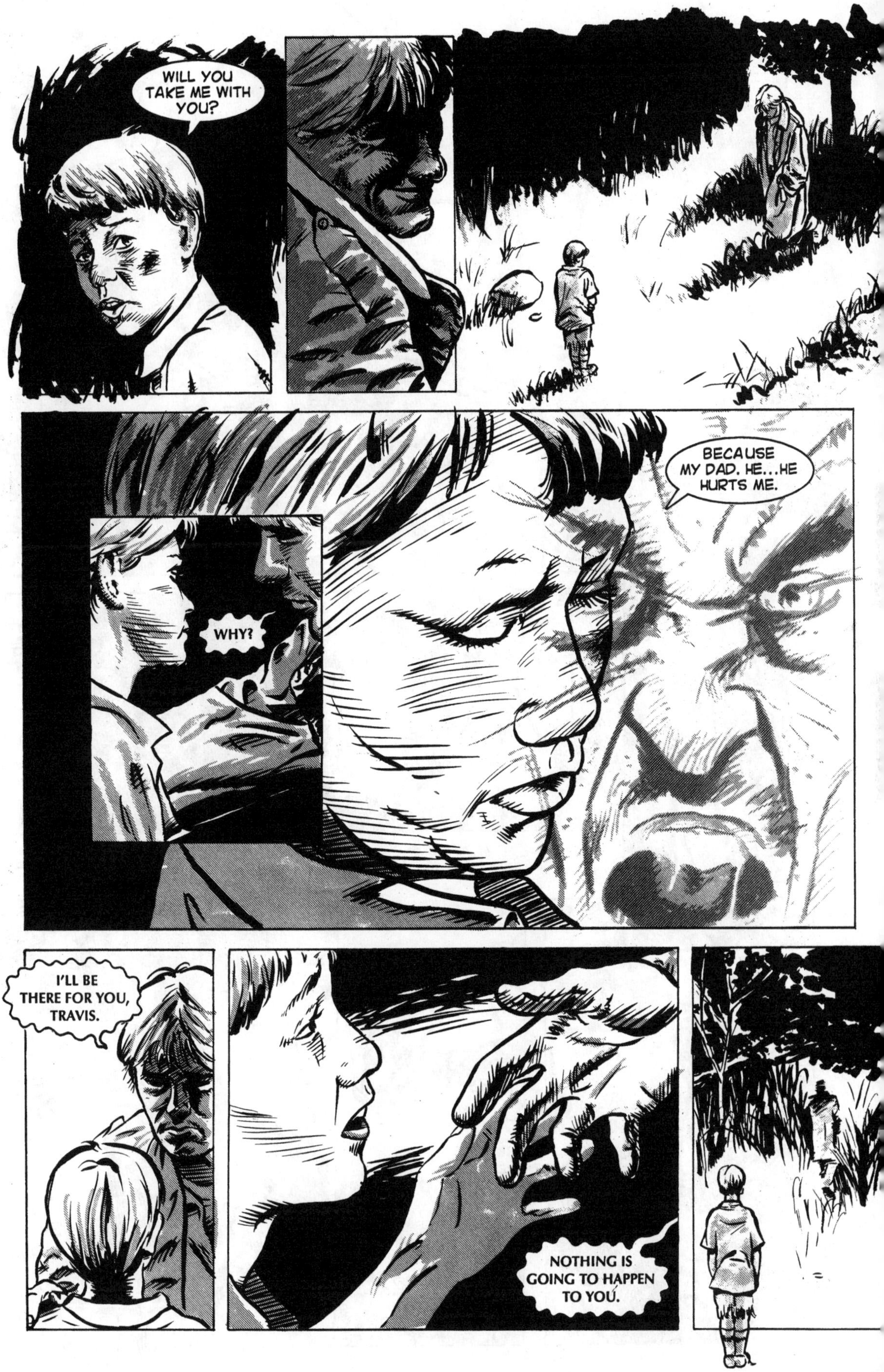

WILL YOU TAKE ME WITH YOU?
WHY?
BECAUSE MY DAD. HE...HE HURTS ME.
I'LL BE THERE FOR YOU, TRAVIS.
NOTHING IS GOING TO HAPPEN TO YOU.

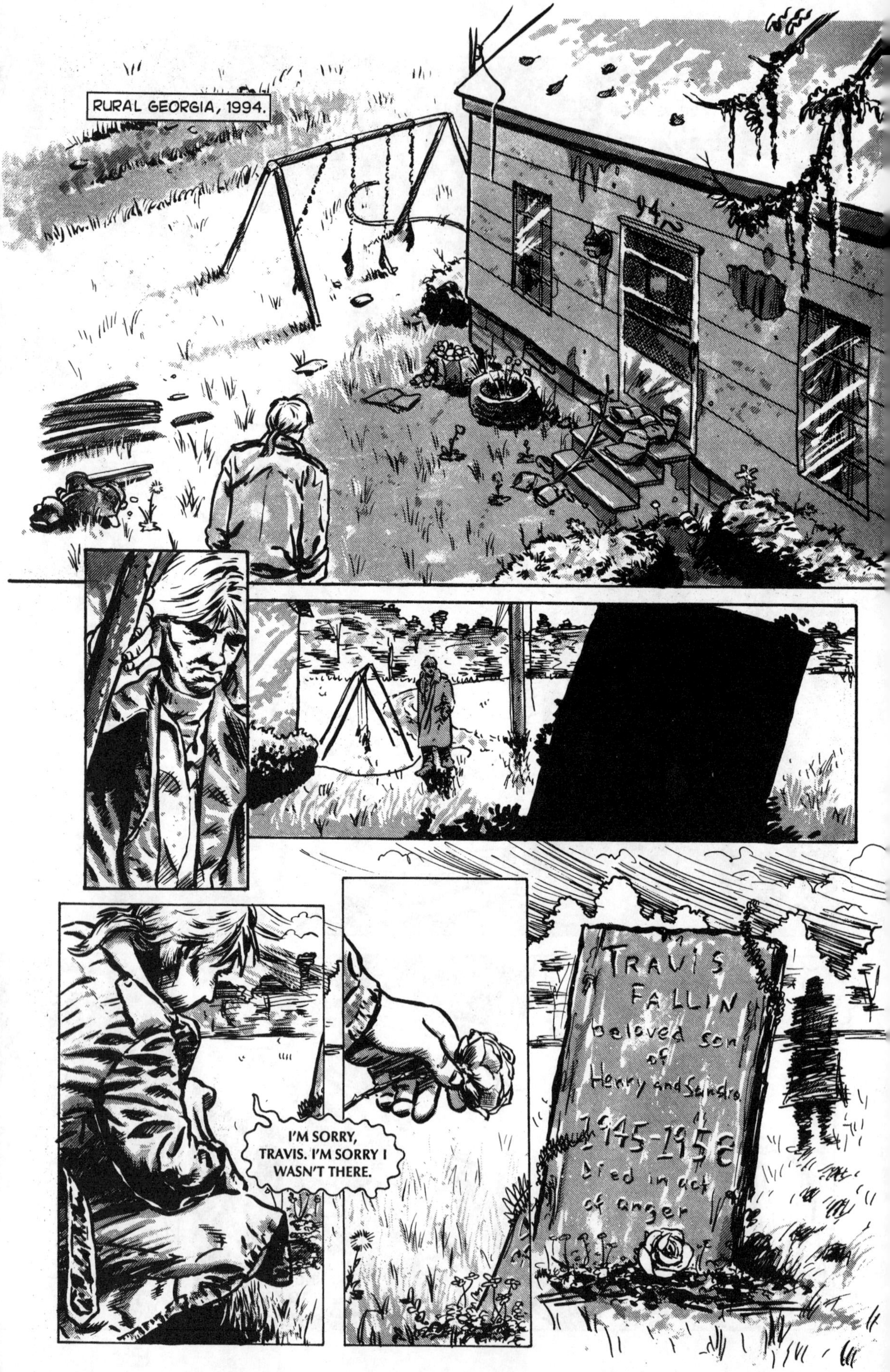
RURAL GEORGIA, 1994.
I'M SORRY, TRAVIS. I'M SORRY I WASN'T THERE.
TRAVIS FALLIN
beloved son of
Henry and Sandra
1945-1958
Died in act of anger

"Living in Hell"

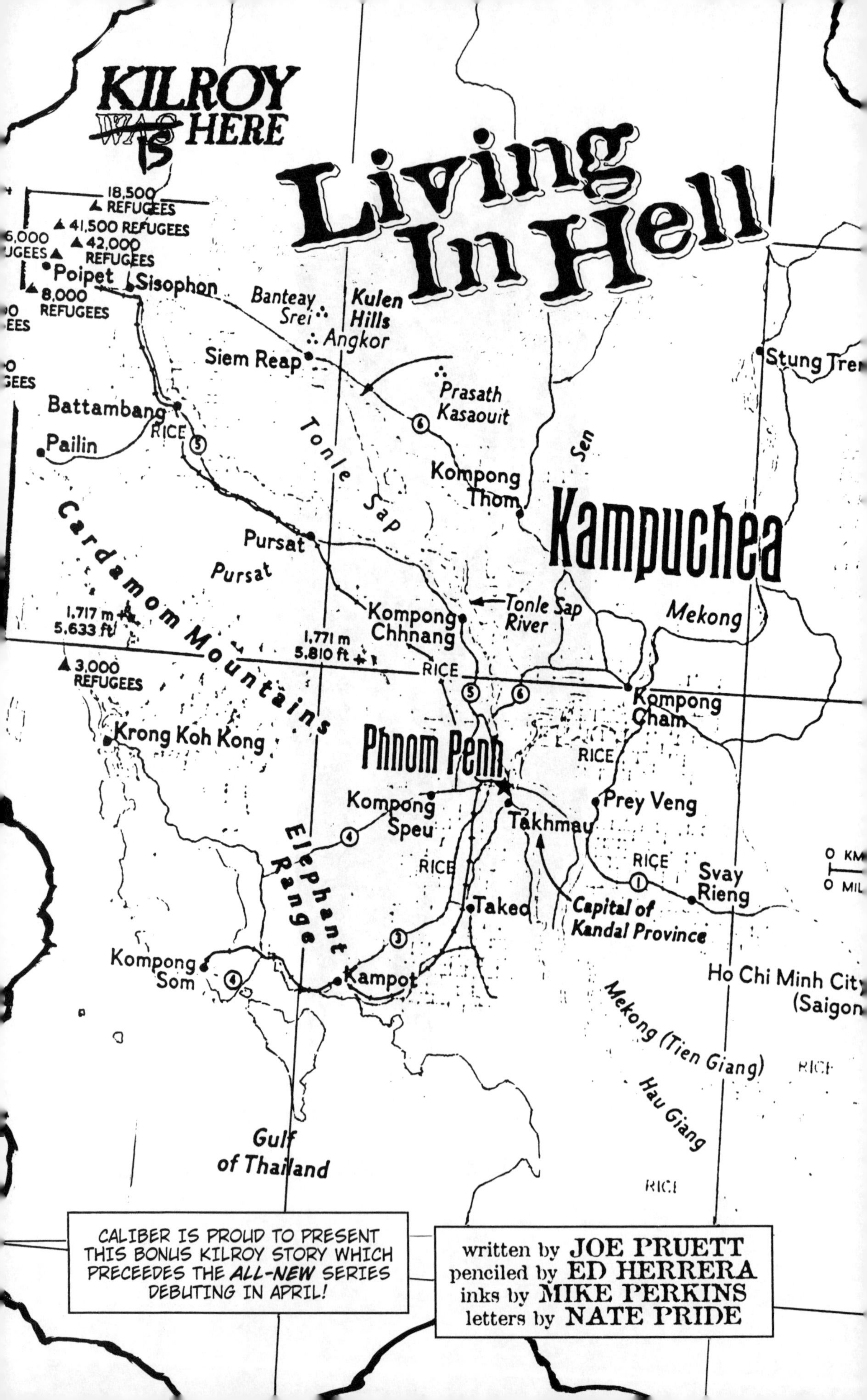KILROY WAS IS HERE
Living In Hell
18,500 REFUGEES
41,500 REFUGEES
42,000 REFUGEES
8,000 REFUGEES
3,000 REFUGEES
Poipet
Sisophon
Banteay Srei
Kulen Hills
Angkor
Siem Reap
Prasath Kasaouit
Stung Treng
Battambang
RICE
Pailin
Tonle Sap
Sen
Kompong Thom
Kampuchea
Pursat
Pursat
Cardamom Mountains
1,717 m 5,633 ft
1,771 m 5,810 ft
Kompong Chhnang
Tonle Sap River
Mekong
Kompong Cham
Phnom Penh
Krong Koh Kong
Kompong Speu
Takhmau
Prey Veng
Elephant Range
Svay Rieng
Takeo
Capital of Kandal Province
Kompong Som
Kampot
Ho Chi Minh City (Saigon)
Mekong (Tien Giang)
Hau Giang
Gulf of Thailand
CALIBER IS PROUD TO PRESENT THIS BONUS KILROY STORY WHICH PRECEEDES THE ALL-NEW SERIES DEBUTING IN APRIL!
written by JOE PRUETT
penciled by ED HERRERA
inks by MIKE PERKINS
letters by NATE PRIDE

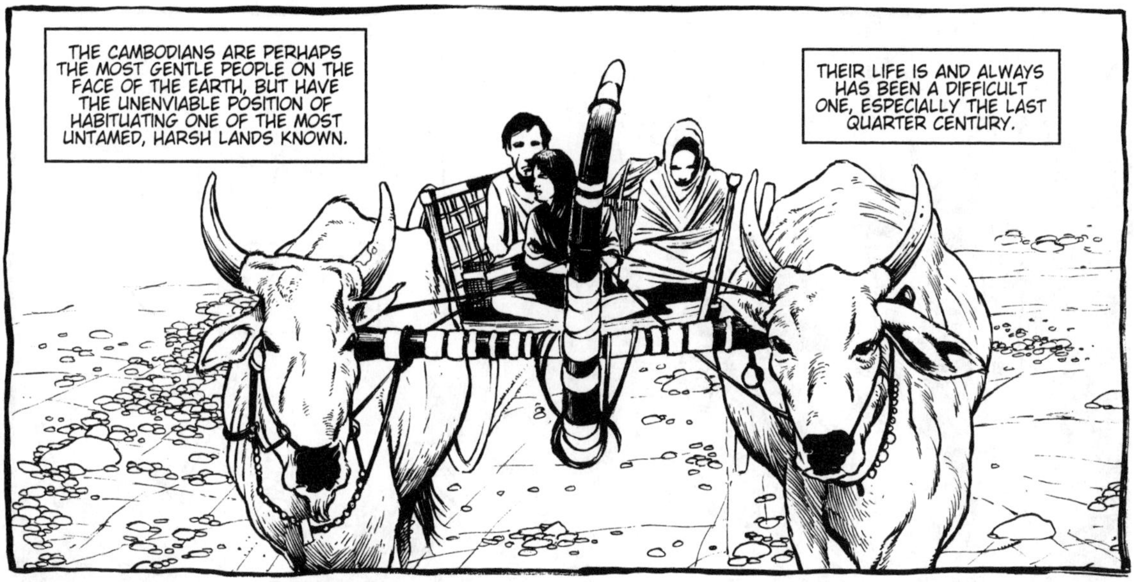
THE CAMBODIANS ARE PERHAPS THE MOST GENTLE PEOPLE ON THE FACE OF THE EARTH, BUT HAVE THE UNENVIABLE POSITION OF HABITUATING ONE OF THE MOST UNTAMED, HARSH LANDS KNOWN.
THEIR LIFE IS AND ALWAYS HAS BEEN A DIFFICULT ONE, ESPECIALLY THE LAST QUARTER CENTURY.

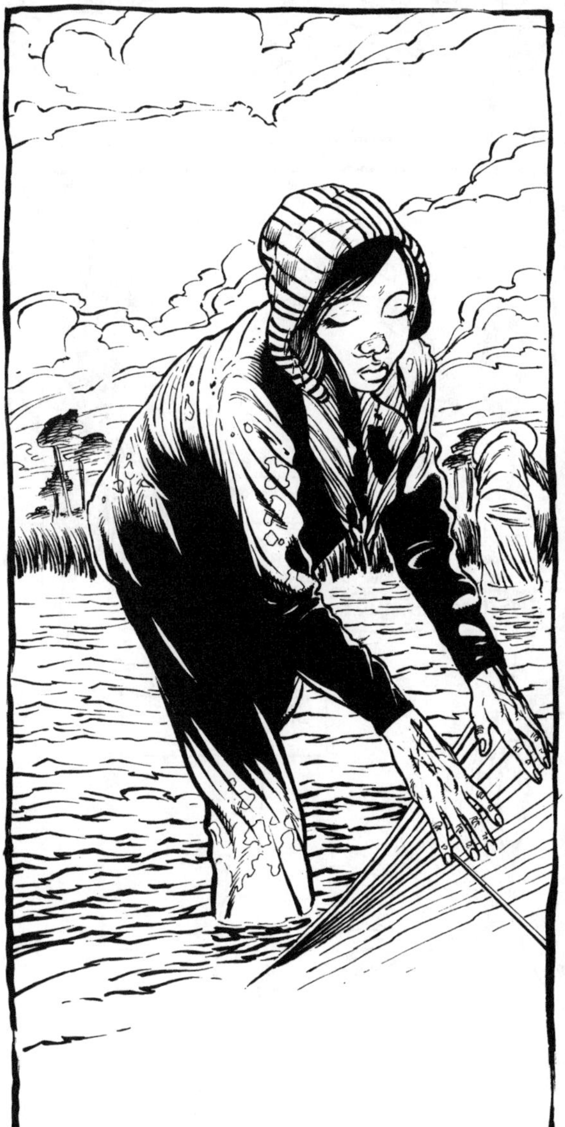

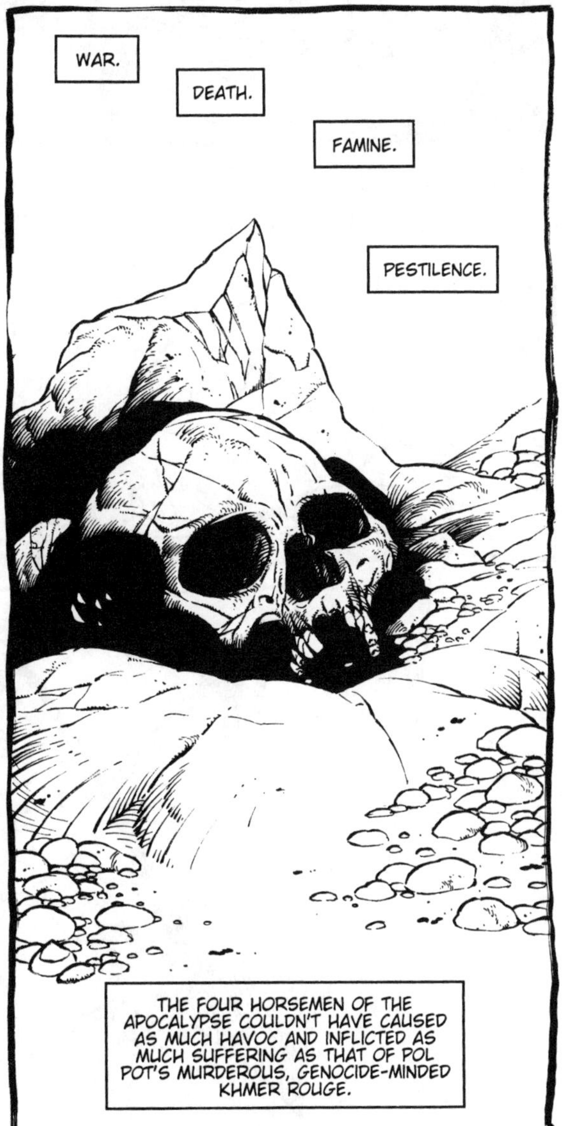
WAR.
DEATH.
FAMINE.
PESTILENCE.
THE FOUR HORSEMEN OF THE APOCALYPSE COULDN'T HAVE CAUSED AS MUCH HAVOC AND INFLICTED AS MUCH SUFFERING AS THAT OF POL POT'S MURDEROUS, GENOCIDE-MINDED KHMER ROUGE.

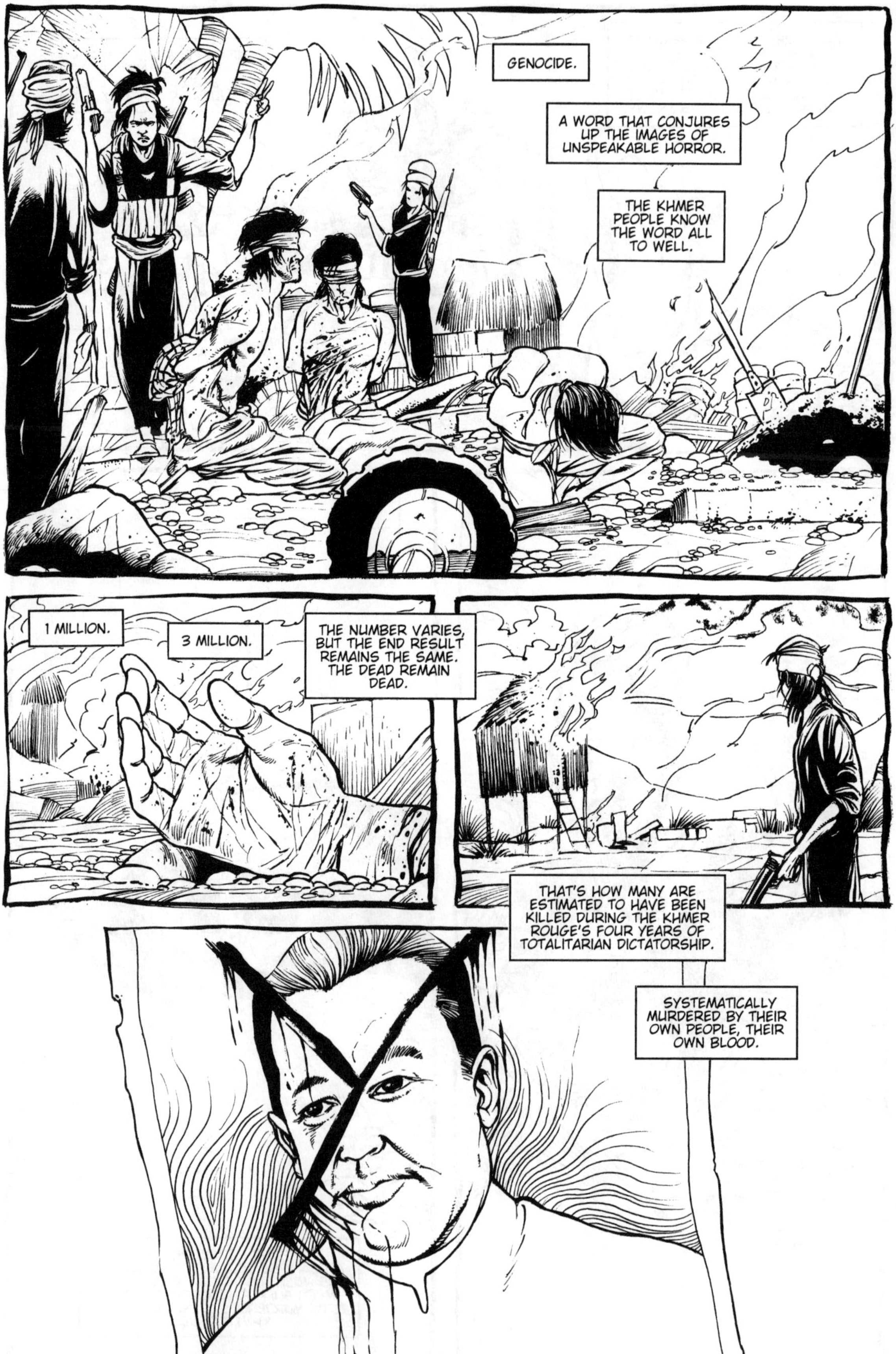
GENOCIDE.
A WORD THAT CONJURES UP THE IMAGES OF UNSPEAKABLE HORROR.
THE KHMER PEOPLE KNOW THE WORD ALL TO WELL.
1 MILLION.
3 MILLION.
THE NUMBER VARIES, BUT THE END RESULT REMAINS THE SAME. THE DEAD REMAIN DEAD.
THAT'S HOW MANY ARE ESTIMATED TO HAVE BEEN KILLED DURING THE KHMER ROUGE'S FOUR YEARS OF TOTALITARIAN DICTATORSHIP.
SYSTEMATICALLY MURDERED BY THEIR OWN PEOPLE, THEIR OWN BLOOD.

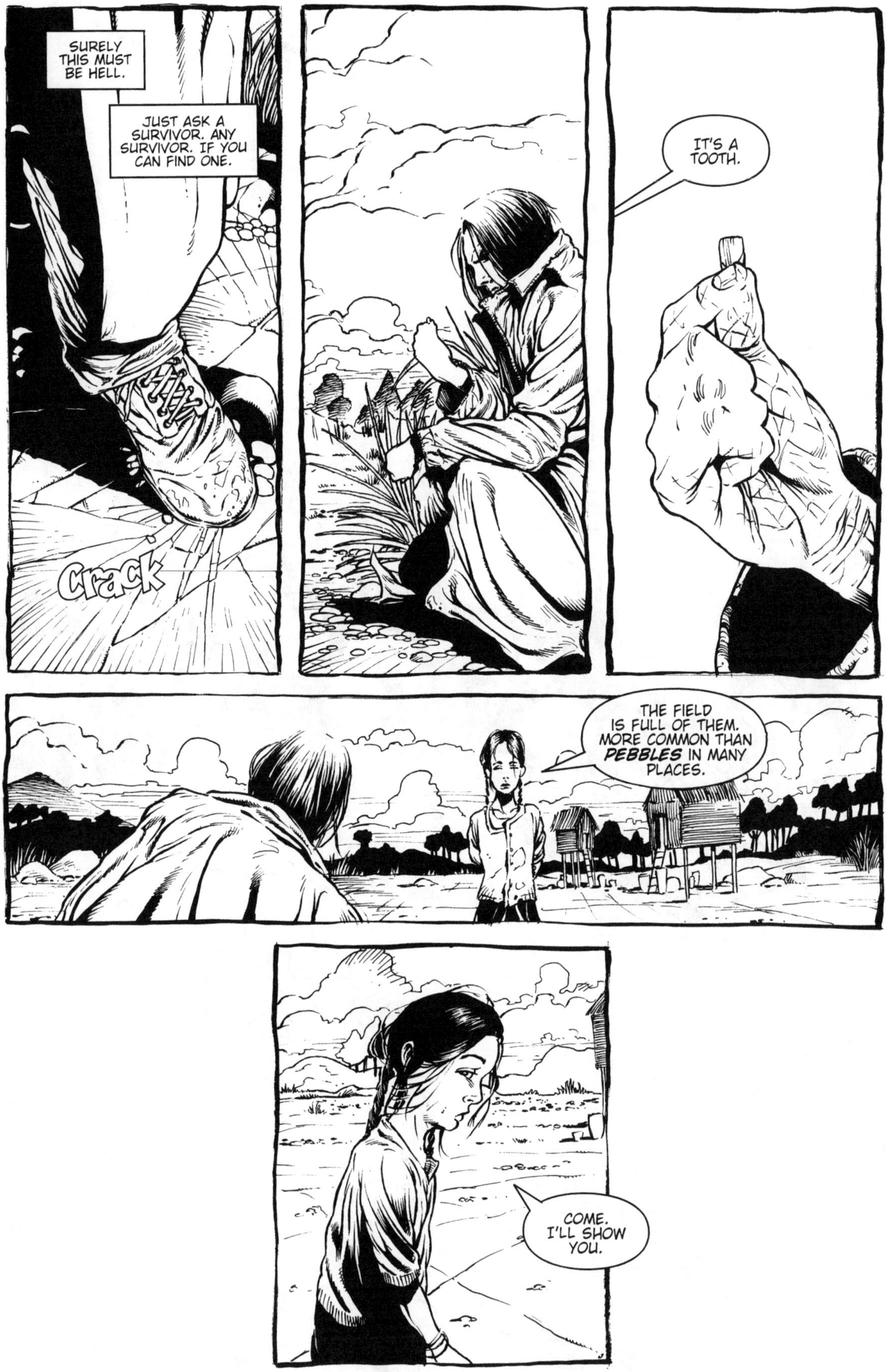
SURELY THIS MUST BE HELL.
JUST ASK A SURVIVOR. ANY SURVIVOR. IF YOU CAN FIND ONE.
Crack
IT'S A TOOTH.
THE FIELD IS FULL OF THEM. MORE COMMON THAN PEBBLES IN MANY PLACES.
COME. I'LL SHOW YOU.

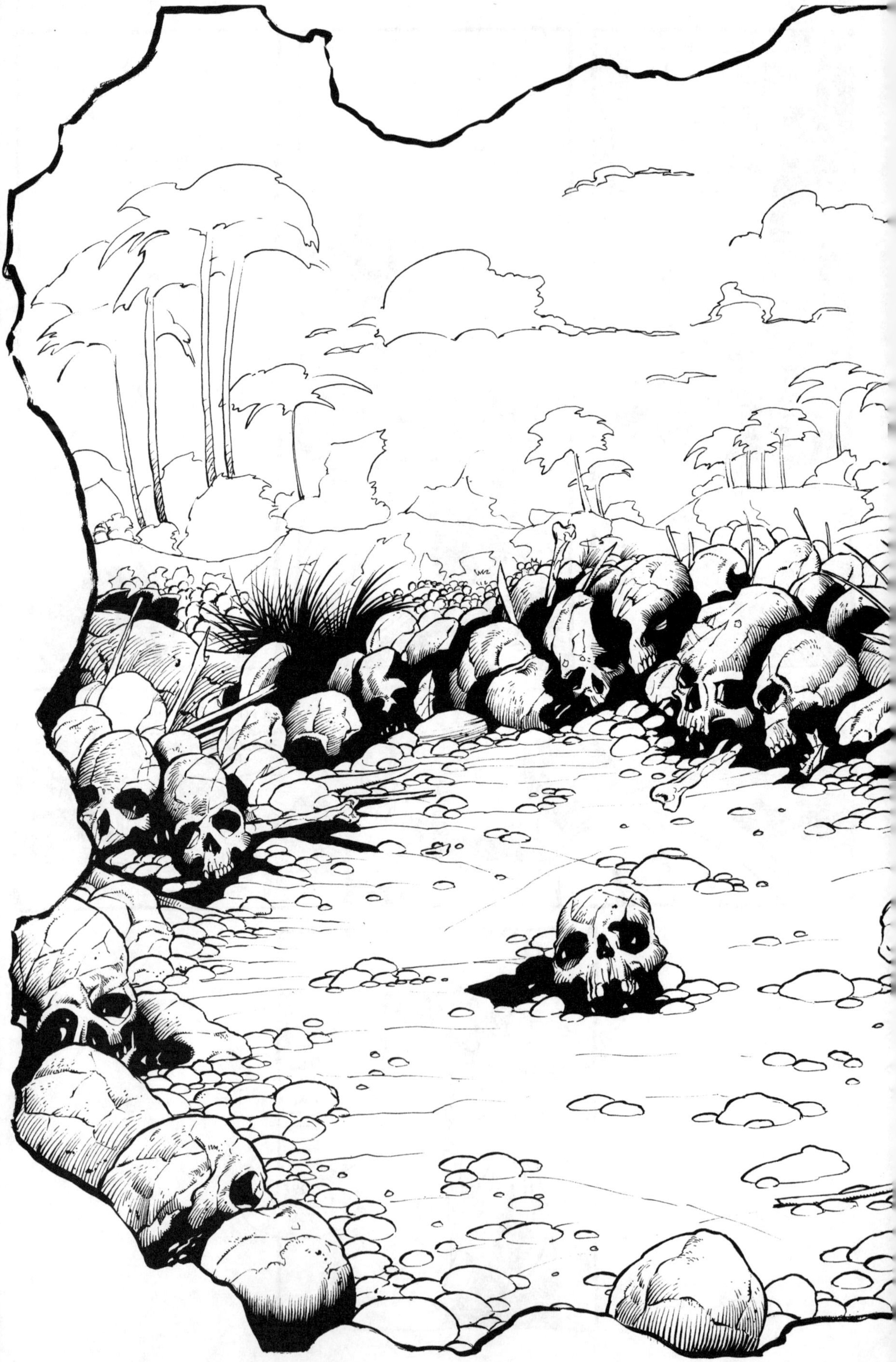

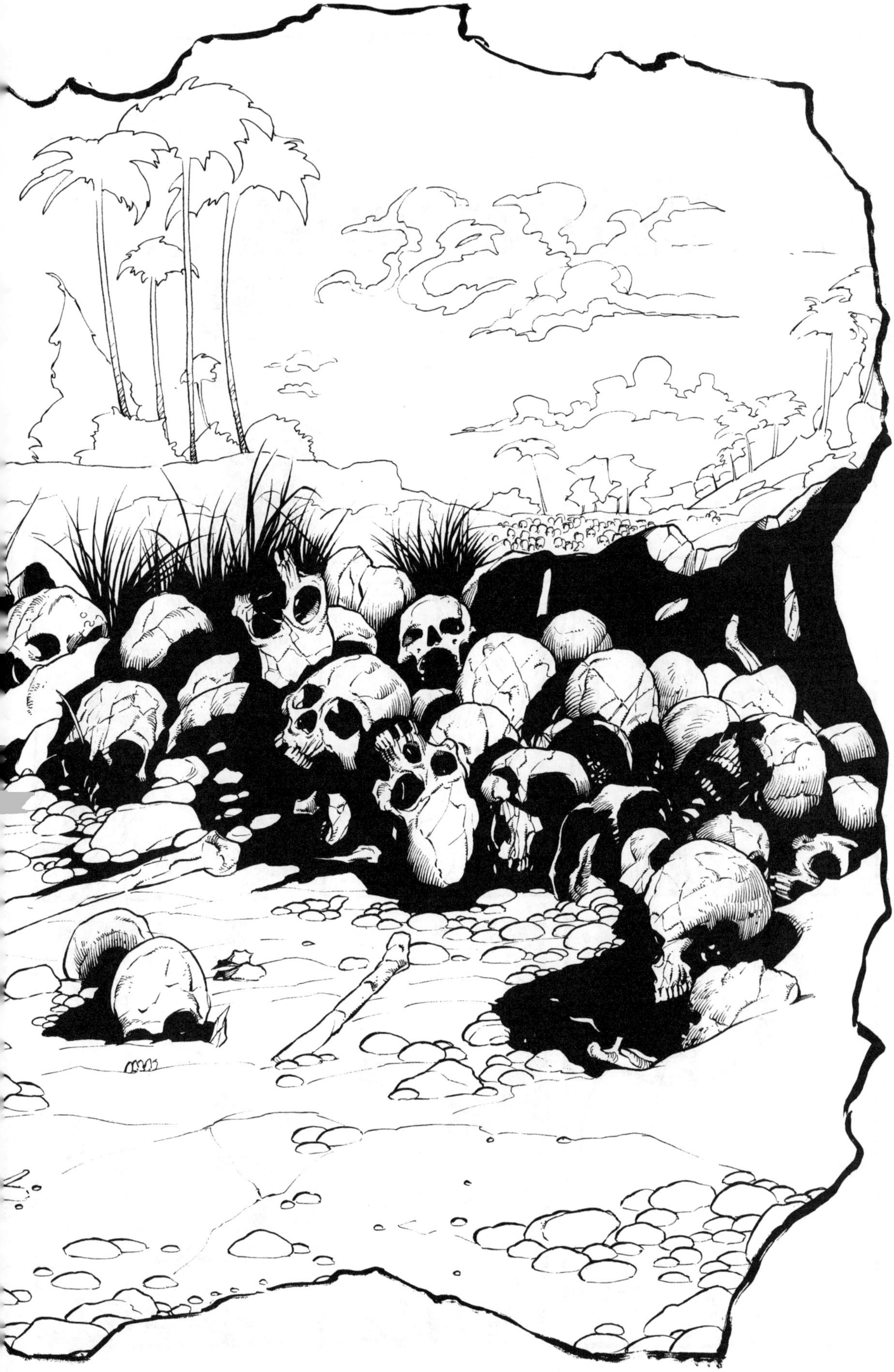

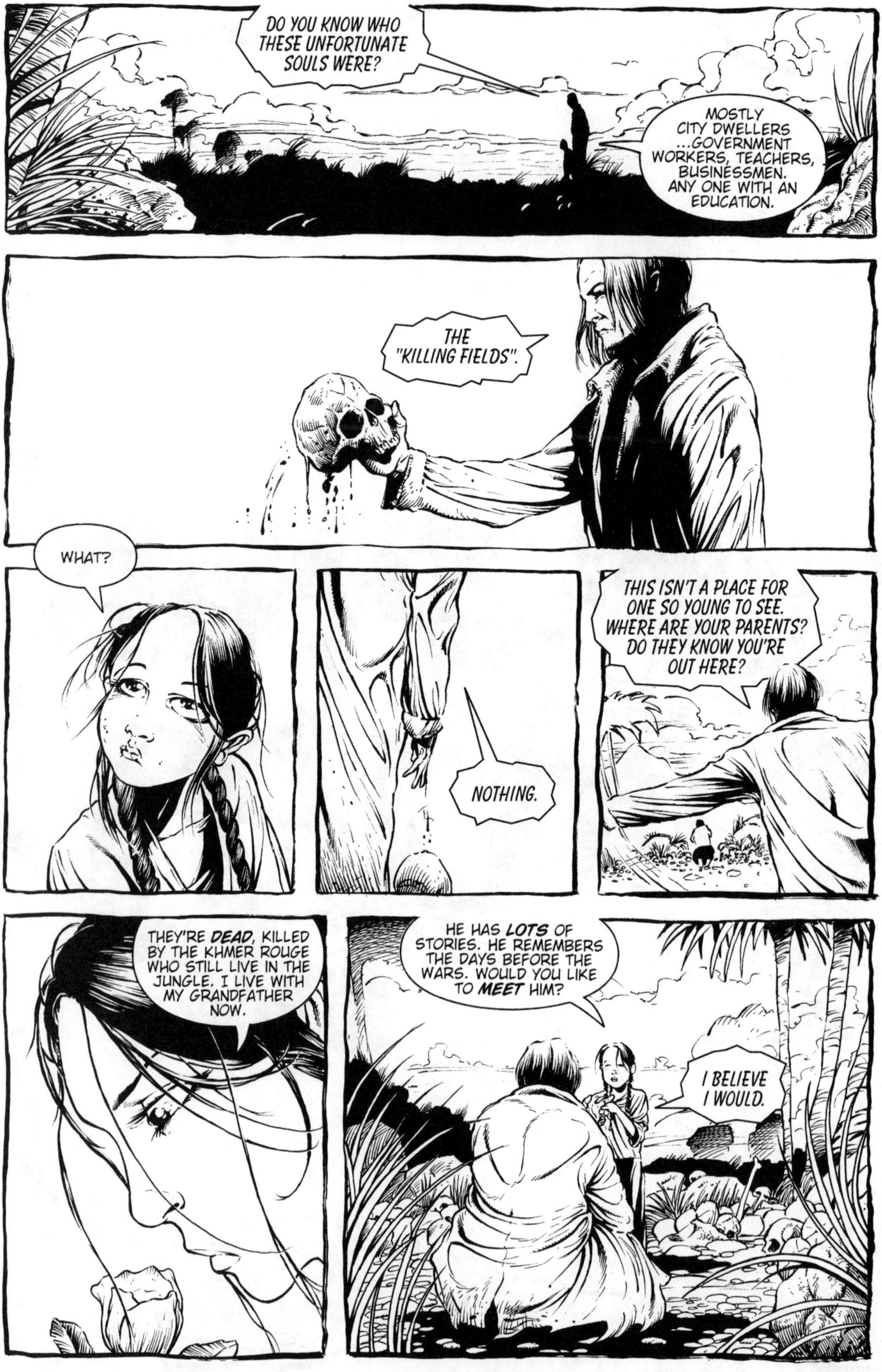
DO YOU KNOW WHO THESE UNFORTUNATE SOULS WERE?
MOSTLY CITY DWELLERS ...GOVERNMENT WORKERS, TEACHERS, BUSINESSMEN. ANY ONE WITH AN EDUCATION.
THE "KILLING FIELDS".
WHAT?
NOTHING.
THIS ISN'T A PLACE FOR ONE SO YOUNG TO SEE. WHERE ARE YOUR PARENTS? DO THEY KNOW YOU'RE OUT HERE?
THEY'RE DEAD, KILLED BY THE KHMER ROUGE WHO STILL LIVE IN THE JUNGLE. I LIVE WITH MY GRANDFATHER NOW.
HE HAS LOTS OF STORIES. HE REMEMBERS THE DAYS BEFORE THE WARS. WOULD YOU LIKE TO MEET HIM?
I BELIEVE I WOULD.

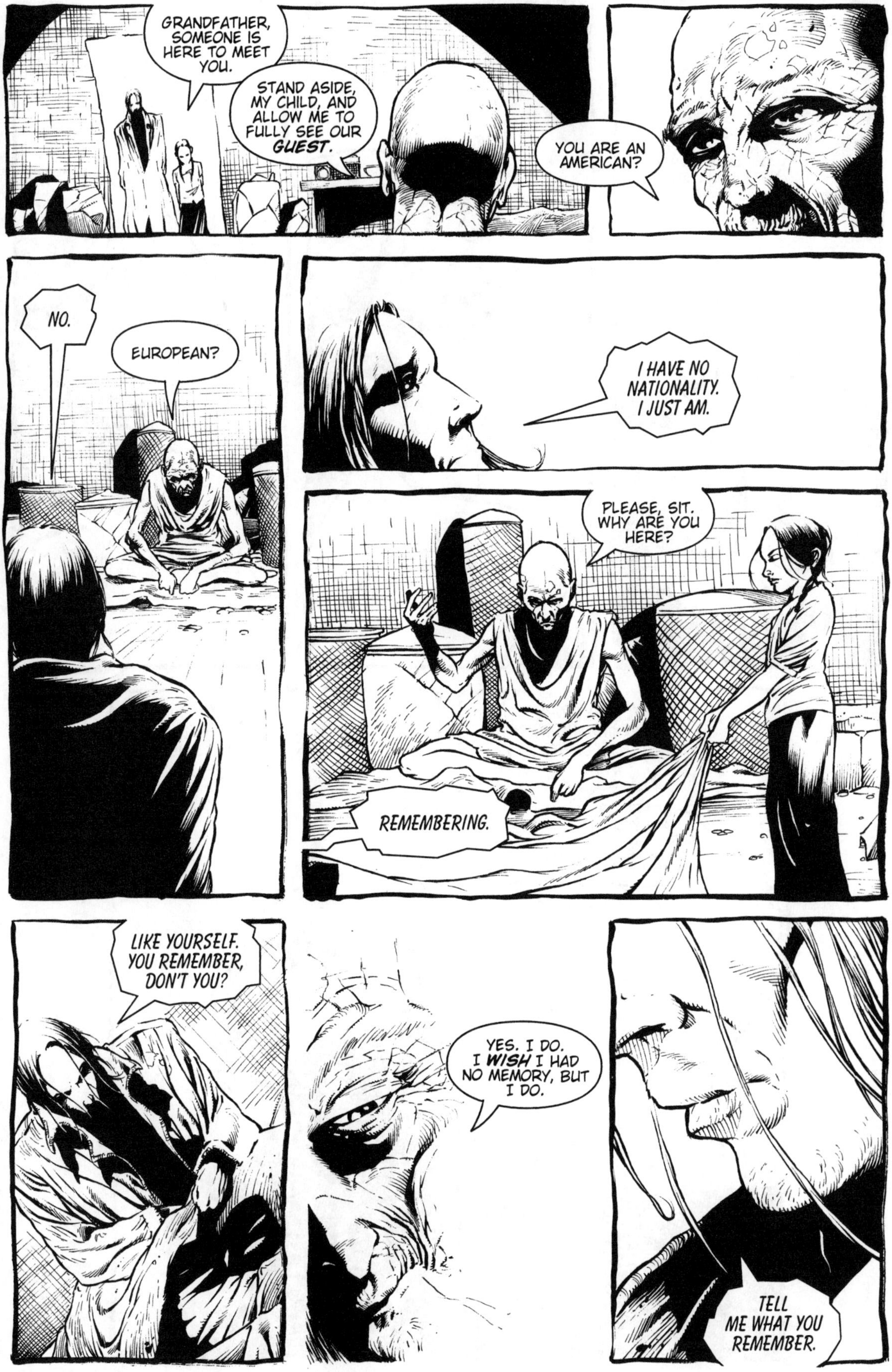
GRANDFATHER, SOMEONE IS HERE TO MEET YOU.
STAND ASIDE, MY CHILD, AND ALLOW ME TO FULLY SEE OUR **GUEST**.
YOU ARE AN AMERICAN?
NO.
EUROPEAN?
I HAVE NO NATIONALITY. I JUST AM.
PLEASE, SIT. WHY ARE YOU HERE?
REMEMBERING.
LIKE YOURSELF. YOU REMEMBER, DON'T YOU?
YES. I DO. I **WISH** I HAD NO MEMORY, BUT I DO.
TELL ME WHAT YOU REMEMBER.

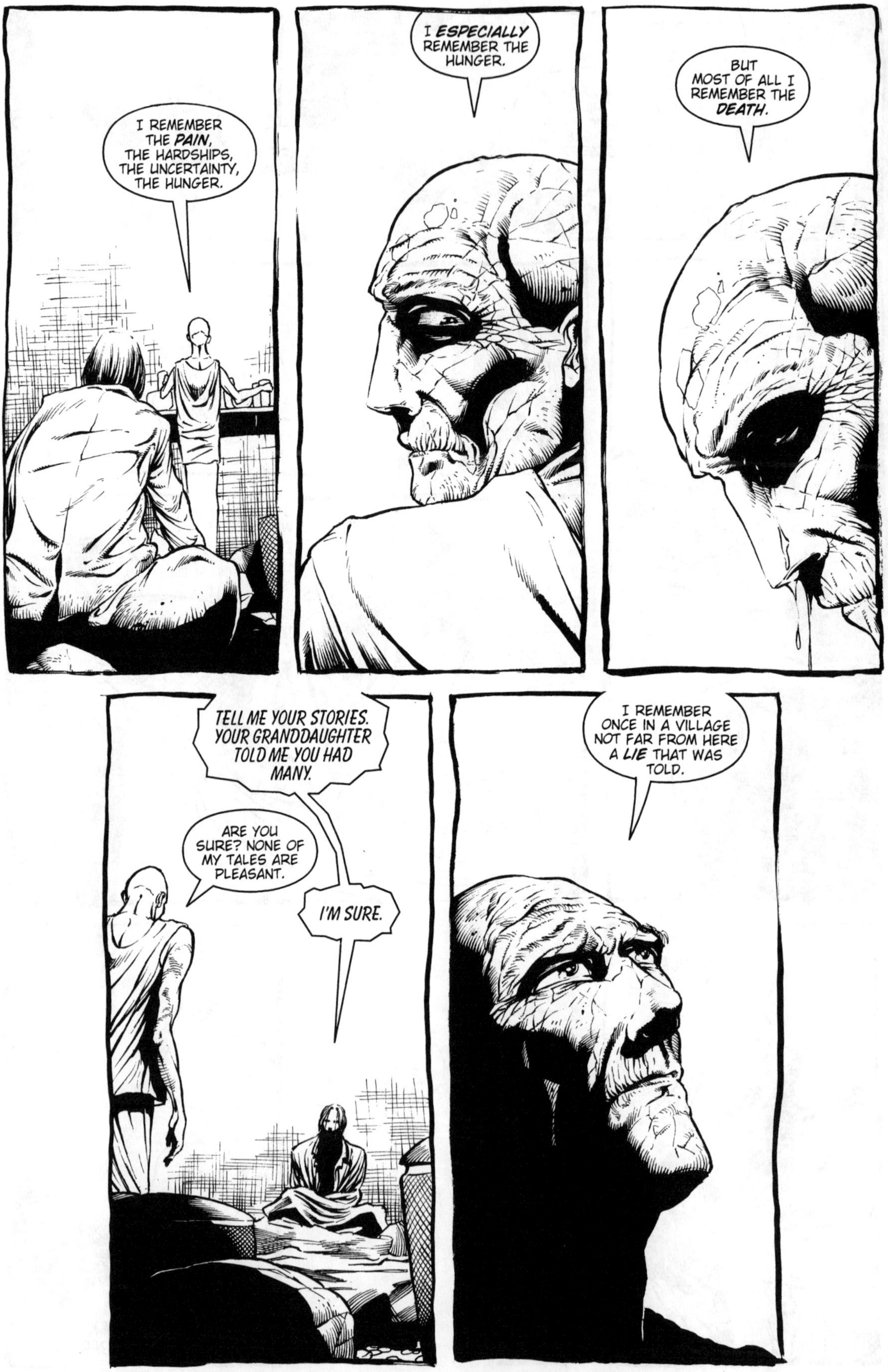
I REMEMBER THE PAIN, THE HARDSHIPS, THE UNCERTAINTY, THE HUNGER.
I ESPECIALLY REMEMBER THE HUNGER.
BUT MOST OF ALL I REMEMBER THE DEATH.
TELL ME YOUR STORIES. YOUR GRANDDAUGHTER TOLD ME YOU HAD MANY.
ARE YOU SURE? NONE OF MY TALES ARE PLEASANT.
I'M SURE.
I REMEMBER ONCE IN A VILLAGE NOT FAR FROM HERE A LIE THAT WAS TOLD.

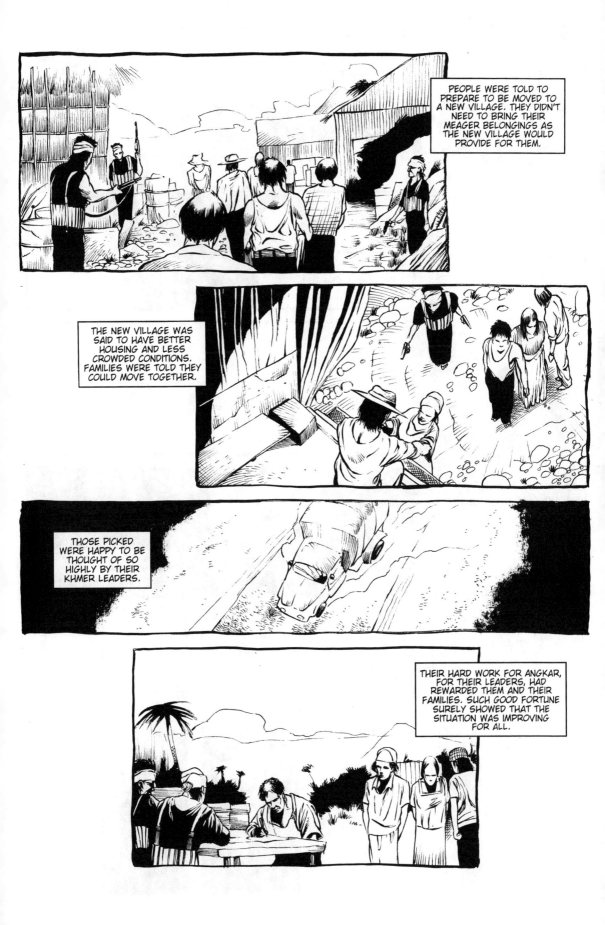

PEOPLE WERE TOLD TO PREPARE TO BE MOVED TO A NEW VILLAGE. THEY DIDN'T NEED TO BRING THEIR MEAGER BELONGINGS AS THE NEW VILLAGE WOULD PROVIDE FOR THEM.

THE NEW VILLAGE WAS SAID TO HAVE BETTER HOUSING AND LESS CROWDED CONDITIONS. FAMILIES WERE TOLD THEY COULD MOVE TOGETHER.

THOSE PICKED WERE HAPPY TO BE THOUGHT OF SO HIGHLY BY THEIR KHMER LEADERS.

THEIR HARD WORK FOR ANGKAR, FOR THEIR LEADERS, HAD REWARDED THEM AND THEIR FAMILIES. SUCH GOOD FORTUNE SURELY SHOWED THAT THE SITUATION WAS IMPROVING FOR ALL.

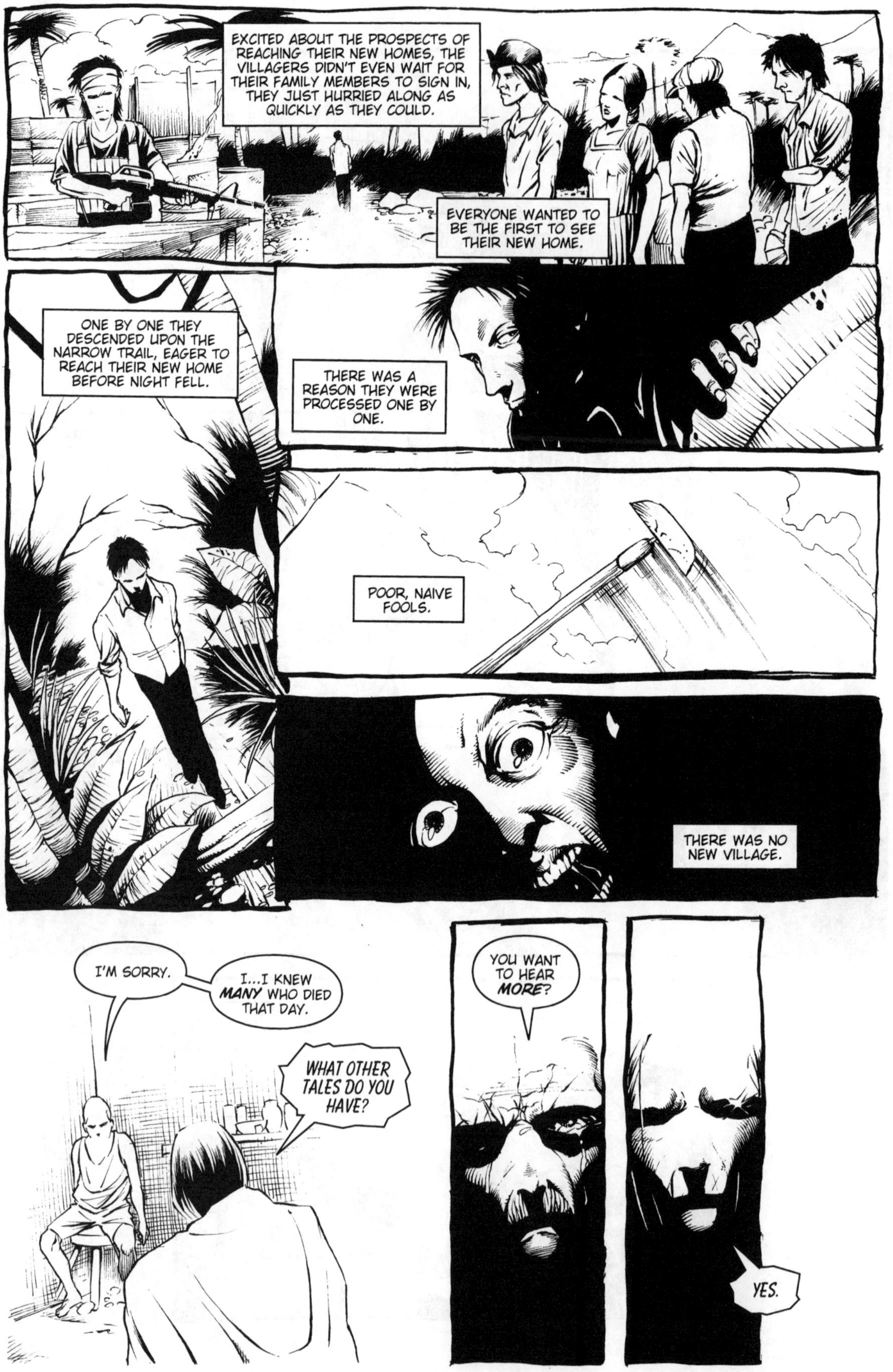
EXCITED ABOUT THE PROSPECTS OF REACHING THEIR NEW HOMES, THE VILLAGERS DIDN'T EVEN WAIT FOR THEIR FAMILY MEMBERS TO SIGN IN, THEY JUST HURRIED ALONG AS QUICKLY AS THEY COULD.
EVERYONE WANTED TO BE THE FIRST TO SEE THEIR NEW HOME.
ONE BY ONE THEY DESCENDED UPON THE NARROW TRAIL, EAGER TO REACH THEIR NEW HOME BEFORE NIGHT FELL.
THERE WAS A REASON THEY WERE PROCESSED ONE BY ONE.
POOR, NAIVE FOOLS.
THERE WAS NO NEW VILLAGE.
I'M SORRY.
I...I KNEW MANY WHO DIED THAT DAY.
WHAT OTHER TALES DO YOU HAVE?
YOU WANT TO HEAR MORE?
YES.

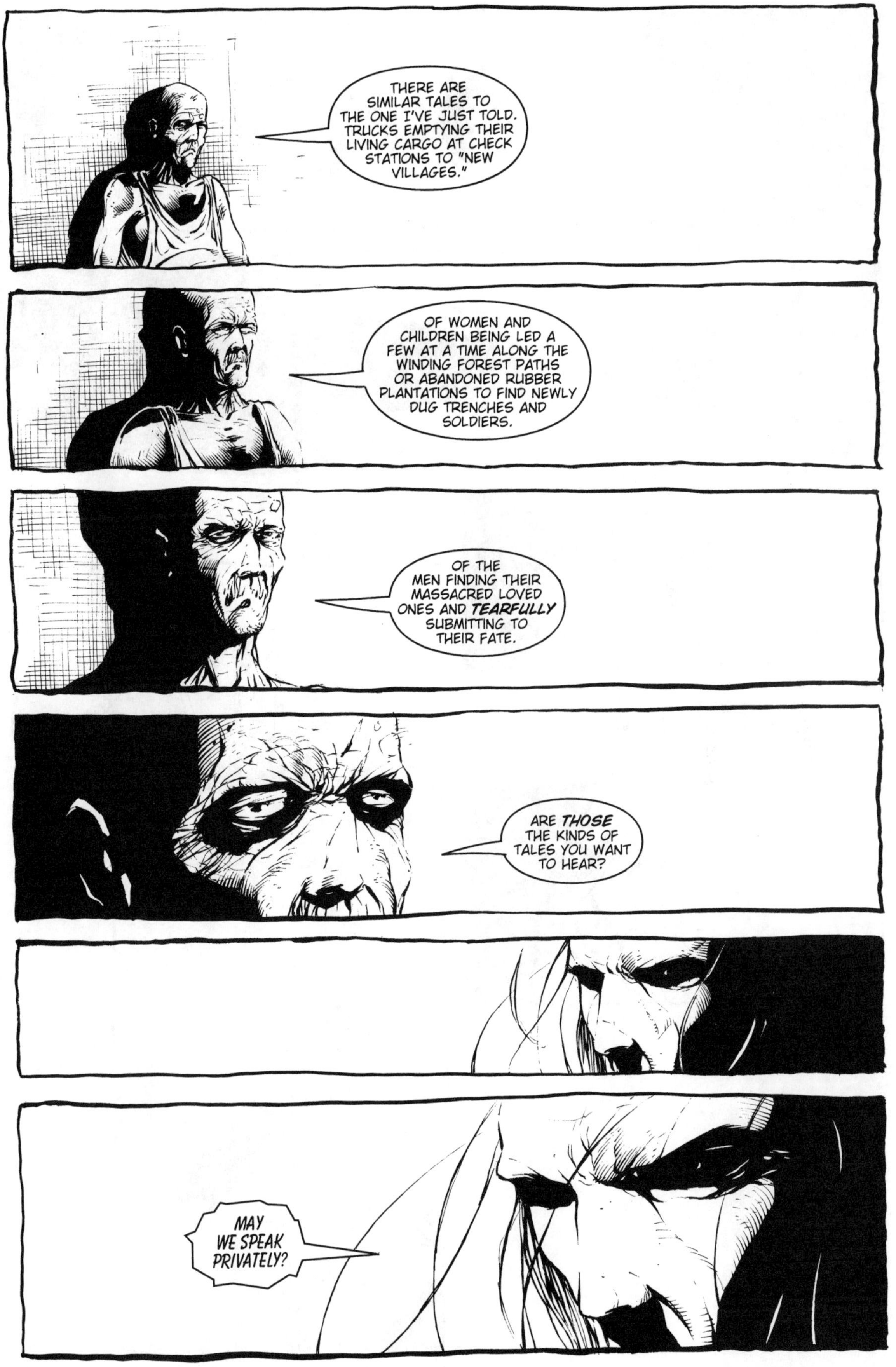
THERE ARE SIMILAR TALES TO THE ONE I'VE JUST TOLD. TRUCKS EMPTYING THEIR LIVING CARGO AT CHECK STATIONS TO "NEW VILLAGES."
OF WOMEN AND CHILDREN BEING LED A FEW AT A TIME ALONG THE WINDING FOREST PATHS OR ABANDONED RUBBER PLANTATIONS TO FIND NEWLY DUG TRENCHES AND SOLDIERS.
OF THE MEN FINDING THEIR MASSACRED LOVED ONES AND *TEARFULLY* SUBMITTING TO THEIR FATE.
ARE *THOSE* THE KINDS OF TALES YOU WANT TO HEAR?
MAY WE SPEAK PRIVATELY?

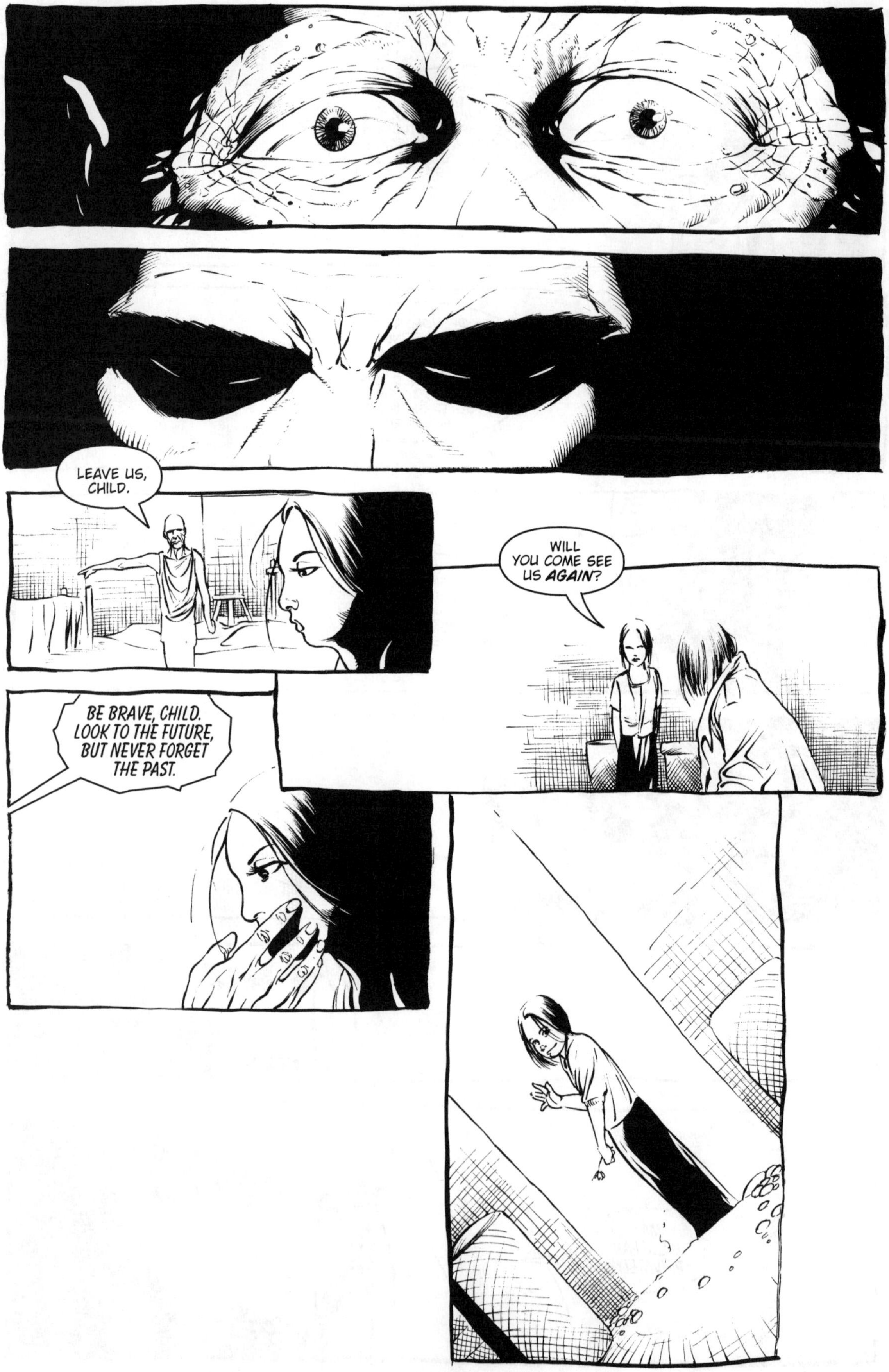
LEAVE US, CHILD.
WILL YOU COME SEE US AGAIN?
BE BRAVE, CHILD. LOOK TO THE FUTURE, BUT NEVER FORGET THE PAST.

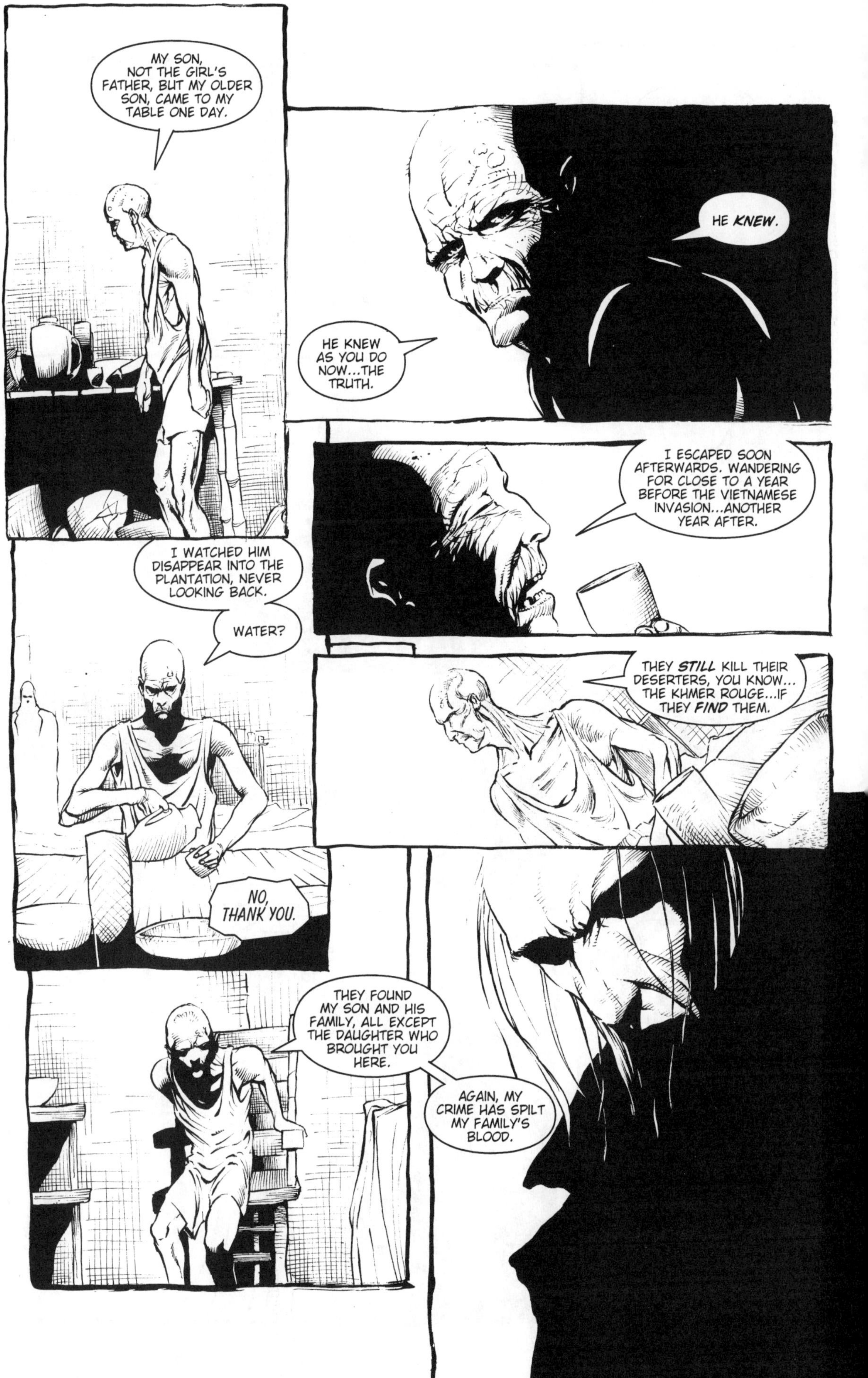
MY SON, NOT THE GIRL'S FATHER, BUT MY OLDER SON, CAME TO MY TABLE ONE DAY.
HE KNEW.
HE KNEW AS YOU DO NOW...THE TRUTH.
I ESCAPED SOON AFTERWARDS. WANDERING FOR CLOSE TO A YEAR BEFORE THE VIETNAMESE INVASION...ANOTHER YEAR AFTER.
I WATCHED HIM DISAPPEAR INTO THE PLANTATION, NEVER LOOKING BACK.
WATER?
NO, THANK YOU.
THEY STILL KILL THEIR DESERTERS, YOU KNOW... THE KHMER ROUGE...IF THEY FIND THEM.
THEY FOUND MY SON AND HIS FAMILY, ALL EXCEPT THE DAUGHTER WHO BROUGHT YOU HERE.
AGAIN, MY CRIME HAS SPILT MY FAMILY'S BLOOD.

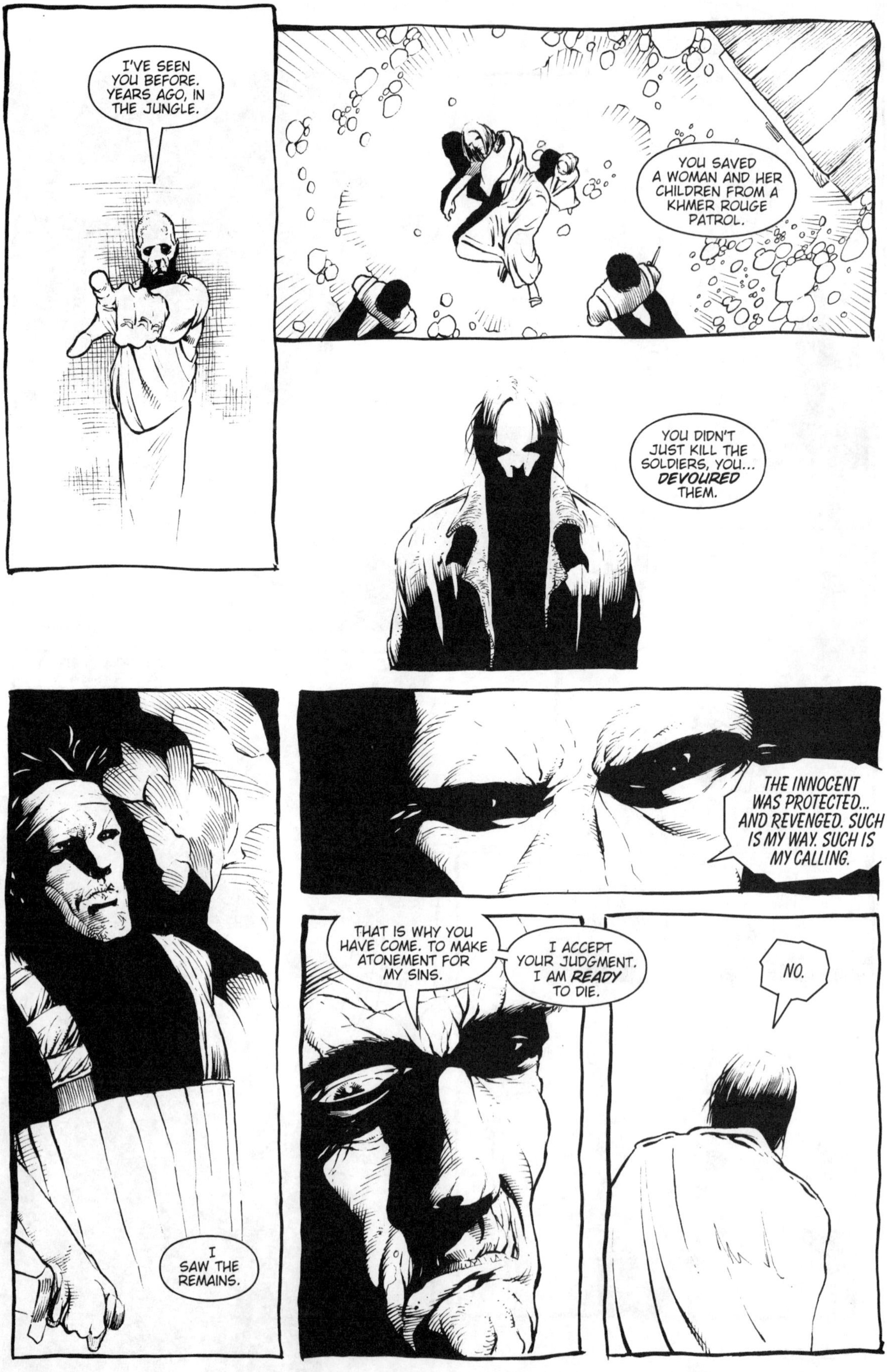
I'VE SEEN YOU BEFORE. YEARS AGO, IN THE JUNGLE.
YOU SAVED A WOMAN AND HER CHILDREN FROM A KHMER ROUGE PATROL.
YOU DIDN'T JUST KILL THE SOLDIERS, YOU... ***DEVOURED*** THEM.
I SAW THE REMAINS.
THE INNOCENT WAS PROTECTED... AND REVENGED. SUCH IS MY WAY. SUCH IS MY CALLING.
THAT IS WHY YOU HAVE COME. TO MAKE ATONEMENT FOR MY SINS.
I ACCEPT YOUR JUDGMENT. I AM ***READY*** TO DIE.
NO.

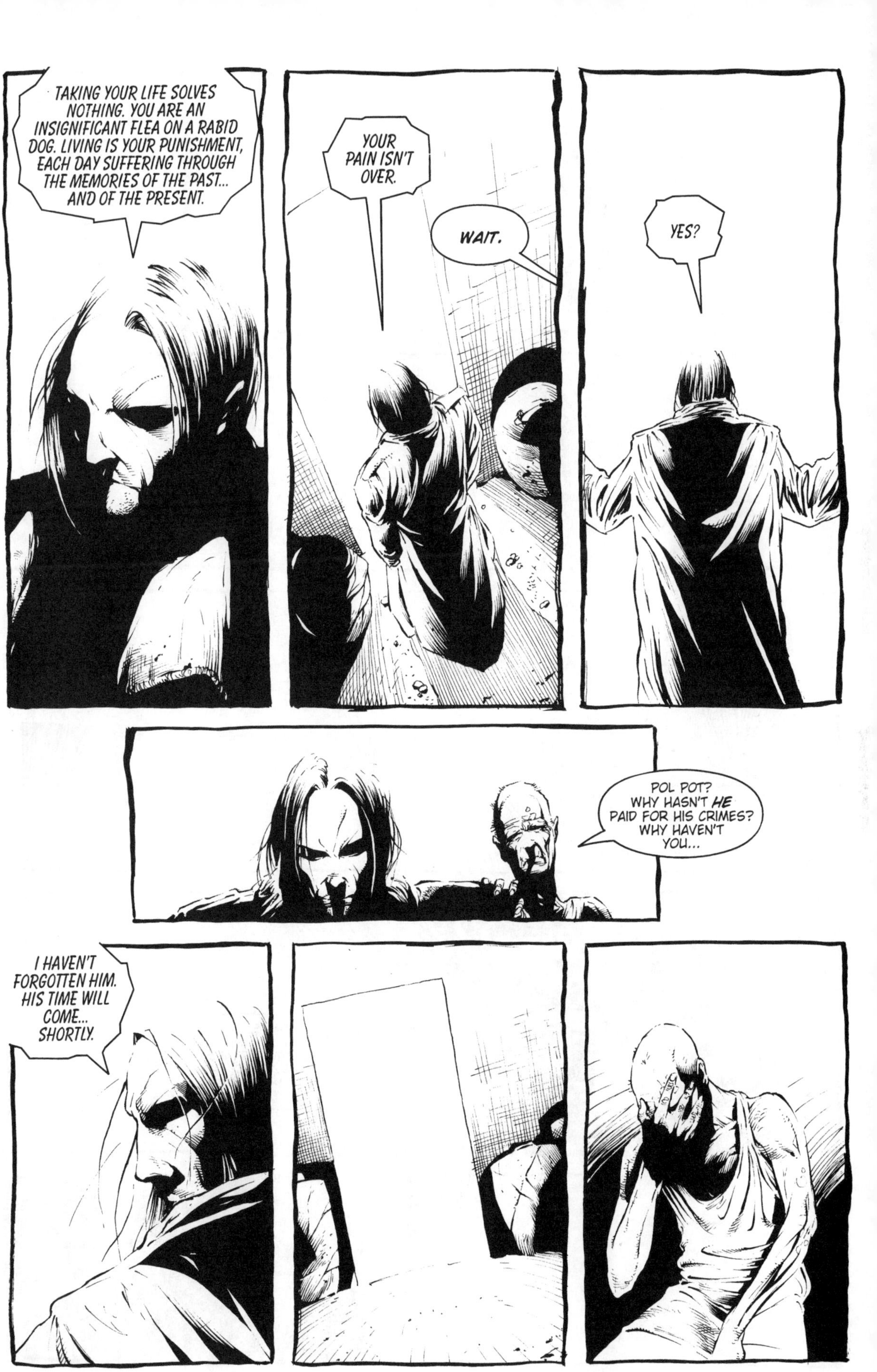
TAKING YOUR LIFE SOLVES NOTHING. YOU ARE AN INSIGNIFICANT FLEA ON A RABID DOG. LIVING IS YOUR PUNISHMENT, EACH DAY SUFFERING THROUGH THE MEMORIES OF THE PAST... AND OF THE PRESENT.
YOUR PAIN ISN'T OVER.
WAIT.
YES?
POL POT? WHY HASN'T HE PAID FOR HIS CRIMES? WHY HAVEN'T YOU...
I HAVEN'T FORGOTTEN HIM. HIS TIME WILL COME... SHORTLY.

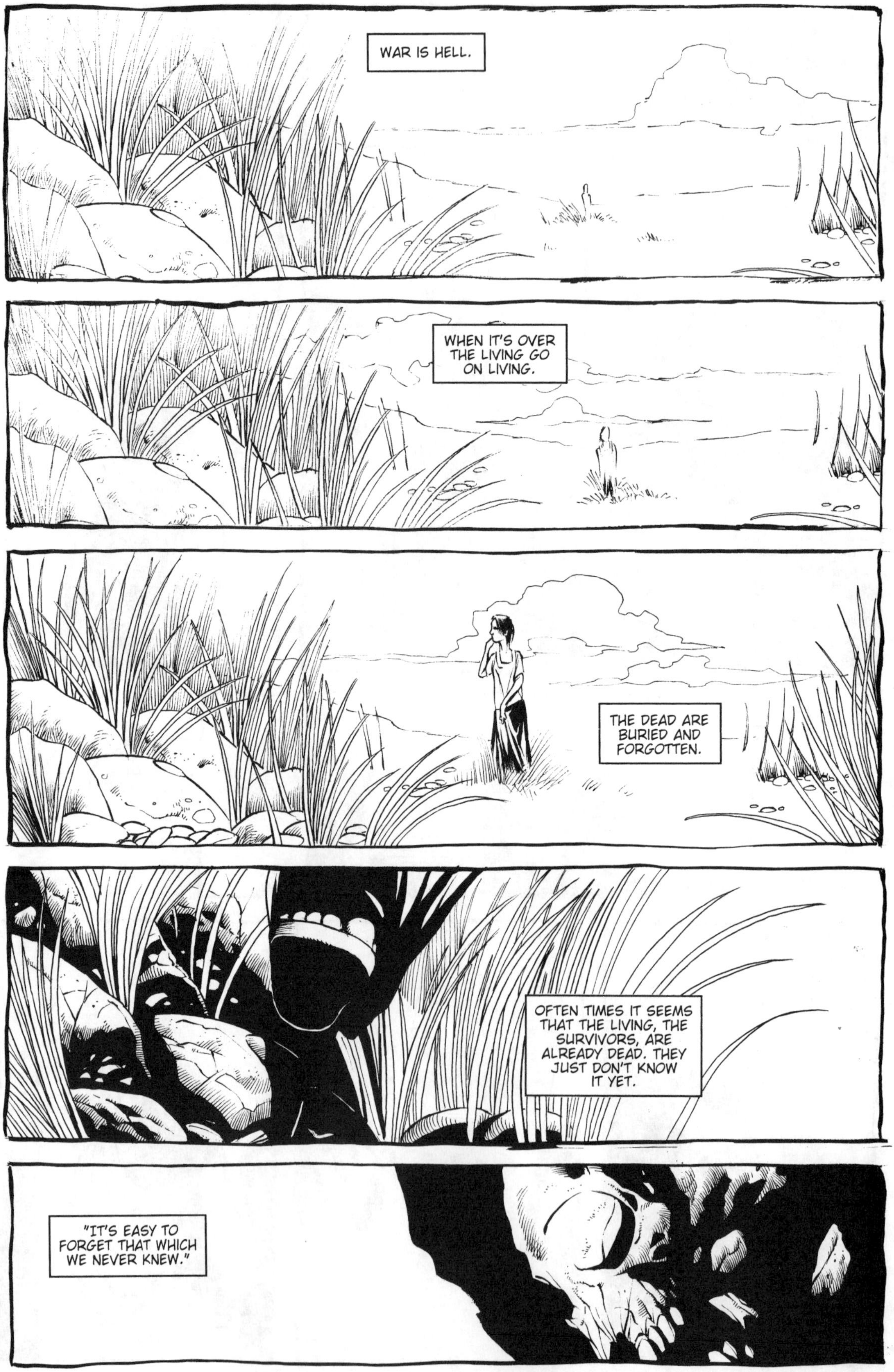
WAR IS HELL.
WHEN IT'S OVER THE LIVING GO ON LIVING.
THE DEAD ARE BURIED AND FORGOTTEN.
OFTEN TIMES IT SEEMS THAT THE LIVING, THE SURVIVORS, ARE ALREADY DEAD. THEY JUST DON'T KNOW IT YET.
"IT'S EASY TO FORGET THAT WHICH WE NEVER KNEW."

Short Stories

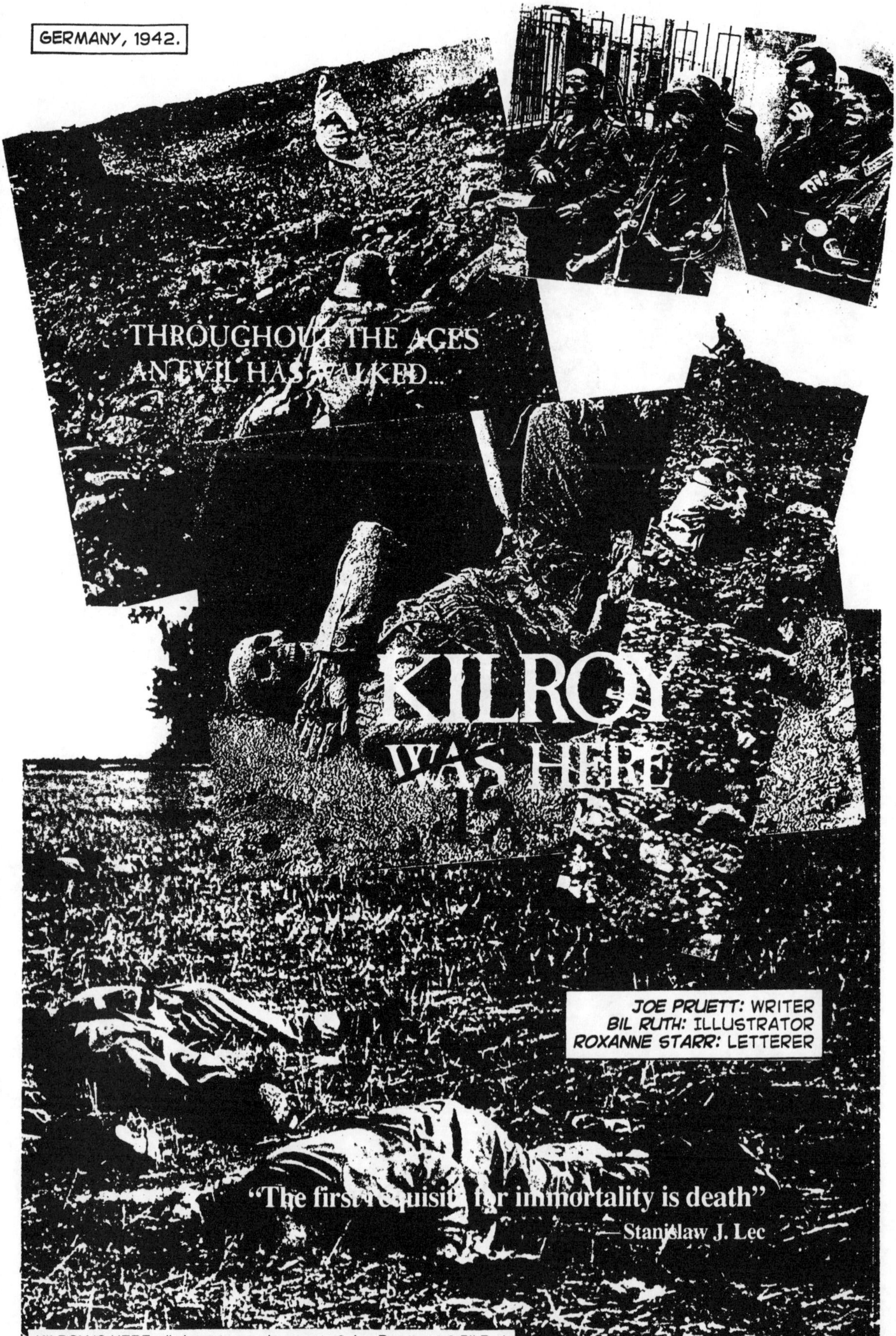
GERMANY, 1942.
THROUGHOUT THE AGES AN EVIL HAS WALKED...
KILROY WAS HERE
JOE PRUETT: WRITER
BIL RUTH: ILLUSTRATOR
ROXANNE STARR: LETTERER
"The first requisite for immortality is death"
—Stanislaw J. Lec
KILROY IS HERE, all characters and concepts © Joe Pruett, art © Bil Ruth

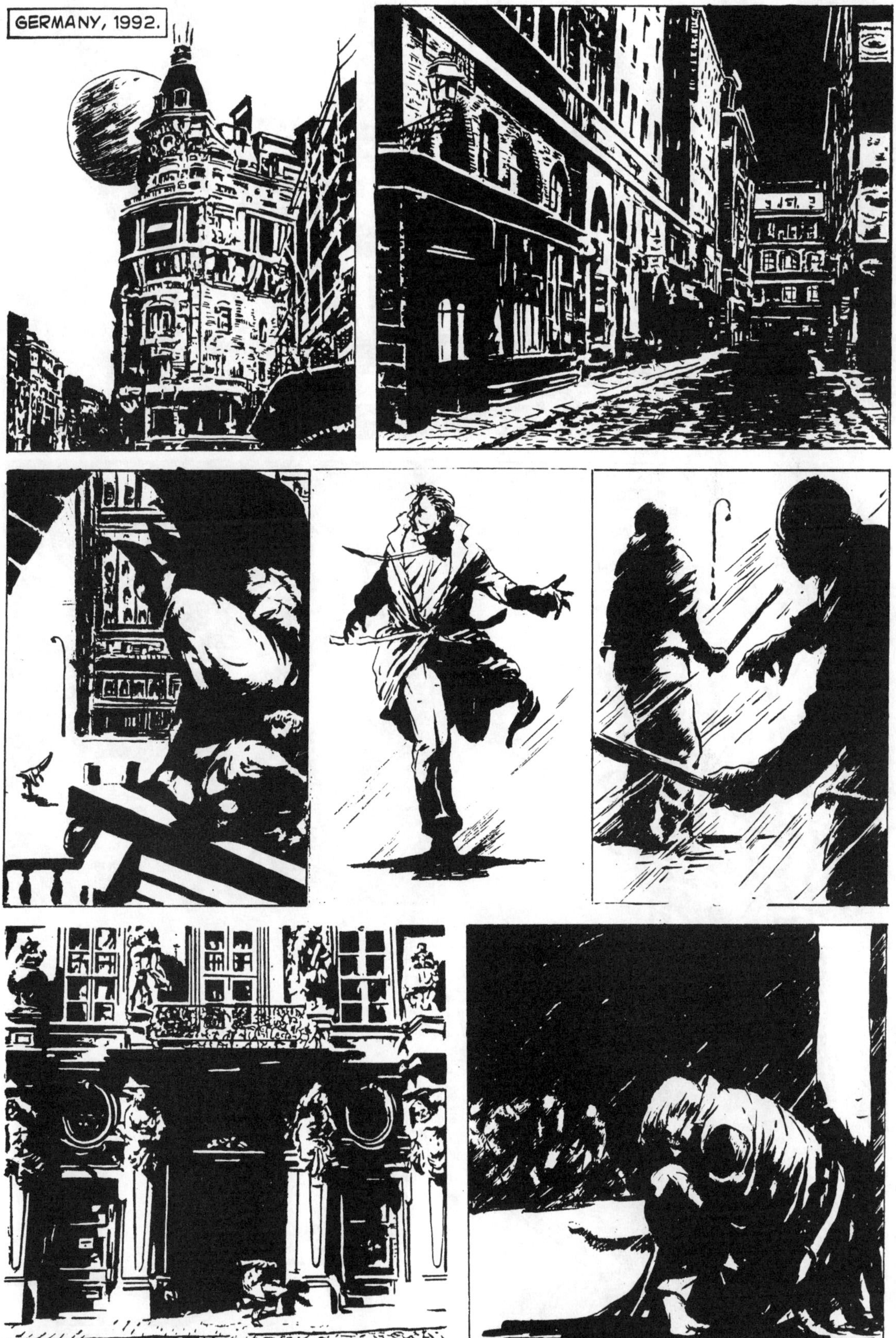
GERMANY, 1992.

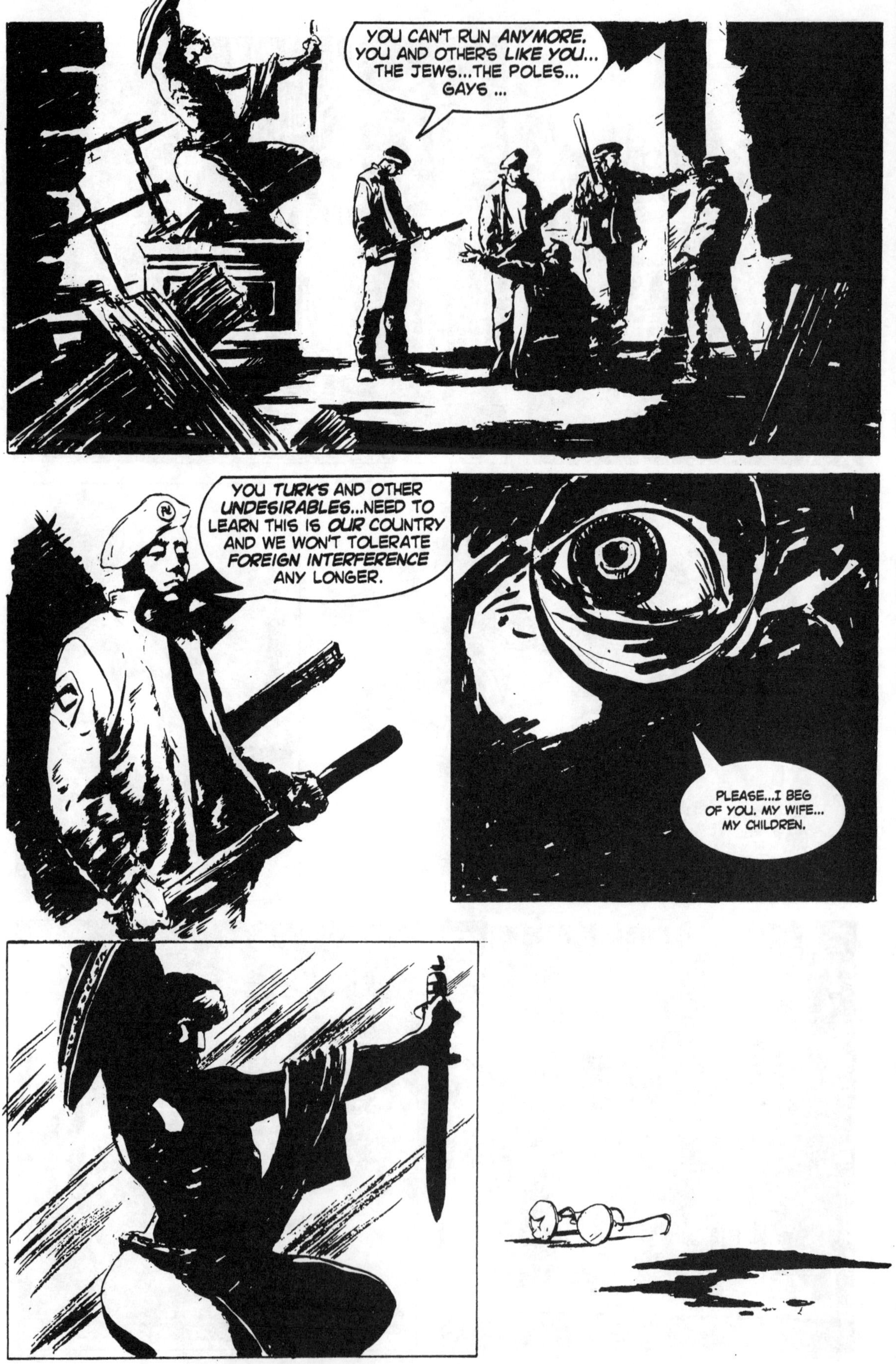
YOU CAN'T RUN ANYMORE. YOU AND OTHERS LIKE YOU... THE JEWS...THE POLES... GAYS ...
YOU TURKS AND OTHER UNDESIRABLES...NEED TO LEARN THIS IS OUR COUNTRY AND WE WON'T TOLERATE FOREIGN INTERFERENCE ANY LONGER.
PLEASE...I BEG OF YOU. MY WIFE... MY CHILDREN.

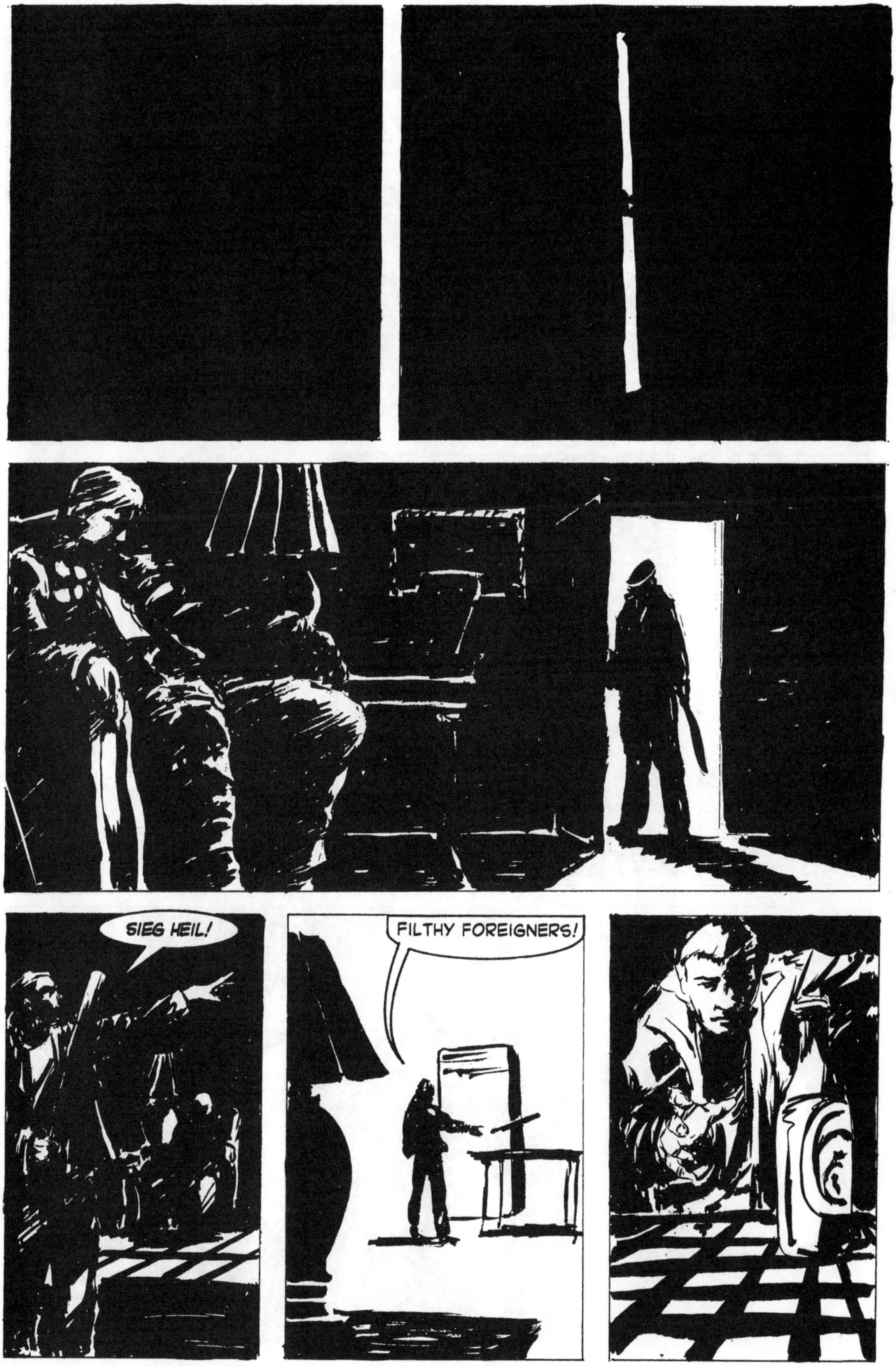
SIEG HEIL!
FILTHY FOREIGNERS!

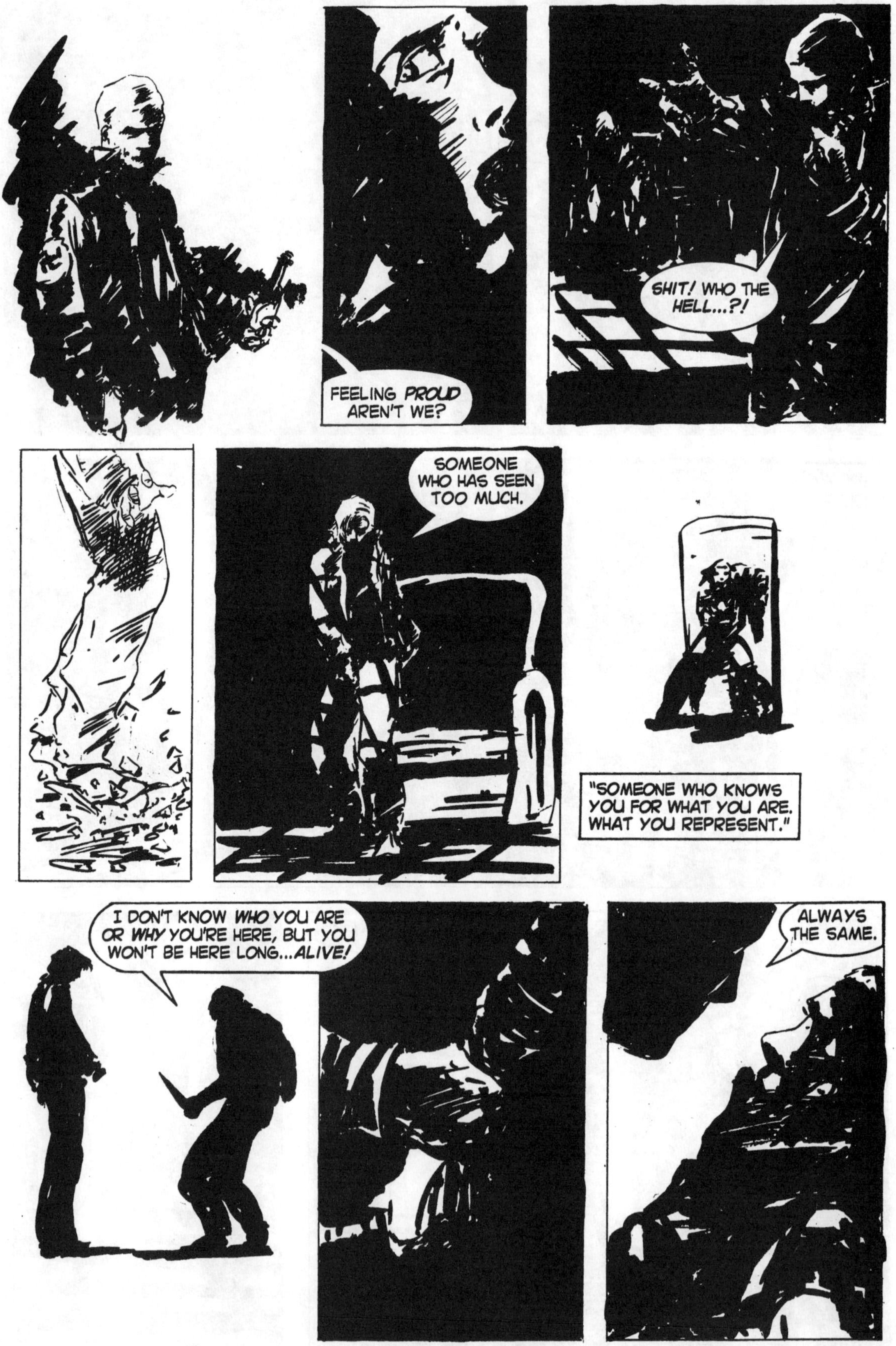
FEELING *PROUD* AREN'T WE?
SHIT! WHO THE *HELL...?!*
SOMEONE WHO HAS SEEN TOO MUCH.
"SOMEONE WHO KNOWS YOU FOR WHAT YOU ARE. WHAT YOU REPRESENT."
I DON'T KNOW *WHO* YOU ARE OR *WHY* YOU'RE HERE, BUT YOU WON'T BE HERE LONG...*ALIVE!*
ALWAYS THE SAME.

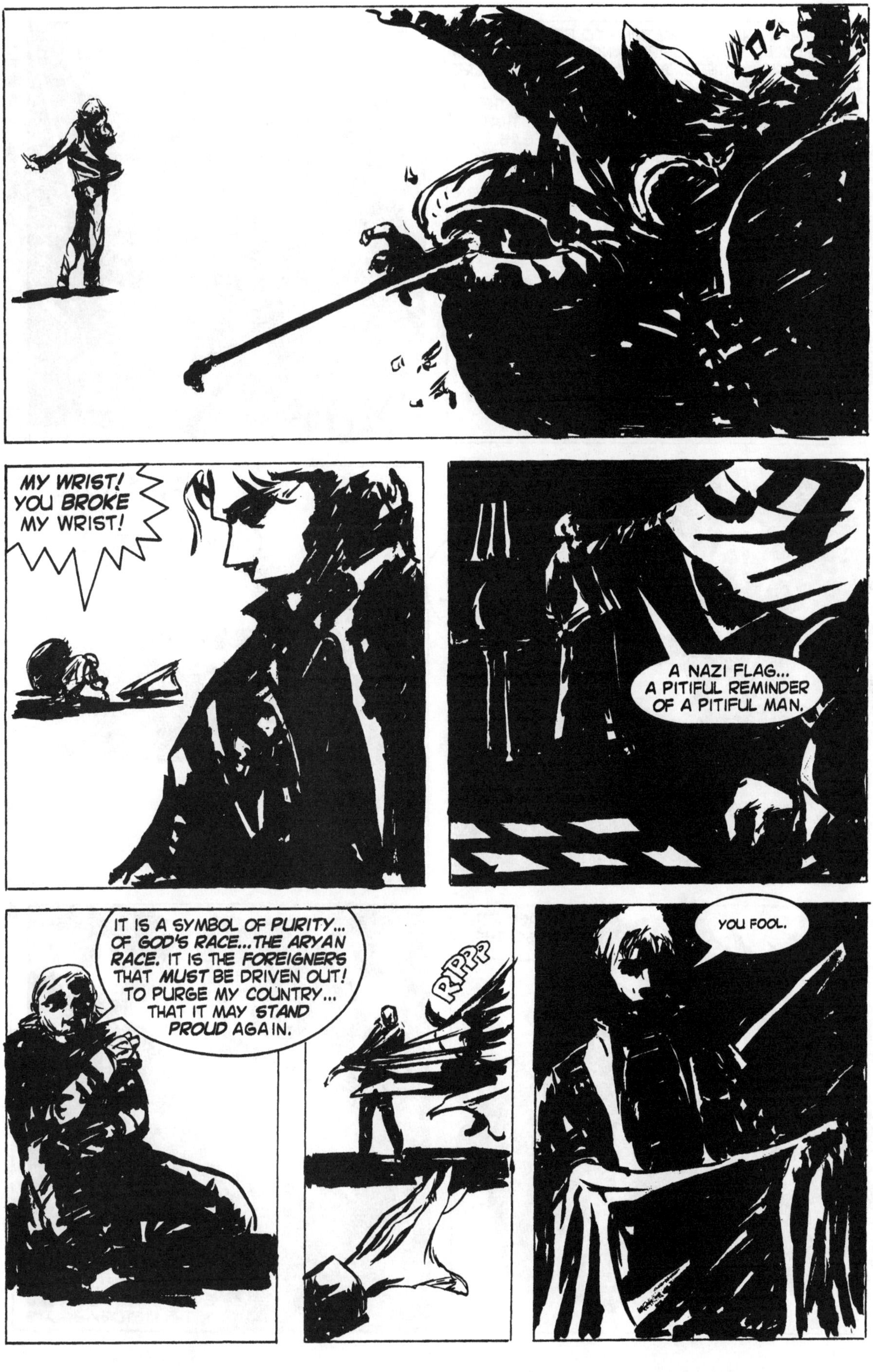
MY WRIST! YOU BROKE MY WRIST!
A NAZI FLAG... A PITIFUL REMINDER OF A PITIFUL MAN.
IT IS A SYMBOL OF PURITY... OF GOD'S RACE...THE ARYAN RACE. IT IS THE FOREIGNERS THAT MUST BE DRIVEN OUT! TO PURGE MY COUNTRY... THAT IT MAY STAND PROUD AGAIN.
RIPPP
YOU FOOL.

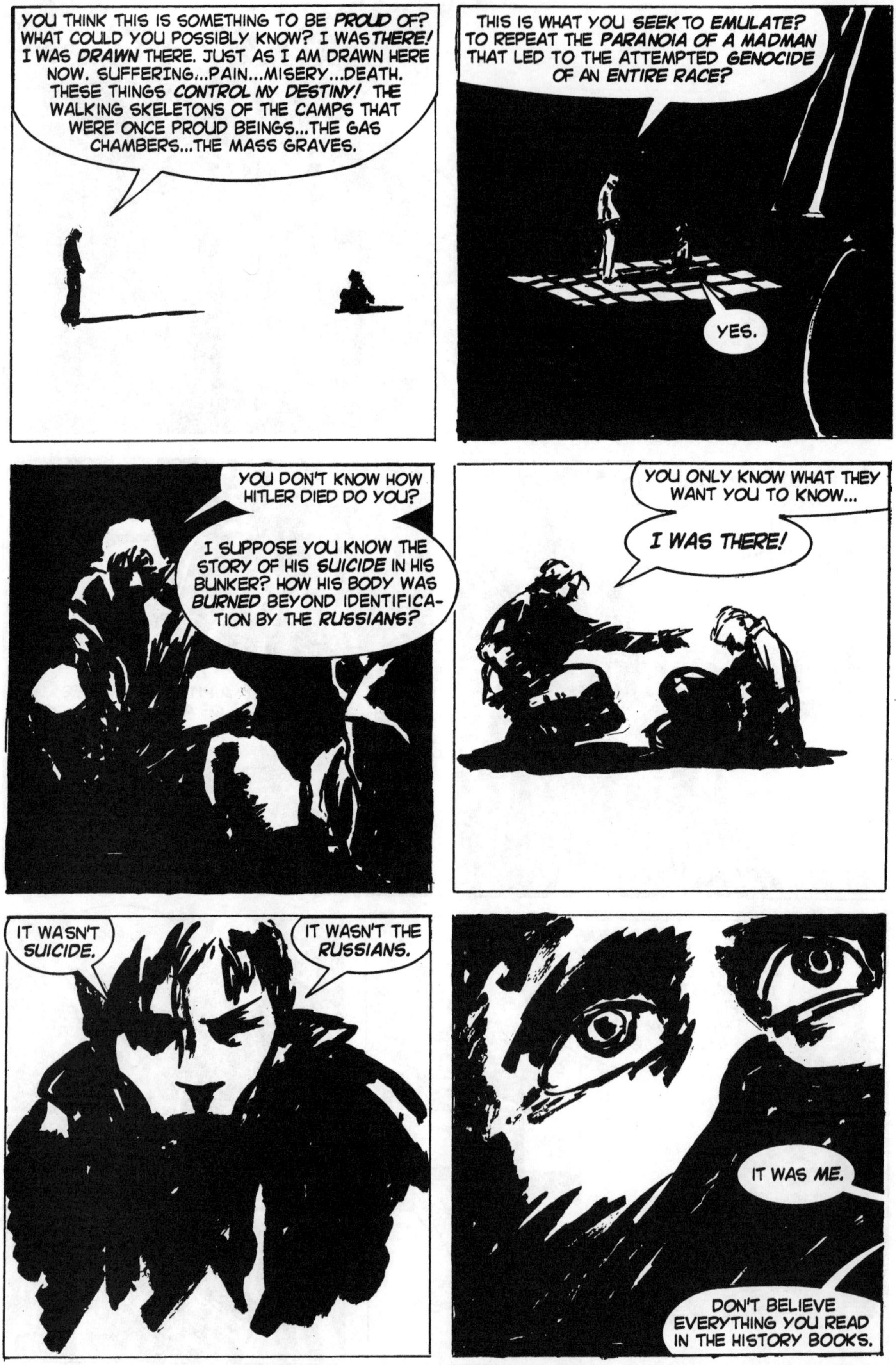
YOU THINK THIS IS SOMETHING TO BE PROUD OF? WHAT COULD YOU POSSIBLY KNOW? I WAS THERE! I WAS DRAWN THERE. JUST AS I AM DRAWN HERE NOW. SUFFERING...PAIN...MISERY...DEATH. THESE THINGS CONTROL MY DESTINY! THE WALKING SKELETONS OF THE CAMPS THAT WERE ONCE PROUD BEINGS...THE GAS CHAMBERS...THE MASS GRAVES.
THIS IS WHAT YOU SEEK TO EMULATE? TO REPEAT THE PARANOIA OF A MADMAN THAT LED TO THE ATTEMPTED GENOCIDE OF AN ENTIRE RACE?
YES.
YOU DON'T KNOW HOW HITLER DIED DO YOU?
I SUPPOSE YOU KNOW THE STORY OF HIS SUICIDE IN HIS BUNKER? HOW HIS BODY WAS BURNED BEYOND IDENTIFICATION BY THE RUSSIANS?
YOU ONLY KNOW WHAT THEY WANT YOU TO KNOW...
I WAS THERE!
IT WASN'T SUICIDE.
IT WASN'T THE RUSSIANS.
IT WAS ME.
DON'T BELIEVE EVERYTHING YOU READ IN THE HISTORY BOOKS.

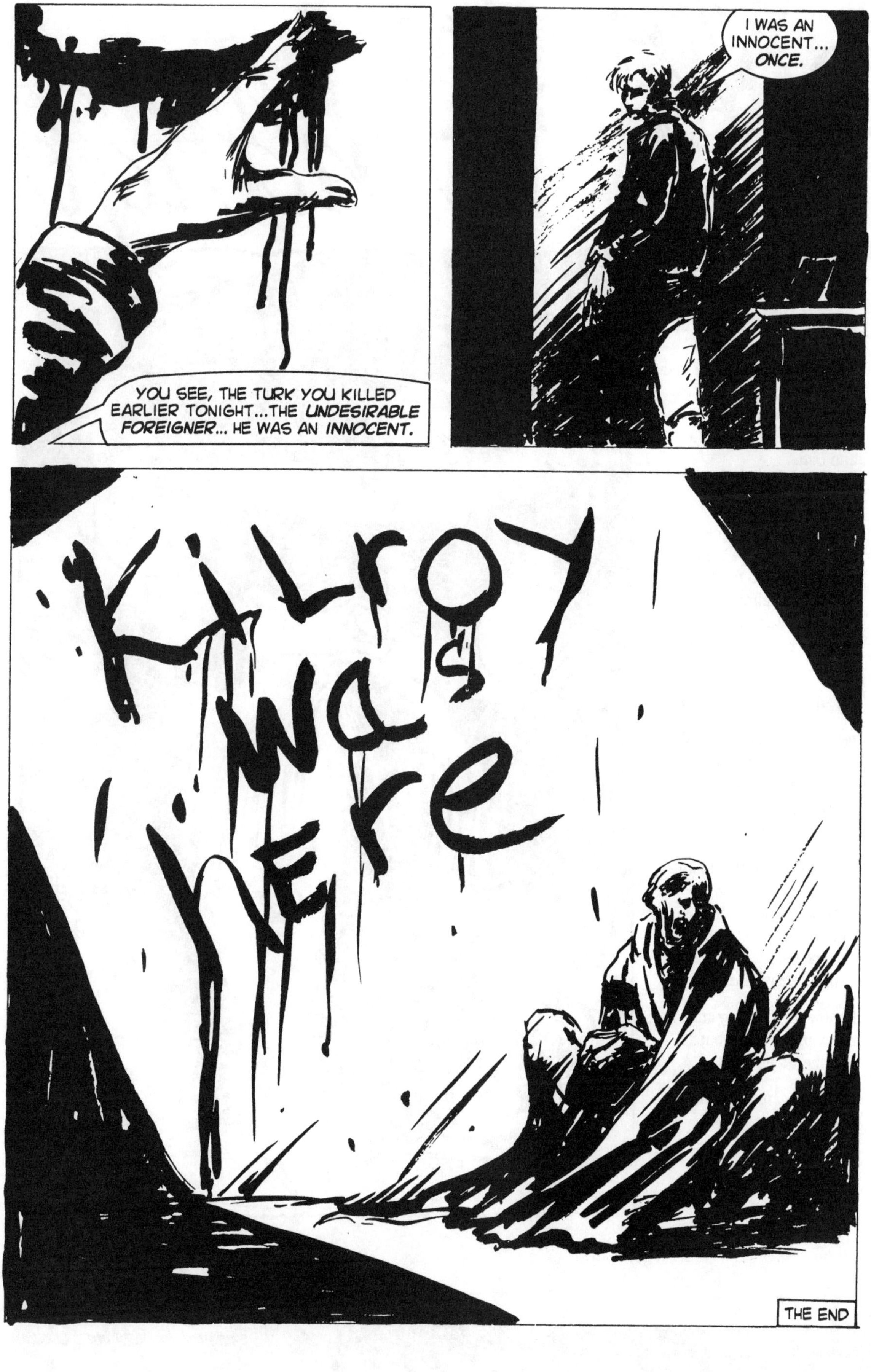
YOU SEE, THE TURK YOU KILLED EARLIER TONIGHT...THE UNDESIRABLE FOREIGNER... HE WAS AN INNOCENT.
I WAS AN INNOCENT... ONCE.
Kilroy was here
THE END

Seasons Change

I can remember when I still enjoyed Christmas.

Just last year I couldn't wait to open my presents. I'd sneak downstairs in the middle of the night, careful to be as quiet as possible, so as not to wake up my Mom and Dad.

This year is different.

The presents don't mean the same. Not because I didn't get what I asked for. I always, well, almost always, get what I want. No, this year there's something missing.

My Mom's not here.

Poor Dad. He's tried so hard to make Christmas go on as usual. Actually, he's probably worked twice as hard as any year before.

It's not his fault that Mom isn't here anymore. Grandma says that "Mom is in a better place." I don't understand that. Wasn't she happy here with us?

I know I'm a big boy and I'm not suppose to cry, but... I miss her so much.

"It's normal to fill sorrow and emptiness, Christopher."

Written by Joe Pruett
Illustrated by Andrew Robinson
Designed by Shinn Uehara

Kilroy is Here

I glanced up and there stood a tall man with long blonde hair, tied in a ponytail, like a girl. He wore a trenchcoat, similar to my Dad's, except his appeared kinda worn out, like my first baseball mitt. He didn't look really old, but, at the same time, he didn't seem too young.

"How' d you know my name?"

"I know much. I know how you feel. You feel hollow... betrayed. Someone you loved has left you suddenly alone. No one talks to you since no one knows what to say. They only want to tell you that they love you, but don't know how."

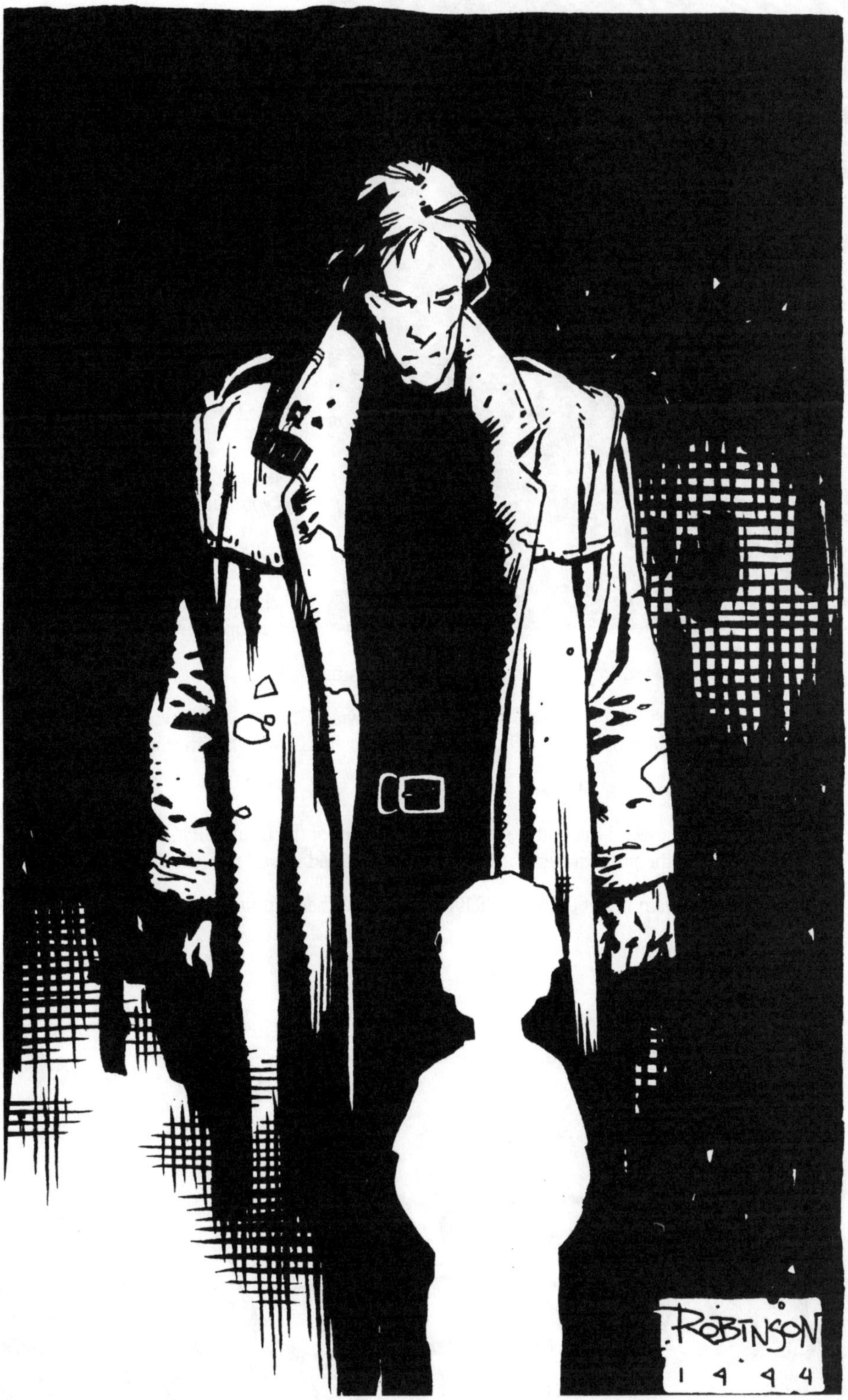
ROBINSON

"Why did Mom have to go?"

"She didn't want to, Christopher. No, your mother would give anything to be with you. She just isn't able. Each person only has an infinite amount of time that they have on this plane. When their time is up, they move on."

"Where did she go?"

"To a place where she no longer has any worries. To a place of eternal peace and solitude."

"Is she in Heaven?"

"You could say that."

"She's far away from here, yet, she's still close. She sees you, Christopher, and she watches over you. She doesn't want to see you unhappy."

"Christmas was her favorite time of the year, wasn't it?"

"Yes."

"She would want it to be your favorite time as well. Just remember, although she may not be here in person, she is here in spirit. Part of her spirit will always be with you...

...deep in your heart...

...and in your memories."

"Treasure your memories, Christopher. They are worth more than any present you could ever receive."

After saying that, the strange man in the dirty, raggedy coat turned to walk away. As if he had someplace else he needed to be.

"Wait!"

I ran over to him and looked into his eyes. There was so much hurt and pain there. I think he needed a friend more than I did.

"You never told me your name?"

"My name? My name is Kilroy."

"Christopher! Time to come in! Dinner's on the table!"

"My Dad is calling me. I have to go."

"I know."

"Thank you. What you said meant a lot to me."

"You mean a lot to your mother... and your father. You have people that love and care for you. Don't ever forget that. You're very lucky."

"Christopher! Hurry up! After we eat we can open presents!"

I turned towards my Dad's voice to answer. "Coming, Dad!"

Kilroy wasn't there anymore. It was like that movie on TV last week when the Invisible Man unwrapped his bandages and disappeared. It was like he vanished in thin air.

"Merry Christmas, Kilroy."

I ran back toward the house, skipping up the steps of the front porch, and paused and looked at the porch-swing where me and Mom would sit and rock the afternoons away.

I can't explain it, but I suddenly felt like Mom was there, smiling at me.

I love you, Mom.

I always will.

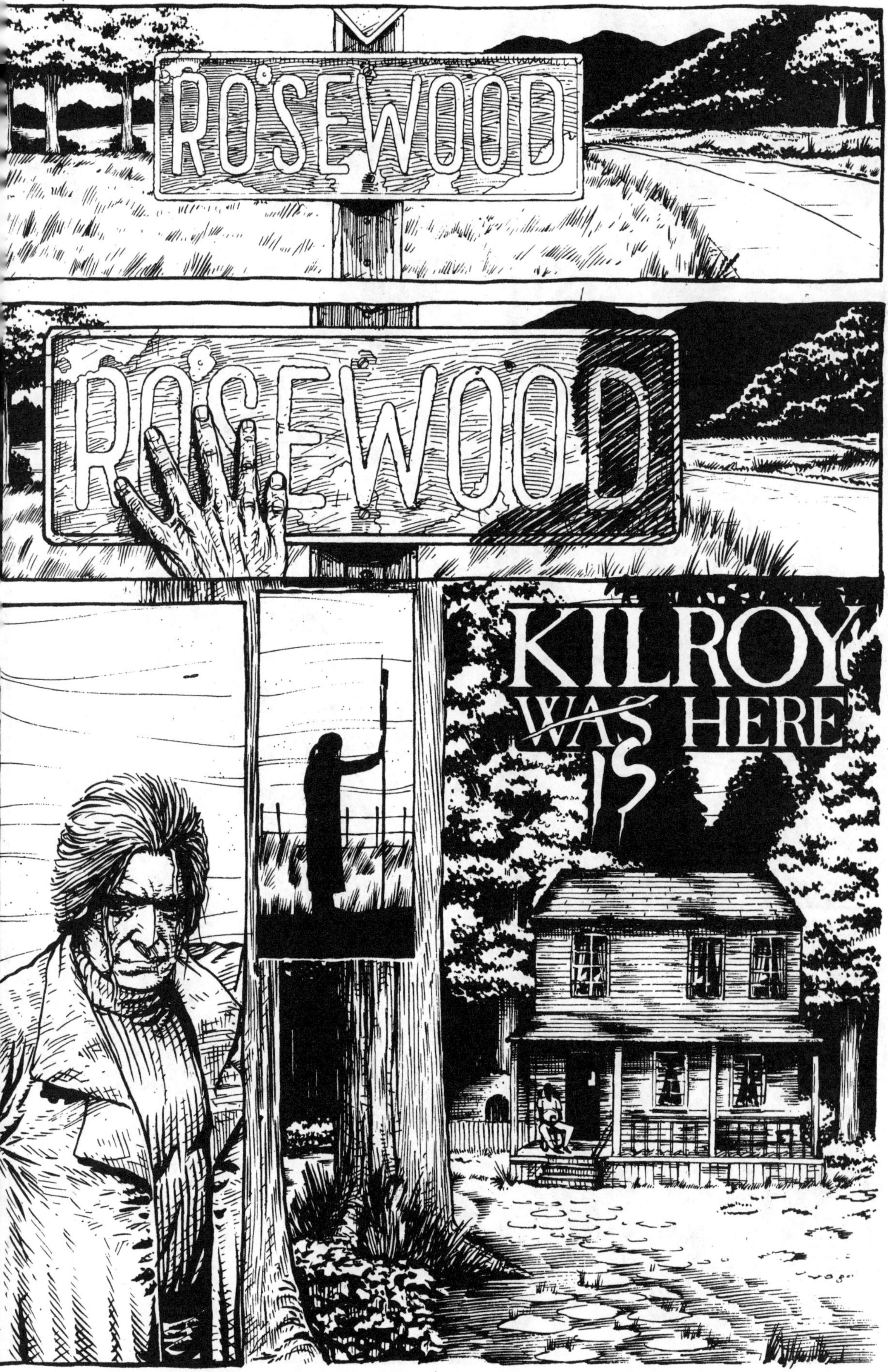
ROSEWOOD
ROSEWOOD
KILROY
WAS HERE
IS

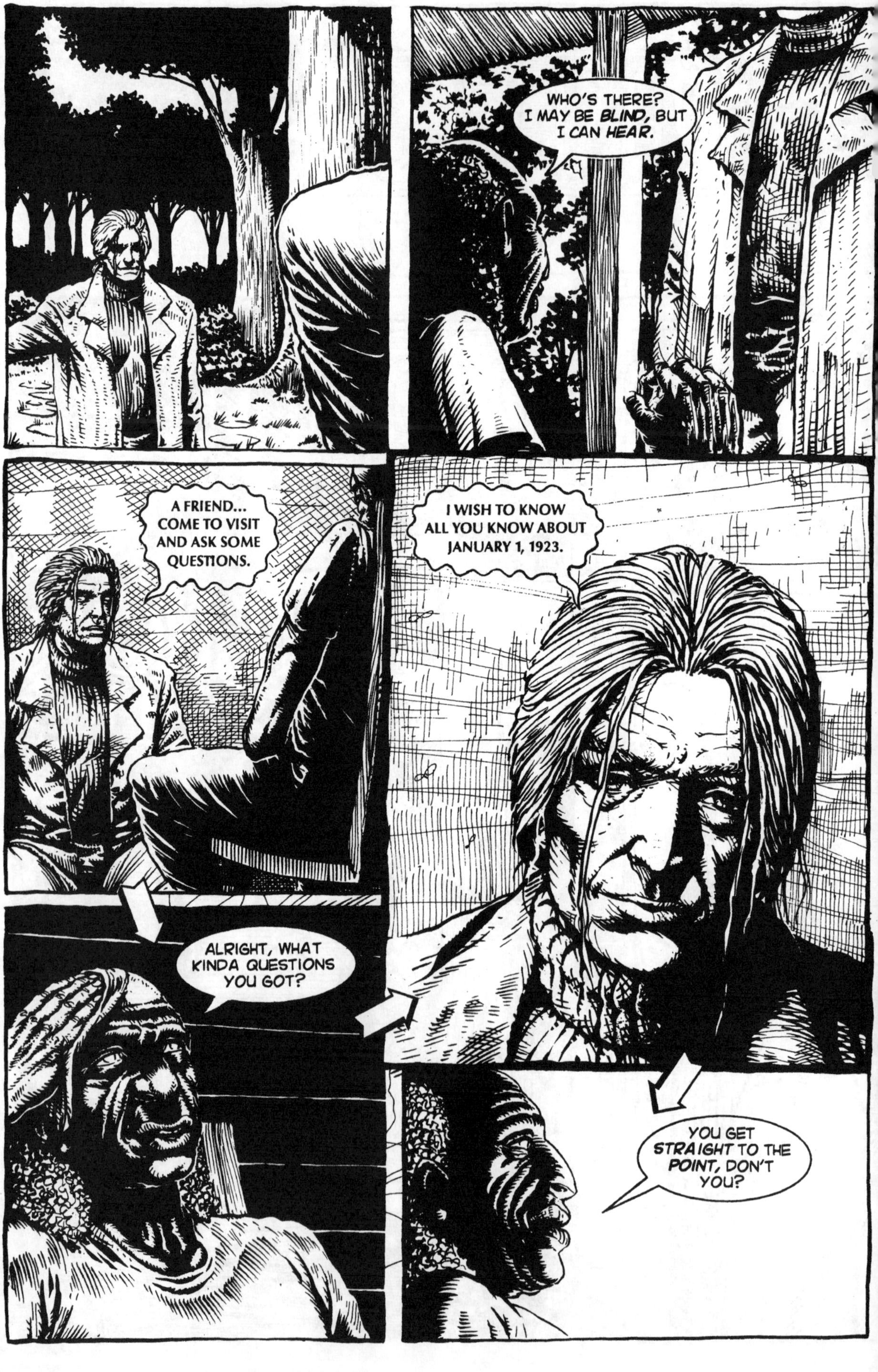
WHO'S THERE? I MAY BE BLIND, BUT I CAN HEAR.
A FRIEND... COME TO VISIT AND ASK SOME QUESTIONS.
ALRIGHT, WHAT KINDA QUESTIONS YOU GOT?
I WISH TO KNOW ALL YOU KNOW ABOUT JANUARY 1, 1923.
YOU GET STRAIGHT TO THE POINT, DON'T YOU?

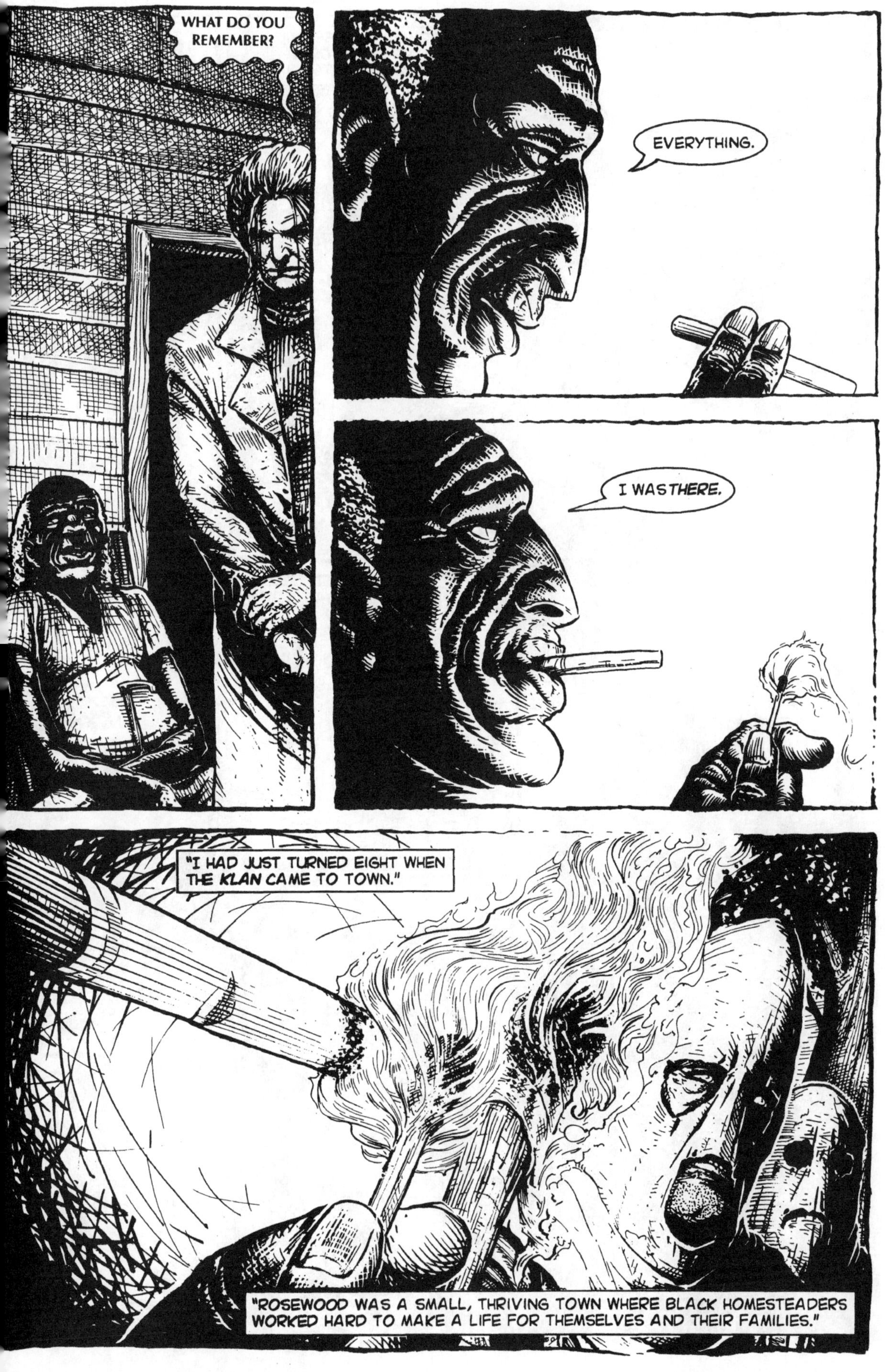

WHAT DO YOU REMEMBER?
EVERYTHING.
I WAS THERE.
"I HAD JUST TURNED EIGHT WHEN THE KLAN CAME TO TOWN."
"ROSEWOOD WAS A SMALL, THRIVING TOWN WHERE BLACK HOMESTEADERS WORKED HARD TO MAKE A LIFE FOR THEMSELVES AND THEIR FAMILIES."

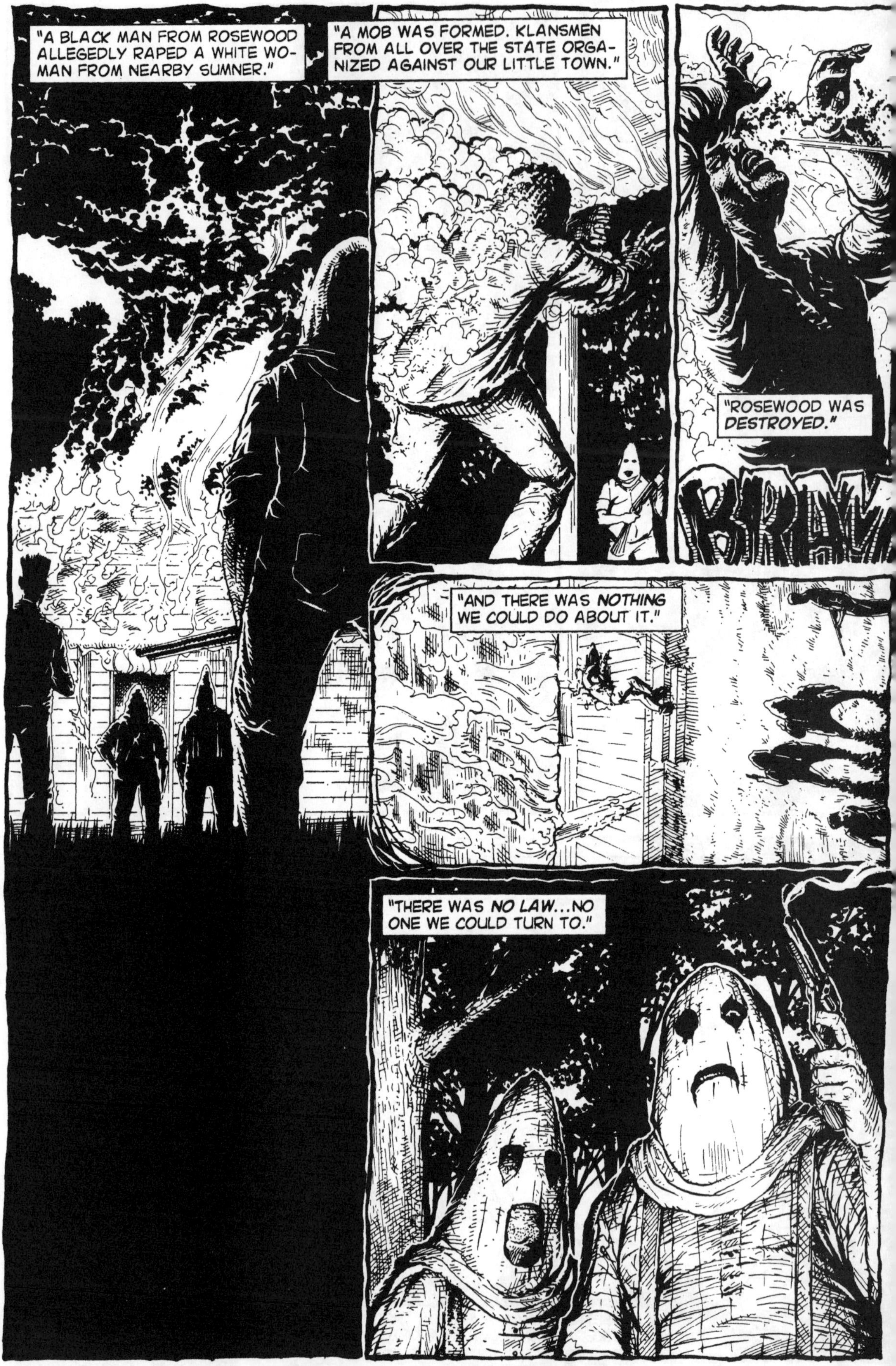
"A BLACK MAN FROM ROSEWOOD ALLEGEDLY RAPED A WHITE WO-MAN FROM NEARBY SUMNER."
"A MOB WAS FORMED. KLANSMEN FROM ALL OVER THE STATE ORGA-NIZED AGAINST OUR LITTLE TOWN."
"ROSEWOOD WAS DESTROYED."
"AND THERE WAS NOTHING WE COULD DO ABOUT IT."
"THERE WAS NO LAW...NO ONE WE COULD TURN TO."

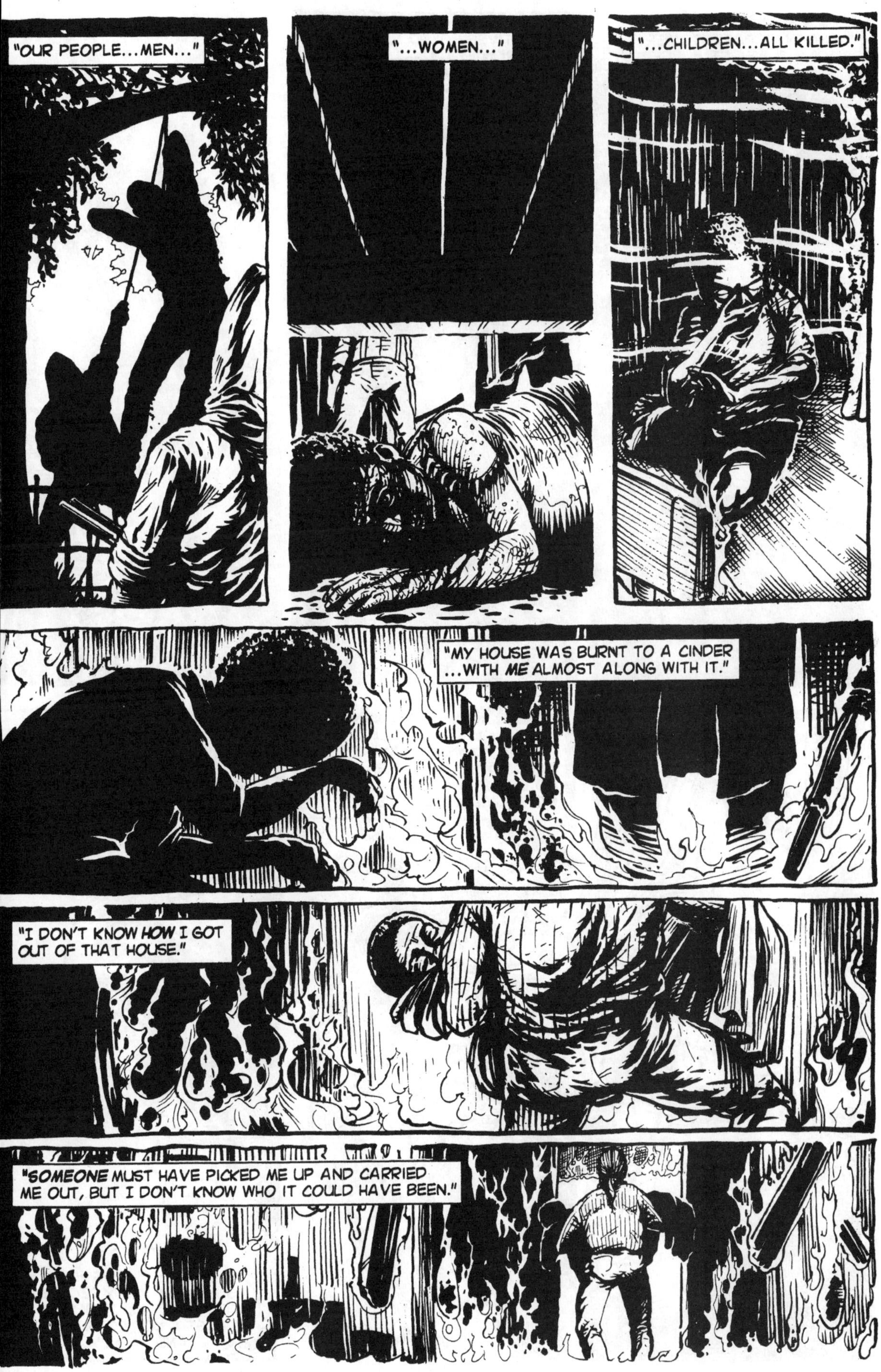
"OUR PEOPLE...MEN..."
"...WOMEN..."
"...CHILDREN...ALL KILLED."
"MY HOUSE WAS BURNT TO A CINDER ...WITH ME ALMOST ALONG WITH IT."
"I DON'T KNOW HOW I GOT OUT OF THAT HOUSE."
"SOMEONE MUST HAVE PICKED ME UP AND CARRIED ME OUT, BUT I DON'T KNOW WHO IT COULD HAVE BEEN."

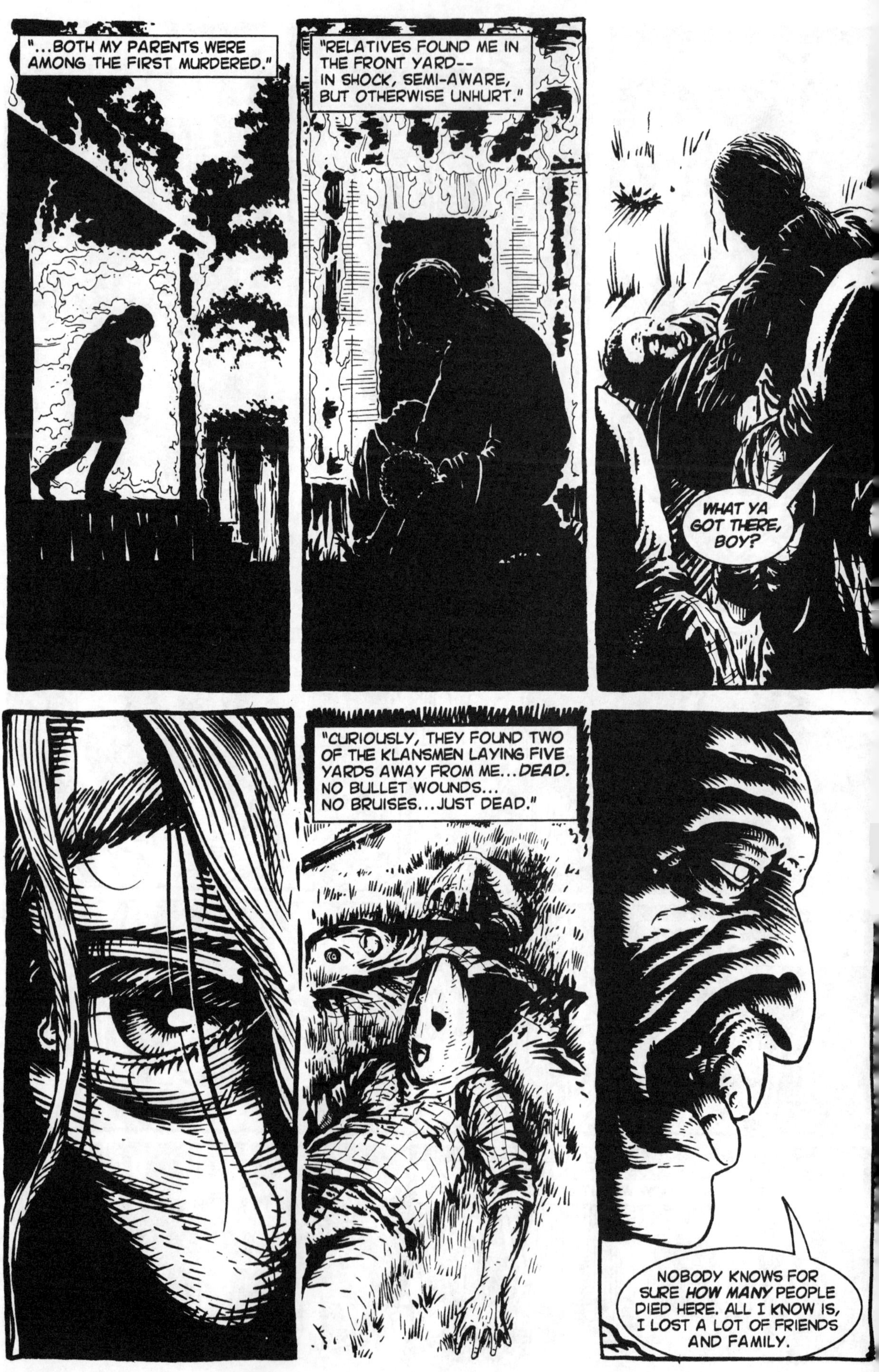
"...BOTH MY PARENTS WERE AMONG THE FIRST MURDERED."
"RELATIVES FOUND ME IN THE FRONT YARD-- IN SHOCK, SEMI-AWARE, BUT OTHERWISE UNHURT."
WHAT YA GOT THERE, BOY?
"CURIOUSLY, THEY FOUND TWO OF THE KLANSMEN LAYING FIVE YARDS AWAY FROM ME...DEAD. NO BULLET WOUNDS... NO BRUISES...JUST DEAD."
NOBODY KNOWS FOR SURE HOW MANY PEOPLE DIED HERE. ALL I KNOW IS, I LOST A LOT OF FRIENDS AND FAMILY.

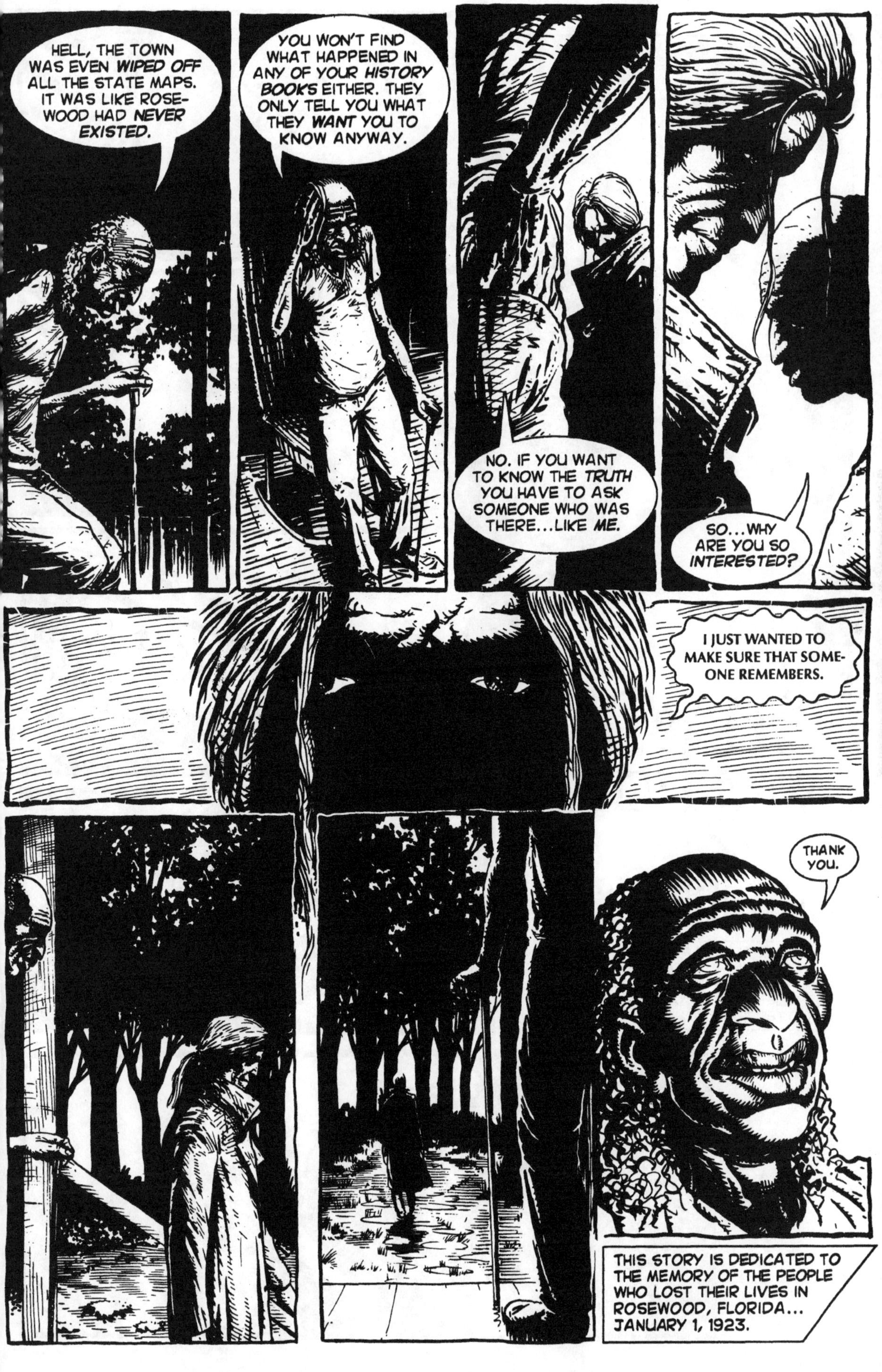
HELL, THE TOWN WAS EVEN WIPED OFF ALL THE STATE MAPS. IT WAS LIKE ROSE-WOOD HAD NEVER EXISTED.
YOU WON'T FIND WHAT HAPPENED IN ANY OF YOUR HISTORY BOOKS EITHER. THEY ONLY TELL YOU WHAT THEY WANT YOU TO KNOW ANYWAY.
NO. IF YOU WANT TO KNOW THE TRUTH YOU HAVE TO ASK SOMEONE WHO WAS THERE...LIKE ME.
SO...WHY ARE YOU SO INTERESTED?
I JUST WANTED TO MAKE SURE THAT SOME-ONE REMEMBERS.
THANK YOU.
THIS STORY IS DEDICATED TO THE MEMORY OF THE PEOPLE WHO LOST THEIR LIVES IN ROSEWOOD, FLORIDA... JANUARY 1, 1923.

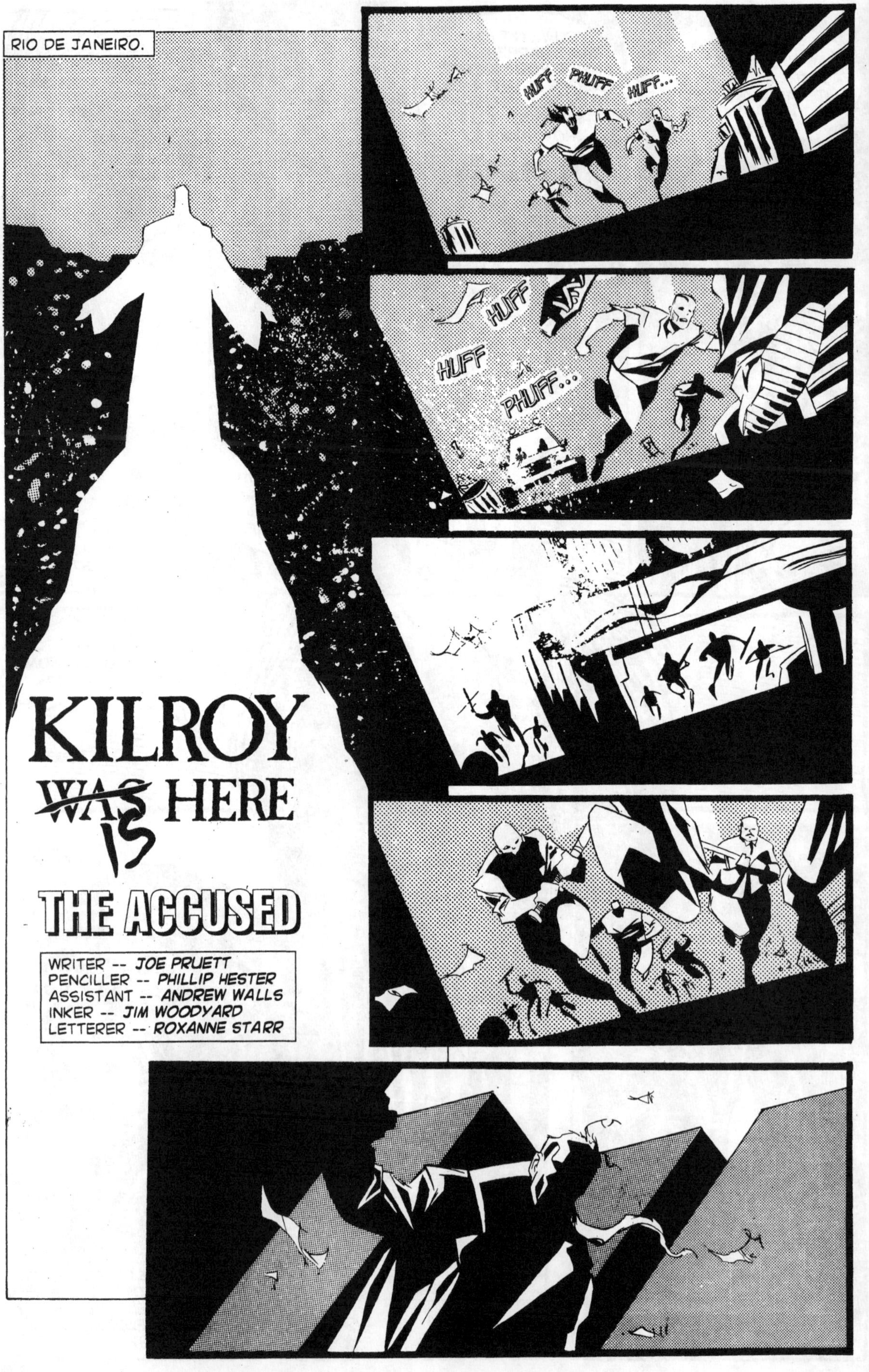

RIO DE JANEIRO.
KILROY
WAS IS HERE
THE ACCUSED
WRITER -- JOE PRUETT
PENCILLER -- PHILLIP HESTER
ASSISTANT -- ANDREW WALLS
INKER -- JIM WOODYARD
LETTERER -- ROXANNE STARR
HUFF PHUFF HUFF...
HUFF
HUFF
PHUFF...

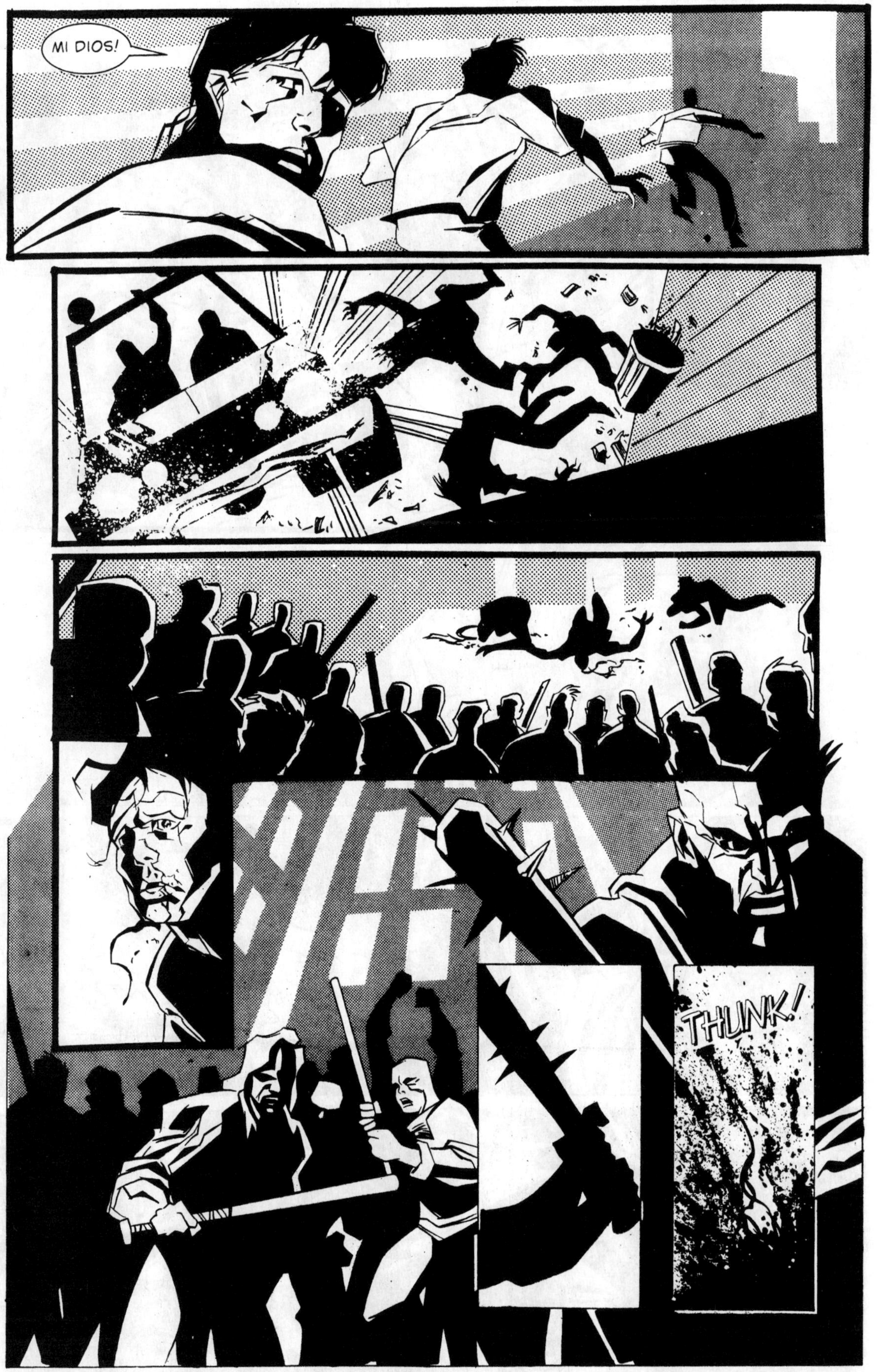
MI DIOS!
THUNK!

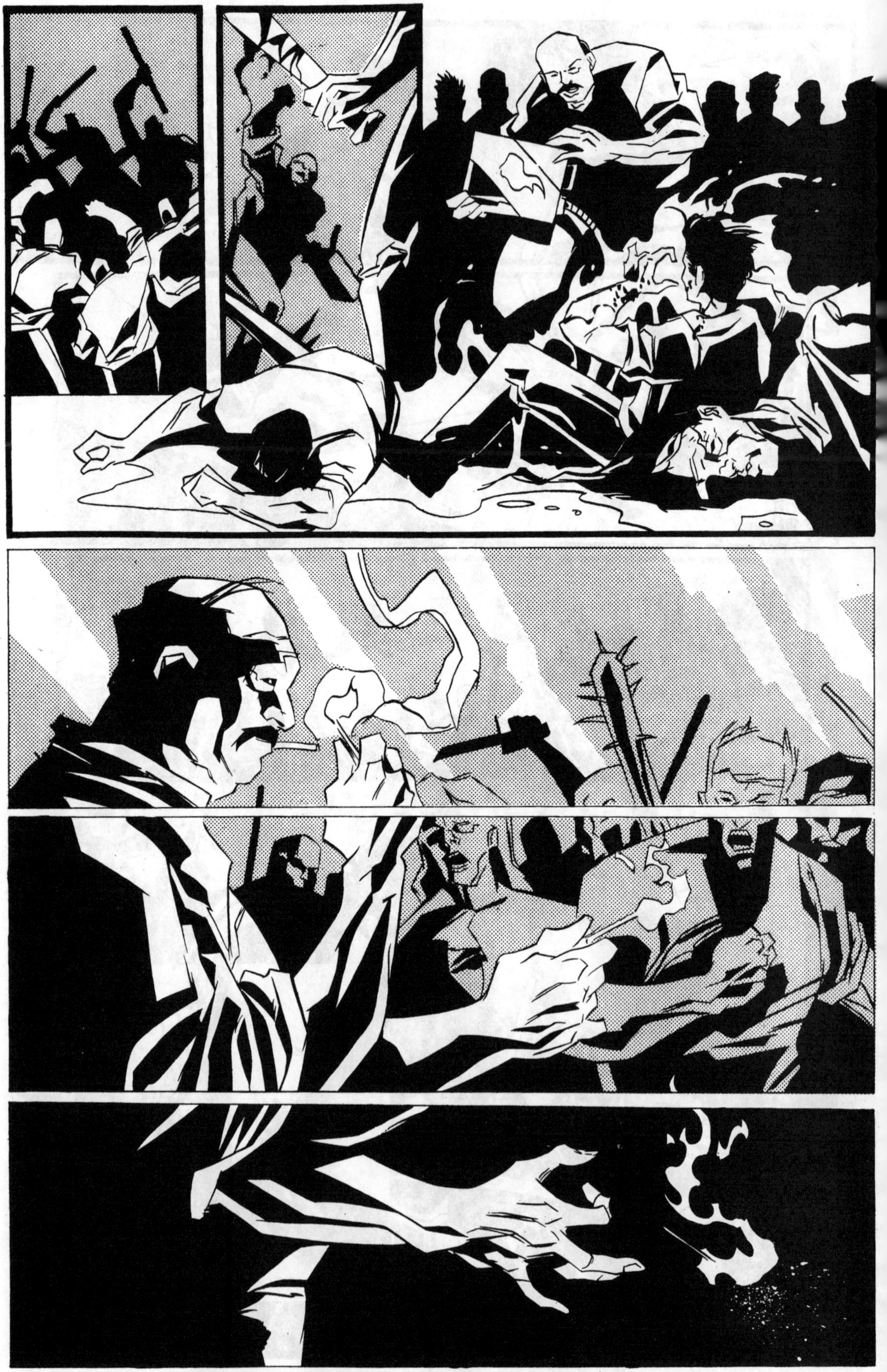

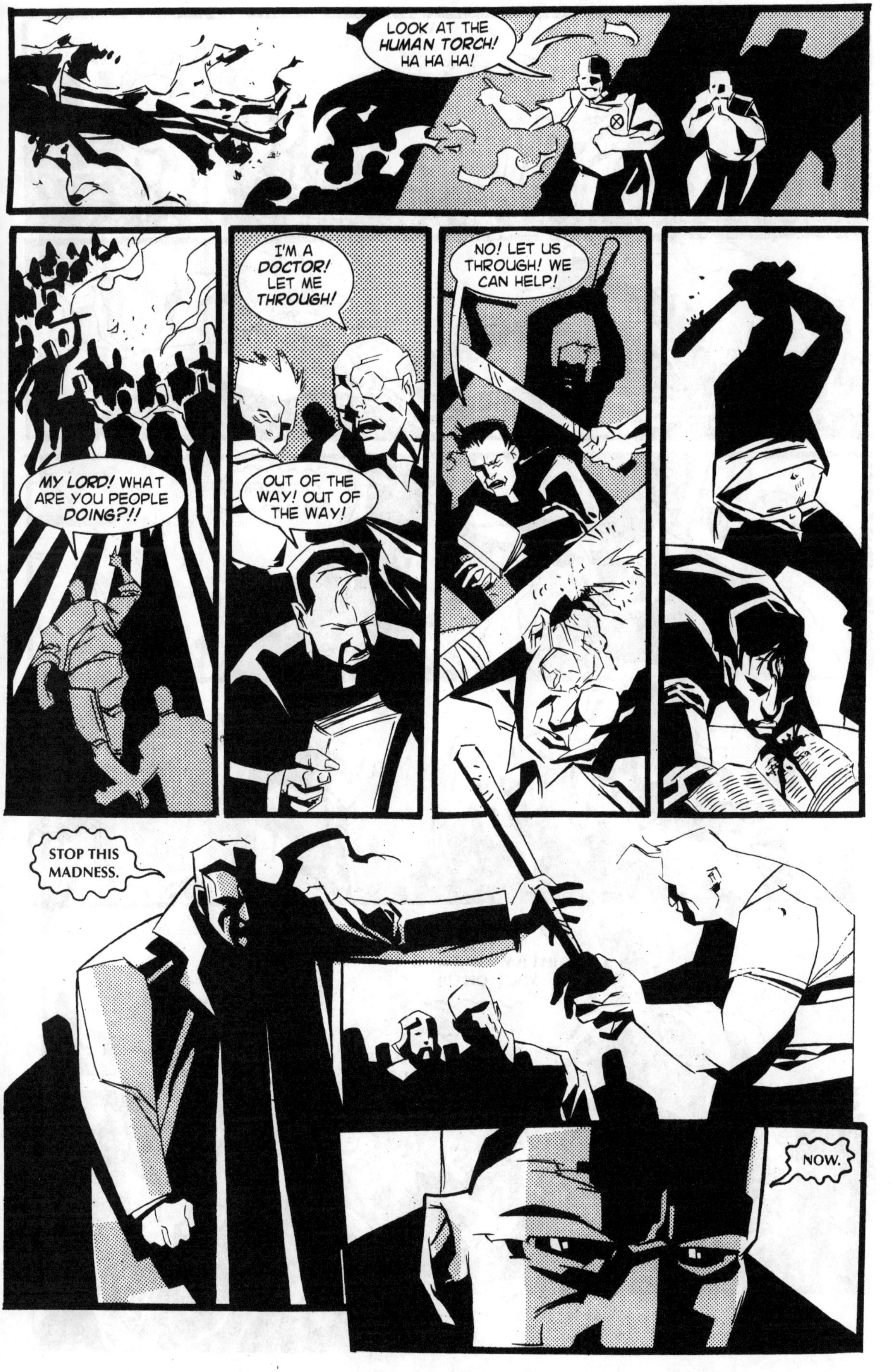
LOOK AT THE HUMAN TORCH! HA HA HA!
MY LORD! WHAT ARE YOU PEOPLE DOING?!!
I'M A DOCTOR! LET ME THROUGH!
OUT OF THE WAY! OUT OF THE WAY!
NO! LET US THROUGH! WE CAN HELP!
STOP THIS MADNESS.
NOW.

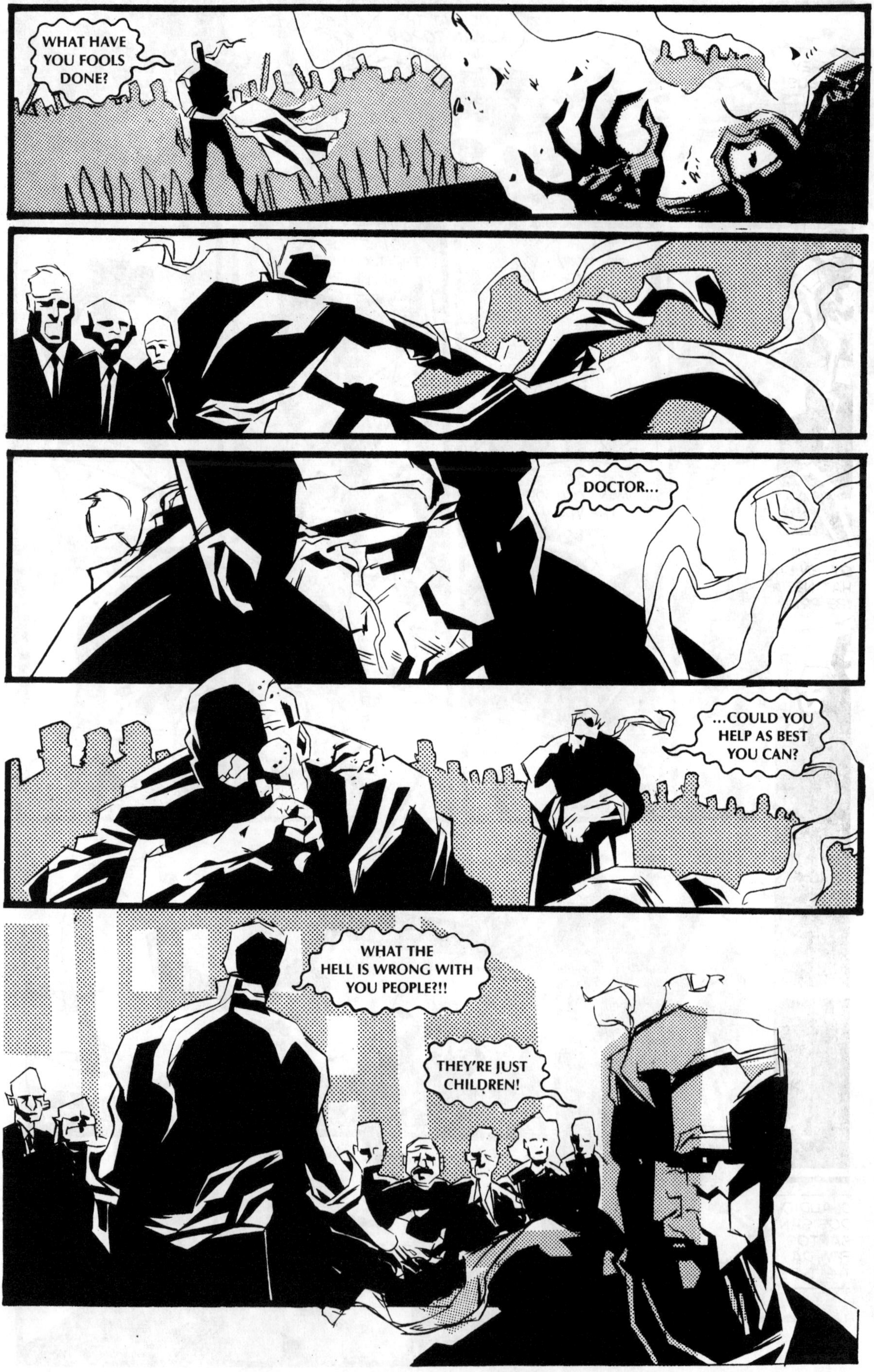
WHAT HAVE YOU FOOLS DONE?
DOCTOR...
...COULD YOU HELP AS BEST YOU CAN?
WHAT THE HELL IS WRONG WITH YOU PEOPLE?!!
THEY'RE JUST CHILDREN!

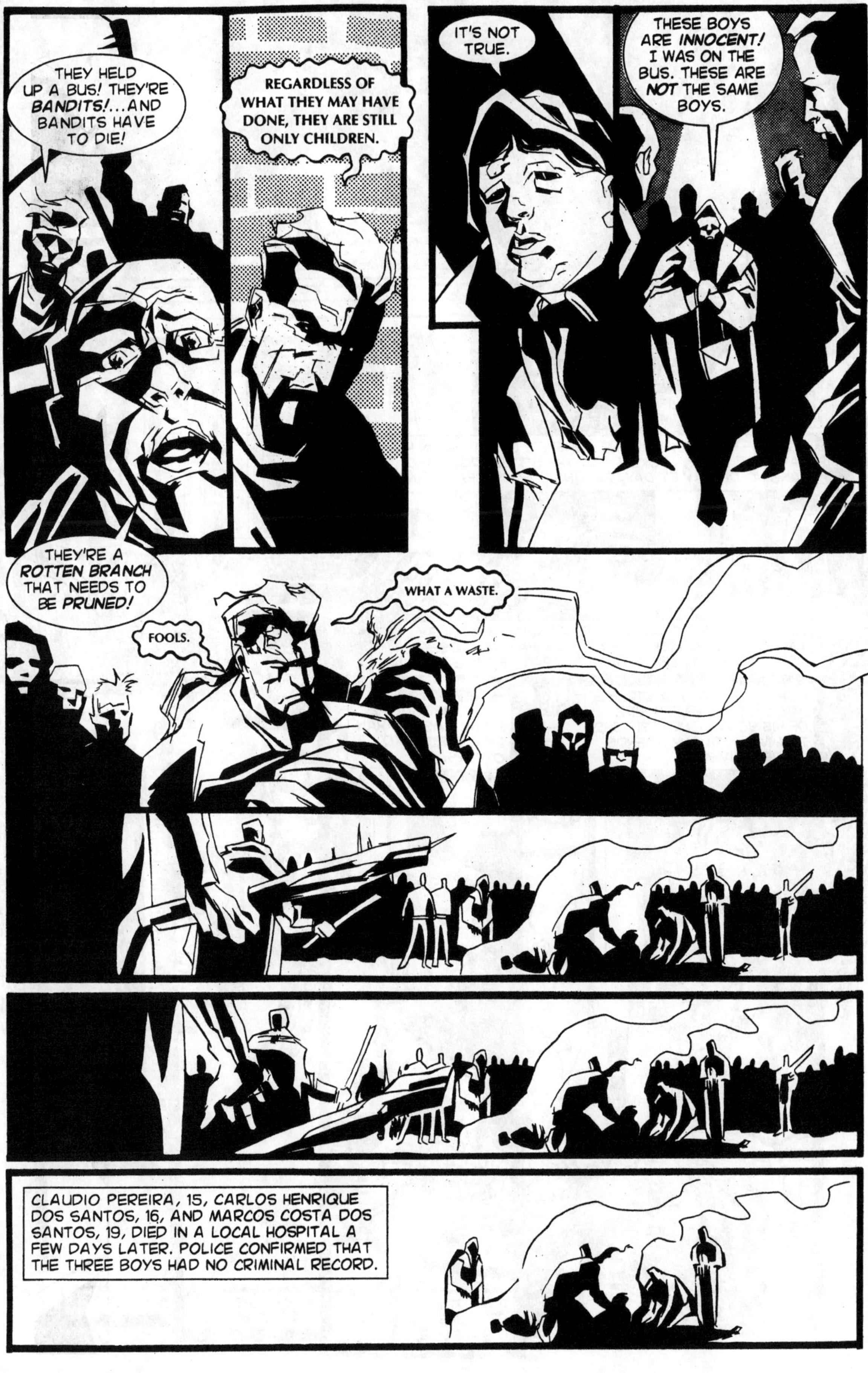
THEY HELD UP A BUS! THEY'RE BANDITS!...AND BANDITS HAVE TO DIE!
REGARDLESS OF WHAT THEY MAY HAVE DONE, THEY ARE STILL ONLY CHILDREN.
IT'S NOT TRUE.
THESE BOYS ARE INNOCENT! I WAS ON THE BUS. THESE ARE NOT THE SAME BOYS.
THEY'RE A ROTTEN BRANCH THAT NEEDS TO BE PRUNED!
FOOLS.
WHAT A WASTE.
CLAUDIO PEREIRA, 15, CARLOS HENRIQUE DOS SANTOS, 16, AND MARCOS COSTA DOS SANTOS, 19, DIED IN A LOCAL HOSPITAL A FEW DAYS LATER. POLICE CONFIRMED THAT THE THREE BOYS HAD NO CRIMINAL RECORD.

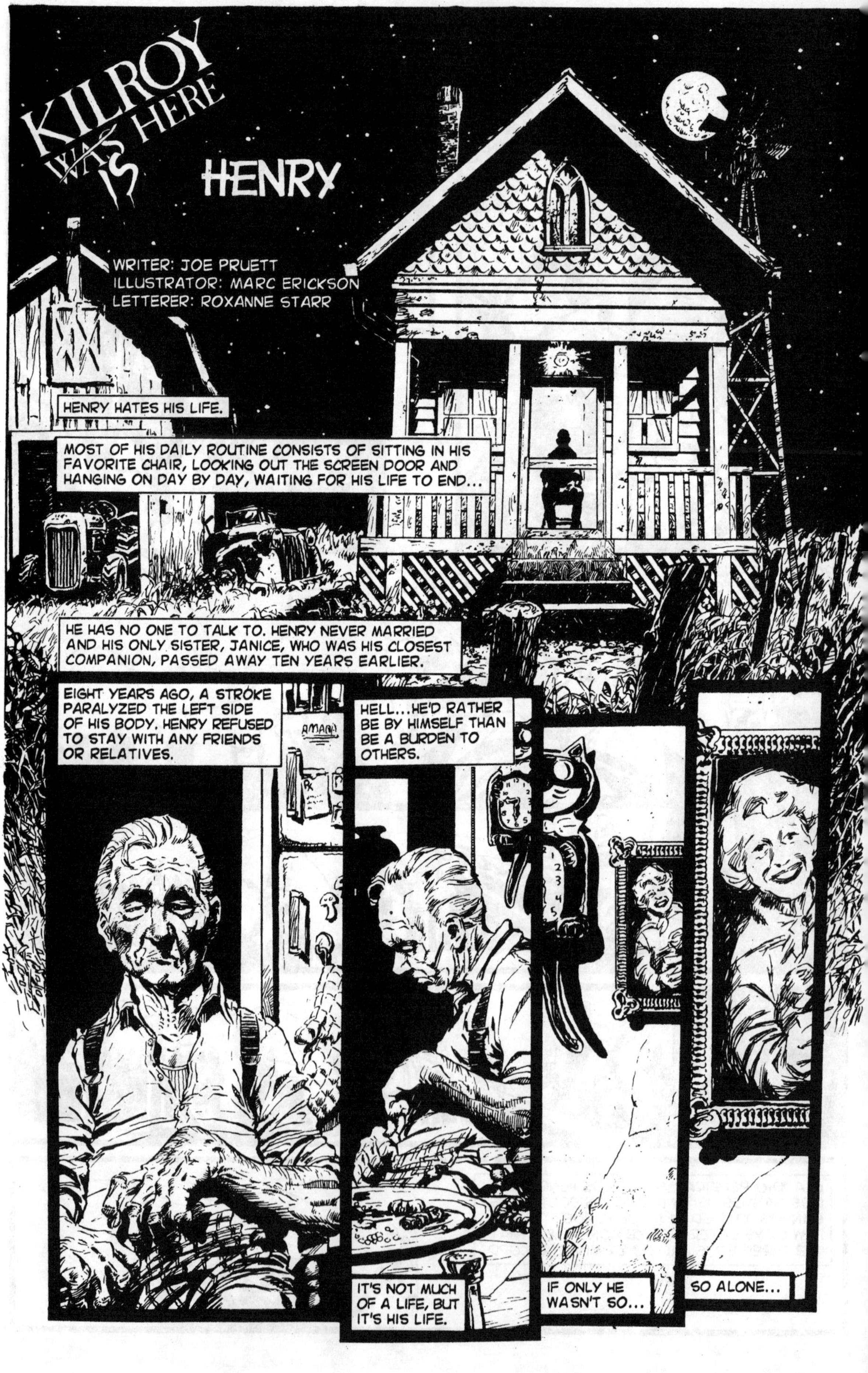
KILROY WAS IS HERE
HENRY
WRITER: JOE PRUETT
ILLUSTRATOR: MARC ERICKSON
LETTERER: ROXANNE STARR
HENRY HATES HIS LIFE.
MOST OF HIS DAILY ROUTINE CONSISTS OF SITTING IN HIS FAVORITE CHAIR, LOOKING OUT THE SCREEN DOOR AND HANGING ON DAY BY DAY, WAITING FOR HIS LIFE TO END...
HE HAS NO ONE TO TALK TO. HENRY NEVER MARRIED AND HIS ONLY SISTER, JANICE, WHO WAS HIS CLOSEST COMPANION, PASSED AWAY TEN YEARS EARLIER.
EIGHT YEARS AGO, A STROKE PARALYZED THE LEFT SIDE OF HIS BODY. HENRY REFUSED TO STAY WITH ANY FRIENDS OR RELATIVES.
HELL...HE'D RATHER BE BY HIMSELF THAN BE A BURDEN TO OTHERS.
IT'S NOT MUCH OF A LIFE, BUT IT'S HIS LIFE.
IF ONLY HE WASN'T SO...
SO ALONE...

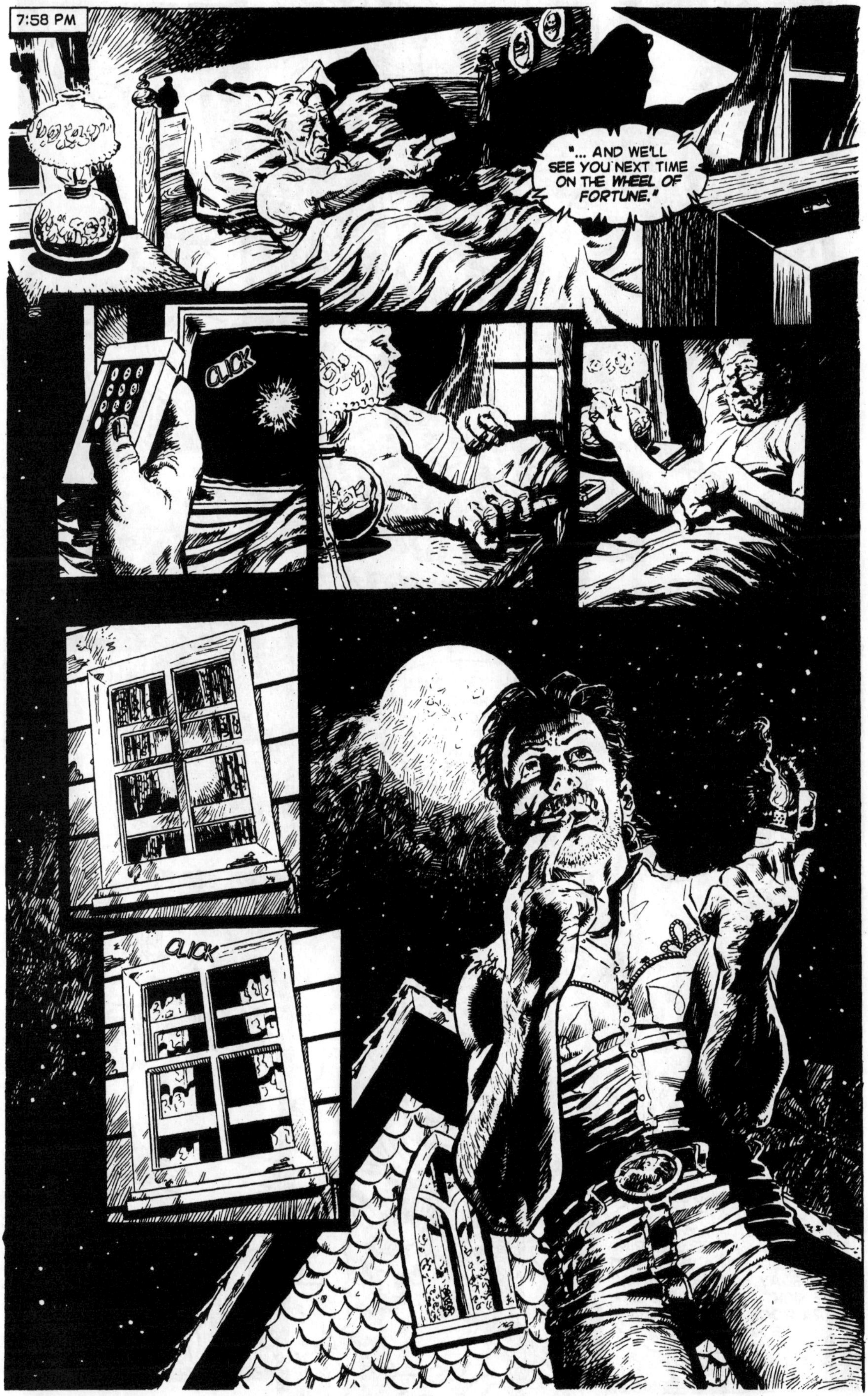
7:58 PM
"... AND WE'LL SEE YOU NEXT TIME ON THE *WHEEL OF FORTUNE.*"
CLICK
CLICK

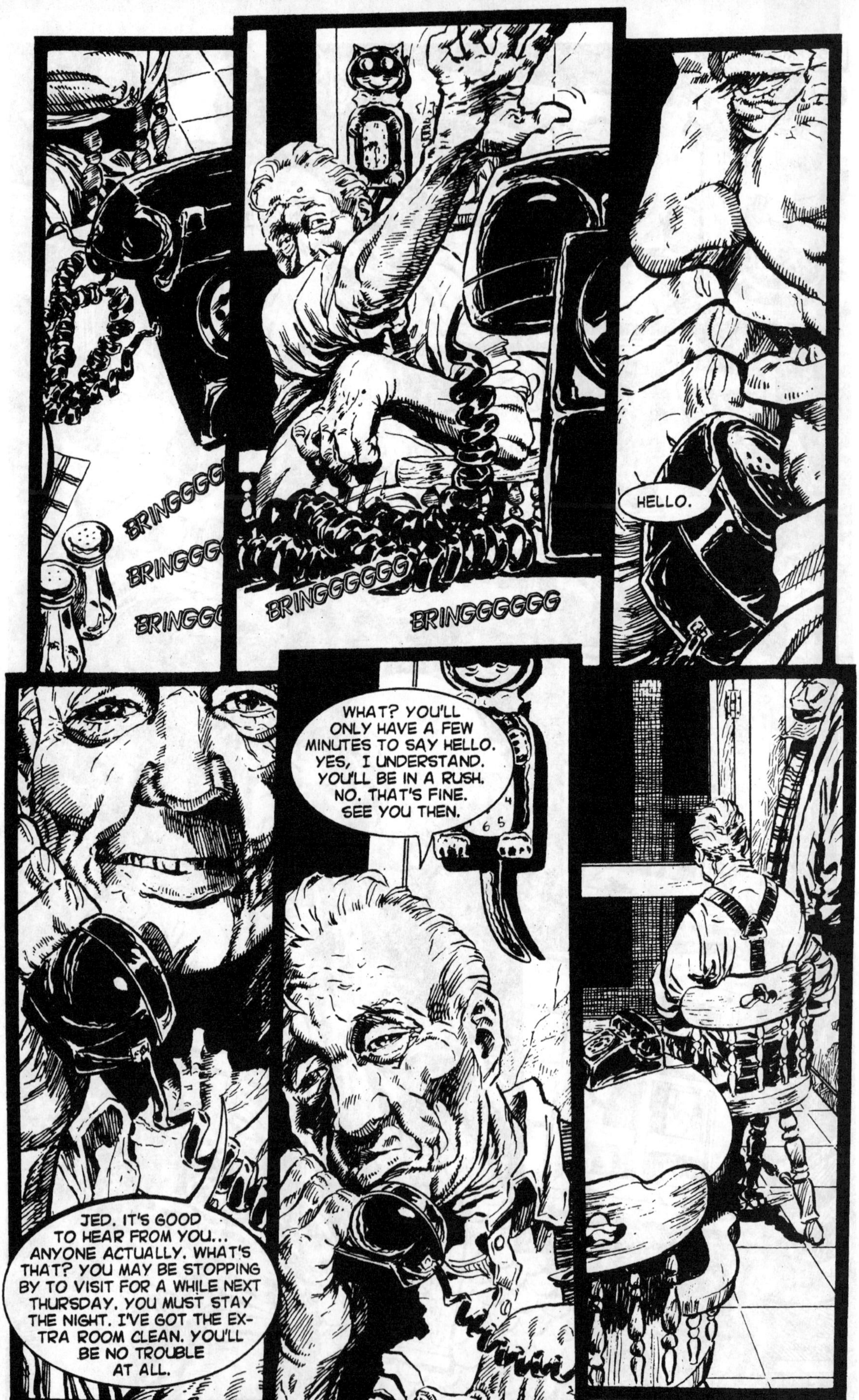
BRINGGGG
BRINGGGG
BRINGGG
BRINGGGGGG
BRINGGGGGG
HELLO.
JED. IT'S GOOD TO HEAR FROM YOU... ANYONE ACTUALLY. WHAT'S THAT? YOU MAY BE STOPPING BY TO VISIT FOR A WHILE NEXT THURSDAY. YOU MUST STAY THE NIGHT. I'VE GOT THE EXTRA ROOM CLEAN. YOU'LL BE NO TROUBLE AT ALL.
WHAT? YOU'LL ONLY HAVE A FEW MINUTES TO SAY HELLO. YES, I UNDERSTAND. YOU'LL BE IN A RUSH. NO. THAT'S FINE. SEE YOU THEN.

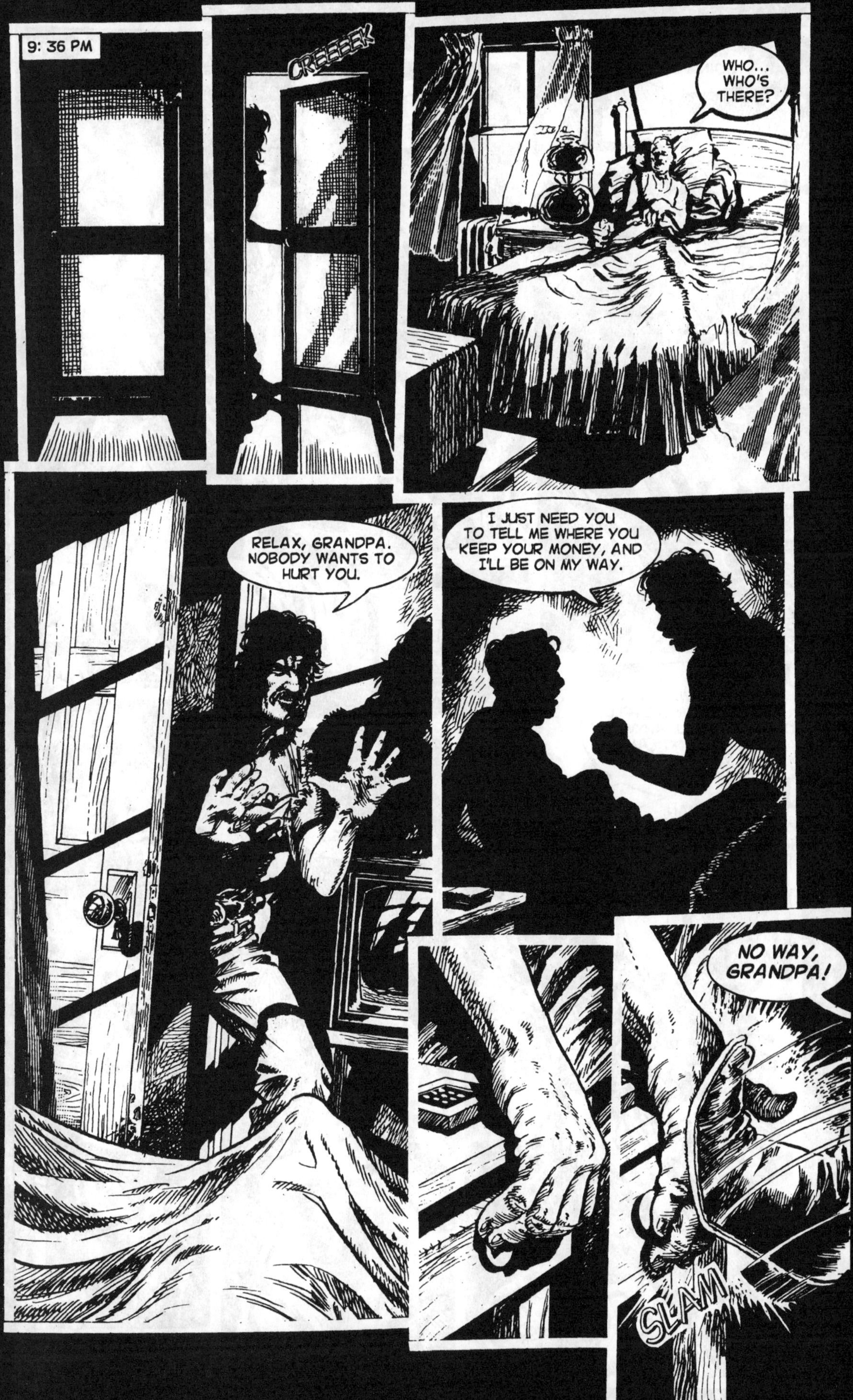
9: 36 PM
CREEEEK
WHO... WHO'S THERE?
RELAX, GRANDPA. NOBODY WANTS TO HURT YOU.
I JUST NEED YOU TO TELL ME WHERE YOU KEEP YOUR MONEY, AND I'LL BE ON MY WAY.
NO WAY, GRANDPA!
SLAM

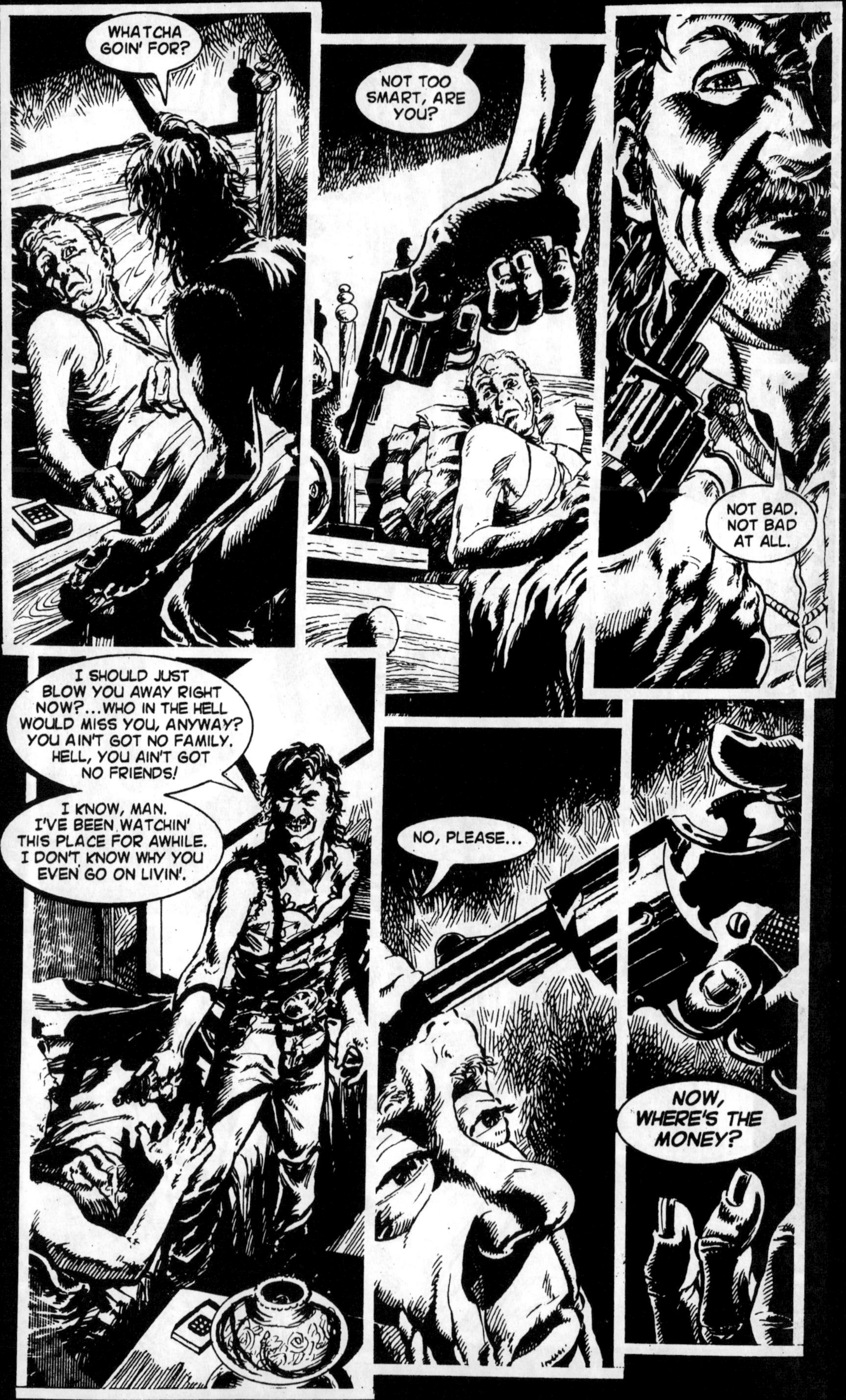

WHATCHA GOIN' FOR?
NOT TOO SMART, ARE YOU?
NOT BAD. NOT BAD AT ALL.
I SHOULD JUST BLOW YOU AWAY RIGHT NOW?...WHO IN THE HELL WOULD MISS YOU, ANYWAY? YOU AIN'T GOT NO FAMILY. HELL, YOU AIN'T GOT NO FRIENDS!
I KNOW, MAN. I'VE BEEN WATCHIN' THIS PLACE FOR AWHILE. I DON'T KNOW WHY YOU EVEN GO ON LIVIN'.
NO, PLEASE...
NOW, WHERE'S THE MONEY?

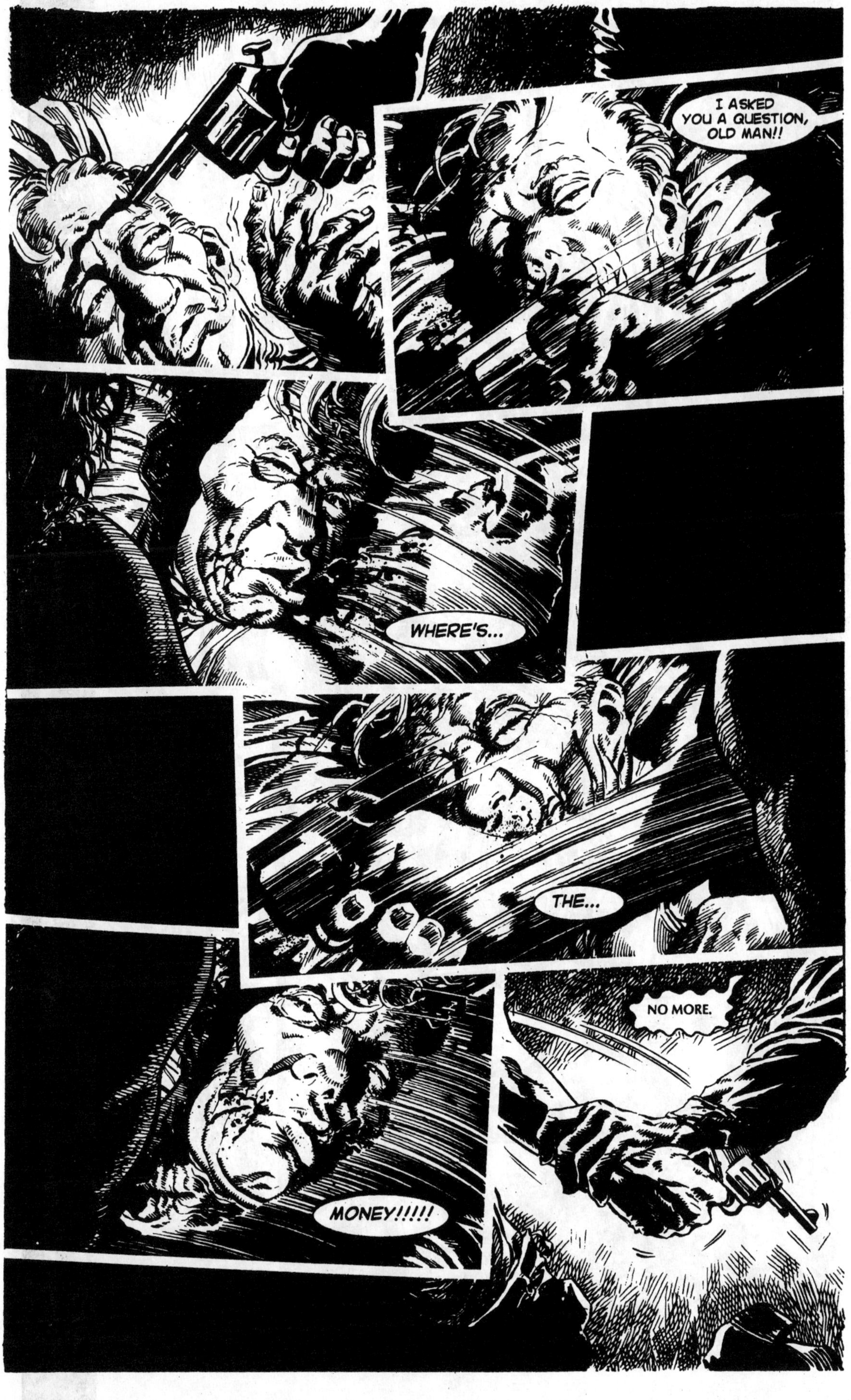
I ASKED YOU A QUESTION, OLD MAN!!
WHERE'S...
THE...
MONEY!!!!!
NO MORE.

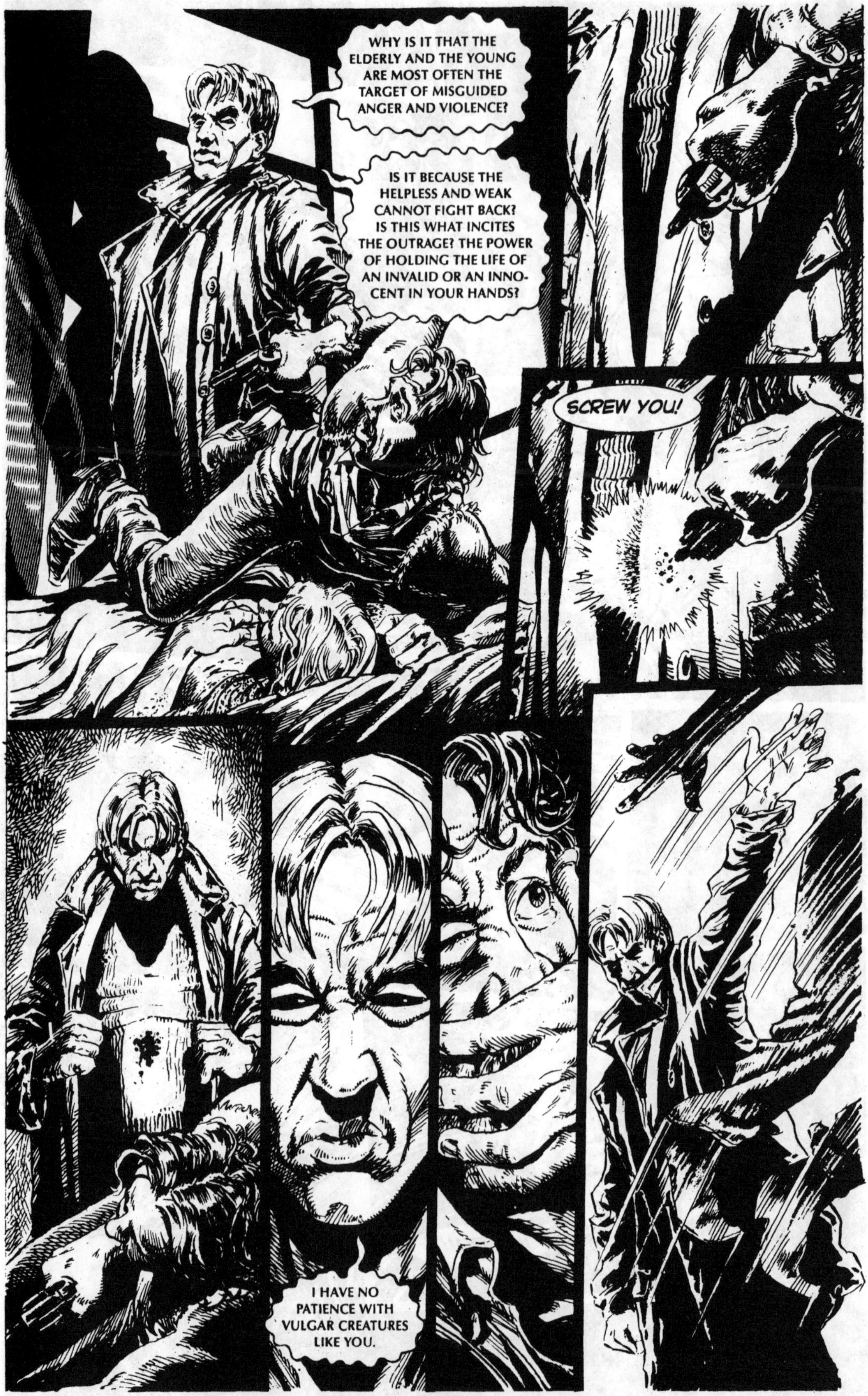
WHY IS IT THAT THE ELDERLY AND THE YOUNG ARE MOST OFTEN THE TARGET OF MISGUIDED ANGER AND VIOLENCE?
IS IT BECAUSE THE HELPLESS AND WEAK CANNOT FIGHT BACK? IS THIS WHAT INCITES THE OUTRAGE? THE POWER OF HOLDING THE LIFE OF AN INVALID OR AN INNO-CENT IN YOUR HANDS?
SCREW YOU!
I HAVE NO PATIENCE WITH VULGAR CREATURES LIKE YOU.

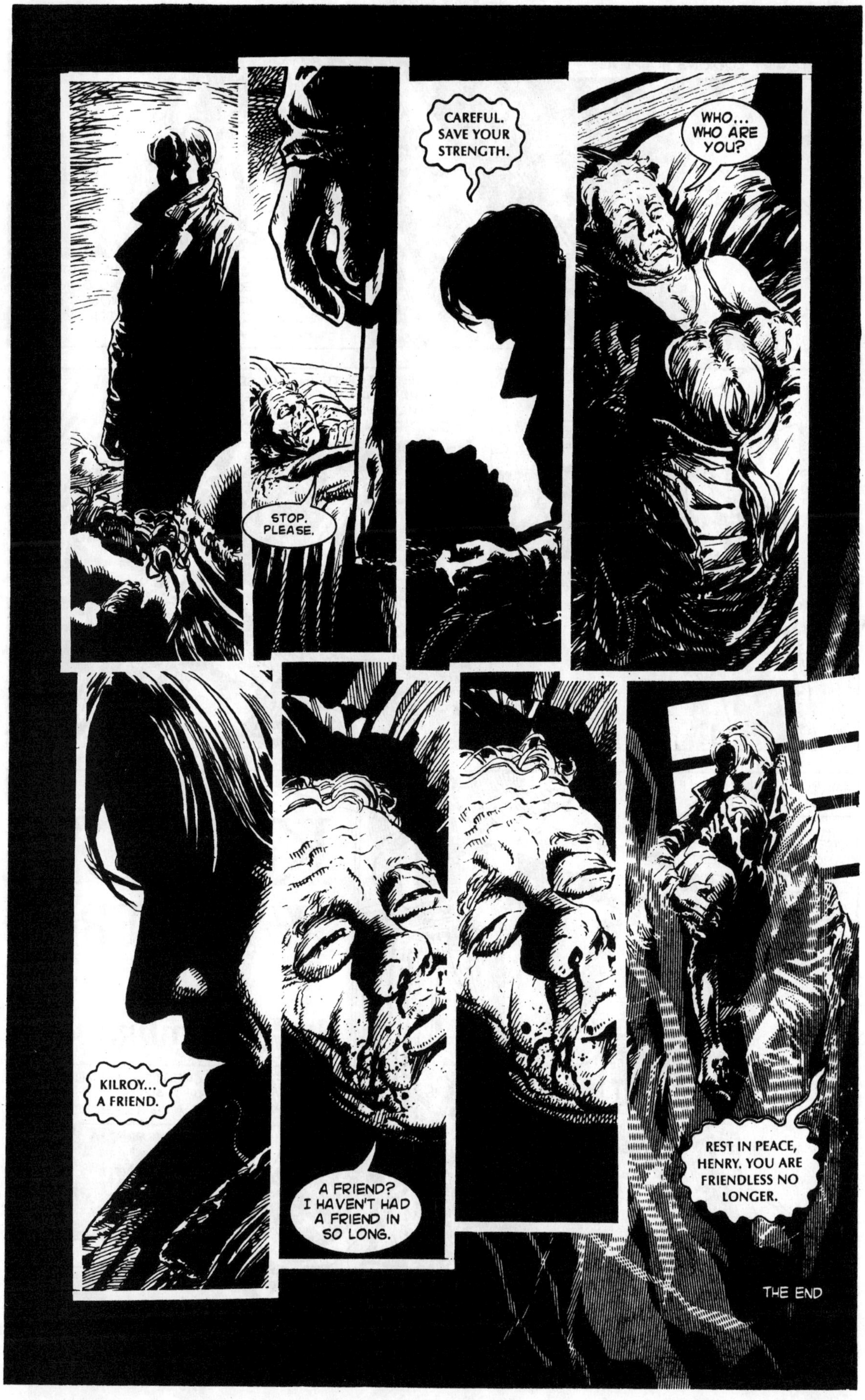
STOP. PLEASE.
CAREFUL. SAVE YOUR STRENGTH.
WHO... WHO ARE YOU?
KILROY... A FRIEND.
A FRIEND? I HAVEN'T HAD A FRIEND IN SO LONG.
REST IN PEACE, HENRY. YOU ARE FRIENDLESS NO LONGER.
THE END

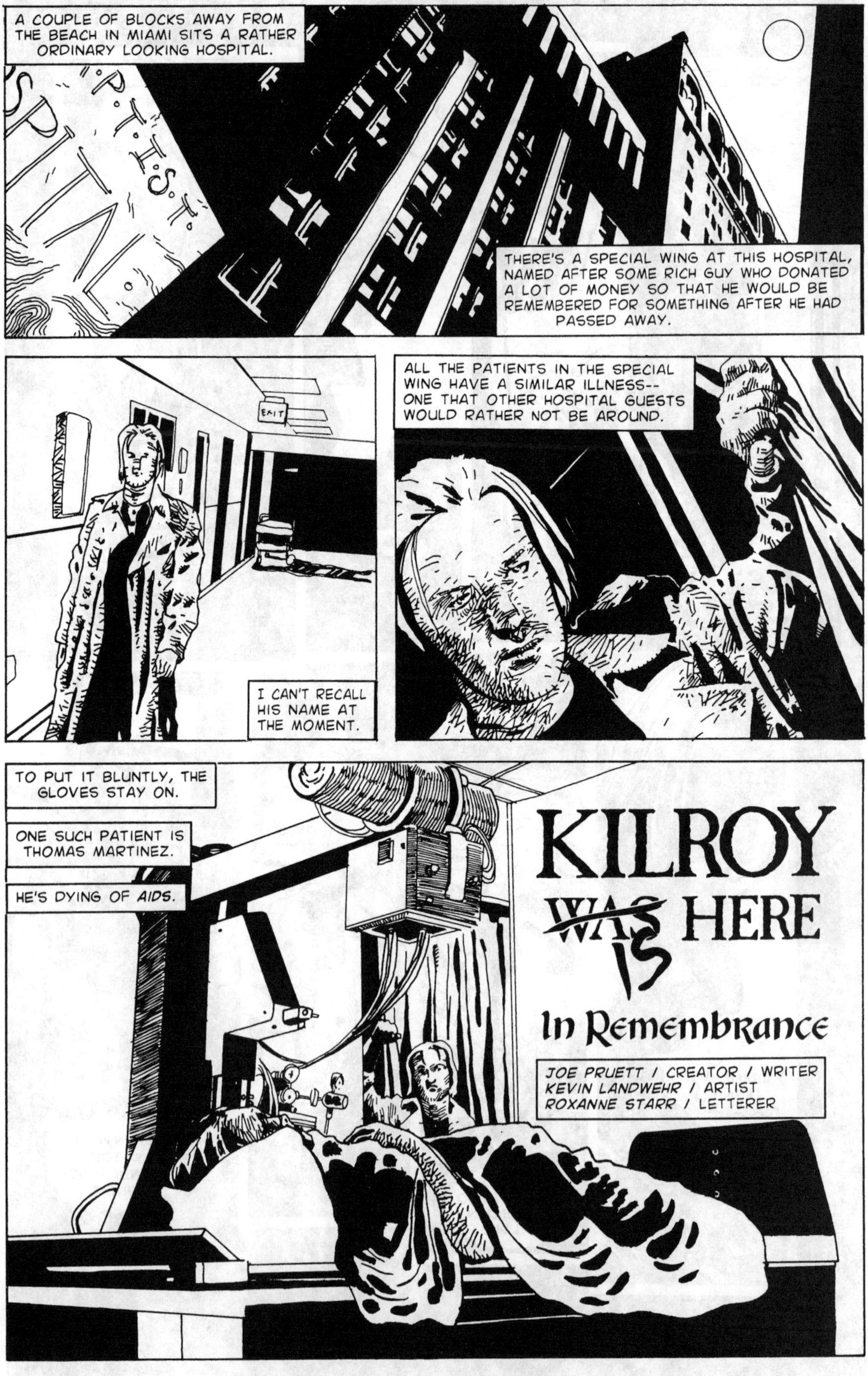
A COUPLE OF BLOCKS AWAY FROM THE BEACH IN MIAMI SITS A RATHER ORDINARY LOOKING HOSPITAL.
THERE'S A SPECIAL WING AT THIS HOSPITAL, NAMED AFTER SOME RICH GUY WHO DONATED A LOT OF MONEY SO THAT HE WOULD BE REMEMBERED FOR SOMETHING AFTER HE HAD PASSED AWAY.
EXIT
I CAN'T RECALL HIS NAME AT THE MOMENT.
ALL THE PATIENTS IN THE SPECIAL WING HAVE A SIMILAR ILLNESS-- ONE THAT OTHER HOSPITAL GUESTS WOULD RATHER NOT BE AROUND.
TO PUT IT BLUNTLY, THE GLOVES STAY ON.
ONE SUCH PATIENT IS THOMAS MARTINEZ.
HE'S DYING OF AIDS.
KILROY ~~WAS~~ IS HERE
In Remembrance
JOE PRUETT / CREATOR / WRITER
KEVIN LANDWEHR / ARTIST
ROXANNE STARR / LETTERER

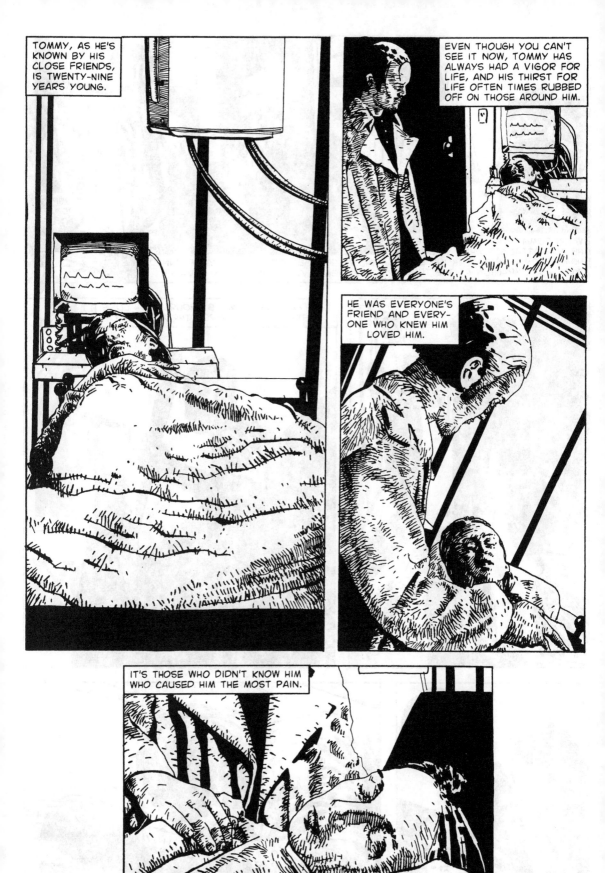

TOMMY, AS HE'S KNOWN BY HIS CLOSE FRIENDS, IS TWENTY-NINE YEARS YOUNG.

EVEN THOUGH YOU CAN'T SEE IT NOW, TOMMY HAS ALWAYS HAD A VIGOR FOR LIFE, AND HIS THIRST FOR LIFE OFTEN TIMES RUBBED OFF ON THOSE AROUND HIM.

HE WAS EVERYONE'S FRIEND AND EVERY-ONE WHO KNEW HIM LOVED HIM.

IT'S THOSE WHO DIDN'T KNOW HIM WHO CAUSED HIM THE MOST PAIN.

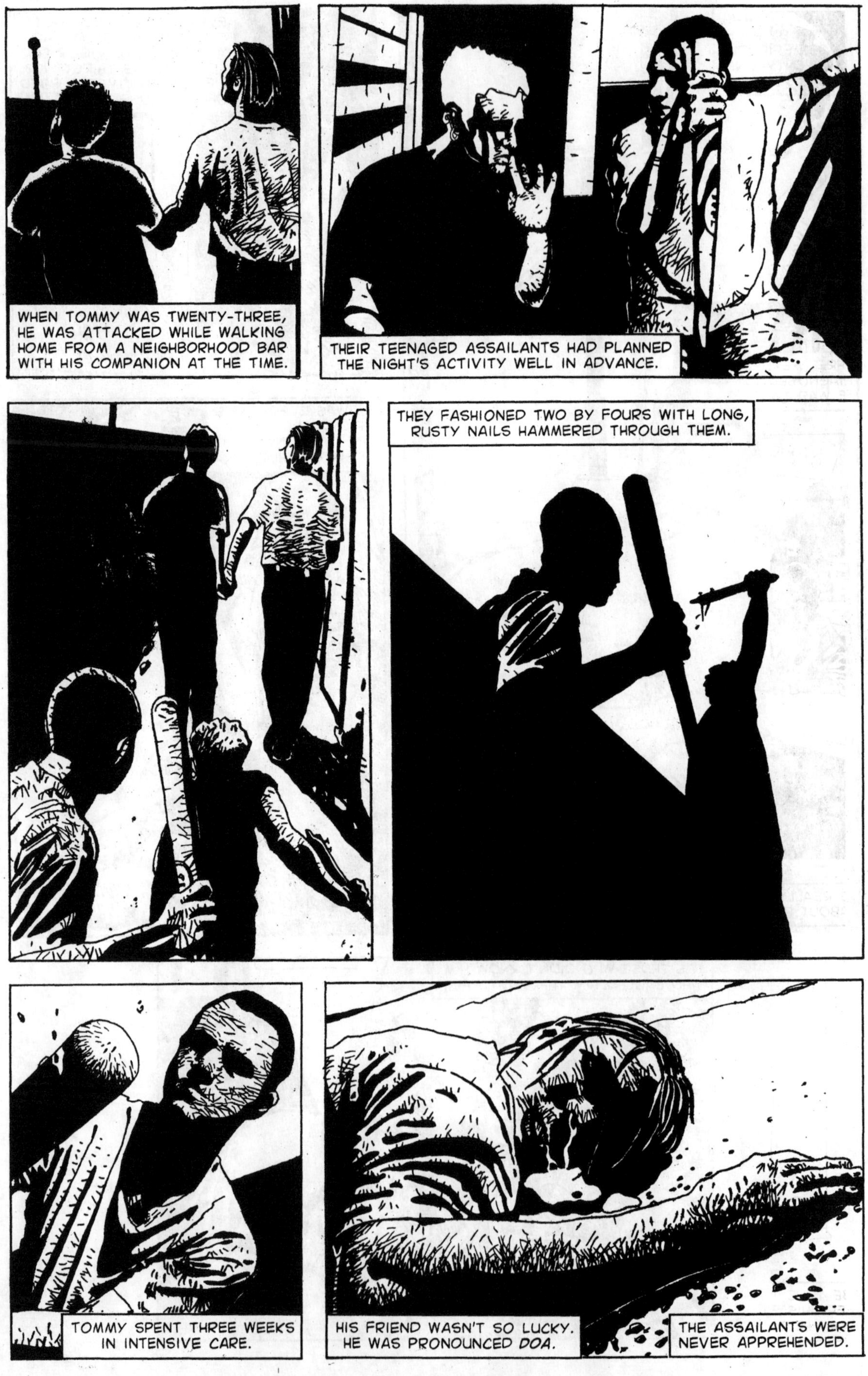

WHEN TOMMY WAS TWENTY-THREE, HE WAS ATTACKED WHILE WALKING HOME FROM A NEIGHBORHOOD BAR WITH HIS COMPANION AT THE TIME.
THEIR TEENAGED ASSAILANTS HAD PLANNED THE NIGHT'S ACTIVITY WELL IN ADVANCE.
THEY FASHIONED TWO BY FOURS WITH LONG, RUSTY NAILS HAMMERED THROUGH THEM.
TOMMY SPENT THREE WEEKS IN INTENSIVE CARE.
HIS FRIEND WASN'T SO LUCKY. HE WAS PRONOUNCED *DOA*.
THE ASSAILANTS WERE NEVER APPREHENDED.

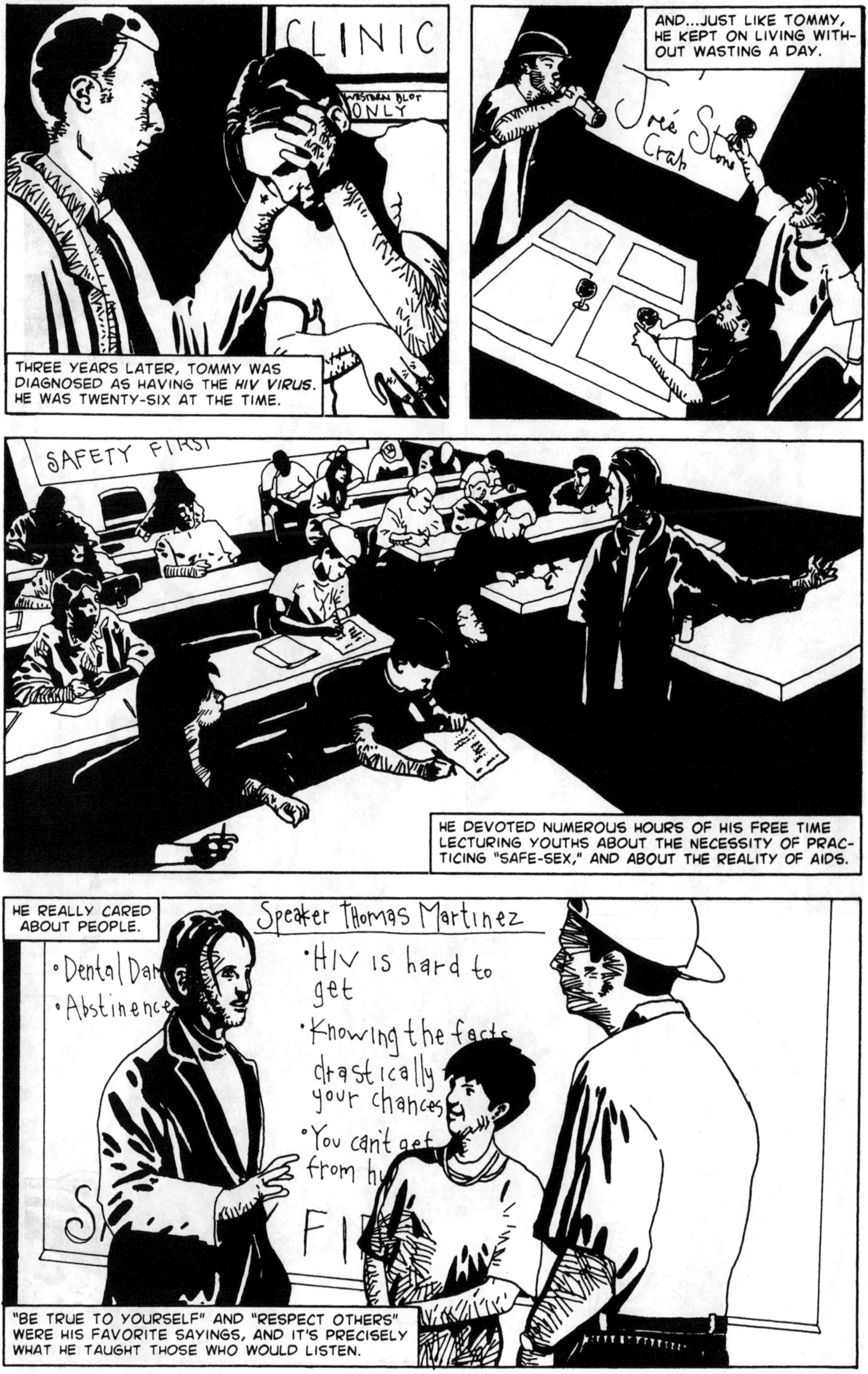
CLINIC
WESTERN BLOT
ONLY
THREE YEARS LATER, TOMMY WAS DIAGNOSED AS HAVING THE *HIV VIRUS*. HE WAS TWENTY-SIX AT THE TIME.
AND...JUST LIKE TOMMY, HE KEPT ON LIVING WITHOUT WASTING A DAY.
SAFETY FIRS
HE DEVOTED NUMEROUS HOURS OF HIS FREE TIME LECTURING YOUTHS ABOUT THE NECESSITY OF PRACTICING "SAFE-SEX," AND ABOUT THE REALITY OF AIDS.
HE REALLY CARED ABOUT PEOPLE.
Speaker Thomas Martinez
•Dental Dar
•Abstinence
•HIV is hard to get
•Knowing the fact
drastically
your chances
•You can't get
from hu
"BE TRUE TO YOURSELF" AND "RESPECT OTHERS" WERE HIS FAVORITE SAYINGS, AND IT'S PRECISELY WHAT HE TAUGHT THOSE WHO WOULD LISTEN.

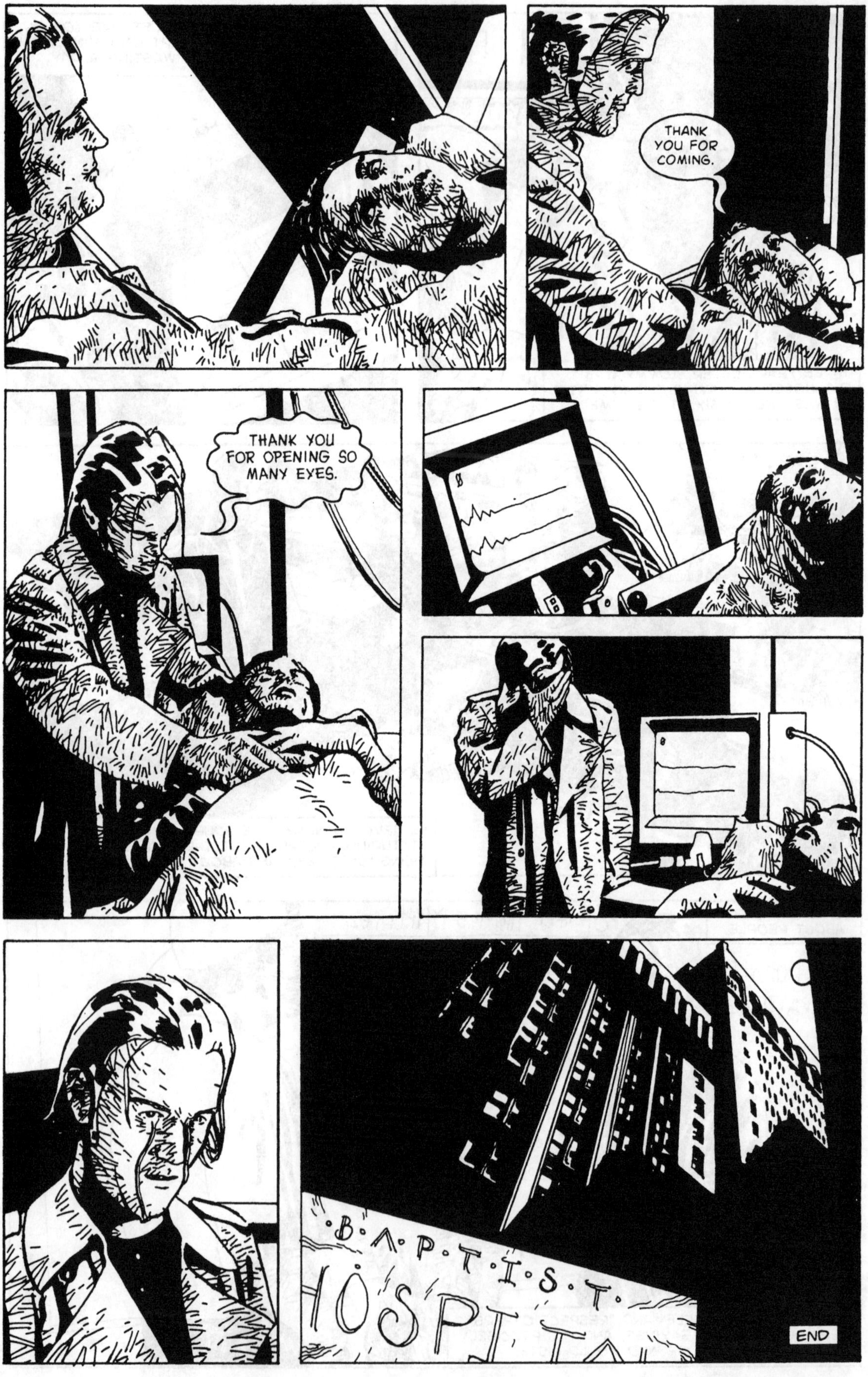
THANK YOU FOR COMING.
THANK YOU FOR OPENING SO MANY EYES.
BAPTIST HOSPITAL
END

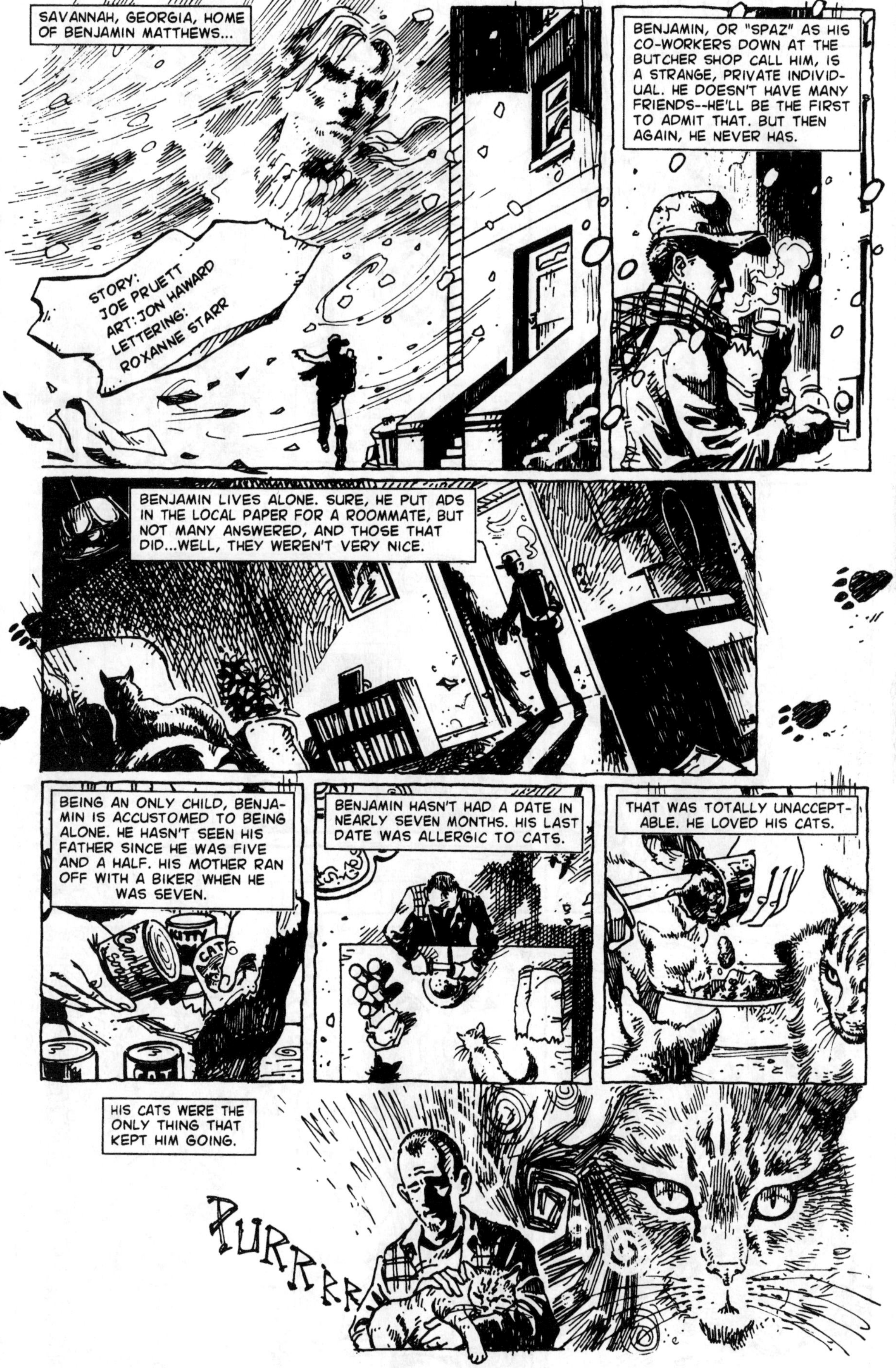

SAVANNAH, GEORGIA, HOME OF BENJAMIN MATTHEWS...
STORY: JOE PRUETT
ART: JON HAWARD
LETTERING: ROXANNE STARR
BENJAMIN, OR "SPAZ" AS HIS CO-WORKERS DOWN AT THE BUTCHER SHOP CALL HIM, IS A STRANGE, PRIVATE INDIVIDUAL. HE DOESN'T HAVE MANY FRIENDS--HE'LL BE THE FIRST TO ADMIT THAT. BUT THEN AGAIN, HE NEVER HAS.
BENJAMIN LIVES ALONE. SURE, HE PUT ADS IN THE LOCAL PAPER FOR A ROOMMATE, BUT NOT MANY ANSWERED, AND THOSE THAT DID...WELL, THEY WEREN'T VERY NICE.
BEING AN ONLY CHILD, BENJAMIN IS ACCUSTOMED TO BEING ALONE. HE HASN'T SEEN HIS FATHER SINCE HE WAS FIVE AND A HALF. HIS MOTHER RAN OFF WITH A BIKER WHEN HE WAS SEVEN.
BENJAMIN HASN'T HAD A DATE IN NEARLY SEVEN MONTHS. HIS LAST DATE WAS ALLERGIC TO CATS.
THAT WAS TOTALLY UNACCEPTABLE. HE LOVED HIS CATS.
HIS CATS WERE THE ONLY THING THAT KEPT HIM GOING.
PURRRR

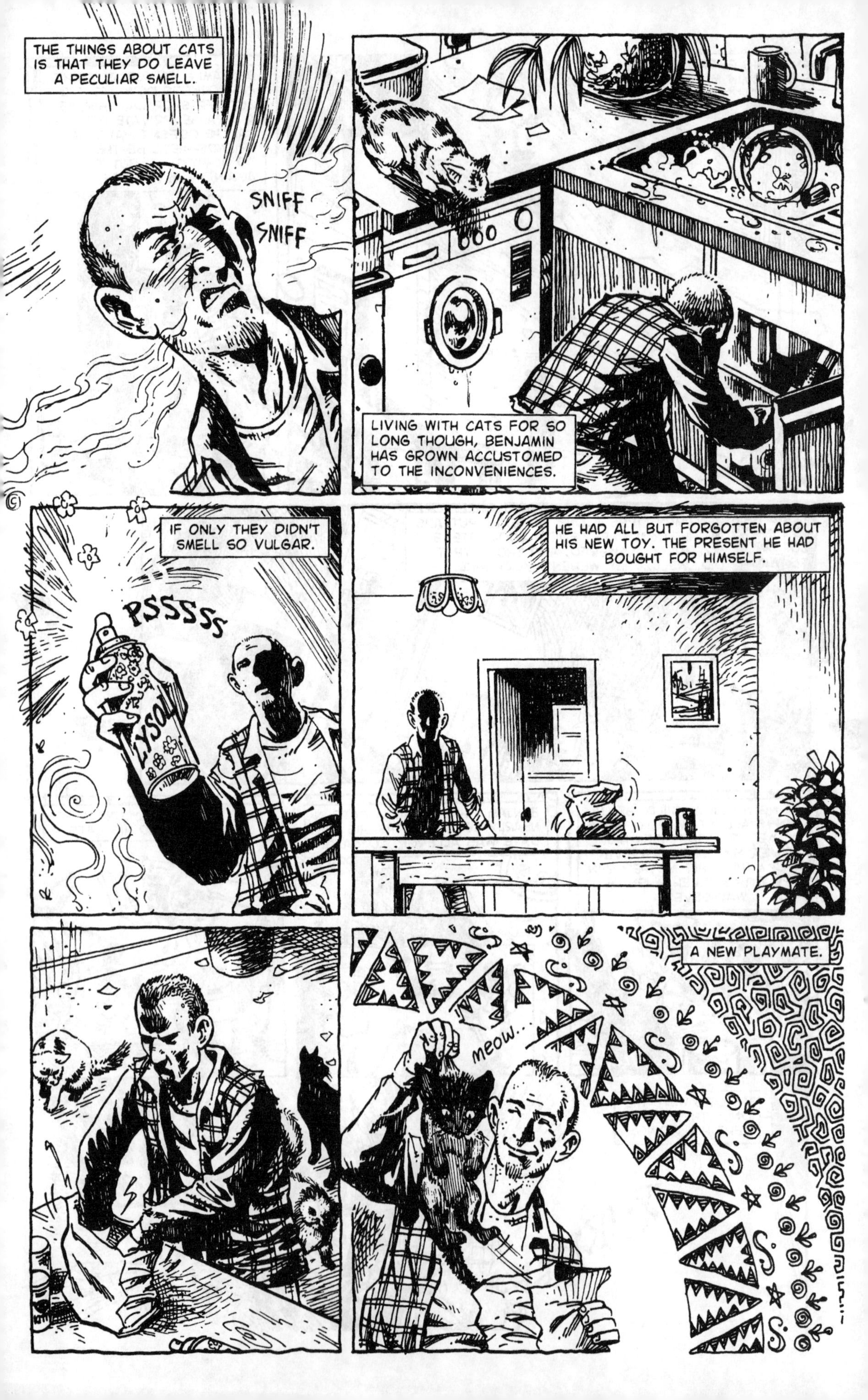
THE THINGS ABOUT CATS IS THAT THEY DO LEAVE A PECULIAR SMELL.
SNIFF SNIFF
LIVING WITH CATS FOR SO LONG THOUGH, BENJAMIN HAS GROWN ACCUSTOMED TO THE INCONVENIENCES.
IF ONLY THEY DIDN'T SMELL SO VULGAR.
PSSSSS
LYSOL
HE HAD ALL BUT FORGOTTEN ABOUT HIS NEW TOY. THE PRESENT HE HAD BOUGHT FOR HIMSELF.
A NEW PLAYMATE.
MEOW...

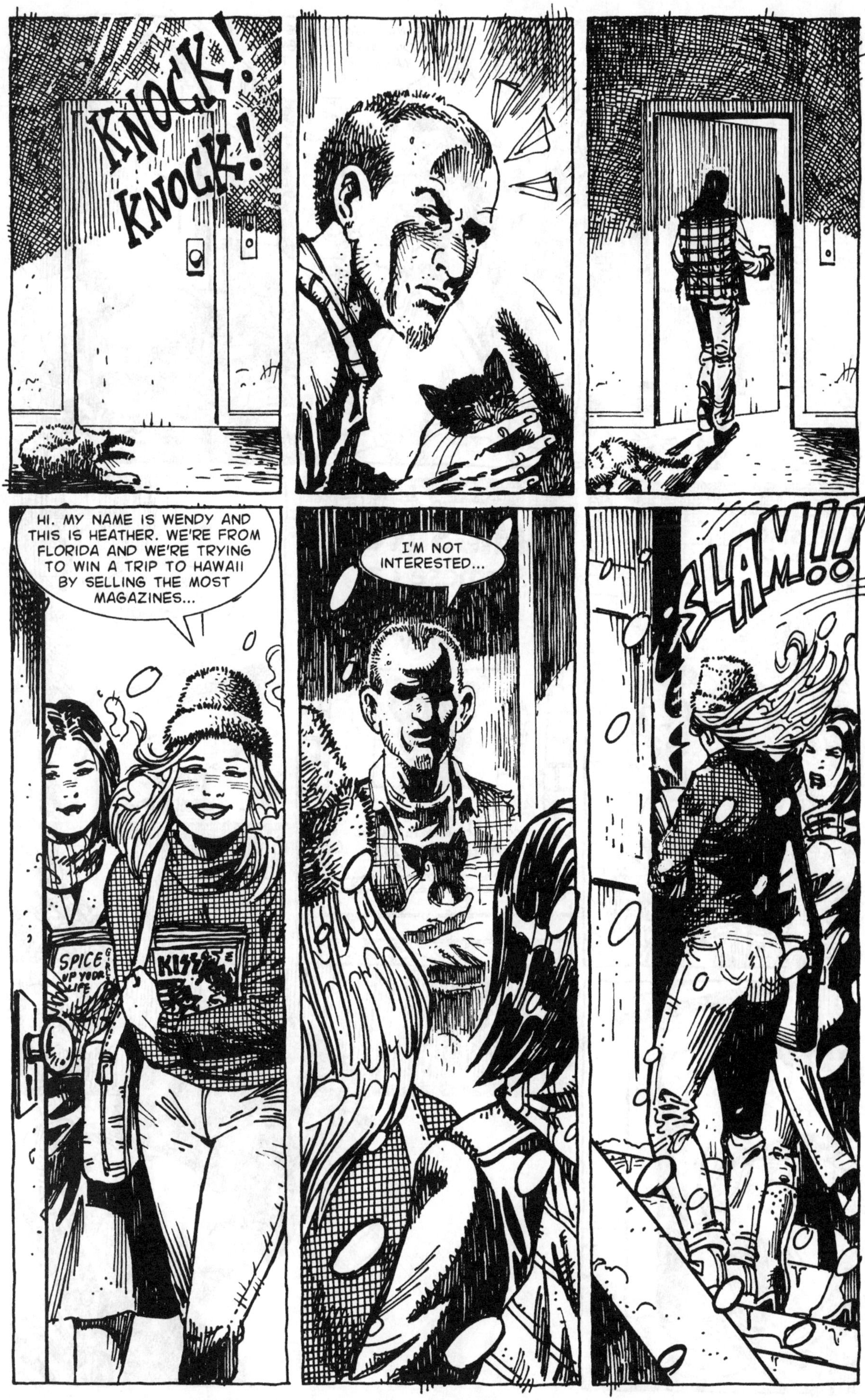
KNOCK! KNOCK!
HI. MY NAME IS WENDY AND THIS IS HEATHER. WE'RE FROM FLORIDA AND WE'RE TRYING TO WIN A TRIP TO HAWAII BY SELLING THE MOST MAGAZINES...
SPICE UP YOUR LIFE
KISS
I'M NOT INTERESTED...
SLAM!!!

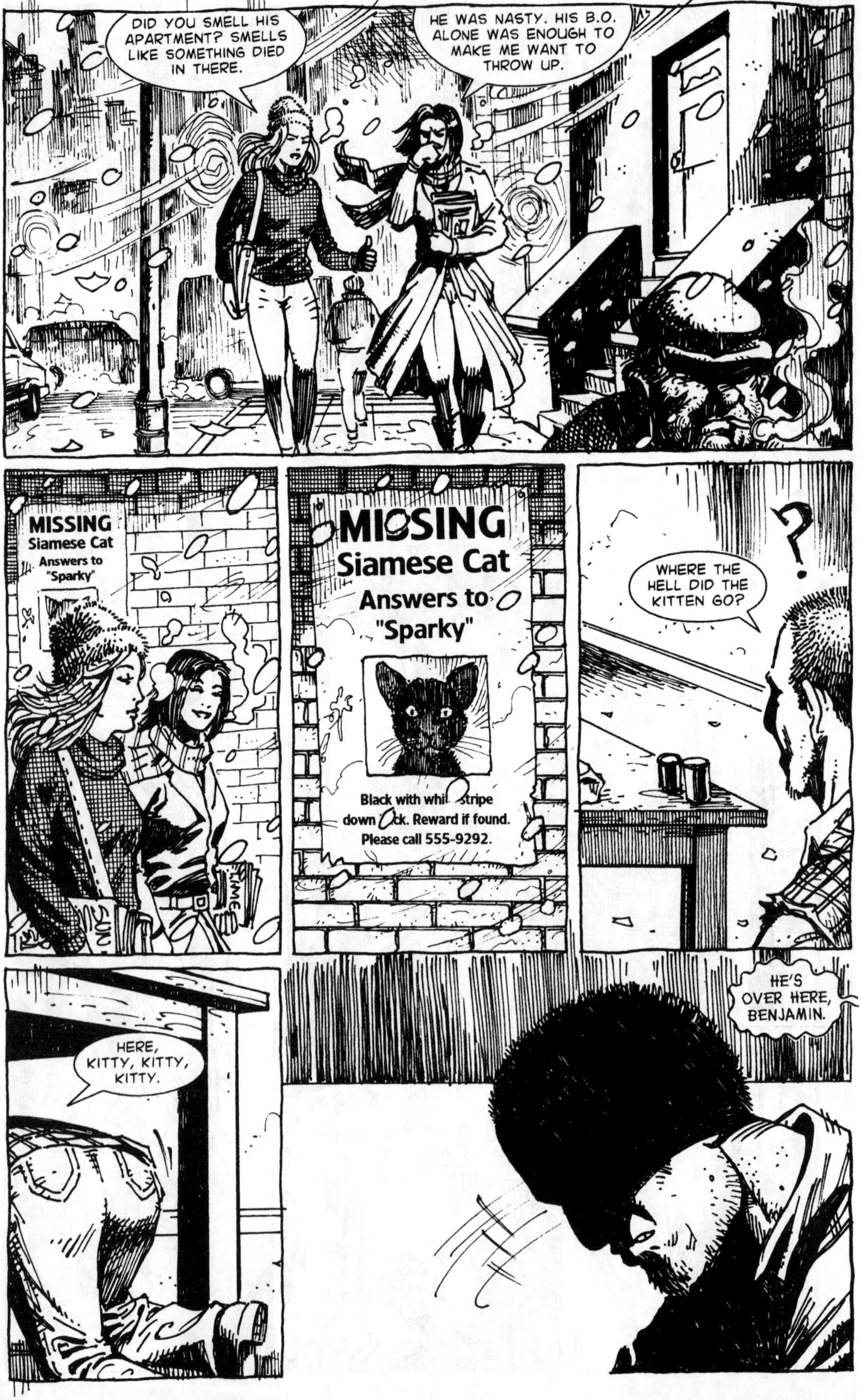
DID YOU SMELL HIS APARTMENT? SMELLS LIKE SOMETHING DIED IN THERE.
HE WAS NASTY. HIS B.O. ALONE WAS ENOUGH TO MAKE ME WANT TO THROW UP.
MISSING Siamese Cat Answers to "Sparky"
MISSING Siamese Cat Answers to "Sparky"
Black with whi stripe down ck. Reward if found. Please call 555-9292.
WHERE THE HELL DID THE KITTEN GO?
HERE, KITTY, KITTY, KITTY.
HE'S OVER HERE, BENJAMIN.

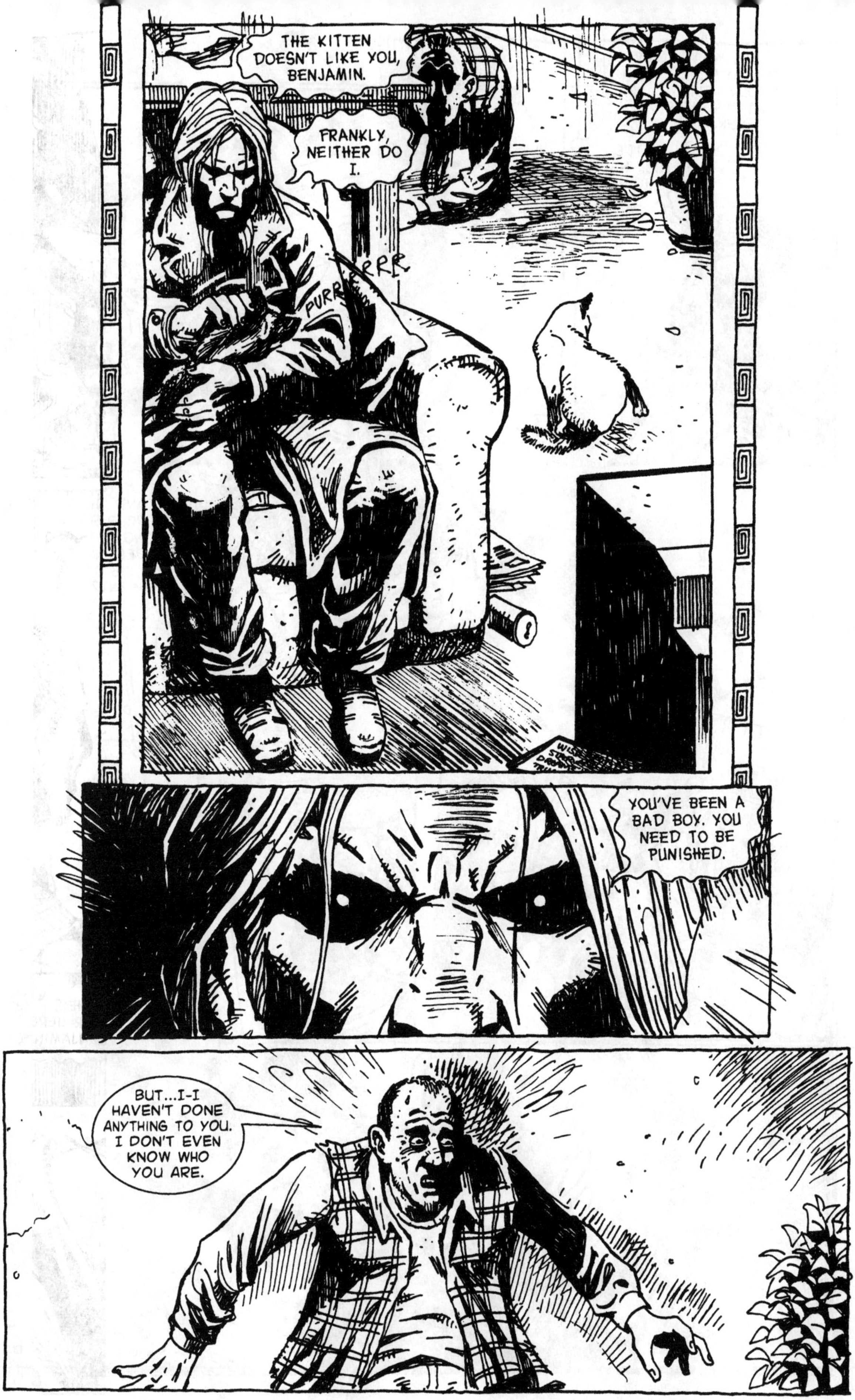
THE KITTEN DOESN'T LIKE YOU, BENJAMIN.
FRANKLY, NEITHER DO I.
PURRRRRR
YOU'VE BEEN A BAD BOY. YOU NEED TO BE PUNISHED.
BUT...I-I HAVEN'T DONE ANYTHING TO YOU. I DON'T EVEN KNOW WHO YOU ARE.

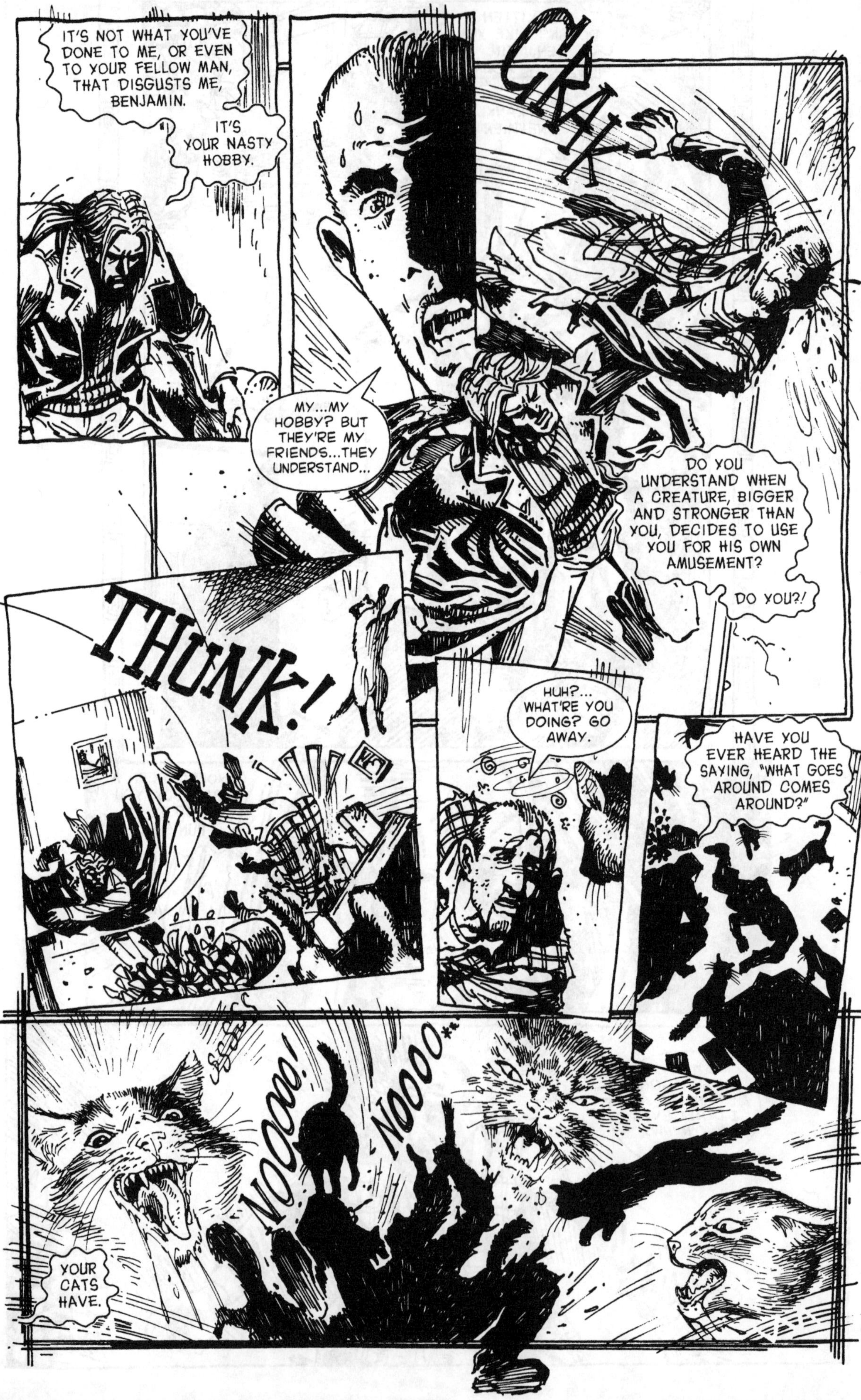
IT'S NOT WHAT YOU'VE DONE TO ME, OR EVEN TO YOUR FELLOW MAN, THAT DISGUSTS ME, BENJAMIN.
IT'S YOUR NASTY HOBBY.
CRAK
MY...MY HOBBY? BUT THEY'RE MY FRIENDS...THEY UNDERSTAND...
DO YOU UNDERSTAND WHEN A CREATURE, BIGGER AND STRONGER THAN YOU, DECIDES TO USE YOU FOR HIS OWN AMUSEMENT?
DO YOU?!
THUNK!
HUH?... WHAT'RE YOU DOING? GO AWAY.
HAVE YOU EVER HEARD THE SAYING, "WHAT GOES AROUND COMES AROUND?"
NOOOOO!
NOOOO
YOUR CATS HAVE.

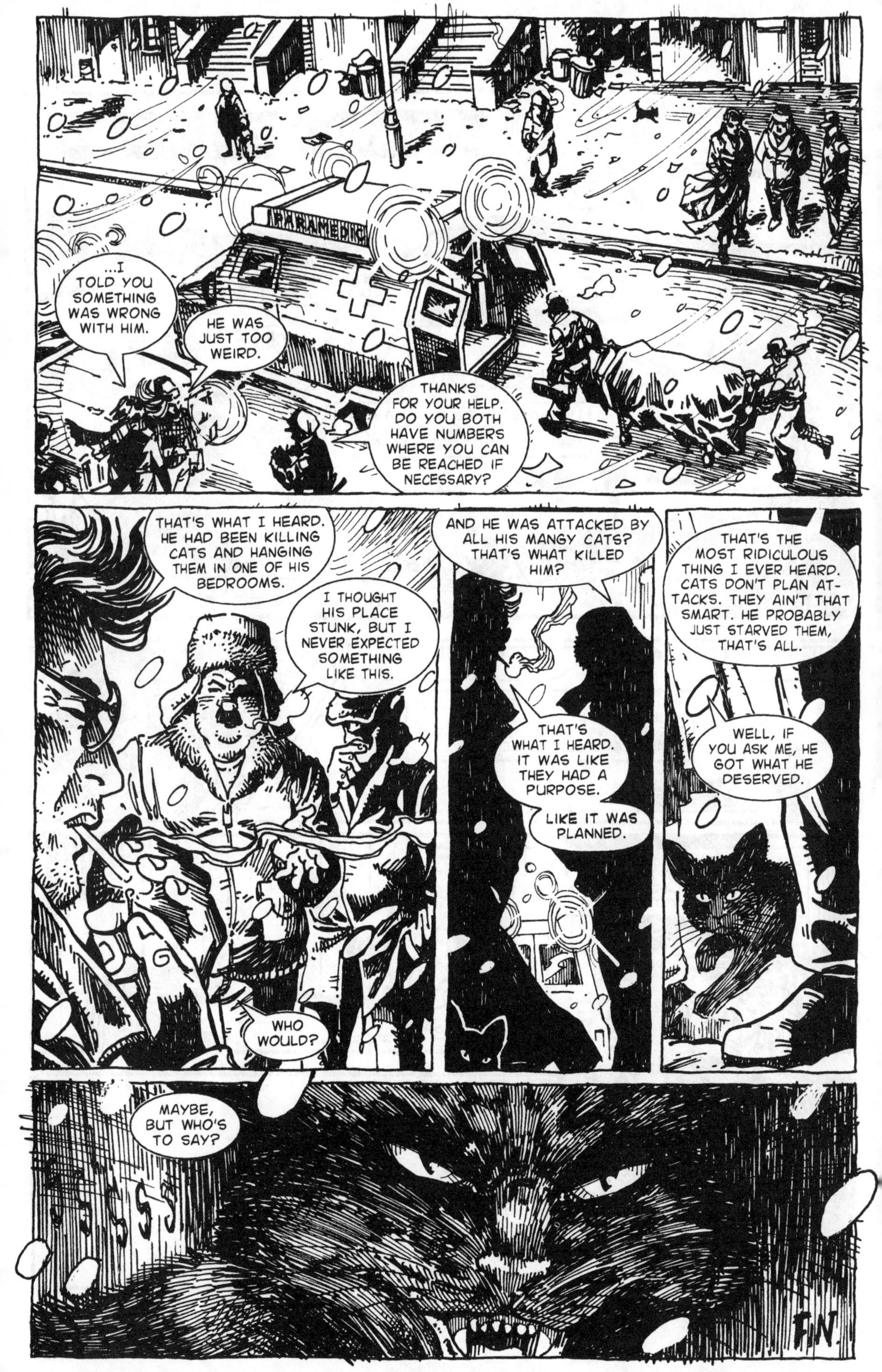
PARAMEDIC
...I TOLD YOU SOMETHING WAS WRONG WITH HIM.
HE WAS JUST TOO WEIRD.
THANKS FOR YOUR HELP. DO YOU BOTH HAVE NUMBERS WHERE YOU CAN BE REACHED IF NECESSARY?
THAT'S WHAT I HEARD. HE HAD BEEN KILLING CATS AND HANGING THEM IN ONE OF HIS BEDROOMS.
I THOUGHT HIS PLACE STUNK, BUT I NEVER EXPECTED SOMETHING LIKE THIS.
WHO WOULD?
AND HE WAS ATTACKED BY ALL HIS MANGY CATS? THAT'S WHAT KILLED HIM?
THAT'S WHAT I HEARD. IT WAS LIKE THEY HAD A PURPOSE.
LIKE IT WAS PLANNED.
THAT'S THE MOST RIDICULOUS THING I EVER HEARD. CATS DON'T PLAN AT-TACKS. THEY AIN'T THAT SMART. HE PROBABLY JUST STARVED THEM, THAT'S ALL.
WELL, IF YOU ASK ME, HE GOT WHAT HE DESERVED.
MAYBE, BUT WHO'S TO SAY?
SSSS
F.N.

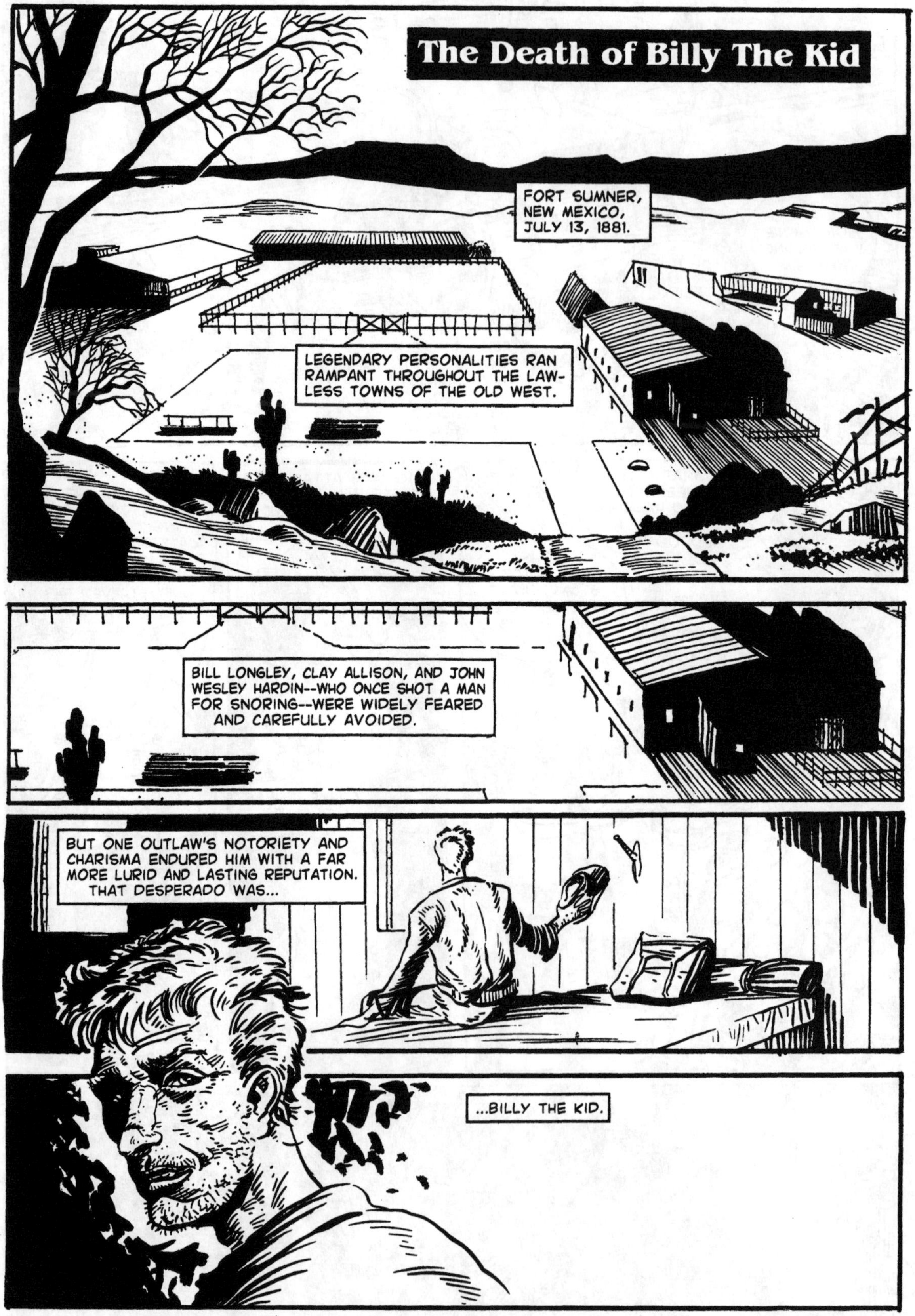
The Death of Billy The Kid
FORT SUMNER, NEW MEXICO, JULY 13, 1881.
LEGENDARY PERSONALITIES RAN RAMPANT THROUGHOUT THE LAWLESS TOWNS OF THE OLD WEST.
BILL LONGLEY, CLAY ALLISON, AND JOHN WESLEY HARDIN--WHO ONCE SHOT A MAN FOR SNORING--WERE WIDELY FEARED AND CAREFULLY AVOIDED.
BUT ONE OUTLAW'S NOTORIETY AND CHARISMA ENDURED HIM WITH A FAR MORE LURID AND LASTING REPUTATION. THAT DESPERADO WAS...
...BILLY THE KID.

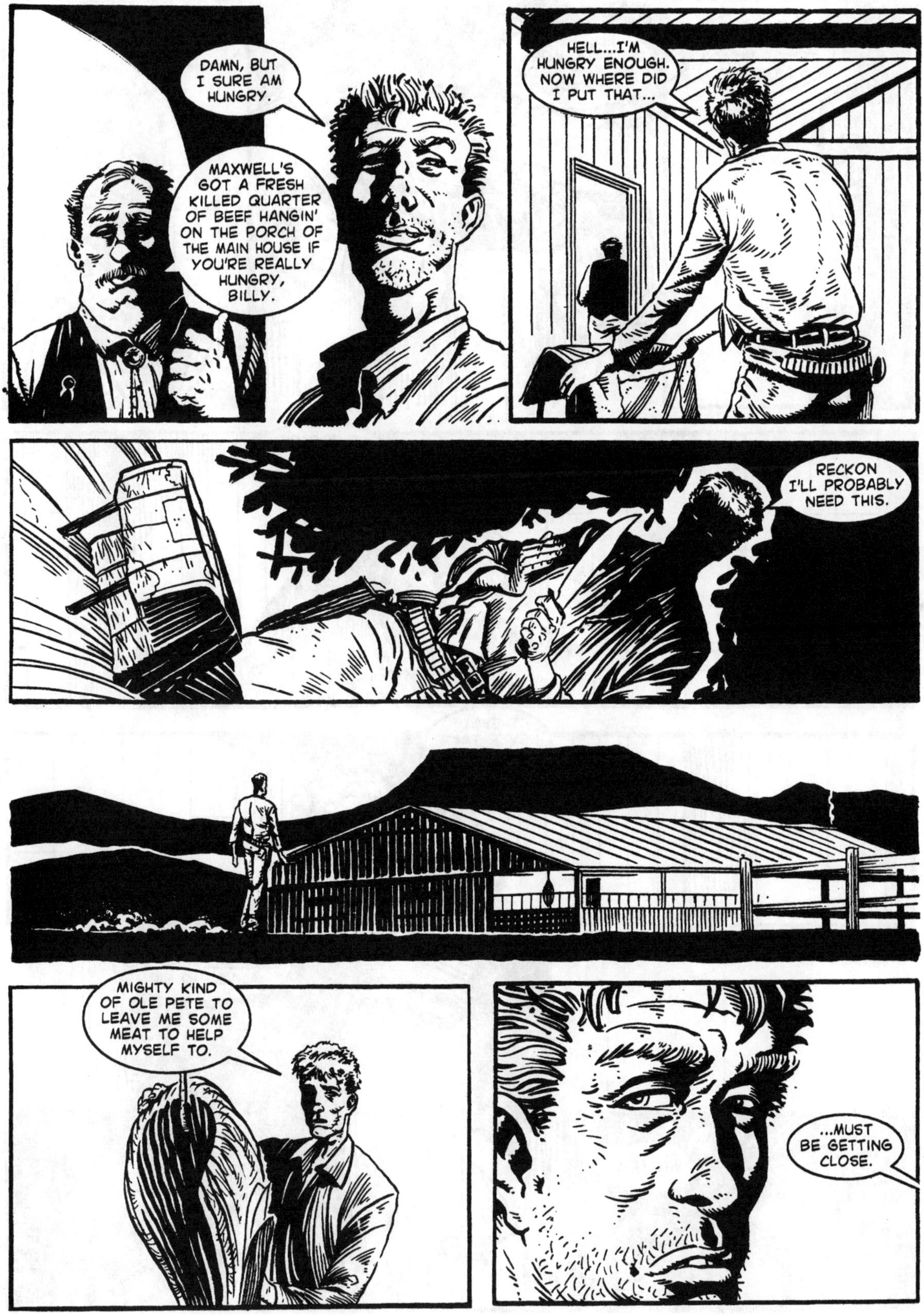
DAMN, BUT I SURE AM HUNGRY.
MAXWELL'S GOT A FRESH KILLED QUARTER OF BEEF HANGIN' ON THE PORCH OF THE MAIN HOUSE IF YOU'RE REALLY HUNGRY, BILLY.
HELL...I'M HUNGRY ENOUGH. NOW WHERE DID I PUT THAT...
RECKON I'LL PROBABLY NEED THIS.
MIGHTY KIND OF OLE PETE TO LEAVE ME SOME MEAT TO HELP MYSELF TO.
...MUST BE GETTING CLOSE.

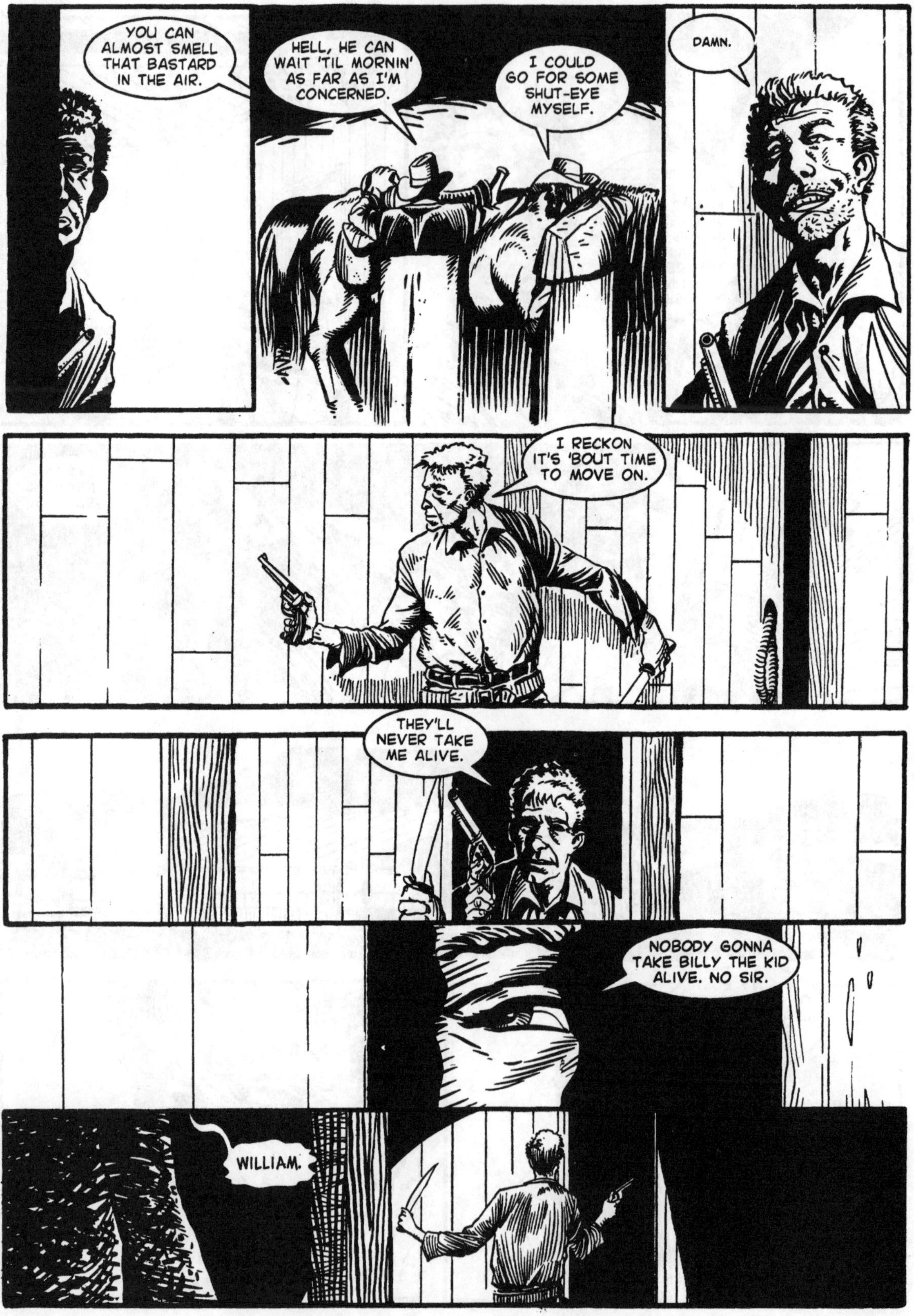
YOU CAN ALMOST SMELL THAT BASTARD IN THE AIR.
HELL, HE CAN WAIT 'TIL MORNIN' AS FAR AS I'M CONCERNED.
I COULD GO FOR SOME SHUT-EYE MYSELF.
DAMN.
I RECKON IT'S 'BOUT TIME TO MOVE ON.
THEY'LL NEVER TAKE ME ALIVE.
NOBODY GONNA TAKE BILLY THE KID ALIVE. NO SIR.
WILLIAM.

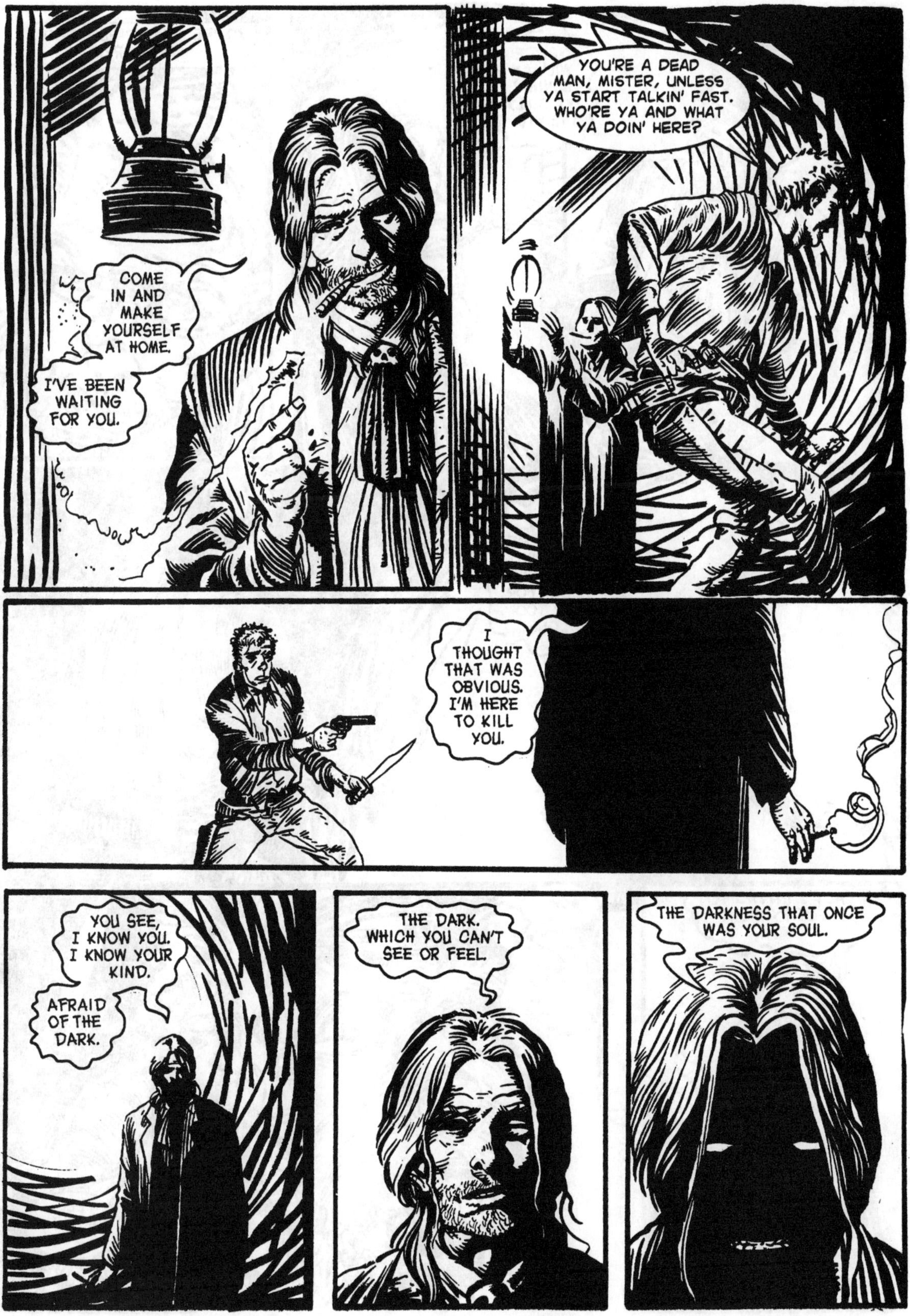
COME IN AND MAKE YOURSELF AT HOME.
I'VE BEEN WAITING FOR YOU.
YOU'RE A DEAD MAN, MISTER, UNLESS YA START TALKIN' FAST. WHO'RE YA AND WHAT YA DOIN' HERE?
I THOUGHT THAT WAS OBVIOUS. I'M HERE TO KILL YOU.
YOU SEE, I KNOW YOU. I KNOW YOUR KIND.
AFRAID OF THE DARK.
THE DARK. WHICH YOU CAN'T SEE OR FEEL.
THE DARKNESS THAT ONCE WAS YOUR SOUL.

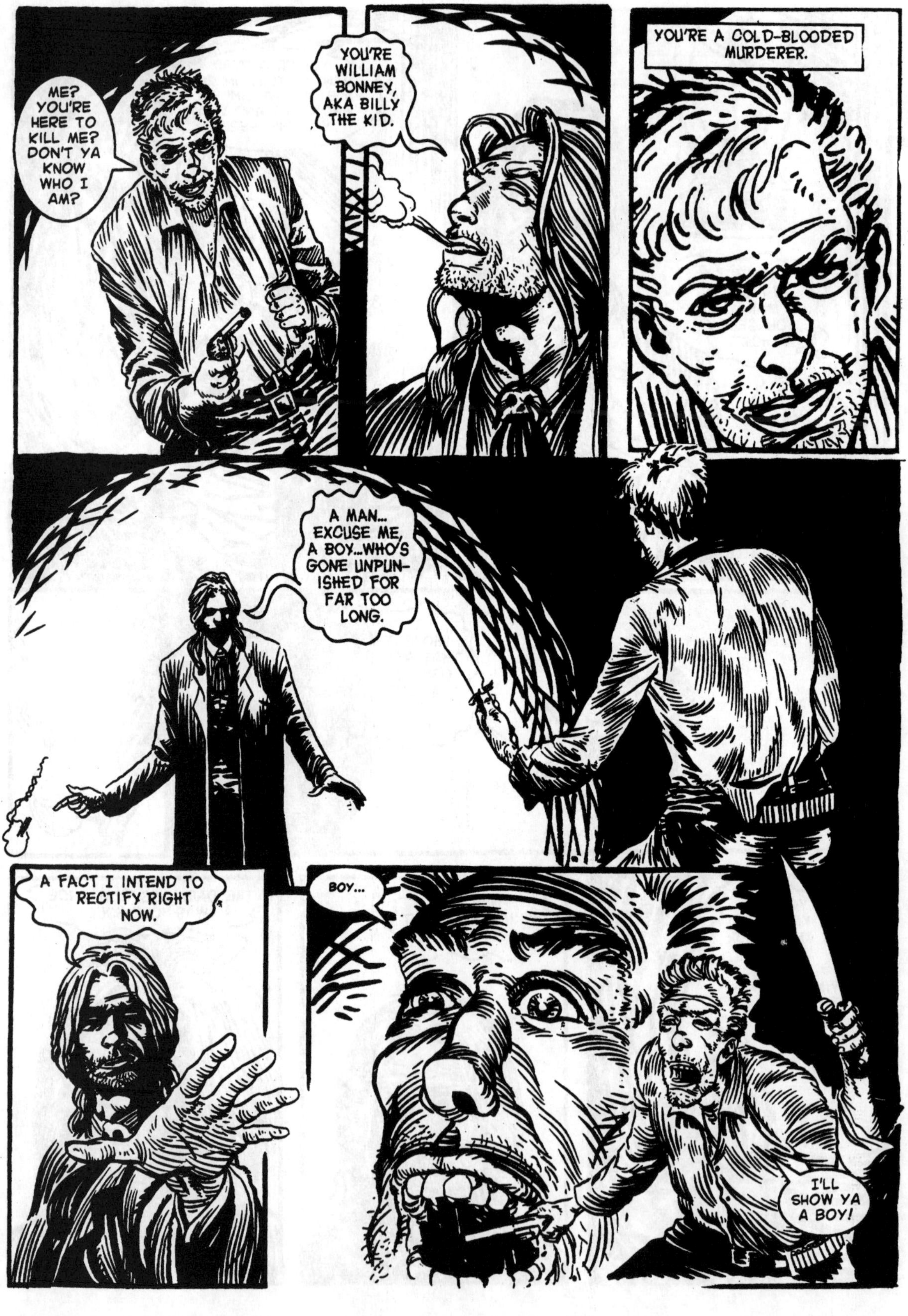
ME? YOU'RE HERE TO KILL ME? DON'T YA KNOW WHO I AM?
YOU'RE WILLIAM BONNEY, AKA BILLY THE KID.
YOU'RE A COLD-BLOODED MURDERER.
A MAN... EXCUSE ME, A BOY...WHO'S GONE UNPUNISHED FOR FAR TOO LONG.
A FACT I INTEND TO RECTIFY RIGHT NOW.
BOY...
I'LL SHOW YA A BOY!

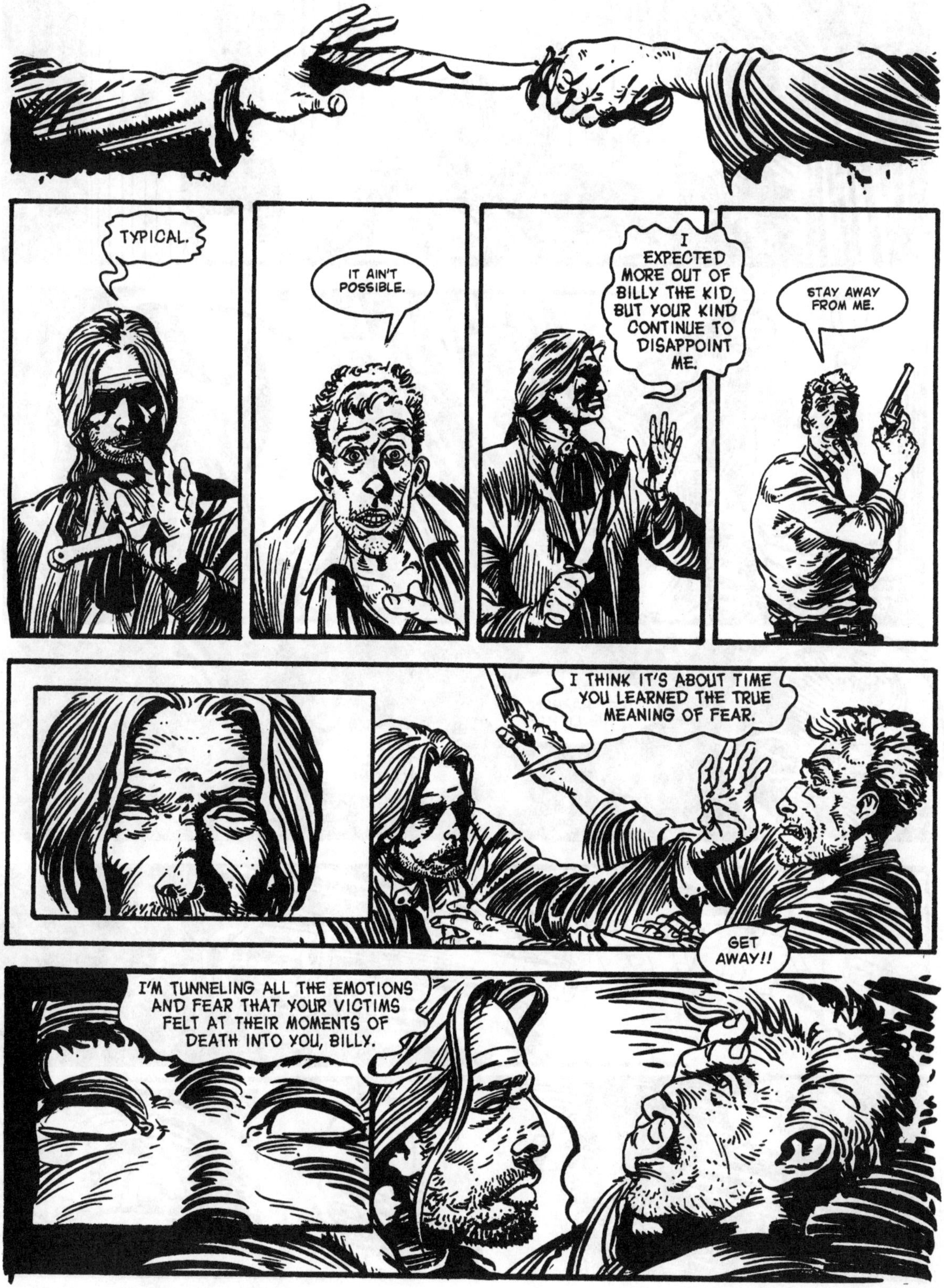
TYPICAL.
IT AIN'T POSSIBLE.
I EXPECTED MORE OUT OF BILLY THE KID, BUT YOUR KIND CONTINUE TO DISAPPOINT ME.
STAY AWAY FROM ME.
I THINK IT'S ABOUT TIME YOU LEARNED THE TRUE MEANING OF FEAR.
GET AWAY!!
I'M TUNNELING ALL THE EMOTIONS AND FEAR THAT YOUR VICTIMS FELT AT THEIR MOMENTS OF DEATH INTO YOU, BILLY.

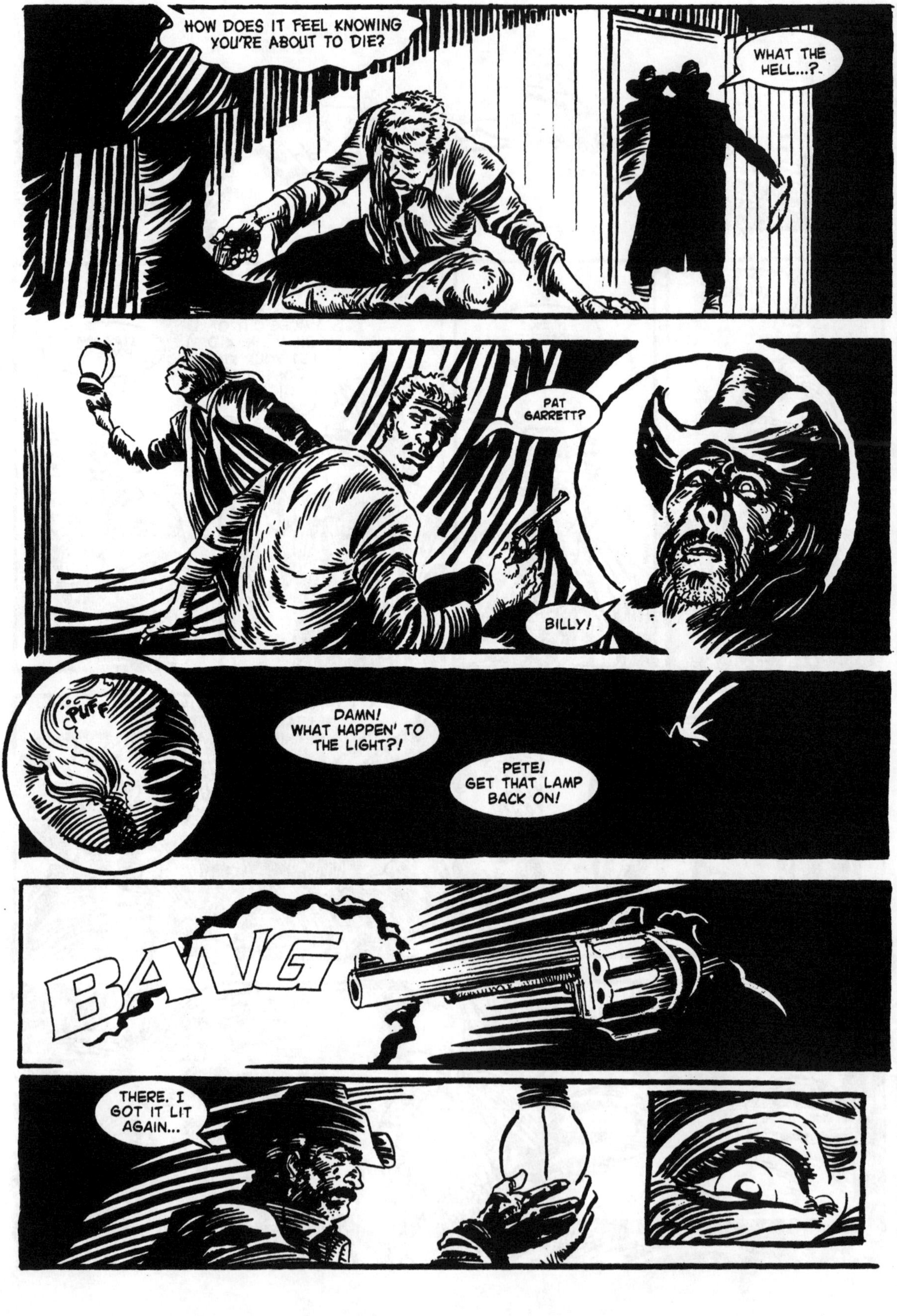
HOW DOES IT FEEL KNOWING YOU'RE ABOUT TO DIE?
WHAT THE HELL...?
PAT GARRETT?
BILLY!
PUFF
DAMN! WHAT HAPPEN' TO THE LIGHT?!
PETE! GET THAT LAMP BACK ON!
BANG
THERE. I GOT IT LIT AGAIN...

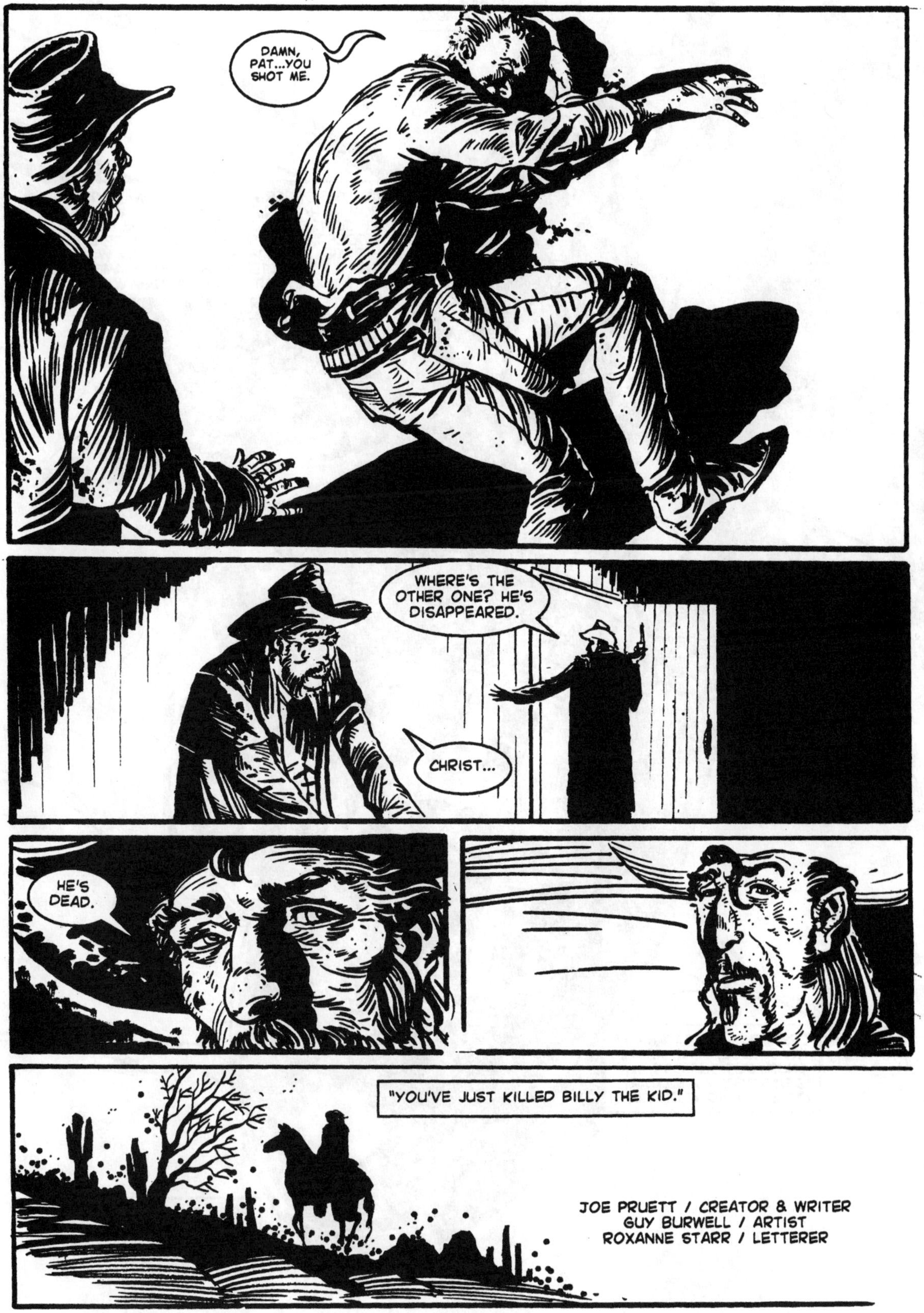
DAMN, PAT...YOU SHOT ME.
WHERE'S THE OTHER ONE? HE'S DISAPPEARED.
CHRIST...
HE'S DEAD.
"YOU'VE JUST KILLED BILLY THE KID."
JOE PRUETT / CREATOR & WRITER
GUY BURWELL / ARTIST
ROXANNE STARR / LETTERER

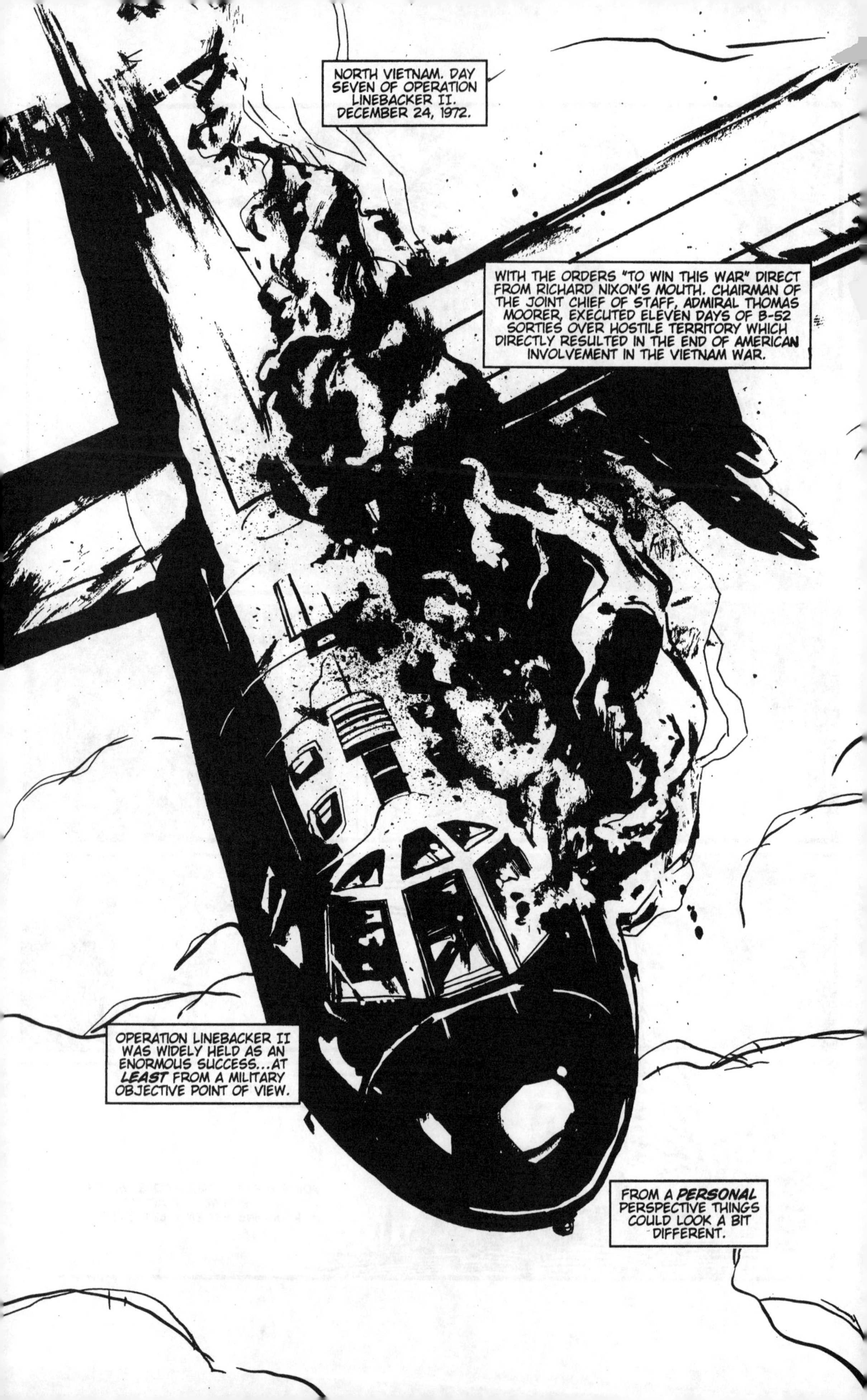
NORTH VIETNAM. DAY SEVEN OF OPERATION LINEBACKER II. DECEMBER 24, 1972.
WITH THE ORDERS "TO WIN THIS WAR" DIRECT FROM RICHARD NIXON'S MOUTH. CHAIRMAN OF THE JOINT CHIEF OF STAFF, ADMIRAL THOMAS MOORER, EXECUTED ELEVEN DAYS OF B-52 SORTIES OVER HOSTILE TERRITORY WHICH DIRECTLY RESULTED IN THE END OF AMERICAN INVOLVEMENT IN THE VIETNAM WAR.
OPERATION LINEBACKER II WAS WIDELY HELD AS AN ENORMOUS SUCCESS...AT *LEAST* FROM A MILITARY OBJECTIVE POINT OF VIEW.
FROM A *PERSONAL* PERSPECTIVE THINGS COULD LOOK A BIT DIFFERENT.

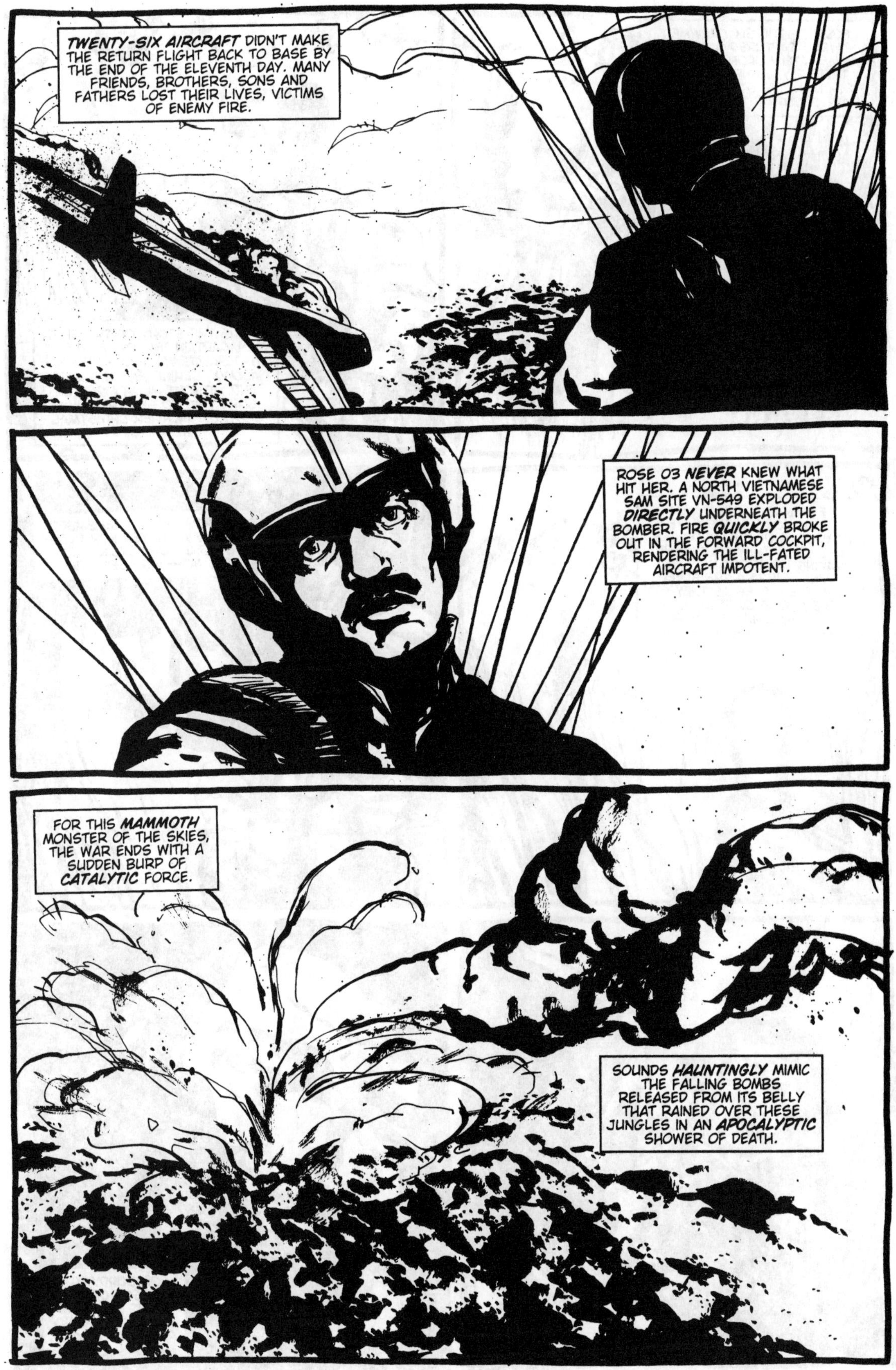
TWENTY-SIX AIRCRAFT DIDN'T MAKE THE RETURN FLIGHT BACK TO BASE BY THE END OF THE ELEVENTH DAY. MANY FRIENDS, BROTHERS, SONS AND FATHERS LOST THEIR LIVES, VICTIMS OF ENEMY FIRE.
ROSE 03 NEVER KNEW WHAT HIT HER. A NORTH VIETNAMESE SAM SITE VN-549 EXPLODED DIRECTLY UNDERNEATH THE BOMBER. FIRE QUICKLY BROKE OUT IN THE FORWARD COCKPIT, RENDERING THE ILL-FATED AIRCRAFT IMPOTENT.
FOR THIS MAMMOTH MONSTER OF THE SKIES, THE WAR ENDS WITH A SUDDEN BURP OF CATALYTIC FORCE.
SOUNDS HAUNTINGLY MIMIC THE FALLING BOMBS RELEASED FROM ITS BELLY THAT RAINED OVER THESE JUNGLES IN AN APOCALYPTIC SHOWER OF DEATH.

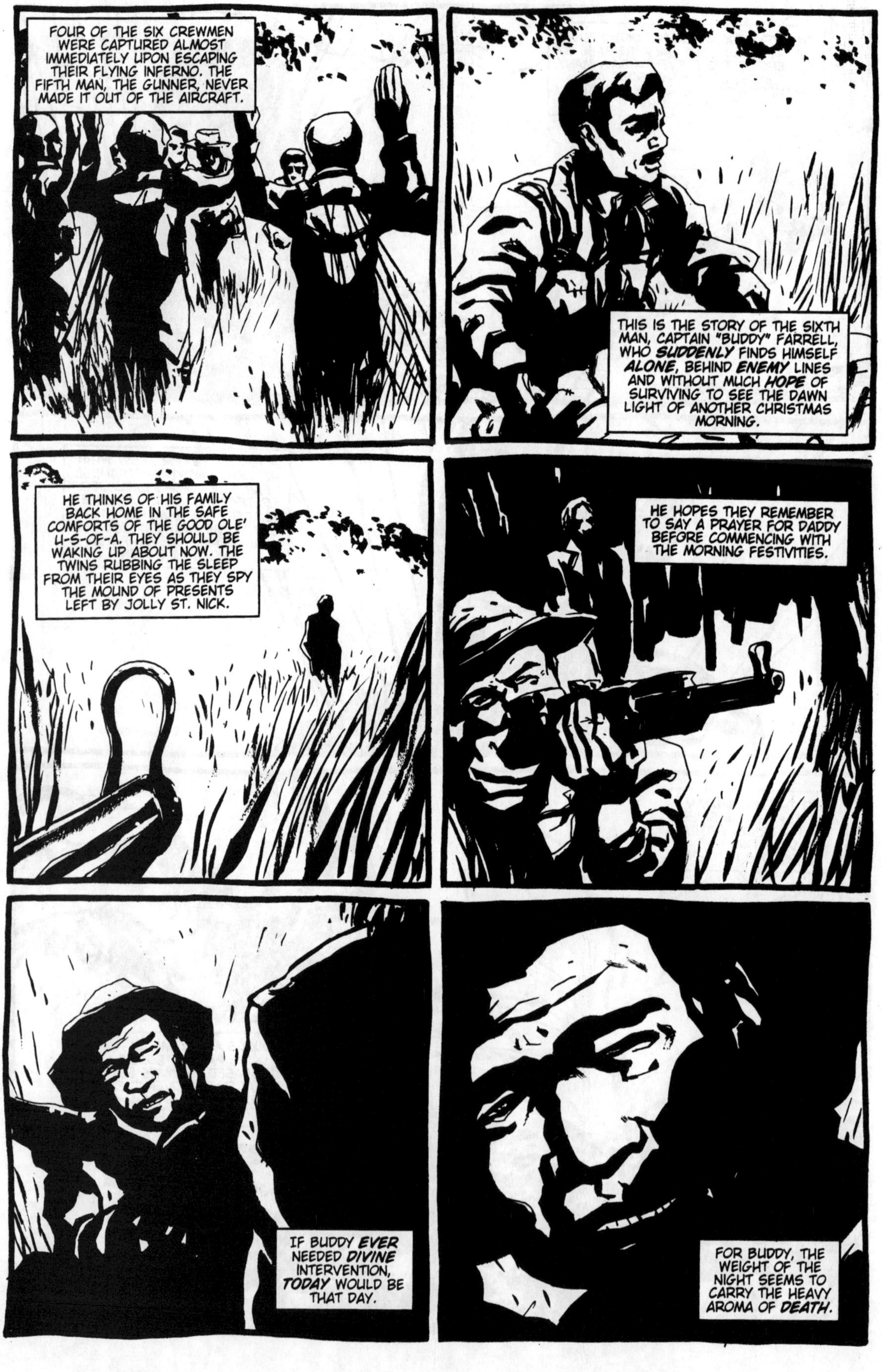
FOUR OF THE SIX CREWMEN WERE CAPTURED ALMOST IMMEDIATELY UPON ESCAPING THEIR FLYING INFERNO. THE FIFTH MAN, THE GUNNER, NEVER MADE IT OUT OF THE AIRCRAFT.
THIS IS THE STORY OF THE SIXTH MAN, CAPTAIN "BUDDY" FARRELL, WHO SUDDENLY FINDS HIMSELF ALONE, BEHIND ENEMY LINES AND WITHOUT MUCH HOPE OF SURVIVING TO SEE THE DAWN LIGHT OF ANOTHER CHRISTMAS MORNING.
HE THINKS OF HIS FAMILY BACK HOME IN THE SAFE COMFORTS OF THE GOOD OLE' U-S-OF-A. THEY SHOULD BE WAKING UP ABOUT NOW. THE TWINS RUBBING THE SLEEP FROM THEIR EYES AS THEY SPY THE MOUND OF PRESENTS LEFT BY JOLLY ST. NICK.
HE HOPES THEY REMEMBER TO SAY A PRAYER FOR DADDY BEFORE COMMENCING WITH THE MORNING FESTIVITIES.
IF BUDDY EVER NEEDED DIVINE INTERVENTION, TODAY WOULD BE THAT DAY.
FOR BUDDY, THE WEIGHT OF THE NIGHT SEEMS TO CARRY THE HEAVY AROMA OF DEATH.

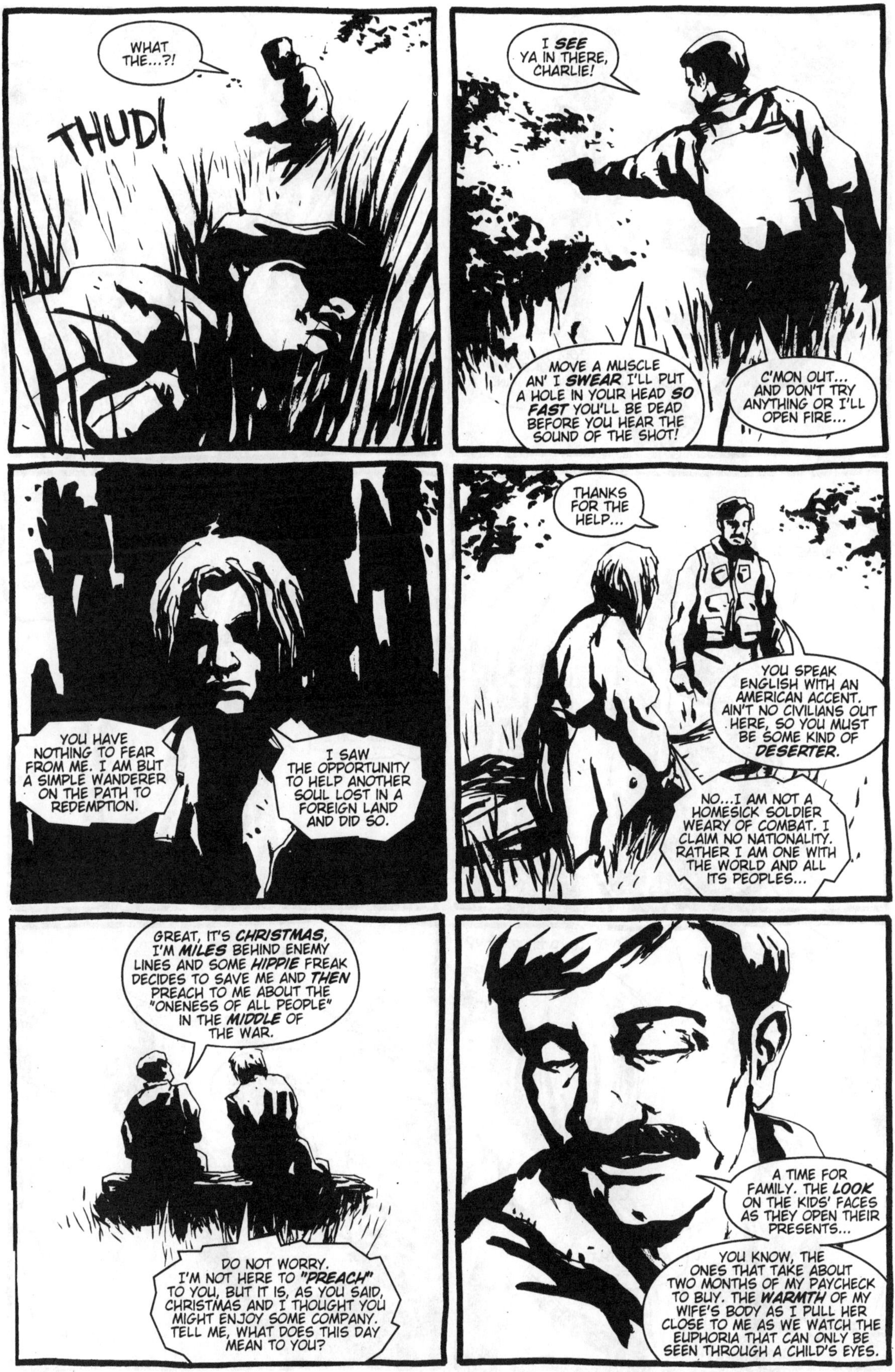
WHAT THE...?!
THUD!
I SEE YA IN THERE, CHARLIE!
C'MON OUT... AND DON'T TRY ANYTHING OR I'LL OPEN FIRE...
MOVE A MUSCLE AN' I SWEAR I'LL PUT A HOLE IN YOUR HEAD SO FAST YOU'LL BE DEAD BEFORE YOU HEAR THE SOUND OF THE SHOT!
YOU HAVE NOTHING TO FEAR FROM ME. I AM BUT A SIMPLE WANDERER ON THE PATH TO REDEMPTION.
I SAW THE OPPORTUNITY TO HELP ANOTHER SOUL LOST IN A FOREIGN LAND AND DID SO.
THANKS FOR THE HELP...
YOU SPEAK ENGLISH WITH AN AMERICAN ACCENT. AIN'T NO CIVILIANS OUT HERE, SO YOU MUST BE SOME KIND OF DESERTER.
NO...I AM NOT A HOMESICK SOLDIER WEARY OF COMBAT. I CLAIM NO NATIONALITY. RATHER I AM ONE WITH THE WORLD AND ALL ITS PEOPLES...
GREAT, IT'S CHRISTMAS, I'M MILES BEHIND ENEMY LINES AND SOME HIPPIE FREAK DECIDES TO SAVE ME AND THEN PREACH TO ME ABOUT THE "ONENESS OF ALL PEOPLE" IN THE MIDDLE OF THE WAR.
DO NOT WORRY. I'M NOT HERE TO "PREACH" TO YOU, BUT IT IS, AS YOU SAID, CHRISTMAS AND I THOUGHT YOU MIGHT ENJOY SOME COMPANY. TELL ME, WHAT DOES THIS DAY MEAN TO YOU?
A TIME FOR FAMILY. THE LOOK ON THE KIDS' FACES AS THEY OPEN THEIR PRESENTS...
YOU KNOW, THE ONES THAT TAKE ABOUT TWO MONTHS OF MY PAYCHECK TO BUY. THE WARMTH OF MY WIFE'S BODY AS I PULL HER CLOSE TO ME AS WE WATCH THE EUPHORIA THAT CAN ONLY BE SEEN THROUGH A CHILD'S EYES.

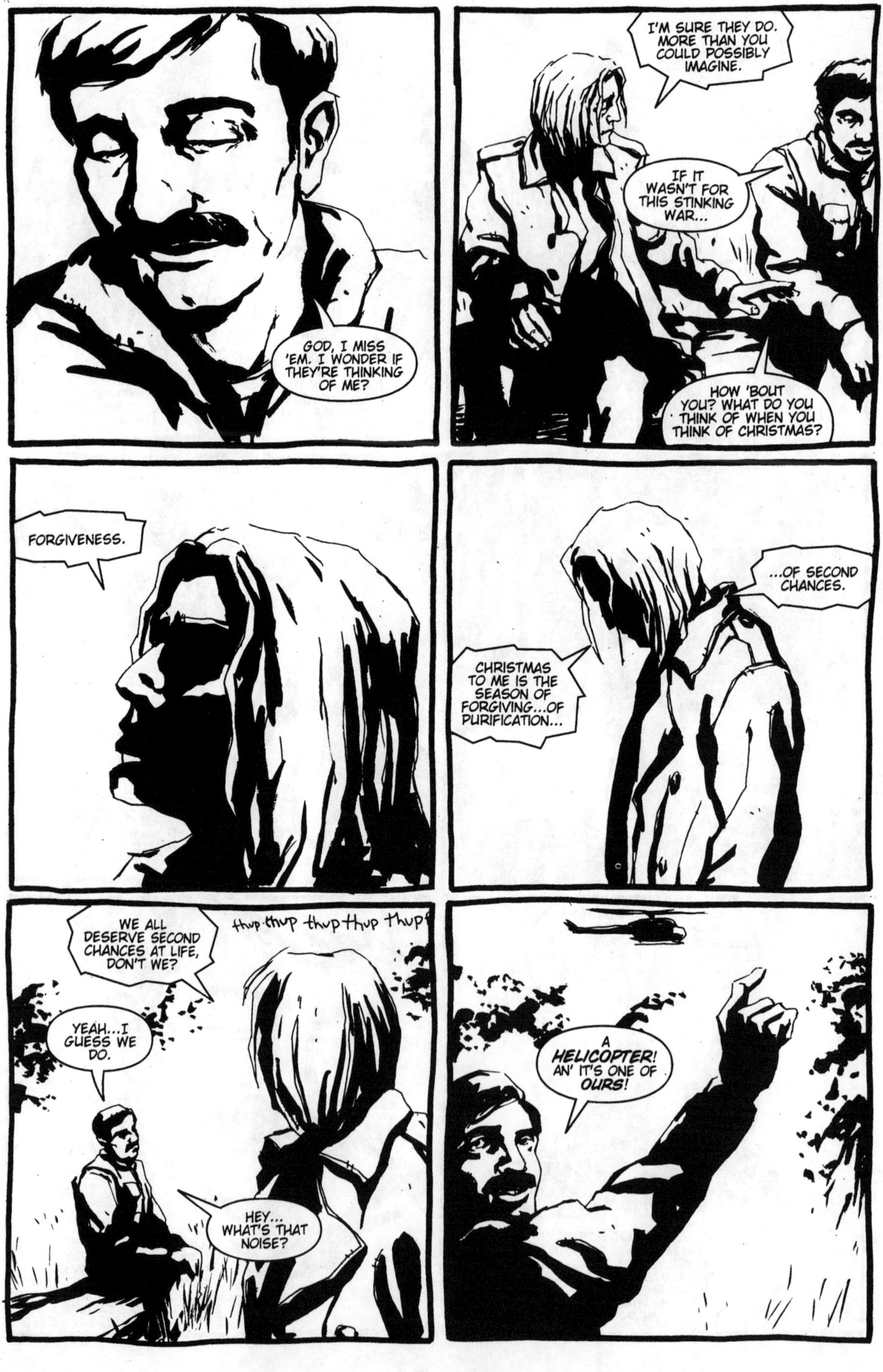
GOD, I MISS 'EM. I WONDER IF THEY'RE THINKING OF ME?
I'M SURE THEY DO. MORE THAN YOU COULD POSSIBLY IMAGINE.
IF IT WASN'T FOR THIS STINKING WAR...
HOW 'BOUT YOU? WHAT DO YOU THINK OF WHEN YOU THINK OF CHRISTMAS?
FORGIVENESS.
CHRISTMAS TO ME IS THE SEASON OF FORGIVING...OF PURIFICATION...
...OF SECOND CHANCES.
WE ALL DESERVE SECOND CHANCES AT LIFE, DON'T WE?
thup thup thup thup thup
YEAH...I GUESS WE DO.
HEY... WHAT'S THAT NOISE?
A HELICOPTER! AN' IT'S ONE OF OURS!

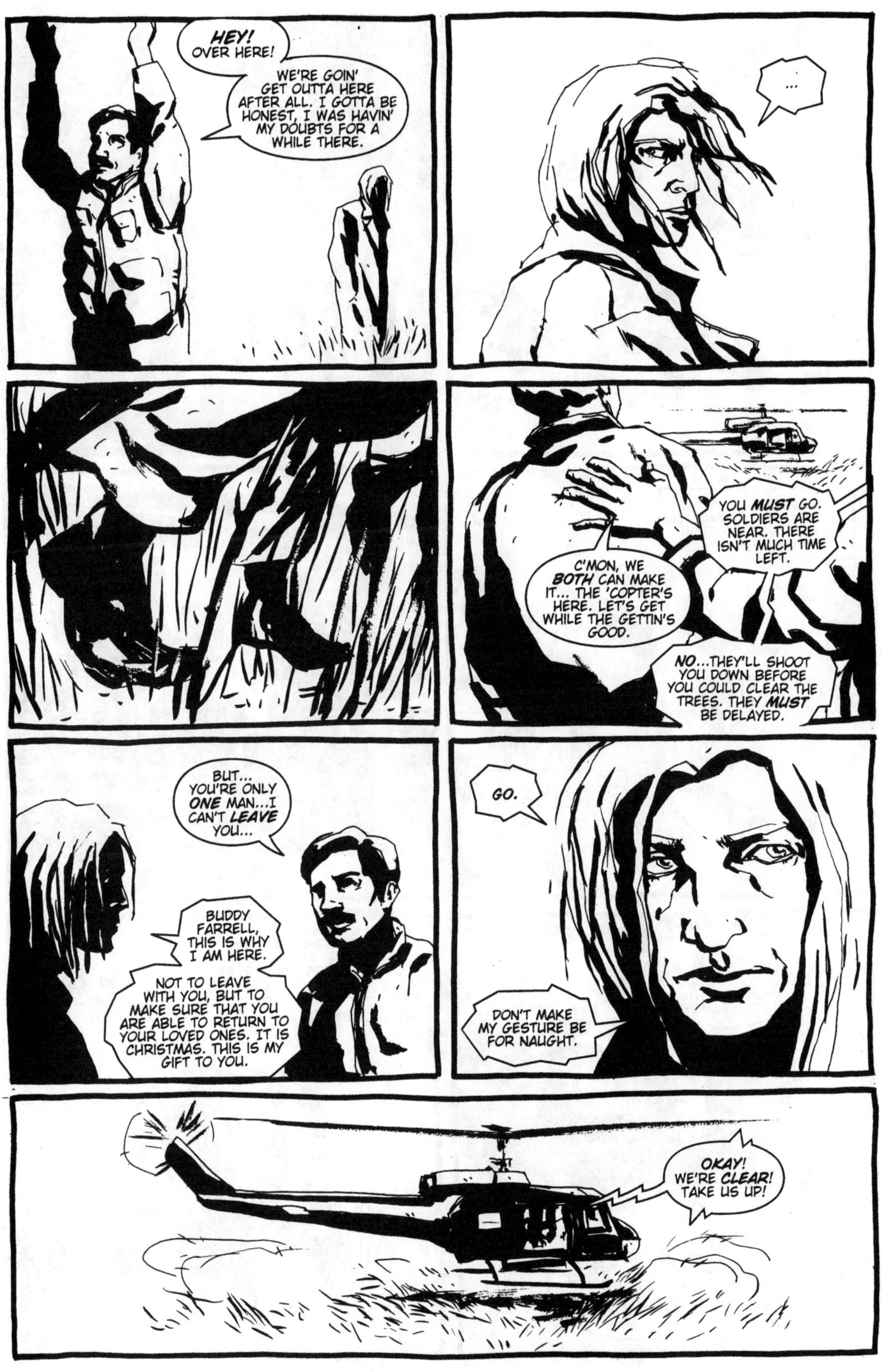
HEY! OVER HERE!
WE'RE GOIN' GET OUTTA HERE AFTER ALL. I GOTTA BE HONEST, I WAS HAVIN' MY DOUBTS FOR A WHILE THERE.
...
YOU MUST GO. SOLDIERS ARE NEAR. THERE ISN'T MUCH TIME LEFT.
C'MON, WE BOTH CAN MAKE IT... THE 'COPTER'S HERE. LET'S GET WHILE THE GETTIN'S GOOD.
NO...THEY'LL SHOOT YOU DOWN BEFORE YOU COULD CLEAR THE TREES. THEY MUST BE DELAYED.
BUT... YOU'RE ONLY ONE MAN...I CAN'T LEAVE YOU...
BUDDY FARRELL, THIS IS WHY I AM HERE.
NOT TO LEAVE WITH YOU, BUT TO MAKE SURE THAT YOU ARE ABLE TO RETURN TO YOUR LOVED ONES. IT IS CHRISTMAS. THIS IS MY GIFT TO YOU.
GO.
DON'T MAKE MY GESTURE BE FOR NAUGHT.
OKAY! WE'RE CLEAR! TAKE US UP!

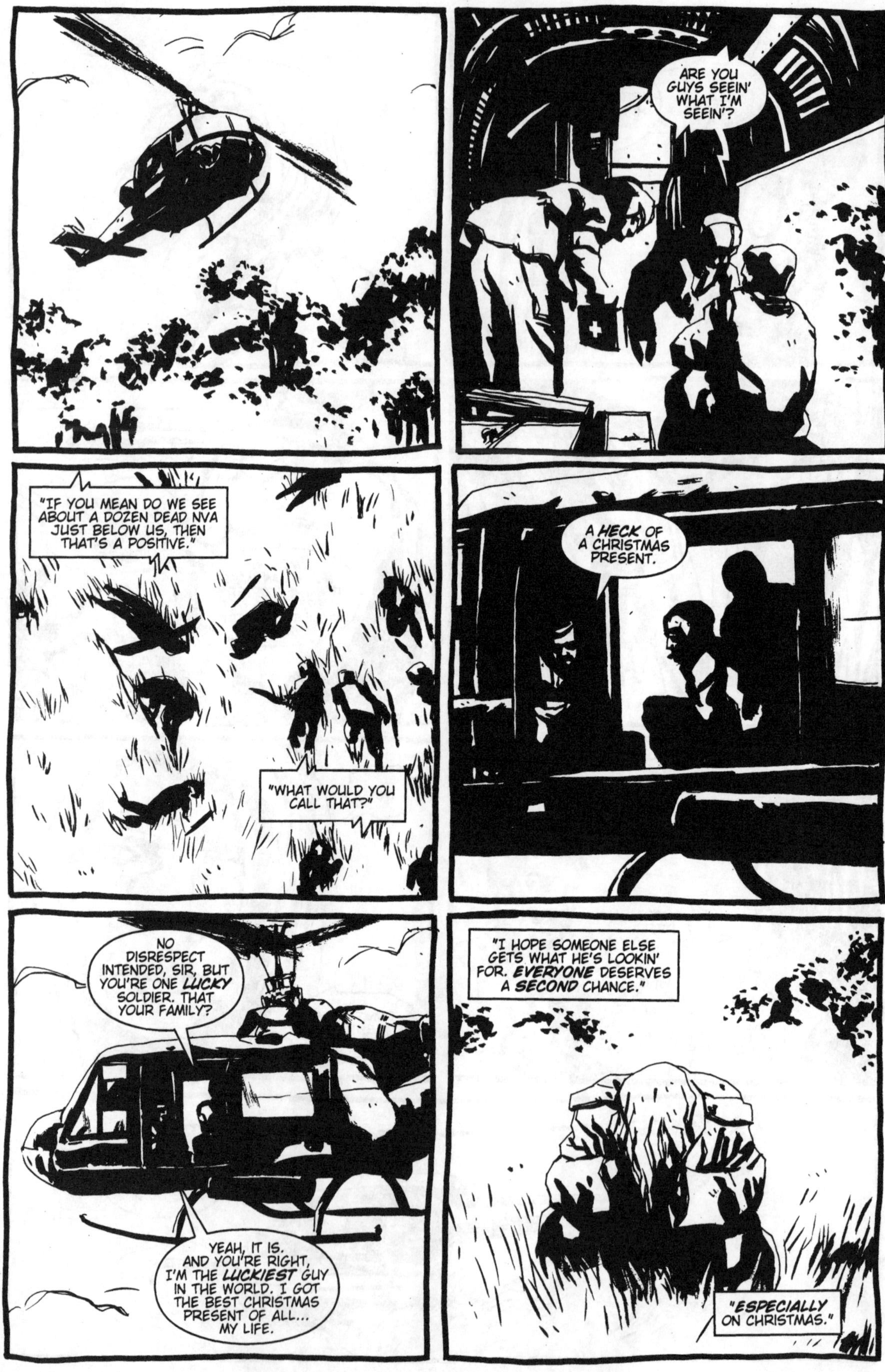
ARE YOU GUYS SEEIN' WHAT I'M SEEIN'?
"IF YOU MEAN DO WE SEE ABOUT A DOZEN DEAD NVA JUST BELOW US, THEN THAT'S A POSITIVE."
"WHAT WOULD YOU CALL THAT?"
A HECK OF A CHRISTMAS PRESENT.
NO DISRESPECT INTENDED, SIR, BUT YOU'RE ONE LUCKY SOLDIER. THAT YOUR FAMILY?
YEAH, IT IS. AND YOU'RE RIGHT, I'M THE LUCKIEST GUY IN THE WORLD. I GOT THE BEST CHRISTMAS PRESENT OF ALL... MY LIFE.
"I HOPE SOMEONE ELSE GETS WHAT HE'S LOOKIN' FOR. EVERYONE DESERVES A SECOND CHANCE."
"ESPECIALLY ON CHRISTMAS."

Pin Ups and Covers

page 354 — Brian Bolland
(cover to Kilroy: Daemonstorm Special)
page 355 — Joe Quesada
(exclusive cover to Kilroy #1 second series for AnotherUniverse.Com)
page 356 — Don Kramer
(cover to Kilroy: The Origin #1)
page 357 — Phil Hester
(pin up from Kilroy: Revelations #1)
page 358 — Matthew Smith
(pin up from Kilroy Is Here #2)
page 359 — D. Alexander Gregory and Andrew Robinson
(cover to Kilroy: The Short Stories)

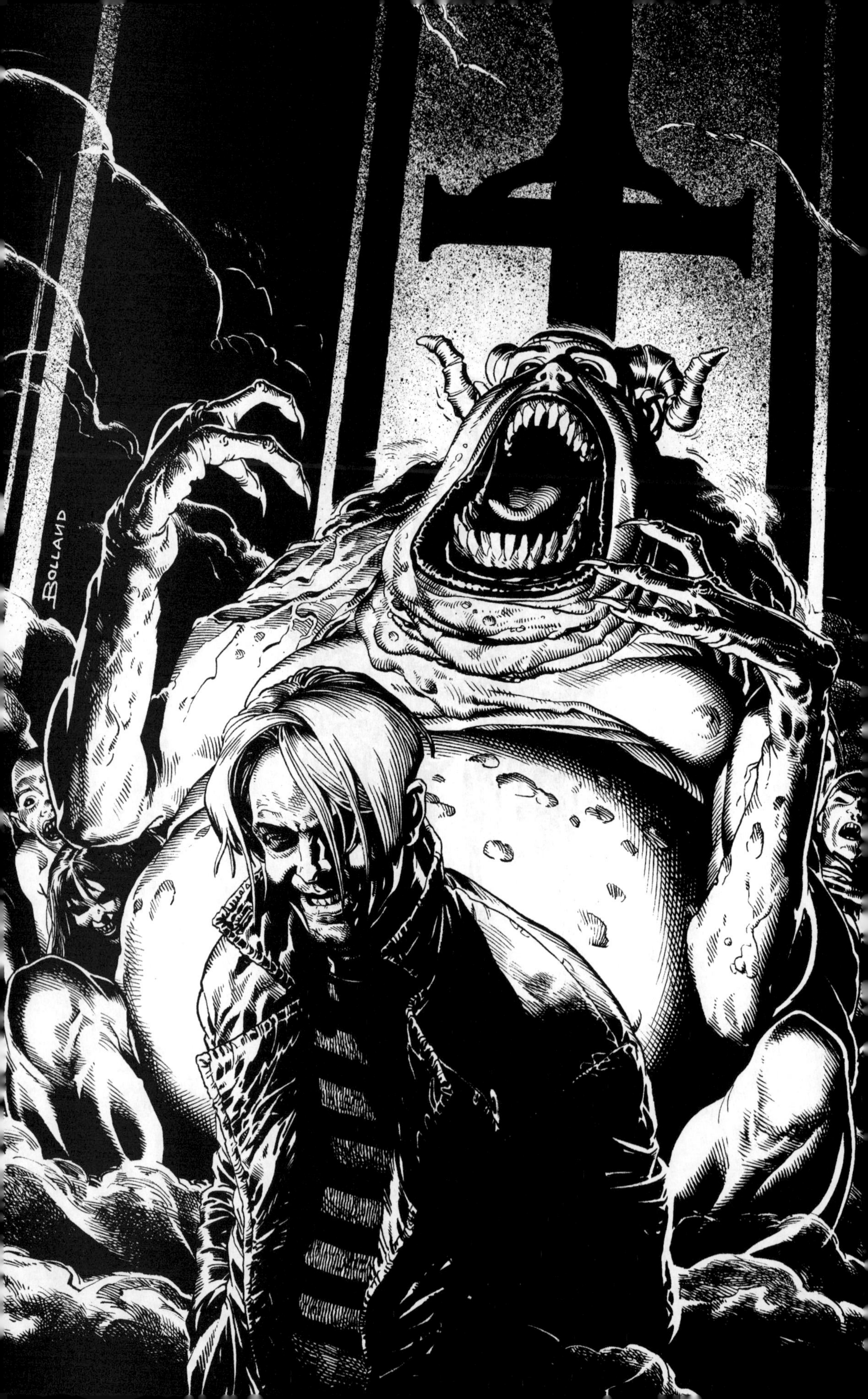
BOLLAND

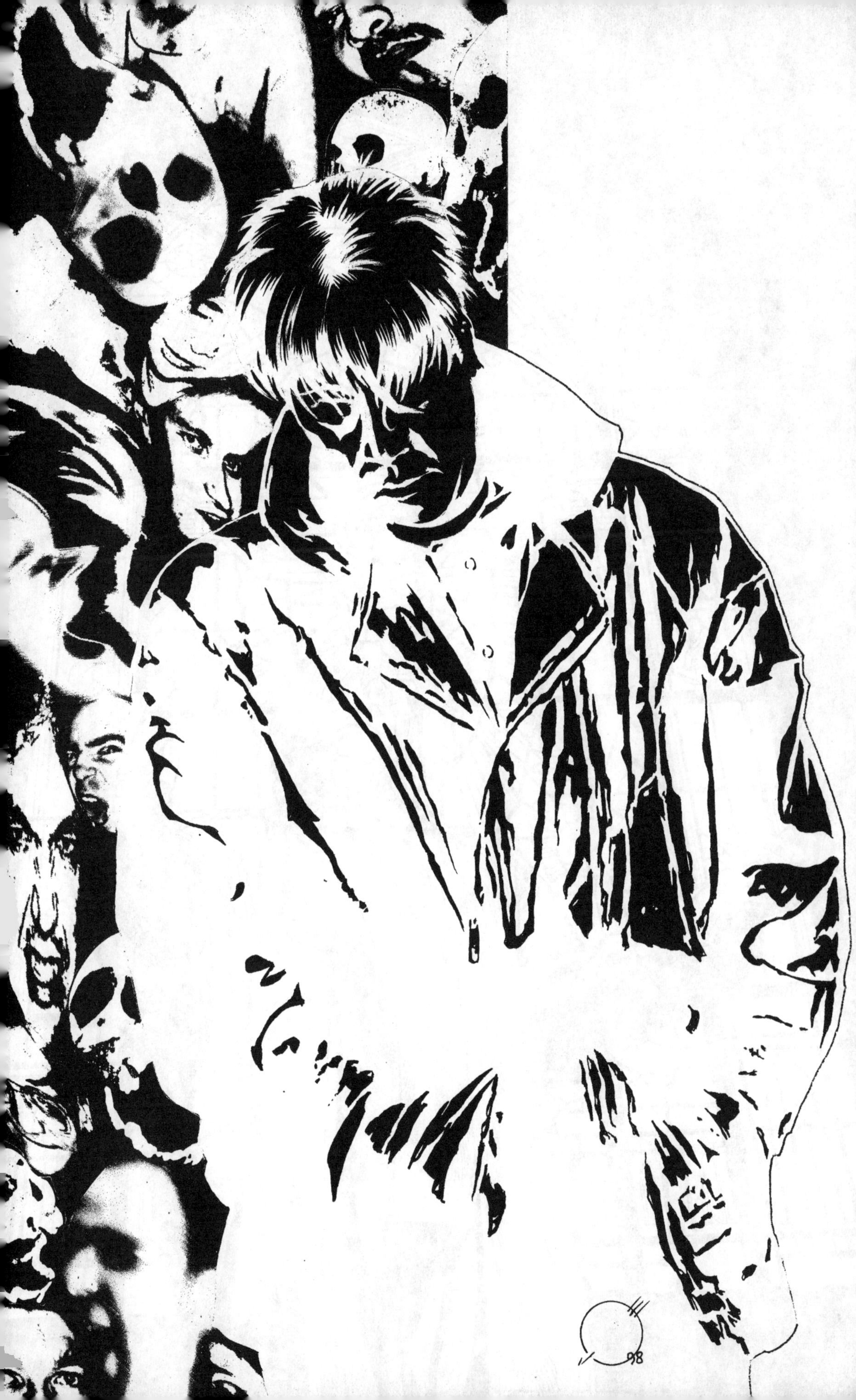

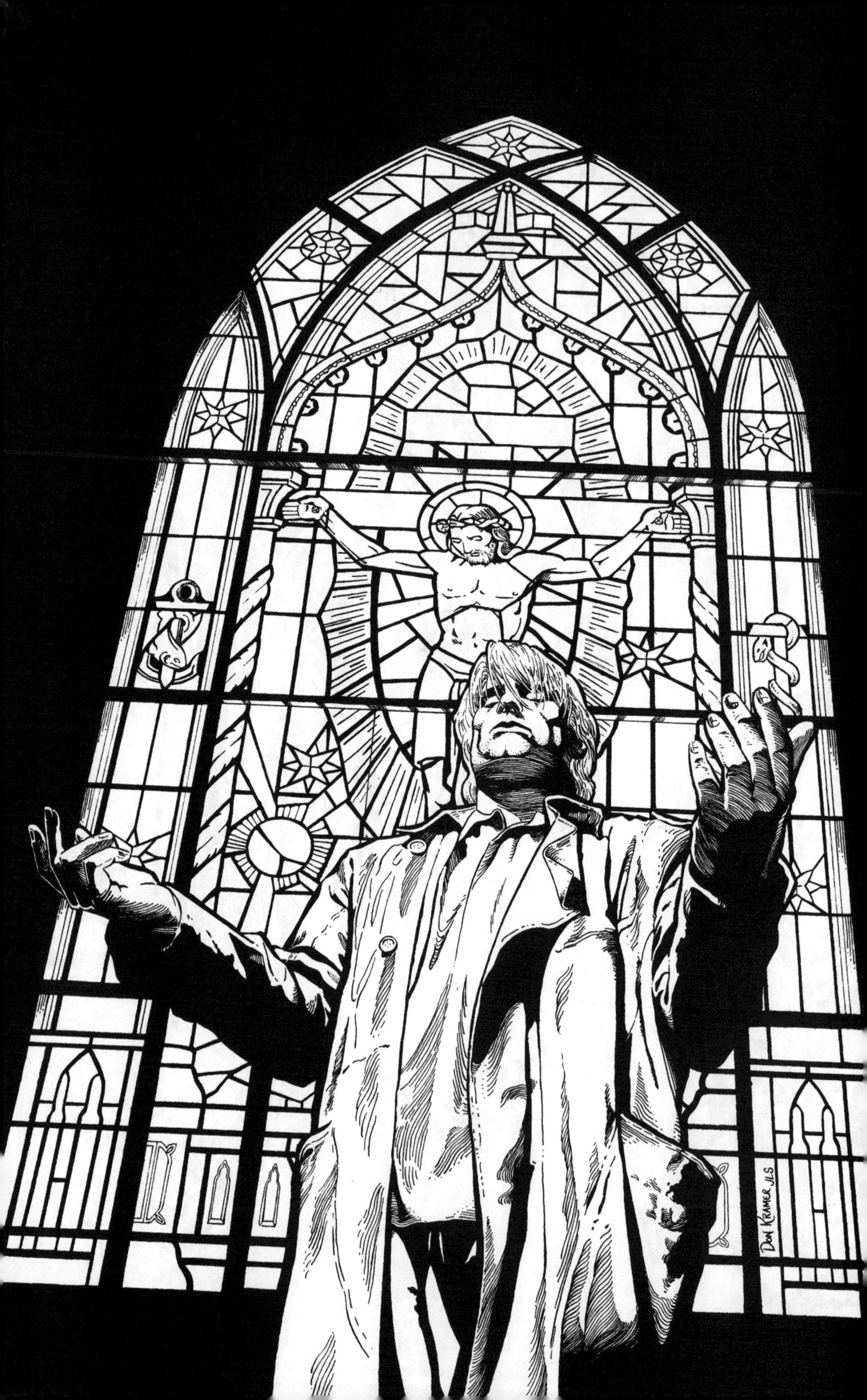
DON KRAMER JLS

Body found
Fisherman spots
body from bridge
(AP) — A body
found in the Des Moines River
matches the description of
Asian woman who was reported
missing this week, police
but officials are waiting
topsy results before
identification.
Shaken baby ca
The Sept. 12 trial of a
man accused of shaki
baby has been conti
in November,
Man hurt in stab
Aurora, Ill., man
counts of child endangerm
counts of willful injury ste
two separate incidents in No
1993.
Fight erupts at ba
A Cedar Falls bar fig
landed a Waterloo m
Police charge
Attempted murder alleg
According to court documents,

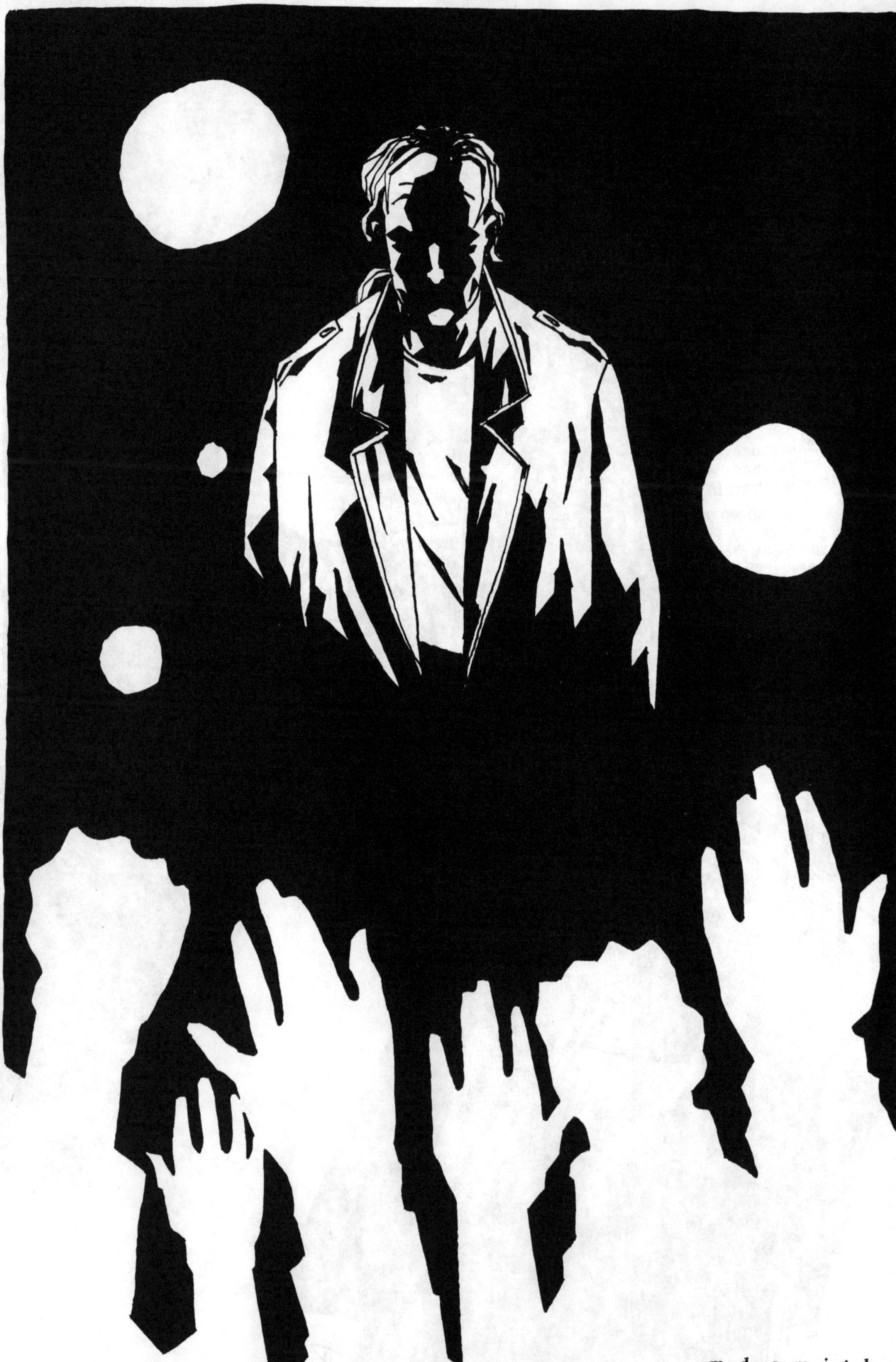
m d s m i t h

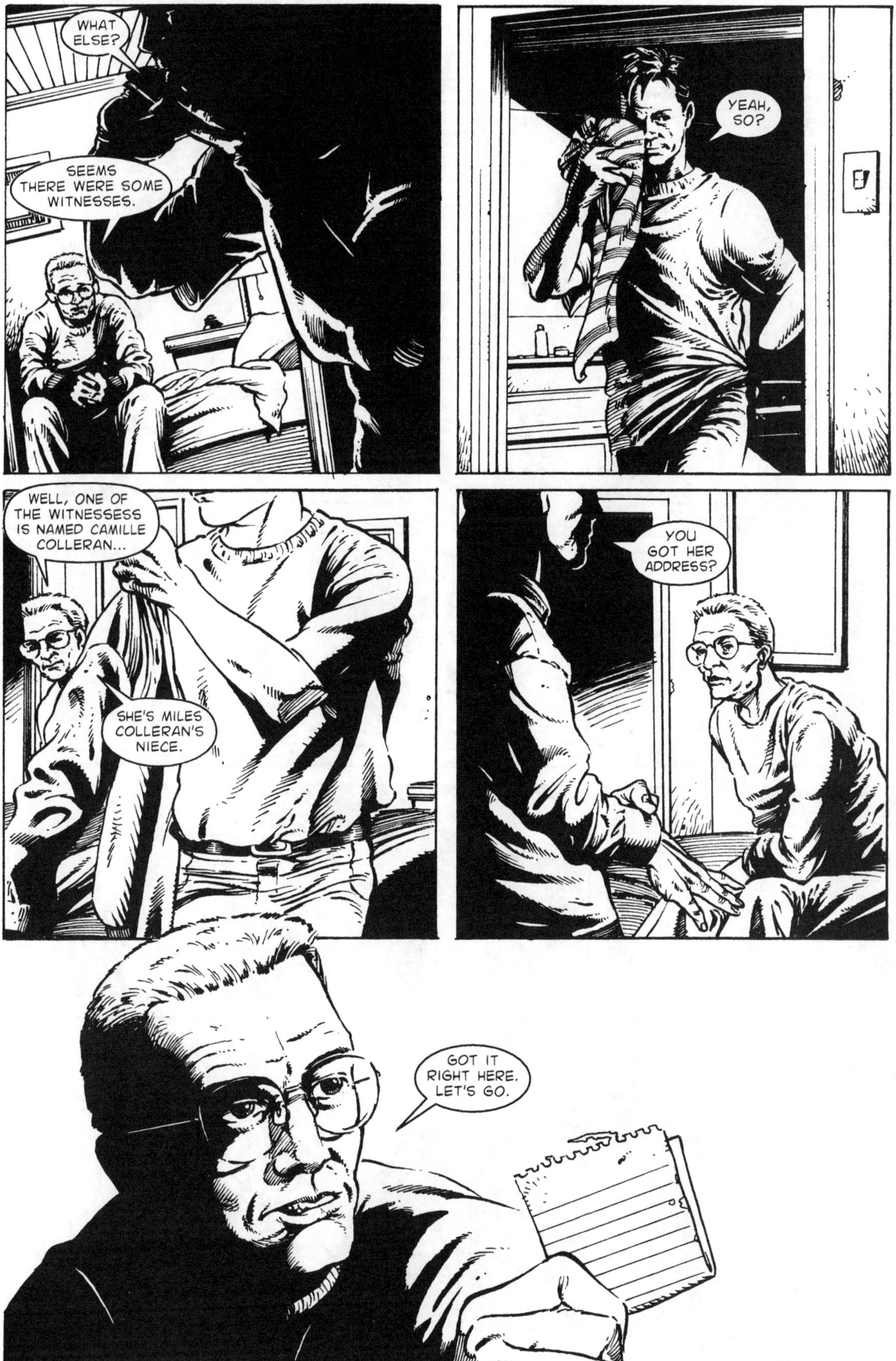
WHAT ELSE?
SEEMS THERE WERE SOME WITNESSES.
YEAH, SO?
WELL, ONE OF THE WITNESSESS IS NAMED CAMILLE COLLERAN...
SHE'S MILES COLLERAN'S NIECE.
YOU GOT HER ADDRESS?
GOT IT RIGHT HERE. LET'S GO.

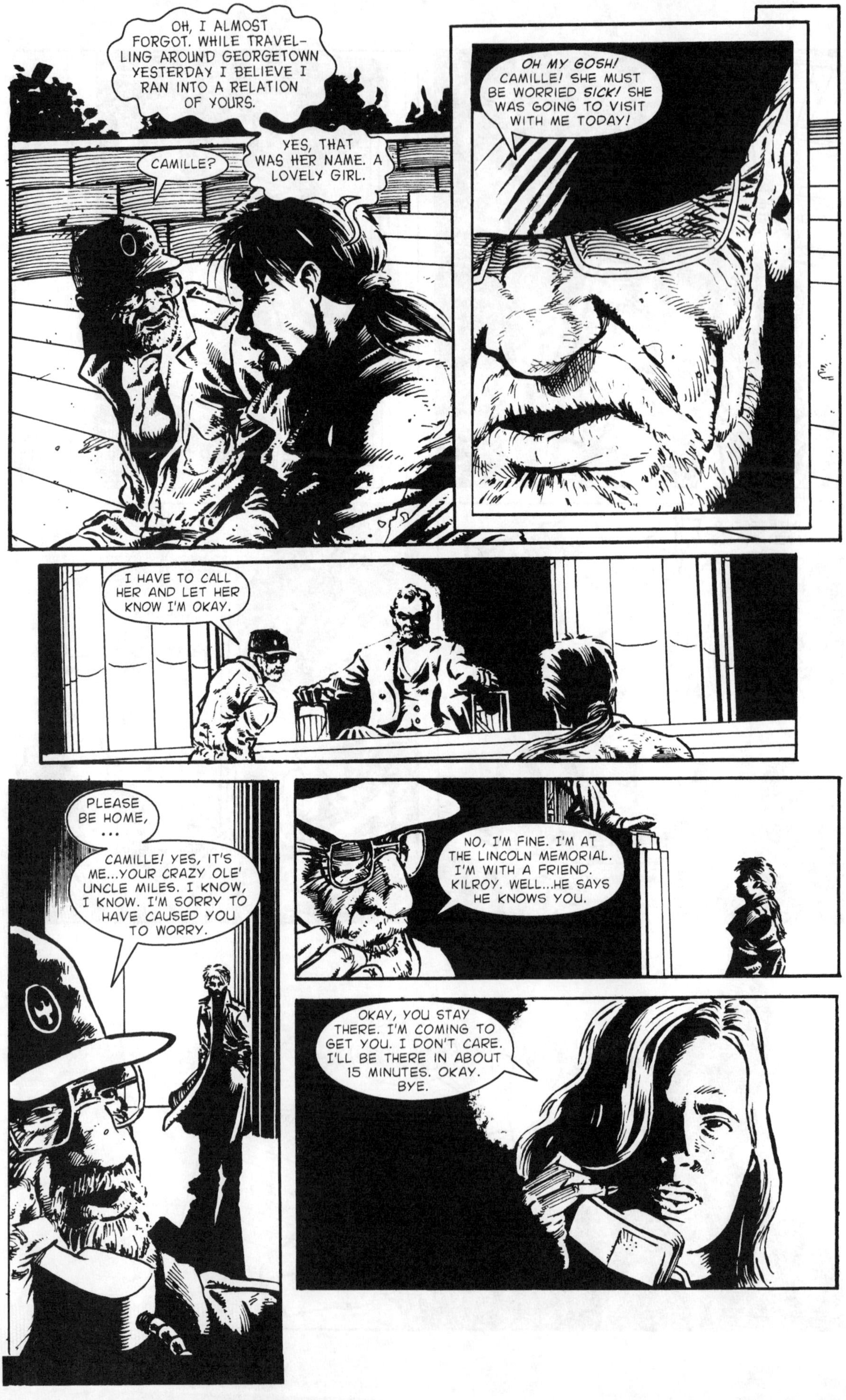
OH, I ALMOST FORGOT. WHILE TRAVELLING AROUND GEORGETOWN YESTERDAY I BELIEVE I RAN INTO A RELATION OF YOURS.
CAMILLE?
YES, THAT WAS HER NAME. A LOVELY GIRL.
OH MY GOSH! CAMILLE! SHE MUST BE WORRIED SICK! SHE WAS GOING TO VISIT WITH ME TODAY!
I HAVE TO CALL HER AND LET HER KNOW I'M OKAY.
PLEASE BE HOME, ...
CAMILLE! YES, IT'S ME...YOUR CRAZY OLE' UNCLE MILES. I KNOW, I KNOW. I'M SORRY TO HAVE CAUSED YOU TO WORRY.
NO, I'M FINE. I'M AT THE LINCOLN MEMORIAL. I'M WITH A FRIEND. KILROY. WELL...HE SAYS HE KNOWS YOU.
OKAY, YOU STAY THERE. I'M COMING TO GET YOU. I DON'T CARE. I'LL BE THERE IN ABOUT 15 MINUTES. OKAY. BYE.

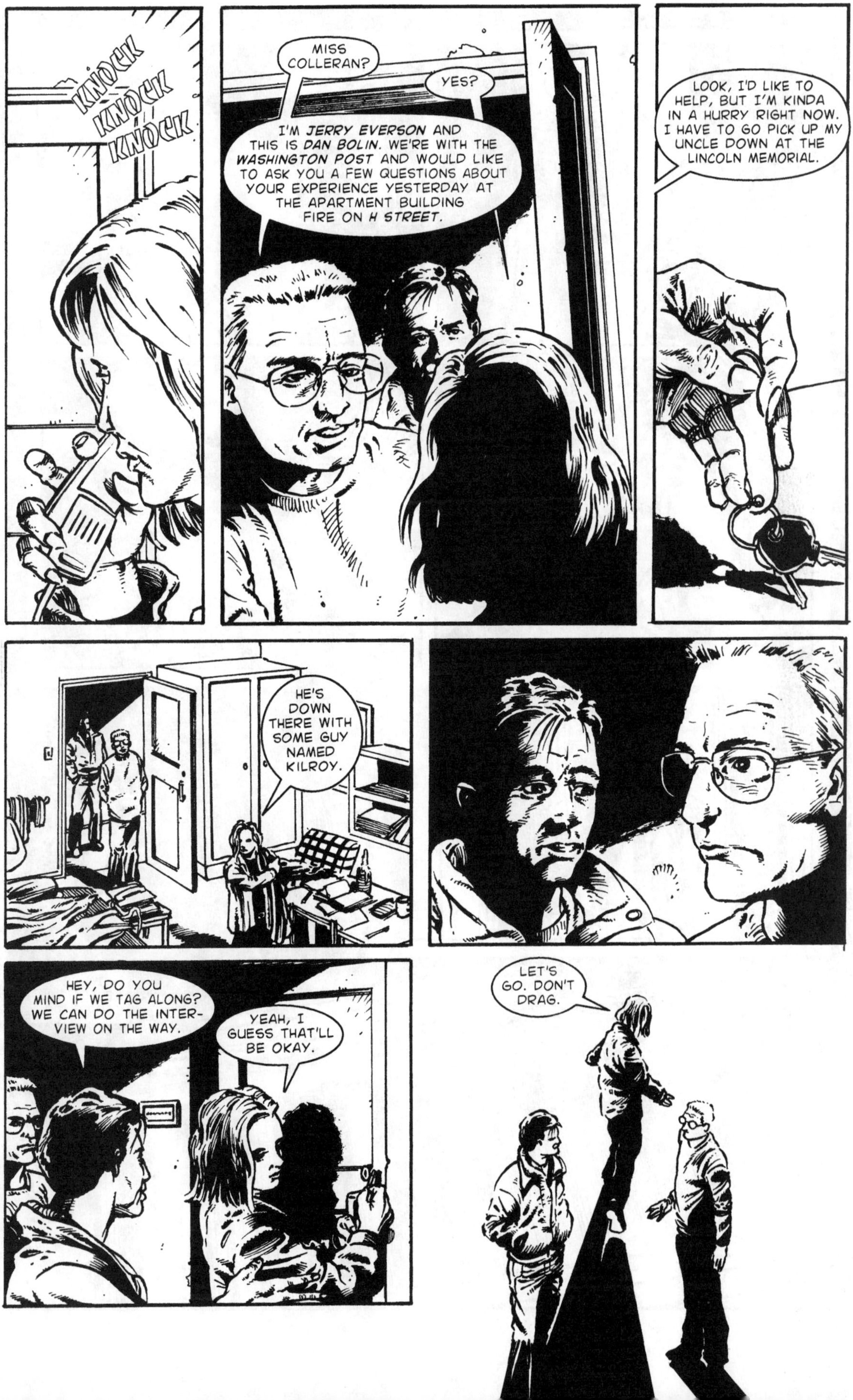
KNOCK
KNOCK
KNOCK
MISS COLLERAN?
YES?
I'M JERRY EVERSON AND THIS IS DAN BOLIN. WE'RE WITH THE WASHINGTON POST AND WOULD LIKE TO ASK YOU A FEW QUESTIONS ABOUT YOUR EXPERIENCE YESTERDAY AT THE APARTMENT BUILDING FIRE ON H STREET.
LOOK, I'D LIKE TO HELP, BUT I'M KINDA IN A HURRY RIGHT NOW. I HAVE TO GO PICK UP MY UNCLE DOWN AT THE LINCOLN MEMORIAL.
HE'S DOWN THERE WITH SOME GUY NAMED KILROY.
HEY, DO YOU MIND IF WE TAG ALONG? WE CAN DO THE INTER- VIEW ON THE WAY.
YEAH, I GUESS THAT'LL BE OKAY.
LET'S GO. DON'T DRAG.

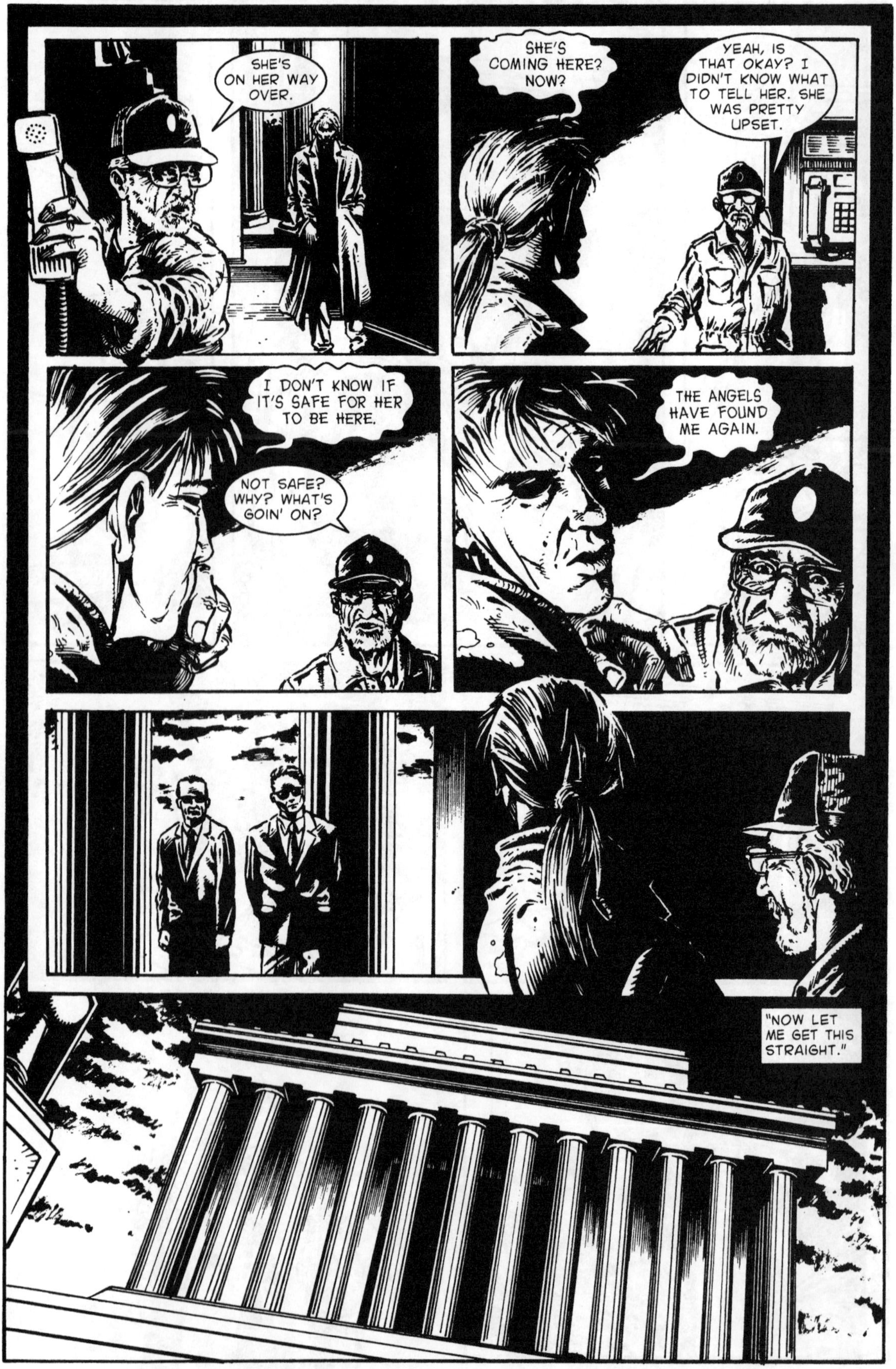
SHE'S ON HER WAY OVER.
SHE'S COMING HERE? NOW?
YEAH, IS THAT OKAY? I DIDN'T KNOW WHAT TO TELL HER. SHE WAS PRETTY UPSET.
I DON'T KNOW IF IT'S SAFE FOR HER TO BE HERE.
NOT SAFE? WHY? WHAT'S GOIN' ON?
THE ANGELS HAVE FOUND ME AGAIN.
"NOW LET ME GET THIS STRAIGHT."

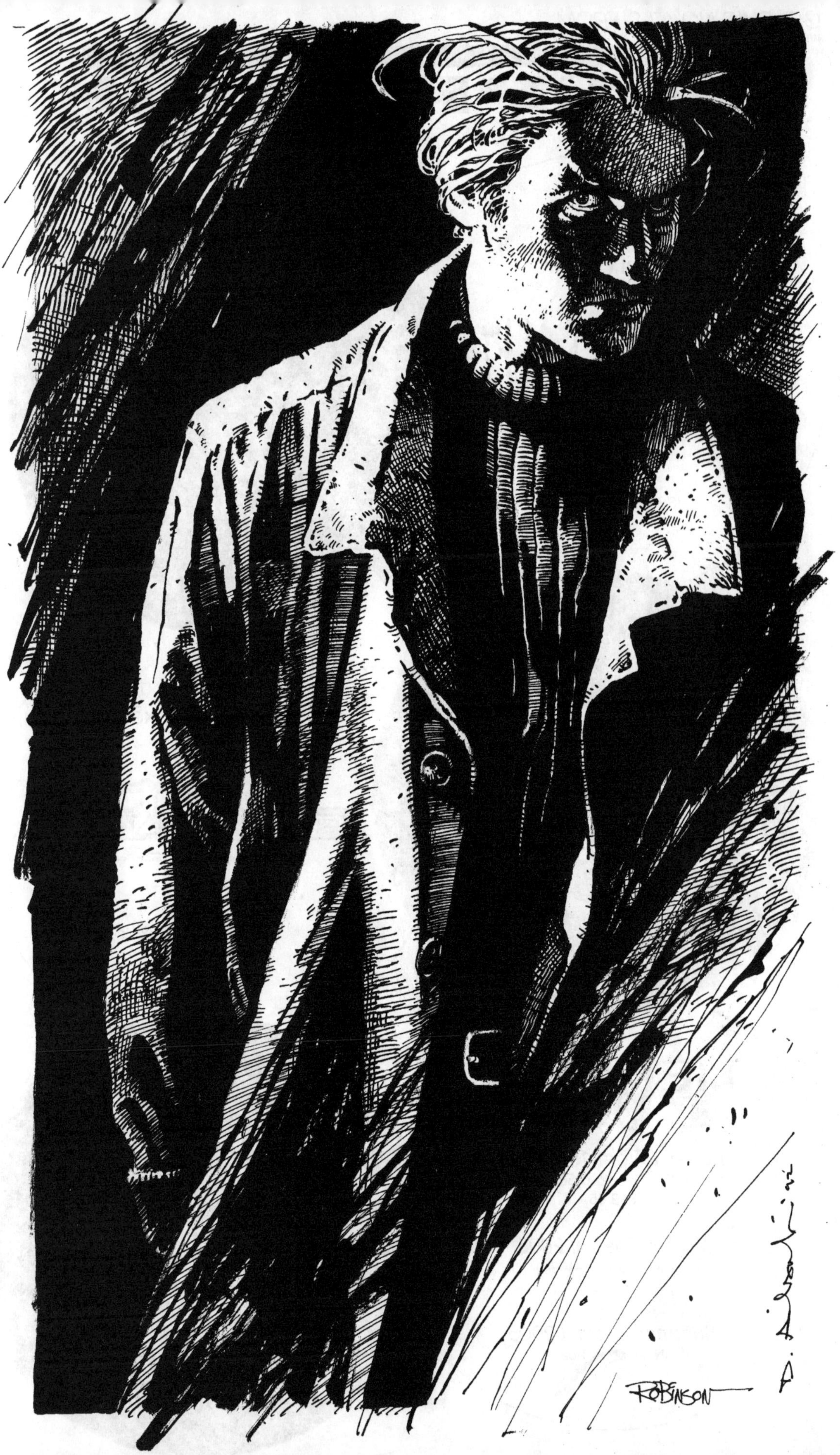
ROBINSON

GRAPHIC NOVELS FROM

DESPERADO

www.desperadopublishing.com

Phil Hester

OVERSIGHT

SHORT STORIES 1990-2005

ISBN #1-58240-577-8
$19.99

Bruce Jones
Bernie Wrightson

ISBN #1-58240-466-6
$14.95
ISBN #1-58240-467-4
$24.95
(signed)

Joe Pruett
Phil Hester
Bruce McCorkindale

THE
NAMELESS

ISBN # 1-58240-499-2
$15.95

Gary Reed
Vince Locke

Saint
GERMAINE
Shadows Fall

ISBN #1-58240-562-x
$14.99

NEGATIVE
BURN

The Best From 1993-1998
ISBN #1-58240-562-x
$19.95

Winter Special 2005
ISBN #1-58240-469-0
$9.95

Summer Special 2005
ISBN #1-58240-524-7
$9.95

Joe Pruett
Ken Meyer Jr.
Mike Perkins
and others

KILROY
IS HERE

ISBN # 1-58240-587-5
$24.99